Fragmentation and
the international relations
of Micro-States

At a time when nearly all armed conflicts are related to self-determination, and frequently to claims for secession, this meticulous study examines the legal issues at stake in the light of the existence of the European Micro-States: Liechtenstein, San Marino, Monaco, Andorra and the Vatican City. Jorri Duursma makes a thorough analysis of the origins, meaning and faults of the modern right of self-determination, addresses and asks several fundamental questions: What constitutes a people with a right to self-determination? How small a people has this right? Who is allowed to secede? What is a State according to international law? Jorri Duursma's book provides an up-to-date and informed account of these important issues which also draws on recent experiences in Eastern Europe and Yugoslavia. It is the first book to provide a thorough international legal account of the European Micro-States, and develops a novel approach to the problems of fragmentation.

CAMBRIDGE STUDIES IN INTERNATIONAL AND COMPARATIVE LAW

This series (established in 1946 by Professors Gutteridge, Hersch Lauterpacht and McNair) is a forum for studies of high quality in the fields of public and private international law and comparative law. Although these are distinct legal sub-disciplines, developments since 1946 confirm their interrelationship. Comparative law is increasingly used as a tool in the making of law at national, regional and international levels. Private international law is increasingly affected by international conventions, and the issues faced by classical conflicts rules are increasingly dealt with by substantive harmonisation of law under international auspices. Mixed international arbitrations, especially those involving state economic activity, raise mixed questions of public and private international law. In many fields (such as the protection of human rights and democratic standards, investment guarantees, international criminal law) international and national systems interact. National constitutional arrangements relating to 'foreign affairs' and to the implementation of international norms are a focus of attention.

Professor Sir Robert Jennings edited the series from 1981. Following his retirement as General Editor, an editorial board has been created and Cambridge University Press has recommitted itself to the series, affirming its broad scope.

The Board welcomes works of a theoretical or interdisciplinary character, and those focusing on new approaches to international or comparative law or conflicts of law. Studies of particular institutions or problems are equally welcome, as are translations of the best work published in other languages.

General Editors James Crawford
Whewell Professor of International Law, University of Cambridge
David Johnston
Regius Professor of Civil Law, University of Cambridge

Editorial Board Professor Hilary Charlesworth   *University of Adelaide*
Mr John Collier   *Trinity Hall, Cambridge*
Professor Lori Damrosch   *Columbia University Law School*
Professor John Dugard   *Director, Research Centre for International Law, University of Cambridge*
Professor Mary-Ann Glendon   *Harvard Law School*
Professor Christopher Greenwood   *London School of Economics*
Professor Hein Kötz   *Max-Planck-Institut, Hamburg*
Dr Vaughan Lowe   *Corpus Christi College, Cambridge*
Professor D. M. McRae   *University of Ottawa*
Professor Onuma Yasuaki   *University of Tokyo*

Advisory Committee Professor D. W. Bowett QC
Judge Rosalyn Higgins QC
Professor Sir Robert Jennings QC
Professor J. A. Jolowicz QC
Professor Eli Lauterpacht QC
Professor Kurt Lipstein
Judge Stephen Schwebel

Fragmentation and the international relations of Micro-States

Self-determination and statehood

Jorri Duursma

CAMBRIDGE UNIVERSITY PRESS
Cambridge, New York, Melbourne, Madrid, Cape Town, Singapore, São Paulo, Delhi

Cambridge University Press
The Edinburgh Building, Cambridge CB2 8RU, UK

Published in the United States of America by Cambridge University Press, New York

www.cambridge.org
Information on this title: www.cambridge.org/9780521563604

© Cambridge University Press 1996

This publication is in copyright. Subject to statutory exception
and to the provisions of relevant collective licensing agreements,
no reproduction of any part may take place without the written
permission of Cambridge University Press.

First published 1996

A catalogue record for this publication is available from the British Library

ISBN 978-0-521-56360-4 hardback

Transferred to digital printing 2009

Cambridge University Press has no responsibility for the persistence or
accuracy of URLs for external or third-party Internet websites referred to in
this publication, and does not guarantee that any content on such websites is,
or will remain, accurate or appropriate. Information regarding prices, travel
timetables and other factual information given in this work are correct at
the time of first printing but Cambridge University Press does not guarantee
the accuracy of such information thereafter.

Contents

Table of cases		viii
Table of treaties		xi
List of abbreviations		xxii

Introduction		1

PART I
The general international legal context — 5

1	Right of self-determination	7
	Documents on self-determination	7
	Debates on self-determination	37
	Judicial decisions	56
	Peoples in doctrine	73
	Self-determination versus *territorial integrity*	77
2	Criteria for statehood	110
	Recognition	110
	Territory	116
	Population	117
	Government	118
	Independence	120
	Illegal entities	127

3	The general question of Micro-States in international organizations	133
	Micro-States and the League of Nations	133
	Micro-States and the United Nations	134

PART II
Five case studies of European Micro-States — 143

Introduction — 145

4	The Principality of Liechtenstein	147
	Territory, population and economy	147
	History	148
	Constitutional and legal order	150
	Relations with States	160
	Relations with international organizations	170
	Application of the criteria for statehood	200
	Self-determination of the Liechtenstein people	204
	Conclusions	205
5	The Republic of San Marino	207
	Territory, population and economy	207
	History	208
	Constitutional and legal order	211
	Relations with States	222
	Relations with international organizations	233
	Application of the criteria for statehood	255
	Self-determination of the San Marinese people	259
	Conclusions	260
6	The Principality of Monaco	261
	Territory, population and economy	261
	History	262
	Constitutional and legal order	264
	Relations with States	274
	Relations with international organizations	291
	Application of the criteria for statehood: first analysis	304

	Self-determination of the Monégasque people	310
	Application of the criteria for statehood: final analysis	311
	Conclusions	314
7	The Principality of Andorra	316
	Territory, population and economy	316
	History	317
	Constitutional and legal order	320
	Relations with States	334
	Relations with international organizations	352
	Application of the criteria for statehood	366
	Self-determination of the Andorran people	372
	Conclusions	373
8	The State of the Vatican City	374
	Territory, population and economy	374
	History	375
	Constitutional and legal order	376
	Relations with States	386
	Relations with international organizations	397
	Application of the criteria for statehood	410
	Self-determination of the Vatican population	417
	Conclusions	418

PART III
General conclusions   421

9	General conclusions	423
	Bibliography	434
	Index	451

Table of cases

A. Laupper v. Switzerland, Liechtenstein and Austria (1986) 158
A. B. et al. v. Italy (1990) 64
A. D. on behalf of Mikmaq Tribal Society v. Canada (1984) 63
Aaland Islands Case (1919) 56–57
Austro-German Customs Union Case (1931) 121

Barcelona Traction, Light and Power Company, Limited (Second Phase) (1970) 103, 128, 129, 132
Bernard Omivayak Chief of the Lubicon Lake Band v. Canada (1990) 64, 66

Certain Phosphate Lands in Nauru (Preliminary Objections) (1992) 127, 141
Cour de Cassation, Judgment (1971) 346

Deutsche Continental Gas Gesellschaft v. Polish State (1929) 115, 116
Drozd and Janousek v. France and Spain (1992) 273, 284, 285, 332
Duedra (1905) 344

E. P. et al. v. Colombia (1990) 64
East Timor Case (1995) 62–63, 103
Eastern Carelia Advisory Opinion (1923) 58
Elsen et autres v. Boudet (1972) 346

Frontier Dispute Case (1986) 68–69, 84, 109

Gerliczy Case (1939) 174

Greco-Bulgarian 'Communities' Advisory Opinion (1930) 59, 79

H. v. Liechtenstein (1993) 159
Herman v. UK (1984) 384

Island of Palmas Case (1928) 116, 121

J. M. v. France (1993) 272, 273, 284
Jordi Drozd and Pavel Janousek against France and Spain (1990) 284–285, 331–332, 344, 371

L. v. Liechtenstein (1993) 158
Land, Island and Maritime Frontier Dispute Case (1992) 108–109
Legal Consequences for States of the Continued Presence of South Africa in Namibia (South West Africa) notwithstanding Security Council Resolution 276 (1970) Advisory Opinion (1971) 59–60, 128, 314

M. v. Liechtenstein (1993) 158
Mandement v. Consorts Gianesini (1977) 346
Massip v. Cruze (1952) 344

North Sea Continental Shelf Cases (1969) 116
Nottebohm Case (Second Phase) (1955) 177, 203
Nuclear Tests Case (1974) 308

Opinion no. 1 (1991) Arbitration Commission on Yugoslavia 67–68, 97, 115, 119
Opinion no. 2 (1992) Arbitration Commission on Yugoslavia 69–70, 79
Opinion no. 3 (1992) Arbitration Commission on Yugoslavia 68, 97
Opinion no. 4 (1992) Arbitration Commission on Yugoslavia 72, 91

Porché v. Société de Gérance et de Publicité (1949) 343

x   TABLE OF CASES

Radio Andorre (1950) 343
Reparation for Injuries Suffered in the Service of the United Nations Advisory Opinion (1949) 115
Right of Passage over Indian Territory (1960) 85
Rights of Minorities in Upper Silesia (Minority Schools) Case (1928) 58, 71

Sieur Chabaud (1931) 270
Sieur Jama et autres (1964) 270
Société 'Le Nickel' (1933) 343

Tinoco Concessions Arbitration (1923) 120

W. v. Liechtenstein (1991) 158
Western Sahara Advisory Opinion (1975) 60–62, 84–85
Whispering Pines Indian Band v. Canada (1991) 64
Wimbledon Case, The (1923) 121

X v. Liechtenstein (1993) 158
X v. Liechtenstein (1994) 158
X v. Liechtenstein (1995, 26981/95) 158
X v. Liechtenstein (1995, 27630/95) 158
X v. San Marino (1993) 221
X v. San Marino (Febr. 1995) 221
X v. San Marino (Apr. 1995) 221
X v. San Marino (Sept. 1995) 221
X and Y v. Switzerland (1977) 168, 194

Table of treaties

Bilateral and trilateral political treaties

Additional Agreement to the 1897 Treaty of Friendship (1914) Italy/San Marino 226

Additional Agreement to the 1939 Treaty of Friendship (1953) Italy/San Marino 226

Additional Agreement to the 1939 Treaty of Friendship (1971) Italy/San Marino 222, 210, 224, 233, 243

Agreement on the Establishment of the Republic of Yemen (1990) North Yemen/South Yemen 82

Agreement on the Joint Administration of Walvis Bay and the Off-Shore Islands (1992) Namibia/South Africa 87

Agreement on the Status of the Episcopal Co-Prince (1994) Andorra/Spain 348–349, 368

Compact of Free Association (1983) Marshall Islands/USA 139–140, 425

Compact of Free Association (1982) Micronesia/USA 139–140, 425

Compact of Free Association (1986) Palau/USA 139–140, 425

Convention (1627) Holy See/San Marino 208

Convention regulating Bilateral Relations (1883) France/Tunisia 124

Convention for establishing a Conventional Regime in Upper Silesia (Minorities Treaty) (1922) Germany/Poland 58

Convention respecting an Extension of Hong Kong Territory (1898) China/UK 88

Convention of Friendship (1860) China/UK 88

Convention of Vicinage (1963) France/Monaco 269, 289, 290, 306

Joint Declaration on the Question of Hong Kong (1984) China/UK 87

xii   TABLE OF TREATIES

Joint Declaration on the Question of Macao (1987) China/Portugal 87
Lateran Treaty (1929) Holy See/Italy 376, 380–381, 386–391, 393–397, 401, 406–407, 410, 412, 414–416
New York Agreement (1962) Indonesia/Netherlands 84
Peace Treaty (1920) Finland/Russia 58
Peace Treaty of Frederikshamn (1809) Russia/Sweden 56
Safeguard Agreement (1972) IAEA/Vatican City 403
Treaty (1861) France/Monaco 263, 305, 310
Treaty (1881) France/Tunisia 123–124
Treaty on the Establishment of German Unity (1990) FRG/GDR 78, 81–82
Treaty of Fez (1969) Morocco/Spain 86
Treaty of Friendship (1897) Italy/San Marino 210, 223, 226
Treaty of Friendship and Commerce (1887) China/Portugal 88
Treaty of Friendship and Commerce (1798) Roman Republic/San Marino 209
Treaty on Friendship, Extradition and Commerce (1862) Italy/San Marino 210, 223, 231, 255
Treaty of Friendship and Good Neighbourhood (1939) Italy/San Marino 222–231, 243, 246, 250, 252, 255–257
Treaty and Interpretative Exchange of Letters (1918) France/Monaco 140, 263, 274–282, 284, 290–291, 295–296, 298–304, 307–309, 311–315
Treaty of Nanking (1842) China/UK 88
Treaty of Péronne (1641) France/Monaco 262–263
Treaty of Vicinage, Friendship and Cooperation (1993) Andorra/France/Spain 140, 335–339, 344–347, 350, 364, 367, 369–373
Treaty on Walvis Bay and the Off-Shore Islands (1994) Namibia/South Africa 87

Border treaties

Border Treaty (1863) Andorran General Council/Spain 316, 350, 366
Border Treaty (1960) Austria/Liechtenstein 170
Convention on Air Traffic (1991) France/Monaco 305

Convention on Maritime Delimitation (1984) France/Monaco 261, 305, 310

Concordats

Agreement on Juridical Questions (1979) Holy See/Spain 348
Concordat (1984) Holy See/Italy 395
Concordat (1941) Holy See/Spain 348
Concordat (1953) Holy See/Spain 348
Lateran Concordat (1929) Holy See/Italy 380–381, 389, 393, 395

Customs, trade and fiscal treaties

Act of Accession of the Kingdom of Spain to the EC (1985) 360–361
Additional Agreement to the 1972 ECSC/Switzerland Free Trade Agreement (1972) ECSC States/Liechtenstein/Switzerland 185–186
Additional Agreement to the 1972 EEC/Switzerland Free Trade Agreement (1972) EEC/Liechtenstein/Switzerland 185–186
Additional Protocol to the 1923 Customs Union Treaty on Product Liability (1994) Liechtenstein/Switzerland 165
Agreement relating to the Creation of the European Economic Area (1992) 153–154, 157, 159–160, 186–191, 195, 201–202
Agreement on Customs Union (1990) Andorra/EEC 302, 340–341, 348, 361–363
Agreement on Customs Union and Cooperation (1991) EEC States/San Marino 229, 248–253, 286, 302
Agreement relating to the 1923 Customs Union Treaty (1994) Liechtenstein/Switzerland 165, 195
Agreement revising the 1978 Treaty on Patent Protection (1994) Liechtenstein/Switzerland 165
Agreement relating to the 1994 Treaty on Value-Added Tax (1994) Liechtenstein/Switzerland 165–166
Agreement establishing the World Trade Organization (1994) 200
Convention (1951) France/Monaco 277
Convention establishing the European Bank for Reconstruction and Development (1990) 200

Convention establishing the European Free Trade Association (1960) 184–186, 193, 201
Convention on Exchange Control (1945) France/Monaco 289–290
Convention on Financial and Currency Relations (1991) Italy/San Marino 219, 231–232, 257
Convention on Insurances (1963) France/Monaco 290
Convention on the Payment of Debts in Ancient Austrian or Hungarian Crowns (1924) Hungary/Romania 174
Convention on Pharmacy (1952) France/Monaco 277
Convention on Pharmacy (1963) France/Monaco 290
Convention on Road Traffic (1949) 356
Convention on Transport by Road (1955) France/Monaco 277
Convention establishing the WIPO (1967) 402–403
Currency Treaty (1980) Liechtenstein/Switzerland 166–167, 189, 202
Customs Convention (1963) France/Monaco 286–287, 297, 301–302
Customs Convention (1930) Italy/Vatican City 391–392, 410
Customs Union Treaty (1852) Austria/Liechtenstein 149, 161, 169
Customs Union Treaty (1923) Liechtenstein/Switzerland 149, 164–165, 167, 170, 172, 180, 184–187, 192–194, 201–202
Exchange of Letters (1867) Andorra/France 340
Exchange of Letters (1967) Andorra/France 340
Exchange of Letters (1920) Austria/Liechtenstein 170, 172
Exchange of Letters on the Control of Medicines (1994) Liechtenstein/Switzerland 165
Exchange of Letters on the 1963 Convention on Insurances (1963) France/Monaco 290
Exchange of Letters on the 1963 Customs Convention (1994) France/Monaco 286
Exchange of Letters on Exchange Control (1963) France/Monaco 289
Exchange of Letters on Exchange Control (1987) France/Monaco 289, 290
Exchange of Letters on the 1963 Fiscal Convention (1963) France/Monaco 288
Exchange of Notes (1972) Italy/San Marino 230, 250

TABLE OF TREATIES   xv

Exchange of Notes constituting a Commercial *Modus Vivendi* (1948) Canada/Italy 229
Fiscal Convention (1963) France/Monaco 277, 278, 287-288
Free Trade Agreement (1972) ECSC States/Switzerland 185, 193
Free Trade Agreement (1972) EEC/Switzerland 185, 193
Free Trade Agreement (1992) EFTA States/Czechoslovakia 179
General Agreement on Tariffs and Trade (1947) 199-200, 340
General Agreement on Tariffs and Trade (1994) 200
Intercantonal Agreement on Financial Contributions to the 'Hochschule' (1982) Liechtenstein/Swiss Cantons 425
Intercantonal Agreement on Medicines (1973) Liechtenstein/Swiss Cantons 424-425
Interim Agreement on Trade and Customs Union (1992) EEC/San Marino 249-250, 252-253
International Convention for the Protection of Performers (1961) 356
Monetary Convention (1930) Italy/Vatican City 392
Monetary Convention (1951) Italy/Vatican City 392
Monetary Convention (1931) San Marino/Vatican City 231
Protocol adjusting the Agreement on a Committee of Members of Parliament of the EFTA States (1993) 188
Protocol adjusting the Agreement relating to the Creation of the European Economic Area (1993) 187
Protocol adjusting the Agreement on a Standing Committee of the EFTA States (1993) 188
Protocol relating to the Application of the Convention establishing the European Free Trade Association to the Principality of Liechtenstein (1960) EFTA States/Liechtenstein 185, 193
Protocol adjusting the EFTA Agreement on the Establishment of a Surveillance Authority and a Court of Justice (1993) 188
Trade Agreement (1978) China/EEC 230
Treaties on Double Taxation (1955, 1969) Austria/Liechtenstein 170
Treaty revising the 1923 Customs Union Treaty (1994) Liechtenstein/Switzerland 164
Treaty establishing the European Coal and Steel Community (1951) 249

Treaty establishing the European Economic Community (1957) 191, 230, 248, 359, 361, 371, 410
Treaty on European Union (1992) 232, 410
Treaty on Extradition, Import, Salt and Tobacco (1802) Italian Republic/San Marino 209
Treaty on Extradition, Import, Salt and Tobacco (1808) Kingdom of Italy/San Marino 209
Treaty on Trade and Navigation (1963) Albania/France 287
Treaty on Value-Added Tax (1994) Liechtenstein/Switzerland 165
Treaty on the Zone of Cooperation in an Area between the Indonesian Province of East Timor and Northern Australia (1989) Australia/Indonesia 62
Universal Copyright Convention (1952) 354–355, 370
Wheat Trade Convention (1986) 401

General multilateral treaties

Agreement establishing the Commonwealth of Independent States (1991) 96
Agreement between the UN and UNESCO (1945) 294–295
Charter of the United Nations (1945) 12–17, 21, 29, 31, 33, 36, 68, 77, 85–86, 97, 136–138, 140–141, 310, 407
Constitution of FAO (1945) 138
Constitution of ILO (1919) 242
Constitution of UNESCO (1945) 138, 239
Constitution of WHO (1946) 240
Convention on Conciliation and Arbitration within the CSCE (1992) 299
Convention for the Peaceful Settlement of International Conflicts (1899) 398
Covenant of the League of Nations (1919) 10, 56, 59, 133–134, 170–171, 173, 234, 291
General Treaty for the Renunciation of War as an Instrument of National Policy (Briand–Kellogg Pact) (1928) 353
International Opium Convention (1925) 352–354
London Treaty (1915) 398

Montevideo Convention on the Rights and Duties of States (1933) 112, 118

Statute of the Council of Europe (1949) 180–183, 246, 299–300

Statute of the IAEA (1957) 297, 403

Statute of the International Court of Justice (1945) 175–178, 181, 197, 203, 205, 227, 235, 294, 407

Statute of the Permanent Court of International Justice (1920) 174, 234, 293–294, 353–354

Statute of the World Tourism Organization (1970) 365

Treaty on the Non-Proliferation of Nuclear Weapons (1968) 199, 403

Treaty of Saint-Germain (1919) 121, 172

Treaty of Utrecht (1713) 52–53, 86

Treaty of Versailles (1919) 282

United Nations Convention on the Law of the Sea (1982) 116

Vienna Convention on the Law of Treaties (1969) 102–103, 114, 128, 192–194, 276, 308, 311–312

Vienna Convention on Succession of States in respect of Treaties (1978) 68, 114

Human rights treaties

African Charter on Human and Peoples' Rights (1981) 35

Convention concerning Emigration (1919) Bulgaria/Greece 59

Convention on the Prevention and Punishment of the Crime of Genocide (1948) 157, 270

Convention on the Rights of the Child (1989) 157, 218, 383, 414

Convention relating to the Status of Refugees (1951) 383, 414

Convention against Torture and other Cruel, Inhuman or Degrading Treatment or Punishment (1984) 157, 218

European Charter of Local Self-Government (1985) 108

European Convention for the Protection of Human Rights and Fundamental Freedoms (1950) 105, 155–156, 158–159, 168, 218, 221, 272–273, 331–332, 359, 384–386

Framework Convention for the Protection of National Minorities (1995) 44, 104–105, 157

ILO Convention no. 87 on Freedom of Association and Protection of the Right to Organise (1948) 221
ILO Convention no. 98 on the Right to Organise and Collective Bargaining (1949) 221
International Convention for the Abolition of Slavery (1926) 270
International Covenant on Civil and Political Rights (1966) 27–35, 38, 40–43, 45, 63–66, 70, 78, 80–81, 91, 100, 104, 218–220, 271–272, 384–386
International Covenant on Economic, Social and Cultural Rights (1966) 27–35, 78, 81, 218–219
Optional Protocol to the International Covenant on Civil and Political Rights (1966) 30, 63–66, 104, 218

Postal, telegraph and telephone treaties
Additional Regulation to the 1923 Postal Convention (1924) Italy/San Marino 228
Administrative Postal Agreement on Andorra (1930) France/Spain 339–340, 347
Agreement relating to the 1978 Treaty on the Maintenance of PTT Services (1994) Liechtenstein/Switzerland 163–164, 170, 202
Convention for the Maintenance of Postal Services (1929) Italy/Vatican City 390–391, 401–402, 413, 415
Convention on the Maintenance of PTT Services (1920) Liechtenstein/Switzerland 149, 163
Convention for the Maintenance of Telegraph and Telephone Services (1929) Italy/Vatican City 391, 401–402, 413, 415
Convention on PTT Relations (1963) France/Monaco 285
Exchange of Letters (1952) Italy/Vatican City 391
Postal Agreement (1920) Austria/Liechtenstein 170, 172
Postal Convention (1923) Italy/San Marino 228
Postal Union Treaty (1912) Austria/Liechtenstein 149
Stockholm Postal Convention (1924) 401
Telegraph Convention (1875) 401
Treaty on the Maintenance of PTT Services (1978) Liechtenstein/Switzerland 163–164, 192–194, 201

Treaty revising the 1978 Treaty on the Maintenance of PTT Services (1994) Liechtenstein/Switzerland 163–164
Universal Postal Convention (1874) 199, 365

Treaties on diplomatic relations

Additional Agreement to the 1939 Treaty of Friendship (1968) Italy/San Marino 228
Exchange of Letters (1940) Holy See/Italy 390
Exchange of Letters (1919) Liechtenstein/Switzerland 161
Vienna Convention on Diplomatic Relations (1961) 258, 339, 367

Treaties on foreigners

Convention (1930) France/Monaco 265, 268, 271, 282–283, 285
Exchange of Letters (1981) Liechtenstein/Switzerland 167
Exchange of Letters on the 1930 Convention (1973) France/Monaco 265, 268, 271, 283
Exchange of Letters on the 1930 Convention (1978) France/Monaco 268
Exchange of Letters on the 1930 Convention (1985) France/Monaco 265
Extradition Treaty (1902) Netherlands/San Marino 222
Extradition Treaty (1906) San Marino/USA 222
Treaty (1923) Liechtenstein/Switzerland 167
Treaty on Swiss/Liechtenstein Nationals (1963) Liechtenstein/Switzerland 167
Treaty on Third-State Nationals (1963) Liechtenstein/Switzerland 167–168

Treaties on judicial cooperation

Agreement revising the 1968 Agreement on the Recognition and Execution of Civil Judicial Judgements (1994) Liechtenstein/Switzerland 165
Treaties on Judicial Cooperation (1955, 1968, 1983) Austria/Liechtenstein 170

Treaty on the Use of Austrian Judges (1884) Austria/Liechtenstein 154, 170

Treaties on sciences and culture

Agreement on the International Laboratory of Marine Radioactivity (1986) IAEA/Monaco 297
Agreement on the International Laboratory of Marine Radioactivity (1961) IAEA/Monaco/Oceanographic Institute 297
Berne Convention on the Conservation of European Wildlife and Natural Habitat (1979) no. 104 301
Convention for the Protection of Cultural Property in the Event of Armed Conflict (1954) 354–355, 369, 396
European Convention on the Academic Recognition of University Qualifications (1959) no. 32 409
European Convention on the Protection of the Archaeological Heritage (1969) no. 66 409
European Cultural Convention (1954) no. 18 301, 409
Treaty on Post-Doctoral Education (1980) Austria/Liechtenstein 170

Treaties on social security

Administrative Agreements on Social Security (1968, 1971, 1978) Andorra/Spain 350
Agreement on Disablement Benefits (1965) Liechtenstein/Switzerland 159
Agreement on Family Allowances (1969) Liechtenstein/Switzerland 159
Agreement on Social Security (1965) Liechtenstein/Switzerland 159
Agreement on Unemployment Benefits (1980) Liechtenstein/Switzerland 159
Exchange of Letters (1932) Liechtenstein/Switzerland 159
Exchange of Letters on Family Allowances (1958) France/Italy 241
Treaties on Social Security (1968, 1974, 1977, 1987) Austria/Liechtenstein 159, 170
Treaty on Social Security (1977) FRG/Liechtenstein 159
Treaty on Social Security (1976) Italy/Liechtenstein 159

Treaties on telecommunication

Agreement of Cooperation in the Field of Radio and Television (1987) Italy/San Marino 231, 257–258
European Convention on Transfrontier Television (1989) no. 132 409
Exchange of Letters on the Establishment of a Radio-Television Station (1987) Italy/San Marino 231, 245
International Telecommunication Convention (1932) 401
International Telecommunication Convention (1973) 365, 370
Radiotelegraph Convention (1927) 401

Abbreviations

AAS	Acta Apostolicae Sedis
AAS Suppl.	Acta Apostolicae Sedis: Supplemento per le Leggi e Disposizioni dello Stato della Città del Vaticano
AD	Annual Digest of Public International Law Cases
AFDI	Annuaire Français de Droit International
AJIL	American Journal of International Law
All-Eur. HR Yearb.	All-European Human Rights Yearbook
ASDI	Annuaire Suisse de Droit International
AYIL	Australian Yearbook of International Law
BA	Bericht und Antrag der Regierung an den Landtag des Fürstentums Liechtenstein
BOPA	Butlletí Oficial del Principat d'Andorra
Bull. EC	Bulletin of the European Communities
BURSM	Bollettino Ufficiale della Repubblica di San Marino
BYIL	British Yearbook of International Law
CMLR	Common Market Law Reports
CSCE	Conference on Security and Cooperation in Europe
CSO	Committee of Senior Officials of the CSCE
D & R	Decisions and Reports of the European Commission of Human Rights
EC	European Community
ECE	Economic Commission for Europe
ECHR	European Convention for the Protection of Human Rights and Fundamental Freedoms
ECOJ	Official Journal of the European Communities
ECOSOC OR	Official Records of the Economic and Social

	Council of the United Nations
ECR	European Court Reports (EU)
ECSC	European Coal and Steel Community
EEA	European Economic Area
EFTA	European Free Trade Association
EJIL	European Journal of International Law
EP	European Parliament
EPC	European Political Cooperation
ETS	European Treaty Series
EU	European Union
EuGRZ	Europäische Grundrechte Zeitschrift
FAO	Food and Agriculture Organization
FAO Doc.	Document of the Food and Agriculture Organization
GA	General Assembly of the United Nations
GAOR	Official Records of the General Assembly of the United Nations
GATT	General Agreement on Tariffs and Trade
GURI	Gazzetta Ufficiale della Repubblica Italiana
GYIL	German Yearbook of International Law
Hague Recueil	Recueil des Cours (Collected Courses), Hague Academy of International Law
Harv. Int'l LJ	Harvard International Law Journal
HRLJ	Human Rights Law Journal
HRY	Human Rights Yearbook
IAEA	International Atomic Energy Agency
ICAO	International Civil Aviation Organization
ICCPR	International Covenant on Civil and Political Rights
ICESCR	International Covenant on Economic, Social and Cultural Rights
ICJ	International Court of Justice
ICJ Reports	Reports of Judgments, Advisory Opinions and Orders of the International Court of Justice
ICLQ	International and Comparative Law Quarterly
ILC Yearbook	Yearbook of the International Law Commission
ILM	International Legal Materials
ILO	International Labour Organisation
IMF	International Monetary Fund

Int'l Fin. Law Review	International Financial Law Review
Int'l JGR	International Journal of Group Rights
Int'l L.	International Lawyer
Israel Yrb. HR	Israel Yearbook on Human Rights
ITU	International Telecommunication Union
JORF	Journal Officiel de la République Française
Jur.	Jurisprudence of the Court of Justice of the European Communities
League of Nations Doc.	Document of the League of Nations
League of Nations Off.J.	League of Nations Official Journal
LGBl	Liechtensteinisches Landesgesetzblatt
LJIL	Leiden Journal of International Law
LNTS	League of Nations Treaty Series
LQR	Law Quarterly Review
mtg	Meeting
NILR	Netherlands International Law Review
NJCM Bulletin	Nederlands Juristen Comité voor de Mensenrechten Bulletin
NQHR	Netherlands Quarterly of Human Rights
OAS	Organization of American States
OSCE	Organization on Security and Cooperation in Europe
PASIL	Proceedings of the American Society of International Law
PCIJ Reports	Collection of Judgments and Collection of Advisory Opinions of the Permanent Court of International Justice
RBDI	Revue Belge de Droit International
RDI	Revue de Droit International de Sciences Diplomatiques et Politiques
RDP	Revue du Droit Public et de la Science Politique en France et à l'Etranger
Res.	Resolution
RGDIP	Revue Générale de Droit International Public
RIAA	Reports of International Arbitral Awards
SC	Security Council of the United Nations
SCOR	Official Records of the Security Council of the United Nations

Stb.	Staatsblad van het Koninkrijk der Nederlanden
Suppl.	Supplement
Suppl. AJIL	Supplement to the American Journal of International Law: Official documents
SWRO	Recueil Officiel des Lois et Ordonnances de la Confédération Suisse
UMJLR	University of Michigan Journal of Law Reform
UN	United Nations
UN Doc.	Document of the United Nations
UN Yearbook	Yearbook of the United Nations
UNCIO	Documents of the United Nations Conference on International Organization, San Francisco, 1945
UNCTAD	United Nations Conference on Trade and Development
UNESCO	United Nations Educational, Scientific and Cultural Organization
UNESCO Doc.	Document of the United Nations Educational, Scientific and Cultural Organization
UNIDO	United Nations Industrial Development Organization
UNMC	United Nations Monthly Chronicle
UNTS	United Nations Treaty Series
UPU	Universal Postal Union
WHO	World Health Organization
WHO OR	Official Records of the World Health Organization
WIPO	World Intellectual Property Organization
WTO	World Trade Organization

Introduction

'[I]f every ethnic, religious or linguistic group claimed statehood, there would be no limit to fragmentation, and peace, security and economic well-being for all would become ever more difficult to achieve.'[1] 'Les micro-états, de par leur nature profonde, possèdent de façon innée et essentielle les valeurs du respect de la diversité et de la convivialité ... Puissent les grandes puissances de la terre se guider par les règles de comportement que les micro-états ont été obligés d'adopter.'[2] These citations show well, on the one hand, that the world community fears unlimited disintegration and secessions, while, on the other hand, Micro-States themselves do not perceive the disadvantage of the existence of very small States for world peace. In a changing world where practically all armed conflicts are related to either internal or external self-determination, often linked to claims for secession, it is worth while examining the legal aspects involved in the existence of Micro-States. Can anything be learned from the already established Micro-States? How do they survive politically and juridically in the international community of States? What problems may future very small States be faced with? Is micro-statehood better than autonomy?

Although few international lawyers have gone deeply into the subject, looking into the problems of Micro-States can clarify certain rules of international law. Three fields of international law most affect Micro-States: the right of self-determination, statehood and the laws governing international relations. These three domains are interrelated and are of the utmost importance for the creation, maintenance and survival of Micro-States. Conversely, Micro-States can

[1] An Agenda for Peace, UN Doc. A/47/277 (1992), para. 17.
[2] Speech by the Head of the Andorran Government, UN Doc. A/49/PV.6 (1994).

help to improve significant definitions of law. Especially in the fields of self-determination and the criteria for statehood, key-terms are left vague and ambiguous. What is a people with the right of self-determination? How small a people still has this right? Who is allowed to secede and under what circumstances? What is a State according to international law? What are the minimum requirements? Micro-States are at the margins of the international community of States. If one wants to clarify the above questions and search for the smallest unit, the minimum criteria, one has at least to look at those margins.

An in-depth analysis of the development of the right of self-determination and the criteria for statehood in relation to micro-peoples and Micro-States is therefore required. Liechtenstein, San Marino, Monaco and Andorra are European Micro-States which have emerged from longstanding traditional units, outside the colonial context, and which are confronted with a growing European integration. Their international legal and political life is not always obvious and convenient. After centuries of relative inactivity, their international relations have recently come into a new and more significant period. The Vatican City is a Micro-State which stands alone in international legal history, but is an example of the highest degree of independence an enclaved Micro-State can obtain.

Micro-States are special entities of public international law. What distinguishes them from other subjects of law is their, comparatively speaking, extremely small territories and populations. When writing about Micro-States, learned scholars have set up a definition which suited the purposes of their study. Ehrhardt's definition, the most cited and followed, describes a Micro-State as 'eine unabhängige, effektive politische Einheit auf zugehörigem Gebiet mit weniger als 300.000 zugehörigen Einwohnern, die völkerrechtliche Rechten und Pflichten von Staaten nicht hinreichend wahrnehmen kann'.[3] The effect of the chosen definition is to outline the subject and to restrict the number of cases falling within the analysis. The definition as such will not entail any changes in the existence, applicability and legal consequences of a rule of international law. As Micro-States are not distinct legal persons, there is no need to try to find a detailed definition of the term 'Micro-State'. Without giving quantitative limits, it suffices to note that Micro-States are entities with exceptionally small

---

[3] D. Ehrhardt, *Der Begriff des Mikrostaats im Völkerrecht und in der internationalen Ordnung* (1970) p. 102.

territories and populations. This means that their human and natural resources are limited too.

What are the consequences of the presence of these diminutive States in the world community? Putting it briefly, how do Micro-States function in the international community and what can international law learn from their existence?

PART I

The general international legal context

1 Right of self-determination

Documents on self-determination
Historical background

The concept of self-determination has gained more and more attention and support during this century. For Micro-States the right or principle of self-determination is of particular importance, because they can be created through the exercise of that right and rely on the respect of it in order to defend their independence which finds itself under continuous pressure. The fundamental philosophical thought behind the concept of self-determination has historically been that every human being is entitled to control his own destiny.[1] However, this line of thought was not always generally accepted in the past. Individuals were considered subjects of their monarchs who ruled by divine right and thus decided upon their common fate. Only in the periods of history when there was no such exclusive authority residing in the Church or the king did the notion of self-determination appear. Self-government and the consent of the governed are principles adhered to by Greek philosophers like Aristotle and seventeenth- and eighteenth-century thinkers such as John Locke and Jean-Jacques Rousseau.

The political destiny of a group of individuals gathered in a community or State was decided by the aggregate rights and wishes of self-determination of each person. It was the group as a whole which legitimized the government and its form. This notion of self-determination comes close to what in contemporary international law is

---

[1] A. M. Connelly, 'The Right of Self-Determination and International Boundaries', in D. S. Constantopoulos, ed., *Thesaurus Acroasium*, vol. XIV (1985) p. 549.

understood as internal self-determination. It was derived from a natural law in the medieval sense.[2]

Another implication of the concept of self-determination was the question of secession of parts of communities or States. In principle, no such right of separation was conceded. Hugo Grotius maintained that no segment of a State's population could detach itself 'unless it is evident that it cannot save itself in any other way'.[3] Conversely, no part of a State's territory could be ceded without the inhabitants' consent.[4]

Returning to the legitimacy of governments rather than the withdrawal or secession from States, we find similar conditions to those that Grotius had set. In the United States Declaration of Independence (1776) the natural right of individuals to choose their own form of government is activated in case of clear oppression. Even though it could be argued that the United States' independence was a matter of secession from the British State, the drafters of the Declaration preferred to emphasize the change in the form of government.

The Declaration reads:

all men ... are endowed by their Creator with certain inalienable Rights ... That whenever any Form of Government becomes destructive of these ends, it is the Right of the People to alter or abolish it, and to institute new Government ... when a long train of abuses and usurpations ... evinces a design to reduce them under absolute Despotism, it is their right, it is their duty, to throw off such Government.[5]

At this stage of development of the right of self-determination, the subtle difference between change of government within the same community and change of community, combined with a new form of government legitimized by overriding interests, had already become evident.

French revolutionary thinking was characterized by the refusal of a right to independence of secessional fractions, limiting itself to the right of already existing nations to abandon monarchical regimes.[6] According to Article 3 of the French Declaration of the Rights of Man

---

[2] L. C. Buchheit, *Secession: The Legitimacy of Self-Determination* (1978) p. 46.
[3] H. Grotius, *De Jure Bellis Ac Pacis Libri Tres*, vol. II (1651) ch. 6, para. 5.
[4] Ibid., ch. 6, para. 4.
[5] 51 *British and Foreign State Papers*, p. 847.
[6] J. F. Guilhaudis, *Le Droit des Peuples à disposer d'eux-mêmes* (1976) p. 19.

and the Citizen, it is the nation which is essentially the source of all sovereignty, not a fraction of the nation.[7]

The term 'self-determination' was first used in the mid-nineteenth century as a translation for 'Selbstbestimmungsrecht', first employed by German theorists.[8] As so often with philosophical concepts, it is rather difficult to determine who was the first to propagate the principle of self-determination. The right of self-determination appears in Marxist doctrine as a right of the working class only, to liberate themselves from capitalism and unify themselves for the proletarian revolution. This would enable the unification of socialist nations.[9] Lenin and President Woodrow Wilson were the greatest advocates of the right of self-determination at the beginning of this century. The exact meaning of the right and its holders remained unclear.[10] This is not surprising if we look at the interests which were at stake.

Wilson launched his ideas of 'free option of peoples',[11] and 'self-government'[12] in messages and speeches. According to him, a people should not be forced 'under a sovereignty under which it does not want to live'.[13] His principles, however, were to apply only to the territory of the defeated Powers after the First World War, for the aim was to dismember the Habsburg and Ottoman empires. His further endeavours were to use the principle of self-determination in Eastern and Southern Europe to undercut potential Bolshevik regimes.[14] This political consideration forces Fenet to conclude 'c'est donc le souci d'équilibre qui détermine la politique de Wilson, et non l'autodétermination des peuples'.[15] Fenet argues that Wilson never preconized independence for the different national groups within the Austro-Hungarian empire, but incited them against German domination.[16]

---

[7] Text in Y. Mény, *Textes constitutionnels et Documents politiques* (1989) p. 2. Political decisions are to be taken by the nation. Any community which does not constitute a nation has no such freedom of its own. The concept of nation becomes very important, as it is the sole holder of the right to form a government.
[8] Connelly, 'The Right of Self-Determination', p. 552.
[9] Ibid.
[10] J. Verhoeven, 'Peuples et Droit international', in F. Rigaux, ed., *Le Concept de Peuple* (1988) p. 41.
[11] Speech made at Monument Grounds, Washington, 14 June 1917, cited in Guilhaudis, *Le Droit des Peuples*, p. 17.
[12] Message from President Wilson to Russia, 9 June 1917, cited in Buchheit, *Secession*, p. 63.
[13] Ibid.
[14] A. Fenet, ed., *Droits de l'Homme, Droits des Peuples* (1982) p. 36.
[15] Ibid., p. 35.
[16] Ibid., p. 39.

He was searching for an equilibrium in Europe, a guarantee against future wars. The peoples of the Austro-Hungarian empire should have attained some form of self-government within a federal framework.[17] Wilson's underlying intentions were, however, not explicitly expressed and the oppressed peoples of the empire had to be disappointed, for their hopes had been raised too high. Because of all the political interests at stake, an atmosphere of confusion about the true meaning of self-determination resulted. Nevertheless, an imperative principle of action was born out of a mere slogan.[18]

It was still Wilson's wish to insert the principle of self-determination in the Covenant of the League of Nations. His draft Article 3 provided that territorial readjustments would be made 'pursuant to the principle of self-determination'.[19] But this very principle in accordance with which Wilson wanted to create a stable political balance was feared by others to be a source of political instability and rebellion. They apprehended its world-wide consequences. Even within the United States delegation at the Paris Peace Conference of 1919, self-determination was considered politically unmanageable and utterly misleading to minority groups within established States.[20] A British Foreign Office memorandum, instructing the British delegation at the Paris Conference, indicated the clear inadvisability 'to go even the smallest distance in the direction of admitting the claim of American negroes, or the Southern Irish, or the Flemings or Catalans',[21] one of the expected results of including the principle of self-determination in the Covenant. Not surprisingly, the principle was not accepted.

The first written official document embodying the principle of self-determination, though not explicitly calling it that, is the Joint Declaration of the President of the United States and the Prime Minister of the United Kingdom of 14 August 1941, better known as the Atlantic Charter.[22] The second principle enunciated is their desire 'to see no territorial changes that do not accord with the freely expressed wishes of the peoples concerned'.[23] First of all, we must observe the imperativeness of the wishes of peoples, not of nations,

---

[17] Ibid., p. 40.
[18] Ibid., p. 41.
[19] Text of Wilson's draft in D. Miller, *The Drafting of the Covenant*, vol. II (1928) p. 12.
[20] Opinion of Robert Lansing, Wilson's Secretary of State, as cited in Buchheit, *Secession*, p. 65.
[21] Ibid., p. 65 at n. 60.
[22] Text of the Joint Declaration of the President and the Prime Minister in 35 Suppl. AJIL (1941) pp. 191–192.
[23] Ibid., p. 192.

States or communities. The principle is centred in 'peoples'. Secondly, the method of approach must be noted, for the principle is formulated in a negative sense. It does not say: 'through their freely expressed wishes, peoples can decide territorial changes'. It merely indicates that a territorial change can only be effective if the accord of the people concerned has been obtained, thus leaving open the possibility that a body other than the people initiates the territorial change. The accord of the people has to be sought by this body, usually a State. The role of the people is a passive one. It seems they do not have the right of initiative for boundary changes. The supremacy of the people is neither complete nor unconditional.

This passivity contrasts sharply with the third principle of the Atlantic Charter, proclaiming 'the right of all peoples to choose the form of government under which they will live'.[24] The drafters go much further than in the second principle. They speak of a 'right', not just of a 'desire' on their part. Here again it is the 'peoples' who are holders of the right. They play an active part, for they have the right of initiative. No other body can impose a form of government, certainly not by force. The third principle goes on to state that 'sovereign rights and self-government [should be] restored to those who have been forcibly deprived of them'.[25] What is meant by the first part of principle three is that all peoples, and no distinction seems to be made as to the geographical position or other characteristics of the people, have the right to choose their form of government. Within a defined community the form of government can be changed at will. What is meant by the 'peoples concerned' in the case of territorial adjustments? Does that mean, in matters of secession, the people living on the territory which is the object of the change, or does it also include the people from whom the separation is sought? The question cannot be answered on the basis of the text of the Charter.

At the end of the Second World War internal self-determination – the right to choose a form of government within a community, without changing the boundaries – was an accepted principle. External self-determination – deciding one's international status – was limited to the passive right of approval or rejection of territorial changes by a people. According to the Atlantic Charter, self-determination is a principle which contributes to 'a better future of the world',[26] if understood as in principles two and three.

[24] Ibid.
[25] Ibid.
[26] Ibid.

Charter of the United Nations

The term 'self-determination of peoples' is mentioned officially for the first time in the Charter of the United Nations. The insertion of the principle of self-determination into the Charter has been attributed to an initiative of the Soviet Union which was taken up by the United States, the United Kingdom and France.[27] The principle as such is referred to twice, namely, in Article 1, paragraph 2 and Article 55 of the Charter. Article 1, paragraph 2 states: 'The Purposes of the United Nations are: ... 2. To develop friendly relations among nations based on respect for the principle of equal rights and self-determination of peoples, and to take other appropriate measures to strengthen universal peace.' Article 55 is a logical continuation of Article 1, paragraph 2 for it enumerates the objectives the United Nations shall promote '[w]ith a view to the creation of conditions of stability and well-being which are necessary for peaceful and friendly relations among nations, based on respect for the principle of equal rights and self-determination of peoples'. According to Cassese the principle of self-determination in the Charter was formulated 'only as a goal, a political policy of the Organization and its members', not as a definite obligation.[28] Examining Article 1, paragraph 2 and Article 55, it is clear that the drafters consider that respect for the principle of equal rights and self-determination of peoples contributes to peaceful and friendly relations among nations and strengthens universal peace. Logically, one should therefore know of what the respect for this principle consists. The text of the Charter does not elucidate the exact meaning of self-determination. The *travaux préparatoires* show, however, the ambiguity and uncertainty surrounding the content of the subject among the founding members of the United Nations.

The principle of self-determination has been stated together with the principle of equal rights of peoples. Are those two separate principles? In Article 1, paragraph 2 and Article 55, 'principle' has been deliberately stated in the singular form. At the United Nations Conference on International Organization in San Francisco, the report of Committee I/1 explains that 'the principle of equal rights of peoples and that of self-determination' were two complementary parts of one standard of conduct, and that the respect for that prin-

---

[27] Buchheit, *Secession*, p. 73 and Verhoeven, 'Peuples et Droit international', p. 50.
[28] A. Cassese, 'Political Self-Determination – Old Concepts and New Developments', in A. Cassese, ed., *UN Law/Fundamental Rights: Two Topics in International Law* (1979) p. 138.

ciple was a basis for the development of free relations and one of the measures to strengthen universal peace'.[29] Does this indicate that all peoples are equal before the law? Or does it even go further to include the equal right of peoples, without distinction, to self-determination? The mention of equal 'rights' of peoples combined with the 'principle' of self-determination of peoples is confusing. What rights do peoples then share on terms of equality? Surely not the right of self-determination, because it was not formulated as a right but as a principle or a policy?[30] Kelsen found the following interpretation of Article 1, paragraph 2. The term 'nations' used in Article 1, paragraph 2 must have the same meaning as the word 'nations' in the Preamble of the Charter, which states: 'We, the peoples of the United Nations' and 'equal rights ... of nations large and small', and in this formula 'nations' means, probably, 'States'.[31] Article 1, paragraph 2 refers thus to relations among States, 'therefore the term "Peoples", too – in connection with "equal rights" – means probably states, since only states have "equal rights" according to general international law'.[32] The fact that the principles of equal rights and self-determination are complementary and that equal rights can only mean equality of States, leads Kelsen to conclude that only States enjoy the principle of self-determination, that is the principle of sovereignty of States.[33]

Were the terms 'nations' and 'peoples' really used as equivalents for the word 'States'? The Belgian delegation pointed out that in Article 1, paragraph 2 the term 'peoples' could be used instead of 'States', but was open to some confusion with regard to the principle of self-determination where 'peoples' could mean 'the national groups which do not identify themselves with the population of a State'.[34] He preferred to attribute equal rights to States only. In the debate on the correct use of the terms 'States', 'nations' and 'peoples', one delegate

---

[29] Report of the Rapporteur of Committee I/1, Doc. 944. Statement made by the Associate Secretary of Committee I/1, CO/170, XVII UNCIO (1945) p. 142.
[30] The French text of Art. 1 (2) of the Charter speaks of a principle of the right of self-determination: 'le respect du principe de l'égalité de droits des peuples et de leur droit à disposer d'eux-mêmes'.
[31] H. Kelsen, *The Law of the United Nations: A Critical Analysis of its Fundamental Problems* (1950) p. 51.
[32] Ibid., p. 52.
[33] Ibid., pp. 52-53.
[34] Doc. 343, VI UNCIO (1945). The Belgian delegation proposed a new text in which reference was made to 'respect for the essential rights and equality of the *States* [emphasis added] and of the peoples' *right* [emphasis added] of self-determination', in Doc. 374, VI UNCIO (1945).

suggested using the word 'nations' throughout Article 1, paragraph 2, because the use of 'peoples' seemed to introduce the right of secession, an effect he apparently wanted to avoid.[35] It was decided to ask the Secretariat for a special justification for the use of 'States', 'nations' and 'peoples'.[36] The Secretariat in its memorandum explained the use of 'States' 'to indicate a definite political entity'.[37] The word 'nation' was referred to in 'a broad and non-political sense', so as 'to include colonies, mandates, protectorates and quasi-States as well as States. It also has a poetical flavour that is lacking in the word "State"'.[38] The interpretation of 'peoples' is even wider, for it reflects 'the idea of "all mankind" or "all human beings"'.[39] Used in the formulation 'self-determination of peoples', the term is justified as a 'phrase [of] such common usage that no other word seems appropriate'.[40] 'Nations' are 'political entities, States and non-States, whereas "peoples" refers to groups of human beings who may, or may not comprise States or nations'.[41] Peoples are therefore not necessarily States, nor nations. The drafters of the Charter maintained the use of these terms in this sense. This then undercuts Kelsen's interpretation of Article 1, paragraph 2 that 'nations' and 'peoples' are equivalents for 'States'.

What was meant by the principle of equal rights and self-determination of peoples? The word 'and' does not suggest any equal rights 'of' self-determination of peoples. The Coordination Committee agreed to consult the Chairman, Rapporteur and Secretary of the Technical Committee I/1 on whether self-determination meant the capacity of peoples to govern themselves and whether it included a right of secession on the part of peoples within a State.[42] He replied that 'the right of self-determination meant that a people may establish any regime which they favour'.[43] Does this also mean that a people can establish its own State? The answer does not exclude this possibility, for a people may choose a regime of its own, separate from those of other peoples, thus redefining governments not according to

---

[35] CO/170, XVII UNCIO (1945) p. 142.
[36] Ibid.
[37] CO/156, XVIII UNCIO (1945) p. 657.
[38] Ibid.
[39] Ibid., p. 658.
[40] Ibid.
[41] Ibid.
[42] CO/170, XVII UNCIO (1945) p. 143.
[43] Doc. WD 424, XVII UNCIO (1945), Doc. 163.

the number of States but according to the number of peoples in the world.

On the basis of the given information, Kelsen concluded that self-determination is 'a principle of internal policy, the principle of democratic government'.[44] Emerson believes that the principle implies 'the right of self-government of peoples and not the right of secession',[45] whereas Buchheit finds no right of secession can be 'supported or discredited by reference to the *travaux préparatoires* of the San Francisco Conference'.[46] Cassese deduces 'a generic right to self-government'.[47] As one delegate put it during the debates, was self-determination 'the right of a State to have its own democratic institutions or the right of secession?'.[48] It should be recalled that no delegate could give an unambiguous answer to that question or wanted to answer it. The delegations were 'reluctant to encourage a debate of many days on the meaning of "self-determination"' since they were not sure that there could be agreement.[49]

One can deduce from the debates that the principle of a people, constituting a State, choosing its own form of government is generally accepted. This was not an innovation considering the historical development of self-determination and the Atlantic Charter.[50] Carefully, we maintain the use of the word 'principle', for although the term 'equal rights' is mentioned in Article 1, paragraph 2 of the Charter, no bridge has been constructed between these rights, yet of uncertain tenor, and self-determination. One even wonders about the juridical necessity of the inclusion of the principle of equal rights. When the Charter was drafted no specific rights belonging to peoples existed in international law. Two interpretations of the phrase 'the principle of equal rights and self-determination of peoples' are possible. First, no 'right' of self-determination is accepted and as no other 'rights' of peoples exist, the addition of 'equal rights' is incorrect and contradictory. Secondly, a certain 'right' of self-determination exists on the footing of equality between peoples, but then the formula 'principle' of self-determination is too weak. Hence, mentioning the principle of equal 'rights' and

---

[44] Kelsen, *The Law of the United Nations*, pp. 51–52.
[45] R. Emerson, *From Empire to Nation: The Rise to Self-Assertion of Asian and African Peoples* (1960) p. 301.
[46] Buchheit, *Secession*, p. 73.
[47] Cassese, 'Political Self-Determination', p. 139.
[48] CO/170, XVII UNCIO (1945) p. 143.
[49] Ibid.
[50] See p. 11 above.

the 'principle' of self-determination in one phrase and saying they are complementary is a *contradictio in terminis*.

The term 'self-government' is referred to twice in the Charter of the United Nations: in Article 73 (b) and Article 76 (b). In Article 73 (b) the administering Member States of Non-Self-Governing Territories agree '(b) to develop self-government, to take due account of the political aspirations of the peoples, and to assist them in the progressive development of their free political institutions, according to the particular circumstances of each territory and its peoples and their varying stages of advancement'. Nothing leads us to conclude that an absolute right to self-government, let alone to independence, exists, and the obligation of the administering Powers is largely left to their discretion and their interpretation of the circumstances.

According to Article 76 (b) a basic objective of the trusteeship system is to promote 'progressive development towards self-government or independence as may be appropriate to the particular circumstances of each territory and its peoples and the freely-expressed wishes of the peoples concerned and as may be provided by the terms of each trusteeship agreement'. Here again no unconditional right to self-government exists though the possibility of independence is expressly mentioned. The administering States have not taken any commitments upon themselves to offer full external self-determination to the peoples of Non-Self-Governing and Trust Territories. In order to grant self-government, it is not the wish of the people which is the imperative and sole condition, but other social, political or economic circumstances can also be taken into account by the administrator.

Does self-government include independence? Following the text of Articles 73 and 76 literally, the answer would be in the negative. In Article 73 (b) 'Self-government' is set apart from the 'development of their free political institutions'. Article 76 (b) refers to the 'development towards self-government *or* [emphasis added] independence'. The terms seem to be alternatives and different from each other. But not all States would have agreed with this differentiation. The communist States were very much in favour of granting independence to the Trust and Non-Self-Governing Territories. Whether this was out of true belief in the right of self-determination or to weaken the colonial Powers is quite another matter. It was therefore not uncommon to understand self-government as including independence.[51]

---

[51] M. Pomerance, *Self-Determination in Law and Practice: The New Doctrine in the United Nations* (1982) p. 10. See Principle VI (a) of GA Res. 1541 (XV).

At the time of the drafting of the Charter of the United Nations no right to full self-determination could be proved to exist in international law. Only the right of a people living within a State to choose the form of government of that State seems to have been accepted. Nevertheless, the principle found its place for the first time in a legally binding document and could begin to develop and define itself in international law through the activities of the United Nations.

General Assembly Resolutions

On the basis of Articles 1, paragraph 2 and 55 of the Charter of the United Nations, the General Assembly formulated a number of recommendations in the form of resolutions which, though not legally binding, have helped to form the notion of self-determination. These resolutions marked the new era of decolonization.[52] The most famous resolution on the right to self-determination to which numerous later resolutions have referred is General Assembly Resolution 1514 (XV) of 14 December 1960, called the Declaration on the Granting of Independence to Colonial Countries and Peoples. The main reason behind Resolution 1514 is, as the preamble explains, 'the necessity of bringing to a speedy and unconditional end colonialism in all its forms and manifestations'. Colonialism is seen to militate against the United Nations' ideal of universal peace and human rights.

Paragraph 2 of the Declaration reads: 'All peoples have the right to self-determination; by virtue of that right they freely determine their political status and freely pursue their economic, social and cultural development.' A special reference to Trust and Non-Self-Governing Territories is made in paragraph 5 of the Declaration stating: 'Immediate steps shall be taken, in Trust and Non-Self-Governing Territories or all other territories which have not yet attained independence, to transfer all powers to the peoples of those territories ... in order to enable them to enjoy complete independence and freedom.' No other conditions but the 'freely expressed will and desire' of the peoples lead to independence. Paragraph 3 specifies: 'Inadequacy of political, economic, social or educational preparedness should never serve as a pretext for delaying independence.'

---

[52] The first resolution mentioning the right of peoples and nations to self-determination as a fundamental human right is GA Res. 421 D (V). A later Res. 545 (VI) asked for the inclusion in the International Covenants on Human Rights of the phrase: 'All peoples shall have the right of self-determination.' GA Res. 637 (VII) laid down a right of self-determination of the peoples of Non-Self-Governing and Trust Territories.

Resolution 1514 extends clearly the scope of Articles 1, paragraph 2, 55, 73 (b) and 76 (b) of the Charter of the United Nations. It is even said to be an attempt to revise the Charter in a binding manner.[53] Compared with the Charter, Resolution 1514 sets a 'right' of self-determination for all peoples and interprets that right in paragraph 2. The wishes of the peoples are the only condition determining the political status. No other conditions or reservations may be invoked (paragraphs 3 and 5). Furthermore, it is incompatible with the purposes and principles of the Charter to aim 'at the partial or total disruption of the national unity and territorial integrity of a country' (paragraph 6).

Although the title of Resolution 1514 could make us think otherwise, the right proclaimed in the Declaration is formulated as a general one. Paragraph 2 aims at a universal application of the right of self-determination of *all* peoples, not just of all colonial peoples. Paragraph 1 declared that 'the subjection of peoples to alien subjugation, domination and exploitation constitutes a denial of fundamental human rights'. Subsequently, and constructed as one element or consequence of the general right to self-determination, the Trust and Non-Self-Governing Territories are granted the right to independence (paragraph 5). These territories were named separately, as the United Nations considered it had an important role to play in the decolonization process. On the basis of Resolution 1514 it cannot be alleged that a right to self-determination exists exclusively for colonial peoples.

Whether a 'right' of self-determination was accepted as a customary rule in international law is another question. In general, the colonial Powers had abstained from voting on the Declaration, because they thought it imposed too many obligations on them which were not justified by the Charter. They continued, however, to support a right to self-government of the colonial territories, but taking into account all specific circumstances of these territories.[54]

In the debates in the General Assembly on draft Resolution 1514, special attention was paid to small Non-Self-Governing Territories. In general, the delegates emphasized the special circumstances of these numerically small peoples in deciding their future political status.

---

[53] Pomerance, *Self-Determination*, p. 11.
[54] UN Doc. A/15/PV.925 (1960) p. 985, para. 45. GA Res. 1514 (XV) was passed by eighty-nine votes to nil with nine abstentions: Australia, Belgium, Dominican Republic, France, Portugal, South Africa, Spain, the United Kingdom and the United States.

The British representative (talking about populations of less than 100,000) mentioned the possible geographical isolation of small territories and their insufficient economies.[55] He also advanced the case of a small territory threatened by a large and powerful neighbour. 'They fear that their independence might not long endure and that they might, unprotected, lose the political freedom which they now enjoy', so he said.[56] The decision concerning the form of independence should, in these small British colonies, not be taken immediately, but be worked out by the United Kingdom with the people concerned.[57] The Jordanian delegate observed that 'to some small States ... the question of how to maintain and safeguard independence is perhaps as difficult as how to achieve it'.[58]

On 24 October 1970, the General Assembly adopted Resolution 2625 entitled the Declaration on Principles of International Law concerning Friendly Relations and Co-operation among States in accordance with the Charter of the United Nations (hereafter, Declaration on Friendly Relations). According to the Preamble of the Declaration on Friendly Relations, the principles enunciated are codified and constitute basic principles of international law. The drafters have been inspired by the principles embodied in the Charter of the United Nations and have elaborated upon them.[59] One of the principles included in the Declaration on Friendly Relations is the principle of equal rights and self-determination of peoples. Discussions on this principle started in 1966.

A Special Committee on Principles of International Law concerning Friendly Relations and Co-operation among States (hereafter, Special Committee) was established to prepare the Declaration on Friendly Relations. Furthermore, the drafts were discussed in the Sixth Committee of the General Assembly. The final text on self-determination with which we shall concern ourselves reads as follows (numbers of paragraphs added):

1 By virtue of the principle of equal rights and self-determination of peoples enshrined in the Charter of the United Nations, all peoples have the right freely to determine, without external interference, their political status and to pursue their economic, social and

---

[55] Ibid., pp. 984–985, para. 39.
[56] Ibid., p. 985, para. 40.
[57] Ibid., p. 985, paras. 41 and 45.
[58] UN Doc. A/15/PV.930 (1960) p. 1057, para. 50.
[59] Paras. 2 and 3, General Part of the Declaration on Friendly Relations.

cultural development, and every State has the duty to respect this right in accordance with the provisions of the Charter.

2   Every State has the duty to promote, through joint and separate action, realization of the principle of equal rights and self-determination of peoples, in accordance with the provisions of the Charter ... and bearing in mind that subjection of peoples to alien subjugation, domination and exploitation constitutes a violation of the principle, as well as a denial of fundamental human rights, and is contrary to the Charter.

...

6   The territory of a colony or other Non-Self-Governing Territory has, under the Charter, a status separate and distinct from the territory of the State administering it; and such separate and distinct status under the Charter shall exist until the people of the colony or Non-Self-Governing Territory have exercised their right of self-determination in accordance with the Charter, and particularly its purposes and principles.

7   Nothing in the foregoing paragraphs shall be construed as authorizing or encouraging any action which would dismember or impair, totally or in part, the territorial integrity or political unity of sovereign and independent States conducting themselves in compliance with the principle of equal rights and self-determination of peoples as described above and thus possessed of a government representing the whole people belonging to the territory without distinction as to race, creed or colour.

The first paragraph is a clear combination of Article 1, paragraph 2 of the Charter, General Assembly Resolution 1514 and Article 1 of the International Covenants on Human Rights of 1966. 'By virtue of the principle ... all peoples have the right' of self-determination. There were four main draft declarations of which two proclaimed only the right and two only the principle of self-determination.[60] The adherents of the 'principle' of self-determination defended their choice by arguing that if it was expressed as a right, it was difficult to determine in which category of persons such a right inhered.[61] Others believed that the principle included the right of self-determination.[62]

---

[60] The Czechoslovakian proposal read: 'All peoples have the right to self-determination': UN Doc. A/7326 (1968) pp. 52–53. The joint proposal by Algeria, Burma, Cameroon, Dahomey, Ghana, India, Kenya, Lebanon, Madagascar, Nigeria, Syria, the United Arab Republic and Yugoslavia stated: 'All peoples have the inalienable right to self-determination'; ibid., p. 53. The proposals by the United States and by the United Kingdom both read: 'Every State has the duty to respect the principle of equal rights and self-determination of peoples': ibid., pp. 54–56.
[61] Ibid., p. 60, para. 157.
[62] Ibid., p. 60, para. 160.

Czechoslovakia stated that the principle was no longer to be considered a mere moral or political postulate, but rather a settled principle of modern international law.[63] Eventually a compromise was reached in paragraph 1 of the Declaration on Friendly Relations: by virtue of the principle of self-determination, all peoples have a right to self-determination. Under paragraph 2 every State has the duty to *promote* the realization of the *principle* of equal rights and self-determination of peoples, while they have to *respect* the *right* of self-determination under the first paragraph.

The second major point raised concerned the definition of 'peoples' and consequently the situations where the right of self-determination was applicable. For the first time the argument was heard that the right of self-determination did not apply to all peoples, but only to colonial peoples or peoples living under alien subjugation, domination and exploitation.[64] Others did not go that far, but nevertheless believed that the right of self-determination applied essentially to peoples living under colonial domination.[65] Some delegates protested against this narrow interpretation, stressing the universal applicability of the principle.[66] Giving the principle of self-determination any other meaning would be contrary to the Charter, according to them. Conversely, the States which understood the right as a right of colonial peoples only, based their interpretation on the same Charter and subsequent resolutions on self-determination.[67] As we have seen, the principle of equal rights and self-determination of peoples embodied in the Charter was meant to be a universally applicable principle.[68] In all the debates that followed the universal value of the principle or right of self-determination was emphasized. It is true that the United Nations has given a good deal of attention to the peoples of Non-Self-Governing and Trust Territories, but it did not intend to limit the right of self-determination to these peoples. The argument that only colonial peoples have the right to self-determination cannot be upheld if in addition one states that the Declaration on Friendly Relations is a codification based on the principles of the Charter. The Declaration on Friendly Relations

---

[63] UN Doc. A/AC.125/SR.40 (1966) p. 4, para. 2.
[64] Indian delegate: UN Doc. A/AC.125/SR.43 (1966) p. 16, para. 40.
[65] Ghanaian delegate: UN Doc. A/AC.125/SR.40 (1966) p. 8, para. 11 and United Arab Republic delegate: UN Doc. A/AC.125/SR.44 (1966) p. 12, para. 23.
[66] British delegate: UN Doc. A/AC.125/SR.44 (1966) p. 8., para. 14 and Australian delegate: ibid., p. 14, para. 28.
[67] Indian delegate: UN Doc. A/AC.125/SR.43 (1966) p. 16, para. 40.
[68] See pp. 12–14 above.

even explains that '[n]othing in this Declaration shall be construed as prejudicing in any manner ... the rights of peoples under the Charter, taking into account the elaboration of these rights in this Declaration'.[69] In interpreting the Declaration we must therefore not oppose the principles of the Charter. The Declaration on Friendly Relations mentions the colonial problem twice: in paragraph 2 the duty 'to bring a speedy end to colonialism' and in paragraph 6 the separate status of colonies and Non-Self-Governing Territories.

This brings us to another point. Although not limited to colonial peoples, the term 'peoples' could have been understood by the drafters in another limitative way. The Czechoslovakian proposal first enunciates the (general) right to self-determination and spends the subsequent paragraphs on the elimination of colonialism and racial discrimination.[70] The joint proposal submitted by Algeria and other non-aligned States also begins with the affirmation of the inalienable right of all peoples to self-determination.[71] The second paragraph states that in accordance with that principle, '[t]he subjection of peoples to alien subjugation, domination and exploitation as well as any other forms of colonialism, constitutes a violation of the principle of equal rights and self-determination of peoples'. Paragraph 2 seems a specification of the general right to self-determination. There may be other situations which constitute a violation of the principle of self-determination, but alien subjugation, domination and exploitation in any case violate this principle. The Algerian delegate explained that he distinguished three situations to which the right of self-determination applied.

The first one was the case of independent peoples in their relations between each other, hence the freedom of action of States. The second situation concerned self-determination of peoples within States. He did not accept a right of secession as he believed it fell entirely under the domestic jurisdiction of States to grant peoples such a right or not. The only exceptions made were entities established and maintained by force and in violation of international law. The third and last case in which the right of self-determination could be invoked was oppressed peoples, namely those living under colonial or racial domination.[72] One can see that the joint proposal of the non-aligned

---

[69] Para. 2, second sentence, General Part of the Declaration on Friendly Relations.
[70] Full text in UN Doc. A/7326 (1968) pp. 52–53.
[71] Ibid., p. 53.
[72] UN Doc. A/AC.125/SR.43 (1966) pp. 6–7, paras. 13–15.

States does not restrict the right of self-determination to peoples under alien subjugation, domination and exploitation. Other peoples, namely independent peoples, also have this right, though they are not considered to be under any form of domination. The view that the right of self-determination extended to dependent and independent peoples was shared by many delegates.[73]

There appeared to be agreement in the Special Committee that it would be unduly narrow to consider that States were the only beneficiaries of the principle.[74] There seemed to be general consensus that the peoples of existing independent States had the right of self-determination.[75] Furthermore, all four draft proposals provided for a right of self-determination of colonial peoples or peoples under alien subjugation, domination and exploitation.[76]

The next question is whether, besides independent peoples of existing States and colonial peoples, there are other peoples who hold the right of self-determination. Some States accepted the right of secession from existing States as inherent in the right of self-determination.[77] Others opposed this view, stating that it was doubtful whether such a right existed and could be codified.[78] They were cautious not 'to plant seeds of insurrection and secession within individual States'.[79] Under the United States and British drafts a limited right of secession was accepted. The United States proposal included 'a zone of occupation ensuing upon the termination of military hostilities' and 'a territory geographically distinct and ethnically diverse from the remainder of that State's territory, even though not as a colony or

---

[73] Yugoslavia: UN Doc. A/AC.125/SR.40 (1966) p. 10, para. 17. Canada and Nepal: A/C.6/SR.899–955 (1966) p. 166, para. 5 and p. 186, para. 19.
[74] UN Doc. A/6799 (1967) p. 98, para. 194.
[75] Only Nigeria interpreted Art. 1 (2) of the Charter of the United Nations as only applicable to colonial peoples and not States: UN Doc. A/AC.125/SR.41 (1966) p. 14, para. 27. This is an incorrect interpretation: see pp. 13–15 above.
[76] The Czechoslovakian proposal mentioned 'colonialism'. The Algerian and other Non-Aligned Countries' joint proposal stated 'subjection of peoples to alien subjugation, domination and exploitation as well as any other forms of colonialism'; the United States proposal provided for 'a colony or other Non-Self-Governing Territory' and 'a Trust territory'; the British proposal included 'peoples [under] alien subjugation, domination and exploitation' as well as 'a colony or other Non-Self-Governing Territory' and 'a Trust Territory'. UN Doc. A/7326 (1968) pp. 52–56.
[77] Yugoslavia: UN Doc. A/AC.125/SR.40 (1966) p. 11, para. 19 and Chile: UN Doc. A/AC.125/SR.43 (1966) p. 7, para. 44.
[78] France: UN Doc. A/AC.125/SR.41 (1966) p. 9, para. 13 and India: UN Doc. A/AC.125/SR.43 (1966) p. 16, para. 40. See also UN Doc. A/6799 (1966) pp. 98–99.
[79] French delegate: UN Doc. A/C.6/SR.932 (1966) p. 193, para. 33.

other Non-Self-Governing Territory'.[80] However, if a State possessed 'a representative Government, effectively functioning as such to all distinct peoples within its territory' the principle of self-determination was satisfied.[81] The requirement of representative government was criticized for the fact that it imposed political views on the constitutional law and practice of other States and could be used as a pretext to subvert the territorial integrity of existing States.[82] In general, the United States and British attempts to define in a more precise way all the situations to which the principle of self-determination applied were received with mixed feelings. The adherents of these drafts welcomed their clarity and believed they codified existing principles.[83] Others either did not accept the proposed cases of secession or thought it undesirable to draft precise texts, while 'the world might experience new and as yet unforeseeable ground swells'.[84] Concern was also expressed that the reference to a geographically distinct territory might deny the right of self-determination to a number of oppressed peoples.[85] The general spirit of the debates unambiguously emphasized the relationship between a territory and a people inhabiting it.

In the end, a compromise was reached. Paragraph 2 of the Declaration on Friendly Relations, after recalling that every State has to promote the realization of the principle of equal rights and self-determination of peoples, states 'and bearing in mind that subjection of peoples to alien subjugation, domination and exploitation constitutes a violation of the principle'.[86] Considering the preceding discussion, the 'bearing in mind' formula does not intend to restrict violations of the right of self-determination to cases of alien subjugation, domination and exploitation. Independent peoples of existing States can see their right of self-determination violated too, though this does not necessarily imply that they are under alien subjugation,

---

[80] Para. 2, A (1)(b) and (2) of the United States draft. This proposal was supported by Australia, Canada, Lebanon, the Netherlands and Venezuela. The British draft mentioned 'a zone of military occupation' and 'a territory which is geographically distinct and ethnically or culturally diverse from the remainder of the territory of the State administering it' (para. 4).
[81] Para. 2, B of the United States draft and para. 4 of the British draft.
[82] UN Doc. A/6799 (1967) p. 99, para. 195.
[83] E.g. the Netherlands: UN Doc. A/AC.125/SR.44 (1966) p. 10, para. 18.
[84] French delegate: UN Doc. A/C.6/SR.932 (1966) p. 193, para. 33.
[85] UN Doc. A/6547 (1966) p. 33, para. 69.
[86] This appeared both in the Non-Aligned Countries' draft and in the British draft.

domination and exploitation. The problem is then to know what 'alien' means and what degree of oppression is necessary to violate the right of self-determination. The *travaux préparatoires* do not make us much wiser on this subject, but the Sub-Commission on Prevention of Discrimination and Protection of Minorities has tackled the problem in the studies of Gros Espiell and Cristescu.[87] We shall refer to this in a subsequent section.[88]

Paragraph 6 of the Declaration on Friendly Relations declares that a colony or other Non-Self-Governing Territory has a separate and distinct status from the territory of the State administering it.[89] The function of this stipulation was to undercut the argument that the colonial territory constituted an integral part of the territory of the colonial Power, as was, for example, claimed by Portugal vis-à-vis its colonies. The administering State can thus not rely on the respect for its territorial integrity. The independence of a colony cannot be a case of secession, for it never constituted a part of the metropolitan State.

The territorial integrity and political unity of a State is inviolable under paragraph 7 of the Declaration on Friendly Relations if the State complies with the principle of equal rights and self-determination of peoples 'and [is] *thus* [emphasis added] possessed of a government representing the whole people belonging to a territory without distinction as to race, creed or colour'. This is a variation of the exoneration clause we found in the United States and British drafts. 'The whole people' of paragraph 7 of the Declaration means either that one State can have but one people, or that within a State more than one people can coexist. The latter meaning seems correct if we read it in combination with the prohibition of discrimination on grounds of race, creed or colour. Only if such a representative government does not exist can the territorial integrity and political unity of a State be disregarded and secession allowed. The obligation of representative government seems to form part of the internal right of self-determination. A representative government is set up as an ideal result of internal self-determination. If this form of internal self-determination is denied, the peoples have the right to external self-determination. This is historically speaking nothing new.[90]

---

[87] Study by Gros Espiell: UN Doc. E/CN.4/Sub.2/377 (1976) and study by Cristescu: UN Doc. E/CN.4/Sub.2/404/Rev. 1 (1981).
[88] See pp. 37–40 below.
[89] This was in conformity with the Czechoslovakian and Non-Aligned Countries' drafts.
[90] See pp. 7–11 above.

Although at times confusingly phrased, the Declaration adds to the concept of self-determination the peoples subjected to alien subjugation, domination and exploitation. The holders of the right of self-determination are therefore the peoples of independent States, peoples under alien subjugation, domination and exploitation (whether or not colonial) and peoples without representative governments. Only populations living under these conditions are recognized as 'peoples' with the right of self-determination. The subsequent years have shown that States have not consistently adhered to these principles.[91]

After the Declaration on Friendly Relations of 1970, no major resolutions, covenants or declarations on the right of self-determination have been adopted by the General Assembly of the United Nations. This does not mean that self-determination has lost its interest. Every year, since 1980, the General Assembly of the United Nations has adopted a resolution on the universal realization of the right of peoples to self-determination.[92] Paragraph 1 of these resolutions, the text of which is reiterated each time, reads: '1. Reaffirms that the universal realization of the rights of all peoples, *including* [emphasis added] those under colonial, foreign and alien domination, to self-determination is a fundamental condition for the effective guarantee and observance of human rights and for the preservation and promotion of such rights.' In these resolutions, the General Assembly demands special attention to the violation of the right to self-determination 'resulting from foreign military intervention, aggression or occupation'.[93] The right of self-determination is formulated as a general and universal right. Peoples living under 'colonial, foreign and alien domination' are one group of peoples in whom the right of self-determination is vested. 'Colonial, foreign and alien domination' does not refer only to colonies but also to any other territory in the world where peoples are subjected to 'foreign military intervention, aggression or occupation'. Any reference to the 'principle' of self-determination has disappeared. Henceforth, the General Assembly speaks solely of the 'right' of self-determination as a human right and a fundamental condition for the effective guarantee, observance, preservation and promotion of all other human rights.[94] The 1993

---

[91] See pp. 94–95 below.
[92] See, e.g., GA Res. 47/84.
[93] Paras. 2–5 of the GA Resolutions on universal realization of the right of peoples to self-determination.
[94] Paras. 1 and 5 of the GA Resolutions on universal realization of the right of peoples to self-determination.

Vienna Declaration and Programme of Action adopts the same formula concerning the right of peoples to self-determination as the Declaration on Friendly Relations.[95]

International covenants on human rights

Under this heading, the right of self-determination appearing in two international covenants on human rights drafted by the United Nations will be discussed. Those two covenants are the International Covenant on Civil and Political Rights (hereafter, ICCPR) and the International Covenant on Economic, Social and Cultural Rights (hereafter, ICESCR), both of 16 December 1966.

The initiative for including the right of self-determination in the Covenants came from the General Assembly. In its Resolution 545 (VI) of 5 February 1952 the Assembly decided to include in the Covenants an article to be drafted in the following terms: 'All peoples shall have the right of self-determination.'[96]

Eventually, the adopted article on self-determination, identical in both Covenants, became Article 1, reading as follows:

> 1 All peoples have the right of self-determination. By virtue of that right they freely determine their political status and freely pursue their economic, social and cultural development.
> 2 All peoples may, for their own ends, freely dispose of their natural wealth and resources, without prejudice to any obligations arising out of international economic co-operation, based upon the principle of mutual benefit, and international law. In no case may a people be deprived of its own means of subsistence.
> 3 The States Parties to the present Covenant, including those having responsibility for the administration of Non-Self-Governing and Trust Territories, shall promote the realization of the right of self-determination, and shall respect that right, in conformity with the provisions of the Charter of the United Nations.[97]

---

[95] Para. 2 of the Vienna Declaration and Programme of Action, UN Doc. A/CONF.157/24 (Part I) (1993).
[96] GA Res. 545 (VI) was adopted by 42 votes to 7 with 5 abstentions.
[97] Art. 1 was adopted by the Third Committee of the General Assembly on 29 Nov. 1955. Voting results were as follows: Art. 1, first sentence of para. 1 – 41 to none, 17 abstentions. Art. 1, second sentence of para. 1 – 30 to 5, 23 abstentions. Art. 1 (1) as a whole – 31 to 9, 18 abstentions. Art. 1 (2) – 26 to 13, 19 abstentions. Art. 1 (3) – 32 to none, 26 abstentions. Art. 1 as a whole – 33 to 12, 13 abstentions. UN Doc. A/C.3/SR.676 (1955) pp. 260–262. It should be noted that para. 2 of GA Res. 1514 (XV) copies the adopted draft Art. 1 (1) of the Human Rights Covenants.

During the drafting procedure of Article 1 many uncertainties were raised as to the nature, scope and limits of the right of self-determination. Due to these ambiguities, some States tried to find other solutions. The Soviet Union had preferred to form a committee of experts composed of, among others, jurists and historians charged to study the subject of self-determination thoroughly.[98] Australia, the Netherlands and the United Kingdom proposed to delete Article 1 completely.[99] Brazil submitted an amendment to the effect that the right of self-determination would only appear in the preamble of the Covenants. Article 1 was to be included in a separate protocol.[100] China suggested the introduction of the right of self-determination in a third separate covenant so as to gain a wider support for the first two covenants.[101] Even the Secretary-General of the United Nations put forth the idea of inserting the right of self-determination in a declaration attached to the Covenants.[102]

None of these suggestions and amendments was followed. Instead, on the joint proposal of Cuba, Ecuador and El Salvador, a Working Party was established.[103] It was finally the text which the Working Party submitted for consideration which was adopted as revised under the amendment of Yugoslavia.[104] The amendment put forward by Yugoslavia was a most significant one.[105] The Working Party's draft Article 1, paragraph 3 stipulated that '[t]he States parties to the Covenant having responsibility for the administration of Non-Self-Governing and Trust Territories shall promote the realization of the right of self-determination in such Territories'.[106] The Yugoslavian amendment aimed at widening this State duty to 'all' the States Parties, 'including' administering States. Furthermore, they were not only to promote the realization of the right, but were also to 'respect that right'.[107] Thus, all States have to respect and promote the right of self-determination.

---

[98] UN Doc. A/3077 (1955) p. 14, para. 41.
[99] Ibid., p. 16.
[100] UN Doc. A/C.3/L.460 (1955) and UN Doc. A/C.3/SR.650 (1955) p. 129.
[101] UN Doc. A/C.3/SR.642 (1955) p. 89.
[102] UN Doc. A/C.3/SR.633 (1955).
[103] UN Doc. A/C.3/L.477/Rev.1 (1955) and UN Doc. A/3077 (1955) p. 17. The nine States represented in the Working Party were all supporters of the right of self-determination: Brazil, Costa Rica, El Salvador, Greece, India, Pakistan, Poland, Syria and Venezuela.
[104] Ibid., p. 20.
[105] Ibid., p. 21.
[106] Ibid., p. 20.
[107] Yugoslavian amendment to Art. 1 (3) adopted by 32 votes to none, with 26 abstentions. See also n. 97, p. 27 above.

In order to draw a clearer picture of the meaning and applicability of the right of self-determination, we shall set some of the arguments brought forward in the debates alongside each other. Not surprisingly, it was the administering and European States which opposed the inclusion of Article 1 in the Covenants.

The first objection raised was the fact that in 1948 the Universal Declaration of Human Rights had made no mention of the right of self-determination.[108] Although not every human right was included in the Universal Declaration, nor every human right of the Declaration was to be adopted in the Covenants, it was thought strange that the right of self-determination had been omitted from the Declaration. The adherents of Article 1 regarded self-determination as a fundamental right and essential for the enjoyment of all other human rights. The opposers wondered therefore why this corner-stone of human rights had not been included in the Universal Declaration of Human Rights. They concluded that the fundamental character of the right of self-determination was open to question.[109]

The second counter-argument concerned the legal nature of self-determination. It was argued that only a principle of self-determination existed, not a right under the Charter of the United Nations. Self-determination was regarded as a political principle[110] of very strong moral force, but too complex to translate into legal terms in an instrument which was to be legally enforced.[111] The majority of States wanted the right of self-determination to appear at the forefront of the Covenants.[112] The General Assembly had already decided to include an article on that right. They contested the fact that an attempt was made to broaden and distort the provisions of the Charter. It was only a reaffirmation. Accepting the principle meant that peoples had the right to ask that the principle in question should be applied to them – it amounted therefore to a right.[113] Others regarded the inclusion as a premature codification, and argued that, as Article 1 was not mentioned in Chapters XI and XII of the Charter, the obligations could not be accepted without amending the Charter.[114] All States agreed with the principle of self-determination,

---

[108] British delegate: UN Doc. A/C.3/SR.642 (1955) p. 90, para. 13.
[109] UN Doc. A/C.3/SR.644 and 652 (1955) p. 100, para. 12 and p. 143, para. 18.
[110] British delegate: UN Doc. A/C.3/SR.642 (1955) p. 90, para. 11.
[111] UN Doc. A/3077 (1955) p. 12, para. 31.
[112] Ibid., p. 13.
[113] Byelorussian delegate: UN Doc. A/C.3/SR.644 (1955) p. 101, para. 19.
[114] Ecuadorean delegate: UN Doc. A/C.3/SR.650 (1955) p. 131, para. 14.

a majority supported the right of self-determination[115] and some believed in a combination of both: the principle of the right of self-determination.[116]

The third point of opposition was that the right of self-determination was a collective human right, and therefore had no place in a covenant on individual rights.[117] It was a collective right to be exercised by a people as a whole. Others considered this argument unacceptable. The distinction between collective and individual rights was misleading. Here it was only the expression of individual will through collective methods.[118] Where was the difference between the right to elect and be elected and the right of self-determination?[119] The distinction was artificial, so it was said. Individuals enjoyed the right of self-determination, but it had a meaning only because individuals lived in a society.[120] No delegate foresaw difficulties which the distinction between collective and individual rights could make under Article 1 of the Optional Protocol to the ICCPR. This article only accepts communications from 'individuals' claiming to be victims of a violation of 'any' of the rights set forth in the Covenant. We shall come back to this problem later on.[121]

The fourth and most decisive reason for opposing the inclusion of Article 1 in the Covenants was its vague and ambiguous provisions. The vagueness, especially of the term 'peoples', was the main explanation for the negative votes cast on Article 1.[122] It was feared that a

---

[115] Amongst these were also States which voted against Art. 1, for example Denmark: UN Doc. A/C.3/SR.676 (1955) p. 262, para. 33.

[116] Luxembourg and France: UN Doc. A/C.3/SR.677 (1955) p. 265, para. 6 and p. 267, para. 24, respectively. This was probably due to the fact that the French text of Art. 1 (2) of the Charter states: '*principe* de l'égalité de droits des peuples et de leur *droit* à disposer d'eux-mêmes' (emphasis added).

[117] Swedish, Dutch and Canadian delegates: UN Doc. A/C.3/SR.641, 642 and 645 (1955) pp. 86, 91 and 103. The Belgian delegate also believed it to be a collective right, but did not consider that a major obstacle to the inclusion of Art. 1 in the Covenants: UN Doc. A/C.3/SR.643 (1955) p. 94, para. 8.

[118] Czechoslovak and El Salvadorean delegates: UN Doc. A/C.3/SR.645 (1955) pp. 104–105, paras. 12 and 21.

[119] Ibid., p. 105, para. 22.

[120] Soviet delegate: UN Doc. A/C.3/SR.646 (1955) p. 109, para. 21.

[121] See pp. 63–66 below.

[122] UN Doc. A/C.3/SR.676 (1955), pp. 262 ff. This reason was invoked by Australia, Belgium, Canada, Denmark, France, Luxembourg, Netherlands, New Zealand, Sweden, Turkey and the United Kingdom. It should be noted that the United States did not participate too actively in the debates, as it had decided not to sign the Covenants. It voted against Art. 1 because it did not find enough guarantees for a prompt, adequate and effective compensation in Art. 1 (2).

vague and imprecise formulation would threaten the very existence of certain States, lead to abuses and encourage manipulations by totalitarian regimes.[123] The centre of the problem was the right to secession, meaning the withdrawal of a group of individuals from an existing State. The effects were feared to be appalling for world peace. The right of self-determination was said to be 'political dynamite'.[124] The opposing States also worried about who would have to interpret the term 'peoples'. The entire responsibility was left to the Human Rights Committee.[125] The Human Rights Committee could be confronted with problems of the same magnitude as those with which the Security Council had to deal.[126] And so it was alleged, if a dispute had to be settled by the International Court of Justice or some other judicial body, 'some countries would probably be surprised at the Court's interpretation of those texts'.[127] As one delegate stated: 'the word [people] would be as difficult to define as the word "State"'.[128]

The adherents of Article 1 did not think the problem of definition had to be solved finally in the Covenants.[129] The word 'peoples' had not been specified in the Charter of the United Nations either, which was a more important document than the Covenants.[130] It was not thought necessary to define 'peoples', for Article 1 was a timeless principle.[131] The signatories of the Charter understood the meaning of the phrase perfectly well, so it was said, they only showed a fear of the true meaning of those words.[132] Eight States clearly pronounced themselves against the right of secession from existing States.[133] According to them the right of self-determination did not apply to separatist movements and minorities. Seven participating States believed the right to secession was inherent in the right of self-determination and belonged also to minorities.[134] Not all of these States

---

[123] French delegate: UN Doc. A/C.3/SR.677 (1955) p. 267, para. 24.
[124] British delegate: UN Doc. A/C.3/SR.644 (1955) p. 101, para. 15.
[125] Israeli delegate: UN Doc. A/C.3/SR.643 (1955) p. 96, para. 31.
[126] New Zealand delegate: UN Doc. A/C.3/SR.649 (1955) p. 124, para. 9.
[127] Ibid., p. 125, para. 16.
[128] Egyptian delegate: UN Doc. A/C.3/SR.651 (1955) p. 139, para. 36.
[129] Yugoslavian delegate: UN Doc. A/C.3/SR.647 (1955) p. 117, para. 40.
[130] El Salvadorean delegate: UN Doc. A/C.3/SR.674 (1955) p. 248, para. 7.
[131] Syrian delegate: UN Doc. A/C.3/SR.673 (1955) p. 245, para. 20.
[132] Guatemalan delegate: ibid., p. 246, para. 26.
[133] Australia, Colombia, Egypt, Greece, Iraq, Saudi Arabia, Syria and Venezuela: UN Doc A/C.3/SR.646–675 (1955) pp. 111–120, 227, 233, 239 and 254.
[134] Denmark, Lebanon, New Zealand, Philippines, Soviet Union, United Kingdom and United States: UN Doc. E/CN.4/SR.369 (1953) pp. 5 and 16, UN Doc. E/CN.4/SR.370 (1953) p. 8, UN Doc. A/C.3/SR.642–670 (1955) pp. 90, 94, 124–126, 143, 225 and 231.

accepted secession unconditionally or without limits. Most States which recognized the right of secession as a part of the right to self-determination were States voting against Article 1, whereas those denying the right of secession were adherents of Article 1. The division was however not an absolute one.[135] No attempt was made on either side of these groups of States to introduce into Article 1 a phrase expressly denying or recognizing secession.

The debate on secession shifted from the discussion on the existence of such a right to the definition of the term 'peoples'. Some delegates tried to define 'peoples' in such a way so as to include or exclude the possibility of minorities or other groups withdrawing from existing States.[136] India explained that the 'word "peoples" was to apply only to large compact national groups ... who made a conscious demand' for the right of self-determination.[137] Yugoslavia understood the term 'peoples' in its widest meaning. The essential prerequisite was, according to them, that 'such a group should inhabit a compact territory the members of which should be related ethnically or in some other way'.[138] The Lebanese delegate criticized those definitions by stating that the Yugoslavian description was inadequate, for it would imply that 'a thousand people inhabiting the same village could call themselves a people'.[139] He described the Indian definition as 'vague and not sufficiently comprehensive'.[140] Of the more restrictive definitions, we cite the one of Venezuela which understands 'the term "peoples" in the most general and unqualified sense, and therefore as not applicable to racial, religious, or other groups or minorities'.[141] Greece saw the right of self-determination as

---

[135] Australia, voting against Art. 1, did not accept the right of secession of minorities; Lebanon, the Philippines and the Soviet Union accepted both Art. 1 and the right of secession of (national) minorities.

[136] Belgium, India, Lebanon, the United States and Yugoslavia produced definitions of 'peoples', leaving open the possibility of secession: UN Doc. E/CN.4/SR.252 (1952) pp. 7–9, UN Doc. E/CN.4/SR.256 (1952) pp. 5 and 7, UN Doc. A/C.3/SR.649 (1955) p. 126, para. 30 and UN Doc. A/C.3/SR.670 (1955) p. 231, para. 28. Greece, Iraq and Venezuela limited the definition of 'peoples' so as not to include the right of secession: UN Doc. A/C.3/SR.646–647 (1955) pp. 111 and 113, UN Doc. A/C.3/SR.671 (1955) p. 233, para. 8. Syria gave a definition of the term 'nation' which strictly speaking would include the possibility of secession; nevertheless Syria adapted its definition later on and interpreted it so as not to apply the right of self-determination to minorities or similar groups: UN Doc. A/C.3/SR.648 and 672 (1955) pp. 120 and 239.

[137] UN Doc. E/CN.4/SR.256 (1952) p. 5.

[138] Ibid., p. 7.

[139] UN Doc. E/CN.4/SR.257 (1952) p. 9.

[140] Ibid.

[141] UN Doc. A/C.3/SR.646 (1955) p. 111, para. 42.

'a right of ethnic and cultural groups which, owing to circumstances beyond their control, had been unable to achieve political independence'.[142] It only applied 'to national *majorities* [emphasis added] living in their own territory but unable freely to determine their political status'.[143]

In the end, as no general consensus would have been found, a definition of the word 'peoples' was deemed unnecessary. It should be understood in 'its most general sense' and mean 'peoples in all countries and territories, whether independent, trust or non-self-governing'.[144] The drafting States could easily have specified the right of self-determination by granting it only to the population of existing States and to the inhabitants of Trust and Non-Self-Governing Territories. They did however nothing of the sort, preferring to vest the right in peoples, a more universal and general concept. What a people was, was not clarified. Thus a legally binding instrument was created, without the knowledge of who the precise holders of the right were. India, while ratifying the ICCPR, made a reservation to the effect that 'peoples' are understood as 'peoples under foreign dominations'. Three objections were raised however to this interpretation.[145]

Does the right of peoples to freely determine their political status include the internal right of self-determination, in other words the right to choose their own form of government? According to the Danish representative, Article 1 had 'the serious defect of omitting any reference to the right of peoples and nations freely to choose their own form of government'.[146] He considered Article 1 therefore incomplete. It should not be forgotten however that Article 1 certainly did not have the intention of narrowing the principles of the Charter. This would be contrary to the intentions of General Assembly Resolution 545 (VI). Article 1 is a reaffirmation of Articles 1, paragraph 2 and 55 of the Charter and even more than that for it establishes a right. As we have concluded before, the Charter accepts the principle that a people may choose its own form of government.[147] *A fortiori*, the internal right of self-determination forms an integral

---

[142] UN Doc. A/C.3/SR.647 (1955) p. 113, para. 4.
[143] Ibid., p. 113, para. 6.
[144] Annotations on the text of the Draft International Covenants on Human Rights, GAOR, Annexes, UN Doc. A/2929 (1955).
[145] Objections raised by the Netherlands, France and the Federal Republic of Germany. UN Doc. CCPR/C/2 Add.5 (1982) p. 3 and UN Doc. CCPR/C/2 Add.4 (1980) p. 4.
[146] UN Doc. A/C.3/SR.644 (1955) p. 99, para. 2.
[147] See p. 15 above.

part of the right to determine one's political status under Article 1 of the Covenants. The General Assembly did not intend to go back in time.

Another problem of a quite different nature is the relationship in both Covenants between Article 1 on the one hand and Article 2 on the other hand. Article 2, paragraph 1 of the ICCPR imposes on the States Parties the obligation 'to respect and to ensure ... the rights recognized in the present Covenant', whereas Article 2, paragraph 1 of the ICESCR obliges the signatories 'to take steps ... with a view to achieving progressively the full realization of the rights recognized in the present Covenant'. As the right of self-determination appears in both Covenants, there are two ways of implementing it: immediate respect (ICCPR) and progressive realization (ICESCR). If a State is a party to both Covenants, the most far-reaching obligation imposes itself. If a State adheres only to one of the Covenants, a discriminatory duty to respect Article 1 manifests itself. Some States will have to take more measures under Article 1 than others. The Lebanese representative was not favourable to this divergence. He suggested that '[o]nly the provision relating to the Non-Self-Governing and Trust Territories should be progressively applied; in all other cases the right of self-determination should be implemented immediately'.[148] Progressively, the right of self-determination has turned into a customary rule of international law demanding in any case an immediate respect of the right by all States, irrespective of whether or not they are party to the ICCPR.

In contrast with General Assembly Resolution 1514 (XV), the international Covenants on human rights do not specify that the right of self-determination should not lead to a partial or total disruption of the national unity and the territorial integrity of a State. However, Article 4, paragraph 1 of the ICCPR provides for the possibility of a derogation from the obligations under the Covenant, '[i]n time of public emergency which threatens the life of the nation'. The disruption of national unity and territorial integrity may be covered by this provision.[149]

The great force of the inclusion of Article 1 in both human rights Covenants, despite its yet undefined scope, is that for the first time the right, and not the principle, of self-determination has a binding

---

[148] UN Doc. A/C.3/SR.668 (1955) p. 223, para. 34.
[149] The outbreak of war was recognized as one of the most important public emergencies: UN Doc. A/2929 (1955) p. 6.

force for the States Parties. Both Covenants have been ratified by a considerable number of States. Even the States previously opposed to Article 1 have adhered to one or both Covenants.[150] Furthermore, the formulation of the right of self-determination in a legally binding instrument permitted the development of State practice and the interpretation of the right. A general customary rule of international law could emerge.

Other documents

Besides the General Assembly Resolutions mentioned above, one should also refer to Resolution 3281 (XXIX) of 12 December 1974 entitled the Charter of Economic Rights and Duties of States. Chapter I (g) of this Charter cites the principle of equal rights and self-determination of peoples as one of the principles governing relations among States. Furthermore, the General Assembly included a reference to the right of self-determination in Article 7 of Resolution 3314 (XXIX) of 14 December 1974, giving the definition of aggression. It states: 'Nothing in this Definition ... could in any way prejudice the right of self-determination ... of peoples forcibly deprived of that right ... particularly peoples under colonial and racist regimes or other forms of alien domination.'

Outside the United Nations context, the right of self-determination was not introduced in many legally binding international instruments. The African Charter on Human and Peoples' Rights of 1981 sets forth the equality of peoples in Article 19 and the right of self-determination in Article 20. Paragraph 1 of Article 20 reads: 'All peoples shall have the right to existence. They shall have the unquestionable and unalienable right to self-determination. They shall freely determine their political status and shall pursue their economic and social development according to the policy they have freely chosen.' The right to self-determination is stated as a general right of all peoples. Paragraph 2 of Article 20 refers to 'colonized and oppressed peoples' who shall have 'the right to free themselves from the bonds of domination'.

In the Final Act of the Conference on Security and Cooperation in Europe, the Helsinki Declaration of 1975, principle VIII, guiding relations between the participating States, contains the equal rights and

---

[150] The ICCPR entered into force on 23 Mar. 1976 and the ICESCR on 3 Jan. 1976. As at 1 Jun. 1994 there were 127 parties to the former and 129 parties to the latter Covenant: NJCM Bulletin (Oct./Nov. 1994) pp. 940–943 and NQHR (1994) pp. 343–351.

self-determination of peoples. The first paragraph of principle VIII runs as follows: 'The participating States will respect the equal rights of peoples *and* [emphasis added] their right to self-determination, acting at all times in conformity with the purposes and principles of the Charter of the United Nations and with the relevant norms of international law, including those relating to territorial integrity of States.' The chosen formula is kept in accordance with Article 1, paragraph 2 of the Charter of the United Nations, but elucidates the relation between equal rights and self-determination through the addition of the word 'and'. Peoples have thus equal rights and the right of self-determination. No mention is made of the term 'principle' in this first paragraph. The original phrase 'principle of equal rights and self-determination of peoples' in the Charter of the United Nations returns in the second paragraph of principle VIII. By virtue of this principle '*all* [emphasis added] peoples *always* [emphasis added] have the right, in full freedom, to determine, *when and as they wish* [emphasis added], their internal and external political status'. Note the supremacy of the will of the peoples and their unconditional exercise of the right to self-determination. They have this right always, when and as they wish, provided that the norms on territorial integrity of States are respected. No preceding alien subjugation, domination, exploitation or other form of oppression is required. Moreover, both the external and the internal right of self-determination are specified. The third paragraph of principle VIII sets forth 'the universal significance of respect for and effective exercise of equal rights and self-determination of peoples' and 'the importance of the elimination of any form of violation of this principle'. Thus, the United States, Canada, Western and Eastern European States have accepted this wide scope of the right of self-determination in a legally non-binding instrument. The Charter of Paris for a New Europe of 1990 also reaffirms 'the equal rights of peoples and their right to self-determination in conformity with the Charter of the United Nations and with the relevant norms of international law, including those relating to territorial integrity of States'.[151]

---

[151] 30 ILM (1991) p. 197.

Debates on self-determination
Sub-Commission on Prevention of Discrimination and Protection of Minorities
Peoples

In 1974 the Sub-Commission on Prevention of Discrimination and Protection of Minorities, a Sub-Commission of the Commission on Human Rights of the United Nations, appointed a Special Rapporteur, Héctor Gros Espiell, to prepare a study on the right of self-determination of peoples under colonial and alien domination. He produced three studies which in accordance with his mandate only involve the right of self-determination of peoples under colonial and alien domination.[152] The Special Rapporteur requested the view of all Member States of the United Nations and its specialized agencies on, among other things, the meaning of the term 'peoples under colonial and alien domination'.[153] Few replies were received.[154] In general, the replying governments emphasized the aggressive element of the domination. The 'colonial and alien' element was understood as 'any kind of domination, whatever form it may take, which the people concerned freely regards as such'.[155] No colonial and alien domination existed 'where a people lives freely and voluntarily under the legal order of a State, whose territorial integrity must be respected, provided it is real and not merely a legal fiction'.[156] The legal fiction is the argument that a colony forms an integral part of the territory of the administering State.

According to Gros Espiell, the United Nations has established the right of self-determination as a right belonging to peoples under colonial and alien domination and not to peoples already organized in the form of a State.[157] This conclusion contrasts with what we have found earlier.[158] The United Nations' State practice does accept a right of self-determination outside the colonial context, namely the right of independent peoples. This view is shared by another Special Rapporteur of the Sub-Commission, Aureliu Cristescu. According to

---

[152] UN Docs. E/CN.4/Sub.2/377 (1976), E/CN.4/Sub.2/405 (1978) vol. I and E/CN.4/Sub.2/405/Rev.1 (1980).
[153] UN Doc. E/CN.4/Sub.2/377 (1976) pp. 12–13.
[154] Replies of Afghanistan, German Democratic Republic, Iraq, Mexico, Pakistan, the Philippines and New Zealand. Ibid., pp. 15–16, nn. 9–14.
[155] Ibid., p. 16.
[156] Ibid.
[157] Ibid., p. 22.
[158] See pp. 12–35 above.

him, peoples, whether or not constituted as a State, are the holders of the right of self-determination.[159] Moreover, the equal rights of peoples entail that the right of self-determination should not be confined to a particular category of peoples.[160] It seems contradictory to understand the right of self-determination of peoples under colonial and alien domination as 'a condition or prerequisite for the existence and enjoyment of all the other rights and freedoms of the individual' and still restrict the right to colonial peoples.[161] In principle, every human being in the world is the holder of human rights, but if non-colonial peoples do not have the right of self-determination, the existence and enjoyment of their human rights will be endangered. Why then deprive them of this fundamental 'prerequisite'?

As to the meaning of the term 'peoples', the study by Gros Espiell reveals that some governments believed it did not encompass minorities, while one government recognized the right of self-determination of all peoples.[162] Cristescu concludes that there are three general elements which are to be considered in the definition of 'peoples'. Basing himself on the various opinions expressed in United Nations organs, these common and returning elements are: a 'people' denotes a social entity possessing a clear identity and its own characteristics, it implies a relationship with a territory and, lastly, peoples should not be confused with ethnic, religious and linguistic minorities.[163] From the fact that peoples and minorities should not be confused, it does not follow that a minority can never be a people and therefore never have the right of self-determination. Ethnic, religious and linguistic minorities enjoy a special protection by virtue of Article 27 of the ICCPR. We have seen that in the various United Nations organs opinions have been divided as to the granting of the right of self-determination to minorities. The positions varied from a categorical denial, to considering the right of self-determination as also belonging to minorities.[164] If one introduces the notion of 'minority' into the concept of 'peoples', one has to define the term 'minority', which could be as complex as finding a definition of 'peoples'.[165] According

---

[159] UN Doc. E/CN.4/Sub.2/404/Rev.1 (1981) p. 37, para. 260.
[160] Ibid., p. 39, para. 268.
[161] UN Doc. E/CN.4/Sub.2/405/Rev.1 (1980) p. 9, para. 52.
[162] The Philippines and Iraq and the German Democratic Republic respectively: UN Doc. E/CN.4/Sub.2/377 (1976) p. 22.
[163] UN Doc. E/CN.4/Sub.2/404/Rev.1 (1981) p. 41, para. 279.
[164] See pp. 31–33 above.
[165] See pp. 40–42 below.

to Cristescu, 'nations' are also covered by the term 'peoples'.[166] He warns however against an abusive interpretation of the right of self-determination. Peoples might be used, against their real interests, to support aggressive or subversive designs for the benefit of foreign interests.[167] No State would be free from the danger of dismemberment.[168] The Special Rapporteur does not suggest any definition of the word 'peoples', but states 'that whenever in the course of history a people has become aware of being a people, all definitions have proved superfluous'.[169] Gros Espiell found that the Member States of the United Nations did not generally accept that there was a right of secession. This would be a misapplication of the principle of self-determination and contrary to the Charter.[170] In its reply, Pakistan denied the right of secession 'unless the association in question had been accomplished illegally against the wishes of the people concerned'.[171] Cristescu, though applying the principle of self-determination to all peoples, does not interpret it so as to encourage secessionist or irredentist movements.[172]

Special Rapporteur Gros Espiell characterizes the right of self-determination both as an individual and as a collective right. It is a collective right in the sense that peoples as such are entitled to the right of self-determination.[173] The Commission on Human Rights has, according to Gros Espiell, repeatedly pointed out that the right of self-determination is a right of the individual, by virtue of which it is every person's right that the people of which he is a member (if it is under colonial and alien domination) should be recognized as having the right to determine freely its own political, economic, social and cultural condition.[174]

Gros Espiell also dealt with the question of very small States. He found 'no legal basis for denying the right of self-determination on the ground that the population of which a people is composed, or the territory which it inhabits, is small'.[175] But he stressed the problems they might encounter in forming real free, independent and

---

[166] UN Doc. E/CN.4/Sub.2/404/Rev.1 (1981) p. 41, para. 280.
[167] Ibid., p. 40, para. 275.
[168] Ibid.
[169] Ibid., p. 40, para. 274.
[170] UN Doc. E/CN.4/Sub.2/405/Rev.1 (1980) pp. 13–14, para. 90.
[171] UN Doc. E/CN.4/Sub.2/405 (1978) vol. I, p. 20, n. 22.
[172] UN Doc. E/CN.4/Sub.2/404/Rev.1 (1981) p. 39, para. 268.
[173] UN Doc. E/CN.4/Sub.2/405/Rev.1 (1980) pp. 9–10, paras. 56–57.
[174] Ibid., p. 10, para. 58.
[175] Ibid., p. 16, para. 108.

sovereign entities as they would be vulnerable to external influences and 'dangerous manifestations of neo-colonialism'. The Special Rapporteur did not believe very small States would be able to discharge the duties flowing from United Nations membership. He feared moreover, that 'the proliferation of very small States might have the effect of destroying or seriously undermining the very foundations of the existing community of nations'.[176] The very small (potential) States which the Special Rapporteur alludes to are the small island colonies, which will be discussed later.[177]

Minorities

Minorities do not have the right of self-determination, unless they are also peoples. Yet, the concept of minorities, which is inherently a relative one, can help to clarify the notion of peoples. There are various interpretations of the characteristics distinguishing one people from another and of the kind of relationship between the people in question and the territory. If one alleges that minorities do not hold the right of self-determination, the reason would be either because minorities are not peoples or because they do not fulfil other conditions, for example they are not under colonial or alien domination or they are not independent peoples. We shall discuss the suggested definitions of minorities and compare them with the elements of definition of 'peoples'.

In the ICCPR both the terms 'peoples' and 'minorities' appear. Article 27 of the Covenant confers upon persons belonging to ethnic, religious or linguistic minorities the right 'in community with the other members of their group, to enjoy their own culture, to profess and practise their own religion, or to use their own language'. Our attention will be focused on the definition of minorities under Article 27 and not so much on the exact content of their rights deriving from it. We recall that the Soviet Union was one of the States which considered Article 1 of the ICCPR applicable to minorities. During the discussion on the protection of minorities in the Commission on Human Rights, the Soviet delegate defined the term 'national minority' in conformity with the term 'nation', namely 'an historically formed community of people characterized by a common language, a common territory, a common economic life and a common psychological structure manifesting itself in a common

[176] Ibid.
[177] See pp. 48–51 below.

culture'.[178] Another delegate emphasized that only national minorities incorporated in a multi-national State against their will should be given the right of secession – a right which ethnic, religious and linguistic minorities did not have.[179] Eventually the rights of Article 27 of the Covenant were granted to ethnic, religious and linguistic minorities only. No mention is made of 'national minorities', but these minorities can be covered by the terms 'ethnic, religious or linguistic minorities'. Especially the Latin-American States stressed that immigrants should not be considered as minorities needing protection.[180] Only residents of the State who are long-established minorities would fall under Article 27. The article was to cover 'only separate or distinct groups, well-defined and long-established on the territory of a State'.[181] In subsequent years, the Human Rights Committee did not however exclude that non-nationals would be protected under Article 27.[182]

The definition of the term 'minority' was also the subject of study and debate in the Sub-Commission on Prevention of Discrimination and Protection of Minorities. In 1977 the Sub-Commission appointed Francesco Capotorti as Special Rapporteur and charged him to prepare a study on the rights of persons belonging to ethnic, religious and linguistic minorities.[183] Subsequent Special Rapporteurs like Deschênes[184] and Eide[185] also reported on the question of minorities. Capotorti suggested a definition of minorities upon which he asked the governments to make observations.[186] The relative numerical

---

[178] Soviet delegate: UN Doc. E/CN.4/SR.369 (1953) p. 16.
[179] Philippine delegate: UN Doc. E/CN.4/SR.370 (1953) pp. 8–9.
[180] Uruguay: UN Doc. E/CN.4/SR.369 (1953) p. 7, Chile: UN Doc. E/CN.4/SR.370 (1953) p. 5, Brazil: UN Doc. A/C.3/SR.1103 (1961) pp. 213–214, para. 12.
[181] UN Doc. A/2929 (1955) p. 63, para. 184.
[182] In its General Comment on Art. 27, the Human Rights Committee noted that 'the quality of a community as a minority under Article 27 does not necessarily depend on a formed bond of citizenship of its members with the host state', UN Doc. CCPR/C/23/CRP.1 (1984) para. 4. See also M. N. Shaw, 'The Definition of Minorities in International Law', 20 Israel Yrb. HR (1990) pp. 38–39 and M. Nowak, 'The Right of Self-Determination and Protection of Minorities in Central and Eastern Europe in the Light of the Case Law of the Human Rights Committee', 1 Int'l JGR (1993) p. 12.
[183] UN Doc. E/CN.4/Sub.2/384 (1977) and UN Doc. E/CN.4/Sub.2/384/Add.1–5 (1977).
[184] UN Doc. E/CN.4/Sub.2/1985/31.
[185] UN Doc. E/CN.4/Sub.2/1990/46.
[186] Capotorti's suggested definition ran as follows: 'an ethnic, religious or linguistic minority is a group numerically smaller than the rest of the population of the State to which it belongs and possessing cultural, physical or historical characteristics, a religion or a language different from those of the rest of the population'. UN Doc. E/CN.4/Sub.2/384/Add.1 (1977) p. 10, para. 9.

factor was stressed by all governments. The group should be numerically inferior to the rest of the population living in a specific area[187] or less than the majority population of the whole State.[188] The Sub-Commission itself and UNESCO added that account should be taken of oppressed majority populations living under powerful minority regimes. The non-dominant majority would then deserve a protection as if it were a minority.[189] Capotorti agreed not to extend minority protection to dominant minority groups, but believed that oppressed majorities had rights which far exceeded the limited contents of Article 27 of the Covenant, namely the right of self-determination.[190] As to the characteristics which should distinguish a minority from the rest of the population, the governments took into account both objective and subjective elements, though some emphasized one element more than the other.[191] The Special Rapporteur found that the objective factor comprised several elements: the group must possess stable ethnic, religious or linguistic characteristics differing sharply from those of the rest of the population; the group should be numerically inferior to the rest of the population or of equal numerical size; and the group should be in a non-dominant position and consist of nationals of the State.[192] The subjective criterion is defined as the will of the group in question to preserve its own characteristics. This will is presumed when a given group has kept its distinctive characteristics over a period of time.[193] These conclusions correspond to the observations made by the replying governments, and Capotorti readjusted his definition in that light.[194] The difficulty of finding a consensus on the definition of 'minorities' was rooted in the divergence of terms used by various governments for this

---

[187] Yugoslavian Government: ibid., p. 19, para. 20.
[188] Indian Government: ibid., p. 18, para. 19.
[189] Ibid., pp. 21–23.
[190] The Special Rapporteur alluded to the oppressed South African black population. Ibid., p. 30, para. 35.
[191] Yugoslavia attached less importance to the subjective factor, often interpreted as civil disloyalty, than, for example, Finland, Italy and Sweden. Ibid., pp. 15–17.
[192] UN Doc. E/CN.4/Sub.2/384/Add.5 (1977) pp. 5–6.
[193] Ibid., p. 6.
[194] His new definition of 'minority' runs: 'A group numerically inferior to the rest of the population of a State, in a non-dominant position, whose members – being nationals of the State – possess ethnic, religious or linguistic characteristics differing from those of the rest of the population and show, if only implicitly, a sense of solidarity, directed towards preserving their culture, traditions, religion or language.' Ibid., p. 7, para. 10. Deschênes came to an almost identical definition in 1985: UN Doc. E/CN.4/Sub.2/1985/31.

concept[195] and their concern to interpret the term so as not to be obliged to extend protection to any population groups in their own State. Discussing the national policies towards minority protection, Capotorti calls it a legitimate concern of any government to safeguard the integrity of the State and to avoid encouraging separatism. This is regarded as a natural limit to any policy of protection for minorities.[196]

Capotorti believes that the international protection of minorities depends on official recognition of their existence.[197] Their existence as such does not depend on recognition but the effective realization of their protection does. Special Rapporteur Asbjørn Eide in his 1990 progress report on protection of minorities stresses that the existence of a minority is a matter of fact depending on objective and subjective factors.[198] His study does not make use of a precise definition of 'minorities', though he distinguishes between 'settled minorities' and 'recent immigrant groups', the latter meaning aliens, refugees, asylum seekers and migrant workers.[199] The Special Rapporteur suggests a special protection and approach for 'recent immigrant' minorities who, due to the fact that they are not long-established minorities in the State, are not covered by Article 27 of the ICCPR. Eide asked the governments to furnish information on their policies concerning minorities protection. In exceptional cases minorities were granted the right to autonomy, for example in the case of indigenous populations. The Special Rapporteur did not look into their possible right of self-determination as this would be beyond the scope of his mandate.[200] Self-determination and secession were however subjects of discussion in the Sub-Commission. It was asked to what extent minorities had the right and the capacity to dismantle a State. If the principle of equality was respected, demands for secession would be

---

[195] In the Philippine Constitution the term 'National Cultural Communities' is used to indicate minorities. The Romanian Constitution employs the term 'co-inhabiting nationality', whereas the 1974 Yugoslavian Constitution mentioned 'nationalities' to designate minority groups. UN Doc. E/CN.4/Sub.2/384/Add.1 (1977) pp. 13–15.
[196] UN Doc. E/CN.4/Sub.2/384/Add.5 (1977) p. 12, para. 23.
[197] UN Doc. E/CN.4/Sub.2/384/Add.1 (1977) p. 32, para. 41.
[198] UN Doc. E/CN.4/Sub.2/1990/46, p. 5, para. 16. Progress report 1990 by Mr Asbjørn Eide approved by the Sub-Commission on Prevention of Discrimination and Protection of Minorities, Res. 1990/5.
[199] Ibid., p. 8.
[200] The Sub-Commission in its Res. 1989/44 entrusted Eide with the preparation of a report on national experience regarding peaceful and constructive solutions of problems involving minorities.

less heard, for 'it was when populations were deprived of their rights ... that the desire for separation manifested itself most strongly'.[201] Another member of the Sub-Commission held that self-determination of minorities could prove dangerous if it remained external, but very fruitful if it resulted in participation in internal affairs.[202] Although the terms 'secession' and 'self-determination' were used in the Sub-Commission, a right of self-determination was certainly not envisaged for minorities. Suggestions were made to accord a right to autonomy or a right to participation in national or regional legislative bodies. These were not however rights flowing from the right of self-determination, but special rights for minorities.

In the 1992 'Declaration on the rights of persons belonging to national or ethnic, religious or linguistic minorities', adopted by the General Assembly, no definition of 'minorities' is given.[203] Article 8, paragraph 2 of this Declaration states that the 'Declaration shall not prejudice the enjoyment by all persons of universally recognized human rights and fundamental freedoms'. The right of self-determination is covered by this article. Paragraph 4 of Article 8 goes on to state that nothing in the Declaration 'may be construed as permitting any activity contrary to the purposes and principles of the United Nations, including sovereign equality, territorial integrity and political independence of States'. The 1995 Council of Europe Framework Convention for the Protection of National Minorities does not present a definition of the term 'national minorities' either.[204] This Convention does not allow any acts contrary to, *inter alia*, 'the territorial integrity and political independence of States'.[205]

It follows from the above discourse that minorities do not automatically have the right of self-determination. Any political rights they may possess result from the willingness of the State's government to grant them and not from a right of self-determination of minorities. What then are the differences and similarities between a minority and a people? Considering the definitions we have found so far, peoples and minorities have in common that they are distinguished by their own characteristics. One people differs from another people, because of its diverging characteristics, as one minority has distinctive charac-

---

[201] Mr Khalifa: UN Doc. E/CN.4/Sub.2/SR.9 (1990) pp. 2-3, para. 8.
[202] Mrs Palley: ibid., p. 9, para. 45.
[203] UN Doc. A/Res/47/135 (1993) Annex, approved by the GA on 8 Dec. 1992.
[204] 34 ILM (1995) pp. 351 ff.
[205] Art. 21 of the 1995 Framework Convention for the Protection of National Minorities.

teristics from the rest of the population of the State. It remains uncertain which elements have to be taken into account to constitute a people. Objective and subjective elements are to be taken into account when defining a minority. This will also be the case for a people, but we do not know yet what degree of distinction is needed. Does a minority have to possess a less clear identity than a people? And is the balance between the objective and subjective elements similar for minorities and for peoples?[206] A second point of similarity between peoples and minorities is that no numerical limits exist. In principle, the number of people of which the group is composed is not seen as an essential element. This was pointed out by the replying governments in the study of Capotorti, with the proviso that the minority group was not so small that protection would amount to a disproportionate duty.[207] The number of individuals who can constitute a people with the right of self-determination is not conditioned either, considering the existence of very small Non-Self-Governing island Territories.[208] Thirdly, peoples and minorities do not necessarily have to be nationals of the State in which they live. Minorities, in order to be covered by Article 27 of the ICCPR, have to be long established in the territory of the State concerned, but probably do not have to have any bond of nationality with the host State. A people is not necessarily identical to all the nationals of a State. It is the inherent characteristics which distinguish a people, not their passports. Never in the debates in the United Nations organs has the concept of people been treated in the light of the nationality of the members of the people.

One of the main differences between a minority and a people is the fact that in the definition of minorities no relationship with a territory is demanded. A minority may well be long established in the territory of a State, but it need not have a particular attachment to a specific area. The origins of minority groups can be very different. They may have lived in a particular territory for ages or find themselves in a specific area due to forced or voluntary transfers. They may form compact or scattered groups. A certain relationship with a territory is therefore possible though not necessary. The longer a minority is established in a given territory, the more chance there is that it will develop a particular attachment to the territory. If a relationship exists, a minority could well constitute a people.

---

[206] See pp. 79–80 below.
[207] UN Doc. E/CN.4/Sub.2/384/Add.5 (1977) p. 6, para. 8.
[208] See pp. 48–51 below, but also pp. 84–88.

Lastly, a minority has to be numerically inferior to the rest of the population, whether taken as a whole or in a specific area. No similar condition is laid down for a people.

Indigenous peoples

Indigenous populations are considered to be special minority groups to whom, apart from the universal human and minority rights, specific indigenous rights should be granted. On 8 September 1981, the Sub-Commission on Prevention of Discrimination and Protection of Minorities established a Working Group on Indigenous Populations.[209] This Working Group has drafted a Universal Declaration on the Rights of Indigenous Peoples.[210] Although the Declaration does not define the term 'indigenous peoples', the Working Group often referred to a working definition elaborated by a Special Rapporteur.[211]

Indigenous populations are special minorities in the sense that they have a strong attachment to their lands. They often have a land-based religion, and possession of or access to land traditionally held by them is of fundamental importance to them.[212] An essential point

---

[209] Res. 2 (XXXIV) of 8 Sept. 1981 of the Sub-Commission. The Commission on Human Rights established a new intergovernmental Working Group with the purpose of elaborating a draft declaration for consideration and adoption by the GA within the International Decade of the World's Indigenous People: Res. 1995/32 of the Commission.

[210] Latest version of the Draft Declaration in UN Doc. E/CN.4/Sub.2/1993/29, pp. 50–60, E/CN.4/1995/2, E/CN.4/Sub.2/1994/56 or 34 ILM (1995) pp. 546 ff.

[211] The so-called Cobo definition runs: 'Indigenous communities, peoples and nations are those which, having a historical continuity with pre-invasion and pre-colonial societies that developed on their territories, consider themselves distinct from other sectors of the societies now prevailing in those territories, or parts of them. They form at present non-dominant sectors of society and are determined to preserve, develop and transmit to future generations their ancestral territories, and their ethnic identity, as the basis of their continued existence as peoples, in accordance with their own cultural patterns, social institutions and legal systems', UN Doc. E/CN.4/Sub.2/1986/7/Add.4, para. 379.

[212] See further R. L. Barsh, 'The Challenge of Indigenous Self-Determination', 26 UMJLR (1993) pp. 277–312; on Nordic indigenous peoples, J. Broested et al., eds., *Native Power: The Quest for Autonomy and Nationhood of Indigenous Peoples* (1985); I. Brownlie, *Treaties and Indigenous Peoples* (1992); J. Burger and P. Hunt, 'Indigenous Peoples' Rights', 12 NQHR (1994) pp. 405–423; R. Falk, 'The Rights of Peoples (in particular Indigenous Peoples)', in J. Crawford, ed., *The Rights of Peoples* (1988) pp. 17–37; B. R. Howard, 'Human Rights and Indigenous People: On the Relevance of International Law for Indigenous Liberation', 35 GYIL (1992) pp. 105–156; C. J. Iorns, 'Indigenous Peoples and Self-Determination: Challenging State Sovereignty', 24 *Case Western Reserve Journal of International Law* (1992) pp. 199–348; G. Nettheim, 'Peoples and Populations: Indigenous Peoples and the Rights of Peoples', in J. Crawford, ed., *The*

of discussion in the Working Group was whether indigenous populations have the right of self-determination. This issue was first raised with regard to the terminology used in the Declaration. Should one speak of indigenous populations or of indigenous peoples? Would the use of the term 'peoples' entail that they possess the right of self-determination? The members of the Working Group and the indigenous populations themselves preferred the term 'peoples'. Most governments were prepared to support the word 'peoples' on the understanding that a distinction was made between internal self-determination of indigenous peoples and the rights contained in General Assembly Resolution 1514 (XV) of 14 December 1960.[213] The governments did not want the Declaration to be interpreted as implying separate statehood for indigenous peoples or extra-citizenship rights. The indigenous peoples claimed a recognition of their right of self-determination in order to remain a distinct group and to arm themselves against forced integration. They wished some degree of autonomy and considered the right of self-determination essential for preventing continued human rights abuses. Some added 'that fear of indigenous self-determination leading to secession is unfounded because of the general approach and understanding of international legal instruments'.[214] Several indigenous representatives in the Working Group demanded a clear and explicit recognition of their right to self-determination in the Declaration. Although a 1989 draft[215] did not include an explicit reference to this right, the 1993 Draft Declaration eventually met the wishes of the indigenous groups. Article 3 states that '[i]ndigenous peoples have the right to self-determination. By virtue of that right they freely determine their political status and freely pursue their economic, social and cultural development.' Autonomy and self-government are specific forms of the exercise of this right which are explicitly mentioned.[216] The exercise of the right can probably not lead to secession, without the consent of the State, as no group or person has 'the right to engage in

Rights of Peoples (1988), pp. 107–126; J. T. Paxman, 'Minority Indigenous Populations and their Claims for Self-Determination', 21 *Case Western Reserve Journal of International Law* (1989) pp. 185–202; and M. E. Turpel, 'Indigenous Peoples' Rights of Political Participation and Self-Determination: Recent International Legal Developments and the Continuing Struggle for Recognition', 25 *Cornell International Law Journal* (1992) pp. 579–602.

[213] UN Doc. E/CN.4/Sub.2/1989/36, p. 17, paras. 54 and 55.
[214] Ibid.
[215] Ibid., Annex II, pp. 31–35.
[216] Art. 31 of the 1993 Draft Declaration.

any activity or perform any act contrary to the Charter of the United Nations'.[217]

Special Committee of Twenty-Four
Small Non-Self-Governing Territories and peoples

At present there are seventeen Non-Self-Governing Territories under the supervision of the Special Committee of Twenty-Four.[218] For the purpose of this study, we shall consider the elements of the right of self-determination of the smallest territories which are discussed in the Sub-Committee on Small Territories.[219] At the moment the largest Non-Self-Governing Territory covered by the Sub-Committee's mandate is Guam, with a territorial area of 549 square kilometres and 139,000 inhabitants.[220] The territory is administered by the United States. The smallest Non-Self-Governing Territory is the island of Pitcairn with an area of five square kilometres and fifty-two inhabitants, administered by the United Kingdom.[221] Every year since its establishment, the Special Committee of Twenty-Four has reaffirmed the inalienable right of the peoples of all these Non-Self-Governing Territories to self-determination and independence. The text of these resolutions is virtually the same each year. Besides recalling the right of self-determination and independence of the Non-Self-Governing peoples, the General Assembly 'reaffirms its conviction that the questions of territorial size, geographical isolation and limited resources should in no way delay the implementation of the Declaration [on the Granting of Independence to Colonial Countries and Peoples] with respect to the Territories concerned'.[222] This point was especially emphasized for the small territories. The Special Committee stressed however that in deciding their future political status, the people of Pitcairn should take into account 'the Territory's tiny size, its small and decreasing population, mineral resources and dependence on

---

[217] Art. 45 of the 1993 Draft Declaration. See pp. 12–17 above.
[218] New Caledonia, Tokelau, East Timor, Western Sahara, Anguilla, Bermuda, British Virgin Islands, Cayman Islands, Falkland Islands, Gibraltar, Montserrat, Pitcairn, St Helena, Turks and Caicos Islands, American Samoa, Guam and United States Virgin Islands.
[219] Anguilla, Bermuda, British Virgin Islands, Cayman Islands, Montserrat, Pitcairn, St Helena, Turks and Caicos Islands, Tokelau, American Samoa, Guam and the United States Virgin Islands.
[220] Last official estimate of 1 Jul. 1992, *Population and Vital Statistics Report, UN Statistical Papers*, Series A, vol. 46, no. 3, as of 1 Jul. 1994, p. 14.
[221] Ibid. Latest population census of 31 Dec. 1990.
[222] See, e.g., GA Res. 3156 (XXVIII), 3157 (XXVIII), 3289 (XXIX), and 3290 (XXIX).

postage stamps for the bulk of its revenue'.²²³

The Special Committee of Twenty-Four has not fixed any limit as to the size of the colonial population or the territory. The right of self-determination is recognized without numerical conditions and all options – association, integration or independence – are left open. In principle, the administering States did not contest the right of self-determination of these small colonial peoples. There were only some differences of opinion on the realization of that right. The main problems raised involved the fragile economy, political unawareness, military bases and other political or economic interests. In order to advance the self-determination of these small populations, the Special Committee urged the administering States to strengthen the local economy and to encourage local political leadership.²²⁴ The purpose was to bring the territories to a stable and less dependent position so that independence could be accomplished and not ruled out in advance. The Special Committee pursued this policy for thirty years, but came under severe criticism in 1990. A number of States in the General Assembly questioned whether the Special Committee still served a useful purpose. Some States criticized the Committee's 'excessively harsh criticism' in repetitive resolutions with 'outdated formulas'.²²⁵ The Special Committee was reproached for its 'tired rhetoric of previous decades' which did not take into account the realistic interests of the remaining colonial peoples.²²⁶ The old policies were not targeted on the specific needs of the remaining Non-Self-Governing Territories.²²⁷ Too much attention was paid to independence as if it were the only possibility for the small territories. One delegate argued that the presence of military bases and the inflow of foreign investments were welcomed by the population for financial reasons.²²⁸ The majority of the States continued to appreciate the work of the Special Committee of Twenty-Four. They believed the presence of military bases constituted a threat to the security of the colonial peoples and neighbouring States.²²⁹ They rejected the arguments according to which the remaining Non-Self-Governing Territories could not survive as independent entities.²³⁰ It was generally felt that

---

²²³ UN Doc. A/9623/Add.5 (Part III) (1974) pp. 6–7.
²²⁴ UN Doc. A/31/23/Rev.1 (1977) vol. III and IV, pp. 193–194 and 161–171, respectively.
²²⁵ Czechoslovakian delegate: UN Doc. A/45/PV.44 (1990) pp. 7–8.
²²⁶ British delegate: ibid., pp. 71–72.
²²⁷ Australian delegate: ibid., pp. 82–83.
²²⁸ United States delegate: ibid., p. 14.
²²⁹ Ukrainian delegate: ibid., p. 18 and Syrian delegate: UN Doc. A/45/PV.43 (1990) p. 56.

50   THE GENERAL INTERNATIONAL LEGAL CONTEXT

independence was not always necessary, but that the peoples in question should at least have a complete freedom of choice. The Special Committee of Twenty-Four recalled that colonialism itself was an outdated phenomenon, which should disappear by the year 2000, the end of the International Decade for the Eradication of Colonialism.[231]

New dangers had arisen. The (small) remaining Non-Self-Governing Territories were often used for drug-trafficking, money-laundering, dumping of toxic wastes, drift-net fishing as well as abuse of natural resources.[232] At present, the Special Committee of Twenty-Four and its Sub-Committee on Small Territories draw more attention to these new problems and make recommendations accordingly. The right of self-determination and independence is still reaffirmed, but more attention is paid to the economic fields that have to be promoted.[233] As to the military bases, the Committee recommends administering States to avoid the involvement of the territories in offensive acts or interference against neighbouring States.[234]

These small island territories were granted the right of self-determination because of their inclusion on the list of Chapter XI territories. This did not however imply that all colonial islands were considered as Non-Self-Governing Territories. Thus the Cocos (Keeling) Islands were treated as a Chapter XI territory, whereas Christmas Island, notwithstanding its similar political history and administrative relation to Australia, was never considered a Non-Self-Governing Territory.[235] As a consequence, some small colonial peoples were and others were not encouraged to exercise a right of self-determination. The Special Committee has often looked into the origins of the populations of other Non-Self-Governing Territories. The inhabitants of the Turks and Caicos Islands were mostly of African descent, the remainder being of mixed or European origin.[236] Their right of self-determination, including those inhabitants of European origin, was never contested. The population of the Cocos (Keeling) Islands, which in 1976 numbered 548,[237] was formed by the descendants of original

---

[230] Syrian delegate: ibid., pp. 56–57.
[231] UN Doc. A/45/PV.44 (1990) p. 92.
[232] Ibid., pp. 92–93.
[233] E.g., question of Pitcairn, St Helena and Tokelau in UN Doc. A/AC.109/2000, 2001 and 2010 (1994) respectively.
[234] See, e.g., Question of St Helena: UN Doc. A/AC.109/1094 (1991).
[235] Both territories are integrated in Australia. See J. Crawford, 'Islands as Sovereign Nations', 38 ICLQ (1989) p. 284, n. 22.
[236] UN Doc. A/31/23/Rev.1 (1977) vol. IV, p. 161.

RIGHT OF SELF-DETERMINATION 51

Malayan settlers brought to the territory in 1827 by John Clunies Ross, a Scottish seaman, and Europeans, including descendants of Clunies Ross. The right of this population to self-determination was not questioned either. Though of recent and mixed origin, the settlers of the Cocos (Keeling) Islands were the first people to inhabit the territory. No other indigenous people had a relationship with the territory.

The Falkland Islands and Gibraltar

The Falkland Islands and Gibraltar are Non-Self-Governing Territories of a special nature. The General Assembly and the Special Committee of Twenty-Four did not explicitly recognize the right of self-determination of the inhabitants of these two territories. The population of the Falkland Islands numbers 1,916 nearly all of British descent, with about 67 per cent born in the Islands.[238] Argentina claims sovereignty over the Islands since 1816 when it proclaimed its own independence from Spain.[239] Until the present day, talks have been going on between the United Kingdom and Argentina which have not changed the present international status of the Falklands Islands as a Non-Self-Governing Territory of the United Kingdom.[240] The Special Committee of Twenty-Four never refers to the right of self-determination of the inhabitants of the Islands and demands instead a peaceful and negotiated settlement of the dispute over sovereignty.[241] On 2 April 1982 Argentina invaded and occupied the Falkland Islands and was forced to surrender on 14 June 1982 after British resistance. The Security Council demanded an immediate withdrawal of all Argentine forces.[242] The Security Council did not mention a right of self-determination of the inhabitants of the Islands either, but condemned the use of force as a means to settle territorial disputes. In 1989 an agreement was reached between the two parties ending officially all

[237] UN Doc. A/32/23/Rev.1 (1979) vol. III, p. 5.
[238] Last census of 1986, B. Hunter, *The Statesman's Year-Book*, 127th edn (1991–1992) p. 467.
[239] See further D. W. Greig, 'Sovereignty and the Falkland Island Crisis', AYIL (1986) pp. 20–70 and L. S. Gustafson, *The Sovereignty Dispute over the Falkland (Malvinas) Islands* (1988). From the Argentinian point of view: A. B. Bologna, *Los Derechos de la Republica Argentina sobre las Islas Malvinas, Georgia de Sur (San Pedro) y Sandwich del Sur* (1989).
[240] See on the exploration and exploitation of hydrocarbons in the EEZ of the Falkland Islands: Joint Declaration on Cooperation over Offshore Activities in the South West Atlantic of 27 Sept. 1995, 35 ILM (1996) pp. 304 ff.
[241] See, e.g., UN Doc. A/AC.109/2003 (1994) offering the good offices of the Secretary-General in order to assist the parties in complying with the GA Resolutions.
[242] SC Res. 502 (1982).

remaining hostilities and granting Argentina certain fishing rights in the Falkland Islands' Exclusive Economic Zone.[243]

Neither party has so far abandoned sovereignty claims on the Islands. Argentina maintains that the population of the Islands does not constitute the original, indigenous people and therefore cannot claim a right to self-determination. The Islands belong, according to Argentina, to its territory. Any other status is contrary to paragraph 6 of General Assembly Resolution 1514 (XV) protecting the national unity and territorial integrity of a country. The United Kingdom and the inhabitants of the Islands have always believed that the right of self-determination was applicable to the Falkland Islands.[244] The General Assembly and the Special Committee continue to recommend to Argentina and the United Kingdom the settlement of the dispute through negotiations 'bearing in mind ... the interests [not wishes] of the inhabitants'.[245] The resolutions make no reference to paragraph 6 of General Assembly Resolution 1514 (XV). The Special Committee, though dealing with a colonial Non-Self-Governing Territory, did not qualify the inhabitants of the territory as a colonial people. The reason for this was the fact that the inhabitants were of British descent and had therefore no indigenous link with the territory. This was also quite clear in the case of the population of Gibraltar.

Gibraltar has a population numbering 30,689 of which there are 20,425 British Gibraltarians, 5,782 other British and 4,482 non-British.[246] The inhabitants are mostly of Genoese, Portuguese and Maltese as well as British descent. The United Kingdom acquired the territory from Spain by the 1713 Treaty of Utrecht which contained a clause which gave Spain the first option to regain its sovereignty over Gibraltar if the United Kingdom sovereignty ended.[247] Virtually all original Spanish inhabitants at the time left Gibraltar and settled in the vicinity of San Roque. In 1946 the United Kingdom reported

---

[243] Joint Statements of 19 Oct. 1989 and 15 Febr. 1990 'on confidence-building measures, including an information and consultation system and safety measures for air and maritime navigation', 29 ILM (1990) pp. 1291–1304.

[244] In hearings before the Special Committee of Twenty-Four, island representatives stressed that they were a long-established people with their own identity: UN Doc. A/AC.109/PV.1369 (1990) pp. 14–15 ff. and UN Doc. A/AC.109/PV.1433 (1994) pp. 13–15.

[245] See, e.g., GA Res. 2065 (XX) and 3160 (XXIII).

[246] Estimate of 31 Dec. 1989: Hunter, *The Statesman's Year-Book*, p. 568.

[247] Treaty of Utrecht of 13 Jul. 1713, 1 *British and Foreign State Papers*, pp. 611 ff. See further D. S. Morris and R. H. Haigh, *Britain, Spain and Gibraltar 1945–90: The Eternal Triangle* (1992).

Gibraltar as a Non-Self-Governing Territory on which it would submit information under Article 73 (e) of the Charter. From 1957 Spain reserved its rights over Gibraltar and considered it was an integral part of its territory.[248] The subject was discussed in the Special Committee of Twenty-Four, which adopted on 16 October 1964 a 'consensus', declaring General Assembly Resolution 1514 (XV) applicable to Gibraltar, and invited both States 'to begin talks without delay ... in order to reach a negotiated settlement ... bearing in mind the interests [not wishes, just as in the Falkland Islands question] of the people of the territory'.[249] The General Assembly repeated this formula in its Resolution 2231 (XXI) of 20 December 1966. Some States which voted in favour of this resolution stated that this did not imply that the people of Gibraltar did not have the right of self-determination.[250]

As the negotiations between Spain and the United Kingdom were progressing, the United Kingdom decided to hold a referendum on the future status of Gibraltar. The population of Gibraltar was asked whether it wanted to remain linked to Britain or pass under Spanish sovereignty. A large majority voted to retain the British connection.[251] The General Assembly declared the holding of the referendum to be in contravention of the provisions of General Assembly Resolution 2231 (XXI).[252] The States opposing the referendum believed that General Assembly Resolution 1514 (XV) was applicable to Gibraltar as it constituted a colonial territory. They did not classify it solely as a territorial dispute.[253] As they did not consider the British Gibraltarians the indigenous population of Gibraltar, they denied them the right of self-determination. They were seen as aliens imported by a colonial regime.[254] The expelled Spanish population who settled in San Roque

---

[248] Spain considers that now that the United Kingdom has to decolonize the territory, Gibraltar should be returned to Spain also by virtue of the retrocession clause of the 1713 Treaty of Utrecht. See A. Cassese, *Self-Determination of Peoples: A Legal Reappraisal* (1995) pp. 206–214; J. Diez-Hochleitner, 'Les Relations hispano-britanniques au Sujet de Gibraltar', 35 AFDI (1989) pp. 167–187; and H. S. Levie, *The Status of Gibraltar* (1983) p. 30.
[249] UN Doc. A/5800/Rev.1 (1964) p. 314.
[250] New Zealand: UN Doc. A/C.4/SR.1745 (1967) p. 461, para. 136 and Finland: UN Doc. A/C.4/SR.1753 (1967) p. 546, para. 35.
[251] Referendum held on 10 Sept. 1967. In favour of British sovereignty 12,138 votes were cast against 44 voting for Spain: Hunter, *The Statesman's Year-Book*, p. 568.
[252] GA Res. 2353 (XXII). The draft resolution was adopted by the Fourth Committee of the General Assembly by 70 votes to 21, with 25 abstentions: UN Doc. A/C.4/SR.1754 (1967) p. 555, para. 52.
[253] Spain: UN Doc. A/C.4/SR.1749 (1967) p. 499, para. 37 and Colombia: UN Doc. A/C.4/SR.1745 (1967) p. 462, para. 140.

in 1704 and its descendants were alleged to constitute the true Gibraltarians.[255] The people should have 'deep roots in the Territory's soil' so that '[t]he people and the territory thus formed an indissoluble whole', with the peoples as 'sole master of the Territory'.[256] Although the population of Gibraltar was not granted the right of self-determination, the solution of the question was not sought in the exercise of the right to self-determination of the 'true Gibraltarians of San Roque' either. Instead, the opposers of the referendum preferred to apply paragraph 6 of General Assembly Resolution 1514, which safeguards the national unity and territorial integrity of a country. General Assembly Resolution 2353 (XXII) refers therefore to this stipulation in its preamble. This resolution invites Spain and the United Kingdom to resume the negotiations 'with a view to putting an end to the colonial situation in Gibraltar and to safeguarding the interests of the population'.[257] The United Kingdom and other States also applied General Assembly Resolution 1514 to the question of Gibraltar. They believed it was a colony and that the Gibraltarian population as a colonial people had the right to self-determination. The State delegates did not thoroughly explain why they had this right, but generally referred to the Gibraltarians as a colonial people who, like all other peoples of Non-Self-Governing Territories, had the right of self-determination under Resolution 1514.[258] The Chief Minister of Gibraltar emphasized that the Gibraltarian population was 'an indigenous, a long-established and distinct population' with its own religious, cultural, economic and social identity which Spain had recognized by promising to safeguard it.[259]

The difficulty of ascertaining the relationship between a population and a territory is even more obvious when we look at the length of time a people has to live in a given territory. From the early eighth century until 1462, Gibraltar was occupied by the Moors, then it came under Spanish sovereignty until 1704, when it became British territory.[260] Therefore, in 1967 the United Kingdom had held Gibraltar thirty-seven years less than Spain had. In the nineteenth century mostly non-British subjects of mixed origins settled in Gibraltar,

---

[254] Sudanese delegate: UN Doc. A/C.4/SR.1754 (1967) p. 553, para. 19.
[255] Mr Hidalgo, mayor of San Roque: UN Doc. A/C.4/SR.1747 (1967) pp. 480–481, para. 35.
[256] Ecuadorean delegate: UN Doc. A/C.4/SR.1746 (1967) p. 467, para. 40.
[257] Para. 3 of GA Res. 2353 (XXII).
[258] Malaysian delegate: UN Doc. A/C.4/SR.1753 (1967) p. 548, para. 48.
[259] UN Doc. A/C.4/SR.1747 (1967) p. 479, para. 22 and UN Doc. A/AC.109/PV.1433 (1994) p. 4.
[260] Gambian delegate: UN Doc. A/C.4/SR.1750 (1967) p. 503, para. 16.

forming the core of the future Gibraltarians.²⁶¹ A part of the population was in this period occasionally compelled to leave because of wars and epidemics, but the population level re-established itself.²⁶² The General Assembly and the Special Committee of Twenty-Four found however no evidence of 'indigenous' links between the 'new' Gibraltarians and the territory of Gibraltar.

It can be concluded from the debates and recommendations of the Special Committee of Twenty-Four and the General Assembly that the right of self-determination is granted to the indigenous people of a colonial territory irrespective of its size.²⁶³ If the inhabitants are imported by the colonial regime and are not the first settlers of the territory, they do not constitute a people for the purposes of the right of self-determination. However, it should be borne in mind that this interpretation met with considerable resistance and that the right of self-determination was denied to this kind of inhabitants only during the discussions, but was not explicitly excluded in the relevant resolutions. Theoretically, a non-indigenous people could in the coming years or centuries cultivate a stronger relationship with the territory and thus become a people with the right of self-determination. The condition that a people must have strong roots in the territory it inhabits is more easily fulfilled for the first settlers than for an imported population which expels the original inhabitants. The Special Committee prefers the application of the rule protecting the national unity and territorial integrity of a country in cases where the right of self-determination is not valid. The interests of the population may then be taken into account, but they are not the only guiding principle. The small size of the population and the territory, as well as the limited resources, does not stand in the way of independence. The fact that a small people may have a low standard of living and be vulnerable to external political influences is a situation to be avoided, but no obstacle to the right of self-determination. It may however constitute a practical problem for real independence.

---

²⁶¹ See Gibraltar Population Table 1704–1979 in Levie, *The Status of Gibraltar*, p. 126.
²⁶² Ibid., p. 94.
²⁶³ But see on small colonial enclaves pp. 84–88 below.

Judicial decisions
League of Nations
Council of the League of Nations

Although not a judicial body, the Council of the League of Nations was called upon to decide a juridical question between Finland and Sweden in which the principle of self-determination was invoked. The dispute concerned the territorial sovereignty over the Aaland Islands, some 6,500 islands with a total land area of 1,481 square kilometres, the population of which was almost entirely of Swedish origin.[264] After having been controlled by Sweden, Aaland and Finland came under Russian sovereignty in 1809.[265] In 1917 Finland struggled for its independence and a separatist movement arose in the Aaland Islands. Finland wanted Aaland to be under its sovereignty, while Sweden and the inhabitants of the Islands preferred it to become Swedish territory. The dispute was submitted for recommendations to the Council under Article 15, paragraph 1 of the Covenant of the League of Nations. Sweden favoured a solution of the Aaland question in conformity with the principle of free self-determination 'which, although not recognized as a part of international law, has received so wide an application in the formation of the New Europe'.[266] Sweden emphasized the just aspirations of the inhabitants. They were not called a 'people', but a population who had a common origin, history and national spirit with Sweden.[267] Island representatives explained they wanted to preserve their Swedish traditions, which they would be unable to do under Finnish sovereignty. If a reunion with Sweden did not succeed, they would endeavour to secure complete independence.[268] Finland considered Aaland an integral part of its territory and a question of domestic jurisdiction.[269] The Council referred the matter first of all to an International Commission of Jurists for a legal advisory opinion. It was recognized 'that it belongs to the sovereign rights of a definitely constituted State to accord or refuse to a fraction of the population the right of determining its political destiny by plebiscite or otherwise'.[270] According to the Commission, international law did not recognize 'the right of national

---

[264] R. Bernhardt, ed., *Encyclopedia of Public International Law* (1990) vol. XII, p. 1.
[265] Ibid. The Islands were renounced by Sweden to Russia under the peace treaty of Frederikshamn of 17 Sept. 1809.
[266] League of Nations Off. J. (1921) no. 7, p. 700.
[267] Ibid., p. 699.
[268] Ibid., p. 694.
[269] Ibid., p. 704.
[270] League of Nations Off. J. (1920) no. 7, pp. 394–395.

groups, as such, to separate themselves from the State of which they form part by the simple expression of a wish, any more than it recognizes the right of other States to claim such a separation'.[271]

The Council then established a Commission of Rapporteurs to prepare a solution to the question. The Rapporteurs were of the opinion that Finland constituted a State by the sole fact of its declaration of independence and that the Aaland Islands were incorporated definitely *de jure* in the new Republic of Finland.[272] The Rapporteurs also denied a legal right to separatist self-determination. They could not concede 'to minorities either of language or religion, or to any fractions of a population, the right of withdrawing from the community to which they belong, because it is their wish or their good pleasure'.[273] Because the Aaland Islands were seen as a *de jure* integral part of Finland, secession could not be realized unless Finland approved. No 'right' of self-determination was accepted in international law in the period of the League of Nations, as we have seen before.[274] Whether a right to self-determination was conceded was left to the discretion of the government of the State concerned. The Council adopted a resolution recognizing Finnish sovereignty over the Aaland Islands. It however demanded certain guarantees for the preservation of the Swedish traditions in the Islands.[275] Sweden and Finland reached an agreement in which certain guarantees were laid down relating to the use of the Swedish language, special Aaland citizenship, revenues and autonomous political institutions.[276] Thus, the wishes of the population of the Islands were not taken as the only principle governing the territorial sovereignty, but nevertheless were given a certain importance considering the negotiated guarantees. Instead of granting a right to self-determination, the Aaland question was solved through a special minority protection.

---

[271] League of Nations Off. J. (1920) Spec. Suppl. 3, p. 5.
[272] League of Nations Off. J. (1921) no. 7, p. 693.
[273] League of Nations Doc. B.7.21/68/106 (1921).
[274] See p. 10 above.
[275] Council Res. of 24 Jun. 1921, League of Nations Off. J. (1921) no. 7, p. 699.
[276] Ibid., p. 701. The present status of the Aaland Islands is governed by the Autonomy Act for Aaland of 28 Dec. 1951 under which Aaland has its own parliament, executive council and governor. Foreign affairs, defence and state finance remain under national Finnish jurisdiction (para. 19 of the Autonomy Act). See T. Eriksson, *Åland an Autonomous Province* (1978).

Permanent Court of International Justice

The Permanent Court of International Justice never pronounced on the right of self-determination. On one occasion the Council of the League of Nations asked for an advisory opinion on the obligations flowing from Articles 10 and 11 of the Peace Treaty signed between Finland and Russia on 14 October 1920, under which the population of Carelia was granted 'the right of nations to self-determination'.[277] The request for an advisory opinion was however declared inadmissible. The interpretation of the right of self-determination seemed to be restrictive even for the Carelian delegation, which declared before the Council that the right did not imply a right of secession from Russia, but a right to be reunited with an autonomous province.[278]

The Permanent Court of International Justice was able to pass judgments on questions relating to minority protection. The interest of the analysis of these judgments lies in the definitions the Permanent Court gives of minority groups. Furthermore, the international minority protection of the League of Nations was sometimes thought to be founded on the principle of self-determination.[279] We should however be cautious with this argument, as the right of self-determination was not accepted by the League of Nations and the minority protection system was established as a solution for the denial of self-determination.

In the *Rights of Minorities in Upper Silesia (Minority Schools)* case of 26 April 1928, the Permanent Court interpreted Article 74 of a Minorities Treaty between Germany and Poland.[280] This article stated that 'whether a person does or does not belong to a racial, linguistic or religious minority may not be verified or disputed by the authorities'. The German Government alleged that whether a person belonged to a minority was a question of intention alone (the subjective principle), whereas Poland considered it a question of fact with which the declaration of intention must accord. The Court declared that 'the declaration must on principle be in conformity with the facts'.[281] Whether a person belonged to a minority group depended therefore on the facts, relating to racial, linguistic or religious

---

[277] Case of *Eastern Carelia*, PCIJ Reports (1923) Series B, no. 5, p. 6.
[278] PCIJ Reports (1923) Series C, no. 3-II, pp. 156–157. See also Verhoeven, 'Peuples et Droit international', pp. 48–49.
[279] D. Thürer, *Das Selbstbestimmungsrecht der Völker* (1976) pp. 159 ff.
[280] PCIJ Reports (1928) Series A, no. 15, Judgment no. 12.
[281] Ibid., p. 35. If the declaration did not conform with the facts, this still did not give the authorities the right to verify the legality of the declaration according to the Court.

characteristics, and on his declaration of intention. Both subjective and objective elements were of importance.

On 31 July 1930, the Permanent Court of International Justice gave an advisory opinion on some legal questions arising out of the Greco-Bulgarian Convention of 27 November 1919. This convention regulated the reciprocal and voluntary emigration of minorities in Greece and Bulgaria. Under the convention it was also possible to take away movable property or receive compensation for immovable property belonging to communities (collective property). What then constituted a community? In this *Greco-Bulgarian 'Communities'* case, the Court defined a community as:

> a group of persons living in a given country or locality, having a race, religion, language and traditions of their own and united by this identity of race, religion, language and traditions in a sentiment of solidarity, with a view to preserving their traditions, maintaining their form of worship, ensuring the instruction and upbringing of their children in accordance with the spirit and traditions of their race and rendering mutual assistance to each other.[282]

The existence of a community was, according to the Court, a question of fact, not of recognition by (national) law. Furthermore, the communities were of an exclusively minority character.[283] The definition given by the Court should, in principle, be regarded as a definition of a minority group. It shows again the relation between objective and subjective elements, by which a group of persons distinguishes itself from another group of persons.

United Nations

International Court of Justice

The principle of self-determination was for the first time referred to by the Court in its advisory opinion concerning *Legal Consequences for States of the Continued Presence of South Africa in Namibia (South West Africa) notwithstanding Security Council Resolution 276 (1970)*.[284] The Court recalled that under Article 22, paragraph 1 of the Covenant of the League of Nations 'the well-being and development of such peoples [i.e., peoples of mandated territories] form a sacred trust of civilisation'.[285] It emphasized furthermore that 'the subsequent development of international law in regard to non-self-

---

[282] PCIJ Reports (1930) Series B, no. 17, p. 21.
[283] Ibid., pp. 21–22 and 30.
[284] ICJ Reports (1971) pp. 15 ff.
[285] Ibid., p. 28, para. 45.

governing territories, as enshrined in the Charter of the United Nations, made the principle of self-determination applicable to all of them.'[286] As the Court believed that the concept of 'sacred trust' was 'not static' and 'by definition evolutionary', it went on to state: 'These developments leave little doubt that the ultimate objective of the sacred trust was self-determination and independence of the peoples concerned. In this domain, as elsewhere, the *corpus iuris gentium* has been considerably enriched, and this the Court, if it is faithfully to discharge its functions, may not ignore.'[287] The application of the principle of self-determination was confirmed for all Non-Self-Governing Territories, though the Court made no explicit reference to a *right* of self-determination.

The relationship between the principle of self-determination and the territorial integrity of a State was the point at issue in the Court's advisory opinion on *Western Sahara*.[288] Both Morocco and Mauritania claimed that Western Sahara was a part of their national territory. The General Assembly addressed an enquiry to the Court as to the nature of the legal ties between the territory of Western Sahara and the Kingdom of Morocco and the Mauritanian entity, respectively. Morocco believed that the request would place the General Assembly in a better position to choose the process best suited for the decolonization of Western Sahara.[289] Mauritania preferred to give priority to territorial integrity instead of the application of the principle of self-determination.[290] According to Spain the questions put to the Court were irrelevant and without practical effect, as Western Sahara should be decolonized in accordance with the wishes of its population only.[291] The Court declared:

The validity of the principle of self-determination, defined as the need to pay regard to the freely expressed will of peoples, is not affected by the fact that in certain cases the General Assembly has dispensed with the requirement of consulting the inhabitants of a given territory. Those instances were based either on the consideration that a certain population did not constitute a 'people' entitled to self-determination or on the conviction that a consultation was totally unnecessary, in view of special circumstances.[292]

---

[286] Ibid., p. 31, para. 52.
[287] Ibid., p. 31, para. 53.
[288] ICJ Reports (1975).
[289] Ibid., p. 29, para. 49.
[290] Ibid., pp. 29–30, para. 50.
[291] Ibid., p. 29, para. 48.
[292] Ibid., p. 33, para. 59.

Judge Nagendra Singh explained these 'special circumstances' in his declaration as situations in which 'the will of the people was found to be axiomatic in the sense that the result was known to be a foregone conclusion or that consultations had already taken place in some form or that special features of the case rendered it unnecessary'.[293]

The Court examined whether there was evidence of an 'effective display of authority' by Morocco in Western Sahara at the time of its colonization and the period immediately preceding that time. The Court did not find such legal ties of State sovereignty, only legal ties of allegiance between the Sultan of Morocco and some tribes living in the territory of Western Sahara.[294] As a Mauritanian State did not exist at the time of Western Sahara's colonization, the Court looked for 'other legal ties' between Mauritania and Western Sahara than legal ties of State sovereignty. Mauritania had pleaded, among other things, that the tribal groups wandering on Mauritanian and Western Saharan territory constituted one nation or people: the Shinguitti people, a 'distinct human unit, characterized by a common language, way of life and religion'.[295] The territory of Western Sahara did not form an entity of its own.[296] The Court admitted that between various tribes and emirates dwelling in the territories of Mauritania and Western Sahara there 'existed many ties of a racial, linguistic, religious, cultural and economic nature', but concluded that 'no common institutions or organs even of a quite minimal character' existed.[297] Therefore, Mauritania did not enjoy some form of sovereignty in Western Sahara. Neither Morocco nor Mauritania had any tie of territorial sovereignty with Western Sahara. The Court added that '[t]hus [emphasis added] the Court has not found legal ties of such a nature as might affect the application ... of the principle of self-determination through the free and genuine expression of the will of the peoples of the territory'.[298]

What if the Court had concluded that Western Sahara did constitute an integral part of the territory of either Morocco or Mauritania? Would the right of self-determination of the inhabitants of Western Sahara then be disregarded? The General Assembly believed that the advisory opinion would help, facilitate and accelerate the

---

[293] Ibid., p. 81, para. II.
[294] Ibid., p. 43, para. 93 and p. 68, para. 162.
[295] Ibid., pp. 58 and 60, paras. 132 and 138.
[296] Ibid., p. 60, para. 139.
[297] Ibid., p. 63, para. 149.
[298] Ibid., p. 68, para. 162.

decolonization of Western Sahara.²⁹⁹ It seems probable that, had the Court certified the existence of legal ties with any of the parties, the General Assembly would have taken this element into account. The Court established a causal connection by using the word 'thus'. *A contrario* we could argue that the principle of self-determination would have been affected if ties of territorial sovereignty had been proved. It remains uncertain to what extent the application of the principle of self-determination would have been affected. Judge Nagendra Singh stressed in his declaration, that 'even if integration of territory was demanded ... it could not be had without ascertaining the freely expressed will of the people – the very *sine qua non* of all decolonization'.³⁰⁰ But if integration would have been subject to the approval of the peoples concerned, then their right of self-determination would not be affected at all. In case of a refusal, they would still have the choice of independence or some other international status. The Court's advisory opinion does not clarify to what degree the principle of self-determination is affected in case the territorial integrity of a country has to be respected under paragraph 6 of General Assembly Resolution 1514.

A question of self-determination also underlay the proceedings brought before the International Court of Justice by Portugal against Australia concerning East Timor. It was *inter alia* alleged by Portugal that by concluding the Treaty on the Zone of Cooperation in an Area between the Indonesian Province of East Timor and Northern Australia,³⁰¹ Australia had infringed the right of the people of East Timor to self-determination.³⁰² Although the Court found that in this case it could not exercise jurisdiction, it unequivocally declared that 'Portugal's assertion that the right of peoples to self-determination,

---

[299] Point 3 of GA Res. 3292 (XXIX) stressed that the General Assembly would decide on the policy to be followed with respect to Western Sahara, in the light of the advisory opinion to be given by the ICJ. Argentina, Cameroon, Spain and Syria emphasized explicitly that the advisory opinion could not prejudice the right of self-determination of the people of Western Sahara: UN Doc. A/C.4/SR.2125 (1974) paras. 43, 57, 66 and 71.

[300] ICJ Reports (1975) p. 81, part II.

[301] 29 ILM (1990) pp. 469 ff.

[302] See C. Chinkin, 'The Merits of Portugal's Claim against Australia', 15 *University of New South Wales Law Journal* (1992) p. 423; C. Chinkin, 'East Timor moves into the World Court', 4 EJIL (1993) pp. 206–222; R. S. Clark, 'Some International Law Aspects of the East Timor Affair', 5 LJIL (1992) pp. 265–271; R. S. Clark, 'Timor Gap: The Legality of the "Treaty on the Zone of Cooperation in an Area between the Indonesian Province of East Timor and Northern Australia"', *Pace Yearbook of International Law* (1992) pp. 69–95; and M. C. Maffei, 'The Case of East Timor before the International Court of Justice', 4 EJIL (1993) pp. 223–238.

as it evolved from the Charter and from United Nations practice, has an *erga omnes* character, is irreproachable' and that 'it is one of the essential principles of contemporary international law'.[303]

Human Rights Committee

Under Article 1 of the Optional Protocol to the ICCPR, the Human Rights Committee can 'receive and consider communications from individuals who claim to be victims of a violation of any of the rights set forth in the Covenant'. Article 1 of the Covenant sets forth the right of all peoples to self-determination. So far the Human Rights Committee has received five communications of persons claiming a violation of their right of self-determination. The first one concerned an individual, the Grand Captain of the Mikmaq Tribal Society, who accused Canada of violating Article 1.[304] He presented his claim on his own behalf and on behalf of the Mikmaq people. The Human Rights Committee declared the communication inadmissible for procedural reasons. The Grand Chief of the Grand Council of the Mikmaq had denied that the Grand Captain was entitled to present the claim on behalf of the Mikmaq Tribal Society. The Human Rights Committee therefore concluded that 'the author has not proven that he is authorized to act as a representative on behalf of the Mikmaq Tribal Society'.[305] In addition, the Committee did not find facts 'supporting his claim that he is personally a victim of a violation of any rights contained in the Covenant'.[306] This decision contrasts with later judgments, for in this case the Committee still leaves open the possibility that a representative leader of a people may present communications, if so authorized by his own laws, and that an individual can be a victim of a violation of Article 1, if he can advance sufficient facts supporting this violation.

The four following communications relating to claimed violations of Article 1 were all declared inadmissible. The claims were no longer dismissed on the grounds that the author of the communication was non-representative, but because under Article 1 of the Optional Protocol 'the author, as an individual, could not claim ... to be a victim of a violation of the right of self-determination enshrined in article 1

---

[303] Case concerning *East Timor (Portugal v. Australia)*, ICJ Reports (1995) p. 102, para. 29. There were no separate or dissenting opinions on this point.
[304] Communication no. 78/1980, *A. D. on behalf of Mikmaq Tribal Society v. Canada*: UN Doc. A/39/40 (1984) pp. 200 ff.
[305] Ibid., p. 203.
[306] Ibid.

of the Covenant, which deals with rights conferred upon peoples, as such'.[307] In the opinion of the Committee, '[t]he Optional Protocol provides a procedure under which individuals can claim that their *individual* [emphasis added] rights have been violated'.[308] The Committee did not consider the right of self-determination as an individual right, though it did not state expressly that it was a collective right either. Although Article 1 of the Optional Protocol speaks of '*any* [emphasis added] of the rights set forth in the Covenant', the Human Rights Committee interprets this formula as only 'individual rights', namely Articles 6 to 27 inclusive of the Covenant.[309] Therefore, no claim for self-determination may ever be brought under the Optional Protocol.[310]

Why then does Article 1 of the Optional Protocol refer to 'any of the rights set forth in the Covenant'? As we have seen, the *travaux préparatoires* reveal a discussion on whether the right of self-determination is a collective or an individual right.[311] The majority of States believed it was an individual right, though exercised collectively. But even those States which were of the opinion that it was a collective right did not therefore exclude the possibility of the Human Rights Committee having to consider it. They even feared it.[312] Such a fear was nevertheless not transmitted to Article 1 of the Optional Protocol. The text does not lead us to believe that 'any of the rights' means 'the rights of Articles 6 to 27 inclusive'. In addition, Article 7 of the Protocol recalls that the Protocol shall in no way limit the right of petition of colonial peoples, 'pending the achievement of the objectives of resolution 1514 (XV)'. Obviously, this right of petition also, and primarily, includes the right to petition about the violation of the right of self-determination. The Optional Protocol as a whole therefore does not exclude all claims of violations of Article 1 of the Covenant.[313] Moreover, in the framework of Article 41 of the Covenant,

---

[307] Communication no. 167/1984, *Bernard Omivayak Chief of the Lubicon Lake Band v. Canada*: UN Doc. A/45/40 (1990) vol. II, p. 9, para. 13.3.
[308] Communication no. 318/1988, *E. P. et al. v. Colombia*: ibid., p. 187, para. 8.2. and Communication no. 358/1989, *Whispering Pines Indian Band v. Canada*: UN Doc. A/46/40 (1991) p. 321, para. 6.2.
[309] Ibid., p. 27, para. 32.1.
[310] Communication no. 413/1990, *A. B. et al. v. Italy*: 12 HRLJ (1991) nos. 1–2, p. 25, para. 3.2.
[311] See p. 30 above.
[312] British delegate: UN Doc. A/C.3/SR.642 (1955) p. 90, para. 14.
[313] See also J. Crawford, 'Outside the Colonial Context', in W. J. A. Macartney, ed., *Self-Determination in the Commonwealth* (1988), p. 4.

which gives one State Party the right to claim that another State Party has violated its obligations under the Covenant, the right of self-determination was unambiguously included in the obligations the violation of which could be brought to the attention of the Human Rights Committee. A proposal to exclude matters arising out of Article 1 of the Covenant from being submitted to the Human Rights Committee was rejected.[314] The Secretary-General had expressed the opinion that 'the implementation measures included in the two draft Covenants ... should apply to the article [i.e. Article 1 of the Covenants]'.[315] Subsequently, the Netherlands had proposed an optional Article 41 bis, which was to become Article 1 and following articles of the Optional Protocol, according to which the Committee could receive petitions from 'individuals or groups of individuals' which were victims of the violation 'of the rights set forth in this Covenant'.[316] This proposal was later changed, without being officially discussed in the Third Committee, by deleting the words 'or groups of individuals' and replacing 'the rights set forth in this Covenant' with 'any of the rights set forth in this Covenant', which became the final text of Article 1 of the Optional Protocol.[317] The opponents of draft Article 41 bis (Article 1 of the Optional Protocol) never invoked an argument to exclude the right of self-determination from the right of individual petition. It is noteworthy that the word 'any' of the rights was included without objections. Nonetheless, the words 'groups of individuals' were deleted without stating the reasons for this amendment. This change does not implicitly mean that complaints concerning a violation of the right of self-determination can no longer be received, nor that 'any of the rights' signifies only 'individual rights'. Individuals may very well comprise a great number of individuals or a person representing a group of individuals.

The fact that Article 1 of the Covenant has been included in a separate Part I does not necessarily imply that the article is therefore excluded from Article 1 of the Protocol. The distinct place of Article 1 of the Covenant emphasizes its importance as a fundamental right and prerequisite of all other human rights. It does not emphasize its exclusion. The drafters of the Covenant did not intend to exclude the

---

[314] French amendment UN Doc. E/CN.4/L.235/Rev.1 (1953) and Belgium amendment UN Doc. E/CN.4/L.244 (1953) rejected by the Commission on Human Rights by 10 votes to 5, with 3 abstentions, UN Doc. E/CN.4/SR.361 (1953) p. 5.
[315] UN Doc. A/5411 (1963) p. 34, para. 81.
[316] UN Doc. A/C.3/L.1355 (1966) para. 3 and UN Doc. A/6546 (1966) para. 474.
[317] UN Doc. A/C.3/L.1402/Rev.2 (1966) and UN Doc. A/6546 (1966) para. 477.

right of self-determination from Article 1 of the Optional Protocol. The decisions on Article 1 of the Covenant made by the Human Rights Committee are contrary to the intentions of the drafters and not in conformity with the text of Article 1 of the Optional Protocol. Canada was one of the States which from the beginning had considered the right of self-determination a collective right.[318]

A collective right distinguishes itself from an individual right in the sense that, where collective rights are concerned, the right has to be exercised by the group as a whole, even if this or that individual could not join in the exercise of the right. An individual right has to be respected in each individual case.[319] Thus, the right of self-determination as formulated in Article 1 of the Covenant indeed is a collective right. It is not however correct to interpret Article 1 of the Optional Protocol so as to exclude collective human rights. Some individuals could be considered as authorized representatives of their people and therefore as individuals able to transmit communications under Article 1 of the Protocol.

The Human Rights Committee was thus never required to decide on whether a group constituted a people within the meaning of Article 1 of the Covenant.[320] It seems in some cases possible for a group of persons claiming to be a 'people' to satisfy their demands as a 'minority' under Article 27 of the Covenant. The Human Rights Committee may give an extensive interpretation of Article 27, but this excludes any claims relating to the political status of the group.[321]

---

[318] The Commission on Human Rights has repeatedly pointed out that the right of self-determination is a right of the individual, by virtue of which it is every person's right that the people of which he is a member should be recognized to have the right of self-determination: UN Doc. E/CN.4/Sub.2/405/Rev.1 (1980) p. 10, para. 58.

[319] Y. Dinstein, 'Collective Human Rights of Peoples and Minorities', 25 ICLQ (1976) p. 103.

[320] In Communication no. 167/1984, the Lubicon Lake Band stated that it was 'a self-identified, relatively autonomous, socio-cultural and economic group' who inhabited a certain area 'since time immemorial' and maintained 'its traditional culture, religion, political structure and subsistence economy'. In the view of Canada, they did not constitute a people, because they were only 'a small portion of a larger group of Cree Indians residing in Northern Alberta'. Interestingly enough, Canada did not exclude the possibility that this larger group of Cree Indians could constitute a people, denying the status of 'people' to a fraction of a people. Canada did not attack the Band's arguments about the essential elements of the definition of a 'people'. UN Doc. A/45/40 (1990) vol. II, p. 2, para. 2.2. and p. 6, para. 6.2.

[321] Communication no. 167/1984 was solved in this way. The Human Rights Committee did not test the Lubicon Lake Band against the definition of 'minority': ibid., pp. 10 ff. See further D. McGoldrick, 'Canadian Indians, Cultural Rights and the Human Rights Committee', 40 ICLQ (1991) pp. 658–669.

Arbitration Commission on Yugoslavia

Within the framework of the Conference on Yugoslavia, organized by the European Communities in order to solve the problems surrounding the disintegration of the Socialist Federal Republic of Yugoslavia (hereafter, SFRY) a special Arbitration Commission was established in 1991.[322] The Arbitration Commission was asked to give its opinion on several legal questions which are of importance for the interpretation of the right of self-determination.

The first legal question the Arbitration Commission had to solve was addressed to it by Lord Carrington, President of the Conference on Yugoslavia, on 20 November 1991. The President requested 'an opinion or recommendation' which the Commission 'might deem useful' to solve the following dispute: Serbia considered that those Republics which had declared themselves independent had seceded from the SFRY which would otherwise continue to exist. The other Republics on the contrary considered that there was no question of secession, but that the question was one of a disintegration or breaking-up of the SFRY as the result of the concurring will of a number of Republics. According to them, the six Republics were to be considered equal successors to the SFRY, without any of them or any group of them being able to claim to be the continuation thereof. The problem referred to a question of State succession, but is interesting from the point of view of the right of self-determination, because of the use of the term 'secession'. In its Opinion No. 1 of 29 November 1991, the Arbitration Commission concluded:

The composition and workings of the essential organs of the Federation ... no longer meet the criteria of participation and representativeness inherent in a Federal State ... the authorities of the Federation and the Republics have shown themselves to be powerless to enforce respect for the succeeding cease-fire agreements ... consequently, the Arbitration Committee is of the opinion: that the Socialist Federal Republic of Yugoslavia is in the process of dissolution.[323]

In the opinion of the Commission, the Republics which had declared their independence had not seceded from an existing State. The State itself was in a process of dissolution, because it had ceased

---

[322] EPC Declaration of 27 Aug. 1991, EPC Press Release 82/91.
[323] Text in 31 ILM (1992) pp. 1496–1497, paras. 2 (b, c) and 3. For more information on the events in Yugoslavia see C. Spencer, *The Former Yugoslavia: Background to Crisis* (1993) and M. Weller, 'The International Response to the Dissolution of the Socialist Federal Republic of Yugoslavia', 86 AJIL (1992) pp. 569–607.

to exist. As the Commission put it: 'the existence of the State implies that the Federal organs represent the components of the Federation and wield effective power'. The Commission established the disappearance of the representativeness of the Federal organs and the loss of power to even enforce the cease-fire agreements. It should therefore be noted that the Republics, which had declared their independence on the basis of their right of self-determination, had not provoked a secession.[324] A secession is a withdrawal from a State which continues to exist on a diminished territory, whereas in the Yugoslavian case, the whole State dissolved. The Arbitration Commission did not pronounce on the legitimacy of this dissolution.

In its Opinion No. 3 of 11 January 1992, the Arbitration Commission laid down the international rules to be observed in the process of dissolution concerning the internal and external frontiers. In the first place, the external frontiers should be maintained in accordance with the principles set forth in the Charter of the United Nations, General Assembly Resolution 2625 (XXV), the Helsinki Declaration and Article 11 of the Vienna Convention of 23 August 1978 on State succession. In the second place, the internal frontiers of the Republics can only be modified by free and mutual consent. In the third place, if such a consent does not exist, the internal borders become protected by international law. The Commission based this rule on the principle of *uti possidetis juris*. This principle was originally used in the colonial context. If, in the decolonization process, a colony acquired independence, the 'colonial' frontiers were maintained. As the International Court of Justice explained in the case concerning the *Frontier Dispute (Burkina Faso/Republic of Mali)* of 22 December 1986, the principle of *uti possidetis juris* is 'a general principle, which is logically connected with the phenomenon of the obtaining of independence, whenever it occurs. Its obvious purpose is to prevent the independence and stability of new States being endangered by fratricidal struggles provoked by the challenging of frontiers.'[325] The

---

[324] The Republics declaring independence were: Slovenia, by referendum Dec. 1990, declaration of independence 25 Jun. 1991, confirmed 8 Oct. 1991; Croatia, by referendum May 1991, declaration of independence 25 Jun. 1991, confirmed 8 Oct. 1991; Macedonia, by referendum Sept. 1991 for independence within an association of Yugoslav States; Bosnia-Herzegovina, by parliamentary sovereignty resolution 14 Oct. 1991 and referendum of 1 Mar. 1992 (See n. 338 below). In addition, a new Serbian Republic of Bosnia-Herzegovina by decision of the Assembly of the Serbian people of Bosnia-Herzegovina, 9 Jan. 1992, was declared.

[325] ICJ Reports (1986) p. 565, para. 20.

principle was to be observed 'both for the frontiers deriving from international agreements, and for those resulting from mere internal administrative divisions'.[326] Administrative boundaries are being transformed into international frontiers in the full sense of the term. The Court admitted that '[a]t first sight this principle conflicts outright with another one, the right of peoples to self-determination', but the requirement of stability and the consolidation of their independence have induced colonial countries 'judiciously to consent to the respecting of colonial frontiers, and to take account of it in the interpretation of the principle of self-determination of peoples'.[327] 'The obligation to respect pre-existing international frontiers in the event of State succession derives from a general rule of international law', affirms the Court.[328]

The right of self-determination does not seem to prevail in all circumstances. The right of self-determination is conceded to all peoples, but under the principle of *uti possidetis juris* only those peoples will be able to establish a State in a delimited area who are already living within certain international or internal frontiers. This will create difficulties for peoples who live in a territory crossed by internal or international boundaries. This is the case, for example, with the Serbian population living in Croatia and Bosnia-Herzegovina. With the declaration of independence of these two Republics, the Serbs found themselves enclosed in another State. The Republic of Serbia therefore asked the Arbitration Commission on 20 November 1991: 'Does the Serbian population in Croatia and Bosnia-Hercegovina, as one of the constituent peoples of Yugoslavia, have the right to self-determination?'[329] The Arbitration Commission in its Opinion No. 2 of 11 January 1992, started by saying that:

international law as it currently stands does not spell out the implications of the right to self-determination. However, it is well established that, whatever the circumstances, the right to self-determination must not involve changes to existing frontiers at the time of independence (*uti possidetis juris*) except where the States concerned agree otherwise.[330]

---

[326] Ibid., p. 565, para. 21.
[327] Ibid., p. 567, para. 25.
[328] Ibid., p. 566, para. 24.
[329] 31 ILM (1992) p. 1498. The memorials, observations and documents provided by Bosnia-Herzegovina, Croatia, Macedonia, Montenegro, Slovenia, Serbia and the Presidency of the SFRY were non-communicable.
[330] Ibid., p. 1498, para. 1.

It is clear that, whatever the circumstances, the right of self-determination cannot prevail over the principle of *uti possidetis juris*. The Arbitration Commission then continued by affirming that

> Where there are one or more groups within a State constituting one or more ethnic, religious or language communities, they have the right to recognition of their identity under international law ... The Serbian population in Bosnia-Hercegovina and Croatia must therefore be afforded every right accorded to minorities.[331]

Thus, the Commission recognizes that the Serbs in Croatia and Bosnia-Herzegovina are 'minorities', within the meaning of general international law. According to the Commission, the right of self-determination, established in Article 1 of the ICCPR, 'serves to safeguard human rights. *By virtue of that right* [emphasis added] every individual may choose to belong to whatever ethnic, religious or language community he wishes.'[332]

One of the consequences of this principle can be, in the opinion of the Commission, that on the basis of agreements between the Republics and the Serbian populations of Bosnia-Herzegovina and Croatia, the members of these populations might 'be recognized ... as having the nationality of their choice'.[333] Hence, the members of the Serbian populations in question are recognized as minorities to whom minority rights have to be conceded, because they are an ethnic, religious or linguistic community. The Commission implicitly recognizes the applicability of the right of self-determination to these Serbian minorities, because the principle may be applied to them in potential agreements and imply a right to choose their nationality. It is however left to the discretion of the Republics to grant them this right, for 'the Republics must afford the members of those minorities and ethnic groups all the human rights and fundamental freedoms recognized in international law, including, *where appropriate* [emphasis added], the right to choose their nationality'.[334]

As the principle of *uti possidetis juris* is applied, the right of self-determination can only be granted to the Serbian populations if the Republics agree. Furthermore, the Commission has construed the right of self-determination in a quite original way. By virtue of this right, every human being may claim he belongs to the ethnic,

---
[331] Ibid., p. 1498, para. 2.
[332] Ibid., p. 1498, para. 3.
[333] Ibid.
[334] Ibid., p. 1499, para. 4 (ii).

religious or linguistic community of his choice and may choose his nationality. Is an ethnic, religious or linguistic community a people or a minority? The formula was used by the Commission to determine that the Serbian populations were 'minorities'. It uses the same formula in connection with the right of self-determination, a right which is only conceded to 'peoples'. Should we therefore conclude that both minorities and peoples are ethnic, religious or linguistic communities? The use of the word 'communities', a neutral term, suggests this possibility. The question is more confusing if we consider the right to choose one's own nationality. In the vocabulary of the last Yugoslavian Constitution of 1974, the term 'nationalities' meant those ethnic groups which have a State outside Yugoslavia, normally used as an equivalent for 'minorities'. The term 'nations' indicated the Slavic nations founding the SFRY and thus having Yugoslavia as their only form of statehood. Article 170, paragraph 1 of the Yugoslavian Constitution stresses that: 'Citizens shall be guaranteed the right to opt for a nation or nationality.'[335] The Commission's Opinion was probably inspired by this article and, if understood in this sense, the right to choose one's nationality implies the right to choose one's ethnic affiliation or the right to choose to what minority group one belongs. This then is no more than the subjective element of the definition of a minority. It is up to the members of the minority to declare to which minority group they belong, possibly justified by objective factors.[336] Such a right cannot be derived from and should not be based on the right of peoples to self-determination. The right to choose a nationality is inherent in the recognition of minority rights. It should always be recognized, not just 'where appropriate'. The right of self-determination has to do not with the choice of nationality, but rather with the choice of peoplehood.

The Arbitration Commission formulated the right of self-determination as an individual right by virtue of which every human being may choose his ethnic, religious or linguistic community, that is, his people. The subjective element of the definition of 'people' is stressed. From the fact that 'ethnic, religious or language communities' are used both in the context of minorities rights and in the context of the right of peoples to self-determination, it can be deduced that

---

[335] English translation: Cross-Cultural Communications, *The Constitution of the Socialist Federal Republic of Yugoslavia* (1976).
[336] Cf. case of *Rights of Minorities in Upper Silesia (Minority Schools)*, PCIJ Reports (1928) Series A, no. 15, Judgment no. 12. See p. 58 above.

minorities and peoples are ethnic, religious or linguistic communities. Independently of other conditions that may be fixed, this element appears in both the definition of 'minority' and the definition of 'people'. In both cases the subjective element is of importance. The Arbitration Commission did not however answer the question put to it. Implicitly it recognized the application of the principle of self-determination to the Serbian populations of Croatia and Bosnia-Herzegovina, but it remains uncertain whether these populations may have the right of self-determination themselves or may only exercise it in community with the rest of the Serbian people, namely those living in Serbia. The question whether a fraction of a people has the right of self-determination, which it can exercise independently of the rest of the people, has not been resolved.

Some indications are nevertheless to be found in the Commission's Opinion No. 4 of 11 January 1992. The Serbian population in Bosnia-Herzegovina had contested the Parliamentary Sovereignty Resolution of 14 October 1991 deciding the independence of Bosnia-Herzegovina. Although the Government of Bosnia-Herzegovina had accepted all obligations which the European Communities had fixed to recognize its independence, the Arbitration Commission declared that 'the will of the peoples of Bosnia-Hercegovina to constitute the SRBH [Socialist Republic of Bosnia-Herzegovina] as a sovereign and independent State cannot be held to have been fully established'.[337] This was due to the fact that the 'Assembly of the Serbian people of Bosnia-Hercegovina' had declared the independence of a Serbian Republic of Bosnia-Herzegovina. The Commission had preferred a referendum in which all citizens of Bosnia-Herzegovina could participate. A fraction of a people – the Serbian population in Bosnia-Herzegovina – could thus decide, together with other peoples or fraction of peoples, the political status of a territory. They could do this independently of the wishes of the rest of the people, namely the other Serbs in Serbia. In this view, the right of self-determination is not a right of peoples as such, but a right of peoples living within certain internal and/or external frontiers.[338]

---

[337] 30 ILM (1992) p. 1503, para. 4.
[338] As a consequence, on 1 Mar. 1992 a referendum was held in Bosnia-Herzegovina which was boycotted by many Serbs. Nevertheless almost 63 per cent of the electorate opted for independence, which prompted the recognition of Bosnia-Herzegovina by the European Communities' Member States.

Peoples in doctrine

Doctrine is the most extensive resource in establishing a definition of the term 'peoples' within the meaning of the right of self-determination. One group of learned publicists pays attention to both subjective and objective criteria, which they give equal value.[339] Their position can be summarized as follows: A people is a group of persons who have a distinct character on the basis of objective and subjective elements. The objective criteria generally comprise race, ethnicity, culture, tradition, history, language and religion.[340] Some scholars include in these elements a common territory,[341] while others lay it down as a separate condition.[342] These common characteristics are not cumulative nor limitative, though some writers consider the criterion of language the most important as it reflects the other objective characteristics the best.[343] The language of a group is then seen as the product of all the other elements a group has in common. It could even be regarded as a sole criterion, replacing all the others, including the subjective elements, for it combines them all.[344] The problem of confining everything to one criterion raises however the problem of determining what a language is compared to a dialect or subdialect. The subjective characteristic bears upon the psychological group thinking. A group possessing the required objective characteristics must in addition have the will to live together as a group, be conscious of its identity and want to preserve its distinctive characteristics. The 'we-consciousness' is therefore based on objectively recognizable factors.[345] The objective and subjective elements are

---

[339] See, e.g., Connelly, 'The Right of Self-Determination', p. 557; I. Brownlie, 'The Rights of Peoples in Modern International Law', in J. Crawford, ed., *The Rights of Peoples* (1988) p. 5; Dinstein, 'Collective Human Rights', p. 104; Guilhaudis, *Le Droit des Peuples*, p. 43; M. van Haegendoren, 'Ethnicity, Language and State', 13 *Plural Societies* (1982) nos. 1–4, p. 48; Secretariat of the International Commission of Jurists, *The Events in East Pakistan* (1972) p. 70; A. N'Kolombua, 'L'Ambivalence des Relations entre le Droit des Peuples à disposer d'eux-mêmes et de l'Intégrité territoriale des Etats en Droit international contemporain', in M. Lachs et al., *Mélanges offerts à Charles Chaumont: Le Droit des Peuples à disposer d'eux-mêmes* (1984) pp. 461–462; and J. A. de Obieta Chalbaud, *El Derecho Humano de la Autodeterminación de los Pueblos* (1985) pp. 37 ff.
[340] These are best reflected by Secretariat of the International Commission of Jurists, *The Events in East Pakistan*, p. 70.
[341] Dinstein, 'Collective Human Rights', p. 104 and N'Kolombua, 'L'Ambivalence', p. 461.
[342] De Obieta Chalbaud, *El Derecho Humano*, p. 47.
[343] G. Héraud, 'Les Communautés linguistiques en quête d'un Statut', 13 *Plural Societies* (1982) nos. 1–4, p. 99 and de Obieta Chalbaud, *El Derecho Humano*, p. 39.
[344] Héraud, 'Les Communautés', p. 94.
[345] Van Haegendoren, 'Ethnicity, Language and State', p. 48.

interrelated. In the view of these publicists, it is the group which determines whether it is or is not a people. It does not have to be recognized by other peoples or States and settles the criteria for individuals for belonging to the group itself.[346]

Unfortunately, these scholars have not always clearly explained the reasons for choosing these criteria and not others. They may well have demonstrated the advantages of considering both objective and subjective elements instead of just one of them, but why these criteria were used in the first place is not always evident. Some learned writers have justified their findings with the work of psychologists, sociologists, ethnologists and linguists,[347] while others base themselves on history.[348]

In modern publications, very few lawyers can be found who define a people exclusively on objective grounds. This concept has been defended by German theorists in the nineteenth and the beginning of the twentieth century.[349] Their philosophy was especially propagated in the territorial dispute with France over Alsace-Lorraine. Certain contemporary scholars stress the objective elements. Although they do not exclude the subjective factor, they attach less value to it.[350] Opposed to the German philosophy, we can find the French theory which defined a nation or people solely on the subjective factor. This definition was maintained in the late nineteenth century.[351] At present, we find publicists who emphasize the subjective element, without setting aside the objective criteria.[352] One scholar identifies a people with a nation entitled to statehood.[353]

---

[346] Dinstein, 'Collective Human Rights', p. 105 and N'Kolombua, 'L'Ambivalence', p. 463.
[347] Héraud, 'Les Communautés', p. 94.
[348] De Obieta Chalbaud, *El Derecho Humano*, p. 34 and Brownlie, 'The Rights of Peoples', pp. 4–5.
[349] See Guilhaudis, *Le Droit des Peuples*, p. 37.
[350] See, e.g., Héraud, 'Les Communautés', p. 94 and de Obieta Chalbaud, *El Derecho Humano*, pp. 47–48 and 60, who defines a people on objective and subjective grounds but with a weakly developed 'consciencia étnica', whereas a nation has a strongly developed subjective element. Both peoples and nations have the right to self-determination according to this author.
[351] E. Renan, *Qu'est-ce qu'une Nation?* (1882) p. 52, who defined a nation as 'une âme, un esprit, une famille spirituelle, résultant, dans le passé, de souvenirs, de sacrifices, de gloires, souvent de deuils et de regrets communs; dans le présent, du désir de continuer à vivre ensemble. Ce qui constitue une nation, ce n'est pas de parler la même langue ou d'appartenir au même groupe ethnographique, c'est d'avoir fait ensemble de grandes choses dans le passé et de vouloir en faire encore dans l'avenir.'
[352] V. P. Nanda, 'Self-Determination under International Law: Validity of Claims to Secede', 13 *Case Western Reserve Journal of International Law* (1981) no. 1, p. 276.
[353] S. R. Chowdhury, 'The Status and Norms of Self-Determination in Contemporary International Law', 24 NILR (1977) p. 77. On the basis of the scheme of the Charter of

Common characteristics are not the *conditio sine qua non*, but the common feeling of a group that it is a people is the deciding factor.[354]

Another group of learned publicists does not tackle the problem in the light of objective or subjective criteria, but determines the 'unit of self-determination', which is generally the inhabitants of 'those territories established and recognized as separate political units'.[355] The recognition of a political unit as a people remains then the decisive criterion for the applicability of the right of self-determination, although it is not said that the recognition is always of a constitutive nature rather than just declaratory.

The State practice of recognizing certain units as peoples within the meaning of the right of self-determination has been used by certain writers to find general rules which can be applied to identify a people. If the United Nations practice in this field is considered, especially in the decolonization process, some general norms were established, but these did not always bear a relation to objective or subjective criteria.[356] They resulted in conditions which did not affect the peoplehood as such. The conditions laid down were not inherent to a people, but were to be fulfilled by peoples or fractions of peoples in order to see their full right of self-determination realized. These are what shall be called 'subsequent conditions', particularly used to justify a secession. The juridical correctness of these findings will be verified below.[357]

One of the first such conditions is the requirement that a people, as defined by objective and subjective factors, be living under a regime which denies it its human rights.[358] Only then will the people

---

the United Nations, he regards a nation as 'secular, multi-racial and multi-lingual where different communities share a larger national identity derived from a feeling of common history and common destiny'.

[354] S. Pierré-Caps, *Nation et Peuples dans les Constitutions modernes*, vol. II (1987) pp. 490–493.

[355] J. Crawford, *The Creation of States in International Law* (1979) p. 101. Also in this line of thought: Pomerance, *Self-Determination*, p. 23; K. Klüpfel, *Selbstbestimmung durch Assoziation* (1987) pp. 84–88; and L. Rohr, 'El Principio de la Auto-Determinación de los Pueblos en el Derecho Internacional', 1 *Annuario de Derecho Internacional Publico* (1981) p. 67.

[356] See, e.g., G. T. Morris, 'In Support of the Right of Self-Determination for Indigenous Peoples under International Law', 29 GYIL (1986) pp. 277–316.

[357] See pp. 89–103 below.

[358] S. J. Anaya, 'The Capacity of International Law to advance Ethnic or Nationality Rights Claims', 75 *Iowa Law Review* (1990) no. 4, pp. 841 ff.; L. S. Eastwood, 'Secession: State Practice and International Law after the Dissolution of the Soviet Union and Yugoslavia', 3 *Duke Journal of Comparative and International Law* (1992–93) p. 346;

in question enjoy the right of self-determination and secession be allowed. This approach is based on the fact that the right of self-determination is a right derived from the notions of freedom, equality and peace and from the will to be free from outside domination.[359] A severe denial of the group's human rights is usually demanded, which means either subjugation, domination and exploitation or the denial of those human rights which are the guarantee of the preservation of the group's identity.[360] Others only grant a right of self-determination to a people which is not only deprived of its human rights, but also living under a non-representative or undemocratic government.[361] They base themselves on paragraph 7 of General Assembly Resolution 2625 (XXV) on Friendly Relations among States. Some authors elaborate additional requirements such as the condition that the people is able to attain viable and responsible statehood.[362] It was also suggested that, in case of secession, the people does not have any alternative in order to preserve its values and that the interests of secession override the interests of the dominant State.[363]

Another group of publicists, though not very numerous, consider that a people can only exercise a right of self-determination if it lives in a geographically separate territory, in other words, a territory separated from the metropolitan State by the sea.[364] This condition is also called the 'salt water theory' and is derived from principle IV of

---

Nanda, 'Self-Determination', p. 278; de Obieta Chalbaud, El Derecho Humano, pp. 156 ff.; E. Suzuki, 'Self-Determination and World Public Order: Community Response to Territorial Separation', 16 Virginia Journal of International Law (1976) no. 4, pp. 798 ff.; C. Tomuschat, 'Self-Determination in a Post-Colonial World', in C. Tomuschat, ed., Modern Law of Self-Determination (1993) pp. 9–10; and R. C. White, 'Self-Determination: Time for a Re-assessment?', 28 NILR (1981) pp. 162–164.

[359] Anaya, 'The Capacity', p. 841.

[360] Nanda, 'Self-Determination', p. 278 and de Obieta Chalbaud, El Derecho Humano, p. 157. Cassese, Self-Determination, p. 359 allows secession of ethnic groups and minorities in 'exeptional cases where factual conditions render self-determination impracticable'. Those are cases of armed conflict where it would be 'too late to plead for a peaceful solution based on internal self-determination' or when a multinational State is 'irremediably oppressive and despotic, persistently violate[s] the basic rights of minorities and no peaceful and constructive solution can be envisaged'.

[361] Buchheit, Secession, pp. 92–93 and Connelly, 'The Right of Self-Determination', p. 548.

[362] Suzuki, 'Self-Determination', p. 862 and White, 'Self-Determination', pp. 163–164.

[363] Nanda, 'Self-Determination', p. 277 and Suzuki, 'Self-Determination', pp. 861–862.

[364] J. F. Guilhaudis, 'Le Droit positif à l'Autodétermination' and G. Héraud, 'Modèle pour une Application générale du Droit d'Autodétermination', both in Institut Européen des Hautes Etudes Internationales, Le Droit à l'Autodétermination: Actes du Colloque international de Saint-Vincent (1980) pp. 29 and 53, respectively.

General Assembly Resolution 1541 (XV) of 15 December 1960, which determines whether or not an obligation to transmit information under Article 73 (e) of the Charter exists.

Though not necessarily excluding the conditions just mentioned, some lawyers require that certain procedural rules are respected.[365] These may include norms on the holding of a referendum, on the use of peaceful means, on the duration of a conflict and on finding solutions for consequential problems such as power stations, water resources and access to the sea.[366] These procedural requirements are designed to minimize the possible negative effects which a secession may cause to a metropolitan State and to ascertain the genuineness of the claims.

In general, the theories of learned publicists can be classified along the above-mentioned lines of thought, though several variations and combinations can be found. It is however difficult to deduce a solid consensus among these writers.

Self-determination *versus* territorial integrity
Holders of the right

The ambiguity of the applicability of the principle or right of self-determination is rooted in the political interests which are at stake at a given moment in time. It was launched as a principle applicable to all peoples, but because of certain political objectives it was in the end only effectively applied to certain peoples. The positions were nevertheless taken in a universal manner. States therefore feared that the principle would be invoked by peoples for whom they had not intended it. This especially concerned peoples within an existing State, for a secession would lead to 'a diminution of the State's wealth, resources and power, thereby lowering its economic stamina, defensive capability and potential international influence'.[367]

As we have seen in the preceding paragraphs, the principle of self-determination developed into a right of all peoples to self-determination. There is little doubt that the phrase 'all peoples have the right of self-determination' is an accepted customary rule of international law. After having been proclaimed as a right relating to peoples of

---

[365] Héraud, 'Les Communautés', pp. 111–116 and Suzuki, 'Self-Determination', pp. 794–797.
[366] Ibid.
[367] Buchheit, *Secession*, p. 27.

Trust and Non-Self-Governing Territories,[368] the right was formulated as a universal right for all peoples in the subsequent General Assembly Resolutions.[369] Such resolutions are not legally binding, but they have gained substantial support over the years. The right of self-determination of all peoples became binding between all States Parties to the ICCPR and the ICESCR. These Covenants are now ratified by a large majority of the world's States. Despite initial political motives, the right of self-determination of all peoples is regarded at present as a juridical rule. It is not just a pragmatic principle, but a right which has to be respected. An *opinio juris sive necessitatis* has been formed and proved not only in the colonial context but also more recently in a non-colonial European context.[370] Only very few learned publicists maintain that the right of self-determination is not a rule of international law.[371]

Even if the right of self-determination is accepted in international law, the precise content and scope of the right needs to be considered. Bearing in mind the *travaux préparatoires*, debates and judicial decisions discussed above, the following can be concluded:

First, the right of self-determination is conceded to all peoples, whether or not under 'colonial, foreign or alien domination'[372] or under 'alien subjugation, domination and exploitation'.[373]

Secondly, all peoples should be treated equally. They have an equal right to self-determination.[374] All peoples, in similar circumstances, should enjoy the same possibilities which the right of self-determination offers. The right of self-determination aims at eliminating the imposition of a 'foreign will' upon a people. It is therefore contrary to the nature of this right to allow a discriminatory application of the right of self-determination to peoples fulfilling the same conditions.

---

[368] GA Res. 637 (VII).

[369] GA Res. 1514 (XV), GA Res. 545 (VI), GA Res. 2625 (XXV) and GA Res. 35/35B with subsequent resolutions: see pp. 17–27 above.

[370] See, e.g., Art. 4 of the Treaty on the Establishment of German Unity of 31 Aug. 1990 under which the unity of Germany is achieved 'in free self-determination' of the German people: 30 ILM (1991) pp. 457 ff. and the Declaration on the State Sovereignty of the Russian Soviet Federated Socialist Republic of 12 Jun. 1990, paras. 7–8, in W. E. Butler, *Basic Documents on the Soviet Legal System*, 2nd edn (1991) pp. 139–141.

[371] J. H. W. Verzijl, *International Law in Historical Perspective*, vol. I (1968) p. 325; R. Emerson, *From Empire to Nation*, n. 45, p. 303; Guilhaudis, 'Le Droit positif', p. 39 and Pierré-Caps, *Nation et Peuples*, p. 506.

[372] GA Res. 35/35B and subsequent Resolutions.

[373] GA Res. 1514 (XV) and GA Res. 2625 (XXV) See pp. 17–27 above.

[374] Arts. 1 (2) and 55 of the Charter of the United Nations and GA Res. 2625 (XXV) See pp. 12–16 and 19–26 above.

Thirdly, the result of the exercise of the right of self-determination is dependent upon the value attributed to a clashing principle: the inviolability of a State's territorial integrity.

The right of self-determination was for the first time effectively invoked by the peoples living in Trust and Non-Self-Governing Territories. Why were they granted this right? The inhabitants of these territories were considered to be 'peoples' living under 'alien subjugation, domination and exploitation'. They had been deprived of the freedom to decide the fate of the territory they inhabited. From the practice of the General Assembly and the Special Committee of Twenty-Four, it can be concluded that the population in question must constitute the indigenous population or first settlers.[375] One of the characteristic features of the inhabitants of Non-Self-Governing Territories is the fact that they are ethnically and/or culturally distinct from the administering State.[376] Thus, the colonial practice of the United Nations shows, in principle, the same adherence to the characteristics of a people and its relationship with a territory as was deduced from the discussions on the general definition of a 'people'.[377]

What then are the characteristics which distinguish a people from another people? Peoples are groups of persons who, whatever their appellation, have been separated from each other on ethnical, racial, linguistic, cultural, religious, traditional or historical grounds. Whether they are called communities, minorities or peoples, these elements have always been enunciated.[378] According to the Arbitration Commission on Yugoslavia, a people and a minority are ethnic, religious or linguistic communities.[379] The subjective element was set forth by the Arbitration Commission on Yugoslavia which left it

---

[375] See pp. 50–55 above. In cases where the indigenous population had been removed from the territory, as in Gibraltar, the right of self-determination was not automatically applied. If the population consisted of indigenous and non-indigenous peoples, either the whole population, only the non-European population or all inhabitants except immigrants were allowed to vote. See Pomerance, *Self-Determination*, pp. 18–23. It is not ruled out that other settlers may in the course of time establish a relation with the territory which is strong enough to make them an indigenous population. This argument could be sustained for the populations of the American and Australian continents as well as of South Africa who are of mixed origins.

[376] Principle IV of GA Res. 1541 (XV).

[377] See, pp. 38–39 above.

[378] Cf. 'community' in *Greco-Bulgarian 'Communities'* case, PCIJ Reports (1930) Series B, no. 17, p. 21, p. 59 above; Opinion No. 2 of the Arbitration Commission on Yugoslavia, pp. 69–70 above. See also pp. 40–46 above.

[379] Opinion No. 2 of 11 Jan. 1992, see pp. 70–72 above.

to every individual to decide to which community he/she belongs.[380] The subjective factor can never be neglected, for the objective characteristics of a group will only be maintained if the members of the group endeavour to maintain them. If a group does not try to preserve its objective characteristics, it does not intend to distinguish itself as a separate group. The existence of objective factors presupposes an underlying subjective will. In addition, a people needs to have roots in a given territory. It has to have an attachment to the territory on which it is established for a certain time.[381] The concept of peoplehood is however also a relative one, as one can only be a people in comparison with another people. This makes the question of delimitation very complicated and no one has so far managed to trace the exact distinctive lines between population groups, for how strong would the objective, subjective and territorial attachment elements have to be? Refuge is therefore sought in the delimitation of territories.

The fundamental approach to the question remains that all peoples, as defined by objective and subjective factors, have a full right of self-determination, that is a free choice of internal and external self-determination. This is the basic rule which does not take into consideration existing international and administrative frontiers. The borders of these self-determination units are determined by the dimensions of the people and its corresponding territory, although these are difficult to assess. No subsequent conditions are imposed on a people in order to be the holder of the right of self-determination. This basic rule is however counterbalanced by the rule that the territorial integrity of an existing State is inviolable. In each case the right of self-determination has to be weighed against respect for the territorial integrity of a State. It is in this weighing process that international recognition becomes relevant. Recognition does therefore not imply that a right of self-determination exists, but that the right of self-determination offsets the inviolability of the territorial integrity in the given case. The partial or total disruption of the national unity and territorial integrity of a country has been forbidden under paragraph 6 of General Assembly Resolution 1514 (XV) and paragraph 7 of the principle on self-determination of General Assembly Resolution 2625 (XXV). States Parties to the ICCPR may take measures derogating from their obligations, also relating to the right of self-determination in Article 1, 'in time of public emergency which threatens the life of

---

[380] Ibid.
[381] See pp. 38–39 and 46–48 above. On the time element see pp. 53–55 above.

the nation'.³⁸² If the territorial integrity is threatened through the exercise of the right of self-determination, this clause can be invoked.

The problems with regard to the application of the right of self-determination are thus shifted from the question of who are the holders of the right, to the question of when does the right of self-determination take precedence over the obligation to respect the territorial integrity of a State. It is on the latter question that one should look for a consistent State practice and *opinio juris sive necessitatis*.

First, we have concluded that an independent people, that is the permanent population of an existing State, has the right to self-determination.³⁸³ This population may well comprise one homogeneous people or a collection of different peoples and fractions of peoples. In the latter case, the right of self-determination of the inhabitants of a State is the compilation of the right of self-determination of the different peoples living in the State's territory. The international community accepts the exercise of the right of self-determination of fractions of peoples which find themselves within the borders of an existing State. These peoples who have a relationship with the territory of an existing State may exercise a full right of self-determination over the whole of the territory. The principle of inviolability of territorial integrity is respected and does not clash with the right of self-determination as long as the decisions concern the whole territory. The population of an existing State may therefore decide its form of government and determine its international status. Thus, if by virtue of the right of self-determination a State decides to merge, associate or reunite with another State, the territorial integrity of both States remains untouched. International practice has never protested against such unifications, providing that it is the free choice of the peoples or their parliamentary representatives and that the external frontiers of the union are confirmed. This practice was followed when the 'Länder' of the German Democratic Republic joined the Federal Republic of Germany on 3 October 1990, through accession, as a 'result of a peaceful democratic process in which the entire German nation exercised its right of free self-determination'.³⁸⁴ Existing frontiers with neighbouring States were maintained. Another case of

---

³⁸² Art. 4 (1) of the ICCPR. Under Art. 4 of the ICESCR, States Parties may subject the rights, including the right of self-determination, to limitations by law 'for the purpose of promoting the general welfare in a democratic society'.
³⁸³ See p. 26 above.
³⁸⁴ Permanent representative of Germany: UN Doc. A/45/PV.18 (1990) p. 21. Treaty on the Establishment of German Unity of 31 Aug. 1990, 30 ILM (1991) pp. 457 ff. Interestingly,

unification concerns the merger of the Yemen Arab Republic (North Yemen) and the People's Democratic Republic of Yemen (South Yemen) on 22 May 1990, to form a unified Republic of Yemen.[385] In the agreement regulating the merger, no reference is made to the right of self-determination. The decision was however taken by the North and South Yemen Parliaments which were democratically elected.

Secondly, peoples living under colonial domination were granted full self-determination, irrespective of the territorial integrity principle. The inhabitants of Non-Self-Governing and Trust Territories were granted the right of self-determination because they were a people. As remarked with respect to the inhabitants of existing States, the right of self-determination of colonial territories is the combination of the right of self-determination of the different peoples, fractions of peoples or one homogeneous people living in the territory. It was therefore unnecessary for the General Assembly and the Special Committee of Twenty-Four to ascertain the homogeneity of the population of the territories.[386] They did however, in general, assure themselves of the indigenous ties existing between the people and the territory.[387] As the inhabitants of Trust and Non-Self-Governing Territories had a full right of self-determination, their choice for independence would in principle clash with the respect for the territorial integrity of the administering States to which they were attached. The territory of a colony was therefore given 'a status separate and distinct from the territory of the State administering it'.[388] The integration of a colony was considered a 'legal fiction'.[389] As a consequence, the

the Unification Treaty between the Federal Republic of Germany and the German Democratic Republic mentions the self-determination of the Germans living in each individual 'Land' of East and West Germany as the basis of the free self-determination of the entire German people. A subdivision of the German people seems to be made: Art. 4 (1) of the Treaty on the Establishment of German Unity.

[385] Agreement on the Establishment of the Republic of Yemen of 22 April 1990, 30 ILM (1991) pp. 820 ff.

[386] This argument has sometimes been turned around, suggesting that the United Nations did not want to define a people with the right of self-determination, because as only colonial peoples were granted this right and as such peoples were not homogeneous, no univocal characteristics of 'a people' could be accepted. If these characteristics were adopted, some colonial peoples would not and others for whom they were not intended would have the right of self-determination. See, e.g., Guilhaudis, *Le Droit des Peuples*, p. 66. This approach disregards the fact that self-determination units can consist of several peoples.

[387] See p. 55 above.

[388] Para. 6 of the principle on self-determination of GA Res. 2625 (XXV).

[389] See p. 37 above at n. 156.

independence of a colony could not result in a partial disruption of the territorial integrity of the metropolitan State.

Peoples who find themselves in similar circumstances as colonies[390] will enjoy a complete right of self-determination even if they are not specifically mentioned on the list of Non-Self-Governing or Trust Territories. This has probably been the case of the Bengali people in East Pakistan, which was geographically separate from West Pakistan. The Bengalis were moreover culturally and ethnically distinct from the other part of Pakistan and suffered human rights violations. They could be considered arbitrarily placed in a position of subordination, as they had, for example, no right of equal participation in elections and governmental affairs.[391] This led the Bengalis to proclaim their own independent State of Bangladesh.[392] Because of Bangladesh's special circumstances, international recognition followed promptly. The situation of Bangladesh has however also been treated as a case of secession legitimized by paragraph 7 of the principle on self-determination in General Assembly Resolution 2625 (XXV), namely the absence of a representative government.[393] Recognition could also have been prompted because Bangladesh was able to maintain effective control over its territory with Indian armed reinforcement.[394] It is nevertheless undeniable that the recognition of Bangladesh was influenced by the fact that it fulfilled all conditions which normally applied to Non-Self-Governing Territories.

The balance of self-determination and territorial integrity is not decided completely, for a colony may well be geographically separate from the administering State and yet have historical ties of territorial sovereignty with a neighbouring State or colony. In such a case, might independence disrupt the neighbouring country's territorial integrity? As a basic rule, State practice has preferred to apply the

---

[390] GA Res. 1541 (XV) defines, in principles IV and V, a Non-Self-Governing Territory as geographically separate from the country administering it (the salt-water theory), whose peoples are ethnically and/or culturally distinct from the administering country and arbitrarily placed in a position or status of subordination by the administering power.

[391] See also Crawford, *The Creation of States*, p. 116.

[392] Bangladesh Proclamation of Independence, 11 ILM (1972) p. 119.

[393] The justification for the secession was contested by the International Commission of Jurists which noted that the 1970 election was no longer based on the principle of discrimination against the Bengalis: Secretariat of the International Commission of Jurists, *The Events in East Pakistan*, p. 73. Suzuki maintains that the 1970 elections were held 'under conditions of severe value deprivations to the Bengalis': Suzuki, 'Self-Determination', p. 805.

[394] Suzuki, 'Self-Determination', p. 806.

principle of *uti possidetis juris*. Old colonial frontiers were respected before and after independence. This was considered a juridical necessity, not a political solution.[395] Even if the colony was claimed to have formed an integral part of another country or colony before colonization, reintegration was not always admitted without the exercise of the right of self-determination.[396] In some cases, historical ties of sovereignty were not accepted and the strict application of the *uti possidetis juris* principle was disregarded.[397] As we have seen in the advisory opinion concerning *Western Sahara*, the International Court of Justice did not pronounce on the effects of the existence of historical ties of territorial sovereignty on the application of the right of self-determination, though it was not excluded that, had such ties existed, the General Assembly would have taken them into account when deciding on the future decolonization of Western Sahara.[398] The principle of territorial integrity was effectively exercised in the case of small colonial enclaves.

Small colonial enclaves

Some Non-Self-Governing Territories listed under Chapter XI of the Charter of the United Nations were incorporated into another State

[395] Case concerning *Frontier Dispute (Burkina Faso/Republic of Mali)* of 22 Dec. 1986, ICJ Reports (1986). Administering States were asked not to change the colonial borders prior to independence. Independence was valid for the whole territory and not per island. See for a discussion on the Island of Mayotte, which according to the GA should remain with the Comores by virtue of the *uti possidetis juris* rule: A. Oraison, 'Quelques Réflections critiques sur la Conception française du Droit des Peuples à disposer d'eux-mêmes à la Lumière du Différend franco-comorien sur l'Ile de Mayotte', 17 RBDI (1983) pp. 655–698.
[396] This was the case of East Timor, a Portuguese colony, which Indonesia claimed to be historically a part of pre-colonial Indonesia. The GA recognized the right of self-determination of the people of East Timor and rejected Indonesia's annexation of 1975: GA Res. 3485 (XXX) and subsequent yearly resolutions until 1983. See also K. N. Blay, 'Self-Determination versus Territorial Integrity in Decolonization Revisited', 25 *Indian Journal of International Law* (1985) pp. 395–398.
[397] West Irian and Belize were integral parts of the Netherlands East Indies and the former Spanish colony of Guatemala respectively. Indonesia claimed West Irian as an integral part of its territory, although the Netherlands maintained that it was a distinct territory. After a plebiscite, West Irian was incorporated into Indonesia pursuant to a New York Agreement of 1962 between Indonesia and the Netherlands: 1 ILM (1962) pp. 231 ff. Belize, which was now under British administration, had not joined in Guatemala's independence and was later claimed by Guatemala on the principle of *uti possidetis juris*. In the case of Belize the GA gave preference to the right of self-determination: GA Res. 35/20 and UN Doc. A/C.4/SR.2122 (1974).
[398] ICJ Reports (1975), see pp. 61–62 above.

without prior consultation of the local population.³⁹⁹ This was the case of small colonial enclaves, very small bits of territory, usually harbour cities of economic and/or strategic importance enclaved by another State, which are 'ethnically and economically parasitic upon or derivative of that State and ... cannot be said in any legitimate sense to constitute separate territorial units'.⁴⁰⁰

The first time the issue of small colonial enclaves emerged was in 1960–1961 in India. When in 1954 France had *de facto* transferred the administration of its enclaves to India, India expected the same from Portugal which possessed three enclaves in Indian territory: Goa, Daman and Diu. Portugal refused however to proceed to a retrocession. An insurrection broke out in the enclaves and a *de facto* government was installed by the local population.⁴⁰¹ India subsequently prohibited the passage of Portuguese troops between Daman and the other two enclaves. The dispute was brought before the International Court of Justice by Portugal which claimed the restoration of its ancient right of passage.⁴⁰² India justified its action by pleading 'at least a moral obligation' under Article 1, paragraph 2 of the Charter of the United Nations of every Member State not to lend 'their aid or have any part in or give any assistance to any action calculated to suppress by force the efforts of peoples who either seek to establish or have in fact established their liberty'.⁴⁰³ In India's opinion, the Portuguese troops aimed at suppressing the principle of self-determination applicable to the enclaves. The Court made no reference to the right or principle of self-determination, solving the question on the basis of long-standing transit practice between India and the United Kingdom on the one hand and Portugal on the other. It nevertheless recognized the unaffected sovereignty of Portugal over the enclaves.⁴⁰⁴

---

³⁹⁹ The ICJ, though not necessarily referring to small colonial enclaves, foresaw the dispensation with consulting the inhabitants of a given territory, *inter alia*, 'in view of special circumstances', Case of *Western Sahara*, ICJ Reports (1975) p. 33, para. 59.
⁴⁰⁰ Crawford, *The Creation of States*, p. 384.
⁴⁰¹ India did not recognize the *de facto* governments as the governments of a new State, though Portugal alleged that the insurrections were instigated by India. See H. Wright, 'The Goa Incident', 56 AJIL (1962) p. 618 and from the Indian point of view M. Sarin, *The Case of Goa (1961) and the Controversy regarding Gandhian Non-Violent Resistance (Satyagraha) and International Law Involved in it* (1973).
⁴⁰² See also on rights of passage in general F. E. Kranz, *International Enclaves and Rights of Passage* (1961) and P. Raton, 'Les Enclaves', 4 AFDI (1958) pp. 186–195.
⁴⁰³ Case of the *Right of Passage over Indian Territory*, ICJ Pleadings, Oral Arguments, Documents (1960) II, p. 151.
⁴⁰⁴ ICJ Reports (1960) p. 40. Only Judge Spiropoulos declared that 'the establishment of a new power in the enclaves must be regarded as having *ipso facto* put an end to the

A year later, India annexed the Portuguese enclaves by force, an act considered as a liberation of the enclaves.[405] This annexation was not officially condemned by the Security Council due to a veto of the Soviet Union and has subsequently never been the object of repeated international protest.[406] In fact Portugal had the choice of either using counter-force or accepting the *fait accompli*, bearing in mind that in the long term the integration of the enclaves would probably have been considered a just way of decolonization.[407]

In all other cases, the incorporation of small colonial enclaves was brought about by negotiation. Thus, in the case of Ifni, a Spanish colonial enclave of 1,920 square kilometres located on the Atlantic coast of Morocco, the General Assembly had asked Spain and Morocco, which claimed retrocession of the territory, to settle the territorial question through negotiations.[408] By the 1969 Treaty of Fez the retrocession was agreed by Spain and endorsed by the General Assembly.[409] No plebiscite had been organized.

Gibraltar is sometimes equally regarded as a small colonial enclave.[410] Although the Special Committee of Twenty-Four has generally approached this question by denying the existence of a genuine colonial people entitled to the right of self-determination,[411] it seems possible that even if there did exist a true Gibraltarian colonial people, preference would still be given to integration into Spain, considering the geographical position of Gibraltar and its political status prior to the 1713 Treaty of Utrecht. The Falkland Islands on the other hand cannot be qualified as a small colonial enclave, in the first place because they are not situated on the mainland and, in the second place, because the historical background and pre-colonial territorial

---

right of passage': ibid., p. 53. In his dissenting opinion, Sir Percy Spender stated that 'it was not disputed by India that Portugal still had sovereignty over the enclaves': ibid., p. 99.

[405] India claimed that Goa was a part of its territory and that the Goans had the same language and ethnic traditions as the Indians: UN Doc. S/PV.987 (1961) para. 60.

[406] States like Chile, China, Ecuador, France, Turkey, the UK and the USA qualified the annexation as a breach of Art. 2 (4) of the Charter, while Ceylon, Liberia, the United Arab Republic and the USSR believed that it was Portugal who violated GA Res. 1514: UN Doc. S/PV.987–988 (1961). See also A. M. Scholz, *Die Behandlung der Goa-Frage durch die Vereinten Nationen* (1970).

[407] See Greig, 'Sovereignty and the Falkland Island Crisis', p. 61.

[408] GA Res. 2078 (XX), 2229 (XXI), 2354 (XXII) and 2428 (XXIII).

[409] GA Res. 2354 (XXII). See also Blay, 'Self-Determination versus Territorial Integrity', p. 407.

[410] M. Shaw, *Title to Territory in Africa: International Legal Issues* (1986) p. 136.

[411] See pp. 53–54 above.

status cannot be proved beyond doubt.[412] When Argentina invaded the Islands in 1982, the Security Council, unlike during the Indian annexations, did condemn the use of force.[413]

The United Nations also dispensed with the need for a free choice on the part of the inhabitants of the enclave of Walvis Bay. The Security Council had officially called for the reintegration of this territory within Namibia of which it was believed to form an integral part, although in the end the exact terms of the retrocession were left to a negotiated settlement between Namibia and South Africa.[414] Walvis Bay did not join in the independence of Namibia, but was progressively returned by South Africa under an Agreement of 1992[415] and a Treaty of 28 February 1994.[416]

Hong Kong and Macao are also treated as small colonial enclaves which will revert to China on 1 July 1997 and on 20 December 1999, to conform to Joint Statements between China and the United Kingdom[417] and China and Portugal, respectively.[418] In 1972, the Special Committee of Twenty-Four removed both territories from the list of Non-Self-Governing Territories, after complaints by China that they were 'occupied territories'.[419] The fact that these territories were

---

[412] Greig, 'Sovereignty and the Falkland Island Crisis', pp. 35–40 and 61–63.

[413] SC Res. 502 (1982).

[414] SC Res. 432 (1978). Walvis Bay was never classified as a Non-Self-Governing Territory as it formed an administrative unit of Namibia until 1977. See for the facts L. Berat, *Walvis Bay: Decolonization and International Law* (1990) and comments of J. Dugard, 'Walvis Bay and International Law: Reflections on a Recent Study', 108 *South African Law Journal* (1991) pp. 82–92.

[415] Agreement on the Joint Administration of Walvis Bay and the Off-Shore Islands, exchange of notes of 30 Oct./9 Nov. 1992, establishing a joint Namibian–South African administration pending the final settlement of the Walvis Bay question, 32 ILM (1993) pp. 1152–1158.

[416] Namibian–South African Treaty on Walvis Bay of 28 Febr. 1994 transferring Walvis Bay to Namibia on 1 Mar. 1994, 33 ILM (1994) p. 1528.

[417] Sino-British Joint Declaration on the Question of Hong Kong of 19 Dec. 1984, 23 ILM (1984) pp. 1366 ff. See also J. Allan, 'Hong Kong's Future and the Uncertainty Principle', 21 *Anglo-American Law Review* (1992) pp. 372–385 and P. Wesley-Smith, *Unequal Treaty, 1898–1997: China, Great Britain and Hong Kong's New Territories* (1983).

[418] Sino-Portuguese Joint Declaration on the Question of Macao of 13 Apr. 1987, 68 RDI (1990) pp. 139–155. See also R. Afonso and F. Gonçalves Pereira, 'The Political Status and Government Institutions of Macao', 16 *Hong Kong Law Journal* (1986) pp. 28–57 and L. Foscaneanu, 'La Déclaration conjointe du Gouvernement de la République populaire de Chine et du Gouvernement de la République du Portugal sur la Question de Macao', 91 RGDIP (1987) pp. 1279–1303.

[419] Endorsed by GA Res. 2908 (XXVII) and 2978 (XXVII). Most States supported the Chinese territorial integrity argument, except for Sweden who reserved its position on the issue: 9 UNMC (1972) no. 7 and UN Doc. A/8730 (1972).

easily classified as constituting a part of China's territorial unity was strengthened by the existence of lease or similar conventions.[420] The retrocession of both territories was negotiated without the participation of the local population. This was not raised as a legal objection by the international community.[421]

The result of the practice followed with regard to small colonial enclaves is:

First, once it has been ascertained that a small enclave used to constitute a part of the territory of another State before its colonization, the argument that the inhabitants of the enclave have over the years formed a distinct people no longer holds good.[422]

Secondly, the absence of the requirement of consultation in the case of small colonial enclaves depends on the geographical connection and smallness of the territory.

Thirdly, outside the colonial context, it is not excluded that small enclaves will not have a full right of self-determination either. The only exceptions are micro-entities which have formed a clear distinct territory over the centuries, the political history of which cannot be assimilated to that of other States.[423]

---

[420] Hong Kong Island was ceded in perpetuity by China to the UK under the Treaty of Nanking of 1842, the Kowloon Peninsula and Stonecutters Island were acquired by the UK by the Convention of Peking of 1860, the New Territories were granted to the UK on lease by a Convention of 1898: C. Parry, ed., *The Consolidated Treaty Series*, vols. 93, 123 and 186 respectively. Portugal obtained perpetual jurisdiction over Macao by a Treaty of 1887, under which it could not transfer this right to another power without China's consent: ibid., vol. 170 (1887–1888) p. 81.

[421] Some writers argue that the people of Hong Kong and Macao should have been consulted and that if China does not respect their rights under the Joint Declarations they have the option to secede. This reasoning however does not take into account that the territories fall into the category of small colonial enclaves, which cannot claim an absolute right of self-determination: E. M. Amberg, 'Self-Determination in Hong Kong: A New Challenge to an Old Doctrine', 22 *San Diego Law Review* (1985) pp. 839–858; R. Y. Chuang, 'The Joint Declarations on Hong Kong and Macao and the Draft Basic Law for Hong Kong', 68 RDI (1990) pp. 139–155; P. A. Dagati, 'Hong Kong's Lost Right to Self-Determination: A Denial of Due Process in the United Nations', 13 *New York Law School Journal of International and Comparative Law* (1992) pp. 153–179; and R. W. McGee and D. King-Kong Lam, 'Hong Kong's Option to Secede', 33 Harv. Int'l LJ (1992) pp. 427–440.

[422] This argument is repeatedly used by Gibraltar, the Falkland Islands and in a sense Hong Kong: McGee and King-Kong Lam, 'Hong Kong's Option', p. 436.

[423] Such as Liechtenstein, San Marino, Monaco and Andorra, see pp. 204–205, 259, 310–311 and 372–373 below.

Secession

Have guiding rules been accepted in State practice relating to the full exercise of the right to self-determination of peoples living within an existing State and wishing to secede? Considering the fact that the disruption of the territorial integrity of an existing State can be either partial or total, and that the same international rules apply to either of those effects, it serves no legal purpose to distinguish between secession, dissolution, separation or disintegration. The same balancing process between the right of self-determination and the respect for territorial integrity applies, whether in case of a secession or in case of a dissolution. This is without prejudice to any different legal consequences which might arise from State succession. We have seen in the preceding paragraphs that positions of States have varied. Some accepted the right of secession of minorities, that is a distinct people or fraction of a people in a State, while others have denied it.[424] The only textual reference to a justification of the partial or total disruption of the territorial integrity of an existing State can be found in paragraph 7 of the principle on self-determination of General Assembly Resolution 2625 (XXV). The full right of self-determination takes precedence if the government does not represent 'the whole people belonging to the territory without distinction as to race, creed or colour'.

It should first of all be observed that the rules governing secession from an existing State do not fall under the exclusive domestic jurisdiction of that State. It is not up to one State to decide whether to reject the secession of a part of its territory, for such a decision involves the balancing of two principles of international law which should therefore be decided on the basis of international law as well. International law determines whether a people has the right to self-determination and also decides whether the territorial integrity of a State deserves protection. If each State is able to decide how much value it should attach to either principle, there would result a disparity in the decision making. The decision whether this or that rule of international law should be applied must be based on international law itself. If this were left to the discretion of individual States, it would result in the denial of the international character of the competing rules in question.[425] When the Yugoslavian delegation

---

[424] See, e.g., p. 31 above at nn. 133 and 134.
[425] The dissolution of Yugoslavia was discussed in the EC and UN. The situations in Nagorno Karabakh and Abkhazia are conciliated by the OSCE and the UN. The attempted secession of Biafra from Nigeria (1968 to 1970) did not inspire a UN involve-

requested the Security Council of the United Nations to impose an arms embargo against it,[426] the members of the Security Council generally considered the Yugoslavian dispute an internal affair.[427] The conflict had nevertheless a strong international dimension in that it could have a 'dangerous impact on Yugoslavia's neighbours'[428] and thus represent a threat to the peace. The fact that the Security Council, at this stage, qualified the secession dispute as internal, except for its implications on neighbouring States, does not preclude that the 'internal' conflict should be governed by international law. It is the lack of clarity of international law in matters of secession which, unjustly, leads to the qualification of the dispute as internal.

The right of secession has been incorporated in some national constitutions, which, in all cases, did not require justificative reasons. These clauses were however frequently deleted from the constitution.[429] Under Soviet law, secession was possible without justification, providing that certain procedural rules were respected.[430]

According to State practice two situations of secession should be distinguished: the case in which the State from which secession is sought agrees and the case in which the State from which secession is sought does not agree with the secession. If the secession has been realized after an amicable agreement between the secessional and remaining parties, the international community has always endorsed

---

ment. Secretary General U Thant declared it was 'purely an internal problem': UN Press Release No. SG/SM/1062 (1969).

[426] UN Doc. S/23069 (1991).
[427] Indian delegate: UN Doc. S/PV.3009 (1991) p. 46.
[428] United States delegate: ibid., p. 58.
[429] Chapter 10 of the Constitution of the Union of Burma (1947) included a right of secession for the States of the Union, provided that certain procedural requirements were met. Text in M. Maung, *Burma's Constitution* (1961) pp. 258–301. This right was deleted in the 1974 Constitution of the Socialist Republic of the Union of Burma. The 1931 Chinese Constitution also adopted a right of secession for all national minorities, but the 1975 Constitution of the People's Republic of China refers to the 'inalienable parts' of its territory. See for the 1931 text C. Brandt et al., *A Documentary History of Chinese Communism* (1952) pp. 220 ff. See for the 1975 text A. P. Blaustein and G. Flanz, eds., *Constitutions of the Countries of the World* (1975) China. For the legality of the secession of the Yugoslavian republics according to municipal law see B. Bagwell, 'Yugoslavian Constitutional Questions: Self-Determination and Secession of Member Republics', 21 *Georgia Journal of International and Comparative Law* (1991) pp. 489–523.
[430] The 1977 Constitution of the USSR laid down 'the right of free secession ... for each union republic' (Art. 72). A law adopted on 3 Apr. 1990 laid down the 'Procedure for deciding Questions connected with the Secession of a Union Republic from the USSR'. See for both documents Butler, *Basic Documents*, pp. 3–44 and 57–63.

this situation.⁴³¹ The separation of the Slovak and Czech Republics in 1993 has been conducted on friendly terms and on the basis of a mutual agreement. This disintegration was however decided by the respective parliaments, without there being a guarantee that it was backed by public opinion. International practice shows that the parliamentary exercise of the right of self-determination is accepted if the elections fulfil the requirements of Article 25 of the ICCPR.⁴³² Thus Yemen was united in 1990 by parliamentary decision, which could not be altered by claims of South Yemen to leave the Republic in 1994.⁴³³ It should be noted that in these cases a Federal State structure was involved, not strongly centralized and unitary States. This has probably facilitated the internal acquiescence in the demanded secession or separation.

If the authorities of the central State oppose the secession of a part of the territory or the total disruption of its territorial integrity, the reactions of other States are of great influence on the solution of the problem. The fact is that other States may recognize the newly established State created in the exercise of the right of self-determination of the seceding people. Through the act of recognition, a preference is expressed for the full right of self-determination of the secessionists. It is the territorial integrity of the newly recognized State which has to be respected. The State from which the territory was withdrawn can no longer claim that the seceded territory constitutes an integral part of its territory. As from recognition, the 'old' State is under the obligation to respect the territorial integrity of the 'new' State. This conclusion can be drawn as soon as it can be demonstrated

---

[431] Such a secession on the basis of mutual accord was accomplished by Senegal, which left the Mali Federation in 1960, by Singapore, which seceded from the Malaysian Federation in 1965 and by Syria, which separated from the United Arab Republic in 1961. The dissolution of the union between Norway and Sweden in 1905 (established in 1815) can also be cited, but is not strict evidence of State practice relating to self-determination and territorial integrity, as at that time the principle of self-determination was not yet accepted in international law. See Buchheit, *Secession*, pp. 89–99.

[432] Art. 25 of the ICCPR does not impose an electoral system, apart from the requirement that non-discrimination norms should be respected. See D. McGoldrick, *The Human Rights Committee: Its Role in the Development of the ICCPR* (1991) pp. 250 and 263, n. 42 and H. J. Steiner, 'Political Participation as a Human Right', 1 HRY (1988) pp. 105–108.

[433] See R. Goy, 'La Réunification du Yémen', 36 AFDI (1990) pp. 249–265. The Security Council called upon the belligerent parties to come to a cease-fire, SC Res. 931 (1994). However, the Arbitration Commission on Yugoslavia preferred to have the Bosnian parliamentary resolution on independence confirmed by referendum, Opinion No. 4 of 11 Jan. 1992.

that the international recognition of the 'new' State is sufficient under international law to remedy the possible non-fulfilment of a criterion for statehood. If world-wide recognition does not exist, the seceding territory may still constitute a State in the light of international law, for recognition is generally not considered a *conditio sine qua non*.[434] However, if the central State regains effective control over the non-recognized seceding State, the world community will most likely not regard this action as an act of international aggression or the infringement of a State's territorial integrity.

State practice relating to opposed secession shows the following pattern:

The secession must be supported by a large, genuine popular will. It cannot be established on the sole wish of an elite group or foreign State. For this reason recognition was withheld from Katanga, the secession of a small claimant group said to be encouraged by Belgium, from Congo.[435] The General Assembly of the United Nations called upon the Member States not to recognize Southern Rhodesia's declared independence of 1965, because its racist minority rule 'would continue the denial of the African majority of their fundamental rights to freedom and independence'.[436] Even in the period of the League of Nations, the Japanese-created State of Manchuria was not recognized, because it was found not to be in accordance with the free will of the inhabitants of Manchuria.[437]

The denial of a people's fundamental human rights does not as such legitimize a secession automatically. As we have seen, this justificative reason was advanced by some learned publicists who derived this principle from the general purpose and nature of the right of self-determination.[438] However morally acceptable this finding may be, it has so far not been proved to be a customary rule of international law by a consistent State practice.

The denial of a group's human rights has been invoked in a number of cases. It should be noted that only violations of human rights prior to demands of secession can be taken into account, not inhuman treatments due to a conflict on secession. Thus, the systematic riots and massacres of Ibos living in Nigeria can be mentioned. The Ibo people was also denied an equal participation in the election process.

---

[434] See pp. 110–115 below.
[435] See further Suzuki, 'Self-Determination', pp. 816, 822–825.
[436] GA Res. 2022 (XX), UN Doc. A/6014 (1965) p. 54.
[437] League of Nations Doc. C.66.M.320 (1932) pp. 97 ff.
[438] See pp. 75–76 above.

RIGHT OF SELF-DETERMINATION 93

All of this led the Ibos to flee to their eastern homeland in Nigeria.[439] In May 1967, they seceded from the Federation of Nigeria and created the Republic of Biafra.[440] Biafra did not however receive world-wide recognition and in January 1970 it was forcefully regained by the Nigerian army.[441] The secession was not discussed by the United Nations, nor by the Organization of African Unity, which termed the situation an internal affair under Nigerian responsibility.[442] In this secession many political and economic interests were at stake. The Ibos were in general a highly skilled and educated group, forming 'the human currency of Nigeria's economic development'.[443] Furthermore, Biafra's oil resources amounted to two-thirds of Nigeria's total oil exports.[444]

Another claim for secession is advanced by the Armenian community of Nagorno Karabakh, a former autonomous region of the Soviet Republic of Azerbaijan.[445] Initially, the Armenian community of Nagorno Karabakh voted on 20 February 1988 for an attachment of the region to the Republic of Armenia. After the August 1991 coup in Moscow, this turned into the proclamation of an independent Republic of Nagorno Karabakh (comprising Nagorno Karabakh and the neighbouring Shaumyan district), which was confirmed by referendum and formalized on 6 January 1992 by a newly elected parliament.[446] The underlying reason for this secession was the long-standing resentment in the Armenian community of Nagorno Karabakh against serious limitations of its cultural and religious freedom by central Soviet and Azerbaijani authorities.[447] The statehood of Nagorno Karabakh has so far only been recognized by Armenia. Azerbaijan's National Assembly cancelled on 26 November 1991 the autonomy of the Nagorno Karabakh region, placing it under its direct control.[448] Azerbaijan regards the issue primarily as one of

---

[439] Suzuki, 'Self-Determination', pp. 799–804.
[440] Proclamation of the Republic of Biafra, 6 ILM (1967) pp. 673 ff.
[441] Suzuki, 'Self-Determination', p. 804.
[442] Statement by the Secretary-General of the UN; UN Press Release No. SG/SM/1062 (1969) and OAU Res. AHG/Res.51 (IV) reprinted in 6 ILM (1967) p. 1243.
[443] Cited by Suzuki, 'Self-Determination', p. 799.
[444] Ibid., p. 825.
[445] Chapters 10 and 11 on autonomous regions of the 1977 USSR Constitution, in Butler, *Basic Documents*, pp. 18–19.
[446] CSCE Doc. (Febr. 1992), Interim Report of the CSCE Rapporteur Mission on the situation in Nagorno Karabakh, 7–CSO/Journal no. 2/Annex 1, pp. 3–4.
[447] Ibid., p. 2.
[448] Ibid., p. 4.

territorial integrity and condemns any Armenian intentions of annexation of the region as unlawful interference in internal Azerbaijani affairs.[449] Armenia says it has no authority to determine the status of Nagorno Karabakh, while the Armenians in this autonomous region claim that they are still entitled to determine the status of their region under Soviet laws and Constitution.[450] They believe they are fighting for their independence based on the right of self-determination.[451] The Committee of Senior Officials of the CSCE urged the interested parties, *inter alia*, to impose a cease-fire on all forces and to continue the 'dialogue among all interested parties, including the views of the inhabitants of Nagorno Karabakh'.[452]

These examples show that secession will not automatically be recognized in the absence of an accord even if a group's human rights are seriously violated. There are many other cases in the world where a group endeavours to protect and maintain its national identity by demanding a larger autonomy, secession or independence.[453] These claims have not however always led to the official proclamation of independent States and therefore have not been the object of international recognition. In all cases where an independent State was declared due to human rights violations international recognition was withheld.[454]

It is doubtful whether an accepted customary rule of international law exists which permits the total or partial disruption of a State's territory in case of a non-representative government based on the

---

[449] Ibid.
[450] Ibid., p. 6.
[451] Ibid., p. 11.
[452] Ibid., p. 15. In para. 4 of Budapest Summit Decision II of Dec. 1994, the OSCE expressed its will to send an international peacekeeping force to Nagorno Karabakh.
[453] Of the contemporary conflicts on this issue, we can cite the situations in Southern Sudan, the Indian States of Punjab, Kashmir and Assam, the Tamils in Sri Lanka, Tibet and the Kurds. See for more information on these and other self-determination conflicts: D. Hermant and D. Bigo, eds., *Approches polémologiques: Conflits et Violence politique dans le Monde au tournant des Années quatre-vingt-dix* (1991).
[454] The Somali National Movement (Isaq people) proclaimed the independence of the Somaliland Republic on 18 May 1991 due to human rights violations and dissatisfaction with the unequal distribution of certain financial burdens (as a result of the facilities granted to Ogadeni refugees). See A. J. Caroll and B. Rajagopal, 'The Case for the Independent Statehood of Somaliland', 8 *American University Journal of International Law and Policy* (1992–93) pp. 653–681; J. Klabbers and R. Lefeber, 'Africa: Lost between Self-Determination and *Uti Possidetis*', in C. Brölmann et al., eds., *Peoples and Minorities in International Law* (1993), pp. 66–68; and J. Dugard, 'Secession: Is the Case of Yugoslavia a Precedent for Africa?', 5 *African Journal of International and Comparative Law* (1993) pp. 163–175.

distinction of race, creed or colour. This principle was set forth in paragraph 7 of the principle of self-determination of General Assembly Resolution 2625 (XXV). Although fighting against such a government, the Ibo people of Biafra did not see its secession recognized. Bangladesh did succeed in being recognized, after basing its secession from Pakistan on the principle of a non-representative government, but the question remains whether it was recognized because of this justification or because Bangladesh managed to keep control over its territory.[455] Nevertheless, Bangladesh's geographical separateness and ethnic distinction from West Pakistan have undoubtedly contributed to its international recognition. Other situations which could be brought into this category have not always led to demands for secession, but rather to attempts at overthrowing the non-representative government.[456]

Secession has frequently been caused by the dissatisfaction of a people with the political ideology of the government it is living under. This government may or may not at the same time deny the group's fundamental human rights and be non-representative. In general, opposition to the communist ideology and its economic implications largely prompted the secession of the Soviet and Yugoslavian Republics in 1990 and 1991. It cannot however be sustained that the former Soviet and Yugoslavian Republics have been recognized because they opposed an unwanted political ideology. The reasons for recognition have been of a quite different nature, based on practical grounds and subject to certain conditions. Other cases of opposition to a certain form of government either have not yet led to an effective secession or are being fought on the basis of internal self-determination only.[457] Resistance against any political ideology, or communism in particular, has not been advanced as a justification

---

[455] See however n. 393, p. 83 above, and R. Sisson and L. E. Rose, *War and Secession: Pakistan, India and the Creation of Bangladesh* (1990).

[456] Without judging the correctness of the invoked justification, we can cite the ethnic conflict between Gios, Manos and Krahns in Liberia (1990). See, e.g., P. Chapleau, 'Entre le Renouveau et le Chaos: Une Analyse des Situations conflictuelles en Afrique du Sud en 1990' and A. Guillaume-Gentil, 'Le Liberia: Un Pays déchiré par une Année de Guerre civile', both in Hermant and Bigo, eds., *Approches polémologiques*, pp. 109–121 and 132–144 respectively.

[457] The rebel movements in Somalia combated the dictatorial regime of General Siad Barre and the civil war of 1982–1985 in Mozambique was directed against communist rule. See G. Prunier, 'Les Conflits de la Corne de l'Afrique 1989–1990' and M. Cahen, 'Mozambique 1990: Dernière Année de Guerre civile?', ibid., pp. 99–108 and 122–131 respectively.

96 THE GENERAL INTERNATIONAL LEGAL CONTEXT

for secession in the debates on the right of self-determination. The only exception made is the case of a non-representative government based on distinction of race, creed or colour, discussed above. A communist government is not founded on such a distinction.

It should be concluded that State practice has not established an *opinio juris sive necessitatis* under which a material justification for secession has been accepted in international law. There is therefore no material customary rule of international law which can decide the balance process between the right of self-determination and the principle of respect for the territorial integrity of a State. This does not decide the question whether procedural rules are fixed if a secession is demanded.

If a secession leads to a total disruption of a State's territorial integrity and thus to a dissolution of the pre-existing State, international recognition of the newly established States will be given more easily than if a secession implies only a partial disruption of a State's territorial integrity. This seems a paradoxical practice, for a partial disruption is a less drastic change than a total disruption. Nevertheless, if a State is completely dismembered due to secessions and its central authorities do not exercise any effective control any more over the whole of the territory, the State has ceased to exist as an international entity. The international community is left no choice but to accept and, if it so wishes, to recognize the newly seceded entities. This course of action is followed not because States believe in its juridical necessity or because total disruptions are deemed more justified than partial disruptions, but because the factual situation leaves no other possibility. The dissolution of a State due to secessions causes the *de facto* and *de jure* disappearance of a pre-existing State. The international community has to determine whether to accept the newly formed entities, bearing in mind that the pre-existing State cannot be re-established without the accord of the seceding parts. The declaration of independence of all fifteen Republics of the Union of Soviet Socialist Republics in 1990–1991 led to the dissolution of the Soviet Union. Thereupon, eleven Republics established the Commonwealth of Independent States.[458] The secession of the Yugoslavian Republics of Slovenia, Croatia, Macedonia and Bosnia-Herzegovina in 1991 was regarded as a dissolution of the Yugoslavian Federation by

---

[458] Agreement establishing the Commonwealth of Independent States of 8 Dec. 1991, between Armenia, Azerbaijan, Belarus, Kazakhstan, Kyrgyzstan, Moldova, Russian Federation, Tajikistan, Turkmenistan, Uzbekistan and Ukraine: 31 ILM (1992) pp. 138 ff.

the Arbitration Commission on Yugoslavia and by the Security Council and the General Assembly of the United Nations.[459]

The Council of the European Communities set up a declaration on the 'Guidelines on the Recognition of New States in Eastern Europe and in the Soviet Union'.[460] The Member States of the European Communities 'affirmed their readiness to recognise, subject to the normal standard of international practice and the political realities in each case, those new States which ... have constituted themselves on a democratic basis, have accepted the appropriate international obligations and have committed themselves in good faith to a peaceful process and to negotiations'.[461] In particular, these new States were asked to respect the provisions of the Charter of the United Nations, the Final Act of Helsinki and the Charter of Paris; to guarantee the rights of ethnic and national groups and minorities; to respect the inviolability of all frontiers; to accept relevant commitments with regard to disarmament, nuclear non-proliferation, security and regional stability; and to settle by agreement questions concerning State succession and regional disputes. In addition, entities which are the result of aggression would not be recognized. The new entities were granted recognition not only because they were States under international law ('the normal standard of international practice'), but also because they fulfilled certain fixed conditions.

In the case of a total disruption of a State's territorial integrity, it can be accepted in international law that the international and internal frontiers are maintained, unless they are modified by mutual accord (*uti possidetis juris*).[462] All other conditions concerning respect for minority rights and the settlement of disputes by peaceful means flow from the general obligations of States under customary international law. Reaffirming these obligations as a pre-condition for recognition may guarantee the effective observance of these State duties.

It is doubtful whether a rule of international law which accepts the secession of federal republics but prohibits the secession of

---

[459] Opinion No. 1 of 29 Nov. 1991 of the Arbitration Commission on Yugoslavia: see pp. 67–68 above; SC Res. 777 (1992) declaring that the SFRY 'has ceased to exist', endorsed by GA Res. 47/1. See also Weller, 'The International Response', pp. 586–596.
[460] Declaration of the European Council of Foreign Ministers of 16/17 Dec. 1991: 31 ILM (1992) pp. 1486–1487.
[461] Ibid.
[462] See also Opinion No. 3 of 11 Jan. 1992 of the Arbitration Commission on Yugoslavia, p. 68 above.

autonomous regions can be proved.[463] Under the former Soviet law on secession, autonomous republics and regions could decide independently whether or not to join the secession of the Union Republic in which they were situated.[464] In the end, this right could not be exercised by the autonomous republics of Abkhazia and Checheno-Ingush nor by the autonomous region of South Ossetia.[465] When these territories declared their independence,[466] armed conflicts broke out with the 'host' Republic, which in general did not lead to international recognition of the newly proclaimed States.[467] As these secessions are always aimed at independence, the better view is probably that federal States can establish their statehood more easily than less autonomous regions. In general, the State structure of a federal republic has been founded before the secession. Such republics will therefore have less difficulty in proving their effective government and independence according to the criteria for statehood. This can be a reason why federal States are more easily recognized as States than autonomous regions. Thus the question is not whether federal republics have the right of self-determination and autonomous regions do not have this right, or whether the secession of federal republics is allowed whereas that of autonomous regions is not. The

---

[463] O. Kimminich, 'A "Federal" Right of Self-Determination?', in Tomuschat, *Modern Law*, pp. 83–100 concludes that there is no federal right of self-determination. Weller concludes that the right of self-determination 'was applied only to those inhabiting a region whose territorial limits had previously been defined by an autonomous government and administration (e.g., federal states)': Weller, 'The International Response', p. 606.

[464] Art. 3 of the 1990 USSR Law on the procedure connected with secession. See Butler, *Basic Documents*, p. 57.

[465] By virtue of Art. 85 of the Soviet Constitution, Checheno-Ingush and Abkhazia were autonomous republics of Russia and Georgia respectively. Art. 87 gave South Ossetia the status of an autonomous region in Georgia: ibid., p. 19.

[466] Chechnya declared officially its independence on 27 Oct. 1991, South Ossetia on 1 Jan. 1992 and Abkhazia on 7 Jul. 1992: for more factual information see B. Szajkowski, *Encyclopaedia of Conflicts, Disputes and Flashpoints in Eastern Europe* (1993) pp. 1–3, 61–66 and 254.

[467] Chechnya received diplomatic recognition from Lithuania, Estonia, Azerbaijan, Turkey and Iran: ibid., p. 63. The SC of the UN decided to establish a United Nations Observer Mission in Georgia (UNOMIG) to verify the cease-fire agreement of 27 Jul. 1993 between Georgia and Abkhazia, SC Res. 858 (1993), also UN Doc. S/25188 (1993). On 4 Apr. 1994, under the auspices of the UN and Russia, the parties signed an agreement granting, *inter alia*, to Abkhazia the right to have 'its own constitution and laws, as well as appropriate State symbols – national anthem, emblem and flag', while respecting the relevant SC Resolutions calling for the respect of Georgia's territorial integrity, RGDIP (1994) p. 735.

question becomes one of proof of statehood and its political desirability.[468]

If secession is demanded by an entity which was unlawfully annexed by another State and whose annexation was not internationally recognized, this entity will be more easily recognized. Hence, if a part of a State used to be an independent State itself, which was usurped by the former State, the latter State may reclaim its sovereignty. This seems to have been the case of Lithuania, Estonia and Latvia which declared their independence from the not-yet dissolved Soviet Union in 1990, justifying their action as a restoration of the violated sovereign rights of the people and the State.[469] Lithuania, Estonia and Latvia were independent States before the Soviet Union annexed the territories on 15 June 1940. This action did not receive general international recognition. It could therefore be argued that the revival of the annexed States of Lithuania, Estonia and Latvia through secession is justified.[470] Although this rule may be readily accepted in wartime until a peace treaty has been concluded, State practice in peacetime is still insufficient to accept the norm as customary international law. This can be especially maintained as the initially non-recognized annexation of Lithuania, Estonia and Latvia could well have been legitimized after fifty years during which third States have no longer disputed the issue. In addition, the recognition of the seceded Baltic States by the international community came in most cases only after the Soviet Union had consented to the secession itself.[471] This could imply that the non-recognition of the 1940 annexations was not necessarily the main legal reason for accepting the secession of the Baltic States in 1990.

Contrary to what some distinguished writers have maintained,[472] international State practice does accept a right of secession. Secession

---

[468] See pp. 118–127 below.
[469] Lithuania declared its independence on 11 Mar. 1990, Estonia on 30 Mar. 1990 and Latvia on 4 May 1990.
[470] V. Rudrakumaran, 'The Legitimacy of Lithuania's Claim for Secession', 10 *Boston University International Law Journal* (1992) pp. 33–60.
[471] Iceland was the first to recognize Lithuania on 11 Febr. 1991 (after the Lithuanian referendum of 10 Febr. 1991), followed by the EC countries on 28 Aug. 1991 and the new ruling Council of the USSR (after the August coup d'état) on 6 Sept. 1991. Russia had granted recognition on 12 Jun. 1991: A. Sprudzs, ed., *The Baltic Path to Independence: An International Reader of Selected Articles* (1994).
[472] See, e.g., Blay, 'Self-Determination versus Territorial Integrity', pp. 390–391; Pierré-Caps, *Nation et Peuples*, p. 512 and H. O. Schoenberg, 'Limits of Self-Determination', 6 *Israel Yearbook on Human Rights* (1976) pp. 102–103.

is inherent in the right of self-determination. It is not prohibited by international law to seek secession if one constitutes a people and/or fraction of a people and if in addition one inhabits a certain territory delimited by international and/or internal administrative borders. The latter condition is reflected by the principle of *uti possidetis juris*. No justificative, material conditions are fixed. This has particularly been demonstrated with regard to the secessions in the Soviet Union and Yugoslavia. As to the procedural realization of the secession, the international community demands that the metropolitan State and the seceding part settle the withdrawal by peaceful means and in mutual agreement. This has been the international reaction to the situation in Nagorno Karabakh and the conflicts concerning the contested Serbian Republic of Bosnia-Herzegovina. If an agreement cannot be reached and both parties hold on to their respective positions, the situation becomes precarious. If the seceding entity is not internationally recognized, this territory remains an integral part of the metropolitan State. Central State authorities may therefore regain control of the area by virtue of their right to establish law and order in the whole of the territory. Measures to this end may entail the use of force, provided that they are not contrary to certain fundamental human rights.[473] The seceding people in question may not use force under the municipal legislation as this will generally be prohibited by national criminal law.

Although the international community has urged the belligerent parties in Yugoslavia, Abkhazia and Nagorno Karabakh to use peaceful means to settle their disputes, there have been, in general, no protests against other civil wars relating to the right of self-determination in Africa or Asia. Even if peaceful settlements are preferred, outside the colonial context, the use of force by secessionists has been neither consistently prohibited nor legitimized by international law. It is even more difficult to impose an obligation to use peaceful means in cases of secession, as the dispute cannot be solved by applying positive rules of international law. A secessional movement

---

[473] Even in time of public emergency, Art. 4 (2) of the ICCPR does not permit a derogation from, for example, the right not to be arbitrarily deprived of one's life (Art. 6), freedom from torture (Art. 7) and freedom from slavery (Art. 8). In addition common Art. 3 of the four Geneva Conventions of 1949 applies in case of internal armed conflicts. See also R. W. Gomulkiewicz, 'International Law Governing Aid to Opposition Groups in Civil War: Resurrecting the Standard of Belligerency', 63 *Washington Law Review* (1988) pp. 43–68 and P. H. Kooijmans, 'In the Shadowland between Civil War and Civil Strife', in A. Delissen and G. Tanja, eds., *Humanitarian Law of Armed Conflict: Challenges Ahead* (1991) pp. 225–247.

cannot turn to an international judicial body and, even if it could, what rules should be applied if State practice has not fixed any norms regulating secession? The disputed secession becomes then the object of political negotiations only.

If therefore a secessional movement offers armed resistance against a State's attempt to overrule the secession, the State may use force as well to defend its authority. Conversely, if the State authorities are the first to use violence, breaching fundamental human rights or even the prohibition of genocide, then the secessionists may offer armed resistance. In the absence of international recognition of the seceding State, the civil war, once started, will continue until a *de facto* solution has been imposed by force. Either the metropolitan State has regained effective control over the seceding territory, or the secessionists have stabilized their authority and have managed to secure the exercise of all elements of statehood, that is, they have created an independent State. The same argument applies when the secession is aimed at association or integration with a third State. If the secessionists have vanquished the central State authorities or if in the end the State has acquiesced in the secession, the seceded territory will have acquired an international status. International recognition will be granted more readily. The successful secession of Eritrea and the establishment of its statehood on 24 May 1993 after more than thirty years of combat may serve as an example. Ethiopia has now recognized the new State. The balance between the right of self-determination and the inviolability of the State's territorial integrity has thus been struck not by a rule of law, but by the law of the strongest, one of the first principles to be rejected by international law. Such has been the case of the failed secession of Biafra and the attempted secessions of Krajina, Nagorno Karabakh, the Serbian Republic of Bosnia-Herzegovina and Chechnya. International law may only enter into this process by demanding that the belligerent parties respect the rules of international humanitarian law and the rights of minorities. By virtue of the principle of *uti possidetis juris*, the international frontiers have to be respected and, if they are known, the internal administrative frontiers as well. This flows from the general practice followed during the dissolutions of the Soviet Union and Yugoslavia, in the absence of a mutual accord.

In the absence of internationally accepted rules either prohibiting or regulating secession, in case of disapproval by the metropolitan State, the secession becomes a question of fact dependent on the effective use of armed aggression. The struggle for secession will only legally end when the territorial integrity of a seceding territory deserves international protection, in other words when the territory constitutes a State or part of a third State. The existing State practice encourages the use of force. Attempts made by doctrine to draft justificative reasons for secession, designed to regulate disputed secession, have not been rewarded by State practice.[474]

Can the right of self-determination be regarded as a *jus cogens* under these circumstances? Article 53 of the Vienna Convention on the Law of Treaties of 23 May 1969 defines *jus cogens* as a peremptory norm of general international law 'accepted and recognized by the international community of States as a whole as a norm from which no derogation is permitted and which can be modified only by a subsequent norm of general international law having the same character'. Gros Espiell regards the right of self-determination of peoples under colonial and alien domination as a case of *jus cogens*.[475] At the preceding discussions on the drafting of Article 53 of the Vienna Convention, the principle of self-determination was cited as an example of *jus cogens*.[476] The International Law Commission decided however not to refer to any specific rights in Article 53. In 1976, the International Law Commission adopted a draft article on international crimes in its Draft Articles on State Responsibility, which makes reference to the 'international obligation of essential importance for safeguarding the right of self-determination of peoples, such as that prohibiting the establishment or maintenance by force of colonial domination'.[477] The original draft Article 18, paragraph 3 (a) of Rapporteur Ago mentioned the '[r]espect for the principle of the equal rights of all peoples and of their right of self-determination'.[478] Whatever the difference in formulation of the two draft articles, they both aim at qualifying the violation of essential obligations relating to the right of self-determination of peoples as an international crime. These obligations are therefore regarded as 'essential for the protection of fundamental interests of the international community'.[479]

---

[474] See pp. 73–77 above.
[475] UN Doc. E/CN.4/Sub.2/405/Rev.1 (1980) pp. 11–13. See also I. Brownlie, *Principles of Public International Law*, 4th edn (1990) p. 513.
[476] ILC Yearbook (1963) vol. II, pp. 198–199 and ILC Yearbook (1966) vol. II, pp. 247–249.
[477] Current Art. 19, para. 3 (b), ILC Yearbook (1980) vol. II, part 2. Adopted in 1976, ILC Yearbook (1976) vol. II, part 2, p. 75.
[478] ILC Yearbook (1976) vol. II, part 1, p. 54.
[479] Art. 19 (2) of the 1980 Draft Articles on State Responsibility.

In its well-known *obiter dictum* in the *Barcelona Traction* case, the International Court of Justice refers to 'obligations of a State towards the international community as a whole ... In view of the importance of the rights involved, all States can be held to have a legal interest in their protection; they are obligations *erga omnes*.'[480] The Court gives the example, among other things, of the 'basic rights of the human person', but does not expressly mention the right of self-determination.[481] As the right of self-determination is generally regarded as a fundamental human right and a prerequisite for the effective enjoyment of all other human rights, it can be argued that of all human rights, the right of self-determination must be a *jus cogens*. This was confirmed by the Court in the *East Timor* case when it firmly declared that 'Portugal's assertion that the right of peoples to self-determination, as it evolved from the Charter and from United Nations practice, has an *erga omnes* character, is irreproachable' and that 'it is one of the essential principles of contemporary international law'.[482] Is it also, in the words of Article 53 of the Vienna Convention on the Law of Treaties, a norm from which no derogation is permitted? The answer should be that the right of self-determination is an absolute right from which one cannot derogate, as long as the territorial integrity of an existing State is not partially or totally disrupted by the exercise of this right. As we have seen, derogation from the right of self-determination leading to secession is allowed, for the existing State may try to regain control over the seceding territory, thus overruling the secession. Therefore, it can be concluded that the right of self-determination of peoples living within an existing State and peoples living in Trust, Non-Self-Governing or analogous Territories is a *jus cogens*.[483] If the right of self-determination is used to disrupt the territorial integrity of a State, it will not have the status of *jus cogens*, but that of an ordinary norm of international law.

---

[480] Case concerning *The Barcelona Traction, Light and Power Company, Limited (Belgium v. Spain)*, ICJ Reports (1970) p. 32, para. 33.
[481] Ibid., p. 32, para. 34. The right of self-determination was expressly mentioned as a *jus cogens* in the separate opinion of Judge Ammoun, p. 304.
[482] Case concerning *East Timor (Portugal v. Australia)*, ICJ Reports (1995) p. 102, para. 29. There were no separate or dissenting opinions on this point.
[483] Cf., L. Hannikainen, *Peremptory Norms (Jus Cogens) in International Law* (1988) pp. 357 ff.

Autonomy

Despite new State practice concerning secession or dissolution in Eastern European countries, no rules of international law have been accepted to solve the problem of how to balance the right of secession and respect for territorial integrity. This legal vacuum encourages the use of force to impose a *de facto* situation which can be unstable in the long run. Without excluding the possibility that the justificative reasons or procedural rules suggested by doctrine with respect to secession may come to be accepted by States as customary international law in the future, the development of the right of self-determination and its interpretation already provide a basis for a solution. It should be borne in mind that one of the basic purposes of international law is to eliminate the use of force through the development of the rule of law. The following guiding considerations are relevant for the solution of the balancing process between secession and territorial integrity:

The suggested principle that secession prevails over territorial integrity in case of severe deprivation of a group's human rights will not be tenable in the future, if the mechanisms for international protection of human rights have been strengthened. The protection and development of the rights of minorities are of essential value in this context, as it is particularly the violation of those rights which can engender claims for secession.[484] It can be maintained that States which have accepted international legal control over the implementation of minority rights and which have recognized the right of individuals or groups of individuals to present claims concerning violations of minority rights to an international judicial body are not legally obliged to give in to secessional movements which justify their secession on the deprivation of the group's human rights. The more effective international legal control on minority rights becomes, the less justifiable a secession by reason of human rights violations is. International control on the implementation of minority rights is especially exercised by the Human Rights Committee under Article 27 of the ICCPR, provided that the State in question has accepted the first Optional Protocol, and to a lesser extent by the Committee of Ministers of the Council of Europe.[485]

---

[484] A. Eide, 'In Search of Constructive Alternatives to Secession', in Tomuschat, *Modern Law*, pp. 139–176.

[485] The Committee of Ministers monitors the implementation of the 1995 Council of Europe Framework Convention for the Protection of National Minorities (Art. 24) and

Secession cannot be accepted under international law if the grievances underlying the demands for secession can be removed through the exercise of internal self-determination. In order to have a right of secession, the claimant group must *a priori* have the right to determine its own internal political organization, including a right to autonomy.[486] A high degree of autonomy can legally be demanded by those groups who have a separate right of self-determination. This cannot be refused as long as the territorial integrity of a State is respected. As a consequence, it becomes more difficult to justify a secession by reason of discontent with the political organization of a State. A high degree of autonomy may in some cases prove sufficient to take away a dissatisfaction with an undemocratic central government or a non-representative government based on the distinction of race, creed or colour. In addition, a claim of secession based on the loss or undermining of the cultural or national identity of a group lends itself very well to the use of internal self-determination only.

The justificative grounds for secession which so far have been advanced by doctrine do not take into account other often deeply rooted sentiments which engender demands for secession. Thus, for example, in the case of Croatia it was felt that a secession was justified, *inter alia*, because Croatia was 'an old European nation with a thousand-year-old statehood' and because, due to its higher economic development, Croatia was '[f]orced to give in to the "federal" priorities, [and] ... could not materialize its own priority projects'.[487] Though it cannot be proved that the international community endorsed these justifications, it did not condemn them as insufficient legal grounds

the Contracting Parties have to transmit to the Secretary-General of the Council of Europe a report, on a periodical basis, on the measures taken by them to implement the Convention (Art. 25). Minorities cannot themselves turn to the Committee of Ministers, nor to the European Commission and Court of Human Rights: 34 ILM (1995) pp. 351 ff. Initially, the protection of national minorities was to be framed in a Protocol to the ECHR, which would have guaranteed a legal means of redress for the minority groups. Governments now plan the drafting of a new Protocol on the protection of cultural rights.

[486] See also H. Hannum, *Autonomy, Sovereignty and Self-Determination: The Accommodation of Conflicting Rights* (1990) pp. 473–477. Cassese, *Self-Determination*, pp. 108, 330 and 348–351, is of the opinion that fractions of peoples and minority groups living in sovereign States who are denied equal access to government do not have a right to self-determination. He nevertheless pleads for the expansion in the scope of self-determination to include ethnic minority groups emphasizing a right to internal self-determination, including regional autonomy.

[487] The third dissatisfaction with Yugoslavia lay in the fact that Croatia's national and cultural identity was undermined by a 'Serbicization of Croatian public life': B. Covic, *Croatia between War and Independence* (1991) pp. 39–41.

for secession either. In practice, justificative reasons were not sought. Peoples and fractions of peoples may claim secession for reasons other than those suggested by doctrine, but with no less vigour.

Elaborating on the present interpretation and status of the right of self-determination leads inexorably to the following rule: secession, whether leading to independence or to any kind of integration with another State, should only be achieved, in the absence of the consent of the State from which secession is sought, after a period of maximum autonomy. This rule flows, in the first place, from the already existing right to autonomy which can eliminate to a certain extent the grievances which otherwise would lead to claims for an immediate secession and, in the second place, from the practice that highly autonomous regions have more chance to see their secession recognized and, as the case may be, their statehood established than regions which had no serious autonomy prior to the secession.[488] The advantage of using this procedural rule to weigh the right of self-determination against respect for territorial integrity is that it is built on an already existing customary international norm – the right to autonomy – while combining legal and international political interests. If material justificative grounds for immediate secession develop into customary international law in the future, the procedural law suggested above can be applied for non-justifiable claims for immediate secession. In addition, a right to gradual secession guarantees that demands for a separation are genuine and supported by a large popular will. Problems relating to the territorial delimitation of the seceding unit can be solved before the full accomplishment of the secession through the use of the separate internal right of self-determination. The right to a progressive secession prevents the use of violence in order to force an immediate and unregulated secession and gives not only the secessionists but also the State from which secession is sought the opportunity to take political and economic transitional measures, as secessions are often claimed by the economically most developed regions of a State.[489] The procedural rule suggested is

---

[488] See p. 98 above.
[489] Cf. the example of the preparation of the secession of Quebec: Cassese, *Self-Determination*, pp. 248–254; and G. Marchildon and E. Maxwell, 'Quebec's Right of Secession under Canadian and International Law', 32 *Virginia Journal of International Law* (1992) pp. 583–623. D. Murswiek, 'The Issue of a Right of Secession – Reconsidered', in Tomuschat, *Modern Law*, pp. 38–39 states that a people must have the right of secession if a State fails to grant it autonomy. In the process leading to autonomy, this argument encourages however the withholding of cooperation by the people in question in order to force a secession.

therefore the result of stretching the presently existing right of self-determination to its limits and of exhausting this right before disrupting a State's territorial integrity.

Micro-peoples or very small fractions of peoples who have a right to autonomy and to secession and who wish to become independent can observe during their period of maximum autonomy what practical, political or economic difficulties they might have to face after independence.[490] In general, the small size of a territory does not stand in the way of the full exercise of the right of self-determination, except in the case of small colonial enclaves.[491] Although the case has not yet been put to the test, one may wonder whether the international community will approve secessions of very small entities. Much will depend on the political history of the entity. It is in practice much more difficult for micro-peoples and very small fractions of peoples to preserve their own identity and avoid assimilation, than it is for larger peoples or fractions of peoples. The political history may prove a certain separateness of the micro-entity involved, which seems more evident in the case of islands than of small enclaves.[492]

The right to gradual secession, suggested above, is a fundamental human right which like any political human right should benefit from the development of international control mechanisms regarding the implementation of civil and political rights. It is regrettable that the Human Rights Committee did not use the legal possibility given to it to consider complaints from groups of individuals on the violation of their right of self-determination and more specifically their right to autonomy.[493] The right to gradual secession cannot be brought under the protection of minority rights either, as minorities and peoples should remain separate legal persons with separate rights. As a consequence there is at present no international judicial body to which fractions of a State population can turn in order to have their right to autonomy recognized. Liechtenstein therefore proposed in the Third Committee of the General Assembly to open a debate on the granting of different levels of autonomy to communities living within States, on the understanding that a 'certain initial and very basic level of autonomy should be acknowledged for all communities

---

[490] See Part II below.
[491] See pp. 84–88 above.
[492] The autonomy of the Aaland Islands, a community of Swedish origin in Finland, serves as an example: see pp. 56–57 above.
[493] See pp. 63–66 above.

with a sufficient degree of distinctive identity'.[494] Aware of the fact that these communities could not address themselves to an international authority, one State proposed that an impartial organ be charged with the examination of demands for autonomy, such as a transformed Trusteeship Council or a special committee of the Security Council.[495] Others preferred these kinds of questions to be regulated by municipal law or by negotiations.[496] The majority feared the consequences of any such actions for the territorial integrity of their States. Thus, the plan to tackle the problem of autonomy was wrecked.[497]

By virtue of the principle *uti possidetis juris*, the internal administrative frontiers will become international borders in case of secession. Peoples demanding autonomy have the right to trace their own internal frontiers, a right inherent in the right of self-determination, bearing in mind that these frontiers might one day become internationally protected. In the former Yugoslavia and the Soviet Union, the *uti possidetis* rule has led to investing as international boundaries administrative limits which originally were intended for quite different purposes.[498] Given the fact that these new boundaries cannot be changed except by mutual agreement and that the absence of such agreements has often resulted in the use of force, one notes the importance of tracing these borders *before* secession.[499] An example of how this could be assured by international means is Article 5 of the European Charter of Local Self-Government which stipulates: 'Changes in local authority boundaries shall not be made without prior consultation of the local communities concerned, possibly by means of a referendum where this is permitted by statute.'[500]

---

[494] Liechtenstein Memorandum distributed to the UN delegations, information from the Permanent Mission of the Principality of Liechtenstein to the UN, also UN Doc. A/48/147 (1993), A/48/147/Add.1 (1993) and A/50/492 (1995).

[495] Armenia: UN Doc. A/C.3/48/SR.21 (1993), para. 12.

[496] Philippines and Uruguay respectively: UN Docs. A/C.3/48/SR.21 (1993), para. 13 and A/C.3/48/SR.22 (1993), para. 46.

[497] See also pp. 198 and 426 below. Pleading for international monitoring mechanisms: Cassese, *Self-Determination*, pp. 347–359.

[498] Cf. Case concerning the *Land, Island and Maritime Frontier Dispute (El Salvador v. Honduras, Nicaragua Intervening)*, ICJ Reports (1992) p. 388.

[499] See also R. McCorquodale, 'Self-Determination: A Human Rights Approach', 43 ICLQ (1994) p. 881.

[500] ETS no. 122, ratified by 16 Member States of the Council of Europe. Although R. Jennings and A. Watts, eds., *Oppenheim's International Law*, 9th edn (1992) vol. I, p. 715 argue that a legal principle of self-determination has been injected into the law about acquisition and loss of territory, J. Crawford, *Democracy in International Law*

RIGHT OF SELF-DETERMINATION 109

The seceding unit which acquires independence or which integrates with another State has to respect general international law whether or not this has been demanded by the international community as a condition of recognizing the secession. This implies, *inter alia*, that minority rights should be respected and that displacements of populations and ethnic cleansing are prohibited.

State structures and governmental organizations have always been subject to change. It is not the purpose of international law to maintain the *status quo* and the existing State patterns, but to provide a peaceful alternative for the adoption of modifications. The international community has gradually accepted the notion of self-determination of peoples, thus breaking the hegemony of States in determining the legal status and development of a territory and its people. It is not surprising that States, which are the creators of an *opinio juris sive necessitatis*, have so far been reluctant to accept any international rule concerning the right of self-determination which could facilitate or encourage secessions and thus endanger the continued existence of the States themselves. However, the absence of a rule can engender the use of force and create unstable legal situations. The right of self-determination, and its accepted interpretation, already contains seeds for a solution and a regulation of the balancing process of secession and territorial integrity.

(1994) p. 10 believes that 'the recent cases involving territorial disputes in Africa and Central America have by-passed the principle of self-determination in the interests of stability'. These cases still concerned the delimitation of the colonial borders between States, based on the *uti possidetis* rule, supplemented by the concepts of *effectivités* and acquiescence: *Burkina Faso v. Mali Frontier Dispute*, ICJ Reports (1986) p. 554, para. 25 and Case concerning the *Land, Island and Maritime Frontier Dispute (El Salvador v. Honduras, Nicaragua Intervening)*, ICJ Reports (1992).

2 Criteria for statehood

Recognition

This chapter is devoted to the international rules determining statehood. Special attention will be given to those criteria which are of particular importance to Micro-States, such as the minimum requirements relating to territory, population and independence. For more information on other domains of international law concerning statehood, we refer to the general works of learned publicists on the subject.[1]

In the eighteenth century the existence of a State was believed to be founded on its internal sovereignty and did not require recognition by other States or monarchs.[2] Under the influence of the positivist theory, which bases the obligation to respect international law on the consent of individual States, effective statehood became more dependent on international recognition. A new State would create obligations for existing States and should therefore be accepted by those States.[3] At the end of the nineteenth and the beginning of the twentieth century, this argument developed into the constitutive theory. Thus, according to Oppenheim, '[a] State is, and becomes, an International Person through recognition only and exclusively'.[4] The formation of a State remained a question of fact, but whether it could

---

[1] See especially G. Jellinek, *Allgemeine Staatslehre* (1914); J. Crawford, 'The Criteria for Statehood in International Law', 48 BYIL (1976–1977) pp. 93–182; J. Crawford, *The Creation of States in International Law* (1979); G. Arangio-Ruiz, *L'Etat dans le Sens du Droit des Gens et la Notion du Droit international* (1975); A. James, *Sovereign Statehood: The Basis of International Society* (1986); and J. D. van der Vyver, 'Statehood in International Law', 5 *Emory International Law Review* (1991) pp. 9–102.

[2] Crawford, *The Creation of States*, pp. 10–11. See also S. von Pufendorf, *De Iure Naturae et Gentium Libri Octo* (1672), English translation C. H. and W. A. Oldfather (1934).

[3] Crawford, *The Creation of States*, p. 12.

[4] L. Oppenheim, *International Law: A Treatise*, 8th edn (H. Lauterpacht, ed.) vol. I (1955) p. 125.

become a subject of international law was a question of law, that is of recognition. This theory did not however imply that the act of recognition was completely arbitrary and discretionary. Certain objective criteria were accepted according to which statehood should be tested. Thus, Jellinek demanded a territory, a people and a government to constitute a State and to be recognized as such.[5] Lauterpacht asked for an 'external independence and effective internal government within a reasonably well-defined territory'.[6] If these objective criteria were complied with, he believed that the international community would be under a duty to recognize the new State.[7] Recognition could also be an invalid act in certain circumstances. This led Crawford to conclude: 'If that is possible, then the test for recognition must be extrinsic to the act of recognition; that is, established by general international law. And that is a denial of the constitutive position.'[8] In contemporary international law there are very few lawyers who still adhere to the constitutive theory and see recognition as a *conditio sine qua non* of a State's international personality.[9] The majority of publicists support the declaratory theory under which the international personality of a State is determined by objective criteria of international law only.[10] Even if a State is not recognized, it will have international rights and duties opposable to the international community. Whether an entity is a State is a matter of fact, not of recognition.[11]

In view of today's near universality of membership in the United Nations, Dugard concludes that the 'United Nations has for practical purposes become the collective arbiter of statehood through the process of admission and non-recognition'.[12] Has United Nations membership thus become a criterion for statehood? The answer is in

---

[5] This is the theory of three elements: 'Staatsgebiet, Staatsvolk und Staatsgewalt'; Jellinek, *Allgemeine Staatslehre*, pp. 394–434.
[6] H. Lauterpacht, *Recognition in International Law* (1947) p. 31.
[7] Ibid., p. 6.
[8] Crawford, *The Creation of States*, p. 19.
[9] But see D. J. Devine, 'Recognition, Newly Independent States and General International Law', 10 *South African Yearbook of International Law* (1984) p. 24 and D. J. Devine, 'The Requirements of Statehood Re-examined', 34 *Modern Law Review* (1971) pp. 410–417.
[10] James, *Sovereign Statehood*, p. 147; Crawford, *The Creation of States*, p. 23; J. E. S. Fawcett, *The Law of Nations*, 2nd edn (1971); C. Rousseau, 'L'Indépendance de l'Etat dans l'Ordre international', 2 Hague Recueil (1948) pp. 171–253; I. Brownlie, *Principles of Public International Law*, 4th edn (1990) pp. 88–91; and M. Akehurst, *A Modern Introduction to International Law*, 6th edn (1987) p. 53.
[11] See further P. K. Menon, 'Some Aspects of the Law of Recognition; Part I: Theories of Recognition', RDI (1989) pp. 161–182.
[12] J. Dugard, *Recognition and the United Nations* (1987) p. 126.

the negative. There are entities whose statehood cannot be legally denied who nevertheless are not members of the United Nations. Thus, a Chinese veto bars the Republic of China's (Taiwan's) entry into the Organization, while Nauru does not apply for membership for financial reasons.[13] These reasons are however not related to the absence of statehood. Admission to the United Nations implies that the international community agrees to treat the new member as a State, with all the rights, duties and responsibilities which this entails, inside as well as outside the United Nations. Thus, membership of the United Nations tends to facilitate the entry of States into other international organizations. This was certainly the case with Andorra's admission to the Council of Europe.[14] Although neither affecting nor modifying the criteria for statehood, the admission to the United Nations constitutes a case of collective recognition which may have either a declaratory or a constitutive effect.

The declaratory theory of recognition has gained wide support in State practice. Thus the often-cited Montevideo Convention on Rights and Duties of States of 26 December 1933 defines a State according to objective criteria only, namely, '(a) a permanent population; (b) a defined territory; (c) a government and (d) the capacity to enter into relations with other States'.[15] This definition has been severely criticized, especially points (b) and (d). Scelle observed in the International Law Commission that the Montevideo definition 'did not apply to collectivities which nevertheless were States'.[16] General Assembly Resolution 3314 (XXIX) of 14 December 1974, adopting a definition of aggression, explains in Article 1 that 'the term "State": (a) Is used without prejudice to questions of recognition'. This does not however necessarily imply that a State does not have to be recognized for all other purposes not involving aggression.

One of the fourteen topics selected by the International Law Commission for codification was the recognition of States and governments.[17] But, as one member of the International Law Commission concluded, '[t]he question of recognition of States and governments should be set aside for the time being, for although it had legal consequences, it raised many political problems which did not lend them-

---

[13] See p. 141 below at nn. 44–46.
[14] See pp. 357–359 below.
[15] Art. 1, LNTS, vol. 165, p. 19.
[16] ILC Yearbook (1949) p. 62, para. 70.
[17] UN Doc. A/925, para. 16, GAOR, 1949, 4th Session, Suppl. no. 10.

selves to regulations by law.'[18] The subject was never to be codified. Although a definition of the word 'State' was not set forth in a separate legal instrument, the International Law Commission did concern itself with suggested definitions in the framework of general declarations or conventions.

The first attempt to clarify the meaning of the term 'State' was made in 1949 with regard to a draft Declaration on the Rights and Duties of States. Special Rapporteur Alfaro had not included an article on statehood in his draft, for he thought that 'the definition of the State had no place in a Declaration on the Rights and Duties of States'.[19] He came to this conclusion because 'if a country did not satisfy the conditions required for the existence of a State, it was not a State; on the other hand, if a State existed, that meant that it had fulfilled the conditions necessary for its existence and that it could not be called upon to fulfil those conditions'.[20] India and the United Kingdom had urged the inclusion of a definition of the term 'State', but the International Law Commission did not think it would come to a consensus on this point.[21] The Montevideo definition was criticized by the Special Rapporteur who did not accept the use of the term 'permanent population', because it excluded nomadic peoples.[22] Another question raised was who was to decide whether the conditions for statehood were fulfilled. One member of the Commission believed that, without an impartial authority, it made no sense to lay down criteria for statehood.[23] Another member thought it was not the right of an international authority, but of the international community to decide whether any community was a State or not.[24] The discussions do not show any general preference for the constitutive or for the declaratory theory. The International Law Commission decided not to include a definition of the term 'State' in the draft Declaration, as the word had been used without definition before and as 'no useful purpose would be served by an effort to define the term "State" '.[25] The word 'State' would therefore be used 'in the sense commonly accepted in international practice'.[26]

---

[18] Mr Bilge: ILC Yearbook (1973) vol. I, p. 175, para. 39.
[19] ILC Yearbook (1949) p. 61, para. 69.
[20] Ibid.
[21] Ibid., p. 289, para. 49.
[22] Ibid., p. 68, para. 63.
[23] Sir Bengal Rau: ibid., p. 63, para. 11.
[24] Mr Koretsky: ibid., p. 70, para. 11.
[25] Ibid., p. 259, para. 26.
[26] Ibid.

The same discussion arose at the time of the drafting of the Convention on the Law of Treaties. In the Article 'use of terms' of the draft Convention, Special Rapporteur Fitzmaurice envisaged the definition of the term 'State'. His draft Article 3 of 1956 stated: '(a) In addition to the case of entities recognized as being States on special grounds, the term "State": (i) means an entity consisting of a people inhabiting a defined territory, under an organized system of government, and having the capacity to enter into international relations binding the entity as such, either directly or through some other State; ... (ii) Includes the government of the State'.[27] This reflects clearly the declaratory theory. In addition, recognition is only constitutive when an entity does not otherwise qualify as a State: the States on special grounds. A later draft Article of 1966 aimed at adding to the present Article 6 of the Vienna Convention: 'The term "State" is used in this paragraph with the same meaning as in: (a) the Charter of the United Nations; (b) the Statute of the Court; (c) the Geneva Conventions on the Law of the Sea; (d) the Vienna Convention on Diplomatic Relations, i.e. it means a State for the purposes of International Law.'[28] Neither draft proposition was adopted. The definition of a State remained a controversial and politically loaded subject and the International Law Commission had no hope of finding a generally acceptable definition.

The question was again subject to discussion in the framework of the draft Articles on Succession of States in respect of Treaties. The Special Rapporteur was reluctant to propose that the International Law Commission should introduce any elements of the topic of recognition into the draft Articles. He believed that '[a]ny reference to the effects of recognition or non-recognition of States would inevitably raise controversial issues about the character and effects of recognition in international law'.[29] In its written comments to the draft Articles, the German Democratic Republic noted that by virtue of generally recognized principles of international law 'the international personality of a State exists independently of its recognition'.[30]

A German–Polish Mixed Arbitral Tribunal referring to the existence of the State of Poland stated in 1929 that 'the recognition of a State is not constitutive but merely declaratory. The State exists by itself and

---

[27] ILC Yearbook (1956) vol. II, p. 107, para. 4.
[28] ILC Yearbook (1966) p. 192.
[29] ILC Yearbook (1974) p. 19, para. 76.
[30] Ibid., p. 18, para. 67.

the recognition is nothing else than a declaration of this existence, recognized by the States from which it emanates.'[31] The International Court of Justice never expressly pronounced itself on all criteria for statehood. In its advisory opinion concerning *Reparation for Injuries Suffered in the Service of the United Nations* of 11 April 1949, the Court stated that the United Nations was an international person, but '[t]hat is not the same thing as saying that it is a State, which it certainly is not'.[32] It gives no reasons for this certainty. In its Opinion No. 1 of 29 November 1991, the Arbitration Commission on Yugoslavia declared that 'the existence or disappearance of a State is a question of fact, that the effects of recognition by other States are purely declaratory'.

Doctrine has deduced from the general practice of States some criteria for statehood which seem to have become general rules of international law. In principle, the declaratory view is adopted, although recognition can have a constitutive effect in certain cases. This is the situation of entities which under the general criteria do not possess statehood. The declaratory effect of recognition on the international personality of a State has a relative value. For what are the legal results if the international community refuses to recognize an entity which nevertheless complies with the objective criteria for statehood? As Crawford questioned: 'can States legitimately refuse ... to treat entities as States which do in fact qualify?'.[33] State practice has not accepted a right of recognition nor a duty to recognize.[34] Recognition, being within the discretion of every State, can therefore be withheld, for political or alleged legal reasons, from an entity which qualifies as a State under general international law. This is the consequence of the declaratory theory. As a result, legitimate but non-recognized States will have more difficulties in being accepted as Member States of international organizations. Relations with the international community will be restricted as they cannot enter into diplomatic relations. These are practical, not legal effects.[35]

---

[31] *Deutsche Continental Gas Gesellschaft v. Polish State*, 5 AD (1929–1930) no. 5.
[32] ICJ Reports (1949) p. 179.
[33] Crawford, 'The Criteria for Statehood', p. 110.
[34] See for further elaboration on this topic P. K. Menon, 'Some Aspects of the Law of Recognition; Part II: Recognition of States', RDI (1990) pp. 9–16.
[35] See pp. 91–92 above.

Territory

The functions of a State, a political and legal community of human beings, must first of all be exercised in a given territory. In the *Island of Palmas* case arbitrator Max Huber declared that international law had 'established this principle of the exclusive competence of a State in regard to its own territory' and that 'the functions of a State can be performed by any State within a given zone'.[36] The territory of a State comprises land territory, internal waters, territorial sea and the air space above this territory.[37] The Montevideo definition demands a 'defined territory',[38] Lauterpacht a 'reasonably well-defined territory'[39] and Hyde a 'fixed territory'.[40] In practice, it is required that 'the State must consist of a certain coherent territory effectively governed'.[41] The territory of a State need not be exactly fixed by definite frontiers. Thus, Albania was accepted as a full member of the League of Nations, although its frontiers were still disputed. Israel was also admitted to the United Nations despite uncertainties about its boundaries and claims to its entire territory.[42] As the German–Polish Mixed Arbitral Tribunal stated: 'In order to say that a State exists ... it is enough that this territory has a sufficient consistency, even though its boundaries have not yet been accurately delimited, and that the State actually exercises independent public authority over that territory.'[43] Likewise, the International Court of Justice notes in its *North Sea Continental Shelf* cases that '[t]here is for instance no rule that the land frontiers of a State must be fully delimited and defined'.[44]

Arangio-Ruiz declared that 'la disponibilité d'un territoire dans le sens dans lequel en disposent les Etats en conditions normales non seulement n'est pas une condition *sine qua non* de la personalité mais n'est pas condition *suffisante* pour la solution négative ou positive des

---

[36] Sole arbitrator Max Huber linked the notions of territory, sovereignty and independence in the *Island of Palmas (Netherlands v. USA)* case of 4 April 1928, 2 RIAA (1928) p. 838.
[37] The Exclusive Economic Zone is not taken into account as a State does not exercise full sovereignty over this sea area. See Arts. 56 and 73 of the United Nations Convention on the Law of the Sea (1982).
[38] See p. 112 above.
[39] Lauterpacht, *Recognition*, p. 31.
[40] C. Hyde in M. J. Whiteman, *Digest of International Law*, vol. I (1963) p. 223.
[41] Crawford, *The Creation of States*, p. 40.
[42] SC Res. 70 (1949) of 4 Mar. 1949 and GA Res. 273 (III) of 11 May 1949.
[43] *Deutsche Continental Gas Gesellschaft v. Polish State*, 5 AD (1929–1930) no. 5, pp. 14–15.
[44] ICJ Reports (1969) p. 32, para. 46.

problèmes d'identité'.[45] He bases his conclusion on the fact that statehood does not disappear if the territory is occupied and a government in exile is formed. Furthermore, even if a non-territorial entity acquires control over a territory, it does not change its international personality. Hence, the requirement of territory is not essential for statehood, so he believes. Arangio-Ruiz based his argument on the situation of the Holy See which did not possess a territory between 1870 and 1929. When eventually it did gain control over a certain territory in 1929, the status of the Holy See did not undergo any changes. This argumentation is however incorrect as the Holy See has never been a State in international law, and it disregards the existence of the Vatican City which has been recognized as a State after territorial acquisition.[46]

The existence of Micro-States with minimum land territory such as Monaco (1.95 square kilometres) and the Vatican City (0.44 square kilometres) leads to the conclusion that no minimum size is required for the territory, as this element was never a reason for denying statehood.[47]

Population

A State is an organization of human beings living together as a community. The population of a State comprises all individuals who, in principle, inhabit the territory in a permanent way.[48] It may consist of nationals and foreigners. As has repeatedly been pointed out by doctrine, the requirement of a population is not necessarily an equivalent of the requirement of nationality.[49] The population of a State need not be completely homogeneous in culture, language, race or otherwise. Indeed, it is even rare, except for Micro-States, to find a State with a homogeneous people. International law does not require a minimum number of inhabitants constituting a State. The smallest number of nationals in a Micro-State can be found in Nauru (4,964 Nauruans)[50] and in Monaco (5,070 Monégasques).[51] This figure can be

---

[45] Arangio-Ruiz, L'Etat, p. 58.
[46] See pp. 375–376, 386–388 and 410–417 below.
[47] See Part II below.
[48] Crawford, The Creation of States, pp. 40 ff.
[49] Ibid. and Menon, 'Some Aspects' (Part II), p. 5.
[50] J. Paxton, ed., The Statesman's Year-Book, 126th edn (1989–1990) p. 892.
[51] See p. 261 below.

even lower if we take into account that theoretically Pitcairn with 52 inhabitants has the right to opt for statehood by virtue of its right to self-determination.[52] No reservations have been made by the international community with respect to statehood because of the limited number of nationals of Micro-States, even if the nationals were outnumbered by foreign residents.

Government

The criterion of government is the central requirement of statehood on which all other criteria depend. An organization of individuals inhabiting a certain territory has its *raison d'être* in the display of authority to bring order and stability in the community. The Montevideo Convention demanded a 'government', while Hyde required an 'organized government exercising control over, and endeavoring to maintain justice within, the territory'[53] and Crawford an 'effective government'.[54] A central issue of the government criterion is the degree of effective control demanded. In general, international practice expects 'some degree of maintenance of law and order'.[55] Basing himself on the international reaction to the situation in the Congo after independence in 1960 and the suppressed secession of Katanga, Crawford concludes that the requirement of effectiveness will be more strictly applied if it concerns an entity whose statehood is opposed under title of international law.[56] Such was the situation of Katanga which was not in accordance with the right of self-determination.[57] New States seem to need more effective control over a territory than established States, unless the previous sovereign has granted them the right to govern. This seems to explain the United Nations involvement in the Congo to re-establish law and order, under presumption that the Congo's statehood had not disappeared, despite great lack of effective government.[58]

Statehood is not automatically lost when a State is illegally occupied by a foreign Power or in cases of civil war and secessional disputes.

---

[52] See p. 48 above.
[53] Hyde in Whiteman, *Digest*, p. 223.
[54] Crawford, *The Creation of States*, pp. 42 ff.
[55] Ibid., p. 46.
[56] Ibid.
[57] See p. 92 above.
[58] Crawford, *The Creation of States*, pp. 42–43.

The presumption of continuity is however of relative value. The Arbitration Commission on Yugoslavia concluded in its Opinion No. 1 of 29 November 1991 that the SFRY was in process of dissolution.[59] It stated 'that the State is commonly defined as a community which consists of a territory and a population subject to an organized political authority, that such a State is characterized by sovereignty' and that it had 'to determine the government's sway over the population and the territory', in other words, that the Federal authorities 'wield effective power'. As the Federal organs no longer met 'the criteria of participation and representativeness inherent in a Federal State' and had 'shown themselves to be powerless to enforce respect for the succeeding cease-fire agreements', the Commission concluded that the SFRY was in process of dissolution. It lacked effective power. This conclusion was drawn even before recognition of the seceding republics. The presumption of continuity of power does not seem to be strictly followed. There is no evidence either that in order to be recognized the seceding Yugoslav Republics had to wield more effective power than was demanded of the SFRY itself. On the contrary, with the loss of effective control by the Federal Government, effective authority seemed to be presumed to be in the hands of the seceding entities. Much depended on the internal political organization of the SFRY. Although, for the purposes of statehood, international law does not prescribe any special form of government, the form of internal political organization will affect the possibility of exercising effective power.[60] Thus, a federal-State structure will more easily lose effective control, when the composite communities no longer participate in the exercise of political power, than very centralized State structures. It also depends on the number of communities which terminate their participation in the central power. Effective power will be more difficult to dismantle in State structures which do not depend on the cooperation of composite parts.

The government of a State does not need recognition in order to fulfil the criteria for statehood. Non-recognition of a government may constitute proof that it lacks effective control over the territory and population, but can also be inspired by political reasons and in this

---

[59] 31 ILM (1992) pp. 1494-1497.
[60] Thus, for example, an anarchistic political structure is a denial of governmental power and will therefore exclude statehood. See also T. Baty, 'Can an Anarchy be a State?', 28 AJIL (1934) pp. 444-455.

case has no influence on the *de facto* existence of a government.[61] Furthermore, some States adhere to the policy of recognizing only States, not governments.[62]

It has sometimes been required that the government and the inhabitants of the State in general 'must have attained a degree of civilization, such as to enable them to observe with respect to the outside world those principles of law which are deemed to govern the members of the international society in their relations with each other'.[63] It seems difficult to imagine what 'degree of civilization' is needed to observe international law. So far, regimes which do not observe human rights or international law in general have been condemned, but this has not led to the extinction of statehood.[64] This argument is without prejudice to entities which have been illegally formed and therefore cannot claim statehood.[65]

Independence

The requirement of independence has often been phrased as a criterion of government and sovereignty.[66] Because of its importance for the determination of the statehood of Micro-States, we shall discuss it separately. The independence of a State is demanded in order to prove that the entity can lead a separate existence. It should not be a continuation of another State. It is not so much the independence of States

---

[61] In the *Tinoco Concessions* arbitration, 1 RIAA (1923) p. 369, the arbitrator declared: 'The non-recognition by other nations of a government claiming to be a national personality, is usually appropriate evidence that it has not attained the independence and control entitling it by international law to be classed as such. But when recognition *vel non* of a government is by such nations determined by enquiry, not into its *de facto* sovereignty and complete government control, but into its illegitimacy or irregularity of origin, their non-recognition loses something of evidential weight on the issue with which those applying the rules of international law are alone concerned .... Such non-recognition for any reason ... cannot outweigh the evidence disclosed ... as to the *de facto* character of Tinoco's government, according to the standard set by international law.'
[62] The Estrada doctrine, followed by Mexico, France, Spain, the United Kingdom and the United States. See Akehurst, *A Modern Introduction*, p. 58.
[63] United States practice according to Hyde in Whiteman, *Digest*, p. 223.
[64] In wartime, for example, the aggressor State does not lose its statehood because it commits an illegal act of aggression. Iraq's invasion of Kuwait on 2 Aug. 1990 was condemned in SC Res. 660 (1990), but Iraq's statehood was not questioned. Neither was this the case of the apartheid regime of South Africa. South Africa was still considered a State.
[65] See pp. 127–132 below.
[66] Jellinek, *Allgemeine Staatslehre*, pp. 435 ff.

but of governments that is required. What degree of independence is therefore necessary under general State practice? Arbitrator Huber declared in the *Island of Palmas* case: 'Sovereignty in the relations between States signifies independence. Independence in regard to a portion of the globe is the right to exercise therein, to the exclusion of any other State, the functions of a State.'[67] It should be noted that sovereignty and independence are used as equivalents. This position has sometimes been adopted in doctrine.[68] We prefer to distinguish between the two terms.[69] Sovereignty is considered a consequence of statehood, not a prerequisite thereof. It is the 'totality of international rights and duties recognized by international law' vested in States.[70] Independence concentrates on the rights which an entity has to the exclusion of other States. Sovereignty and independence are interrelated. A substantial limitation of sovereignty in favour of a third State leads to loss of independence and therefore loss of statehood. As Rousseau stated: 'La perte de l'indépendance coïncide nécessairement avec la disparition de l'Etat.'[71]

However, not every alienation of sovereignty will lead to the extinction of statehood. In the *Wimbledon* case, the Permanent Court of International Justice refused 'to see, in the conclusion of a treaty, by which a State undertakes to perform or refrain from performing a particular act, an abandonment of its sovereignty'.[72] The often-cited individual opinion of Judge Anzilotti in the *Austro-German Customs Union* case clarifies the notion of independence in a general sense. He understood the independence of Austria protected under Article 88 of the Treaty of Saint-Germain of 1919 as a 'normal' independence of States. It meant 'the existence of Austria ... as a separate State and not subject to the authority of any other State or group of States. ... it may also be described as sovereignty (*suprema potestas*), or external sovereignty, by which is meant that the State has over it no other authority than that of international law.'[73] With regard to accepted contractual obligations he was of the opinion that '[a]s long as these

---

[67] 2 RIAA (1928) p. 838.
[68] See, e.g., James, *Sovereign Statehood*, p. 22 and F. H. Hinsley, *Sovereignty*, 2nd edn (1986).
[69] See Crawford, *The Creation of States*, pp. 26–27 and 71.
[70] Ibid., p. 26.
[71] C. Rousseau, *Droit International Public*, vol. III (1977) p. 330.
[72] PCIJ Reports (1923) Series A, no. 1, p. 25.
[73] PCIJ Reports (1931) Series A/B, no. 41, p. 57.

122   THE GENERAL INTERNATIONAL LEGAL CONTEXT

restrictions do not place the State under the legal authority of another State, the former remains an independent State however extensive and burdensome those obligations may be'.[74] The six dissident Judges in this case believed a State lost its independence 'if it lost the right to exercise its own judgement in coming to the decisions which the government of its territory entails'.[75] A putative State should therefore not fall under the authority of another State and should keep, in Cavaré's words, 'le pouvoir de décision définitif et originaire'.[76] The government should be able to take decisions without having to abide by external rules and have an original title to power, not delegated by a third State. Some scholars did not deduce very stringent requirements for independence from the practice of States. Okeke notes that '[i]f an entity has its own organs, such as law courts, legal system, and law of nationality, then one could say that there is a *prima facie* case of statehood',[77] while Hyde and Dugard do not always strictly insist on independence.[78] These positions should be approached with caution as they are not borne out by the practice of States taken as a whole.

Independence is generally divided into formal and actual or real independence.[79] According to Crawford's definition, '[f]ormal independence exists where the powers of government of a territory (both in internal and external affairs) are vested in the separate authorities of the putative State',[80] whereas actual independence is defined as 'the minimum degree of real governmental power at the disposal of the authorities of the putative State, necessary for it to qualify as "independent" '.[81] When formal and actual independence exists, the entity may qualify as a State. If only formal independence occurs, Crawford maintains that this is a denial of statehood.[82] Darsow believes however that State practice treats formal independence as the decisive factor of statehood.[83] In case of a lack of formal independence, but substantial

[74] Ibid., p. 58.
[75] Ibid., p. 77. The minority opinion did not differ so much with the majority opinion over the definition of independence as over the disputed questions of fact: see Crawford, *The Creation of States*, p. 51.
[76] L. Cavaré, *Le Droit international public positif*, vol. I (1967) p. 336.
[77] C. N. Okeke, *Controversial Subjects of Contemporary International Law* (1974) p. 30.
[78] Hyde in Whiteman, *Digest*, p. 223 and Dugard, *Recognition*, p. 72.
[79] Rousseau, 'L'Indépendance', pp. 171–253, Crawford, *The Creation of States*, pp. 52–71 and Menon, 'Some Aspects' (Part I), p. 8.
[80] Crawford, *The Creation of States*, p. 52.
[81] Ibid., pp. 56–57.
[82] Ibid., p. 69.
[83] T. Darsow, *Zum Wandel des Staatsbegriffs: Unter besonderer Burücksichtigung der Lehre und Praxis internationaler Organisationen, der Mikrostaaten und der PLO* (1984)

real independence, statehood seems to be generally withheld too.[84]

Crawford mentions two situations which derogate from formal independence:[85]

The first is the existence, as a matter of international law, of a special claim of right, irrespective of consent, to the exercise of governmental powers. One State believes as of right that it has exclusive competence to act for another entity without the latter's consent.

The second is a discretionary authority to determine upon and effect intervention in the internal affairs of the putative State. This power of intervention, we must add, can also affect the external affairs of an entity. Crawford cites the example of 'the undetermined powers of intervention possessed by France in respect of Monaco ... [which] have led to doubts concerning the latter's independence'.[86] He states further that 'a broad discretionary power of intervention could always be used with colour of right to deny local independence. Monaco would thus appear not to have formal independence.'[87] This conclusion cannot be endorsed without a thorough examination of Franco-Monégasque relations. We shall therefore come back to this point.[88]

To illustrate a situation of legal interference by a third State, we can cite the case of protectorates from which statehood has generally been withheld.[89] Under a treaty of 12 May 1881 concluded between France and His Highness the Bey of Tunis, Tunisia was put under a protectoral system. The external sovereignty of Tunisia was restricted, while the Bey was deprived of an active right of legation and had a limited passive right of legation, as foreign diplomats could only be received after consultation with France. The Bey of Tunis had taken up the obligation 'à ne conclure aucun acte ayant un caractère international sans en avoir donné connaissance au gouvernement de la République

---

pp. 86-91. He bases this conclusion on the existence of Micro-States, especially the treatment of Liechtenstein by the League of Nations, without taking into account the general and subsequent treatment of Micro-States by the international community in general. There are in fact no indications that actual independence is not important for Micro-States. On the contrary, this is often the most difficult independence for them to achieve. See pp. 257-258 and 311-314 below.

[84] These cases are however rare. It seems to have occurred in the British Dominions in 1924. Crawford, *The Creation of States*, pp. 69-70.

[85] Ibid., pp. 55-56.

[86] Ibid., p. 56.

[87] Ibid.

[88] See p. pp. 305-310 below.

[89] See A. Kamanda, *A Study of the Legal Status of Protectorates in Public International Law* (1961) pp. 182-183.

française et sans s'être entendu préalablement avec lui'.⁹⁰ In addition, a subsequent convention obliged the Bey 'à procéder aux réformes administratives, judiciaires et financières que le gouvernement français jugera utiles'.⁹¹ A General Resident representing the French Government had large discretionary powers in the internal affairs of Tunisia. He had to approve all the Bey's decrees, acted as Minister of Foreign Affairs and presided over the Council of Ministers.⁹² The Tunisian police force incorporated French chiefs of police put at the disposal of the Bey by the French Government.⁹³ As this legal situation shows certain similarities at first sight with the relations of Monaco and France (except for a guarantee of independence), it has been alleged that Monaco is a protectorate.⁹⁴ For an investigation into the correctness of this statement we refer to our subsequent analysis.⁹⁵

Actual independence is lost in the case of:⁹⁶

Substantial illegality of origin In this case the putative State has been created in violation of basic rules of international law or *jus cogens*. Although the statehood of this entity will probably be denied, because of its illegality of origin alone, the entity will be presumed to lack actual independence. This will especially concern illegal creations of States by third States.⁹⁷

Entities formed under belligerent occupation There is a strong presumption that these entities do not enjoy actual independence from the occupying power.⁹⁸

*Substantial external control of the State*⁹⁹ This category is of the utmost importance for Micro-States, because even if formal independence is proved, they must show sufficient control over their external and internal affairs. Such independence will not be demonstrable in

---

⁹⁰ Art. 6 of the treaty of 12 May 1881 between France and the Bey of Tunis. Full text in E. Rouard de Card, *Les Traités de Protectorat conclus par la France en Afrique 1870–1895* (1897) pp. 159–161.
⁹¹ Art. 1 of the Convention of 8 June 1883 between France and Tunisia regulating the respective relations of the two countries. Ibid., p. 161.
⁹² Ibid., p. 36.
⁹³ Ibid., p. 35.
⁹⁴ P. Guggenheim, *Lehrbuch des Völkerrechts*, vol. I (1948) pp. 252–254.
⁹⁵ See pp. 304–314 below.
⁹⁶ Ibid., pp. 58–69.
⁹⁷ See pp. 127–132 below.
⁹⁸ An example of this was the creation of the State of Manchukuo, presumed to be under Japanese control, although it concerned Chinese occupied territory.
⁹⁹ Crawford, *The Creation of States*, p. 60.

case of 'foreign *control* overbearing the decision-making of the entity concerned on a wide range of matters of high policy and doing so systematically and on a permanent basis'.[100]

Several aspects of independence are relevant for Micro-States:

1 The smallness of a territory, a limited number of nationals and few or no natural resources do not, by definition, have to lead to loss of formal and actual independence. Both the Vatican City and Nauru enjoy a relatively high degree of independence.[101]
2 The degree of independence of Micro-States depends on several elements: the historical evolution of the relations between the Micro-State and any other State, usually a neighbouring State, the negotiation position of the Micro-State and its willingness to stand possible financial losses. These factors are essentially based on the political and economic strength of each Micro-State. Though in this respect every Micro-State is different, one can distinguish three main fields in which some form of cooperation has been sought with another State:
(a) *Practical cooperation* This concerns cooperation for practical purposes which facilitates the everyday functioning of the Micro-State. It comprises postal, telegraph, telephone and customs cooperation as well as practical collaboration for the proper functioning of radio and television stations and schools. Agreements concluded for the purposes of such practical cooperation are not *a priori* prejudicial to the independence of the Micro-State.
(b) *Economic cooperation* This sort of cooperation is not only designed to facilitate the economic survival of the Micro-State, but is also the result of the reconciliation of the economic interests of the Micro-State with those of its neighbouring State and vice versa. Economic collaboration may comprise general financial cooperation and monetary, banking and fiscal coordination. Though the economic agreements between the Micro-State and its neighbouring State do not, in general, substantially limit the independence of a Micro-State, it is often the dissatisfaction of the neighbouring State with the economic cooperation which incites the neighbouring State to put pressure on the Micro-State in order to compel it to make certain concessions. This has, for instance,

---

[100] Brownlie, *Principles of Public International Law*, p. 76.
[101] See for the Vatican City pp. 413–416 below. Nauru and Australia have committed themselves to non-interference in each other's internal affairs and to conducting their relations in accordance with the principles of mutual respect for one another's independence, sovereignty and equality: Principles 2 and 3 of the Joint Declaration of Principles Guiding the Relations between Australia and the Republic of Nauru, 32 ILM (1993) p. 1476.

been the case for San Marino (casino dispute)[102] and for Monaco (fiscal dispute).[103]

(c) *Political cooperation* The international political cooperation between a Micro-State and its neighbouring country comprises defence agreements, general restrictions on external and/or internal political affairs and diplomatic representation. This category does not include the cooperation between a Micro-State and a neighbouring State, without treaty obligation, by reason of political affiliation. Liechtenstein and San Marino sometimes use the diplomatic services of their neighbouring States, but without losing control over the conduct of their international relations.[104] A defence agreement exists between France and Monaco and implicitly between Spain, France and Andorra.[105] Diplomatic representation by a third State, while maintaining control over foreign affairs, does not impair the independence of a Micro-State under general international law; neither do defence agreements. The heart of the problem with regard to the formal independence of a Micro-State is to what extent the internal and/or external policies of the Micro-State have to be brought in line with those of the neighbouring State. This question is especially relevant for Monaco and Andorra, which have undertaken certain obligations in this sense.[106]

3 The actual and formal independence of a State is not impaired if the State in question has been forced, even by legal means of pressure not involving the use of violence, to make concessions to another State leading to an abandonment of independence in violation of the right of self-determination. This rule is based on the principle *ex injuria jus non oritur*. Due to the peremptory nature of a norm of *jus cogens*, the breach of *jus cogens* cannot create a legal title. Consequently if a State violates the right of self-determination of the people of another State by using force or any other means, including legal measures, the statehood of this latter State would not be prejudiced if, without this violation, the State has formal and actual independence. By analogy with a belligerent occupation,[107] it can be accepted in international law that the threat or use of coercive measures, not involving the use of force and irrespective of their legality, cannot derogate from the independence of another State if these measures have compelled that State to give up certain elements of its independence against

---

[102] See pp. 225–227 below.
[103] See pp. 276–278 below.
[104] See for Liechtenstein pp. 161–163 below and for San Marino pp. 227–228 below.
[105] See pp. 290, 345 and 350 below, and in general pp. 169, 233 and 396 below.
[106] See for Monaco pp. 274–282 and 305–310 below and for Andorra pp. 335–338 and 369–370 below.
[107] Crawford, *The Creation of States*, pp. 57–58.

its will and against the wishes of its people. A strong and official protest by the people in question against the concessions it was forced to make is a *conditio sine qua non* in order to preserve its independence and statehood, otherwise its consent to be bound by the imposed obligations can be seen as an expression of its right of self-determination. This principle will apply particularly to Micro-States or any other State the negotiating position of which is particularly weak. The problem is, however, that with the present state of international law, there may well be few or no international forums to which grievances can be addressed by the very weak States.[108] Practice may then prove that the strong State has a discretionary power to impose its will on the weak State. Much therefore depends on the measure of independence a Micro-State manages to draw to itself and on the acceptance by the rest of the international community of these independent actions.[109] Recognition thus acquires a special constitutive effect.

Illegal entities

It is possible that an entity which fulfils the conditions for statehood discussed above is nevertheless not recognized by the international community, because its creation violates a peremptory norm of international law. The problem which arises is whether this entity can be considered a State which violates international law, or whether statehood is precluded by definition because of the illegal origin. In the former case, non-recognition would only function as a political sanction without prejudicing statehood. In the latter case, non-recognition denies the statehood, because it regards the legality of origin as a constitutive criterion for statehood. Both positions have been supported by doctrine.[110] In our opinion, preference should be given to the argument

---

[108] The treaties concluded between France and Monaco or Andorra respectively do not, for example, provide for a denunciation clause, nor for an arbitral procedure. They do not have other judicial means of redress without France's cooperation. See pp. 282 and 338 below, and also pp. 140–141 on the Case concerning *Certain Phosphate Lands in Nauru (Nauru v. Australia)*.

[109] See also J. Crawford, 'Islands as Sovereign Nations', 38 ICLQ (1989) p. 283.

[110] Devine, 'Recognition', pp. 410–417 believes that illegality of origin has no effect on statehood, but it should be noted that he adheres to an absolute constitutive theory of recognition. Dugard, *Recognition*, pp. 127–131 maintains that if the creation of a State breaches the right of self-determination, it still meets the essential requirements of statehood, but the existence of the State violates a peremptory norm of international law. Fawcett, *The Law of Nations*, pp. 38–39 and his comment to Devine, 'Recognition', p. 417 deduced a new 'additional criterion of statehood', namely the right of all peoples to have effective representation in their government. Crawford, *The Creation*

that an entity cannot claim statehood if its creation was founded and made possible by the violation of a rule of *jus cogens*. The condemnation of the illegal creation of Southern Rhodesia by the General Assembly and the General Assembly's call upon the Member States of the United Nations 'not to recognize any form of independence in Southern Rhodesia without the prior establishment of a government based on majority rule in accordance with General Assembly Resolution 1514 (XV)' has been diversely interpreted.[111] Some maintained that Southern Rhodesia was in fact an illegal State,[112] while others denied the existence of Southern Rhodesia's statehood.[113] Although arguments can be found for either position, from an overall legal point of view statehood should not be accepted. If the creation of the entity is rooted in a breach of *jus cogens*, this violation should not have any legal effects. Whatever the value of the maxim *ex injuria jus non oritur* in general, especially in the case of a breach of peremptory norms of international law, no legal consequences should be accepted which are to the advantage of those who infringed the rules of *jus cogens*.[114] Furthermore, even if statehood were accepted, though regarded as illegal in origin, the non-observance of a rule of *jus cogens* entails the international responsibility *erga omnes* of the illegally created State.[115] Consequently, the illegal State is under the obligation to bring the illegal situation to an end.[116] This may have to lead to the dissolution of the State or to a change of government while retaining statehood. In either case problems of State succession and acceptance of obligations already entered into by the former illegal State may arise. Such unwanted commitments can be avoided if the statehood of the illegal entity has not been accepted as from its creation, thus preventing it from performing any international acts until the restoration of the legal situation.

   of States, p. 106 concludes that a new rule 'prohibiting entities from claiming statehood if their creation is in violation of an applicable right of self-determination' has come into being.
[111] GA Res. 2379 (XXIII).
[112] Devine, 'Recognition', pp. 412–415 and Dugard, *Recognition*, p. 130.
[113] Fawcett, *The Law of Nations*, pp. 38–39 and Crawford, *The Creation of States*, p. 104.
[114] Under Art. 53 of the Vienna Convention on the Law of Treaties, a treaty conflicting with a *jus cogens* is void. By analogy, a State created by breaching a *jus cogens* should have no legal existence either.
[115] Case of *Barcelona Traction, Light and Power Company, Limited (Belgium v. Spain)*, ICJ Reports (1970) p. 32, para. 33.
[116] Advisory opinion on *Legal Consequences for States of the Continued Presence of South Africa in Namibia (South West Africa) notwithstanding Security Council Resolution 276 (1970)*, ICJ Reports (1971) p. 54, para. 117.

It has been alleged that new States were asked to respect *jus cogens*, while existing States did not have to fulfil the criteria relating to the respect of peremptory norms of international law. This was criticized as an 'unfortunate double standard of ethical behaviour' with respect to the criteria for statehood.[117] This is however a specious argument, for it is the *act of creating* a State which is regulated by certain rules of *jus cogens*, notwithstanding the respect which all States, new and old, have to show for these rules in general. This is not incompatible with the fact that existing States may be created in the past under circumstances which at present would be regarded as illegal, but which at the time were absolutely justified. It is not a 'double standard', but the evolution of international law. Moreover, the creation of a putative State will only be illegal if it is founded on a breach of international law and made possible by this violation. Any other breaches of rules of international law which as such were not indispensable for the foundation of a State will not affect the statehood, but can entail international responsibility of the new State or entity.

Three norms of general international law have been invoked with respect to the illegality of the creation of States:[118]

The prohibition of aggression and of acquisition of territory by means of force Acts of aggression are generally accepted to be outlawed by a rule of *jus cogens*.[119] It prohibits the use of force between States. In the present context, a State may not forcefully acquire a territory belonging to another State in order to create or help to create a new State on this territory.[120] Thus, the United Nations organs have condemned the occupation by Israel of East Jerusalem, the West Bank and the Golan Heights,[121] the Iraqi invasion of Kuwait[122] and the

[117] Dugard, *Recognition*, p. 129 opposed Crawford's statement that new States could not claim statehood if their creation was in violation of an applicable right of self-determination, while expressly excluding existing States from the application of this principle: Crawford, *The Creation of States*, pp. 105–106.
[118] See also van der Vyver, 'Statehood', pp. 64–65.
[119] Case of *Barcelona Traction, Light and Power Company, Limited (Belgium v. Spain)*, ICJ Reports (1970) p. 32, para. 34. See also L. Hannikainen, *Peremptory Norms (Jus Cogens) in International Law* (1988) pp. 323 ff.
[120] Art. 1 of the Definition of Aggression states: 'Aggression is the use of armed force by a State against the sovereignty, territorial integrity or political independence of another State', while Art. 5 (3) specifies: 'No territorial acquisition or special advantage resulting from aggression is or shall be recognized as lawful': GA Res. 3314 (XXIX).
[121] GA Res. 2253 (ES-V) of 4 Jul. 1967 and subsequent yearly resolutions. See van der Vyver, 'Statehood', p. 46 at n. 187.
[122] SC Res. 660 (1990).

establishment of the Turkish Republic of Northern Cyprus after Turkish armed intervention in Northern Cyprus.[123] The only exception to this rule seems to be a justification under another rule of *jus cogens*. Indian troops aided Bangladesh to become an independent State, which, as we have seen, possessed the right of self-determination with force of *jus cogens*.[124] With regard to the conflicts in Eastern Europe the European Communities recalled that 'its member States will not recognise entities which are the result of aggression'.[125] As a consequence, entities which wish to secede from an existing State and which do not have the right of self-determination with force of *jus cogens* cannot claim statehood if the putative State has been founded with the help of armed force by a third State. The legal situation will be different if the seceding entity can demonstrate its statehood prior to the external help and aggression. The creation of the State would then not have depended on a breach of *jus cogens*.

The right of self-determination A new State cannot be created without the consent of the peoples living in self-determination units which hold the right of self-determination as a rule of *jus cogens*, that is, peoples living in States, Non-Self-Governing and assimilated Territories.[126] Moreover, the practice of States demands that the wishes are observed even of those peoples which have the right of self-determination by virtue of a general rule of international law, for example peoples within an existing State wishing to secede. This is a minimum requirement without prejudice to the balancing process of self-determination and territorial integrity. Thus secessions without popular support are *a priori* illegal and cannot lead to the creation of a State. As we have seen, Southern Rhodesia had been created without the consent of the majority of the population and was not recognized on that ground.[127] Similarly, the creation of Bantustans (South African Homeland States) was condemned by the United Nations. It was considered contrary to the principle of self-determination.[128]

The Arbitration Commission on Yugoslavia considered that the Socialist Republic of Bosnia-Herzegovina did not meet the necessary

---

[123] SC Res. 541 (1983).
[124] See p. 83 above. Bangladesh could be assimilated with a Non-Self-Governing Territory.
[125] EPC Declaration of 16/17 Dec. 1991 on the Guidelines on the Recognition of New States in Eastern Europe and in the Soviet Union, 31 ILM (1992) p. 1486.
[126] See pp. 81–83 above.
[127] See p. 92 above and GA Res. 2022 (XX), UN Doc. A/6014 (1965) p. 54.
[128] GA Res. 2775E (XXVI) and GA Res. 3411D (XXX).

conditions for its recognition, because the 'will of the peoples' had not been fully established.[129] The Serbian populations had protested against the parliamentary decision for independence and had proclaimed their own State within Bosnia-Herzegovina.[130] The European Communities only decided to recognize Bosnia-Herzegovina on 6 April 1992 after a referendum held on 1 March 1992, which resulted in a 63 per cent majority for independence.[131] In this case of secession too, statehood seemed to be precluded if it was not evident that a majority of the population supported it.[132]

The prohibition of racial discrimination and apartheid It has been suggested that the establishment of a racist regime hinders the creation of a State.[133] The General Assembly called upon all States not to recognize Southern Rhodesia 'without the prior establishment of a government based on majority rule'.[134] The establishment of Bantustans was not recognized by the United Nations Member States because it was designed 'to consolidate the inhuman policy of apartheid' and 'to perpetuate white minority domination'.[135] Furthermore, the independence of the Homeland States was rejected as 'invalid'.[136] The Bantustans were not considered independent because of their economic and political reliance on South Africa.[137] One should however be careful in accepting the prohibition of racial discrimination as a rule whose violation will preclude statehood. We are concerned with the illegality of the creation of a putative State. The root of the illegality is the breach of the right of self-determination of the whole population. It is this breach which permits the establishment of a 'State' with a government based on minority rule and which permits the creation of an apartheid system. Thus minority rule is a consequence of the fundamental illegality; it is effect, not

---

[129] Opinion No. 4 of 11 Jan. 1992, 31 ILM (1992) pp. 1501–1503.
[130] Decision by the Assembly of the Serbian People of Bosnia-Herzegovina to create a Serbian Republic of Bosnia-Herzegovina (9 Jan. 1992).
[131] EPC Declaration on Yugoslavia (6 Apr. 1992), EPC Press Release 40/92. The referendum was boycotted by the Serbs who constituted 32 per cent of the total population in Bosnia-Herzegovina.
[132] But see on parliamentary exercise of the right of self-determination p. 91 above.
[133] Van der Vyver, 'Statehood', p. 65; with more differentiation Crawford, *The Creation of States*, pp. 226–227.
[134] Para. 2 of GA Res. 2379 (XXIII).
[135] GA Res. 32/105N.
[136] GA Res. 31/6A.
[137] Crawford, *The Creation of States*, p. 225.

cause. As we are concerned with criteria which are inherent in statehood and its foundation, the principle that the creation of a State should not lead to a minority government and racist regime cannot be accepted as a criterion for statehood. If it were otherwise, an unfortunate double standard would be admitted. Existing States would not lose their statehood when a racist regime came into power, whereas an entity wishing statehood would not constitute a State if it adopted a racist minority rule. In this case, a double standard should be avoided, as the norm does not regulate the creation of a State in itself but applies to the existence of a State. The criterion of effective government leaves the choice of the form of government to the population of the State, but does not punish it with the disappearance of the statehood if the government violates a norm of *jus cogens*.[138] Moreover, the creation of a State in order to establish a government based on racial discrimination will in most cases be in contravention of the right to self-determination of the whole population. On this ground statehood will be excluded. The international responsibility of States following an apartheid regime remains unaffected, for the prohibition of racial discrimination is generally accepted as *jus cogens*.[139]

[138] See pp. 118–120 above. South Africa's statehood was not contested during the apartheid policy.
[139] Case of *Barcelona Traction, Light and Power Company, Limited (Belgium v. Spain)*, ICJ Reports (1970) p. 32, para. 34. See also Hannikainen, *Peremptory Norms*, pp. 471–476.

3   The general question of Micro-States in international organizations

Micro-States and the League of Nations

On 23 April 1919 San Marino submitted a request for admission to the League of Nations,[1] followed by Monaco on 6 April 1920[2] and Liechtenstein on 15 July 1920.[3] The demands for admission were not met, but they led to discussions on alternative membership for very small States.[4] The Assembly of the League of Nations was not prepared to admit these Micro-States as full Members. Under the Covenant of the League of Nations each Member State had one vote and, in general, decisions of the Assembly or the Council required the agreement of all Member States represented at the meetings.[5] It was considered undesirable to accord Micro-States the same right of veto or an equal value in voting procedures as larger States. The Assembly therefore decided on 17 December 1920 that the Committee on Amendments to the Covenant should 'consider whether, and in what manner, it would be possible to attach to the League of Nations sovereign States which, by reason of their small size, could not be admitted as ordinary Members'.[6] This Committee submitted a report which was discussed in Committee No. 5 of the Second Assembly.[7] It was concluded, in the first place, that all States should join the League of Nations equally 'although with less importance, ... States of

---
[1] League of Nations Off. J. (1920) no. 5, p. 264.
[2] Ibid., pp. 265–266.
[3] League of Nations, *Documents of the Assembly* (1920) no. 18.
[4] For a full discussion on the admission procedure of Liechtenstein, San Marino and Monaco, see pp. 170–174, 233–234 and 291–293 below respectively.
[5] Arts. 3 (4) and 5 (1) of the Covenant of the League of Nations.
[6] League of Nations, *Records of the Second Assembly*, Plenary Meetings (1921) p. 685.
[7] 'The Position of Small States', ibid., pp. 685–688.

a very small area' and that 'peace and security would be more readily attained if a certain class of States, even States of secondary importance, were not excluded'.[8] Three different systems were suggested:[9]

'Associated' membership Small States would be given a right of full representation, but without a vote. The disadvantage invoked however was that by allowing them to speak in the Assembly, also on questions in which they had no direct interests, the debates would be prolonged.

'Limited participation' membership Under this system small States would be full Members with the right to participate in the debates and in votes, but limited to cases in which their national interests were involved. Whether this was the case was to be decided by a majority of the Assembly. Complications were however feared in defining the status of the State and the definition of its own particular interests.

'Represented' membership The small State would not become a real Member of the League, but would be represented by some other State which was already a Member of the League of Nations. This system was believed in practice to give rise to serious difficulties which might lead to the possibility of political disputes.

All three systems needed an amendment of the Covenant and as the question remained a theoretical one, for no small State had requested such alternative membership, the Committee decided to postpone further action. Other forms of collaboration between the League of Nations and the Micro-States were encouraged such as participation in conferences convoked by the League. *A priori*, the League had not excluded statehood for the three Micro-States in question, but political equality was far from being accepted.

Micro-States and the United Nations

'To admit all the bits and pieces of former empires as independent States would not only debase the coinage of membership, but would surely be more than the U.N. structure could bear.'[10] This citation

---

[8] Ibid., p. 686.
[9] Ibid., p. 687.
[10] D. W. Wainhouse, *Remnants of Empire: The United Nations and the End of Colonialism* (1964) p. 134.

summarizes the worries which were felt in the United Nations at the end of the sixties and beginning of the seventies. Due to the decolonization process the United Nations was confronted with many potential new States of which a great number were rather small territories. It was not impossible that all small Non-Self-Governing and Trust Territories would opt for independence instead of integration or association, thus considerably augmenting the number of States in the world. What would happen to the United Nations structure if these potential States were admitted as Members? If at the time all potential Micro-States with less than 300,000 inhabitants were to be admitted to the United Nations, it was calculated that they would constitute a two-thirds majority in the General Assembly, cover 10 per cent of the budget and represent 4 per cent of the world's total population.[11] Moreover, they would be capable, in cooperation with other African and Asian countries, of adopting certain measures which had to be financed by a minority of States. In particular, the United States, main contributor to the United Nations budget, considered this situation unacceptable.

The Secretary-General U Thant was the first person to refer to what became known as the 'question of Micro-States' in his annual report of 1965.[12] He continued to draw attention to this problem in subsequent reports.[13] He favoured a solution permitting Micro-States to participate in the work of the United Nations on the basis of an observer status or some form of association. The Secretary-General rejected full membership for these States as '[s]uch membership may, on the one hand, impose obligations which are too onerous for the "Micro-States" and, on the other hand, may lead to a weakening of the United Nations itself'.[14] The permanent representative of the United States frequently proposed that the Security Council should entrust the Committee on the Admission of New Members with the question of associate membership or other solutions for Micro-States.[15] The United States delegate raised the question of Micro-States in the Security Council in

---

[11] D. Ehrhardt, 'Mikrostaaten als UN-Mitglieder? Zum Strukturproblem der Weltorganisation', *Vereinte Nationen* (1970) no. 4, p. 111.

[12] *Introduction to the Annual Report of the Secretary-General on the Work of the Organization (16 Jun. 1964–15 Jun. 1965)*, UN Doc. A/6001/Add.1 (1965).

[13] UN Doc. A/6301/Add.1 (1966); UN Doc. A/6701/Add.1 (1967); UN Doc. A/7201/Add.1 (1968).

[14] UN Doc. A/6701/Add.1 (1967) p. 20, para. 164.

[15] Correspondence between the permanent representative of the United States of America and the President of the Security Council between 1967 and 1969: S/8296 (1967); S/8316 (1967); S/8376 (1968); S/8437 (1968); S/8520 (1968); S/9327 (1969) and S/9397 (1969).

1965 during the discussions on the admission of the Maldive Islands which was to become the then smallest Member State of the United Nations. The delegate stated that by virtue of Article 4, paragraph 1 of the Charter, Member States should not only be willing, but also be able to carry out the Charter obligations. He concluded that 'many of the small emerging entities, however willing, probably do not have the human or economic resources at this stage to meet this secondary criterion'.[16] After a brief introduction in 1968, the Security Council tackled the Micro-States problem in 1969 by establishing a Committee of Experts which was to prepare a study on alternative memberships.[17] In general, the delegates stressed the danger of loss of credibility and effectiveness for the United Nations if all potential Micro-States were to become Member States. There was no clear definition of 'Micro-States', although the United States seemed to suggest States with less than 100,000 inhabitants[18] or States 'exceptionally small in area, population, and human and economic resources'.[19] Moreover, it was believed that Micro-States lacked 'highly qualified manpower and money' for 'a minimum level of representation at the United Nations'.[20] Only the delegation of Nepal did 'not agree with the assumption that increase in the membership of the United Nations as a result of the emergence of what are called the "micro-States" would inevitably lead to the weakening of the Organization'.[21] Nepal emphasized the United Nations' universality and the principle of equality of States. It believed that it was for these States themselves to decide whether United Nations membership was too onerous for them to bear.[22]

The Committee of Experts met eleven times between 1969 and 1971, producing one interim report on 15 June 1970.[23] The Committee

---

[16] UN Doc. S/PV.1243 (1965) p. 14, para. 89.
[17] First discussion: UN Doc. S/PV.1414 (1968) pp. 8-9; second discussion: UN Doc. S/PV.1505 (1969) and S/PV.1506 (1969).
[18] UN Doc. S/PV.1505 (1969) p. 2, para. 12, also suggested by the Secretary-General, i.e., the population of the then existing smallest member (100,000 for the Maldive Islands). See M. M. Gunter, 'The Problem of Ministate Membership in the United Nations System: Recent Attempts towards a Solution', 12 *Columbia Journal of Transnational Law* (1973) p. 464 at n. 1.
[19] S/9327 (1969), also in Secretary-General's Annual Report, UN Doc. A/6701/Add.1 (1967) p. 20.
[20] United States delegate: UN Doc. S/PV.1505 (1969) p. 3, para. 17.
[21] UN Doc. S/PV.1506 (1969) p. 2, para. 15.
[22] Ibid., p. 2, paras. 15-17.
[23] UN Doc. S/9836 (1970) pp. 210-211.

was unable to formulate specific recommendations, but presented two proposals, of the United States and the United Kingdom respectively.[24]

United States proposal The United States suggested the establishment of the status of 'United Nations Associate Member'. Micro-States in this category would 'enjoy the rights of a Member in the General Assembly except to vote or hold office' and 'bear the obligations of a Member except the obligation to pay financial assessments'. In the other United Nations organs Micro-States would enjoy 'appropriate rights'. The proposal was to combine the political, economic and social development of Micro-States and their contribution to 'the broad objectives of the United Nations' with the diminution of the financial burden.

British proposal The United Kingdom delegation submitted a working paper which amounted to the same results as the United States proposal, but had a different legal construction. Micro-States could become normal Members of the United Nations, but would 'voluntarily renounce certain rights, in particular voting and election in certain United Nations bodies', and supply a financial contribution 'at a nominal level'.

Serious obstacles prevented them from being adopted, but both proposals were vividly discussed in doctrine.[25] The Committee of Experts had asked the opinion of the Legal Counsel of the United Nations on the submitted proposals and particularly whether they necessitated an amendment of the Charter.[26] The Legal Counsel

---

[24] See for full text, ibid., p. 211.
[25] See, e.g., R. Adam, 'Micro-States and the United Nations', 2 *Italian Yearbook of International Law* (1976) pp. 80–101; P. W. Blair, *The Ministate Dilemma* (1967); R. Fisher et al., 'The Participation of Microstates in International Affairs', PASIL (1968) pp. 164–188; M. M. Gunter, 'What happened to the United Nations Ministate Problem?', 71 AJIL (1977) pp. 110–124; W. L. Harris, 'Microstates in the United Nations: A Broader Purpose', 9 *Columbia Journal of Transnational Law* (1970) pp. 23–53; M. H. Mendelson, 'Diminutive States in the United Nations', 21 ICLQ (1972) pp. 609–630; B. Saint-Girons, 'L'Organisation des Nations Unies et les Micro-Etats', 76 RGDIP (1972) pp. 446–474; S. M. Schwebel, 'Mini-States and a more Effective United Nations', 67 AJIL (1973) pp. 108–116; R. I. Starr et al., 'The Future Relationship between Small States and the United Nations', 3 Int'l L. (1969) pp. 58–74; Y. van de Steen, 'De Verenigde Naties en de Microstaten: Problemen omtrent de Toetreding van Microstaten tot de Verenigde Naties', 7 RBDI (1971) pp. 578–618; and U. Whitaker, 'Proliferation in the U.N.: Mini-Membership for Mini-States', 7 *War/Peace Report* (1967) pp. 3–5.
[26] UN Doc. S/AC.16/SR.10 (1971) p. 9.

concluded that '[t]he U.S. proposal and the U.K. suggestion cannot, as they presently stand, be implemented within the framework of the United Nations, without amendment of the Charter'.[27] There was a general feeling among the members of the Committee that it was undesirable to amend the Charter, as the opportunity would certainly be seized to insert other questions into the proposals for amendment.[28] An amendment challenging the sovereign equality of States was also feared likely to 'result in the bitterest rancor and suspicion'.[29] Another difficulty was the definition of 'Micro-States' to which the associate membership applied. The French member of the Committee believed 'that the Committee would have great difficulty in producing any definition at all of a Micro-State', for this would necessarily be arbitrary.[30] In the absence of a definition, the associate status could be used by all States. The proposals were however 'not intended to allow countries to have the option not to pay or vote'.[31] In addition, the British proposal had the disadvantage that the 'voluntary' renouncement could always be revoked. More importantly, the potential and existing Micro-States themselves did not advocate an associate membership in the United Nations. UNESCO and FAO had amended their constitutions so as to provide for associate membership for Non-Self-Governing Territories. It was clear that the Micro-States did not favour such a status as it would cast doubt on their statehood.

At present, the so-called 'Micro-States question' has lost practical interest. Opposition to the admission of Micro-States to the United Nations disappeared when it became clear that the world community would not be enriched with a great number of Micro-States. Many small Non-Self-Governing Territories have opted for integration or association, or await a final decision.[32] Liechtenstein, Micronesia, the Marshall Islands, San Marino, Monaco, Andorra and Palau have obtained full membership of the United Nations.[33] Although the

---

[27] UN Doc. S/AC.16/Conf. Room Paper 8 (1971) p. 55.
[28] Soviet representative: UN Doc. S/AC.16/SR.7 (1970) pp. 3–4.
[29] Gunter, 'What happened?', p. 115.
[30] UN Doc. S/AC.16/SR.10 (1971) p. 10. See also J. G. Rapoport et al., *Small States and Territories: Status and Problems*, UNITAR study (1971).
[31] United States delegate: UN Doc. S/AC.16/SR.6 (1970) p. 6.
[32] See pp. 48–51 above.
[33] Micronesia and the Marshall Islands on 17 Sept. 1991 (GA Res. 46/3 and 46/4 respectively), Liechtenstein on 18 Sept. 1990, San Marino on 2 Mar. 1992, Monaco on 28 May 1993, Andorra on 28 Jul. 1993 (see pp. 195–198, 254–255, 303–304 and 364 below respectively) and Palau on 15 Dec. 1994 (GA Res. 49/63).

reluctance to admit very small States to the League of Nations and the United Nations was inspired for different reasons, one point is always emphasized: the statehood of the Micro-States is not disputed, but the international community is not prepared to accord them rights which would permit them to exercise a disproportionate political influence on international affairs. Only when fears of such a consequence had disappeared were some Micro-States admitted to the United Nations.

The entry of Micro-States into the United Nations has been of particular relevance to their international recognition, as well as to the strengthening of their relations with other States.[34] Micronesia, the Marshall Islands, Palau, Monaco and Andorra have concluded agreements with other States under which theoretically their absolute freedom of voting in the United Nations could be restricted. By virtue of their respective Compacts of Free Association with the United States, Micronesia, the Marshall Islands[35] and Palau[36] shall in the conduct of their foreign affairs 'consult' with the Government of the United States.[37] Monaco has to 'exercer ses droits de souveraineté en

---

[34] In the UN it is now a widely established practice to use the term 'small States' instead of 'Micro-States'.

[35] *United States Public Law* no. 99-239, 99 *US Official Statutes* 1770 (1986). See P. W. Manhard, *The US and Micronesia in Free Association: A Chance to do Better?* (1979).

[36] *United States Public Law* no. 99-658, 100 *US Official Statutes* 3672 (1986). See also R. Goy, 'Le dernier Territoire sous Tutelle: Les Iles du Pacifique', 34 AFDI (1988) pp. 454-474; L. A. McKibben, 'The Political Relationship between the United States and the Pacific Islands Entities: The Path to Self-Government in the Northern Mariana Islands, Palau and Guam', 31 Harv. Int'l LJ (1990) pp. 257-293; and J. Hinck, 'The Republic of Palau and the United States: Self-Determination becomes the Price of Free Association', 78 *California Law Review* (1990) pp. 915-971, who argues that the Compact of Free Association for Palau is voidable because it is contrary to the Palauans' right of self-determination, as the USA has limited their free choice in matters of military authority. The Compact for Palau was adopted by referendum, after eight failures, on 9 Nov. 1993. The controversy concerned the right of the USA to transport nuclear or other hazardous material into the jurisdiction of Palau. Because of this stipulation in the Compact, the Palauan Constitution demanded initially an approval by a two-thirds majority. As this level was never reached, the Constitution had to be amended in 1992. See further *1992 Trust Territory of the Pacific Islands*, 45th Annual Report, US Department of State, Report of the UN Visiting Mission to Observe the Plebiscite in Palau, Trust Territory of the Pacific Islands, Nov. 1993, UN Doc. T/1978 (1993) and *Decolonization* (Apr. 1993) no. 44, UN Department of Political Affairs.

[37] Title 1, Art. II, Section 123 (a) of the Compacts for Micronesia and the Marshall Islands; Title 1, Art. II, Section 121 of the Compact for Palau. The USA will in turn consult with the Governments of the Islands on matters which it regards as relating to or affecting any such Government. The Islands have no authority whatsoever in security and defence matters in their territory: Title 3, Art. I, Section 311 of the Compacts for

parfaite conformité avec les intérêts politiques, militaires, navals et économiques de la France'.[38] Under a trilateral treaty with France and Spain, Andorra on the one hand and France and Spain on the other have to 'veiller au respect mutuel de leurs intérêts fondamentaux respectifs'.[39] Even if these agreements are not always clearly phrased, they could nevertheless be invoked by the neighbouring States in question to restrict the absolute freedom of voting of these five Micro-States. Such restricting bilateral (or trilateral) agreements can however not prevail over the Charter obligations.[40] The effect of agreements limiting independence is a complete destabilization of the principle of sovereign equality of the Member States on which the United Nations is based.[41] Member States would no longer be sovereignly equal if some of them were not to have the freedom to vote as they wished in all United Nations organs by virtue of a bilateral treaty. At least within the United Nations such treaties can have no legal effect as they are contrary to Article 2, paragraph 1 of the Charter.[42]

The relevance of the principle of equality applied by the United Nations in its relations with Micro-States is felt in the judicial and political protection offered.[43] Thus, a very small island State like Nauru was

---

Micronesia and the Marshall Islands; Title 3, Art. I, Section 312 of the Compact for Palau. It is not clear what the exact meaning of 'consult' is. A statement of agreed principles for free association signed by US and Micronesian representatives in 1978 laid down that the free association would remain 'as distinguished from independence'. See Manhard, *The US and Micronesia*, p. 73 at point 1. The USA has not expressly recognized the independence of Micronesia, the Marshall Islands and Palau. The Compacts declare the peoples of these islands 'self-governing' which is not necessarily the equivalent of independence: Title 1, Art. I, Section 111 of the Compacts. The USA has declared itself not to be responsible for any actions of the Governments of Micronesia, the Marshall Islands and Palau in the area of foreign affairs 'except as may from time to time be expressly agreed': Title 1, Art. II, Sections 124–125 of the Compacts for Micronesia and the Marshall Islands; Title 1, Art. II, Sections 126–127 of the Compact for Palau. This does not mean that the conduct of foreign affairs cannot be influenced by the USA.

[38] Art. 1, 2nd para. of the Franco-Monégasque treaty of 1918, pp. 274–282 below.
[39] Art. 4, 1st para. of the treaty of vicinage, friendship and cooperation, pp. 335–338 below.
[40] Art. 103 of the UN Charter.
[41] Art. 2 (1) of the UN Charter.
[42] No counter-argument can be found in the fact that the non-independent Byelorussian and Ukrainian Soviet Republics had been admitted to the UN without protest, as this was clearly a result of a package deal based on political considerations. Protests would have been useless. It did not alter the fact that the Soviet Union could be considered to have acted in violation of the Charter by demanding an equal voting pattern from these Republics. See also pp. 111–112 above.
[43] R. P. Anand, 'Sovereign Equality of States in International Law', 2 Hague Recueil (1986) p. 185.

able to settle, before the International Court of Justice, a long-standing dispute with Australia on the rehabilitation of worked-out phosphate lands at the time it was still a Trust Territory under the joint authority of Australia, New Zealand and the United Kingdom.[44] Without this judicial redress and the application of the principle of sovereign equality, Nauru would never have managed to obtain the desired compensation, nor would the case have been settled amicably.[45] In his separate opinion Judge Shahabuddeen recalled that 'the principle of equality of States has always applied as a fundamental principle to the position of States as parties to a case before the Court'.[46]

Sovereign equality does not mean equality in resources (natural, human or financial) or in power. The micro-Member States of the United Nations dispose of only a small delegation, of one or two representatives,[47] and have to make a selection of the subjects they will concentrate on.[48] The delegates of the four European Micro-States on occasion meet and consult each other. The United Nations is not insensible to the specific problems very small States are faced with. The General Assembly recognized that small States were particularly vulnerable to external threats and acts of interference in their internal affairs. It therefore stressed the 'vital importance' of unconditional respect of the Charter principles and the strengthening of

---

[44] Nauru has a land area of 21.3 square kilometres and at the last census of 1983 a population of 8,042 of whom 4,964 are Nauruans: J. Paxton, ed., *The Statesman's Year-Book*, 126th edn (1989–90) p. 892. See also B. Macdonald, *In Pursuit of the Sacred Trust: Trusteeship and Independence in Nauru* (1988) and Y.-L. Sage, 'Le Système juridique de l'île de Nauru', 46 *Revue Juridique et Politique Indépendance et Coopération* (1992) pp. 458–466.

[45] The Case concerning *Certain Phosphate Lands in Nauru* was settled by amicable agreement between the two parties on 10 Aug. 1993. Nauru would receive $A 107 million from Australia: Art. 1 of the agreement, 32 ILM (1993) p. 1474. See further on this case B. Conforti, 'L'Arrêt de la Cour Internationale de Justice dans l'Affaire de certaines Terres de Phosphates à Nauru (Exceptions préliminaires)', 38 AFDI (1992) pp. 460–467; E. M. Fitzgerald, 'Nauru v. Australia: A Sacred Trust Betrayed?', 6 *Connecticut Journal of International Law* (1990) pp. 209–249; I. Scobbie, 'Case concerning Certain Phosphate Lands in Nauru (Nauru v. Australia), Preliminary Objections Judgment', 42 ICLQ (1993) pp. 710–719; and C. Weeramantry, *Nauru: Environmental Damage under International Trusteeship* (1992).

[46] Case concerning *Certain Phosphate Lands in Nauru (Nauru v. Australia)* preliminary objections, ICJ Reports (1992) p. 270.

[47] Australia took the initiative to provide funds for a joint New York office with common support services, established in 1983, to house the permanent missions of the Solomon Islands, Vanuatu, Western Samoa and the Maldives: Anand, 'Sovereign Equality', p. 186.

[48] See for the activities of Liechtenstein, San Marino, Andorra and Monaco in the UN pp. 195–198, 254–255, 303–304 and 364 below.

regional security arrangements.⁴⁹ Furthermore, a global conference was organized in Barbados in 1994 on the sustainable development of small island developing States in order to increase financial and technical assistance to them, to improve their institutional and administrative capacities, to intensify regional arrangements and common services and to help them with their environmental problems.⁵⁰

From the Micro-States' point of view, the United Nations not only offers a recognition of their sovereign equality, but also enhances that sovereignty by providing more judicial and certainly more political protection against external interference in their internal affairs. The United Nations is a forum in which they can make themselves heard and expose their problems to the world community, without sinking into oblivion.

---

[49] GA Res. 46/43. On the agenda of the 49th session of the GA a new item was included entitled 'Protection and security of small States'. See also J. Crawford, 'Islands as Sovereign Nations', 38 ICLQ (1989) pp. 277–298.

[50] Organization of the conference decided by GA Res. 47/189. Agenda 21, Chapter 17, Section G of the 1992 UN Conference on Environment and Development (UN Doc. A/CONF.151/26 (1992) Res. 1, Annex II) already recommended the urgent sustainable development of small island States. UNCTAD in particular acts as a catalyst for responding to the specific needs of these small States. See GA Res. 47/186, UN Docs. A/47/414 and Add.1 (1992) and A/47/718/Add.2 and Corr.1 (1992). Also, RGDIP (1994) pp. 729–730.

PART II

Five case studies of European Micro-States

Introduction

Micro-States, due to their limited territory, population and natural resources, have to adapt themselves and find solutions in order to survive and function optimally in the international community. In this process they have to abide by the rules of international law and accept the consequences for their international status. Depending on their historical development and the attitude of their neighbouring countries, Micro-States have been obliged to regulate their independence in a certain way. Their smallness generally also has implications for other legal domains, as we shall see in this part of the study. Although some general studies have been written on the relationship between Micro-States and the international community, they have not thoroughly focused their attention on the international legal aspects of the behaviour of Micro-States and of the international community as a whole towards these Micro-States.[1] The implications of international law for Micro-States are not identical to those for 'normal' States. This becomes clear in the case of five European Micro-States. The international legal situations of Liechtenstein, San Marino, Monaco, Andorra and the Vatican City will be studied in depth. The order chosen is generally related to the degree of independence of the Micro-States from their neighbouring countries and the

---

[1] See, e.g., C. Amelunxen, *Die kleinstaaten Europas* (1964); A. Astraudo, *Les petits Etats d'Europe*, 3rd edn (1938); P. W. Blair, *The Ministate Dilemma* (1967); J. de Clerq, *Les petites Souverainetés d'Europe* (1936); G. Gschnitzer, 'Lebensrecht und Rechtsleben des Kleinstaates', in A. P. Goop, *Gedächtnisschrift Ludwig Marker* (1963) pp. 19–52; R. O. Keohane, 'Lilliputians' Dilemmas: Small States in International Politics', 23 *International Organization* (1969) pp. 291–310; H. C. Luke, 'Freaks of Freedom', 131 *Fortnightly Review* (1932) pp. 600–621; E. Plischke, *Microstates in World Affairs: Policy Problems and Options* (1977); and G. L. Reid, *The Impact of Very Small Size on the International Behavior of Microstates* (1974).

intensity of their international activities. Thus, Liechtenstein will be treated before San Marino and Monaco before Andorra. The Vatican City, which has probably more independence from its neighbouring State than the other four Micro-States, as well as highly developed international activities, will nevertheless be discussed at the end of the case studies, because of its very special nature and status in the international community. The analysis of this exceptional case permits a comparison with other Micro-States and proves that dependence is not inevitable for and inherent in Micro-States.

4 The Principality of Liechtenstein

Territory, population and economy

The Principality of Liechtenstein has a total land area of 160 square kilometres.[1] It has 30,310 inhabitants of whom 61.4 per cent are of Liechtenstein nationality, the rest being of foreign origin.[2] In 1993, Liechtenstein had an export surplus of 1,024 million Swiss francs.[3] Of the exports of the products of Liechtenstein industry, 13.8 per cent go to Switzerland, 6.2 per cent to the other EFTA countries, 41.6 per cent to the European Community and 38.4 per cent to other countries.[4] The Liechtenstein economy is based on a small agricultural sector, a strongly export-oriented industrial sector and a highly developed service sector comprising banking and tourism.[5]

---

[1] Fürstentum Liechtenstein Amt für Volkswirtschaft, *Statistisches Jahrbuch 1994*, p. 3.
[2] Ibid., p. 21: status as at 31 Dec. 1993, percentages calculated on the basis of the figures represented. Of the total population, 15.7 per cent are Swiss, 7.4 per cent Austrian, 3.7 per cent German, 2.9 per cent Italian and 8.3 per cent of other nationality, forming a foreign population of 38.6 per cent.
[3] Ibid., pp. 188–189. This figure does not take into account imports and exports from and to Switzerland.
[4] Ibid., p. 192: status as at 31 Dec. 1993, percentages calculated on the basis of the figures represented.
[5] Liechtenstein has five banks of which two were established in 1992 and 1993 respectively. In 1994, the balance sheet total of these banks amounted to 23,477.9 million Swiss francs. The main export products are machines, including means of transport and products from the metal industry, comprising 44.6 per cent and 16.6 per cent of exports respectively, excluding the trade with Switzerland: *Statistisches Jahrbuch 1994*, p. 189 (percentages calculated on the basis of the figures represented). See also 'Der internationale Erfolg der Liechtensteinischen Wirtschaft ist kein Zufall', *VN Magazin Extra* (1986); 2.6 per cent of the working population in Liechtenstein was employed in the agricultural sector, against 52.8 per cent in the industrial sector and 44.6 per cent in the service sector; and F. Kneschaurek, 'Entwicklungsperspektiven der liechtensteinischen Volkswirtschaft in den neunziger Jahren', 17 *Liechtenstein Wirtschaftsfragen* (1990) p. 15.

The State budget for 1994 showed surplus receipts of 16.99 million Swiss francs.[6] Liechtenstein's budget is mainly financed by taxes and fees which cover 80.5 per cent of the State receipts.[7] Liechtenstein has a moderate tax system comprising twelve main categories of taxes with relatively low levies.[8] Due to the limited possibilities of internal trade, the Liechtenstein economy is highly dependent on exports and the inflow of foreign capital. Consequently, the economy is more exposed to external influences than those of larger countries.

History

The area which is now Liechtenstein was part of the ancient Roman province of Rhaetia. This province was turned into a county by Charlemagne.[9] The territory of Liechtenstein is composed of the 'Oberland', which used to be the county of Vaduz, and the 'Unterland', which was the seignory of Schellenberg. Both territories were united in 1434 and were 'reichsfrei', which meant that the Count of Vaduz and Seignor of Schellenberg was placed under the immediate authority of the Emperor without the intermediary of another liege lord. The inhabitants were poor and came through a difficult time in the seventeenth century. Their lands were used for battlefields in the Austrian war against the Three Federations and their lives were endangered by the plague and by witch-hunting. The then ruling Count von Hohenems was in deep debt and after complaints by his subjects about his mismanagement, the Emperor divested him of his functions. An imperial Commissioner was appointed who decided to sell the county and seignory. Prince Johann von Liechtenstein bought the seignory of Schellenberg in 1699 and the county of Vaduz in 1712.[10] The Liechtenstein family had held high

---

[6] 'Voranschlag 1996', Annex to BA no. 71/1995, p. 2. For 1995, a surplus of 16.05 million Swiss francs was foreseen.
[7] Predictions for 1995, 'Voranschlag 1995' Annex to BA no. 66/1994, pp. 81–84. Company taxes cover 15 per cent, property and income taxes 9.9 per cent and indirect tax on the sale of goods 11.0 per cent of total receipts.
[8] Property tax is about 0.07 per cent, income tax 1.4 per cent and company taxes vary between 7.5 and 15 per cent. See W. Kranz, ed., *The Principality of Liechtenstein: A Documentary Handbook*, 5th edn (1981) pp. 97–102 and P. Marxer et al., *Companies and Taxes in Liechtenstein*, 4th edn (1988).
[9] O. Seger, *Überblick über die Liechtensteinische Geschichte* (1974) pp. 5–6. For further reading, see P. Kaiser, *Geschichte des Fürstentums Liechtenstein*, 1847 edn (1983).
[10] For 115,000 and 290,000 gulden respectively: P. Raton, *Liechtenstein: History and Institutions of the Principality* (1970) p. 20.

offices in Austria and had acquired the title of Prince in 1608, without however possessing a Principality.[11] The purchase of both territories permitted the Prince to become Elector or 'Reichsfürst' in the Council of Electors or 'Reichsfürstentag' with a seat and right to vote. In order to be seated in this high Council, the Prince von Liechtenstein needed a minimum possession of 'reichsfrei' territory. The acquired territories were raised to an Immediate Imperial Principality and named Principality of Liechtenstein after its Prince.[12]

In 1799, Liechtenstein was briefly occupied by Napoleon's troops and the Austrian army. Napoleon had met General Prince Johann I of Liechtenstein as the Austrian peace negotiator and it is said that, out of esteem for the Prince, Napoleon had included Liechtenstein in his Rhine Confederation as a sovereign State in 1806.[13] The Prince's signature does not appear on the founding document of the Confederation and the inhabitants of Liechtenstein were not informed of the new status.[14] The Principality of Liechtenstein became formally a sovereign State even though it had to accept Napoleon as a protector. After the Congress of Vienna, Liechtenstein was admitted to the new German Federation ('Deutsche Bund') which comprised thirty-nine sovereign German States. The Federation was dissolved in 1866, due to the Austro-Prussian war, which freed Liechtenstein of any alliance. In 1852, Liechtenstein concluded a customs union treaty with Austria, followed by a postal union treaty in 1912.[15]

During the First World War the Principality of Liechtenstein remained neutral, but was nevertheless severely affected. Its textile industry lacked base material and the savings of the Liechtenstein people were lost after the strong devaluation of the Austrian currency. After the War, Liechtenstein severed its links with Austria, seeking a rapprochement with Switzerland. It concluded a postal union convention with Switzerland in 1920 gradually introduced the Swiss franc as legal currency and signed a customs union treaty with Switzerland in 1923.[16]

---

[11] Before 1608 the family held the title of Seignors von Liechtenstein. Seger, *Überblick*, p. 27.
[12] This is in contrast to the usual practice according to which the Prince takes over the name of the territory. Ibid., pp. 9–10.
[13] Ibid., p. 12.
[14] Ibid.
[15] See pp. 169–170 below.
[16] See pp. 163–166 below.

The Liechtenstein population demanded a greater influence on the administration of their country. In 1918, the first direct, male elections of Liechtenstein's Parliament, the 'Landtag', were held. A new Constitution was drafted in 1921. In the Second World War Liechtenstein remained neutral and due to its rapprochement with Switzerland it was not afflicted with famine. After the War, there was a strong growth of the economy due to the development of high-tech industry. Liechtenstein had a friendly tax and trade legislation which attracted foreign enterprises, despite its unfavourable location. Moreover, the country possessed a large labour reserve coming from the agricultural sector, which could be deployed in the industries. Liechtenstein has managed to attain a higher degree of prosperity than most other European countries in the same period.

Constitutional and legal order

Form of government

The State structure of the Principality of Liechtenstein can be described as a constitutional hereditary monarchy upon a democratic and parliamentary basis, according to which the power of the State is vested in the Prince and in the people.[17] The Constitution of Liechtenstein sets forth a complete system of checks and balances between the powers of the Prince, the Government, the Diet (Liechtenstein's Parliament), the people and the judiciary.

The Prince is the Head of State and exercises his authority in conformity with the provisions of the Constitution and of other laws.[18] He represents the State in all its relations with foreign countries.[19] Every law requires the sanction of the Prince in order to acquire validity.[20] The Prince takes care of the execution and administration of the laws, through the Government.[21] Every law, decree or ordinance issued by the Prince has to be countersigned by the Head of the Government.[22] The only exception to this rule concerns the appointment and

---

[17] Art. 2 of the 1862 Constitution as amended by the 1921 reform. Text in LGBl (1921) no. 15, pp. 69 ff. English text in A. P. Blaustein and G. H. Flanz, eds., *Constitutions of the Countries of the World* (1987): Liechtenstein.
[18] Art. 7 of the Constitution.
[19] Art. 8, 1st para. of the Constitution.
[20] Art. 9 of the Constitution.
[21] Art. 10 of the Constitution.
[22] Art. 85 of the Constitution.

dismissal of the Head of the Government.[23] Furthermore, the Prince may take the necessary measures in urgent cases for the security and welfare of the State, subject to the countersignature, but without the cooperation of the Diet.[24] The succession to the throne is determined by the law of the Princely House which also provides for an internal control over the Prince Regnant in the family council.[25] Since 1989, the Prince Regnant has been Prince Hans-Adam II von und zu Liechtenstein who had been charged with the Princely sovereign rights as a representative of the Prince in 1984.[26] In his address of 12 May 1993 from the throne, the Prince Regnant announced his intention to propose an amendment of the Constitution which would make it possible to discharge a Prince Regnant from office and/or to abolish the monarchy.[27] According to this draft amendment, which has not been submitted to the Diet so far, the Liechtenstein nationals could adopt a motion of no-confidence against the Prince by way of referendum. The Princely House would then have to decide on the Prince's deposition or the Diet could submit a new Constitution to the people, to be approved by referendum, installing a Republic.

The Government of Liechtenstein consists of the Head of the Government and four Government Councillors who are appointed by the Prince with the concurrence of the Diet and on the proposal of the latter for a period of four years.[28] The Government conducts the national administration and is responsible both to the Prince and to

---

[23] T. Allgäuer, *Die parlamentarische Kontrolle über die Regierung im Fürstentum Liechtenstein*, Diss. no. 1097 (1989) p. 36 at n. 23.

[24] Art. 10, last sentence of the Constitution. This possibility was used for instance in 1943, when the Prince prolonged the period of session of the Diet to prevent elections and the entrance of a national socialist party, in 1982, in order to declare the Swiss law on narcotics of 1951 applicable in Liechtenstein and on 10 Aug. 1990 to take economic sanctions against Iraq.

[25] Art. 3 of the Constitution and Art. 12 (1) of the law of the Princely House, LGBl (1993) no. 100. The succession to the throne is assured for the male descendants, with priority over the female descendants, of the Prince Regnant. The family council is composed of three members and three substitutes chosen for a period of five years by the members of the Princely House who are allowed to vote: Art. 10 of the law of the Princely House. The law of the Princely House creates an autonomous legal regime which in certain domains (nationality legislation, political rights) derogates from the common legislation.

[26] Art. 13 of the Constitution was amended in 1984 so as to permit the delegation of powers to the hereditary Prince in case of temporary incapacity of the reigning Prince or in preparation for governmental succession. LGBl (1984) nos. 28 and 32.

[27] *Protokoll über die Eröffnungssitzung des Landtages* (12 May 1993) pp. 4-6.

[28] Art. 79 of the Constitution.

the Diet.²⁹ The Prince can dismiss the Government on his own initiative or at the request of the Diet.³⁰ The Government members must have been born with Liechtenstein nationality.³¹ Each member of the Government has one or more portfolios. The Head of the Government is, generally, in charge of internal and external affairs and finance, while his deputy has the responsibility for, among other things, economy and justice.³² The Constitution does not preclude combined membership of the Government and of the Diet. Juridically, the two functions are not incompatible, which is rather logical in a country with a very small population. Nowadays, the combination of both functions is considered politically undesirable in consideration of a greater control and objectivity. Only the Head of the Government and the Government Councillor acting as his deputy are fully employed, whereas the other three Councillors have additional functions.³³

Liechtenstein's Parliament, the Diet, consists of twenty-five members elected by universal and direct suffrage for a period of four years.³⁴ All Liechtenstein citizens who are at least twenty years old and legally residing in the Principality at least one month before the elections are entitled to vote and are eligible for election.³⁵ The Diet can be convened or dissolved by the Prince, or by the people subject to a referendum.³⁶ The Diet participates in the work of legislation and in the conclusion of certain treaties, and establishes the annual

---

²⁹ Art. 78, 1st para. of the Constitution.
³⁰ Art. 80 of the Constitution. This power was used for the first time in 1993. See also Allgäuer, *Die parlamentarische Kontrolle*, p. 82.
³¹ Art. 79, 4th para. of the Constitution. On 17 Jun. 1992, the Diet approved an initiative to amend the Constitution aimed at eliminating the discrimination between born Liechtensteinese and non-born Liechtensteinese in public functions. *Postulat* of 14 May 1992, *Protokoll über die öffentliche Landtagssitzung* (16/17 Jun. 1992) pp. 1131–1132. The Constitution has not yet been amended to this end.
³² See the table in Allgäuer, *Die parlamentarische Kontrolle*, p. 74.
³³ Ibid., pp. 78–79.
³⁴ Arts. 46 and 47 of the Constitution. Before the constitutional amendment of 20 Oct. 1987, LGBl (1988) no. 11, the Diet consisted of fifteen members. There are fifteen seats reserved for the 'Oberland' and ten for the 'Unterland'.
³⁵ LGBl (1985) no. 4, para. 1. On 15 Apr. 1992, the Diet approved an amendment of the law on political rights and of the Constitution lowering the age of eligibility to vote and to be elected to eighteen years, *Protokoll über die Oeffentliche Landtagssitzung* (15/16 April 1992) pp. 362–363 and BA no. 50/1991. The amendment was however rejected in a referendum of 26/28 Jun. 1992.
³⁶ Art. 48 of the Constitution. At least 1,000 Liechtenstein citizens or three communes may request the Diet to convene. A referendum initiated by at least 1,500 citizens or four communes must be held in order to dissolve the Diet. In order to prorogue the Diet for three months or to dissolve it, the Prince must prove warrantable grounds.

budget.³⁷ It has the right of interpellation, of petition and of budgetary control. Moreover, it can initiate a parliamentary inquiry.³⁸ The right of initiative with regard to legislation appertains to the Prince, through the procedure of Government bills, the Diet and the citizens by means of a referendum.³⁹ Decisions are taken by an absolute majority or, in case of constitutional amendments, by a majority of at least three-quarters at two successive sittings.⁴⁰ A law cannot enter into force without the approval of the Diet, the Prince and the Head of the Government. In addition, under certain conditions a law has to be approved by referendum. This constitutional system necessitates a close cooperation between the Prince, the Government and the Diet.

The citizens of Liechtenstein have substantial political rights of which, besides the right to elect the members of the Diet, the right of referendum occupies a substantial place. A referendum may be held in the following cases:

1. At the initiative of 1,000 Liechtensteinese or three communes a draft law can be submitted to a referendum. An initiative aimed at amending the Constitution needs the support of 1,500 citizens or four communes.⁴¹
2. A law or a financial resolution, if it is not declared to be urgent, may be submitted to a referendum if the Diet so decides or at the request of 1,000 citizens or three communes (1,500 citizens or four communes for issues affecting the Constitution).⁴² The Diet may also call for a referendum on certain principles embodied in a law.
3. Treaties which need the approval of the Diet under Article 8 of the Constitution can be submitted to a referendum by the Diet or at the request of 1,500 citizens or four communes.⁴³ This possibility

---

³⁷ Art. 62 of the Constitution. Under Art. 8 only those treaties which cede national territory, alienate national property, dispose of rights of sovereignty or State prerogatives, assume any new burden for the Principality or its citizens or contract any obligation to the detriment of the rights of the people of the Principality have to be approved by the Diet.
³⁸ Allgäuer, *Die parlamentarische Kontrolle*, p. 83.
³⁹ Art. 64 of the Constitution.
⁴⁰ Arts. 58 and 111 of the Constitution.
⁴¹ Art. 64 of the Constitution.
⁴² Art. 66 of the Constitution.
⁴³ Art. 66 bis of the Constitution. An initiative of the people to introduce this new article in the Constitution was submitted on 18 Sept. 1991 and approved by referendum on 13/15 March 1992, BA no. 87/1991. The Diet criticized the initiative, because it would make Liechtenstein's foreign policy less flexible and endanger its position in the EEA, if amendments to the EEA Agreement could be rejected, *Protokoll über die Oeffentliche Landtagssitzung* (11/12 Dec. 1991) pp. 1796–1804.

further democratizes Liechtenstein's foreign policy and gives the people a say in external affairs. This provision was especially drafted with a view to the ratification of the EC–EFTA Agreement relating to the creation of the European Economic Area (hereafter, EEA Agreement).[44] Nevertheless, if a request for a referendum is in contravention of the Constitution or of an existing treaty which has already been ratified, the Diet may declare the initiative invalid.[45]

Judicial system

The system of law regarding the civil and criminal code is based on the Austrian example. Before the entry into force of the 1921 Constitution, the Liechtensteinese could in second instance appeal only to a High Court in Vienna and in last instance to a Supreme Court in Innsbruck.[46] At present, all Liechtenstein's courts are established in the Principality. The judicial organization is based on the principle of independence of the Government and the administration of justice is carried out in the name of the Prince.[47] If the court is composed of a Sole Judge, he will be a professional magistrate appointed by the Prince for life. At present, there are eight Sole Judges of whom three are Austrians and five are Liechtensteinese. If the court consists of more than one judge, the majority will be laymen, whereas foreign judges, that is non-Liechtensteinese, may never constitute a majority.[48] Every citizen can be appointed as judge for a period of four years.[49]

In civil procedures, the Lower Court of Vaduz ('Landgericht') will be competent to decide the dispute in first instance. A Sole Judge ('Einzelrichter') will hear the case. In second instance, appeal is

---

[44] See pp. 187–190 below.
[45] Art. 70 (b) (2) of the law on political rights, LGBl (1973) no. 50. Art. 70 (b) (3) permits appeal to the State Tribunal ('Staatsgerichtshof') against the decision on invalidity. This law has been amended following the adoption of new Art. 66 bis of the Constitution, BA no. 48/1992.
[46] A. Oehry, 'Fürst und Volk bei der Bestellung der liechtensteinischen ordentlichen Gerichte', 7 *Liechtensteinische Juristen Zeitung* (1986) p. 145.
[47] Art. 99 of the Constitution.
[48] Art. 2 of the law on judicial organization ('Gerichtsorganisationsgesetz'), LGBl (1922) no. 16. See also Allgäuer, *Die parlamentarische Kontrolle*, p. 87. By virtue of Art. II of a treaty with Austria signed on 19 Jan. 1884, Austria has promised to place its judges at Liechtenstein's disposal to serve as judges in the Principality, LGBl (1884) no. 8. See also K. Kohlegger, 'Als österreichischer Richter in Liechtenstein', in *Herbert Battliner Festgabe zum 60. Geburtstag* (1988) pp. 281–290.
[49] Art. 21 of the law on judicial organization.

possible to the civil chamber of the High Court ('Obergericht') which is composed of five judges appointed by the Prince on the proposal of the Diet.[50] A third instance is possible by appealing to the Supreme Court of Justice ('Oberster Gerichtshof').[51] Lastly, a case may be brought before the State Tribunal ('Staatsgerichtshof') if a violation of a constitutional right or a breach of a right set forth in the European Convention for the Protection of Human Rights and Fundamental Freedoms is claimed.[52]

In criminal procedures, the course of proceedings is the same as in civil procedures. In first instance, however, there are four different courts which are competent to hear criminal cases depending on the seriousness of the offence.[53] If it concerns an imposed imprisonment of not more than six months, the prison sentence will in general be served in the prison of Vaduz.[54] For punishments exceeding six months of imprisonment, the sentence will be served in a Swiss prison under the agreements concluded with certain Swiss cantons.[55] The Prince possesses the prerogative of remitting, mitigating or commuting pronounced sentences and of quashing initiated prosecutions.[56]

All decisions and orders of the Government are subject to appeal before the Administrative Tribunal ('Verwaltungsbeschwerdeinstanz').[57] The Administrative Tribunal consists of a chairman trained in the law and four appeal judges who are appointed by the Prince on

---

[50] Art. 2 of the law on judicial organization.
[51] Art. 101 of the Constitution.
[52] Art. 104 of the Constitution and Art. 23 of the law on the State Tribunal ('Staatsgerichtshof-Gesetz'), LGBl (1925) no. 8 as amended by LGBl (1982) no. 57. A new law on the State Tribunal, expected to be promulgated in 1996, will enable claims against rights set forth in any convention (Art. 14 (1) of the draft law).
[53] A Sole Judge is competent to deal with all offences punishable by a maximum of six months' imprisonment, a Court of Aldermen judges indictable offences, a Criminal Court more serious crimes and a Juvenile Court all juvenile offences. See Oehry, 'Fürst und Volk', p. 146 and Anon., 'Die Organisation der Strafgerichte und der Strafvollzug im Fürstentum Liechtenstein', 4 *Der Strafvollzug in der Schweiz* (1980) no. 112, pp. 204–206.
[54] The Court may decide the execution of the sentence in a foreign prison in case of an imposed imprisonment of at least one month. Anon., 'Die Organisation', pp. 205–206.
[55] Ibid., p. 206.
[56] Art. 12, 1st para. of the Constitution. If it concerns a member of the Government the prerogative of remission or mitigation can only be exercised at the instigation of the Diet: Art. 12, 2nd para. of the Constitution. The prerogative may not be used in contravention of basic rules and rights laid down in the Constitution and penal code. See Allgäuer, *Die parlamentarische Kontrolle*, p. 91.
[57] Art. 97 of the Constitution.

the proposal of the Diet.[58] In this administrative judicial process, the Administrative Tribunal examines the formal validity of a Government order and considers objections against an unreasonable course of action, a refusal or slowing down of administrative action.[59] The Administrative Tribunal has excecutive power in the sense that it may replace a Government order with its own decision.[60] If one of the parties in civil, penal or administrative proceedings claims that a law or a Government order is contrary to the Constitution, the court or tribunal may request an opinion on this incompatibility from the State Tribunal.[61]

The State Tribunal occupies a special place in Liechtenstein's judicial system.[62] The State Tribunal has different areas of competence, *inter alia*:

1. It examines the constitutionality of (draft) laws and of administrative orders.[63] The Government or the Diet may request an interpretation of a constitutional provision.[64]
2. It is competent to judge claims by the Diet against a member of the Government concerning a violation of the Constitution or other laws.[65]
3. It decides certain administrative cases attributed to it by law in first and last instance.[66] Thus, the law on political rights permits appeal to the State Tribunal if the Diet has declared invalid a people's initiative for a referendum on a treaty.[67]

Human rights situation

The Principality of Liechtenstein has ratified the European Convention for the Protection of Human Rights and Fundamental Freedoms

---

[58] All members of the Tribunal have a substitute. The chairman and his deputy (substitute) must be of Liechtenstein nationality. Art. 97 of the Constitution.
[59] Allgäuer, *Die parlamentarische Kontrolle*, p. 88 at n. 9.
[60] Ibid., p. 88.
[61] Art. 28, 2nd para. of the law on the State Tribunal.
[62] The Tribunal consists of five judges appointed by the Diet for a period of five years. The President of the Tribunal is appointed with the approval of the Prince. The Tribunal must include at least two jurists. The President of the Tribunal and at least two other members must be of Liechtenstein nationality: Arts. 2 and 4 of the law on the State Tribunal.
[63] Art. 11 (2) of the law on the State Tribunal.
[64] Arts. 11 (3) and 29 of the law on the State Tribunal.
[65] Arts. 14 and 44 of the law on the State Tribunal.
[66] Art. 13 of the law on the State Tribunal.
[67] Art. 70 (b) (3) of the law on political rights.

of 1950 (hereafter, ECHR).⁶⁸ It is also a party to the UN Convention against Torture and other Cruel, Inhuman or Degrading Treatment or Punishment of 1984⁶⁹ and the Convention on the Prevention and Punishment of the Crime of Genocide of 1948.⁷⁰

Liechtenstein's Constitution guarantees the exercise of several human rights.⁷¹ The most important reform in the field of human rights was initiated in 1984, when Liechtenstein women were granted the right to vote and to be elected.⁷² The equality of men and women in the eyes of the law has always been a sensitive subject in Liechtenstein. On 16 June 1992, the Diet approved the introduction of a new paragraph to Article 31 of the Constitution guaranteeing equal rights to men and women.⁷³ The introduction of this provision was deemed especially necessary as the principle of equality of men and women was laid down in Articles 69 and 70 of the EEA Agreement.⁷⁴ The Government has listed fourteen laws which have to be adapted to the new principle of equality, among which are the law on nationality and the legislation on social security.⁷⁵

---

⁶⁸ It has also signed Protocols nos. 1, 9, 10 and 11 to this Convention. Only Protocol no. 6 was ratified on 15 Nov. 1990. The others are expected to be ratified soon.

⁶⁹ Ratified on 2 Nov. 1990.

⁷⁰ Ratified on 22 Jun. 1994. It has signed the UN Convention on the Rights of the Child and the European Framework Convention for the Protection of National Minorities.

⁷¹ Chapter IV of the Constitution entitled 'General Rights and Obligations of the Citizens of the Principality', which applies only to Liechtensteinese.

⁷² Introduction of universal suffrage in Art. 29 (2) of the Constitution, LGBl (1985) no. 4. Communes could grant the right to vote or to take part in elections to Liechtenstein women under Art. 110 bis of the Constitution introduced in 1976, LGBl (1976) no. 50.

⁷³ LGBl (1992) no. 81.

⁷⁴ Art. 69 (1) of the EEA Agreement guarantees equal pay for men and women for the same work, whereas Art. 70 and Annex XVIII lay down the general equal treatment of men and women in labour and social security legislation.

⁷⁵ BA no. 58/1994. Until the approval of the amendments, the State Tribunal may not examine the constitutionality of these laws in respect of Art. 31 (2) of the Constitution: Part II of the law amending the Constitution, LGBl (1992) no. 81. Liechtenstein nationality is passed onto the legitimate children of a Liechtenstein father, whereas the legitimate children of a Liechtenstein mother can only acquire Liechtenstein citizenship through naturalization. The foreign spouse of a Liechtenstein man has the right to acquire her husband's nationality through a simple procedure, whereas the foreign husband of a Liechtenstein woman has to apply for citizenship through a more complicated procedure of naturalization: Arts. 4, 5 and 5 bis of the law on nationality, LGBl (1960) no. 23 with subsequent amendments in LGBl (1976) no. 41, LGBl (1984) no. 23 and LGBl (1986) no. 104. As soon as Liechtenstein has adhered to the EEA Agreement, new laws on social security will eliminate the differentiation between men and women, especially with regard to the imposed contributions and the calculation of the social security benefits.

At the ratification of the ECHR, Liechtenstein made three reservations, of which two were withdrawn in 1991, due to a revision of its penal code.[76] The new criminal code also abolished the death penalty in Liechtenstein. It therefore acceded to Protocol no. 6 to the ECHR.

Liechtenstein has recognized the competence of the European Commission of Human Rights to receive petitions from individuals. So far, nine applications against Liechtenstein have been received and decided by the European Commission of Human Rights; all of them were either declared inadmissible or struck off the list of cases.[77] Two applications are considered here: The first application, introduced by a Liechtenstein national on 6 July 1988, concerned the alleged violation of Article 6 of the ECHR and Article 1 of Protocol no. 1 to the Convention.[78] The applicant, who was the former director of a Liechtenstein company which had been declared bankrupt, complained that the civil proceedings before the Liechtenstein courts, instituted against him by the official liquidator for unlawful financial transactions, had been too lengthy, incorrect and unfair. With regard to Article 6 of the Convention, the Commission concluded that the application was manifestly ill-founded. The application in respect of Article 1 of Protocol no. 1 was declared incompatible *ratione personae*, as Liechtenstein was not a party to Protocol no. 1.[79] The

---

[76] BA no. 11/1991, approved by the Diet on 26 Mar. 1991, *Protokoll über die Oeffentliche Landtagssitzung* (25/26 March 1991) p. 253. The penal code of 24 Jun. 1987, entered into force on 1 Jan. 1989, decriminalized homosexual acts between adults, thus the reservation to Art. 8 of the ECHR could be lifted. The reservation which is still valid affects Art. 6 (1) of the ECHR, as the public nature of the court sessions and of the pronouncement of the judgment are limited by the Liechtenstein laws on the subject. See also T. Bruha, 'Liechtenstein and an All-European System of Human Rights Protection', 1 All-Eur. HR Yearb. (1991) pp. 55–61.

[77] Apart from the cases mentioned in nn. 78 and 80 the following applications were considered: Application no. 11399/85 (*A. Laupper v. Switzerland, Liechtenstein and Austria*), decision of the Commission of 6 Oct. 1986 (no appearance of a violation), Application no. 16705/90 (*M. v. Liechtenstein*), decision of the Commission of 10 Febr. 1993 (case struck off list after withdrawal by applicant), Application no. 21139/93 (*L. v. Liechtenstein*), decision of the Commission of 1 Jul. 1993 (non-exhaustion of domestic remedies), Application no. 21657/93 (*X v. Liechtenstein*), decision of the Commission of 14 Oct. 1993 (inadmissible), Application no. 21902/93 (*X v. Liechtenstein*), decision of the Commission of 13 Jan. 1994 (inadmissible), Application no. 26981/95 (*X v. Liechtenstein*), decision of the Commission of 7 Sept. 1995 (inadmissible) and Application no. 27630/95 (*X v. Liechtenstein*), decision of the Commission of 7 Sept. 1995 (inadmissible).

[78] Application no. 14245/88 (*W. v. Liechtenstein*), decision of the Commission of 9 Dec. 1991.

[79] Ibid., pp. 4–6.

second application concerned a Swiss businessman convicted for aggravated fraud under the Liechtenstein penal code. The applicant claimed that his conviction for aggravated fraud had been contrary to Article 7, paragraph 1 of the ECHR as the notion 'particularly serious damage' used under the Liechtenstein penal code was too vague to define the fraud and constituted therefore a violation of the principle of *nulla poena sine lege*. The Commission declared the application manifestly ill-founded as it believed the Liechtenstein penal code had not been unreasonably applied.[80]

Lastly, the differentiation between foreigners and Liechtenstein nationals should be noted in Article 31 of the Constitution. By virtue of this stipulation all nationals ('Landesangehörigen') are equal before the law.[81] This right is not guaranteed to the foreign inhabitants of Liechtenstein, for their rights are determined in the first instance by treaties, or, in the absence of such, on the basis of reciprocity.[82] This difference will have to disappear for the nationals of EU and EFTA countries in consequence of the EEA Agreement. Chapter IV of the Constitution sets forth in its heading the 'allgemeinen Rechten und Pflichten der Landesangehörigen', which implies that the human rights set forth in this Chapter do not apply to aliens. For them the ratification of the ECHR is of special value, as it constitutes the source of their legally protected human rights in Liechtenstein. The place which a Micro-State like Liechtenstein reserves for foreigners in its legal system is of particular interest, as usually a relatively high percentage of Micro-States' inhabitants are aliens. Due to internal efforts and to the ratification of the ECHR and

---

[80] Application no. 19570/92 (*H. v. Liechtenstein*), decision of the Commission of 31 Mar. 1993, p. 5.

[81] An explanatory law of 1971, LGBl (1971) no. 22, declares: 'Unter dem vor der Verfassung verwendeten Begriff "Landesangehörige" sind alle Personen mit liechtensteinischem Landesbürgerrecht ohne Unterschied des Geschlechts zu verstehen.'

[82] Art. 31 (3) of the Constitution. As a consequence, old-age pensions and disablement benefits will only be paid to foreigners after they have paid their contributions for ten years. Certain bilateral treaties have provided for a reduced period of five years: treaty on social security with Austria of 30 Oct. 1968, LGBl (1969) no. 15, treaty with the Federal Republic of Germany of 7 Apr. 1977, LGBl (1982) no. 32 and treaty with Italy of 11 Nov. 1976, LGBl (1980) no. 29. Swiss nationals are in general treated on the same footing as Liechtensteinese: exchange of letters of 31 Dec. 1932, LGBl (1933) no. 4 and subsequent accords on equalization of Swiss and Liechtenstein social security legislation of 3 Sept. 1965, LGBl (1966) no. 13, on family allowances of 26 Febr. 1969, LGBl (1970) no. 16, on disablement benefits of 3 Sept. 1965, LGBl (1966) no. 13, and on unemployment benefits of 11 March 1980, LGBl (1980) no. 19.

the EEA Agreement, the protection of human rights and its national development has been strengthened.

Relations with States
Foreign policy
Liechtenstein's foreign policy is characterized by the following elements:

Recognition of statehood The main purpose of Liechtenstein's foreign policy is the maintenance and protection of its independence and its statehood.[83] It therefore strove for the membership of certain international organizations like the Council of Europe and the United Nations. This was also a means of making diplomatic contacts with a great number of States without going to great expense.[84] In general, it can be concluded that Liechtenstein aims at combining effective steps towards more political or juridical acceptance by the international community with a careful management of its limited financial and human resources.

Neutrality Liechtenstein managed to remain neutral during the First and Second World Wars.[85] Independently of other political factors which might have influenced Liechtenstein's survival as a neutral State during both World Wars, it is evident that its neutrality was indispensable in order to stay outside the conflict. In peacetime, the Principality's neutrality takes on a different practical meaning of non-alignment. It should not be forgotten that Liechtenstein's neighbouring countries are traditionally neutral too. Liechtenstein's neutrality is not necessarily identical with that of its neighbours and at present lacks a specific definition.[86] A practical result of its

---

[83] *Die Aussenpolitik des Fürstentums Liechtenstein: Standort und Zielsetzungen*, Schriftenreihe der Regierung (1988) no. 1, p. 13; D. J. Niedermann, *Liechtenstein und die Schweiz: Eine völkerrechtliche Untersuchung* (1976) p. 60. See also pp. 200–205 below.

[84] See pp. 179–184 and 195–198 below. The expected expenditure in 1995 for foreign affairs activities constitutes 1.8 per cent of total expenditure: 'Voranschlag 1995', Annex to BA no. 66/1994, calculated on the basis of foreign affairs expenditures of the department of foreign affairs, the costs of participation in the Council of Europe, the United Nations, the EEA, the expenditures for the EFTA-UN representation in Geneva, the missions to the EU and the OSCE and the embassy in Berne.

[85] On 20 Sept. 1914 it officially declared its neutrality to the Austro-Hungarian Empire. Later other belligerent parties were also informed of its neutrality. Niedermann, *Liechtenstein und die Schweiz*, pp. 63–67. See also p. 149 above.

neutrality policy can be seen in Liechtenstein's behaviour in international organizations. When voting or speaking in the assembly of an international organization like the OSCE, the Council of Europe or the United Nations, Liechtenstein does not act according to a certain political ideology or 'bloc', but according to what it considers the general interest, where national interests are not prominent.[87] It also implies that Liechtenstein does not necessarily adjust its vote to that of its neighbouring countries.

Relations with Switzerland

Diplomatic representation

When after the First World War the Diet decided to terminate the customs treaty with Austria, thus announcing the withdrawal from Austrian influence and the rapprochement with Switzerland, the Liechtenstein Government sought to secure its international interests through the diplomatic channels of Switzerland.[88] On 21 October 1919 the Liechtenstein Head of Government requested from the Swiss Federal Council 'die Vertretung der Liechtensteinischen Interessen in den Ländern zu übernehmen, wo das Fürstentum keine Vertretung hat, während die Schweiz eine solche besitzt'.[89] The request explained that although only a very small number of Liechtensteinese lived outside the Principality, Liechtenstein attached great value to the representation of its interests in other countries. It should be borne in mind that after the First World War Liechtenstein's State budget did not permit the establishment of a costly diplomatic service. The Swiss Federal Council accepted the mandate and informed the States with which it maintained diplomatic relations of its entrusted agency. Most States accepted Liechtenstein's representation by Switzerland, but Czechoslovakia refused to accept it in 1946.[90]

In the instructions to its embassies and consulates, Switzerland explained that the representation of Liechtenstein consisted of the exercise of diplomatic or consular protection of Liechtensteinese,

---

[87] See pp. 177–184 and 195–198 below.
[88] P. Raton, *Staat und Geschichte* (1969) pp. 76–77.
[89] G. F. de Martens, *Nouveau Recueil Général de Traités*, 3rd series, vol. XXIII (1930) pp. 543–544.
[90] See, for example, the acceptance of Sweden on 18 Nov. 1919: ibid., p. 544. The refusal of Czechoslovakia is mentioned by H. Thévenaz, 'La Suisse, Etat mandataire', 6 ASDI (1949) pp. 15–16. This refusal was probably due to claims of the Liechtenstein Princely family to land properties in Czechoslovakia.

their registration, delivering travel documents and assisting Liechtensteinese in distress.[91] General diplomatic relations between the Principality and third States will only be attended to by Switzerland on a case-by-case basis, after having received specific orders from Liechtenstein.[92] Actions on behalf of Liechtenstein nationals will, in general, only be instituted at Liechtenstein's request, except in case of emergency.[93] Switzerland is not obliged to give effect to all Liechtenstein orders and Liechtenstein always has the freedom to establish its own diplomatic missions or to negotiate directly with a third State.[94]

Since the Second World War, Liechtenstein has increasingly taken care of its own representation, especially in international organizations and at conferences.[95] At present, Liechtenstein has accredited ambassadors to four countries (Austria, Belgium, the Holy See and Switzerland). It maintains diplomatic or consular relations with fifty-three States.[96] In addition, Liechtenstein has a permanent representative mission in Strasbourg for the Council of Europe, a permanent mission in New York to the United Nations, an EFTA–UN mission in Geneva, a mission to the European Union and a permanent representation to the OSCE in Vienna. Considering Liechtenstein's limited human resources it is evident that not all international posts can be held by Liechtenstein nationals. In 1980, for instance, a Canadian was

---

[91] 'Instruktionen des Politischen Departements betreffend die Vertretung der liechtensteinischen Interessen vom 20 Februar 1948 an die schweizerischen Gesandtschaften und Konsulate', full text in P. Guggenheim, 'Völkerrecht', 7 ASDI (1950) pp. 176–184.

[92] Ibid., p. 176.

[93] The Swiss representatives in their dealings with foreign governments will have to specify that in a specific case they represent the Principality of Liechtenstein. Diplomatic or consular protection may be refused to a Liechtenstein national if he has prejudiced Switzerland's interests so that his protection cannot reasonably be demanded: ibid., pp. 177–178.

[94] A Swiss note of 10 March 1920 makes clear that Switzerland's representation of Liechtenstein does not prejudice the Principality's sovereignty and does not entail that the Prince cannot appoint his own delegations: cited by V. Lanfranconi, *Die Staatsverträge und Verwaltungsabkommen zwischen der Schweiz und dem Fürstentum Liechtenstein unter besonderer Berücksichtigung der daraus entstandenen völkerrechtlichen Konsequenzen* (1969) p. 65 and n. 19.

[95] Until Liechtenstein became a member of the United Nations, a member of the Swiss delegation in United Nations conferences was often mandated by the Prince and voted as a Liechtensteinese: Raton, *Staat und Geschichte*, p. 85.

[96] Status as at Jan. 1996. The Liechtenstein ambassador to Switzerland is also accredited to the Holy See. There are no foreign resident ambassadors and thirteen of the forty-one consular representatives have their consulate in Liechtenstein. Diplomatic relations will soon be established with Andorra and Monaco. Information from the Liechtenstein Office for Foreign Affairs.

appointed as the 'Liechtenstein' judge of the European Court of Human Rights.[97] Young Liechtensteinese are however given the opportunity to train in the Swiss or Austrian diplomatic services.[98]

Postal union

On 10 November 1920, Liechtenstein and Switzerland signed a convention relating to the maintenance of postal, telegraph and telephone services in Liechtenstein by the Swiss postal, telegraph and telephone administration.[99] This convention has been replaced by a treaty of 9 January 1978,[100] which now includes provisions on radio and television, and which in turn has been amended and supplemented by a treaty and agreement of 2 November 1994, for the purpose of Liechtenstein's entry into the EEA.[101] After having specified that the postal and telecommunications regalia belong to Liechtenstein,[102] the treaty sets forth that the postal and telecommunications services will be maintained by the Swiss postal and telecommunications office.[103] All Swiss legal and administrative regulations relating to the postal and telecommunications services are applicable in Liechtenstein,[104] though EEA law takes precedence in relation to the EEA States.[105] Conventions which have been or shall be concluded by Switzerland with third States with regard to postal and telecommunications services are equally valid in Liechtenstein.[106] To this end, Liechtenstein has authorized Switzerland to represent it during negotiations with third States on the conclusion of postal and telecommunications treaties, and to conclude such treaties with effect in Liechtenstein.[107] The postal union treaty does not prevent

[97] Council of Europe, *The Protection of Human Rights in Europe* (1981) p. 7.
[98] Interview with HH Prince Hans-Adam II von and zu Liechtenstein of 5 Apr. 1991.
[99] Text in de Martens, *Nouveau Recueil Général de Traités*, vol. xv, pp. 707 ff.
[100] LGBl (1978) no. 37. French text in SWRO (1979) no. 2, pp. 25 ff.
[101] Treaty revising the 1978 postal union treaty and agreement to the 1978 postal union treaty of 2 Nov. 1994, LGBl (1995) nos. 81 and 82.
[102] Arts. 1 and 2 (1) of the postal union treaty.
[103] Art. 3 of the postal union treaty. The expenses are borne by Liechtenstein which also receives the benefits.
[104] Art. 4 (1) of the postal union treaty, for both present and future regulation.
[105] Art. 3 (2) of the 1994 agreement to the 1978 postal union treaty.
[106] Art. 4 (2) of the postal union treaty, which states that those treaties 'haben im Fürstentum Liechtenstein in gleicher Weise Geltung wie in der Schweiz'.
[107] Art. 4 (3) of the postal union treaty, under which treaties are concluded by Switzerland 'mit Wirksamkeit für das Fürstentum Liechtenstein'. Liechtenstein has the right to oppose the inclusion of a new treaty concluded by Switzerland in the annex on applicable regulations of the postal union treaty. In that case recourse to an arbitral tribunal is foreseen: Arts. 4 (4) and 30 of the postal union treaty.

Liechtenstein from concluding international conventions or from becoming a member of an international organization itself.[108] If Switzerland has not adhered to such a convention or organization, a special agreement between the two States has to be concluded.[109] The treaty can be terminated by either State subject to one year's notice.[110]

Customs union

After the termination of the customs relations with Austria, Liechtenstein signed a customs union treaty with Switzerland on 29 March 1923.[111] Under Article 1, the territory of the Principality is attached to the Swiss customs territory and no restrictions on imports and exports can be accepted, unless they are permitted for the commerce between cantons. The Swiss authorities appoint, pay and dismiss the customs officers and border guards in Liechtenstein.[112] As a basic rule, all present and future Swiss customs legislation and regulations on industrial and intellectual property are applicable in Liechtenstein.[113] Treaties relating to these subjects concluded by Switzerland with third States are equally valid for Liechtenstein.[114] Since 1991, Liechtenstein can become a party to an international convention or a member of an international organization to which Switzerland has also adhered.[115] Because of Switzerland's non-ratification of the EEA Agreement, the customs union treaty was amended so as to permit Liechtenstein's accession to this Agreement while upholding the customs union with Switzerland.[116] Special agree-

---

[108] Art. 6 (1) of the postal union treaty.
[109] Art. 6 (2) of the postal union treaty as amended by treaty of 2 Nov. 1994. Thus a special agreement was needed for the accession of Liechtenstein to the EEA. This agreement of 2 Nov. 1994 determines the relation between EEA and Swiss PTT law and establishes a joint commission to ascertain the proper functioning of the agreement (Arts. 5–6 of the 1994 agreement to the 1978 postal union treaty).
[110] Art. 33 (2) of the postal union treaty. After 1989, the treaty is tacitly renewed each time for a period of five years at the end of which, subject to one year's notice, the treaty can be terminated.
[111] For relations with Austria see pp. 169–170 below. Text of the 1923 customs union treaty with Switzerland in 21 LNTS (1924) no. 545, pp. 232 ff. and LGBl (1923) no. 24.
[112] Art. 19 of the customs union treaty.
[113] Arts. 4 and 5 (1) of the customs union treaty.
[114] Arts. 5 (2) and 7 of the customs union treaty.
[115] Art. 8 bis (1) of the customs union treaty, permitting Liechtenstein's full membership of EFTA.
[116] New Art. 8 bis (2) of the customs union treaty, as amended by treaty of 2 Nov. 1994, permits the accession of Liechtenstein to conventions or organizations to which Switzerland has not adhered, subject to a special agreement, LGBl (1995) no. 76.

ments have been concluded to this end, under which, in Liechtenstein, the EEA law takes precedence over the Swiss customs regulations in relation to EEA States.[117] The Swiss customs officers in Liechtenstein have to apply EEA law in relation to products originating from EEA States.[118] A joint commission is established, charged with the supervision of the correct implementation of the agreements.[119] Liechtenstein makes sure that no products are illegally imported into Switzerland, through an internal surveillance and control system.[120] It has created its own customs department to that end.[121] Switzerland pays annually Liechtenstein's share of customs receipts.[122] In case of a conflict relating to the interpretation of the customs union treaty, the dispute can be brought before an arbitral tribunal.[123] Both States parties can terminate the treaty subject to one year's notice.[124]

Following the example of Switzerland, Liechtenstein introduced a VAT (value-added tax) system on 1 January 1995. It concluded a treaty and a supplementary accord with Switzerland under which it committed itself to taking the Swiss VAT law into its own legislation.[125] The Swiss Federal Court will act as the highest court in VAT matters[126] and a mixed commission has been established in which Liechtenstein can defend its interests, subject to an arbitral procedure.[127] For VAT purposes, Liechtenstein and Switzerland will constitute one territory. Their common receipts will be apportioned on the

[117] Art. 3 of the 1994 agreement to the 1923 customs union treaty, LGBl (1995) no. 77. This agreement is supplemented by an additional protocol on product liability, an agreement on the recognition of civil judicial judgments, an exchange of letters on the control of medicines and an accord amending the 1978 treaty on patent protection, LGBl (1995) nos. 78–80 and BA no. 1994/93, Annexes.
[118] Art. 7 and Annex III of the 1994 agreement to the 1923 customs union treaty.
[119] Arts. 9–10 of the 1994 agreement to the 1923 customs union treaty.
[120] Art. 4 and Annex I of the 1994 agreement to the 1923 customs union treaty.
[121] Arts. 6–7 of the law on customs, LGBl (1995) no. 92.
[122] Art. 37 of the customs union treaty as amended in 1994. For 1994, Liechtenstein's share amounted to 26.9 million Swiss francs, which accounted for 5.3 per cent of Liechtenstein's State revenues. See 'Voranschlag 1996', Annex to BA no. 71/1995.
[123] Art. 43 of the customs union treaty.
[124] Art. 41 of the customs union treaty.
[125] Art. 1 (1) of the treaty on VAT of 28 Oct. 1994 and Art. 1 (1) of the agreement to the treaty on VAT of 28 Nov. 1994, LGBl (1995) nos. 30–31. It is the first time that Swiss law is not automatically made applicable in Liechtenstein, but needs to be transformed into Liechtenstein law. Law on VAT, LGBl (1994) no. 84.
[126] Art. 1 (3) of the treaty on VAT.
[127] Arts. 2 and 3 of the treaty on VAT and Arts. 12 and 13 of the agreement to the treaty on VAT.

basis of a distribution code, making border control on goods unnecessary.[128]

Monetary union

Due to the strong devaluation of the Austrian currency after the First World War and the financial losses which this implied for the Liechtenstein inhabitants, Liechtenstein decided to introduce the Swiss franc as legal tender in its territory.[129] By virtue of a 1980 currency treaty,[130] the Swiss legislation relating to money, credit and valuta policy and to the protection of Swiss coins and banknotes is applicable in Liechtenstein.[131] Liechtenstein's sovereignty in currency matters remains untouched.[132] Switzerland's National Bank exercises its rights over banks and companies in Liechtenstein in the same manner as in Switzerland.[133] A violation of the applicable Swiss currency legislation is, in general, judged by the Liechtenstein courts in first and second instance. An appeal for nullification of a sentence of the Liechtenstein High Court can only be lodged with the Swiss Court of Cassation.[134]

A mixed commission is charged with the consideration of interpretation and implementation questions relating to the currency treaty.[135] If a dispute cannot be solved by the mixed commission, an arbitral tribunal can be established.[136] The treaty can be terminated subject to six months' notice. In addition, Liechtenstein can withdraw from the treaty within one month of the enactment of a new Swiss

---

[128] Art. 8 of the agreement to the treaty on VAT.

[129] This decision was based on a verbal agreement with Switzerland and on Liechtenstein laws: LGBl (1920) no. 8 and LGBl (1924) no. 8; see also Raton, *Staat und Geschichte*, p. 79.

[130] LGBl (1981) no. 52. The currency treaty came into force on 25 Nov. 1981.

[131] Art. 1 (1) of the currency treaty. Liechtenstein may oppose the inclusion of a new Swiss regulation in the annex. The currency treaty does not provide for the application of a treaty concluded by Switzerland with third States: Art. 1 (3).

[132] Art. 2 (1) of the currency treaty reads: 'Die liechtensteinische Währungshoheit bleibt unberührt.'

[133] Art. 3 (1) of the currency treaty.

[134] Art. 6 (1) and (5) of the currency treaty. The Swiss National Bank may request the Liechtenstein authorities to institute criminal proceedings against Liechtenstein banks, persons or companies: Art. 6 (2).

[135] Art. 13 (1) of the currency treaty. The mixed commission is composed of three Liechtenstein and three Swiss members: Art. 13 (2).

[136] Art. 14 of the currency treaty. If the parties do not appoint their arbitrators within two months or if the arbitrators fail to appoint the umpire within three months, the parties may ask the President of the European Court of Human Rights to designate the members of the arbitral tribunal.

currency law.[137] Under the currency treaty, Liechtenstein cannot develop its own independent monetary policy. The monetary union with Switzerland facilitates and supplements the postal and customs unions. Liechtenstein retains, however, the possibility of adopting any other legal tender within a relatively short time.

Aliens office

By virtue of Article 33 of the customs union treaty of 1923, Liechtenstein and Switzerland cooperate in the maintenance of the aliens police and border control. Two treaties with Switzerland were concluded on 6 November 1963 which are corollaries of the customs union treaty.[138]

The first treaty regulates the treatment of Swiss and Liechtenstein nationals in Liechtenstein and Switzerland respectively. There are no border controls between Liechtenstein and Switzerland.[139] Liechtenstein and Swiss nationals receive a residence permit and a work permit in the other country upon request.[140] This stipulation has been suspended since 19 October 1981 on the initiative of Liechtenstein which endeavoured to maintain a well-balanced relation between Liechtenstein nationals and aliens in Liechenstein.[141] Nevertheless, Liechtenstein reserves a preferential treatment for Swiss nationals. In certain cases, Swiss residents may exercise a liberal profession[142] and be put on an equal footing with EEA nationals.[143]

---

[137] Art. 15 of the currency treaty.

[138] Both agreements replace an earlier treaty of 20 Dec. 1923. The first treaty relates to the sojourn of Swiss and Liechtenstein nationals, LGBl (1963) no. 38, and the second treaty concerns third-State nationals, LGBl (1963) no. 39. The two treaties terminate as soon as the customs union treaty has been terminated: Art. 10 (2) of the treaty on Swiss/Liechtenstein nationals and Art. 11 (2) of the treaty on third-State nationals.

[139] Art. 1 (1) of the treaty on Swiss/Liechtenstein nationals. Liechtenstein and Swiss nationals can cross the border with Switzerland without travel documents.

[140] Art. 3 (1) of the treaty on Swiss/Liechtenstein nationals. Naturalized Liechtensteinese only receive Swiss residence and work permits if they no longer fall under the Swiss aliens police control or ten years after the naturalization: Art. 3 (2).

[141] Exchange of letters between Liechtenstein and Switzerland of 19 Oct. 1981, LGBl (1981) no. 49. The suspension applies reciprocally, but does not affect, *inter alia*, students, cross-border workers, persons working for certain public services and patients in hospitals and clinics.

[142] Art. 3 bis of the treaty on Swiss/Liechtenstein nationals as amended by agreement of 2 Nov. 1994, LGBl (1995) no. 84 (to the exception of police, lawyers, notaries, trustees and medical professions). See also 'Can Liechtenstein's Lawyers survive the EEA?', 11 Int'l Fin. Law Review (1992) pp. 21–24.

[143] Joint Swiss/Liechtenstein declaration on the question of equal treatment of 2 Nov. 1994, BA no. 1994/93. The equal treatment applies only once Liechtenstein has decided on extra liberalization after the end of the EEA transitional period.

The second treaty of 1963 lays down the general legislation on the sojourn of aliens in Liechtenstein. The Swiss legislation concerning the sojourn and residence of aliens is applicable in Liechtenstein to third-State nationals and, since the suspension of Article 3 of the first treaty, also to Swiss nationals.[144] Liechtenstein can fix its own regulations regarding the expulsion of aliens, which have no effect in Switzerland.[145] Conversely an expulsion from Swiss territory also applies to Liechtenstein territory, unless the Swiss aliens police expressly exclude this territorial effect for Liechtenstein.[146]

In 1977, the European Commission of Human Rights considered a joint application by X and Y against Switzerland, which had prohibited the entry of X on to Swiss and Liechtenstein territory for two years.[147] X, a third-State national, had stayed in Liechtenstein with Y without a residence permit for more than the ninety days which are allowed under the Swiss legislation. The question was raised whether X had been within Switzerland's jurisdiction within the meaning of Article 1 of the ECHR. Switzerland maintained that it was not responsible for the prohibition of entry. The plaintiffs alleged that Liechtenstein had renounced its sovereignty in this matter, for it could not undo Switzerland's decision. The Commission stated that the acts with effect in Liechtenstein brought all those on whom they were applicable within Switzerland's jurisdiction, for 'the Swiss authorities when acting for Liechtenstein do not act in distinction from their national competences. In fact on the basis of the treaty [on third nationals of 1963] they act exclusively in conformity with Swiss law and it is only the effect of this act which extended to Liechtenstein territory.'[148]

If Swiss and EEA laws on the establishment and sojourn of aliens do not coincide, only the EEA law will be applicable in Liechtenstein.[149] In this context, Liechtenstein's restrictive legislation on foreign ownership of immovable properties and on foreign land investments will be adapted for EEA nationals.[150] Both 1963 agreements on the sojourn of aliens can be terminated subject to one year's notice.

---

[144] Art. 1 (1) of the treaty on third-State nationals.
[145] Art. 2 (b) of the treaty on third-State nationals.
[146] Art. 3 of the treaty on third-State nationals.
[147] Applications no. 7289/75 and 7349/76, *X and Y v. Switzerland*, D & R 9, pp. 57 ff.
[148] Ibid., p. 73.
[149] Art. 2 (e) of the treaty on third-State nationals as amended by agreement of 2 Nov. 1994, LGBl (1995) no. 83.
[150] Art. 6 of the draft law on land acquisition provides for ownership permits of land, which are granted to Liechtenstein and other EEA nationals if they prove a valid

Defence

Since the dissolution of the German Federation in 1866, Liechtenstein has had no army. The Constitution however sets forth the civic duty of every man fit to bear arms, up to the completion of his sixtieth year, to serve in the defence of his country in the event of emergency.[151] Apart from this contingent, no armed units may be organized or maintained, except for the provision of the police service.[152] In line with the traditional neutrality of the two countries, Switzerland and Liechtenstein have not concluded a defence treaty with each other. Neither has the Liechtenstein territory been included in the Swiss defence system.[153]

Relations with Austria

Apart from its proximity, Liechtenstein's ties with Austria are related to the Austrian origins of the Princely House. In the nineteenth century the Austrian postal services extended to Liechtenstein. On 5 June 1852 a customs union treaty was concluded with Austria.[154] The commerce between the two countries was free.[155] Austria undertook to extend existing customs treaties to Liechtenstein and to conclude new customs treaties also in the name of Liechtenstein if the Prince approved.[156] The Austrian customs officers swore an oath of allegiance to the Prince and were subject, in first instance, to the Liechtenstein judiciary. This customs union treaty was terminated by the Diet on 2 August 1919 and its termination was approved by Austria on 30 August 1919.[157] The breach with Austria was prompted on the one hand by the financial losses which Liechtenstein had suffered due to the devaluation of the Austrian currency after the First World War and on the other hand by Liechtenstein's desire to accentuate its independence from Austria so as to receive a more favourable political and economic treatment from the Allied Powers.[158]

interest in the acquisition, such as the establishment of an enterprise, the exercise of a profession or for residential purposes, BA no. 118/1992.
[151] Art. 44, para. 1 of the Constitution.
[152] Art. 44, para. 2 of the Constitution.
[153] Raton, *Staat und Geschichte*, p. 165.
[154] H. Neumann, *Recueil des Traités et Conventions conclus par l'Autriche*, vol. v, pp. 686–700.
[155] Art. IX of the Austro-Liechtenstein customs union treaty.
[156] Art. XII of the Austro-Liechtenstein customs union treaty.
[157] Raton, *Staat und Geschichte*, p. 177.
[158] See pp. 148–150 above. See also for a further elaboration E. von und zu Liechtenstein, *Liechtensteins Weg von Oesterreich zur Schweiz: eine Rückschau auf meine Arbeit in der Nachkriegszeit 1918-1921* (1945) pp. 169–243.

Until the coming into force of the postal and customs union treaties with Switzerland, Liechtenstein concluded new, transitional agreements with Austria. On 22 April 1920 an exchange of letters with Austria regulated the new customs regime.[159] A postal agreement was concluded on 1 May 1920 which remained valid until 31 January 1921.[160]

At present, Liechtenstein has concluded certain treaties with Austria in matters of judicial cooperation,[161] education,[162] social security,[163] double taxation[164] and border demarcation.[165] Even if the relations with Austria are not regulated in the same manner as the legal relations with Switzerland, the Government of Liechtenstein has noted an intensification of Austro-Liechtenstein cooperation.[166] Thus, like Switzerland, Austria has supported Liechtenstein's candidature for membership in the Council of Europe and the United Nations.[167]

Relations with international organizations
League of Nations

On 28 August 1919, not long after the conclusion of the Covenant of the League of Nations which would enter into force on 10 January 1920, the Diet discussed the question of whether it was opportune to apply for membership of the League of Nations.[168] Questions were

---

[159] De Martens, *Nouveau Recueil Général de Traités*, vol. xv, p. 630. Liechtenstein promised not to impose customs tariffs on imports and exports from and to Austria, whereas Austria applied a most-favoured-nation clause to Liechtenstein. As this arrangement proved to be too burdensome for Liechtenstein's exports, it unilaterally introduced its own customs tariffs on 1 Dec. 1921: LGBl (1921) no. 25. The customs agreement with Austria was amended on 30 Dec. 1921 so that the most-favoured-nation clause would be used both by Liechtenstein and by Austria: ibid., p. 634.

[160] Raton, *Staat und Geschichte*, pp. 80–81. Under this agreement Liechtenstein issued and sold its own stamps and covered the costs of its postal services.

[161] Treaty of 19 Jan. 1884, LGBl (1884) no. 8 on the use of Austrian judges in Liechtenstein; treaty of 1 Apr. 1955, LGBl (1956) no. 10 and subsequent treaties on legal cooperation, LGBl (1968) no. 14, LGBl (1983) nos. 40 and 41.

[162] See, for example, on post-doctoral education for Liechtenstein doctors, treaty of 31 Oct. 1980, LGBl (1980) no. 74.

[163] Treaties on social security of 26 Sept. 1968, LGBl (1969) nos. 14 and 15, and further LGBl (1974) no. 34, LGBl (1977) nos. 48 and 63 and LGBl (1987) no. 73.

[164] Treaties of 7 Dec. 1955, LGBl (1956) no. 12 and of 5 Nov. 1969, LGBl (1970) no. 37.

[165] Border treaty of 1 Sept. 1960, LGBl (1960) no. 19 as amended on 1 March 1991, LGBl (1991) no. 11.

[166] *Die Aussenpolitik*, p. 22.

[167] See pp. 179–184 and 195–198 below.

[168] N. Jansen, 'Liechtenstein und die Vereinte Nationen', 18 *Liechtenstein Wirtschaftsfragen* (1991) p. 18.

raised concerning the financial and military obligations flowing from League membership, especially under Article 1, paragraph 2 of the Covenant of the League of Nations. Moreover, Liechtenstein wondered whether the League of Nations would accept the maintenance of its neutrality which it had officially declared in the First World War. As, on 11 May 1920, Switzerland had agreed to become a member of the League of Nations, Liechtenstein decided to prepare its application for membership too. On 15 July 1920, Liechtenstein submitted its application through the Swiss Minister in London.[169] In its letter, Liechtenstein recalled its neutrality during the last War and the absence of military forces since 1866.

The request for admission was discussed in the first instance by the second Sub-Committee of Committee No. 5 of the Assembly.[170] The French member of the second Sub-Committee was opposed to granting such a small State as Liechtenstein the same right to vote as a large State.[171] The Sub-Committee considered five questions in order to determine the acceptance or refusal of Liechtenstein's application.[172] After having concluded that the application for admission was in order, the Sub-Committee observed that the Government of the Principality of Liechtenstein was recognized *de jure* by many States. Liechtenstein possessed a stable Government and fixed frontiers with a population between 10,000 and 11,000. Nevertheless, the Sub-Committee's findings under questions 4 and 5 led to the conclusion 'that the Principality of Liechtenstein could not discharge all the international obligations which would be imposed on her by the Covenant'.[173] The Sub-Committee based its conclusion on two

---

[169] League of Nations, *Documents of the Assembly* (1920) no. 18.
[170] League of Nations, *Reports of the First Assembly, 4th–6th Committee* (1920), Report of the Sub-Committee on the admission of Albania, Austria, Bulgaria and Liechtenstein (27 Nov. 1920) Annex 2, p. 217.
[171] Jansen, 'Liechtenstein und die Vereinte Nationen', p. 22.
[172] These questions were:
 '1 Is the application for admission to the League of Nations in order?
 2 Is the Government recognised "de jure" or "de facto", and by which States?
 3 Does the country possess a stable government and settled frontiers? What are its size and population?
 4 Is the country fully self-governing?
 5 What has been the conduct of the government including both acts and assurances with regard to:
 (1) Its international obligations?
 (2) The prescriptions of the League as to armaments?'
 League of Nations, *Reports of the First Assembly* (1920) p. 217.
[173] Ibid.

arguments, namely that Liechtenstein had deputed to others some of the attributes of sovereignty and that it had no army.[174]

The second Sub-Committee's report was endorsed by Committee No. 5 on 6 December 1920.[175] On 17 December 1920, the Assembly voted against the admission of Liechtenstein to the League of Nations by twenty-eight votes to one (Switzerland) and thirteen abstentions.[176] The stated reasons for the League of Nations' refusal to admit Liechtenstein as a full member were however not the real reasons. At the time of the discussions on Liechtenstein's admission to the League of Nations, between 25 November 1920 and 17 December 1920, it could hardly be maintained that Liechtenstein had delegated many attributes of its sovereignty to other Powers. In this period the scarcely restrictive transitional customs agreement, with Austria of 22 April 1920 was in force, as well as a provisional postal agreement, leaving Liechtenstein considerable freedom.[177] The customs union treaty with Switzerland had not yet been concluded, although negotiations had started on this subject in May 1920.[178] As we have seen, the diplomatic and consular representation by Switzerland could only be exercised *ad hoc* and subject to Liechtenstein's orders.[179] Moreover, the same second Sub-Committee had approved Austria's request for membership even if under Article 88 of the Treaty of Saint-Germain of 1919 Austria had restricted its sovereign rights to choose those economic relations which it desired.[180] At that time, Liechtenstein's obligations under its agreements with Austria and Switzerland were less burdensome than Austria's renouncements under the Treaty of Saint-Germain.

---

[174] Ibid. It stated: 'There can be no doubt that juridically the Principality of Liechtenstein is a sovereign State, but by reason of her very limited area, small population, and her geographical position, she had chosen to depute to others some of the attributes of sovereignty. For instance, she has contracted with other Powers for the control of her Customs, the administration of her Posts, Telegraphs and Telephone Services, for the diplomatic representation of her subjects in foreign countries, other than Switzerland and Austria, and for final decisions in certain judicial cases. Liechtenstein has no army.'

[175] League of Nations, *Records of the First Assembly, Plenary Meetings* (1920), Annex C, pp. 667–668.

[176] Ibid., p. 652.

[177] See pp. 169–170 above.

[178] Lanfranconi, *Die Staatsverträge*, p. 77.

[179] See p. 162 above.

[180] See also M. M. Gunter, 'Liechtenstein and the League of Nations: A Precedent for the United Nations' Ministate Problem?', 28 AJIL (1974) p. 499.

It is furthermore doubtful whether the possession of military forces was obligatory under Article 1, paragraph 2 of the Covenant of the League of Nations. This article regulates the deployment of military forces of Member States, but does not necessarily impose the existence of an army in a Member State. It would however have raised considerable political and juridical criticism if the Assembly had officially refused to admit Liechtenstein to the League of Nations on grounds of its small size. The Covenant of the League of Nations did not provide for such an exclusion. In addition, the question of smallness was also discussed at the admission of Luxembourg. The Czechoslovakian delegate declared that 'in practice, the smallness of a State does not prevent its being admitted into the League'.[181] He explained Liechtenstein's non-admission by reason of 'its close connection with another State which is able to defend the interests of Liechtenstein and thus ensure that this little State is not left outside the League of Nations'.[182]

Liechtenstein had weakened its position and had provided the League of Nations with an excuse for non-admission by applying for membership through the mediation of Switzerland. In Committee No. 5, the Swiss President of the Federal Council, Motta, had admitted that 'Liechtenstein est un trop petit Etat pour être admis dans les conditions actuelles'[183] and therefore suggested that the Swiss representative might be allowed to represent Liechtenstein interests in the League.[184] This procedure could have shown a certain dependence of Liechtenstein on another Power, which was immediately emphasized by the League of Nations and given more importance than the real juridical relations with Switzerland or Austria at the time revealed. Nevertheless, the Assembly of the League of Nations did not doubt Liechtenstein's sovereign statehood, although it did not expressly mention the criteria according to which it had tested Liechtenstein's statehood. The true reason for the non-admission of Liechtenstein was its smallness, not its deputation of some sovereign attributes by reason of its smallness.[185] It was thought unacceptable to grant

---

[181] League of Nations, *Records of the First Assembly, Plenary Meetings* (1920) p. 563.
[182] Ibid.
[183] League of Nations, *Records of the First Assembly, 4th–6th Committee* (1920) no. 12, p. 11.
[184] Ibid., p. 217.
[185] See also Gunter, 'Liechtenstein and the League of Nations', pp. 496–501. *Contra*, defending the juridical validity of the non-independence and lack-of-army arguments: A. Rougier, 'La première Assemblée de la Société des Nations (Genève, novembre–

Liechtenstein, or any other Micro-State, the same right to vote, and even a veto right when unanimity was required, as larger States.

International courts
Permanent Court of International Justice

On 17 May 1922, the Council of the League of Nations adopted a resolution which permitted all non-Member States of the League of Nations to become a party to the Statute of the Permanent Court of International Justice.[186] It was left to the Court to decide to which States it would send a letter offering them this option.

Liechtenstein was among the States to receive the Court's communication.[187] It did not respond to the Court's letter until 22 March 1939 when it accepted the Statute of the Court and submitted a declaration to the registry of the Permanent Court of International Justice accepting its general and compulsory jurisdiction under Article 36, paragraph 2 of the Statute for five years.[188] On 17 June 1939, the registrar of the Court received an application from the Government of Liechtenstein instituting proceedings against Hungary, which had also accepted the compulsory jurisdiction of the Permanent Court of International Justice.[189] The case concerned a Liechtenstein national, Gerliczy, who had been ordered by a Hungarian court to pay a considerable amount of money to some Hungarian nationals. Liechtenstein alleged that the court's decision had ruined Gerliczy financially and was contrary to the Hungaro-Romanian Convention of 16 April 1924 which regulated the payment of debts in ancient Austrian or Hungarian crowns. At the time of the entry into force of this Convention, Gerliczy had been a Romanian national. By reason of the invasion of the Netherlands by Germany the proceedings before the Court were discontinued.[190] On 3 September 1945, the registrar of the Court asked the Government of Liechtenstein what its intentions were with regard to the *Gerliczy* case. The letter remained without answer.

 décembre 1920)', 28 RGDIP (1921) pp. 230–231 and G. Scelle, 'L'Admission des nouveaux Membres de la Société des Nations par l'Assemblée de Genève', 28 RGDIP (1921) pp. 136–137.
[186] *Rapport Annuel de la Cour Permanente de Justice Internationale* (1 Jan. 1922–15 Jun. 1925) series E, no. 1, p. 139.
[187] See also pp. 234 and 293 below.
[188] *Seizième Rapport de la Cour Permanente de Justice Internationale* (15 Jun. 1939–31 Dec. 1945) series E, no. 16, p. 348.
[189] *Gerliczy* case: ibid., pp. 144–148.
[190] On 18 Oct. 1939, the President of the Permanent Court of International Justice had fixed the time limits within which the memorials had to be submitted. This term had been extended on 17 Mar. 1940.

International Court of Justice

On 24 March 1949, the Swiss Office for Liaison with the United Nations submitted to the Secretary-General a letter from the Liechtenstein Head of Government concerning Liechtenstein's request to become a party to the Statute of the International Court of Justice.[191] The application was first submitted to the Security Council which referred it to its Committee of Experts. The Soviet delegate did not approve of this procedure, as he did not consider Liechtenstein a 'free and independent' State.[192] On 16 June 1949, the Committee of Experts decided to advise the Security Council to admit Liechtenstein as a party to the Statute of the International Court of Justice.[193] The Soviet and Ukrainian members of the Committee of Experts had stated that '[i]t was apparent that Liechtenstein had yielded important parts of its sovereignty to another State. Liechtenstein was not, therefore, a sovereign and independent State and there was no need to admit it to become a party to the Statute of the International Court of Justice.'[194] The majority of the members of the Committee, however, maintained that Liechtenstein was a State in the sense of Article 93, paragraph 2 of the Charter, 'since it possessed all the qualifications of a State', and added that the jurisdiction of the Court 'should be extended as far as possible'.[195] Moreover, this was considered 'all the more useful for Liechtenstein since it was a small State, and the protection of law was most necessary in such a case'.[196] The Soviet and Ukrainian delegates in the Security Council abstained from voting and the Soviet Union did not exercise its veto against Liechtenstein's admission.[197]

On 26 October 1949, Liechtenstein's application was discussed in the Sixth Committee of the General Assembly.[198] The Australian delegate emphasized that Liechtenstein was 'a State possessing all the necessary qualifications for admission to the Statute of the

---

[191] UN Doc. S/1298 & Corr. 1 (1949) p. 6.
[192] UN Doc. S/PV.423 (1949) no. 26, pp. 16–17. The Soviet and Ukrainian delegates abstained from voting.
[193] By nine votes to nil with two abstentions (USSR and Ukrainian Soviet Socialist Republic). Report of the Committee of Experts, UN Doc. S/1342 (1949) pp. 2–3.
[194] Ibid., p. 3.
[195] Ibid.
[196] Ibid.
[197] UN Doc. S/PV.432 (1949) and UN Doc. A/967 (1949).
[198] UN Doc. A/C.6/L.47 (1949), also report of the Sixth Committee, UN Doc. A/1054 (1949). Australia and Belgium had submitted a draft resolution in favour of Liechtenstein's application, which was approved by forty-two votes to four with one abstention: UN Doc. A/C.6/S/PV.174 (1949) p. 215.

International Court' and advocated 'the greatest possible use of the International Court'.[199] There are no indications that the Sixth Committee applied a more flexible definition of statehood in this case, so as to encourage the use of the International Court of Justice, than is adopted in general international law. Yugoslavia emphasized that '[o]nly independent sovereign States could become parties to the Statute of the International Court' and that '[t]aking into account the particular conditions of the union between Liechtenstein and Switzerland, he was satisfied that Liechtenstein was an independent State'.[200] The Egyptian representative 'believed that the United Nations should apply the principle of universality' and that Liechtenstein satisfied all requirements 'although it was a small State. Moreover, the small States were the ones that most needed the protection of the Court.'[201] The Byelorussian delegate, however, declared: 'A review of the economic and political situation of Liechtenstein would show that it had never been an independent State ... It had formed a customs union with Switzerland, which country took care of Liechtenstein's post and telegraph service and its diplomatic representation ... it must be considered a dependent State', and therefore it could not be a party to the Statute of the International Court of Justice.[202] Under these requirements the Byelorussian delegate should have concluded that the Byelorussian Soviet Socialist Republic was not an independent State either.

The opposition of the Soviet Republics and the Soviet Union is to be understood in the 'cold war' context. The communist countries, in general, did not favour the participation of the European Micro-States which were Western-orientated in international fora. The Egyptian representative defended the opinion of the majority who believed that the fact that Liechtenstein 'had formed a customs union with another State and that Switzerland represented it diplomatically did not make it a dependent State. There were several countries which were represented by other countries in international affairs, and that did not affect their independence.'[203] On 1 December 1950, the General Assembly adopted a resolution enabling Liechtenstein to

---

[199] Ibid., p. 214.
[200] Ibid.
[201] Ibid.
[202] Ibid.
[203] Ibid., pp. 214-215.

become a party to the Statute of the International Court of Justice.[204]

Not long after having been admitted as a party to the Statute of the International Court of Justice, Liechtenstein filed an application in 1951, instituting proceedings against Guatemala. In what was to become the well-known *Nottebohm* case, the Court did not doubt Liechtenstein's statehood either, for it stated: 'It is for Liechtenstein, *as it is for every sovereign State* [emphasis added], to settle by its own legislation the rules relating to the acquisition of its nationality.'[205] Nottebohm had obtained Liechtenstein nationality on 13 October 1939, only four days after his request for naturalization and a few brief visits to Vaduz.[206] The Liechtenstein law on nationality of 1 January 1934 provided for the possibility of naturalization after three years' residence in the territory of the Principality, but this requirement could be dispensed with in circumstances deserving special consideration and by way of exception.[207] The Court concluded in 1955 that Nottebohm had no 'genuine connection' with Liechtenstein, which could therefore not extend its protection to Nottebohm vis-à-vis Guatemala.[208] Interestingly enough, Liechtenstein amended its law on nationality in 1960 so that naturalization is only possible after five years of residence in the Principality, without any possibility of dispensation with this requirement.[209]

OSCE

Liechtenstein participated in the very first conference of the CSCE organized in Helsinki in 1972. The reasons for inviting Liechtenstein to the conferences and the preparatory talks may have been diverse. Von Ledebur suggests that the interest which the Holy See had shown in promoting peace, the right of self-determination and religious freedom had been a motive for including the other European Micro-

---

[204] GA Res. 363 (IV) of 1 Dec. 1949. Liechtenstein has recognized as compulsory *ipso facto* and without special agreement, in relation to any other State accepting the same obligation, the jurisdiction of the International Court of Justice. Declaration of 29 Mar. 1950 under Art. 36 (2) of the Statute of the ICJ.
[205] ICJ Reports (1955) p. 20.
[206] Ibid., pp. 13–16.
[207] Art. 6 (d) of the 1934 law on nationality, LGBl (1934) no. 1. After having made certain financial contributions, Nottebohm was given dispensation from the condition of three years' residence: ibid., p. 15.
[208] Ibid., pp. 25–26.
[209] New Art. 6 (d) as amended on 2 Nov. 1960, LGBl (1960) no. 23.

States in the CSCE negotiations.[210] Prince Regnant Hans-Adam II of Liechtenstein explained that Liechtenstein was invited to the first preparatory talks organized by the Eastern European countries in Romania because they had invited all existing European States which had participated in the Congress of Vienna of 1815.[211] Liechtenstein, which joined the group of neutral and non-aligned States, had several interests in its participation in the CSCE.

In the first place, it allowed Liechtenstein to stand on terms of sovereign equality with other European States, the United States and Canada. The Helsinki Declaration of 1975 could not come into being without the cooperation and consensus of Liechtenstein. This fact was furthermore accepted by the other participating States. In contrast with the Soviet Union's position in the United Nations on Liechtenstein's application to become a party to the Statute of the International Court of Justice, the Eastern European States did not question Liechtenstein's statehood in the CSCE.[212] Despite the small size of its delegation, Liechtenstein could make certain contributions to the work of the Helsinki Conference. Thus, Liechtenstein endeavoured to secure respect for the procedural rules of the conference. In critical phases of the negotiations certain larger States wished to close the list of speakers or to vote by majority rule instead of by consensus. In order to still exert a certain influence, Liechtenstein defended the principle of consensus and its right to speak.[213]

In the second place, Liechtenstein's interest in participating in the CSCE lay in the strengthening of the solidarity between the European States.[214] By reason of its small size and of its sensitivity to external economic and military influences, Liechtenstein attaches great importance to a stable security in Europe.

In the third place, Liechtenstein participated actively in the so-called third Basket, that is, the Helsinki negotiations on cooperation in humanitarian and other fields. In this domain, Liechtenstein's

---

[210] M. von Ledebur, 'Licht und Schatten über der KSZE', 10 *Liechtenstein Politische Schriften* (1984) p. 183.

[211] Liechtenstein was not invited to the second preparatory negotiations organized by the Western European countries. As Liechtenstein objected to this exclusion, it was allowed to re-enter the conferences and thus participated in the Helsinki talks between 1972 and 1975. Interview with HH Prince Hans-Adam II von and zu Liechtenstein of 5 Apr. 1991.

[212] See pp. 175–176 above.

[213] Von Ledebur, 'Licht und Schatten', pp. 187–188.

[214] Ibid., pp. 184–185.

neutrality and wish for security made it a supporter of human rights and the exchange of information.[215]

It is represented in the OSCE Parliamentary Assembly by two members of the Diet[216] and bears 0.20 per cent of the cost of the OSCE institutions.[217] The OSCE has also served as a forum to draw international attention to Liechtenstein's claims against another participating State. Thus it has repeatedly recalled its claims against the Czech and Slovak Republics with respect to the confiscation by the communist Government of certain lands in Czechoslovakia owned by Liechtenstein nationals.[218]

Council of Europe

In May 1948 a conference was organized by the coordination committee of the European movement in the Hague in which Liechtenstein participated. The recommendations of this conference have strongly influenced the establishment of the Council of Europe.[219] Yet, Liechtenstein did not become a founding member of the Council of Europe. It only entered into contact with the Council of Europe in 1969, when it became a party to the first five European conventions.[220] On 27 November 1974, Liechtenstein was given official

[215] As von Ledebur put it: 'In Liechtenstein kann man das kleine Modell einer politischen Gemeinschaft erkennen, die ohne Ideologie Arbeiter und Unternehmer, Bürger mit ihren Familien und einem Monarchen in lebendiger Gemeinschaft vereint. Diese Gemeinschaft strahlt, obwohl sie klein ist, wegen ihrer Menschlichkeit und Würde über ihre Grenzen hinaus': ibid., p. 189.
[216] Art. 1 (I) of the final resolution of the Madrid Conference concerning the establishment of the CSCE Parliamentary Assembly, 3 Apr. 1991, 30 ILM (1991) pp. 1344 ff.
[217] Part III (2) of the Supplementary Document to give effect to certain provisions contained in the Charter of Paris for a New Europe, 30 ILM (1991) p. 220.
[218] At the admission of the Czech and Slovak Republics to the CSCE during the Stockholm Council Meeting of Dec. 1992, Liechtenstein made an interpretative statement reminding them that 'outstanding issues between the Czech and Slovak Federal Republics and the Czech and the Slovak Republic do encompass nationalization of property of Liechtenstein nationals seized without compensation in the years 1945 and thereafter', in A. Bloed, ed., *The Conference on Security and Co-operation in Europe: Analysis and Basic Documents* (1993) p. 896. At the signing of the free trade agreement between the EFTA countries and Czechoslovakia in Mar. 1992, Liechtenstein expressed its reservations to ratifying the agreement as long as the Czechoslovakian Government refused to modify its position. Liechtenstein's proposals to refer the matter to the ICJ and to make major investments in the Czech and Slovak Republics were rejected: Liechtenstein press release no. 118 of 26 Mar. 1992.
[219] N. von Liechtenstein, 'Liechtensteins Mitgliedschaft im Europarat', 10 *Liechtenstein Politische Schriften* (1984) p. 197.
[220] Ibid., p. 205.

permanent observer status at the Parliamentary Assembly.[221] In fact, by becoming an observer, Liechtenstein was able to familiarize itself with the work of the Council of Europe and at the same time to gain the confidence of the Member States of the Council.

Thus, in 1977, exploratory talks began with the Member States and the Secretary-General on the feasibility of Liechtenstein becoming a member of the Council of Europe. At the beginning certain objections were raised concerning the advisability of admitting more small Member States to the Council of Europe which would toughen the decision-making process. Liechtenstein promised that it would respect the justified wishes of the larger States.[222] As a consequence, Liechtenstein deposited its request for admission on 4 November 1977. On 17 March 1978, the Committee of Ministers invited the Consultative Assembly (now called the Parliamentary Assembly) to express its opinion on the matter.[223] The Assembly's Political Affairs Committee and the Committee on European Non-Member Countries both prepared a report on the admission of Liechtenstein and concluded that Liechtenstein fulfilled the conditions for accession to the Council of Europe as laid down in Article 4 of the Statute.[224] The first study, by the Political Affairs Committee, inquired into three main issues:

Does the Principality of Liechtenstein have all the attributes of a sovereign State? After having examined Liechtenstein's history and relations with Switzerland, the rapporteur concluded that '[t]here can therefore be no doubt about Liechtenstein's independence'.[225] Although he gave no general norms according to which Liechtenstein's independence was evaluated, the rapporteur emphasized Liechtenstein's freedom to set up its own diplomatic missions, the Swiss position that the customs union treaty did not prejudice Liechtenstein's sovereignty and the fact that Liechtenstein had proved

---

[221] At the first parliamentary session as an official observer, Liechtenstein explained its difficulties in collaborating seriously with the Council, as it had such a small delegation. Liechtenstein was allowed to have two parliamentary observers, which was extended to four on 7 Mar. 1975 by adding two substitute members. Council of Europe, *Parliamentary Assembly, Official Report* (22–29 Jan. 1975), vol. III, 23rd Session (3rd part), 16th mtg (22 Jan. 1975) p. 495.

[222] Von Liechtenstein, 'Liechtensteins Mitgliedschaft', p. 207.

[223] Council of Europe Doc. 4139, Res. 78 (23) of 17 Mar. 1978, in Council of Europe, *Parliamentary Assembly, Documents: Working Papers* (24–28 Apr. 1978) vol. I, p. 1.

[224] Council of Europe Docs. 4193 and 4211, ibid., vol. III and vol. IV respectively.

[225] Council of Europe Doc. 4193, p. 13, adopted by the Committee on 6 Jul. 1978.

its capacity to sustain international relations.²²⁶ Special attention was given to Liechtenstein's adherence to the Statute of the International Court of Justice and to the Final Act of the CSCE. It should be noted that the rapporteur did not explicitly examine whether Liechtenstein had been recognized by other States according to the constitutive theory of recognition. Rather, he sought confirmation of Liechtenstein's statehood by proving that it had been accepted by certain international fora which are only open to States.²²⁷

Does Liechtenstein recognize its citizens' fundamental freedoms and respect them in practice? The rapporteur concluded that the crucial basic human rights were guaranteed and manifestly observed, that the economic and social rights were in certain respects superior to those of some Member States of the Council of Europe and that the equality of rights of women had not yet become law to the extent considered necessary by the Parliamentary Assembly.²²⁸

Is Liechtenstein, despite its relatively small population, able to fulfil all the obligations and duties arising from the Statute? Liechtenstein's financial position was considered very healthy. Furthermore, the Liechtenstein Government had declared its willingness to respect all obligations flowing from the Statute.²²⁹

The second report, prepared by a rapporteur of the Committee on European Non-Member Countries, was based on a fact-finding visit to Liechtenstein.²³⁰ Three major points were raised:

Sovereignty and independence As all bilateral agreements with Switzerland could be revoked at short notice and as Switzerland could only represent Liechtenstein diplomatically on specific instructions of the latter, the rapporteur reaffirmed Liechtenstein's statehood.²³¹

---

²²⁶ Ibid., pp. 8 and 10.
²²⁷ The rapporteur emphasized, for example, that '[c]olonies, protectorates or other territories which are not independent states are excluded from membership of the ICJ ... the United Nations recognised Liechtenstein's sovereignty'. Ibid. pp. 12–13.
²²⁸ Ibid., p. 17.
²²⁹ The rapporteur rejected the Status of Associate Member of Article 5 of the Statute for Liechtenstein, as this membership 'implies denial, or at least doubt that an area has the character of a state': ibid., p. 20.
²³⁰ Council of Europe Doc. 4211, approved by the Committee on 8 Sept. 1978, and amendments of Doc. 4193.
²³¹ Ibid., pp. 2–6.

Specific problems which had raised discussion in the Council of Europe In the first place, the absence of women's voting rights was not considered a determining factor for the rejection of Liechtenstein's entry into the Council of Europe.[232] In the second place, Liechtenstein had declared its willingness to cooperate with the Member States of the Council of Europe to combat tax offences and evasion.[233] In the third place, Liechtenstein's size and implications for its behaviour in the Council of Europe were considered. It was feared that it would use its vote in such a way as to frustrate the will of other members, although there is no unanimity rule in the Council of Europe as there used to be in the League of Nations. The Government of Liechtenstein had therefore declared that 'in the decision-making of the Council of Europe, Liechtenstein would exercise the vote as a member in a manner appropriate to her size'.[234] The Member States wanted to ascertain that Liechtenstein would not toughen the decision-making process or sell its vote and would vote independently of any other State. In practice, however, the Liechtenstein declaration has no legal meaning. After its accession, Liechtenstein has always voted as it deemed right, even if its vote just tipped the balance.[235] The Statute of the Council of Europe does not provide for two categories of votes. The rapporteur furthermore observed that 'quantity has never been regarded as a criterion in the Council of Europe'.[236]

Liechtenstein's European vocation It was demonstrated that Liechtenstein already belonged 'to the family of advanced democratic European nations, both politically and economically'.[237]

On 28 September 1978, the Parliamentary Assembly voted in favour of Liechtenstein's admission to the Council of Europe.[238] It was the

---

[232] Ibid., pp. 6–7. Switzerland had also been admitted to the Council at a time when women's right to vote had not yet been introduced in all cantons. Furthermore, excluding Liechtenstein could be counterproductive and could disappoint or discourage Liechtenstein's only women's political organization which had declared itself in favour of accession.
[233] Ibid., pp. 8–9.
[234] Letter of 4 Nov. 1977 of the Liechtenstein Head of Government to the Secretary-General of the Council of Europe: ibid., p. 10. See also point 7 of the Assembly's Opinion (28 Sept. 1978), Doc. 4193, p. 2.
[235] Interview with HH Prince Hans-Adam II von und zu Liechtenstein of 5 Apr. 1991.
[236] Council of Europe Doc. 4211, p. 10.
[237] Ibid., p. 12, para. 40.
[238] The Committee of Ministers therefore invited Liechtenstein to become a full member of the Council of Europe on 13 Nov. 1978 and its accession to the Council of Europe

first political international organization of which Liechtenstein became a member. The debates in the Parliamentary Assembly can be summarized as follows: A British parliamentarian wanted to re-examine the two reports on Liechtenstein in the Committees and prepare a general study on the problems of the relations between the Council of Europe and European Micro-States. He feared that if more Micro-States entered the Council of Europe they would have a disproportionate amount of votes.[239] This proposition was rejected as it was thought incorrect after almost one year of discussion to delay a final decision on Liechtenstein's admission. It was also considered contrary to the Statute which does not distinguish between Micro- and Maxi-States.[240] There was a general consensus that the contractual relations with Switzerland did not prejudice Liechtenstein's independence and therefore its statehood.[241] The delegates who opposed Liechtenstein's admission based their argument on the absence of women's voting rights.[242]

Liechtenstein's conduct in the Council of Europe has in certain ways been an advantage for other European Micro-States which wanted to become a member of the Council of Europe, because it has shown the other Member States what a Micro-State can contribute to the work of a political international organization.[243] Liechtenstein considers that it has often a more responsible voting pattern than other Member States, because it has no important national interests and can vote for the general good.[244]

---

followed on 23 Nov. 1978. Committee of Ministers Resolution (78) 48 of 13 Nov. 1978. It has two seats on the Parliamentary Assembly.

[239] Council of Europe, *Parliamentary Assembly, Official Report* (27 Sept.–5 Oct. 1978) vol. II, 30th Session (2nd part), 11th mtg (28 Sept. 1978) p. 381.
[240] Ibid., pp. 382–383.
[241] Ibid., pp. 385, 398 and 402.
[242] Thus, for example, a British, a Danish and a Norwegian delegate: ibid., pp. 389, 391 and 396 respectively. In addition, it was argued that Liechtenstein was a tax haven, but this argument was not sustained as an official reason for rejecting its candidature, because Liechtenstein planned to review its fiscal and company laws. This domain was a matter of internal legislation according to the supporters of Liechtenstein's membership: ibid., p. 401.
[243] See on the application of San Marino pp. 242–246 below.
[244] Liechtenstein keeps close contacts with Switzerland and Austria in matters to which it cannot attend itself, due to the smallness of its delegation. Liechtenstein consults with Switzerland or Austria or any other Member State that has particular expertise in the subject concerned. Interview with HH Prince Hans-Adam II von und zu Liechtenstein of 5 Apr. 1991.

The advantages of its membership are diverse. On a long-term basis, Liechtenstein wanted to strengthen the international, in this case European, recognition of its independence and its statehood. It was also a means of entering into regular diplomatic relations with other European States without having to establish costly diplomatic missions to each of them. It facilitated the conclusion of multilateral treaties which otherwise had to be drafted separately with the neighbouring States. Furthermore, membership of the Council of Europe permits the influencing of the policies of other Member States, self-criticism and participation in the general construction of Europe.

At the beginning, the Liechtensteinese feared that by acceding to the Council of Europe they would be forced to make important concessions in fiscal and company legislation. In practice, however, this has not been the case. Liechtenstein is at a certain disadvantage in the sense that it cannot man all the committees of experts. It also demands time from the non-professional Liechtenstein parliamentarians to attend the Assembly's sessions.

European integration

EFTA

On 4 January 1960, seven European States signed a Convention establishing the European Free Trade Association in Stockholm (hereafter, Stockholm Convention).[245] The problem concerning the legal position Liechtenstein should have in the European Free Trade Association (hereafter, EFTA) when Switzerland ratified the Stockholm Convention was raised. Switzerland maintained that by virtue of Article 7 of the customs union treaty of 1923 with Liechtenstein, the Stockholm Convention would also apply to Liechtenstein, whereas Liechtenstein preferred to become a full member of EFTA.[246] As, however, the field of application of the Stockholm Convention was more extensive than the customs union treaty, Switzerland could not represent Liechtenstein in matters which were not related to customs regulations.[247] Because, at the time, Liechtenstein could not conclude

---

[245] The founding States of EFTA were Austria, Denmark, Norway, Portugal, Sweden, Switzerland and the United Kingdom. Text of the Stockholm Convention in EFTA Secretariat, *The European Free Trade Association* (Jun. 1987) pp. 98 ff.

[246] Interview with HH Prince Hans-Adam II von und zu Liechtenstein of 5 Apr. 1991.

[247] Thus Switzerland lacked the legal power to act for Liechtenstein in certain domains regulated by the Stockholm Convention, such as State subsidies, State enterprises, competition laws and the establishment of enterprises: Arts. 13–16 of the Stockholm Convention.

customs-related treaties independently, it was decided to draft a Protocol to the Stockholm Convention extending Switzerland's mandate.[248] This Protocol of 4 January 1960 was ratified by all signatory States of the Stockholm Convention and by Liechtenstein and proposed to give special powers to Switzerland. The Protocol stated: '1. The Convention shall apply to the Principality of Liechtenstein as long as it forms a customs union with Switzerland and Switzerland is a Member of the Association. 2. ... Liechtenstein shall be represented by Switzerland'.[249]

The special powers are only valid for the Stockholm Convention. Thus, when Switzerland signed free trade agreements with the EEC and the ECSC on 22 July 1972, additional Agreements between the European Communities, Switzerland and Liechtenstein were required in order to make the free trade agreements applicable to Liechtenstein.[250] Liechtenstein could represent its interests through a representative within the Swiss delegation to the Joint Committees.[251] Such Joint Committees were established with the EEC and with the ECSC.[252] When talks between the European Community and EFTA aimed at the creation of a European Economic Area, which would extend well beyond the Swiss mandate under the customs union treaty, Liechtenstein took advantage of this occasion to redefine and strengthen its position vis-à-vis Switzerland, EFTA and the European Community. In order to avoid exclusive negotiations between the European Community and Switzerland, which legally could have

---

[248] Art. 8 (1) of the 1923 customs union treaty. See also p. 164 above.
[249] Protocol relating to the application of the Convention establishing the European Free Trade Association to the Principality of Liechtenstein: EFTA Secretariat, *The European Free Trade Association* (Jun. 1987) pp. 137–138.
[250] European Communities, *Collection of the Agreements concluded by the European Communities*, vol. III (1958–1975) pp. 160–161 for the Additional Agreement between the EEC, Switzerland and Liechtenstein of 22 Jul. 1972, and vol. V (1952–1975) pp. 351–352 for the Additional Agreement between the Members of the ECSC, Switzerland and Liechtenstein of 22 Jul. 1972. Supplementary Protocols with Greece of 17 Jul. 1980, LGBl (1989) no. 23 and with Portugal and Spain of 14 Jul. 1986 extending the ECSC–Switzerland–Liechtenstein free trade Agreement of 22 Jul. 1972 to the new ECSC members. The free trade Agreements with the European Communities were only applicable to Liechtenstein for as long as the customs union treaty with Switzerland of 1923 remained in force: Art. 3 of both additional Agreements of 22 Jul. 1972.
[251] Art. 2 of both additional Agreements of 22 Jul. 1972.
[252] The Liechtenstein observer within the Swiss delegation to the Joint Committees could not take any initiatives, impose sanctions or terminate the free trade Agreement, for he had no right to vote. W. B. Gyger, *Das Fürstentum Liechtenstein und die Europäische Gemeinschaft* (1975) part 4, p. 96.

been possible, as in the case of the additional Agreements of 1972, Liechtenstein managed to be accepted as a separate negotiating partner. Considering the wide implications of the draft EEA Agreement this was believed to be an adequate solution which emphasized Liechtenstein's sovereignty.[253] On 3 April 1990, the EFTA Ministers declared their willingness to accept Liechtenstein as the seventh negotiating partner on the EFTA side in the EEA talks.[254] This declaration was accepted by the European Council on 18 June 1990.[255]

Liechtenstein wanted to become a full party to the EEA Agreement and therefore decided to become a full member of EFTA. This was made possible by the amendment of the Swiss–Liechtenstein customs union treaty of 29 March 1923.[256] The EFTA Council approved Liechtenstein's accession to the Stockholm Convention on 22 May 1991.[257] Liechtenstein's accession to EFTA has not been made conditional upon the maintenance in force of the customs union treaty of 1923.

The question arises whether Liechtenstein may vote independently of the Swiss position in matters which fall within the regulations of the customs union treaty of 1923. All States Parties have one vote in the EFTA Council; although normally voting is by consensus, in certain cases a unanimous vote is requested.[258] Article 8, first paragraph of the customs union treaty forbids Liechtenstein to conclude independently customs treaties with third States. The customs union treaty does not however provide for the concordance of Liechtenstein and Swiss customs and voting policies in international organs. Thus Liechtenstein is legally free to vote in the EFTA Council according to its own policy. This is equally so for the EEA Council and Common EEA Commission as well as the EFTA and Common EEA Parliamentary Committee. In addition, through its full membership of EFTA, Liechtenstein may present at its own initiative a claim against other EFTA Member States before the EFTA Council.[259]

---

[253] BA no. 56/1990, p. 17.
[254] Ibid., p. 18.
[255] BA no. 81/1990, p. 4.
[256] See p. 164 above. An agreement on Art. 8 bis was signed on 26 Nov. 1990, ratified and entered into force on 28 Aug. 1991.
[257] Annex 3 to BA no. 43/91. Liechtenstein officially acceded to the Stockholm Convention on 1 Sept. 1991. As a consequence, the Protocol of 4 Jan. 1960 is no longer valid: Point V of the Council decision of 22 Mar. 1991.
[258] Art. 32 (5) of the Stockholm Convention.
[259] Art. 31 of the Stockholm Convention.

European Economic Area

The EEA Agreement, in the drafting of which Liechtenstein had actively participated, was approved by referendum by the Liechtenstein nationals on 13 December 1992.[260] As Switzerland's referendum on the EEA Agreement held on 6 December 1992 had led to the non-ratification of the EEA Agreement by Liechtenstein's neighbouring State, certain legal questions arose. By virtue of old Article 8 bis of the customs union treaty between Switzerland and Liechtenstein, Liechtenstein could only have become a party to a customs convention if Switzerland was a contracting party itself. In the days following the Liechtenstein referendum, Liechtenstein and Swiss experts met to discuss a solution to the question. According to the EEA Agreement, the regional union between Switzerland and Liechtenstein should not be precluded provided that the good functioning of the Agreement is not impaired.[261] Given the close links between Switzerland and Liechtenstein, special arrangements were needed for the entry into force of the EEA Agreement in Liechtenstein, both on the EC–EFTA side and on the bilateral side. On 17 March 1993, the diplomatic conference of EC and EFTA countries (except Switzerland) approved the Protocol adjusting the EEA Agreement.[262] The Protocol stipulates that for Liechtenstein the EEA Agreement, as adjusted by the Protocol, will come into force on a date to be determined by the EEA Council, provided that the EEA Council has not only decided that the good functioning of the Agreement is not impaired, but has also taken the appropriate decisions in particular as to the application to Liechtenstein of measures already adopted by the EEA Council or the EEA Joint Committee.[263] In addition, the protocols of the EEA Agreement which referred to both Switzerland and Liechtenstein will only apply for Liechtenstein.[264] Certain joint declarations of Switzerland and Liechtenstein are declared void.[265] The EFTA States

---

[260] The referendum held on 11–13 Dec. 1992 showed 55.81 per cent in favour of and 44.19 per cent against the EEA Agreement, BA no. 147/1992.

[261] Art. 121 (b) of the EEA Agreement. Text in ECOJ no. L 1 (3.1.94) pp. 3 ff.

[262] ECOJ no. L 1 (3.1.94) pp. 572 ff.

[263] Art. 1 (2) of the Protocol adjusting the EEA Agreement. Before the entry into force of the EEA Agreement for Liechtenstein, the Principality was already allowed to participate in the decisions of the EEA Council: Art. 1 (3).

[264] Protocols nos. 5, 6, 8, 9, 15 and 16: Arts. 9–14 of the Protocol adjusting the EEA Agreement.

[265] Declarations nos. 2, 14 and 33 to the EEA Agreement: Final Act of the diplomatic conference, EC Doc. AF/EEE/f, ad II.

adjusted their 'internal EFTA Agreements' so as to regulate the number of seats reserved for Liechtenstein in the Court of Justice, the EFTA Standing Committee and the EFTA Parliamentary Committee.[266]

On 2 November 1994, a number of treaties and accords were signed by Switzerland and Liechtenstein, permitting the entry into force of the EEA Agreement in the Principality, without the establishment of borders between the two countries.[267] On 20 December 1994, the EEA Council declared that these arrangements fulfilled the conditions set in Article 121 (b) of the EEA Agreement.[268] The EEA Agreement entered into force for Liechtenstein on 1 May 1995.[269]

The ratification of the EEA Agreement constitutes a considerable economic and political advantage for Liechtenstein even if it has to make certain concessions on its traditional policies. Liechtenstein's industrial sector is strongly export-oriented[270] and since 1987 the export to EC countries has risen proportionately.[271] The Liechtenstein Government believed that long-term economic advantages could only be guaranteed if Liechtenstein's 'Eigenstaatlichkeit' was maintained and strengthened.[272] This necessitated a cooperation in the process of European integration and not a marginalization. The fundamental consequences of the EEA Agreement for Liechtenstein are as follows:

Free movement of persons.[273] Traditionally, Liechtenstein has a restrictive system where the entry and sojourn of foreigners is

---

[266] Protocols adjusting the EFTA Agreement on the Establishment of a Surveillance Authority and a Court of Justice, the Agreement on a Standing Committee of the EFTA States and the Agreement on a Committee of Members of Parliament of the EFTA States. See H. Frennered, 'The Protocols adjusting the EEA Agreement and the EFTA Agreements', *EFTA Bulletin* (1993) no. 2, pp. 9–11.

[267] See pp. 163–168 above.

[268] Point 4 of the EEA Council decision of 20 Dec. 1994, Press release no. 280–G, EEA 1610/94.

[269] After a second referendum of 7–9 Apr. 1995 approving by 55.9 per cent Liechtenstein's participation in the EEA, BA no. 14/1995 and pursuant to the decision of the EEA Council No. 1/95 of 10 Mar. 1995, ECOJ no. L 86 (20.4.95) p. 58.

[270] Liechtenstein's nominal Gross National Product in 1988 was 1,700 million Swiss francs against total industrial exports of 2,417 million Swiss francs. The latter figure does not account for net exports, which explains the gap between Gross National Product and total exports. *Statistisches Jahrbuch 1994*, pp. 110 and 192.

[271] In 1987, 39.3 per cent of total exports was sent to EC countries against 45.4 per cent in 1991 and 41.6 per cent in 1993. Exports to Switzerland and other EFTA countries have decreased in percentage terms in the same period. Figures calculated on the basis of *Statistisches Jahrbuch 1994*, p. 192.

[272] Commentary to the EEA Agreement, BA no. 46/92, p. 238.

[273] Art. 28 (1) of the EEA Agreement.

concerned.[274] Under the EEA Agreement the Liechtenstein labour market will be open to all EEA nationals. New regulations, depending on their subject, will have to be introduced within two to five years. The States Parties will then re-examine the results of the transitional period and possibly extend it.[275] The States Parties have declared that when deciding on a request for an extension, they will take into account Liechtenstein's special geographical situation,[276] that is, its smallness and the problems which that entails. Furthermore, Liechtenstein plans to take protective measures under the general protection clause of the EEA Agreement in the event of an exceptional increase in the number of foreigners.[277] To this end, Liechtenstein issued a unilateral declaration explaining in which cases it understood that it was justified to take protective measures.[278]

Freedom of establishment.[279] This freedom permits the establishment of foreign enterprises, foreign banks and self-employed workers in Liechtenstein. Traditionally, Liechtenstein's laws did not allow the establishment of foreign enterprises with large foreign capital in their territory. Only enterprises under Liechtenstein law could be founded in the Principality. Likewise, a branch of a foreign bank could not be established in Liechtenstein. Doctors, engineers and architects exercising their profession in Liechtenstein had to possess Liechtenstein nationality.[280] After the transitional period of three to five years, Liechtenstein may take protective measures if the inflow of foreign enterprises becomes disproportionate.[281] The bilateral currency treaty is the only agreement which has not been adapted to Liechtenstein's ratification of the EEA Agreement, as it was believed highly unlikely that Swiss currency legislation would become contrary to an EEA regulation.[282]

[274] See pp. 167–168 above.
[275] Art. 9 (1) of Protocol 15 to the EEA Agreement.
[276] Art. 9 (2) of Protocol 15 to the EEA Agreement. This point has been confirmed by express declaration of the EEA Council of 20 Dec. 1994.
[277] Art. 112 (1) of the EEA Agreement.
[278] The declaration of 2 May 1992 concerns especially the residence of foreigners and the foreign ownership of lands. Declaration by the Liechtenstein Government on the country's special situation, Annex 1 to BA no. 46/92, p. 1016. There were no objections raised by the other States Parties to this interpretative declaration.
[279] Art. 31 (1) of the EEA Agreement.
[280] BA no. 46/92, pp. 84 and 94.
[281] The indicative factor, according to Liechtenstein's unilateral declaration to Art. 112 of the EEA Agreement, is an exceptional increase in the number of jobs. Ibid., p. 85.
[282] BA no. 1994/93, p. 5.

Free movement of services.[283] This is of particular importance for the Liechtenstein banks which, although they will have to accept more internal competition, will now be able to offer their services in the other EEA States.[284]

Free movement of capital.[285] Foreign investment in Liechtenstein must be permitted on the basis of non-discrimination vis-à-vis Liechtenstein citizens. The implications for Liechtenstein are especially felt in the ownership of land. Traditionally the ownership of Liechtenstein land could only be acquired after permission from the Liechtenstein authorities. Foreigners could only own land in certain restricted cases. This stipulation was designed to prevent speculation and the concentration of land ownership in the hands of a few persons.[286] By unilateral declaration, Liechtenstein can provide for the establishment of protective measures under Article 112 of the EEA Agreement if the access to the land market for Liechtenstein's inhabitants is jeopardized.[287]

The EU as well as EFTA countries have treated Liechtenstein as a full negotiating partner and, instead of using Liechtenstein's smallness against it, have accepted its special characteristics. Such an understanding will be especially necessary when Liechtenstein requests an extension of the transitional period concerning the free movement of persons and when it unilaterally takes protective measures. It remains to be seen for how long the EEA States will accept these protective measures, especially as they do not have reciprocal effect.[288]

---

[283] Art. 36 (1) of the EEA Agreement.
[284] BA no. 46/92, pp. 94–96. By virtue of EC Regulation no. 91/308, ECOJ no. L 166/77 (28 Jun. 1991), which is part of the *acquis communautaire* and has to be taken over by the EFTA countries, a State's financial system should not be used for money laundering. Liechtenstein has therefore provided for the penalization of actions which obstruct inquiry into the legal origins of money. LGBl (1993) no. 6. See also A. Batliner and R. J. Proksch, 'Changes on the Way for Liechtenstein Banks?', 10 Int'l Fin. Law Review (1991) pp. 28–29.
[285] Arts. 40 ff. of the EEA Agreement.
[286] BA no. 118/1992, p. 10.
[287] BA no. 46/92, p. 125.
[288] Art. 113 of the EEA Agreement provides for consultations in the common EEA Commission aimed at withdrawing the protective measures as soon as possible or limiting their effects.

European Union

All EFTA States, except for Iceland, Liechtenstein and Norway, have joined the EU. The Liechtenstein Government, as a result of the discussions in the Diet on the EEA Agreement, took the position that a request for admission should only be made if there existed a true political will to accede and to accept the complete *acquis communautaire*.[289] The Government nevertheless keeps close contacts with the EU and Switzerland on possible options for Liechtenstein. The Liechtenstein Government believes that its smallness cannot be a reason for not admitting Liechtenstein to the EU, although some problems could be raised with regard to its participation in the EU institutions.[290] From Liechtenstein's point of view, membership of the EU would cause certain financial problems. The Government expects that Liechtenstein would be a net contributor to the EU.[291] Thus it would lose most of its customs revenue and possibly be confronted with higher customs tariffs on imports of raw materials from third States on which Liechtenstein's processing industry is dependent.[292] The EU could doubt, according to the Liechtenstein Government, whether Liechtenstein had the work capacity to participate in its institutions.[293] Moreover, the EEA Agreement sets forth a more extensive protection clause than the EC Treaty.[294] The issue is therefore whether the EU would be willing to make certain concessions in favour of Liechtenstein as was done in the EEA negotiations. Liechtenstein must also be assured that no EC regulation will force it to abandon its moderate tax system, though the Principality has already introduced a VAT system.[295]

As Liechtenstein has become a State Party to the EEA Agreement independently of Switzerland, it has abandoned an absolute assimilation with the Swiss customs regime. When considering an EU membership for Liechtenstein, the question whether or not Switzerland will become a member of the EU is irrelevant, though

---

[289] BA no. 92/1992, p. 16.
[290] Ibid., p. 5.
[291] Ibid., p. 13.
[292] See Gyger, *Das Fürstentum Liechtenstein*, pp. 112–113.
[293] BA no. 92/1992, p. 15.
[294] Art. 112 (1) of the EEA Agreement provides for protective measures in case of serious economic, social or ecological difficulties. Art. 226 of the EC Treaty can be invoked in case of serious economic problems but only in the transitional period, whereas Arts. 223 and 224 are related to national security and war difficulties.
[295] See pp. 165–166 above.

Switzerland would have to agree to a special bilateral arrangement or face the termination of the customs union with Liechtenstein.[296]

International responsibility

Does Liechtenstein have international responsibility for the non-observance of a treaty obligation which is applicable in Liechtenstein by virtue of the postal or customs union treaty with Switzerland? It must first be determined whether Liechtenstein becomes a State Party to the treaties which Switzerland concludes under Article 4 of the postal union treaty and Articles 7 and 8 of the customs union treaty.[297] Special Rapporteur Waldock of the International Law Commission prepared a draft Article 59 to be included in the Vienna Convention on the Law of Treaties. This article, which was specially drafted to cover the Swiss–Liechtenstein relations, ran as follows:

> The application of a treaty extends to the territory of a State which is not itself a contracting party if–
> (a) the State authorized one of the parties to bind its territory by concluding the treaty;
> (b) the other parties were aware that the party in question was so authorized; and
> (c) the party in question intended to bind the territory of that State by concluding the treaty.[298]

The Special Rapporteur emphasized that Liechtenstein did not itself become a party to those treaties and that in case of a violation of the treaty a third State 'would not be able to bring that complaint directly against Liechtenstein, but would have to lodge it through Switzerland'.[299] This position was severely criticized by the members of the International Law Commission. The Chairman thought that 'since Liechtenstein was an autonomous subject of international law, it was the State of Liechtenstein that was bound by a treaty of that kind and not its territory' and that 'if Liechtenstein failed to observe the treaty it was still Liechtenstein that was failing to meet its obligations; consequently Liechtenstein ... must be regarded as a party to the treaty'.[300] These arguments were generally endorsed by the other

---

[296] Ibid.
[297] See pp. 163–166 above.
[298] ILC Yearbook (1964) vol. II, p. 15.
[299] ILC Yearbook (1964) vol. I, pp. 53–54, paras. 2 and 8.
[300] Ibid., p. 53, para. 6 and p. 54, para. 9.

members. Draft Article 59 was believed to deal with a very special and rare case that need not be generalized into a rule.[301] The International Law Commission did not retain the article.

Article 2, paragraph 1 (g) of the Vienna Convention on the Law of Treaties describes a 'party' as 'a State which has consented to be bound by the treaty and for which the treaty is in force'. Liechtenstein has, admittedly, expressed its general consent to be bound by postal and customs treaties which are concluded by Switzerland, by accepting their application in its territory. In this sense one could call Liechtenstein a State Party to the treaties. Nevertheless, the postal and customs union treaties themselves stipulate that Liechtenstein has the right to become a State Party itself to international conventions if Switzerland has ratified these conventions too.[302] This implies that if Liechtenstein does not ratify a convention itself, it is not considered a State Party. As we have seen, the Protocol of 4 January 1960 which made the Stockholm Convention applicable in Liechtenstein did not make Liechtenstein a State Party to the Convention. It only became a full member of EFTA after it had ratified the Stockholm Convention in its own name.[303] Likewise, the free trade Agreements with the European Communities of 22 July 1972 were applied in Liechtenstein, but Liechtenstein had no seat or voting power of its own in the Joint Committees. In fact, only States Parties had the right to vote and have their own representation in the Joint Committees. Liechtenstein could not terminate a treaty, suspend it or invoke any international principle likely to terminate or invalidate the treaty. It must be concluded that Liechtenstein has never been considered or treated as a State Party to the international conventions concluded by Switzerland and applicable in the Principality.

Can Liechtenstein be considered a third State with rights and obligations from a treaty concluded by two or more other States, within the meaning of Articles 35 and 36 of the Vienna Convention on the Law of Treaties?[304] Third States which are not States Parties to a treaty

---

[301] Ibid., p. 63, para. 35 (Conclusion of the Special Rapporteur).
[302] 'Das Recht des Fürstentums Liechtenstein, *selbst Vertragsstaat* [emphasis added] ... zu werden'. Same formula in Art. 6 (1) of the postal union treaty and Art. 8 bis (1) of the customs union treaty.
[303] See p. 186 above.
[304] See C. Chinkin, *Third Parties in International Law* (1993) pp. 32–33 and P. Reuter, *Introduction to the Law of Treaties* (1989) pp. 73–76.

may have certain obligations arising from this treaty if they accept these obligations in writing. It does not seem incompatible with this provision that a third State gives its general consent to be bound by obligations of a treaty without expressly mentioning this or that obligation. In the case of Liechtenstein, such a general consent can be withdrawn by denouncing the postal and customs union treaties. In this respect Liechtenstein could be classified as a third State within the meaning of Article 35 of the Vienna Convention on the Law of Treaties.

It is more controversial whether the parties to a treaty had the intention to accord all the rights of the treaty provisions to Liechtenstein, when they declared that the treaty would apply to the Principality. Considering that under the postal and customs union treaties Liechtenstein has no freedom of action, because Swiss authorities are charged with their implementation, the rights flowing from a treaty will not apply to Liechtenstein in so far as they permit a State action. Such actions can only be performed by Switzerland. Conversely, if the right does not imply an action of the holder of the right but a direct obligation of the other State Party, such as a most-favoured-nation provision, the right will apply to Liechtenstein. It seems therefore logical that if a State Party does not respect its obligations, Liechtenstein has the right to invoke that State's international responsibility. In this sense, Liechtenstein is also a third State within the meaning of Article 36 of the Vienna Convention on the Law of Treaties.

It should be borne in mind that the applicability in Liechtenstein of postal and commercial treaties concluded by Switzerland and the fact that Switzerland does not sign the treaties *in the name of* Liechtenstein are closely related to the execution of those treaties by Swiss authorities. If the Liechtenstein-located Swiss authorities violate a provision of a postal or customs treaty concluded with a third State, they do not act in distinction from the Swiss-located authorities. As they are not put at Liechtenstein's disposal, Liechtenstein cannot be held internationally responsible for the acts of the Swiss postal and customs offices in Liechtenstein territory.[305] This situation will change if Liechtenstein installs its own postal and

---

[305] This position is confirmed by the European Commission of Human Rights with regard to acts of the Swiss Aliens Office with effect in Liechtenstein: Applications no. 7289/75 and 7349/76, *X and Y v. Switzerland*, D & R 9, pp. 57 ff. See p. 168 above at n. 147 and accompanying text.

customs services. Liechtenstein remains internationally responsible for breaches of commercial agreements which do not require an implementation by the Swiss authorities or for the acts of the Swiss customs officers under the express authority of Liechtenstein by virtue of the EEA Agreement.[306]

United Nations

Liechtenstein envisaged United Nations membership at a rather early stage. Preliminary unofficial talks with certain delegations in New York had already begun in the sixties, but the admission of Liechtenstein seemed as yet impossible. At that time the United States and the United Kingdom in particular were against admitting a great number of Micro-States to the United Nations.[307] By 1988, discussions with the permanent representatives of the Security Council, other Security Council members and the representatives of the regional groups showed that all delegations were in favour of Liechtenstein's admission by reason of the principle of universality underlined in the United Nations.[308]

The problems arising from Liechtenstein's application for membership of the United Nations were not so much of an international order, as of a national order. In general, the application for membership lacked popular support. In March 1986, a Swiss people's referendum resulted in a 75 per cent refusal of Switzerland's membership in the United Nations. It was also known that the Liechtenstein population tended to vote in a similar way to the nearby Swiss cantons which had rejected Switzerland's membership in the United Nations with an even higher percentage.[309] It was eventually decided not to consult the Liechtenstein people by way of referendum.[310] On 14

---

[306] By virtue of Art. 7 and Annex III of the 1994 agreement to the 1923 customs union treaty, Switzerland takes certain administrative measures by order of Liechtenstein.
[307] See p. 137 above.
[308] BA no. 41/1989, p. 3.
[309] Interview with HH Prince Hans-Adam II von and zu Liechtenstein of 5 Apr. 1991. An unofficial student opinion poll showed that in 1988 66.3 per cent of the Liechtensteinese were against United Nations membership, with 26.3 per cent in favour and 7.4 per cent undecided: M. Beck et al., *Die Vereinten Nationen – Ein Thema für Liechtenstein* (1988) p. 78.
[310] The possibility of a referendum on treaties instead of laws was not provided for in the Constitution. Arts. 8 and 66 of the Constitution were examined by two legal experts, an Austrian and a Swiss, who came to opposite conclusions as to whether the Constitution permitted a referendum on a treaty. A people's initiative for a referendum on the United Nations membership was rejected by the Diet. Interview with HH Prince Hans-Adam II von and zu Liechtenstein of 5 Apr. 1991.

December 1989, the Diet unanimously approved the application for membership in the United Nations.[311] The main argument against United Nations membership focused on the costs which a United Nations membership would entail and on the fact that the United Nations would not bring anything new or substantial to Liechtenstein.[312]

The reasons for seeking admission to the United Nations were diverse. They included:[313] the reinforcement of Liechtenstein's independence and statehood through an active foreign policy at an international level; a global cooperation and international solidarity on the basis of an international order ruled by international law; the establishment of diplomatic contacts with virtually all States of the world without having to run into disproportionate costs; and participation in the finding of international solutions for environmental, health and food problems.[314]

By letter of 10 August 1990, Liechtenstein applied for membership in the United Nations.[315] On 13 August 1990, the Security Council referred the request for examination to its Committee on the Admission of New Members[316] which issued its report the following day and recommended that Liechtenstein be admitted.[317] On 14 August 1990, the Security Council unanimously recommended the admission of Liechtenstein to membership in the United Nations.[318] Most Security Council members declared that they had no doubt that Liechtenstein was fully capable of carrying out the obligations of a Member State, as it had already effectively participated in several agencies of the United Nations, the CSCE and the Council of Europe.[319] China emphasized that Liechtenstein was a peace-loving country which met the requirements for United Nations membership.[320] Romania believed that Liechtenstein would 'help to

---

[311] *Landtags-Protokolle* (1989) vol. V, *Oeffentliche Landtagssitzung* (13/14 Dec. 1989) p. 1589.
[312] Arguments cited in the Diet, *Landtags-Protokolle* (1989) vol. V, *Oeffentliche Landtagssitzung* (13/14 Dec. 1989) p. 1575.
[313] BA no. 41/1989.
[314] Ibid., p. 7.
[315] UN Doc. S/21486 (1990).
[316] UN Doc. S/PV.2935 (1990).
[317] UN Doc. S/21506 (1990).
[318] SC Res. 663 (1990) and UN Doc. A/45/419 (1990).
[319] UN Doc. S/PV.2936 (1990) pp. 3 and 6, United Kingdom and Finnish delegates respectively.
[320] Ibid., p. 7.

strengthen the quantitative dimension of the universality of [the] Organization'.[321] The Soviet delegate, whose country was previously opposed to Liechtenstein's admission to the Statute of the International Court of Justice,[322] declared that Liechtenstein would 'make a positive contribution to the multifaceted work of the Organization' and that 'all States, large and small, can and should make their contribution to the process of strengthening security and expanding mutual understanding between peoples'.[323]

On 18 September 1990, the General Assembly accepted Liechtenstein's admission by acclamation.[324] The President of the General Assembly stated that 'Liechtenstein brings to the United Nations a rich experience in the ways and means open to small States to foster their well-being and independence. There is much here, I am sure, that other States can learn from.'[325] In general, the delegates declared that 'all members of the international community, even if they are small in terms of geography and population, can contribute decisively to the ... work of the General Assembly and the Organization as a whole'.[326] Thus Liechtenstein became the 160th Member State of the United Nations.[327]

It is remarkable that Liechtenstein's application was not submitted to a thorough investigation into its statehood. Due to the active role which it had played in the CSCE and the Council of Europe there was no room left for doubt about its statehood, nor on its capacity to fulfil the membership obligations. This international attitude stands in glaring contrast to the international reactions which arose in the League of Nations when Liechtenstein applied for membership.[328] Apart from the institutional objections which prompted the League's attitude, the difference in reaction can be explained by the success of Liechtenstein's foreign policy in emphasizing its 'Eigenstaatlichkeit' and in proving that it can provide a valuable contribution to the work of international fora despite its smallness.

---

[321] Ibid., p. 12.
[322] See pp. 175–177 above.
[323] UN Doc. S/PV.2936 (1990) pp. 7–8.
[324] GA Res. 45/1 and UN Doc. A/45/PV.1 (1990) p. 23.
[325] Ibid.
[326] Austrian delegate: ibid., p. 33. Also Sri Lanka, p. 27 and Hungary, pp. 28–30.
[327] Liechtenstein had been admitted to the ECE in a consultative capacity on 30 Mar. 1976: Decision by the ECE M (XXXI) of 30 Mar. 1976, UN Doc. E/5781, E/ECE/909, ECOSOC OR (25 Apr. 1975–9 Apr. 1976) Suppl. no. 8, pp. 93 and 106. In 1993, total costs of UN membership amounted to 1,784,966 Swiss francs: 'Voranschlag 1995', Annex to BA no. 66/1994.
[328] See pp. 170–174 above.

During the forty-eighth session of the General Assembly, Liechtenstein requested the inclusion of a sub-item entitled 'Effective realization of the right of self-determination through autonomy' in the existing item 'Right of peoples to self-determination'. This initiative sought to promote a broader and more flexible application of the right to self-determination, by *inter alia* providing different levels of autonomy for communities living within States and at least a certain initial and very basic level of autonomy for communities with a sufficient degree of distinctive identity.[329] After a lively debate in the Third Committee, some States feared that the initiative would lead to disintegration of existing States, to interference in internal affairs and to difficult discussions on the definition of 'communities'.[330] Armenia and Ecuador were among the States supporting Liechtenstein's ideas and they even envisaged the creation of an impartial organ which would be charged with examining claims for self-determination.[331] It was however decided to defer the consideration of this matter to one of the Committee's future sessions.[332]

The United Nations gives Liechtenstein the opportunity to make its voice heard on a universal political level. The wide range of topics dealt with by this Organization makes it necessary for small delegations like Liechtenstein's to define clear priority areas.[333]

Other international organizations

Liechtenstein participates in other governmental organizations or conferences, besides the ones we have discussed in the preceding paragraphs, of which we name the following:

---

[329] UN Doc. A/48/147 and Add.1 (1993), A/50/492 (1995) and Memorandum (not published). See pp. 107–108 above.
[330] In this spirit: Ghana, India, Indonesia, Iraq, Kenya and Malaysia, UN Doc. A/C.3/48/SR.21–22 (1993).
[331] Armenia proposed to charge the Trusteeship Council or a special committee of the Security Council with this matter, whereas Ecuador thought the Sixth Committee would be more competent to formulate legal answers to present-day self-determination questions: ibid., pp. 4–5.
[332] Liechtenstein is presently developing the initiative further within an academic rather than political framework. The Prince of Liechtenstein has given a grant to Princeton University's Woodrow Wilson School of Public and International Affairs to establish a research programme on self-determination. Information from the Permanent Mission of the Principality of Liechtenstein to the UN.
[333] Information from the Permanent Mission of the Principality of Liechtenstein to the UN. It also protested against the violations of humanitarian law in the former Yugoslavia, UN Doc. S/1387 (1994).

UPU On 17 January 1950 the Liechtenstein Head of Government declared to the UPU that by virtue of Article 2 of the postal union treaty of 1920 with Switzerland, Liechtenstein was a member within the meaning of Article 10 of the Universal Postal Convention. On 13 April 1962, Liechtenstein became a full and independent member of the UPU and therefore was no longer represented by Switzerland.[334]

ITU Liechtenstein became a member of the ITU on 25 July 1963. Liechtenstein was granted a reserved radio frequency which it started using in 1995.[335]

UNCTAD Liechtenstein was invited to the first world conference of UNCTAD held on 23 March 1964. As a member of two United Nations specialized organizations, the UPU and the ITU, Liechtenstein was always invited to United Nations conferences. When on 30 December 1964 UNCTAD became a permanent organ of the United Nations, Liechtenstein remained a Member State.[336]

IAEA Liechtenstein has been a member of the IAEA since 13 December 1968.[337] The Board of Governors of the IAEA[338] and the General Conference[339] had approved Liechtenstein's application without discussion. The Liechtenstein representative explained thereupon his State's interests in the Organization, declaring that '[c]lose co-operation with Switzerland had enabled Liechtenstein to carry out useful research work in the field of atomic energy, to develop new materials for reactors and to train nuclear energy experts'.[340]

WIPO Liechtenstein adhered to the WIPO on 17 February 1972.[341]

GATT When Switzerland ratified GATT on 1 April 1966, it declared that the customs territory of Switzerland included the Principality of Liechtenstein as long as it formed a customs union with Switzerland.[342] Liechtenstein was seen as a part of the 'metropolitan customs

---

[334] Jansen, 'Liechtenstein und die Vereinte Nationen', p. 29. LGBl (1962) no. 22.
[335] The Liechtenstein Government has granted a concession for the establishment of 'Radio L': BA no. 63/1994.
[336] Jansen, 'Liechtenstein und die Vereinte Nationen', pp. 31–32.
[337] LGBl (1969) no. 44. It ratified the Treaty on the Non-Proliferation of Nuclear Weapons on 20 Apr. 1978, following Switzerland's ratification of 9 Mar. 1977.
[338] IAEA Doc. GOV/1268 (18 Apr. 1968) and IAEA Doc. GOV/OR.404 (13 Jun. 1968) p. 8, paras. 35–36.
[339] IAEA Doc. GC (XII) OR.119 (24 Sept. 1968) p. 3, paras. 21–28.
[340] Ibid., para. 28.
[341] LGBl (1972) no. 25.
[342] Point 3 of the Protocol of accession, 570 UNTS (1966) no. 814, p. 276.

territory' of Switzerland within the meaning of Article XXIV, paragraph 1 of the General Agreement. On 29 March 1994, the Liechtenstein Government decided to accede to GATT 1947. It has also signed GATT 1994 and the WTO Agreement, thus enabling it to become an original Member of the new World Trade Organization.[343]

European Bank for Reconstruction and Development Liechtenstein signed the Convention establishing the European Bank for Reconstruction and Development on 29 May 1990. Liechtenstein pays 0.02 per cent of the Bank's total capital.[344] Liechtenstein's participation in the Bank shows its solidarity in the European economic construction and the role it wants to play therein.[345]

Application of the criteria for statehood

Combining our findings, the following can be concluded with regard to the examination of Liechtenstein's statehood:[346]

Territory The relative smallness of Liechtenstein's territory has not precluded its statehood. In addition, it has formally been maintained that its smallness was no reason to exclude it from an international organization or conference. This international position was phrased as a general rule.

Population Liechtenstein possesses a permanent population of which 38.6 per cent are foreigners.[347] This proportion of foreign inhabitants has never led to the international denial of the existence of a State population in Liechtenstein.

Government As we have found, Liechtenstein has an elaborate system of government on a highly democratic basis.[348] There can be no doubt about the effective power which the governmental institutions wield in the territory of Liechtenstein.

---

[343] BA no. 1994/23, p. 4. Acceptance as an 'original Member' under Art. XIV of the WTO Agreement, 33 ILM (1994), pp. 1144 ff.
[344] This amounts to 3.6 million Swiss francs, of which 70 per cent is in the form of a guarantee. It has one seat in the Council of Governors and one seat in the Executive Board shared with Switzerland and Turkey. BA no. 84/90, p. 9.
[345] Ibid.
[346] See for the general criteria for statehood, pp. pp. 116–127 above.
[347] See p. 147 above.
[348] See pp. 150–154 above.

Independence It should be noted that, although prompted by political reasons, the Soviet Union argued that Liechtenstein was not a State only because it lacked independence, and not because it was too small.[349] The most examined and most sensitive aspect of Liechtenstein's legal position has always been its independence from Switzerland and Austria. The following foreign elements are present in Liechtenstein's governmental organization:

1. *Certain Swiss or Austrian judges in the judicial system* They do not comprise the majority of a court's judges.[350] They are independent and therefore by definition not under Swiss or Austrian control.

2. *Some diplomatic relations are maintained by Switzerland* Switzerland can only act under Liechtenstein's orders and is not as such in charge of Liechtenstein's diplomatic missions. Liechtenstein is free to set up its own diplomatic representations.[351] This has been underlined by the Council of Europe.[352] Since Liechtenstein became a member of the Council of Europe, EFTA and the United Nations, Switzerland's political representation on behalf of Liechtenstein has lost much of its value.

3. *Swiss control over postal and customs services* The postal and customs officers in Liechtenstein are under Swiss authority. Swiss postal and customs legislation is applicable in Liechtenstein as well as the treaties concluded by Switzerland with third States. Liechtenstein cannot, in general, oppose the application of a customs treaty in its territory.[353] These restrictions on its independence can however be lifted within one year on denunciation of the postal and customs treaties.[354] Moreover, as a result of its independent ratification of the EEA Ageement, Liechtenstein will have its own specific customs control and can take a different legal course from Switzerland. It has the freedom to act independently of Switzerland within the institutional bodies set up by the EFTA and EEA Agreements.[355]

4. *Swiss monetary control* Liechtenstein cannot develop its own monetary policy and the Swiss National Bank exercises its authority over Liechtenstein-based banks, persons and companies

---

[349] See p. 175 above at n. 194 and accompanying text.
[350] See p. 154 above.
[351] See p. 162 above.
[352] See p. 180 above.
[353] See p. 164 above.
[354] See pp. 164–165 above. This point was also emphasized by the Council of Europe.
[355] See p. 186 above.

virtually as in Switzerland.[356] Liechtenstein's treaty obligations in this matter can be revoked within six months.

5 *Swiss legislation on the residence and sojourn of aliens* Switzerland can expel an alien with effect for Liechtenstein without the latter's cooperation or influence. Liechtenstein maintains its own aliens office and still has a certain freedom to apply the Swiss aliens legislation.[357] The implementation of the EEA Agreement will lead to a disparity in the application of the aliens legislation in Switzerland and Liechtenstein.[358] The ratification of the EEA Agreement by Liechtenstein has thus accentuated Liechtenstein's freedom of action in its relations with Switzerland.

The delegation of certain powers to Switzerland has not prejudiced Liechtenstein's formal independence. The treaty obligations and functions delegated to Switzerland have not been considered by the international community as precluding Liechtenstein's statehood.

Does Liechtenstein also have actual independence from Switzerland? Given its small size, Liechtenstein has, in practice, managed to keep a high degree of real independence. Its actual freedom of political action is for instance reinforced by the fact that Liechtenstein provides for its own water consumption and electricity supply through a hydro-electric power station supplemented by solar energy installations. Liechtenstein can sever its links with Switzerland on twelve months' notice by terminating the postal, customs and monetary union treaties. The effects of such an action would not be dramatic, as 86.2 per cent of industrial exports go to countries other than Switzerland.[359] The Swiss franc could be replaced by any other currency and the postal services could be privatized. Even if the Liechtensteinese prefer to keep their present friendly relations with Switzerland, it is this factual situation which places Liechtenstein in a better negotiating position and makes it less prone to external pressures. It is evident that Liechtenstein possesses actual independence and is not submitted to substantial external control by Switzerland.

Recognition Liechtenstein's international recognition seems to have a purely declaratory nature. The League of Nations had 'no doubt' that juridically the Principality was a sovereign State.[360] A clear

[356] See p. 166 above.
[357] See p. 168 above.
[358] See pp. 168 and 188–189 above.
[359] Status as at 31 Dec. 1993, calculated on the basis of the figures represented in *Statistisches Jahrbuch 1994*, p. 192.
[360] See p. 172 above at n. 174.

distinction should nevertheless be made between the recognition of Liechtenstein's statehood and the admission of Liechtenstein to an international organization, as the former does not guarantee the latter. The League of Nations' refusal to admit Liechtenstein as a full member was not based on the rejection of its statehood, as we have seen.[361] The first post-war recognition came from the Member States of the United Nations, when they approved Liechtenstein's accession to the Statute of the International Court of Justice. The Principality was said to possess 'all the qualifications of a State'.[362] This position was confirmed by the International Court of Justice.[363] The non-recognition by the Soviet, Byelorussian and Ukrainian Republics, though based on legal arguments, seemed to have been mainly inspired by political reasons. The Soviet Union did not object to Liechtenstein's admission in the CSCE.[364]

Liechtenstein's foreign policy aimed at consolidating even further its international recognition by adhering to the Council of Europe and the United Nations. In practice, Liechtenstein's problems were not, at that stage, linked to the recognition of its statehood, but to the reluctance of the international community to admit the Principality with open arms in political organizations. The Council of Europe took more care to examine the statehood of Liechtenstein than it usually did for larger States. It was, in general, concluded that Liechtenstein had enough independence to be qualified as a State. Therefore, Liechtenstein's recognition was not meant to be reparative of a lack of independence. It was nevertheless examined and thought important whether Liechtenstein had been previously admitted to certain international conferences or organizations. This was considered especially by the Council of Europe and to a lesser degree by the United Nations in 1991.[365] The United Nations, when deciding on Liechtenstein's application for membership, did not show any doubts as to Liechtenstein's statehood.[366] The object of these investigations was not so much to search for proof of Liechtenstein's statehood and recognition thereof, but to ascertain the Principality's ability to fulfil its international obligations and to participate in the work of the organization in question.

---

[361] See p. 173 above.
[362] See p. 175 above at n. 195 and accompanying text.
[363] *Nottebohm* case, ICJ Reports (1955) p. 20.
[364] See p. 178 above.
[365] See p. 181 above at n. 227 and p. 196 above at n. 319 and accompanying text.
[366] See p. 197 above.

We can conclude that Liechtenstein is a State in international law and that its degree of formal and actual independence falls within the generally demanded criterion of independence.

Self-determination of the Liechtenstein people

The inhabitants of a State, that is independent peoples, have the right of self-determination with force of *jus cogens*.[367] Now that Liechtenstein's statehood has been ascertained, the Liechtenstein inhabitants undoubtedly have the right of self-determination, provided that they constitute a 'people' or 'fraction of a people' within the meaning of international law. As we have seen, objective and subjective criteria should be taken into account as well as an attachment to the territory.[368] It is noticeable that a small population like that of Liechtenstein cannot clearly distinguish itself on strictly objective criteria from its surrounding populations due to the social 'openness' of its society and frequent interrelations with the neighbouring populations. The objective characteristics of the Liechtenstein inhabitants are therefore especially combined in the historical and traditional togetherness. The origins of their national character can be retraced to the beginning of the eighteenth century when the territory was bought by the Prince of Liechtenstein who gave his name to the Principality and its people.[369] The Liechtenstein nationals are to a great extent the descendants of families which are long established in the Liechtenstein territory. Even if the Liechtenstein inhabitants do not have their own Liechtenstein language and clearly distinct culture, they do have a subjective we-consciousness.[370] The Liechtenstein nationals, to the exclusion of the foreign inhabitants, are also anxious to preserve their own identity so as not to be overwhelmed by foreigners.

It can therefore be sustained that the Liechtenstein nationals possess the objective and subjective characteristics required to be a

---

[367] See the general conclusion on p. 103 above.
[368] See pp. 79–80 above.
[369] See p. 149 above.
[370] Amelunxen notes on this subject that the actual Liechtenstein consciousness of its nationhood was born out of the confrontation with Germany in 1939 when the Liechtenstein people became aware that they did not constitute a part of the German nor of the Swiss nation: C. Amelunxen, 'Schwierige Vaterländer – Aspekte der liechtensteinisch–deutschen Beziehungen in Vergangenheit und Gegenwart', 2 *Liechtenstein Politische Schriften* (1973) p. 60.

people and have an attachment to their territory. If the objective criteria are taken more restrictively, or if less importance is given to the subjective criteria, the Liechtenstein people could be considered a part of a people. This would however not prejudice their right of self-determination, because they constitute a State.

Conclusions

We have set out to investigate the legal consequences of Liechtenstein's smallness, on the basis of which the following can be concluded:

1. Liechtenstein's statehood is well established and recognized.
2. Liechtenstein's foreign policy, which aimed at consolidating its sovereignty in the long term through the membership of several international political organizations, does not as such have any legal consequences for Liechtenstein's international status. Its statehood was juridically unquestionable before its admission to the Council of Europe, and especially fortified by its adherence to the Statute of the International Court of Justice. Liechtenstein's membership of the Council of Europe, the United Nations, EFTA and the OSCE, as well as its adherence to the EEA, have however the effect of proving its political existence, thus preventing a marginalization and an assimilation with Switzerland. It also emphasized Liechtenstein's capacity to cooperate in the work of international organizations and to take an active part in its results.
3. Liechtenstein's international behaviour has been in a certain sense a pioneer work for the other European Micro-States, because it was the first European Micro-State to enter actively into the Council of Europe and the United Nations. In general, its activities inspired confidence from the international community and influenced the behaviour of the international community towards Micro-States in general.
4. Liechtenstein's degree of independence is not only due to legal efforts but has also been determined by its historical development, internal facilities and the political structure of its neighbouring States. It thus seems probable that, and this is not a legal but a political conclusion, Liechtenstein's international actions were facilitated by the fact that Switzerland is, by its very nature, used to small decentralized political units. This could have been different if Liechtenstein had been confronted with a more centralized neighbouring State.[371]

---

[371] See on the situation in San Marino, Monaco and Andorra, pp. 223-233, 274-290 and 335-346 below.

5 In general, it can be observed that Liechtenstein's legal and political status over the years has been fortified to a degree which has lessened the effects of dependence due to its small territory and restricted human and natural resources. In view of these achievements, Liechtenstein has managed to compensate for the inherent disadvantages of being a Micro-State.

5   The Republic of San Marino

Territory, population and economy

The Republic of San Marino is an enclave between the Italian regions of Marche and Emilia-Romagna. The Republic has a territory of 61 square kilometres and there were 25,863 inhabitants in 1991.[1] The San Marinese population comprises 82.3 per cent of the inhabitants, against 17.0 per cent Italian nationals.[2] The San Marinese economy is mainly based on industrial production and the service sector.[3] San Marino has no official statistics on imports, exports and re-exports. There is nevertheless no doubt that the San Marinese economy is strongly export-oriented, whether of original goods or of re-exported products.[4] The provisional State budget for 1995 forecast a deficit of 28,460.5 million lire covered by loans.[5] Direct and indirect taxes cover

---

[1] Status as at Apr. 1991, Centro Elaborazione Dati e Statistica, *Bollettino di Statistica* (Apr./May 1991) nos. 4–5, fig. 2.5, p. 9.

[2] Ibid. Calculated on the basis of the figures represented. The foreign inhabitants comprise 17.7 per cent of the population, of which 17.0 per cent are Italians and 0.7 per cent are other foreigners.

[3] Of the working population 5 per cent are active in the agricultural sector, 32 per cent in industry, 14 per cent are artisans, 15 per cent work in tourism and trade, 7 per cent in other services and 27 per cent in the public administration. Of total industrial productions 34 per cent are machines, 17 per cent clothing, 17 per cent chemical pharmacy, 16 per cent mixed industries, 9 per cent ceramics and 7 per cent food: Associazione Nazionale dell'Industria Sammarinese, *Uno Stato e la sua Industria nel Mondo*, pp. 11 and 13.

[4] Re-exporting seems to be frequent. Thus between 1982 and 1986 San Marinese imports of fresh meat rose by 210 per cent from 742 to 2,300 tons, *Bollettino di Statistica* (Oct./Dec. 1986) p. 28. This could not be justified by an increase of local consumption by more inhabitants or tourists. As San Marino had no meat-tinning factory the meat products must have been re-exported. See P. Giorgeri, *Conflittualità nelle Relazioni Italo – Sammarinesi* (1987–88) pp. 182–183.

[5] No. 7,000 of the 1995 provisional budget, BURSM (1994) no. 12.

72.2 per cent of the State's revenues, of which the tax on imported goods amounts to 68.8 per cent.[6] The San Marinese fiscal system sets forth two main taxes which are at slightly lower rates than in Italy.[7] Numerous limited liability companies have their registered offices in San Marino.[8] Characteristically for a Micro-State, San Marino's economy is highly dependent on the international trade situation and the inflow of foreign capital.

History

According to an ancient legend San Marino was founded by a pious and devout stone cutter, Saint Marinus, in AD 301. A noblewoman of Rimini had given the mountain of Titano and the surrounding area to Saint Marinus in gratitude for his helping to save her son.[9] Although some historians doubt the authenticity of this legend, the Republic of San Marino has existed as a separate entity ever since the foundation of the Papal States and has conserved many of its original institutions. In the middle of the sixteenth century the Community of San Marino was an indirect dominion of the Holy See, with substantial autonomy and undisputed recognition of the papal sovereignty.[10] By a convention of 1627 the Holy See expressly recognized San Marino's autonomy and privileges, while San Marino in turn recognized the Holy See's sovereignty over the territory. In the first half of the eighteenth century the situation in San Marino was characterized by anarchy and the abuse of the right of asylum and the right to grant letters of recommendation which facilitated the refuge of wanted

---

[6] Direct taxes cover 18.6 per cent, indirect taxes 4.0 per cent and tax on imported goods 49.6 per cent of total State revenues. Figures calculated on the basis of categories 1–3 of title no. 1 of the 1995 provisional budget, BURSM (1994) no. 12.

[7] A tax on revenues from capital, land, buildings, independent and dependent work, and a tax on trade benefits: Law relating to the general tax on revenues ('imposta generale sui redditi') of 13 Oct. 1984, No. 91, BURSM (1984) no. 10. The maximum levy of the tax on revenues is 50 per cent. The company tax on commercial activities is 24 per cent against 36 per cent (or 47 per cent including other company taxes) in Italy: Decree of 23 Dec. 1986, No. 154, BURSM (1986) no. 12 and Giorgeri, *Conflittualità*, p. 188.

[8] In contrast with Italian company law, San Marino does not provide for nominative shares. See G. Vedovato, *Le Relazioni Italia–San Marino*, 2nd ser. X (1960) pp. 28–30.

[9] Ufficio di Stato per il Turismo, *San Marino la Leggenda, la Storia, il Paesaggio* (1991) p. 7.

[10] C. Buscarini, 'Dal Comune allo Stato: Note sulla Formazione della Soggettività Internazionale di San Marino', *Storia e Ordinamento della Repubblica di San Marino* (Febr.–Apr. 1982) p. 64. The Papal States were divided into two structures: the direct dominion which was under the direct papal authority and the indirect dominion which had an autonomous government under papal sovereignty.

persons. Due to this situation and the protests of certain San Marinese inhabitants, the papal legate in Romagna, Cardinal Alberoni, convinced Pope Clemens XII to take San Marino by force and turn it into a direct dominion.[11] San Marino was occupied by the armed forces of the Church on 17 October 1739. The majority of the San Marinese population objected to this intervention and gained support of other Cardinals and the Austrian, Spanish and French ambassadors in Rome.[12] An apostolic delegate was therefore appointed by the Pope to organize a plebiscite on the freedom and maintenance of the Republic, which was approved by a more than three-quarters majority. On 5 February 1740 the Republic of San Marino regained its previous status under the Holy See's protection.[13]

On 23 May 1798, the Republic of San Marino concluded a treaty of friendship and commerce with Napoleon's Roman Republic. The preamble of this treaty recalled that San Marino was under the protection of the French Republic.[14] Napoleon's representative, Monge, offered San Marino an enlargement of its territory in 1798,[15] which it graciously refused.[16] San Marino subsequently concluded a treaty on extradition, imports, salt and tobacco with the Italian Republic on 10 June 1802[17] which was renewed with the Kingdom of Italy on 29 October 1808.[18]

The Congress of Vienna did not explicitly concern San Marino. The Holy See therefore concluded that, as the Papal States were re-established in the original pre-Napoleonic status, San Marino had become an indirect dominion again. San Marino claimed however that as the

---

[11] J. M. Le Besnerais, *Le Statut international de la République de Saint-Marin* (no date mentioned, about 1968) pp. 45-48.
[12] Ibid., pp. 48-50.
[13] Ibid., p. 50, also Buscarini, 'Dal Comune allo Stato', p. 67.
[14] The preamble reads: '[la] Repubblica Francese, sotto la cui protezione si ritrova la Repubblica di San Marino'. The treaty laid down the 'buona amicizia e buona intelligenza' between the Roman Republic and San Marino (Art. 1) and regulated trade on the basis of a most-favoured-nation clause (Art. 2). Text in T. Ballarino, 'L'Evoluzione della Personalità Internazionale di San Marino', *Studi Sammarinese* (1987) pp. 21-22.
[15] Monge wrote: 'même si quelque partie des Etats voisins, non contestée, vous était absolument nécessaire, je suis chargé par le Général en chef [Napoleon] de vous prier de lui en faire part'. Cited in Le Besnerais, *Le Statut international*, pp. 58-59.
[16] The Republic stated: 'contente de la circonscription de son territoire et de sa modeste existence, n'a garde d'accepter l'offre généreuse qui lui est faite et de concevoir les vues ambitieuses d'un agrandissement qui pourrait avec le temps compromettre sa liberté'. Ibid., p. 60.
[17] Text in Ballarino, 'L'Evoluzione', pp. 23-24.
[18] Buscarini, 'Dal Comune allo Stato', p. 70.

Congress of Vienna had not decided on its status, this implied a recognition of its independent status acquired between 1798 and 1815.[19] The Holy See never admitted the latter interpretation and held on to San Marino's restrictive autonomous administration. The relations between San Marino and the Holy See deteriorated until the unification of the Italian State in 1861. This unification did not prejudice San Marino's existence as a separate entity: a treaty was concluded with the Italian Kingdom on 22 March 1862 accepting the king's protective friendship ('amicizia protettrice') over San Marino.[20]

During both World Wars, San Marino declared its neutrality.[21] Nevertheless, San Marino's territory was bombed by the Allied Forces between July and September 1944. San Marino subsequently claimed compensation from the United Kingdom for the violation of its neutrality. After several years of negotiations, San Marino received £80,000.[22] Moreover, the reparation was accompanied by a declaration of honour made in the House of Commons on 7 July 1960 which recognized and honoured San Marino's efforts to maintain its neutrality and to prevent a German occupation of its territory.[23] After the Second World War, San Marino's economy developed strongly through the inflow of foreign capital and the establishment of enterprises. This period is also marked by the intensification of San Marino's diplomatic and international relations. The survival of San Marino as a separate entity throughout history is probably due to its political insignificance and its will to preserve its autonomous institutions.

---

[19] Ibid., p. 71.
[20] Art. XXIX of the 1862 treaty: Annex XIX, ibid., pp. 125–129. This protection clause was reaffirmed on 27 Jun. 1897 and remained valid until a treaty of 10 Sept. 1971.
[21] During the First World War, through the mediation of the United States and the Holy See, it tried to liberate certain San Marinese workers who had been interned in an Austrian camp. Austria however refused to release these prisoners because it stated that San Marino was not neutral, as many San Marinese had joined the Italian army. M. A. Bonelli, *I Rapporti Convenzionali Italo-Sammarinesi: Con Notizie sulle Relazione Internazionali della Reppublica di San Marino (1862-1942)* (1985) pp. 366-368.
[22] Ibid., p. 170.
[23] Ibid. See also R. Ago, 'La Neutralità di S. Marino', *Libera Orizzonte* (31 Jul. 1963) no. 7, pp. 7-8.

Constitutional and legal order
Form of government

San Marino does not have an official Constitution as such. The first legal documents which mentioned San Marino's institutional organs were the Statutes of 1600. At present, the Republic's institutional framework is that laid down in a law of 8 July 1974 (hereafter, the fundamental law) which can only be amended by a two-thirds majority in the San Marinese Parliament.[24] The sovereignty is vested in the people which exercises it through a representative democracy.[25]

San Marino's Parliament, the 'Consiglio Grande e Generale' (hereafter, the Great and General Council) has the legislative power.[26] It has been composed of sixty members since at least the Statutes of 1600 and probably even earlier.[27] The Great and General Council appoints the members of the Government – the 'Congresso di Stato' (hereafter, State Congress) – and the Heads of State – the 'Capitani Reggenti' (hereafter, Captains Regent) – from among its members. Apart from its legislative power, the Great and General Council also has the right of interrogation and interpellation and the right to adopt motions in order to discharge the State Congress.[28] It furthermore has the right to approve the State budget and to ratify the decrees promulgated by the Captains Regent.[29] It possesses the judicial power to decide on a *restitutio in integrum* if a private person is unjustly aggrieved by a definite judicial decision, and can give a pardon, an amnesty or change a criminal judgment.[30]

---

[24] Art. 16, law of 8 Jul. 1974, No. 59 called 'Dichiarazione dei diritti dei cittadini e dei principi fondamentali dell'ordinamento sammarinese', BURSM (1974) no. 3.
[25] Art. 2 of the fundamental law.
[26] Art. 3, 1st para. of the fundamental law. The Great and General Council is elected for five years by all San Marinese nationals of at least eighteen years of age, including those living outside San Marino: Art. 8 of the law of 23 Dec. 1958, No. 36 (law on elections). Almost one-third of the San Marinese nationals live outside San Marino.
[27] R. Bonelli, *Gli Organi dei Poteri Pubblici nell'Ordinamento della Repubblica di San Marino* (1984) p. 36. Only in 1739, during the occupation by Cardinal Alberoni, was the Great and General Council composed of twenty-seven surviving members.
[28] Law of 11 Mar. 1981, No. 21. An interrogation concerns questions relating to the correctness of certain facts, Government actions or intentions of the Government. An interpellation aims at questioning the reasons behind the Government's conduct with regard to its policy or to the situation of the State: ibid., p. 40.
[29] Art. 3, 3rd para. of the fundamental law.
[30] Criminal Code, see Bonelli, *Gli Organi*, p. 40.

The function of Head of State is exercised by two Captains Regent according to the principle of collegiality, in other words, a decision has to be approved by both Captains Regent.[31] This institution was referred to in the Statutes of 1600 and was not uncommon at the end of the Roman period and in the Italian States of the Middle Ages.[32] The Captains Regent are appointed by the Great and General Council from among its members for a period of six months on 1 April and 1 October.[33] The Captains Regent cannot resign. They form the presidency of the State Congress, the Great and General Council and the Council of Twelve. The Captains Regent retain their right to vote in the Great and General Council. They help with the nomination and formation of the Government and can adopt decrees.[34] After their term of office, the Captains Regent are traditionally submitted to the jurisdiction of a 'sindicato' which is composed of two members of the Great and General Council and appointed by the latter. The 'sindicato' pronounces itself on the political and legal responsibility of the Captains Regent for their acts during their term of office.[35]

San Marino's Government, the State Congress, exercises the executive power and is responsible to the Great and General Council. The State Congress is composed of ten ministers and is usually based on a coalition of two political parties chosen at the beginning of every legislative period by and from the members of the Great and General Council.[36] The State Congress can resign or be dismissed by the Great and General Council.[37] Decisions taken by the State Congress have to

---

[31] Art. 3, 1st para. of the fundamental law.

[32] This was known as the institution of the 'consules' who could have certain judicial power. Bonelli, *Gli Organi*, p. 52.

[33] They are ineligible for re-election until at least three years after the end of their previous term of office. Only San Marinese by birth, i.e., of San Marinese fathers, can become Captains Regent. Law of 24 Mar. 1945, No. 45.

[34] The latter right can be exercised in emergency cases, after consultation with the State Congress, or if a law provides for such a possibility. In either case the ratification by the Great and General Council has to be sought within three months of their promulgation: Art. 3, 3rd para. of the fundamental law.

[35] E. Spagna Musso and R. Lipparini, 'L'Ordinamento Costituzionale di San Marino', *Archivio Giuridico 'Filippo Serafini'*, vol. CCVI (1986) p. 48.

[36] The most important ministers are the Secretaries of State for foreign affairs, for internal affairs and for finance and budget. There are seven delegates for labour, industry, territorial matters, health and social security, education, communication and commerce.

[37] Thus in Febr. 1992, the State Congress resigned for internal political reasons. The coalition between the Partito Progressista Democratico and the Partito Democratico Cristiano was replaced by a coalition of the Partito Socialista and the Partito Democratico Cristiano: *Notizia* (1992) no. 4, p. 2.

be approved by unanimity. The State Congress prepares draft laws and decrees to be promulgated by the Great and General Council and the Captains Regent respectively. It cannot issue its own regulations, but takes care of the execution of the laws and decrees.[38]

The Great and General Council appoints furthermore twelve members from its parliamentarians at each legislative period who are seated in the Council of Twelve, the 'Consiglio dei XII'.[39] This, in principle, political organ has certain judicial powers.[40]

One of the remnant institutions of the Statutes of 1600 is the 'Arengo', an assembly of all San Marinese heads of families. Historically, the 'Arengo' had the right to present claims or propositions to the Captains Regent who could submit the requests to the Great and General Council. This procedure, known as the 'Istanze di Arengo', is still upheld in the form of a right of petition which at present belongs to all San Marinese citizens.[41] The 'Arengo' convenes to this end every Sunday after the entry into function of the Captains Regent.[42]

The right of initiative can be exercised by the State Congress, by each member of the Great and General Council, by every 'Giunta di Castello' (commune) and since 1981 by at least sixty San Marinese nationals.[43] In any case, the approval of the Great and General Council must be obtained in order to promulgate the draft law. A democratization of San Marino's political system led to the introduction of the possibility of referendum in 1981.[44] A referendum can be held in two cases:

1 An abrogative referendum aimed at the abrogation of an existing law or decree.[45]

---

[38] Bonelli, *Gli Organi*, pp. 68–69.
[39] Art. 1 of the law of 5 Jun. 1923, No. 13 on the Council of Twelve.
[40] See pp. 215–217 below.
[41] Spagna Musso and Lipparini, 'L'Ordinamento Costituzionale', pp. 10–11.
[42] A. Sottile, 'L'Ordinamento Politico e Giuridico della Repubblica di San Marino e la sua Situazione Internazionale', 51 RDI (1973) p. 325.
[43] Arts. 21 and 24 (1) of the law of 11 Mar. 1981, No. 21.
[44] The initiative for a referendum can be taken by fifteen electors and needs the approval of the 'Collegio', a council composed of the appeal judges and three members of the Great and General Council. Five 'Giunte di Castello' can also ask for a referendum. Moreover, in case of a confirmative referendum, the initiative can emanate from at least thirty-one members of the Great and General Council: law of 29 Oct. 1981, No. 82.
[45] With the exception of the fundamental law, fiscal laws, laws approving the State budget, international treaties and pardons: Art. 2 (2) of the law of 29 Oct. 1981, No. 82. On 25 Jul. 1982 a referendum was organized on the abrogation of the law on nation-

2   A confirmative referendum which has the object of approving or rejecting a promulgated law or decree which has not yet entered into force.[46]

As can be observed, San Marino's political system does not respect a strict separation of the legislative, executive and judicial powers. The principal institutional functions are centred around the Great and General Council which represents the people. The Great and General Council has approved in its 1991 session a general line of reform of the institutional organs and has invited the State Congress to present draft laws to this end.[47] The reform intends to reinforce the legal protection and political participation of the citizens, and the balance and separation of powers. At present, only a new law on the judicial organization has been adopted.[48]

Judicial system

The judges in San Marino cannot be San Marinese nationals, unless by virtue of statutory exceptions.[49] In accordance with the present practice, the only exception to the rule is the Conciliatory Judge ('Giudice Conciliatore') who can be a San Marinese citizen. The Great and General Council can nevertheless appoint a San Marinese judge by unanimity or with one vote against.[50] The judges are appointed by the Great and General Council for four years and are subsequently confirmed for an undetermined period.[51] The independence of the judiciary is guaranteed by law.[52] The judges have to swear an oath of allegiance to the Republic and are responsible to the Great and

---

ality of 1974 under which a San Marinese woman who acquired the nationality of her foreign husband lost her San Marinese nationality. The referendum rejected the proposal and the law was maintained: Bonelli, *Gli Organi*, p. 25. Art. 3, 1st para. of a new law on nationality of 27 Mar. 1984, No. 32 sets forth a similar clause for married San Marinese women and men. See p. 221 below and the discussion on this point in the Council of Europe, pp. 244–245 below.

[46] Art. 14 (1) of the law of 29 Oct. 1981, No. 82.
[47] *Notizia* (1992) no. 1, pp. 10–11.
[48] Law of 28 Oct. 1992, No. 83. See pp. 215–216 below.
[49] Art. 15, 3rd para. of the fundamental law. The Statutes of 1600 and subsequent practice until 1974 did not forbid the appointment to judicial office of a San Marinese. The fundamental law seems therefore contradictory: C. Buscarini, 'Gli Organi della Giurisdizione nell'Ordinamento di San Marino', 3 *IGS Miscellanea* (Jul. 1992) pp. 79–107.
[50] Bonelli, *Gli Organi*, p. 104. In practice the judges are of Italian nationality.
[51] Art. 7 of the law on judicial organization of 29 Oct. 1992, No. 83, BURSM (1992) Suppl. to no. 10.
[52] Art. 15, 3rd para. of the fundamental law and Art. 1, 1st para. of the 1992 law on judicial organization.

General Council.[53] Through the action of a Parliamentary Commission, the 'Sindicato', the Great and General Council can remove a judge from his functions if he has compromised the faith, respect and moral and professional esteem to which he is entitled or the prestige of the administration of justice.[54] Although the judges are subject only to the laws and are held to a punctual interpretation and application of the law in force,[55] the aforesaid power of removal is widely phrased and does not necessarily exclude the removal of a judge for pronouncing a politically undesired judgment. It is to be hoped that in practice this provision will not prejudice the judges' independence.

Civil jurisdiction is entrusted to four main judicial organs. Disputes which concern claims of no more than twenty million lire[56] are first submitted to a Conciliatory Judge who tries to come to an amicable agreement. His decisions remain subject to appeal before a Law Commissioner ('Commissario della Legge').[57] The Law Commissioner also acts as a judge in first instance for disputes involving more than twenty million lire and as an appeal judge against decisions of special judicatures.[58] If the Law Commissioner acts as a first instance organ, an appeal can be lodged before the Civil Appeals Judge ('Giudice delle Appellazioni Civili'). In third instance, if the first and second judgments do not concord, the Council of Twelve may choose between the two decisions.[59] San Marino does not have a Civil Code.[60]

Following the judicial reform of 1992 criminal jurisdiction is exercised in first instance by the Law Commissioner, the Criminal Appeals Judge ('Giudice delle Appelazioni Penali') or the Juvenile Court ('Tribunale dei Minori').[61] An appeal against a Law Commissioner's or

---

[53] Art. 1, 2nd para. and Art. 6, 6th para. of the 1992 law on judicial organization.

[54] Art. 14, 4th para. of the 1992 law on judicial organization reads: 'Il Consiglio Grande e Generale può deliberare l'esonero dall'incarico allorchè il Magistrato abbia compromesso la fiducia, il rispetto, l'estimazione morale e professionale che gli competono ovvero il prestigio dell'amministrazione della giustizia.'

[55] Art. 1, 3rd para. of the 1992 law on judicial organization.

[56] Decree of 17 Jul. 1991, No. 88, BURSM (1991) no. 7.

[57] Art. 20, 1st para. of the 1992 law on judicial organization.

[58] The Fiscal Committee, the Conciliatory Labour Committee and the Executive Committee of the Social Security Institute. Bonelli, *Gli Organi*, p. 102.

[59] Art. 5, 2nd para. of the 1992 law on judicial organization.

[60] Its legislation in civil matters is composed of various ordinary laws and common law ('diritto comune'), i.e., the norms of the Statutes of 1600 and before, reflecting ancient Roman law and canon law of the Middle Ages. Bonelli, *Gli Organi*, pp. 107-108 and Spagna Musso and Lipparini, 'L'Ordinamento Costituzionale', p. 19.

[61] Art. 2, 2nd para. of the 1992 law on judicial organization established a Magistrate of a Juvenile Court. The function of Criminal Judge of first instance was abolished and

Juvenile Court's sentence can be lodged before the Criminal Appeals Judge.[62] The sentences of the Criminal Appeals Judge acting in first instance are no longer subject to appeal.[63] A pardon, amnesty or change of sentence can be given by the Great and General Council.[64] The penal legislation has been laid down in the Criminal Code of 1974 and the Code on Criminal Procedure of 1878.[65] An imposed prison sentence will in general be served in the prison of San Marino. The Criminal Code provides for the execution of prison sentences of more than six months in a foreign prison on the basis of international conventions, but these conventions have never been concluded.[66] In both civil and criminal proceedings the Great and General Council can pronounce a *restitutio in integrum* against unjustly damaging judgments and decide on a *querela nullitatis*, that is, a claim of nullity of a court's judgment by an individual.[67] Every judicial organ in San Marino is composed of a sole judge, except for the Council of Twelve which is rather a politico-judicial organ.[68]

The inhabitants of San Marino have recourse to the administrative judicial process against acts or measures taken by the institutional organs of the Public Administration.[69] The jurisdiction is exercised by the Administrative Judge of first instance ('Giudice Amministrativo di primo grado') with the possibility of an appeal before the Administrative Judge of Appeal ('Giudice Amministrativo d'Apello').[70] The Council of Twelve exercises jurisdiction in third instance if the judgments in first and second instance differ.[71] The Administrative Judge of first instance has also in certain cases the right of preventive

---

taken over by the Criminal Appeals Judge: Art. 24, 5th para. The Law Commissioner can judge crimes punishable by up to three years of imprisonment, while the Criminal Appeals Judge considers crimes for which a prison sentence of more than three years is foreseen.

[62] Bonelli, *Gli Organi*, pp. 103–104.
[63] Before 24 Nov. 1992 crimes punishable by more than three years of imprisonment were considered by a Criminal Judge of first instance with the possibility of appeal before the Criminal Appeals Judge. Ibid., p. 104.
[64] Ibid., pp. 48–49.
[65] Criminal Code of 25 Febr. 1974, No. 17 and Code on Criminal Procedure of 2 Jan. 1878 as amended by laws of 18 Oct. 1963, No. 43 and 11 Dec. 1974, No. 86. A new Code on Criminal Procedure is in preparation: *Notizia* (1994) no. 1, p. 11.
[66] Art. 99 of the Criminal Code of 1974.
[67] Art. 5, 1st para. of the 1992 law on judicial organization.
[68] Art. 9 of the 1992 law on judicial organization.
[69] Art. 9 of the law on administrative jurisdiction, 28 Jun. 1989, No. 68, BURSM (1989) no. 6.
[70] Art. 2, 1st–3rd paras. of the law on administrative jurisdiction.
[71] Art. 2, 4th para. of the law on administrative jurisdiction.

control over the legitimacy of administrative decisions.[72] It should be noted that the judges can examine the 'constitutionality' of ordinary norms, that is, their conformity with the stipulations set forth in the fundamental law.[73] In case of doubt, the judges can ask for an opinion from the Great and General Council, which rules on the question after having heard the opinion of experts.[74] As questions of such legitimacy rarely arise, this procedure provides for a simple solution instead of the establishment of a Constitutional Court.[75]

Apart from its judicial function as a third instance in administrative and civil proceedings, the Council of Twelve has several other competences,[76] among which is the granting of permission to foreigners to acquire immovable goods situated in San Marinese territory. This special permission prevents too much external interference and the concentration of economic and financial power in the hands of aliens in the Republic.[77] The Council of Twelve issues permanent residence permits,[78] officially recognizes legal persons and non-profit seeking associations and exercises disciplinary control over solicitors and notaries.[79]

Human rights situation

Before the promulgation of the fundamental law which includes certain human rights, fundamental human rights were protected in San Marino by unwritten customary law. The fundamental law has codified these and other rules. It sets forth, *inter alia*, the inviolability of the home and the right of the freedom of the person, of association, of opinion and of religion without describing their exact meaning. The law can limit the exercise of these rights in exceptional cases, on serious grounds of public order and interest.[80] Moreover, every San Marinese citizen has the right to vote and to be elected.[81] The right to

---

[72] Arts. 22–28 of the law on administrative jurisdiction.
[73] Art. 16, 2nd para. of the fundamental law and the law of 19 Jan. 1989, No. 4.
[74] Ibid.
[75] Spagna Musso and Lipparini, 'L'Ordinamento Costituzionale', p. 16.
[76] Law of 5 Jun. 1923, No. 13.
[77] See for similar measures in Liechtenstein, p. 190 above.
[78] Art. 1, 5th para. of the law of 4 Aug. 1927, No. 23, BURSM (1927) no. 6. See also pp. 230–231 below.
[79] Bonelli, *Gli Organi*, pp. 72–78.
[80] Art. 6, 1st para. of the fundamental law.
[81] Art. 7 of the fundamental law. San Marinese women have had the right to vote since 1958 and the right to be elected since 1973, although San Marinese women who have acquired San Marinese nationality by their marriage with a San Marinese man can only

work, to equal pay, to holidays and to strike is also guaranteed.[82] This has permitted the establishment of trade unions in San Marino.

According to the fundamental law, San Marino recognizes the norms of general international law as an integral part of its own organization and supports international conventions on human rights and freedom.[83] Thus San Marino became a State Party to the ICCPR, the ICESCR,[84] the ECHR[85] and the United Nations Convention on the Rights of the Child.[86] Under Article 40, paragraph 1 of the ICCPR, San Marino submitted its initial report on 14 September 1988.[87] The Human Rights Committee was of the opinion that San Marino's short report was 'restrictive and inaccurate'.[88] Confusion had arisen because of one paragraph in San Marino's report which stated:

> 3 (b) Not all provisions of the International Covenant on Civil and Political Rights can be invoked directly before courts. At present, some of them have still to be included in written laws and administrative regulations in order to be enforced directly by the Courts and by the different bodies of the administrative jurisdiction.[89]

Some members of the Human Rights Committee consequently deduced that the International Covenant did not have the force of law until it was expressly embodied in internal legislation.[90] The San Marinese representative replied however that this passage was confusing and meant that 'after the accession of San Marino to the

---

be elected after five years: law of 23 Dec. 1958, No. 36 and the law of 10 Sept. 1973, No. 29, BURSM (1973) no. 5 on the equalization of the rights of women.

[82] Art. 9, 1st para. of the fundamental law.

[83] Art. 1 of the fundamental law states: 'La Repubblica di San Marino riconosce le norme del diritto internazionale come parte integrante del proprio ordinamento ... aderisce alle Convenzioni internazionali in tema di diritti e di libertà dell'uomo ...'

[84] Both ratified on 18 Oct. 1985; San Marino also accepted the Optional Protocol to the ICCPR.

[85] It became a State Party to the ECHR on 22 Mar. 1989. San Marino is also a Party to Protocols Nos. 1, 4, 6, 7, 9 and 10. See pp. 242–246 below.

[86] Ratified on 30 Sept. 1991.

[87] UN Doc. CCPR/C/45/Add. 1 (1989).

[88] Opinion of Mr Pocar shared by the other members: UN Doc. CCPR/C/SR.980 (1990) p. 6, para. 38 and in general pp. 6–10. It should be noted that the San Marinese representative mentioned that the Republic had ratified the Convention against torture and other cruel, inhuman or degrading treatment or punishment. This is however incorrect, as San Marino is not mentioned on the list of States Parties to this Convention. See *Multilateral Treaties deposited with the Secretary-General* (1994) Status as at 31 Dec. 1993, p. 180.

[89] UN Doc. CCPR/C/45/Add. 1 (1989) p. 1.

[90] UN Doc. CCPR/C/SR.980 (1990) p. 6, para. 37, p. 7, para. 42 and p. 8, para. 49.

Covenant, there has been no special legislation mentioning the principles embodied in the Covenant, only the decree by virtue of which it entered into force and the law No. 59 of 8 July 1974 [the fundamental law]' and furthermore explained that a decree is promulgated in order to make it a State law which can be invoked by all citizens who can demand that it is fully respected.[91] The questioned paragraph of San Marino's report seems therefore incorrect. In fact, under San Marino's legislation, international conventions are ratified by the Captains Regent and are given full and entire enforcement ('piena ed intera esecuzione') in San Marino by decree. This decree can only be promulgated with the approval of the Great and General Council.[92] The rights laid down in a convention which has been given force of law by a decree can therefore be invoked before the courts. Unfortunately, not all international conventions which are applicable in San Marino by virtue of a decree of the Captains Regent are published in the statute book.[93] The texts of the ICCPR and the ICESCR were not officially published in the statute book, although this fact does not prejudice the applicability of the Covenants. The San Marinese inhabitants are therefore not automatically informed of the exact content of their rights under non-published, but applicable human rights conventions.

One member of the Human Rights Committee expressed some concern over the hierarchical status of the ICCPR within San Marino's legislation. He believed that, as the decree promulgating the Covenant was accepted by a simple majority in the Great and General Council and as the fundamental law needed a two-thirds majority, in case of a conflict between the Covenant and the fundamental law the latter would be maintained.[94] As we have seen, the fundamental law permits the test of compatibility for any norm applicable in San Marino and states that the norms of general international law are an integral part of its organization, whereas it is specified that San Marino adheres to human rights conventions.[95] The reference to this

---

[91] UN Doc. CCPR/C/SR.981 (1990) p. 6, para. 28.
[92] Art. 3, 3rd para. 2nd sentence of the fundamental law.
[93] The decree itself is entered into the statute book and adopts always the same formula, but it is not always followed by the content of the convention. Conventions with Italy are usually fully published, e.g., the treaty on financial relations of 2 May 1991, BURSM (1991) no. 5. Conversely, no text of a human rights convention ratified by San Marino has been published.
[94] Mr Pocar: UN Doc. CCPR/C/SR.981 (1990) p. 8, para. 40.
[95] Art. 16, 2nd para. and Art. 1 of the fundamental law. See pp. p. 217 above at nn. 73–75 and accompanying text and n. 83, p. 218 above.

stipulation in the fundamental law could imply that generally recognized rules of international law and human rights conventions which San Marino has ratified have the same hierarchical status as the fundamental law itself, thus taking precedence over ordinary laws.[96]

One of the points emphasized by the Human Rights Committee was the general prohibition on San Marinese nationals becoming judges in their Republic.[97] Considering that the function of judge is a function of 'public service' within the meaning of Article 25 (c) of the ICCPR, it can be questioned whether the prohibition is 'without unreasonable restrictions'. In this case the right to have access on general terms of equality to public service in one's country does not seem to be unreasonably restricted. The foreign nationality of San Marino's judges is seen as a necessity to guarantee their independence in a small society where social relations are close.[98] Moreover, the prohibition is not absolute, as we have seen.[99]

Another question raised in the Human Rights Committee concerned the rule in San Marino that in civil suits foreigners could be required to pay a *cautio judicatum solvi* to appear before court, and the conformity of this rule with, *inter alia*, Article 26 of the Covenant.[100] It is probable that this rule conflicts with the general prohibition of discrimination on the ground of national origin. Article 26 of the Covenant was not invoked in relation to the San Marinese legislation forbidding aliens to acquire immovable property in San Marino without the permission of the Council of Twelve.[101] A discrimination on the ground of sex is apparent in San Marino's law

---

[96] This conclusion is however not a certainty as the fundamental law has no equivalent to Art. 10 of the Italian Constitution which establishes that Italian law shall be in conformity with the generally recognized rules of international law. Moreover, if a rule of international law is put at the same level as the fundamental law, problems arise if other norms of the fundamental law itself are not in conformity with, for example, a human rights convention. In principle, the San Marinese jurisprudence provides for the application of the maxim *lex posterior derogat priori* for laws of hierarchically equal status. This then does not guarantee, in all cases, the primacy of the ICCPR. The San Marinese jurisprudence has not yet solved such possible conflicts.
[97] The Human Rights Committee wanted to know the reasons behind this prohibition: UN Doc. CCPR/C/SR.980 (1990) p. 7, para. 39.
[98] The foreign judges should therefore lead a reserved life in relation to the San Marinese population, may not marry San Marinese nationals or enter into family or friendly ties with the local population on the basis of ancient statutes: Commissione per lo Studio dei Problemi Istituzionali dell'Ordinamento Sammarinese, *Relazione* (1972) p. 120.
[99] See p. 214 above at nn. 49–50 and accompanying text.
[100] UN Doc. CCPR/C/SR.980 (1990) p. 7, para. 44.
[101] Art. 3, 3rd para. of the law on foreigners, law of 4 Aug. 1927, No. 23, BURSM (1927) no. 6.

on nationality.[102] The children of a San Marinese father are San Marinese nationals, whereas the children of a San Marinese mother only acquire her nationality if the father is unknown or stateless.[103] A foreign woman who marries a San Marinese man acquires San Marinese nationality if she renounces her own nationality.[104] A foreign man who marries a San Marinese woman can only acquire San Marinese nationality by naturalization, that is, if he has his residence in San Marino for at least thirty years.[105]

So far, no applications from individuals or claims from other States Parties against San Marino have been received by the Human Rights Committee. The European Commission of Human Rights has received four applications so far, none of them leading to a condemnation of San Marino for violations of the ECHR.[106]

It should furthermore be emphasized that San Marino abolished the death penalty in 1848.[107] The fundamental law distinguishes between human rights which belong to all persons ('tutti') and those which are only held by all the citizens ('tutti i cittadini') which means the San Marinese nationals. The latter category includes the right to hold public office, to participate in elections, to found political parties and trade unions, to social security and the civil duty to be loyal to the laws and institutions of the Republic.[108] After San Marino's accession to ILO, it ratified certain International Labour Conventions.[109] In practice San Marino has always emphasized its long-standing tradition of respect for human rights, like for instance the right of political asylum.[110]

---

[102] Law on nationality of 27 March 1984, No. 32, BURSM (1984) no. 3.
[103] Art. 1 (1) and (2) of the law on nationality.
[104] Art. 3, 2nd para. of the law on nationality.
[105] Art. 1 (1) of the law on nationality.
[106] Application no. 21069/92 (*X v. San Marino*), decision of the Commission of 9 Jul. 1993. The applicant, an Italian national, claimed that the withdrawal of his residence permit by the San Marinese State Congress constituted a violation of Art. 2 Protocol no. 4 and Art. 1 Protocol no. 7 of the ECHR. The Commission considered both claims of violation manifestly ill-founded under Art. 27 (2) of the Convention. Application no. 24243/94 (*X v. San Marino*), decision of the Commission of 22 Febr. 1995 (inadmissible), Application no. 24653/94 (*X v. San Marino*), decision of the Commission of 6 Sept. 1995 (inadmissible) and Application no. 25425/95 (*X v. San Marino*), decision of the Commission of 10 Apr. 1995 (cases struck off list by applicant).
[107] Spagna Musso and Lipparini, 'L'Ordinamento Costituzionale', p. 19. The maximum prison sentence is at present twenty-four years: Art. 81 of the Criminal Code.
[108] Arts. 4, 2nd para., 7, 8, 9 and 13 of the fundamental law.
[109] Such as ILO Convention no. 87 on freedom of association and protection of the right to organize and ILO Convention no. 98 on the right to organize and collective bargaining.
[110] The preamble of the fundamental law emphasizes the 'gloriose tradizioni di libertà e di democrazia della Repubblica'. Art. 1 expressly mentions that the Republic 'riconferma il diritto di asilo politico'.

Relations with States
Foreign policy
The foreign policy of the Republic of San Marino is based on the following principles:

Neutrality San Marino's neutrality is the application of a fundamental and traditional principle which until 1971 remained an unwritten customary rule and which is said to flow spontaneously from the consciousness of the San Marinese people.[111] San Marino reconfirmed its neutrality in an additional agreement of 1971 to the treaty of friendship of 1939 with Italy.[112] The last war in which San Marino was involved was waged against Sigismondo Malatesta, the supreme commander of the Church troops, in 1462.[113] As we have seen, San Marino defended its neutrality in both World Wars.[114] At present, after the cold war, San Marino seeks to redefine its concept of neutrality. It will be taken into account that the Republic will remain at an equal distance from States or blocs and it is generally believed that small neutral States like San Marino can play a mediatory role in conflict situations.[115]

Reinforcement of its international status At the beginning of this century San Marino endeavoured to conclude extradition treaties with other States to accentuate its separateness.[116] In addition, the Republic entered into diplomatic or consular relations with sixty-seven States and gradually tried to raise consular relations to the ambassadorial level.[117] The recognition of San Marino's international status was also obtained through the accession to international organizations.[118]

---

[111] See also Ago, 'La Neutralità', p. 6.
[112] Art. 1, 2nd para. of the treaty of friendship of 1939 as amended on 10 Sept. 1971, BURSM (1972) no. 2.
[113] Le Besnerais, *Le Statut international*, pp. 161–162.
[114] See p. 210 above.
[115] Interview with Mrs M. A. Bonelli, Head of the General Office Politico-Diplomatic Affairs of the Republic of San Marino, 7 Oct. 1991.
[116] Thus it concluded extradition treaties with the Netherlands in 1902 and with the United States in 1906. Texts in G. Ramoino and M. Bonelli, *Supplemento alla Raccolta delle Leggi e Decreti della Repubblica di San Marino*, 1st edn (1915) pp. 372 and 384.
[117] In 1995, San Marino maintained diplomatic relations at the ambassadorial level with thirty-four States, among which, Andorra, Austria, Belgium, Egypt, France, Italy (since 1980), the Holy See, the Sovereign Order of Malta, Sweden and Switzerland. The diplomatic representatives of Italy, the Sovereign Order of Malta and the Holy See are resident in San Marino. Information from the Department of Foreign Affairs of San Marino.
[118] See pp. 233–255 below.

Contributing to the solution of international problems within its capacities[119] San Marino believes that it should contribute to international causes such as peace, the development of peoples and wealth, and the protection of human rights.

Relations with Italy
Friendly relations

The main pillar on which the Italo-San Marinese relations are based is the treaty of friendship of 31 March 1939.[120] This treaty replaced the very first treaties of friendship concluded with the newly established State of Italy on 22 March 1862 and 27 June 1897.[121] The Italian unification, the 'Risorgimento', had not prejudiced San Marino's autonomous status due to the fact that Italy wanted to show its gratitude towards San Marino for offering a refuge to the partisans of the unification movement and for approving the final abolition of the Church's temporal power.[122] As Italy had introduced compulsory military service it wanted to secure the extradition of conscripts and deserters from San Marino by a treaty.[123] The treaty of friendship of 1939 took over the principles set forth in the treaties of 1862 and 1897, emphasizing Italy's protective friendship for the maintenance of San Marino's ancient freedom and independence and San Marino's promise not to accept the protective friendship of any other Power.[124] This clause led to confusion on the degree of protection which Italy could exercise and the juridical nature of San Marino's international status, which could lead to the conclusion that the Republic was a protectorate of Italy.[125] Although this was contested by most

---

[119] Interview with Mrs M. A. Bonelli of 7 Oct. 1991.
[120] 'Convenzione di amicizia e di buon vicinato fra la Repubblica di San Marino e il Regno d'Italia', BURSM (1939) no. 8, entered into force on 30 Sept. 1939. Text also in G. F. de Martens, *Nouveau Recueil Général de Traités*, 3rd series, vol. XL, pp. 635 ff.
[121] Ibid., vol. II, pp. 799 ff.
[122] G. Rossi, 'I Rapporti della Repubblica di San Marino con lo Stato Italiano', in E. R. Iwanejko, ed., *La Tradizione Politica di San Marino: Dalle Origini dell'Indipendenza al Pensiero Politico di Pietro Franciosi* (1988) p. 313.
[123] Seventeen out of thirty articles of the 1862 treaty of friendship were dedicated to terms of extradition.
[124] Art. 1, 2nd para. of the 1939 treaty of friendship read: 'La Repubblica di San Marino, nella certezza che non le verrà mai meno l'amicizia protettrice di S.M. il Re d'Italia per la conservazione della sua antichissima libertà e indipendenza, dichiara che non accetterà quella di nessun'altra potenza.'
[125] In this sense see P. Guggenheim, *Lehrbuch des Völkerrechts*, vol. I (1948) p. 254, who believed that San Marino was a protectorate due to Italy's duty of defence and San Marino's duty not to accept any other alliances.

jurists,[126] it was believed necessary to replace the 'protective friendship' stipulation so as to eliminate any reference to protection by Italy. On 10 September 1971, an additional agreement introduced a new Article 1 in the treaty of friendship which laid down Italy's greatest and widest cooperation for the maintenance of San Marino's ancient freedom and independence, while the duty of non-alliance was replaced by a reconfirmation of San Marino's neutrality.[127]

Under the treaty of friendship the nationals of both Republics may exercise any profession or function, including any public office, in the other Republic under the same conditions as the Republic's nationals.[128] This stipulation seems to imply that the nationality of a San Marinese or an Italian cannot prevent his accession to an employment in Italy or San Marino respectively, even if it concerns a public post. As public offices are in general reserved for a country's own nationals, the treaty provision aims at bringing Italian and San Marinese nationals on a level of equality. In practice however this rule has not been followed in the case of free accession to public posts. A woman of foreign nationality, including an Italian woman, who has acquired San Marinese nationality through marriage and after having renounced her own nationality, can only be eligible for the Great and General Council and consequently for the public office of Secretary of State if she has San Marinese nationality for at least five years. The possibility that an Italian takes up a public office reserved for San Marinese nationals seems in this case excluded. Yet the treaty provision in question provides for free access to whatever ('qualsiasi') public office under the same conditions as the country's nationals. Furthermore, San Marino's fundamental law prohibits, in general,

---

[126] See, e.g., G. Vedovato, *Le Relazioni*, pp. 9–10, who concluded that San Marino was not a protectorate because there did not exist a clear duty of military defence for Italy and a diplomatic representation by Italy, nor a duty for San Marino to accept interference in its internal and external affairs by a protecting State.

[127] Art. 1, 2nd para. of the 1939 treaty of friendship as amended in 1971 reads: 'La Repubblica di San Marino riconferma la sua neutralità ed esprime la certezza che non le verranno mai meno la più viva amicizia e la più ampia cooperazione della Repubblica Italiana per la conservazione della sua antichissima libertà e indipendenza. In questo intento il Governo italiano ed il Governo sammarinese procederanno a regolari consultazioni sui problemi di comune interesse.' BURSM (1972) no. 2 and GURI (1972) no. 336, p. 8380.

[128] Art. 4 of the 1939 treaty of friendship states: 'I cittadini di ciascuno dei due Stati saranno ammessi, nel territorio dell'altro ... e potranno accedere a qualsiasi pubblico impiego a parità di condizioni con i nazionali.'

judges from being of San Marinese nationality.[129] As Italians should hold a public office under the same conditions as the San Marinese, it should therefore also be prohibited, in general, for Italians to become judges in San Marino. Nevertheless, most judges in San Marino are Italians. Conversely, the case has not yet been put to the test whether a San Marinese can take up a public office within Italian governmental institutions. Article 4 of the treaty of friendship is therefore either ill-phrased and contrary to the parties' intentions or not respected by at least the San Marinese practice and rules on parliamentary eligibility.

Due to certain tensions in the relations between Italy and San Marino from 1948 to 1953, San Marino had been constrained to accept the obligation not to permit the establishment of gambling houses on its territory.[130] In 1949, the Great and General Council had officially permitted the establishment of a casino in San Marino in order to attract more tourism and to cover more rapidly the State deficit.[131] This measure, combined with the considerable increase in the number of limited liability companies in San Marino, was considered by Italy to be prejudicial to its fiscal system.[132] Moreover, the conflict with San Marino was also prompted by the facility of annulment of marriages permitted by the San Marinese common law and frequently used by Italian couples.[133] As a consequence, Italy invoked the violation of the spirit of the 1939 treaty of friendship by San Marino and took countermeasures which were maintained for two years.[134] After a shift in San Marino's government coalition and despite the protests of the San Marinese Secretary of State for foreign affairs, the Republic conceded. The countermeasures were lifted and the treaty of friendship was amended so as to prohibit gambling houses in San Marino, prevent an

---

[129] Art. 15, 3rd para. of the fundamental law. See also on this point p. 214 above at nn. 49–50 and accompanying text.

[130] Art. 47 (4) of the 1939 treaty of friendship as amended on 29 Apr. 1953, BURSM (1954) no. 4.

[131] Vedovato, *Le Relazioni*, pp. 34–36.

[132] The financial losses for Italy due to the casino in San Marino were estimated at 800 million lire a year. Of the eighty-six companies registered in San Marino in 1948, eighty companies had been established between 1944 and 1948. Ibid., pp. 28 and 33.

[133] Ibid., pp. 36–37.

[134] Passport controls and frontier posts were established at the Italo-San Marinese borders, paralysing the flow of tourists and disrupting the postal traffic. In addition, Italy suspended the payment of the customs contribution which it was due to pay annually to San Marino. Giorgeri, *Conflittualità*, pp. 118–119. The Italian blockade was upheld from Aug. 1949 to Aug. 1951.

excessive use of the possibility of annulment of marriages by non-resident Italians and include a duty on the part of Italy to reconstruct the railway between Rimini and San Marino.[135]

It is doubtful whether Italy's countermeasures between 1949 and 1951 were permitted under international law. Italy invoked the violation of the spirit of the 1939 treaty of friendship. This treaty however did not prohibit the establishment of gambling houses and did not restrict San Marino's company law or matrimonial legislation. In fact, such provisions were only introduced after an explicit amendment of the treaty of friendship in 1953. San Marino's actions could have been considered contrary to the feelings of mutual friendship and good neighbourliness which, according to Article 1, first paragraph of the 1939 treaty of friendship, inspired the Italo-San Marinese relations, or contrary to Article 47, paragraph 3 of the same treaty which prohibits the adoption of financial measures which could directly or indirectly influence the Italian fiscal regime.[136] The granting of a concession to establish a privately owned casino could probably not be considered a 'financial measure' even if San Marino received more tax revenues due to this concession. Indeed, by concluding the additional agreement introducing the said prohibitions and regulations into the treaty of friendship, Italy seemed to admit that these rules had not been laid down before the amendment.[137] Moreover, Article 1, first paragraph of the 1939 treaty of friendship does not seem to set forth more duties for San Marino than general international law imposes on States in the relations between each other. Customary international law does not prohibit the establishment of gambling houses and, in general, considers the legislation on companies and marriages a matter of domestic jurisdiction. The violation of the

---

[135] Arts. 5, last para., 47 (4) and 52 of the treaty of friendship as amended on 29 Apr. 1953, BURSM (1954) no. 4. The latter obligation was considered to be compensation for San Marino's renunciation of the right to establish radio and television stations in San Marino. Due to unfavourable viability projections the train connection was never re-established: exchange of notes on 23 Oct. 1987, BURSM (1990) no. 4.

[136] Art. 1, 1st para. of the 1939 treaty of friendship read: 'Le relazioni fra il Regno d'Italia e la Repubblica di S. Marino saranno ispirate a sentimenti di mutua amicizia e di buon vicinato.' Art. 47 (3) reads: 'San Marino si impegna: ... 3° a non adottare alcun provvedimento finanziario che possa, direttamente o indirettamente, in qualunque modo o misura, influire sul regime tributario o sulla circolazione monetaria del Regno d'Italia'.

[137] An additional agreement of 10 Febr. 1914 to the 1897 treaty of friendship already prohibited gambling houses in San Marino under Art. 1. This treaty was no longer in force after being replaced by the 1939 treaty of friendship.

spirit of the 1939 treaty of friendship cannot be regarded as a violation of a rule 'expressly recognized' by the two States within the meaning of Article 38, paragraph 1 (a) of the Statute of the International Court of Justice.[138] If therefore it were accepted that San Marino's actions did not involve its international responsibility, Italy's countermeasures were illegal and by themselves a violation of Articles 52 and 55 of the treaty of friendship.

The treaty of friendship can be denounced by either of the contracting parties subject to six months' notice.[139]

Diplomatic representation

Until the beginning of this century San Marino did not have an extensive diplomatic representation abroad due to its restricted financial and human resources. Gradually it was felt that San Marino should fortify its international status by concluding extradition treaties with major countries and by entering into diplomatic and consular relations with a number of States. The development of San Marino's diplomatic relations was also partly justified by the relatively large number of San Marinese nationals who had emigrated from San Marino in the first half of this century because of the Republic's poor economic situation.[140] It was furthermore believed that an expansion of the relations with other States and also with international organizations would improve the relations with Italy.[141] Just after the Second World War membership of international organizations proved to be still too costly for San Marino.[142] The relations with international organizations are of rather recent origin. The treaty of friendship of 1939 initially provided for the absence of diplomatic representation between Italy and San Marino.[143] As this situation was considered unsatisfactory and as San Marino wanted to strengthen its international position vis-à-vis Italy, the treaty was amended on 6 March 1968 in order to permit the establishment of diplomatic relations between

---

[138] Just after the settlement of the dispute with Italy, San Marino applied to become a party to the Statute of the ICJ on 6 Nov. 1953. See p. 235 below.

[139] Art. 58, 3rd para. of the 1939 treaty of friendship.

[140] M. A. Bonelli, 'La Politica Estera e i Rapporti con gli altri Stati Europei', in Iwanejko, La Tradizione Politica, p. 334. In 1990 there were about 18,000 San Marinese nationals living abroad: information given to the Human Rights Committee, UN Doc. CCPR/C/SR.981 (3 Aug. 1990) p. 7, para. 35.

[141] Bonelli, 'La Politica Estera', p. 331.

[142] See pp. 236–242 below.

[143] Art. 2, 1st para. of the 1939 treaty of friendship.

the two countries.[144] The 1939 treaty of friendship stipulates that in third States with which San Marino has not established diplomatic or consular relations, the Italian consulates will provide assistance to San Marinese nationals.[145] The treaty does not explicitly provide for assistance by Italian embassies, although this is not excluded in practice. The efforts to intensify San Marino's international relations accounted for 3.0 per cent of the State's total expenditures in 1995.[146]

Postal union

Italy and San Marino have established a postal union.[147] San Marino maintains its own post offices in its territory and collects the postal tariffs at its own expense.[148] It has the freedom to issue its own stamps and postcards.[149] All the tariffs and norms which are in force in Italy, including the regulations in force for the postal traffic with third States, are applicable to the post emanating from San Marino.[150] The tariffs and norms which are in force in Italy do not distinguish between their national and international origin, given Italy's traditional dualist approach to the incorporation of international law into its national legislation. The norms embodied in a postal convention concluded by Italy with a third State should therefore be extended to San Marino after they have entered into force in Italy. Any change of tariffs and norms applicable in Italy needs a separate incorporation into the San Marinese legislation to have force of law.[151] Therefore San Marino does not become a State Party to a postal convention concluded by Italy with a third State. The postal convention can be terminated by either party subject to six months' notice.[152]

---

[144] Art. 2, 1st para. of the 1939 treaty of friendship as amended on 6 March 1968, BURSM (1970) no. 4. Since 1980 diplomatic relations between Italy and San Marino have been at the ambassadorial level.

[145] Art. 3 of the 1939 treaty of friendship.

[146] Calculated on the basis of the 1995 provisional budget, expenses for the department of foreign affairs, BURSM (1994) no. 12.

[147] Based on a postal convention of 5 May 1923, GURI (1923) no. 294, pp. 7207–7208 and an additional regulation of 7 Jun. 1924, BURSM (1924) no. 8.

[148] Art. 6 of the postal convention. The services regarding cheques and current accounts regulated by Italian law are maintained by San Marinese post offices at the expense of the Italian postal administration: Art. 5 of the postal convention.

[149] Art. 9 of the postal convention.

[150] Arts. 2 and 4, 2nd para. of the postal convention and Art. 1 of the additional regulation.

[151] As an international rule always needs to be transformed into national San Marinese legislation, a tariff or norm entered into force in Italy after the 1923 postal convention can only be applicable in San Marino after explicit adoption by a decree of the Captains Regent.

[152] Art. 11, 2nd para. of the postal convention.

San Marino has been a full member of the Universal Postal Union since 1 July 1915. It was first represented by Italy which ended its representative functions on 20 June 1914.[153] As San Marino has to adopt the postal regulations in force in Italy, it does not seem possible for the Republic to ratify postal conventions in the framework of the Universal Postal Union which have no force of law in Italy.

Customs union

Since 1 December 1992 a customs union has been established between San Marino and the European Community.[154] For an analysis of this customs union we refer to a subsequent paragraph.[155] Before the entry into force of the customs union agreement with the EEC, a customs union existed with Italy which was regulated by the 1939 treaty of friendship. There were no customs tariffs or quantitative restrictions on trade between San Marino and Italy. Imports from third States were subject to the customs regime in force in Italy and customs duties were levied by Italy prior to their entry into San Marinese territory.[156] As a consequence of this legal regime, customs duties flowing from a commercial agreement concluded by Italy or, after its establishment, by the European Community, with a third State were applied to the imported products of San Marino which by necessity had to pass through the Italian territory. These commercial agreements concluded with third States did not make any reference to San Marino.[157] Although their provisions were applied by Italy to San Marino's imported goods, there was no legal guarantee that the third States in question would apply the provisions of their agreement with Italy to the products which they imported from San Marino. The only exceptions to this rule were the Member States of the European Community. According to a regulation of 1968 of the Council of the European Communities, the Republic of San Marino was considered, by virtue of the convention with Italy of 31 March

---

[153] Ballarino, 'L'Evoluzione', p. 45.
[154] Art. 2 of the customs union agreement with the EEC signed on 16 Dec. 1991, ECOJ no. C 302 (22.11.91) pp. 12 ff.
[155] See pp. 246–254 below.
[156] Art. 44, 1st para. of the 1939 treaty of friendship read: 'La Repubblica di San Marino rinuncia al diritto di libero transito, in esenzione da dazi doganali e diritti accessori, attraverso il territorio italiano, di merci e di prodotti di ogni specie che siano importati nel territorio della Repubblica da terzi Stati.'
[157] See, e.g., the exchange of notes constituting a commercial *modus vivendi* between Canada and Italy of 23/28 Apr. 1948, 231 UNTS (1956) no. 3206, which included a most-favoured-nation clause in para. 3.

1939, a part of the customs territory of the Community.[158] Nevertheless, this did not imply that vis-à-vis third States the products originating from San Marino were assimilated with European Community products.[159] The treaty of friendship provided for the payment of an annual customs contribution by Italy which was a fixed amount[160] given by way of compensation for the renouncements made by San Marino.[161]

After the introduction of the VAT system in 1972 in Italy,[162] an exchange of notes with San Marino provided for the establishment in San Marino of a tax on imported goods to be levied by San Marino.[163] Goods entirely manufactured and sold in San Marino were not subject to indirect taxation until January 1996.[164]

Aliens office

Italian and San Marinese nationals can circulate freely without passport obligation in San Marino and Italy respectively.[165] The freedom to enter San Marino does not include the freedom of residence. Permission for a permanent residence or for residence for an undetermined period can only be granted by the Council of Twelve.[166] The Council of Twelve also has the authority to grant its permission to

---

[158] Art. 2 and annex point 3 of the Council Regulation no. 1496/68, ECOJ no. L 238 (28.9.68). Art. 234 of the EC Treaty stipulates that agreements with third States concluded prior to the entry into force of the Treaty are not prejudiced.

[159] A Trade Agreement of 3 Apr. 1978 between the EEC and China established a most-favoured-nation treatment between the two contracting parties (Art. 2). San Marino is not a contracting party and is not mentioned in the Agreement, although Art. 10 states that 'As far as the European Economic Community is concerned, this Agreement shall apply to the territories in which the Treaty establishing the European Economic Community is applied, and under the conditions laid down in that Treaty.' The EC Treaty only partly applies to San Marino, i.e., the customs regime. This does not oblige China to consider San Marino a part of the EC. See European Communities, *Collection of the Agreements concluded by the European Communities* (1978) vol. VIII, part I, pp. 1405 ff. San Marino does not have official statistics on its exports to EC countries and third States.

[160] The amount was reconsidered periodically and amounted to 9,000 million lire since 1986, BURSM (1986) no. 12.

[161] Art. 52 of the treaty of friendship, i.e., compensation for customs duties, for not cultivating tobacco, for not issuing bank notes, for not adopting financial measures which could influence the fiscal or monetary regime of Italy and for not establishing gambling houses.

[162] Presidential Decree of 26 Oct. 1972, No. 633, GURI (1972) no. 292.

[163] Exchange of notes of 21 Dec. 1972, not published. Law on tax on imported goods, BURSM (1972) no. 5.

[164] See p. 250 below.

[165] Art. 55 of the 1939 treaty of friendship.

[166] Art. 1, 5th para. of the regulation on aliens, No. 23, BURSM (1927) no. 6.

foreigners so that they can buy or acquire under any other title immovable goods in the Republic.[167] There is no rule which prohibits the entry into San Marino of a third State national who has been expelled by Italy, although his entry will be complicated as San Marino can only be reached through Italian territory.

Radio and television

San Marino's agreement not to establish or permit the establishment of radio and television stations in its territory was lifted by an exchange of notes with Italy of 23 October 1987 and followed by an agreement of cooperation in the field of radio and television.[168] Under the agreement a San Marinese radio and television station which has the right to broadcast in San Marino and Italy can be established with mixed Italian and San Marinese capital.[169] The Italian Government contributes annually to this broadcasting station, whereas San Marino promises not to seek any other cooperation in the field of radio and television outside its territory.[170] A Joint Committee controls the correct application of the agreement.[171] San Marino's radio and television station has functioned since 1991.

Monetary union

San Marino adopted the Italian lira as legal tender by virtue of the first treaty of friendship of 1862.[172] San Marino has promised not to adopt any financial measures which could, directly or indirectly, in any way, influence Italy's monetary system.[173] This general obligation has been specified further in 1991 by a Convention on financial and currency relations between Italy and San Marino.[174] This Convention establishes that the free movement of goods, services and capital between the two States may not be hampered on currency grounds.[175] Italy accords

---

[167] Art. 3, 3rd para. of the regulation on aliens.
[168] BURSM (1990) no. 4.
[169] Arts. 2 and 3 of the radio and television agreement.
[170] Arts. 4 and 8 of the radio and television agreement.
[171] Art. 9 of the radio and television agreement.
[172] San Marino still issues its own coins, but renounced the issuing of banknotes in 1914. By virtue of the monetary convention with the Vatican City, the San Marinese and Vatican coins are legal tender in the Vatican City and San Marino respectively: monetary convention of 30 Dec. 1931, BURSM (1932) no. 4 (Art. 1).
[173] Art. 47 (3) of the 1939 treaty of friendship.
[174] Convention on financial and currency relations of 2 May 1991 and Additional Act, BURSM (1991) no. 5.
[175] Art. 1 of the Convention on financial and currency relations.

physical and legal persons resident in San Marino the same currency position as physical and legal persons resident in Italy, which implies, *inter alia*, that the San Marinese banks have the same monetary status as the Italian banks.[176] Although they were in practice already adopted in 1987,[177] San Marino is obliged to accept substantially in its own legislation the Italian currency norms including the protection clauses.[178] The Convention furthermore obliges San Marino to prevent such competitive conditions for San Marinese financial institutions in their relations with its Italian residents which are distortive in respect of the conditions presented in Italy.[179]

In 1988, the Great and General Council established the San Marinese Institute of Credit ('Istituto di Credito Sammarinese', hereafter, ICS) which acts not only as a central bank (for example, issuing State bonds), but also as a commercial bank.[180] San Marino's relative currency autonomy has been restricted by the 1991 Convention on financial and currency relations with Italy, although the San Marinese banks can provide more financial services than before. It should furthermore be noted that in the framework of the Maastricht Treaty on European Union of 7 February 1992 a declaration has been made 'on monetary relations with the Republic of San Marino, the Vatican City and the Principality of Monaco' which states that 'the existing monetary relations between Italy and San Marino ... remain unaffected by the Treaty establishing the European Community until the introduction of the ECU as the single currency of the Community', after which '[t]he Community undertakes to facilitate such renegotiations of existing arrangements as might become necessary as a result of the introduction of the ECU as a single currency'.[181] The

---

[176] Art. 2 of the Convention on financial and currency relations.
[177] Circular of the San Marinese credit and currency inspectorate of 22 Jan. 1987. See also T. Masi, 'L'Analisi e il Commento del Testo', *Forum* (1991) no. 1, p. 22.
[178] Art. 3 of the Convention on financial and currency relations. The term 'substantially' ('sostanzialmente') replaced the term 'integrally' ('integralmento') which was initially used in the draft, thus leaving San Marino a greater discretion: ibid., p. 23.
[179] Art. 4, 1st para. of the Convention on financial and currency relations.
[180] Art. 1 of the Additional Act recognizes the ICS' commercial bank status. The ICS has a 70 per cent initial capital under Government control against 20 per cent owned by San Marinese and 10 per cent by Italian banks. A bank can only be established in San Marino with the permission of the ICS subject to the approval of the Italian authorities. The Italian Exchange Office ('Ufficio Italiano dei Cambi') and the ICS may request information from each other on currency transactions made by the ICS, by San Marinese financial institutions or by San Marinese residents: Arts. 2, 2nd sentence and 3.
[181] 31 ILM (1992) p. 365.

Convention on financial and currency relations with Italy can be denounced subject to six months' notice.[182] The newly established ICS and the redefinition of the Italo-San Marinese financial relations facilitated the accession of San Marino to the International Monetary Fund on 23 September 1992.[183]

Defence

There is no military defence agreement between Italy and San Marino as this would probably be contrary to San Marino's policy of neutrality and non-alliance. A clear duty of military defence cannot be deduced from Article 1 of the treaty of friendship, which asserts Italy's greatest friendship and widest cooperation for the maintenance of San Marino's freedom and independence. It is not evident that a military defence action would fall under this duty of greatest friendship and widest cooperation, although it is not excluded either.[184] According to the regulation on military forces the defence of the independence and integrity of San Marino can be maintained by the Militia ('Milizia'), in general after a decision of the Great and General Council.[185] The Militia should be distinguished from the other military or police forces, which have to maintain the respect for the law.[186]

Relations with international organizations

League of Nations

The first contact which San Marino sought with the League of Nations was on 28 January 1919, when it asked the Italian delegate in the Conference of the League of Nations to represent San Marino as well. The Italian delegate answered that as San Marino had not been invited

---

[182] Art. 9 of the Convention on financial and currency relations.
[183] *Notizia* (1992) no. 7, pp. 2–3. See p. 255 below.
[184] Vedovato, *Le Relazioni*, p. 9 does not believe that there is an obligation of defence for Italy by virtue of Art. 1 of the 1939 treaty of friendship as amended by the additional agreement of 10 Sept. 1971.
[185] Art. 4 (1) of the regulation on military forces, law of 26 Jan. 1990, No. 15, BURSM (1990) no. 1. The Militia is composed of the San Marinese men aged between sixteen and sixty, who are subject to military service. Foreigners may only enter into the Militia after at least six years of residence in San Marino: Arts. 3 and 9, 2nd sentence.
[186] There are three other military forces: the 'Guardia di Rocca', the 'Guardia del Consiglio Grande e Generale' and the 'Gendarmeria': Art. 1 of the regulation on military forces. A non-military 'Corpo di Polizia Civile' has certain disciplinary duties: Arts. 1 and 3 of the law of 21 Nov. 1990, No. 142. The members of the military and police forces do not have to be San Marinese or Italian nationals.

to participate in the Conference it should wait for the adoption of the Covenant of the League of Nations before being invited to become a part of the League.[187] On 24 February 1919, the San Marinese State Congress discussed a letter received by its *chargé d'affaires* in Paris from President Woodrow Wilson in which he pointed out that, for the moment, San Marino could not participate in the League of Nations as the list of participating States had been closed for some time, but that the League's Covenant provided for the admission of new members, which would be possible for San Marino at any time.[188] Consequently, San Marino was the first Micro-State to apply for admission to the League of Nations, by letter of 23 April 1919.[189] The Secretary-General of the League of Nations requested more information from San Marino on 22 August 1920. This request was left unanswered and San Marino's application for membership never appeared on the agenda of the League's Assembly. San Marino's application was probably not carried through due to the political unwillingness which was demonstrated in the League of Nations to admit very small States like San Marino on an equal footing with larger Member States.[190] This has not prevented San Marino from participating in international conferences held under the auspices of the League of Nations.[191]

International courts
Permanent Court of International Justice

By letter of 30 June 1922 the registrar of the Permanent Court of International Justice informed the Captains Regent of the possibility for non-Member States of the League of Nations to adhere to the Statute of the Permanent Court of International Justice.[192] As we have seen this possibility was only offered to international entities which were considered as States.[193] San Marino never asked to become a State Party to the Statute of the Permanent Court of International Justice.

---

[187] Information given to the San Marinese Parliament, Session of 15 Febr. 1919, *Atti del Consiglio Principe* (1917–1919), Libro L no. 58.
[188] Session of 24 Febr. 1919, *Verbali del Congresso di Stato* (1917–1920), p. 363.
[189] League of Nations Off. J. (1920) no. 5, p. 264.
[190] Compare with Liechtenstein's application, pp. 170–174 above.
[191] San Marino participated in the International Conference for the unification of the law concerning exchange bills and cheques held in Geneva on 7 Jun. 1930, and also participated in the elaboration of a draft Convention regulating whale hunting: information from the State Archives of San Marino.
[192] Information from the State Archives of San Marino.
[193] See p. 174 above.

International Court of Justice

By letter of 6 November 1953, San Marino applied to become a party to the Statute of the International Court of Justice.[194] The Security Council referred the application to its Committee of Experts.[195] The report of the Committee of Experts does not show any discussions on San Marino's statehood and independence, as had been the case with Liechtenstein's application.[196] The Security Council thereupon adopted the Chilean proposal by ten votes to none, with one abstention from the Soviet Union which had also abstained in the Committee of Experts.[197] The reasons for the abstention by the Soviet delegate are not given.[198] Objections concerning San Marino's statehood do not seem to have been raised. The application was subsequently sent to the General Assembly,[199] which permitted San Marino to become a party to the Statute of the International Court of Justice.[200] The consideration by the General Assembly was extremely brief. San Marino's application was not discussed in any of the Assembly's Committees and no member wished to speak on the item in the plenary meeting.[201] Until now, no case has been brought before the International Court of Justice by or against San Marino.

OSCE

San Marino had already been invited to participate in the preparatory talks of the CSCE in 1972. There seem to have been no protests by other participating States against San Marino's admission to the Conference in Helsinki. San Marino had chosen to join the group of neutral and non-aligned States within the CSCE and over the years

---

[194] UN Doc. S/3137 (1953).
[195] UN Doc. S/PV.641 (1953) and Report of the Chairman of the Committee of Experts, UN Doc. S/3147 (1953) p. 73.
[196] See pp. 175–177 above.
[197] UN Doc. S/PV.645 (1953) pp. 3–4.
[198] R. Higgins, *The Development of International Law through the Political Organs of the United Nations* (1963) p. 49, suggests that the Soviet abstention was founded on San Marino's small size. It should be noted that the Soviet Union also abstained from voting with regard to Japan's application to become a party to the Statute of the International Court of Justice, which was under consideration by the Security Council at the same time as San Marino's application: UN Doc. S/PV.645 (1953) p. 3, paras. 10–11.
[199] UN Doc. A/2601 (1953) p. 1.
[200] GA Res. 806 (VIII) of 9 Dec. 1953, adopted by fifty-one votes to none, with five abstentions.
[201] UN Doc. A/9/PV.471 (1953) p. 456, para. 34. San Marino has not accepted the compulsory jurisdiction of the International Court of Justice under Art. 36, paragraph 2 of the Statute.

has endeavoured to intensify its participation in this group.[202] The main interest for San Marino in its participation in the OSCE is the international acceptance of its sovereign equality by the other participating States. San Marino furthermore emphasizes the relevance of international security and the reduction of the arms race which are especially relevant for a militarily weak Micro-State.[203] Although San Marino's actions in the OSCE are given more political weight through the joint actions of the group of neutral and non-aligned States, they also emphasize its individual strength. Thus, San Marino permitted itself to express a more severe criticism against human rights violation in Yugoslavia in 1991 than most other States, which had more national interests at stake and more relations with Yugoslavia than San Marino.[204] San Marino has two seats in the OSCE Parliamentary Assembly[205] and bears 0.20 per cent of the costs for the OSCE institutions.[206]

FAO

Before the establishment of FAO, San Marino had been a member of its predecessor, the International Agriculture Institute.[207] In 1948, San Marino considered the opportunity to become a member of FAO, but feared that it could not meet the financial contribution which this involved. It also wondered whether Italy had any interest in San Marino's participation in FAO, in order to find more support for its proposals within the Organization.[208] On 20 September 1951, San Marino requested information from FAO concerning the conditions for admission and the minimum contribution. As the annual contri-

---

[202] Discussions in the Great and General Council, 17–19 Oct. 1989, *Notizia* (1989) no. 10, p. 2.
[203] *Notizia* (1989) no. 5, p. 4 on the 1989 CSCE Ministers Conference on security and conventional weapons in Europe.
[204] Interview with Mrs M. A. Bonelli, also acting as senior official to the CSCE for San Marino, 7 Oct. 1991.
[205] Art. 1 (I) of the final resolution of the Madrid Conference concerning the establishment of the CSCE Parliamentary Assembly, 3 Apr. 1991, 30 ILM (1991) pp. 1344 ff.
[206] Part III (2) of the Supplementary Document to give effect to certain provisions contained in the Charter of Paris for a New Europe, 30 ILM (1991) p. 220.
[207] The International Agriculture Institute functioned from 28 May 1908 to 1 Aug. 1946, after which its duties were taken over by FAO. San Marino was a member of the Institute from 27 Nov. 1908. H. Maza, *Neuf Meneurs internationaux: De l'Initiative individuelle dans l'Institution des Organisations internationales* (1965) pp. 213, 220–221.
[208] Letter from the San Marinese Secretary of State for foreign affairs to the former San Marinese delegate to the International Agriculture Institute of 17 Nov. 1948, State Archives of San Marino.

bution amounted to 2,500 US dollars, San Marino preferred to become a permanent observer to FAO, like the Holy See.[209] It requested admission to the most important conferences of the committees and preferred, if possible, to be exonerated from any financial contribution.[210] On 29 November 1951, the Sixth Conference of FAO took San Marino's request for a permanent observer status under consideration and decided that, as the Holy See's permanent observer status was granted under special circumstances, which were not related to the territorial sovereignty over the Vatican City, this could not be invoked as a precedent. The Conference deferred the question until its seventh session and requested a special report on 'the possibility of defining proper methods of associating countries such as San Marino with the activities of the Organization'.[211] On 16 October 1952, the Council of FAO considered the problems which were involved with San Marino's request to become a permanent observer and examined the possibility of Micro-States becoming members of the Organization. It concluded that small States like San Marino '... sont généralement considérés comme souverains, même s'ils ont volontairement conclu avec un grand Etat voisin des accords qui limitent leur faculté d'agir indépendamment de lui'.[212] However, due to the smallness of their territory, their restricted population and agricultural production and trade, 'il est douteux qu'ils puissent utilement souscrire aux obligations du Préambule, ni que les autres Etats Membres aient un intérêt quelconque à les associer à l'oeuvre internationale de la FAO'.[213] The Council of FAO also doubted whether San Marino's agricultural consumption would present important international interests considering that it was embodied in the neighbouring State's customs territory.[214] Moreover, its financial resources were insufficient to cover the annual minimum contribution. Even if the admission of the Holy See to FAO as a permanent observer was not to constitute a precedent, the Council eventually concluded that this was not a reason for refusing the status of permanent observer to any

---

[209] Letter from the San Marinese Secretary of State for foreign affairs to the Director-General of FAO of 18 Oct. 1951, State Archives of San Marino.
[210] Letter from the San Marinese Secretary of State for foreign affairs to the Director-General of FAO of 31 Oct. 1951, State Archives of San Marino.
[211] FAO Doc. 51/11/4137, *Conference of FAO, Sixth Session* (29 Nov. 1951) C 51/PV7, pp. 18–19.
[212] FAO Doc. 52/10/6299, *Conseil de la FAO, 16ème Session* (17 Nov. 1952) CL 16/29, p. 1.
[213] Ibid.
[214] Ibid., p. 2.

other State.²¹⁵ Nevertheless, on 17 March 1953, the Director-General of FAO informed San Marino that 'nos Gouvernements membres ne paraissent pas envisager avec faveur de conférer à des Etats souverains le Statut d'Observateur Permanent auprès de la FAO'.²¹⁶ San Marino therefore agreed to be invited on an *ad hoc* basis to the most important conferences as an observer, as had been the practice since 1949.²¹⁷ The matter was no longer brought under the consideration of the Conference of FAO. San Marino did not apply for membership in the subsequent years.

UNESCO

As early as 1947, San Marino showed a pronounced interest in becoming a member of UNESCO. It was pointed out that UNESCO would give San Marino the possibility to affirm its international position and could serve as a first step to membership of the United Nations.²¹⁸ On 7 June 1947, the San Marinese Secretary of State for foreign affairs officially asked to be admitted as a member of UNESCO.²¹⁹ The application was not to be officially considered by the Executive Board of UNESCO, as San Marino had problems in finding financial resources to cover its contribution. Three years later, in 1950, the application for membership was still considered valid and San Marino wondered whether the company operating its casino could indemnify for part of the contribution costs.²²⁰ As we have seen, the casino was only short lived, leaving San Marino with limited financial resources.²²¹

It was not until 1974 that San Marino submitted a new application for admission to UNESCO.²²² The Executive Board of UNESCO consid-

---

²¹⁵ Ibid., p. 3.
²¹⁶ Letter from the Director-General of FAO to the San Marinese Secretary of State for foreign affairs of 17 Mar. 1953, State Archives of San Marino.
²¹⁷ Letter from the San Marinese Secretary of State for foreign affairs to the Director-General of FAO of 5 Jun. 1953, State Archives of San Marino. San Marino participated in, for example, the Foot-and-Mouth Disease Conference of 1949 and attended the fifth and sixth sessions of the FAO Conference.
²¹⁸ Letter from the Italian delegate of the UN Relief and Rehabilitation Administration (UNRRA) to the representative of San Marino in Switzerland, no date (about 1947), State Archives of San Marino.
²¹⁹ Letter from the San Marinese Secretary of State for foreign affairs to the Executive Board of UNESCO of 9 Jun. 1947, State Archives of San Marino.
²²⁰ Letter from the San Marinese Secretary of State for foreign affairs to the San Marinese *chargé d'affaires* in Paris of 25 Jan. 1950, State Archives of San Marino.
²²¹ See p. 225 above.
²²² UNESCO Doc. 94 EX/54 (1974).

ered the application briefly without going into San Marino's international status. It was reminded that Italy had lent its support to San Marino's application, that San Marino maintained diplomatic relations with several European and American States, and that it was a democratic community which was interested in problems of cultural cooperation.[223] After being sanctioned by the Executive Board, the application was dealt with by the General Conference which approved San Marino's membership by acclamation and without discussion.[224]

WHO

The World Health Organization was one of the United Nations' specialized organizations of which San Marino attempted to acquire membership between 1948 and 1949. Like the failed initial applications in FAO, UNESCO and ILO, the first request for membership of WHO was unsuccessful. San Marino's first application was presented to the Director-General on 26 June 1948 and examined by the Legal Committee of the World Health Assembly. This Committee concluded that San Marino's application was not receivable as it was submitted too late.[225] The application was deferred to the Assembly's next session in 1949, and was this time examined by the Committee on Constitutional Matters of the World Health Assembly. A discussion arose in the Committee concerning San Marino's sovereignty. The Italian, British and Ceylonese delegates did not doubt that San Marino was a sovereign State, whereas the Dutch, Yugoslavian, Egyptian and United States representatives wanted a more thorough examination of San Marino's international status.[226] A Working Party was established to that end which issued a report on 27 June 1949.[227]

---

[223] UNESCO Doc. 94 EX/SR.31 (20 May–25 Jun. 1974) p. 382, paras. 25.1–25.2.
[224] *Records of the General Conference of UNESCO: Proceedings*, 18th Session (1974) vol. III, part 1, p. 31, para. 65.3. San Marino became an official member of UNESCO on 17 Oct. 1974. It established its National Commission for UNESCO in 1980 in accordance with Art. VII of the UNESCO Constitution: law of 13 Febr. 1980, BURSM (1980) no. 2. It was never suggested that San Marino should opt for an associate membership which was a possibility provided for in Art. II (3) of the UNESCO Constitution since 1951.
[225] The provisions of rule 89 of the Rules of Procedure required that an application for membership should reach the Director-General at least thirty days before the opening of the Assembly session during which the application was to be examined. The resolution of the Legal Committee was adopted by the World Health Assembly: WHO OR (1948) 1st Assembly, pp. 76 and 332.
[226] WHO OR (1949) 2nd Assembly, pp. 290–292.
[227] Ibid., p. 312.

The report made it clear that two problems existed with regard to the application of San Marino, namely '(a) that of the international status of San Marino, and (b) the question of the reservation with regard to the financial obligation to be undertaken by San Marino'.[228] Yet again, San Marino had feared the financial implications of its membership of WHO, and had made a reservation in respect of its financial contribution, which it had not withdrawn. Without considering San Marino's international status, the Working Party emphasized this financial reservation and 'was not in a position to recommend the acceptance of the application of San Marino'.[229] San Marino did not aspire to the possibility of associate membership for 'territories ... which are not responsible for the conduct of their international relations'[230]. San Marino remained an *ad hoc* observer until 1980.

On 18 March 1980, San Marino again applied for membership of WHO.[231] The application was communicated to all Member States and was considered by the World Health Assembly on 6 May 1980.[232] San Marino's application did not give rise to any discussion and was approved by the World Health Assembly by acclamation.[233] It is remarkable that San Marino's request for membership had not been submitted to a special committee of the World Health Assembly, nor did the Assembly itself examine San Marino's statehood, financial capacity or willingness to observe the Constitution of WHO. These considerations must have been raised implicitly, but were not the object of an official investigation and report as had been the case in 1949.

---

[228] Ibid.
[229] Ibid. This decision was approved by the World Health Assembly in Res. WHA 2.98, WHO OR (1949) 2nd Assembly, p. 54. It should be remarked that San Marino had informed WHO of its modest financial revenues and that '[w]ith the best will in the world, this small state could not pay such a large annual contribution [2,500 US dollars]'. San Marino pleaded for the universal application of the Constitution of WHO and suggested that the Constitution 'shall be amended so as to fix a maximum but not a minimum limit to annual contributions', which would be assessed according 'to the area of the territory, the population, the economic and financial position and the solvency of the respective States': WHO OR (1949) 2nd Assembly, Doc. A2/CM/4, p. 6.
[230] Art. 8 of the WHO Constitution. The associate membership is less costly than ordinary membership, but casts doubt on the territory's statehood.
[231] WHO Doc. A33/30 (3 Apr. 1980).
[232] *Thirty-Third World Health Assembly, Verbatim Records of Plenary Meetings* (5–23 May 1980) pp. 40–41.
[233] Ibid. Res. WHA 33.1 of 6 May 1980.

ILO

An application for membership of ILO was already in preparation in 1945 in order to reaffirm the principle of San Marino's sovereignty.[234] This project was however soon abandoned for financial reasons and due to the fact that ILO did not yet admit observers to its Conferences. In the fifties, San Marino had established a system of social security. As the social security agreements between Italy and third States were not extended to San Marinese workers in other countries, San Marino reconsidered ILO membership with a view to creating more advantageous working conditions for San Marinese workers in ILO Member States.[235] As a consequence, the San Marinese Secretary of State for foreign affairs submitted an official application for membership on 2 May 1958. The application specified, *inter alia*, that San Marino was willing to contribute to the costs of the Organization with an equitable contribution, to be fixed in mutual agreement, taking into account the modest resources of the San Marinese budget.[236] San Marino was thereupon quickly informed that ILO could not make any exceptions to the minimum contribution of 0.12 per cent, but that San Marino would be accepted as an observer to the annual Conferences.[237] San Marino withdrew its application and accepted the observer status.[238]

In 1982 San Marino again applied for membership of ILO which this time was not barred by financial difficulties. The application was the object of a report from a subcommittee of the Selection Committee of the International Labour Conference.[239] The report considered that the

---

[234] Letter from the San Marinese Secretary of State for foreign affairs to the Consul-General of San Marino in Rome of 10 Nov. 1945, State Archives of San Marino.

[235] Letter from the San Marinese Secretary of State for foreign affairs to a plenipotentiary minister of San Marino of 13 May 1954, and letter from the San Marinese Secretary of State for foreign affairs to a minister of San Marino of 18 Febr. 1957, State Archives of San Marino. Some agreements on social security matters between Italy and third States were extended to San Marinese migrant workers, e.g., through an exchange of notes with France of 12 Nov. 1958 on family allowance.

[236] Point c) of the application for membership of 2 May 1958 annexed to a letter from the Secretary of State for foreign affairs to the plenipotentiary minister of San Marino in Paris of 2 May 1958, State Archives of San Marino.

[237] Letter from the plenipotentiary minister of San Marino in Paris to the San Marinese Secretary of State for foreign affairs of 16 May 1958, State Archives of San Marino.

[238] Letter from the San Marinese Secretary of State for foreign affairs to the plenipotentiary minister of San Marino in Paris of 26 May 1958, State Archives of San Marino.

[239] Report of the Subcommittee of the Selection Committee appointed to study the application of the Republic of San Marino for Membership of ILO, ILO Doc. CP/D.10 (11 Jun. 1982) International Labour Conference, 68th Session.

grounds which had led the League of Nations to reject applications from, *inter alia*, San Marino were no longer relevant. ILO had no reason to reject the membership of very small States which possessed all attributes of sovereignty such as San Marino.[240] Moreover, San Marino had provided ILO with guarantees that it was able to meet the requirements imposed by membership and would include representatives of employers' and workers' organizations in its tripartite delegation.[241]

The General Conference of ILO took note of the Selection Committee's recommendation to admit San Marino to ILO and proceeded to a vote without further discussion.[242] The Government of San Marino believed that membership of ILO would give the Republic international prestige and confirmation.[243]

Council of Europe

In an effort to strengthen its position at the European level and to intensify its international activities, San Marino prepared its admission as a member of the Council of Europe by obtaining observer status in 1982. After getting acquainted with the work of the Council of Europe, San Marino expressed its wish to be invited to become a member on 18 January 1988. Subsequently, the Committee of Ministers asked the Parliamentary Assembly for its opinion on the matter.[244] The request was transmitted to the Political Affairs Committee and the Committee on Relations with European Non-Member Countries, which appointed one rapporteur each who issued a joint report on 15 September 1988.[245] After having carried out a fact-finding mission in San Marino, the two rapporteurs examined three main questions:

Is San Marino a sovereign State? One of the important aspects of San Marino's international status was its relations with Italy, so it was thought.[246] It was emphasized that the reference to the protective

---

[240] Ibid., p. 3, para. 5.
[241] Ibid., p. 3, para. 6.
[242] San Marino received 321 votes in its favour which did not correspond to the minimum 332 votes, i.e., two-thirds of the Member States required under Art. 1 (4) of the ILO Constitution: International Labour Conference, *Record of Proceedings*, 68th Session, 15 Jun. 1982, p. 23/1. A second vote was therefore necessary three days later which resulted in a unanimous approval of San Marino's application for membership.
[243] *Notiziario* (Jun. 1982–Febr. 1983) no. 1, p. 45.
[244] Council of Europe Doc. 5860, Council of Europe, *Parliamentary Assembly, Documents: Working Papers* (2–6 May 1988) vol. I, p. 1.
[245] Council of Europe Doc. 5938, ibid., vol. V, pp. 1–15.
[246] Ibid., p. 5, para. 10.

friendship of Italy had been omitted from the treaty of friendship in 1972[247] and that San Marino had the right to denounce the treaty and conclude any political alliance it wished. Briefly examining the Italo-San Marinese relations, the rapporteurs concluded that they 'cannot be defined as those of protectorate and protector. They are in fact based on equality between sovereign States; they contain nothing of the trusteeship implicit in the concept of a protectorate.'[248] The monetary relations with Italy and the fact that San Marino had agreed not to become a tax haven[249] were considered 'perfectly in line with the request of the Council of Europe Parliamentary Assembly that the creation of tax havens should not be allowed'.[250] Moreover, Italy's consular representation in countries where San Marino has no consulates of its own was based 'exclusively on the free will of the two countries concerned'.[251] The rapporteurs concluded 'that relations between Italy and San Marino are not such as to detract from the latter's sovereignty' and added that 'it is vital to note that the sovereignty and independence of San Marino *also* [emphasis added] derive from recognition of the country by the international community'.[252] It seemed as if the rapporteurs believed that San Marino's statehood is not only based on the sufficient degree of independence vis-à-vis Italy, but also on its international recognition. In this sense, the international recognition of San Marino is given a constitutive effect for its statehood.[253] As we have seen, the international recognition of Liechtenstein was given less importance by one of the rapporteurs, who also treated the San Marinese application. For the case of Liechtenstein he regarded the international recognition more as an evidence of its statehood than as a vital element of it.[254] It is not clear

---

[247] Ibid., p. 5, para. 12. The rapporteurs did not have to examine San Marino's international status prior to the amendment of the treaty of friendship in 1971. See also pp. 223–224 above.
[248] Ibid., p. 6, para. 14.
[249] The report alludes to the obligation of San Marino not to issue financial regulations likely to impinge upon Italy's tax system or fiduciary currency, contained in Art. 47 (3) of the 1939 treaty of friendship. See p. 226 above.
[250] Council of Europe Doc. 5938, Council of Europe, *Parliamentary Assembly, Documents: Working Papers* (3–8 Oct. 1988) vol. V, p. 6, para. 15. Parliamentary Assembly Recommendation 833 (1978) on cooperation between Council of Europe Member States against international tax avoidance and evasion.
[251] Ibid., p. 6, para. 16.
[252] Ibid., p. 6, para. 17.
[253] See p. 115 above.
[254] Mr Reddemann was the rapporteur of Council of Europe Doc. 4193 on Liechtenstein: see p. 181 above. Council of Europe Doc. 5938 on San Marino was also prepared by Mr Reddemann in cooperation with the second rapporteur.

whether the rapporteurs intentionally wanted to make a distinction between the effect of recognition on the international position of Liechtenstein, and its effect on the international status of San Marino. As the rapporteurs had already concluded that San Marino was sufficiently independent to be sovereign and as they did not seem to adhere to a strict constitutive theory of recognition in the case of Liechtenstein which was also sufficiently independent, it is contradictory to insist on a constitutive recognition for San Marino. The relations of San Marino with its neighbouring State are based on a legal construction which is different from the relations of Liechtenstein with its neighbouring State. This difference is however not of such a nature as to justify the acceptance of a constitutive recognition in the former and a declaratory recognition in the latter case. The report of the Council of Europe stands alone where the constitutive recognition of San Marino is concerned, and was not followed by other international organizations.[255] The rapporteurs concluded that 'there is no doubt about the sovereignty of the Republic of San Marino'.[256]

Does San Marino have a democratic constitution and does it respect human rights?[257] It was concluded that San Marino was 'a parliamentary democracy in which the rule of law is respected'.[258] With respect to the human rights situation, the rapporteurs recalled two drawbacks which had been detected by the rapporteur of the Political Affairs Committee during the procedure which culminated in the granting of observer status to San Marino in 1982.[259] The first concerned women's rights and particularly the fact that under San Marino's law on nationality women who married foreigners forfeited their citizenship. This stipulation had however been removed by the law of 27 March 1984, so that the rapporteurs concluded that the amendment 'introduced equality between men and women in respect of nationality'.[260] This is incorrect for, although the stipulation in question has been made applicable to both men and women, the new law on nationality of 27 March 1984 is not based on the equality of men and women in other nationality matters, such as the passing on

---

[255] See, e.g., pp. 238–242 above and pp. 254–255 below.
[256] Council of Europe Doc. 5938, p. 10, para. 28.
[257] Ibid., pp. 10–12.
[258] Ibid., p. 10, para. 31.
[259] Council of Europe Doc. AS/Pol. (34) 4.
[260] Council of Europe Doc. 5938, p. 12, para. 38.

of nationality to children and nationality through marriage.²⁶¹ The second drawback concerned San Marino's freely renounced right to broadcast by radio and television. The rapporteurs observed that this right had been fully restored by a convention with Italy of 23 October 1987.²⁶² Moreover, San Marino now had its own daily newspaper, so that the obstacle to freedom of expression and communication by the press had been removed.²⁶³

*Does San Marino have the ability to face up to the obligations which membership of the Council of Europe entails?*²⁶⁴ There was no doubt about San Marino's capacity to respect its financial obligations, nor of its willingness to play an active part in the work of the Committee of Ministers and the Parliamentary Assembly. The proposed draft opinion also mentioned that San Marino 'intends to exercise its membership rights and duties in a manner compatible with its resources'.²⁶⁵ This is a variant of the Liechtenstein declaration to 'exercise her vote as a member in a manner appropriate to her size'.²⁶⁶ It is clear that, as in the case of Liechtenstein, this cannot imply special membership rights or duties. San Marino may vote as it deems necessary and has to pay the minimum financial contribution.

The rapporteurs thus concluded that '[i]n spite of its small population, the Republic of San Marino does satisfy the pre-conditions for membership of the Council of Europe'.²⁶⁷ They added that '[e]very nation, however small it may be, is capable of playing a valuable, and irreplaceable, part in the Council of Europe's efforts to meet the objectives laid down in its Statute'.²⁶⁸

The Parliamentary Assembly considered San Marino's membership on 6 October 1988 and generally approved the participation of a small State in the work of the Council of Europe.²⁶⁹ The Liechtenstein

---

²⁶¹ See p. 221 above at nn. 102–105 and accompanying text.
²⁶² See p. 231 above.
²⁶³ Council of Europe Doc. 5938, p. 12, paras. 39–41.
²⁶⁴ Ibid., pp. 12–14.
²⁶⁵ Point 4 of the draft opinion, ibid., p. 2, taken over by the Parliamentary Assembly in Opinion no. 143 (1988), Council of Europe, *Parliamentary Assembly, Texts adopted by the Assembly* (3–8 Oct. 1988) p. 1.
²⁶⁶ Council of Europe Doc. 4211, p. 10 and point 7 of the Assembly's Opinion (28 Sept. 1978), Doc. 4193, p. 2. See also p. 182 above at n. 234.
²⁶⁷ Council of Europe Doc. 5938, p. 14, para. 52.
²⁶⁸ Ibid., p. 14, para. 53.
²⁶⁹ Council of Europe, *Parliamentary Assembly, Official Report* (6 Oct. 1988), Doc. AS(40)CR13, Second part, pp. 27–39.

delegate said 'Liechtenstein's membership of the Council of Europe over the past ten years had shown that small countries had a role to play' and could benefit from regular communication with other larger States, with which they could not have relations otherwise.[270] The Parliamentary Assembly adopted an opinion unanimously in favour of San Marino's membership of the Council of Europe.[271] The only problem which exists for San Marino is the search for sufficient, qualified personnel in order to examine all the Council of Europe documents on which a national policy can be based.[272] The attitude of both Liechtenstein and San Marino has convinced the Council of Europe that Micro-States can contribute positively to its work and do not necessarily vote under the influence of other States.

European Community

In 1968, the Council of the European Communities had established by regulation that San Marino constituted a part of the Community's customs territory by virtue of the treaty of friendship of 1939 linking it to Italy.[273] In 1986, in reply to a question raised by an Irish parliamentarian of the European Parliament, the Commission stated more precisely that the free movement of workers, the freedom of establishment and the free movement of services did not apply to, *inter alia*, San Marino which constituted a third State with respect to the Community.[274]

San Marino, which has an observer status to the European Union, started preliminary talks with the Community on a customs union agreement in 1983. It was the first European Micro-State to start such unofficial negotiations. Throughout the negotiations San Marino wanted to state clearly its legal position towards the Community as a third State and emphasized its sovereignty.[275] In the mean time, the Committee on Institutional Affairs of the European Parliament

---

[270] Ibid., pp. 31–33.
[271] Opinion no. 143 (1988), Council of Europe, *Parliamentary Assembly, Texts adopted by the Assembly* (3–8 Oct. 1988) pp. 1–2. San Marino officially ratified the Statute of the Council of Europe on 16 Nov. 1988.
[272] Interview with Mrs M. A. Bonelli of 7 Oct. 1991. The judge reserved for San Marino in the European Court of Human Rights has San Marinese nationality.
[273] Art. 2 and annex point 3 of Council Regulation no. 1496/68, ECOJ no. L 238 (28.9.68). See also pp. 229–230 above at n. 158.
[274] Answer given by Mr Delors in name of the Commission to written question no. 900/86 of 14 Jul. 1986, ECOJ no. C 54 (2.3.87) p. 31.
[275] *Notizia* (1990) no. 4, p. 3.

adopted a 'resolution on the rights of the citizens of small States and territories in Europe'.[276] This resolution, which was particularly prompted by the official negotiations started with Andorra,[277] laid down that Micro-States like Andorra, San Marino and Monaco attached great importance to the maintenance of their political independence, but that the unification of the European market would no doubt have negative results for their economies.[278] Therefore, so it was said, the Community had to take care that the interests of these small States would remain untouched, without prejudicing Community integration.[279] The Committee on Institutional Affairs proposed that the agreements with the Micro-States should not be confined to a customs union but should also comprise the free movement of persons, a closer involvement in the 'Europe of the citizens', and a participation in the Community declaration on fundamental rights and freedoms and should prevent naturalization and establishment with a view to evading tax in the country of origin.[280] The report and resolution of the Committee on Institutional Affairs was to a large extent set aside by the European Commission and the Council.

The opening of the official talks in December 1990 had been preceded by a San Marinese memorandum of April 1990 which was sent to the Commission.[281] On 4 July 1991 the European Commission and San Marino initialled an agreement on customs union and cooperation, which for the greater part met San Marino's wishes laid down in its memorandum.[282]

---

[276] Report of the Committee on Institutional Affairs of 20 Apr. 1989, on the rights of the citizens of small States and territories in Europe, EP Doc. A2 – 86/89, European Parliament, *Session Documents* (1989–90). The report and resolution were adopted by the Committee on Institutional Affairs under the authority of the European Parliament by virtue of Art. 37 of the EP rules of procedure.

[277] See p. 361 below.

[278] EP Doc. A2 – 86/89, point B of the resolution, p. 5.

[279] Ibid., point C of the resolution, p. 5.

[280] Ibid., points 2 and 3 of the resolution, p. 6.

[281] Memorandum not published, information from the San Marinese department of foreign affairs.

[282] Bull. EC 7/8 – 1991, point 1.3.28, p. 88: contrary to what this source mentions, the agreement was not initialled on 5 but on 4 Jul. 1991. The text of the initialled agreement was not officially published. Three San Marinese proposals in the memorandum were not embodied in the agreement: San Marino had not wished to adopt the Community legislation on the characteristics of products, because it could not participate in the creation of this legislation. It therefore preferred to be consulted on this issue in a mixed organ, yet to be established. It had pleaded for the mutual recognition of the titles and diplomas acquired in the European Community and San Marino (the

On 7 November 1991, the Commission presented the initialled agreement to the Council[283] which signed the agreement in the form of an exchange of letters between the European Economic Community and the Republic of San Marino on 16 December 1991.[284] The final agreement differs only on one point from the initialled agreement of 4 July 1991. The Cooperation Committee which is set up by the agreement is composed of representatives of the Commission on the one hand, assisted by, and this is new, delegates of the Member States, and representatives of San Marino on the other hand.[285] This addition can be explained for legal reasons. The agreement on customs union and cooperation not only covers customs regulations, but also certain duties of cooperation and social provisions which do not fall under the exclusive competence of the European Community by virtue of Article 3 of the EC Treaty. It is for this reason that some Member States insisted that the agreement was of a mixed nature and therefore also required to be ratified by every Member State separately.[286] The approval of the European Parliament had to be obtained. The agreement was submitted to four parliamentary Committees which all gave a favourable opinion.[287] On 7 July 1992, the rapporteurs of the Committee on External Economic Relations and of the Committee on Foreign Affairs and Security, both Italians, argued for the approval of the agreement on customs union and cooperation with San Marino in the European Parliament. They briefly recited the content of the agreement and reminded the European Parliament that San Marino 'has been independent since the

---

agreement did not enclose a provision to that effect) and had proposed that the Community's financial means and the corresponding subsidies in favour of initiatives designed to sustain and develop the San Marinese economy should also be fixed for economic, infrastructural and cultural initiatives with the Member States.

[283] Commission proposal for a Council Decision, ECOJ no. C 302 (22.11.91) p. 10. See also COM (91) 429 final of 4 Nov. 1991. Bull. EC 12 – 1991, point 1.3.23, p. 101.

[284] Full and final text of the agreement on customs union and cooperation between the EEC and the Republic of San Marino signed on 16 Dec. 1991 in ECOJ no. C 302 (22.11.91) pp. 12 ff.

[285] Art. 23 (4) of the agreement on customs union and cooperation.

[286] EP Legislative Resolution A3 – 0114/92 of 9 Jul. 1992, ECOJ no. C 241 (21.9.92) p. 169 mentions Arts. 113, 228 and 235 of the EC Treaty as the legal basis of the agreement on customs union and cooperation.

[287] Report of the Committee on External Economic Relations of 23 Mar. 1992, EP Doc. A3 –0114/92, European Parliament, *Session Documents*, including the opinions of the Committee on Agriculture, Fisheries and Rural Development, the Committee on Foreign Affairs and Security and the Committee on Budget. The Committee on Foreign Affairs and Security stated that San Marino 'lived for a long time under the aegis of the

XIth century [sic]' and that 'San Marino is not a tax haven'.[288] On 9 July 1992, the European Parliament approved the conclusion and entry into force of the agreement on customs union and cooperation.[289]

As the agreement on customs union and cooperation had to be ratified by the national parliaments of the EC Member States as well, the entry into force of the agreement was expected to be delayed. Therefore, an interim agreement on trade and customs union was concluded.[290] The interim agreement takes over the customs and trade articles of the agreement on customs union and cooperation, as well as the provisions concerning the establishment of a Cooperation Committee. Under the interim agreement however, the Community representatives in the Cooperation Committee are no longer assisted by delegates of the Member States, as it concerns strictly a matter of Community competence.[291] The interim agreement ceases to apply once the agreement on customs union and cooperation comes into operation.[292]

The agreement on customs union and cooperation has 'the aim of contributing to the social and economic development of San Marino and strengthening relations between the Parties'.[293] The following legal regime has been established to this end:

Customs union A customs union is established between the European Community and San Marino for industrial and agricultural products except for those falling within the scope of the ECSC Treaty.[294] In

---

Italian State as far as development of its external political and trade relations is concerned' and emphasized 'San Marino's wish not to be excluded from the process of European integration'. It also believed that 'the Republic of San Marino today represents an independent political and economic entity, in spite of its small size and consequent strong links with neighbouring Italy', p. 10.

[288] *Debates of the European Parliament* (7.7.92), No. 3 - 420/102, and ECOJ no. C 241 (21.9.92) p. 29.

[289] EP Legislative Resolution A3 - 0114/92 and Council Decision 9541/91, C3 - 0031/92, ECOJ no. C 241 (21.9.92) pp. 138-139 and 168-169.

[290] The interim agreement was concluded and ratified by a Council Decision of 27 Nov. 1992 and came into force on 1 Dec. 1992. Approval of the Great and General Council on 20 Nov. 1992. Decree no. 98 of 2 Dec. 1992, and Council Decision 92/561/EEC of 27 Nov. 1992, ECOJ no. L 359 (9.12.92) pp. 13 ff. with full text of the interim agreement.

[291] Art. 13 (4) of the interim agreement.

[292] Art. 19, 3rd para. of the interim agreement.

[293] Art. 1 of the agreement on customs union and cooperation.

[294] In general, the products covered by Chapters 1 to 97 of the Common Customs Tariff, Art. 2 of the agreement on customs union and cooperation (Art. 1 of the interim agreement).

respect of third States, San Marino applies the EC Common Customs Tariff and other legislation necessary for the proper functioning of the customs union, with the exception of refunds and compensatory amounts accorded for the export of agricultural products.[295] As we have seen,[296] San Marino is committed to levy tax on imported goods pursuant to the exchange of letters with Italy of 21 December 1972. This tax is not applied to national products and therefore constitutes a charge of an equivalent effect to an import duty which had to be abolished by 1 January 1996.[297] This will lead to the introduction of a general VAT system in San Marino, levied by the San Marinese authorities. San Marino has authorized the Community until 1 December 1997 to carry out customs clearance formalities 'on behalf of and for San Marino'.[298] After this period San Marino has the right to carry out customs clearance formalities itself.[299] The Cooperation Committee decides on 'the arrangements for assigning to the San Marino Exchequer the amounts collected ... and the percentage to be deducted by the European Economic Community to cover administrative costs'.[300] This would imply that Italy, in the name of the European Community, has to assign to San Marino the exact amount of imported duties collected on the latter's behalf, subject to a deduction for administrative costs. So far no arrangements have been made to this end and Italy continues to pay its annual and since 1986 fixed customs contribution ('canone doganale') under Article 52 of the treaty of friendship, which does not reflect the exact amounts collected by Italian customs offices on imports to San Marino, but is also given by way of compensa-

---

[295] Art. 7 (1) of the agreement on customs union and cooperation (Art. 6 (1) of the interim agreement). San Marino applies the Community veterinary, plant health and quality regulations vis-à-vis third States, but only the Community veterinary, plant health and quality regulations on agricultural products in its relations with the EC: cf. Art. 6 (4) and Art. 7 (1) 5th para. of the agreement on customs union and cooperation (Arts. 5 (4) and 6 (1) 5th para. of the interim agreement).

[296] See p. 230 above at n. 163 and accompanying text.

[297] Art. 6 (2) of the agreement on customs union and cooperation (Art. 5 (2) of the interim agreement). As of 1 Jan. 1996 San Marino has introduced a supplementary tax corresponding to that currently levied on imported goods, chargeable on domestic products for home consumption.

[298] Art. 8 (1) (a) of the agreement on customs union and cooperation (Art. 7 (1) (a) of the interim agreement).

[299] Art. 8 (1) (b) of the agreement on customs union and cooperation (Art. 7 (1) (b) of the interim agreement).

[300] Art. 8 (3) (b) of the agreement on customs union and cooperation (Art. 7 (3) (b) of the interim agreement).

tion for the concessions made by San Marino.³⁰¹ When in the future Italy's customs contribution ('canone doganale') has to be readjusted, the negotiations will have to take place in the Cooperation Committee as far as the 'customs duties part' of the customs contribution is concerned.

Cooperation   A general clause provides for the institution of 'cooperation with the aim of strengthening existing links between them [the Community and San Marino] on as broad a basis as possible for the mutual benefit of the Parties, taking account of their respective powers'.³⁰² Four priority areas are mentioned: the encouragement of the growth and diversification of the industrial and service sectors of the economy of San Marino, especially small and medium-sized enterprises,³⁰³ environmental protection,³⁰⁴ tourism including the promotion of out-of-season tourism in San Marino³⁰⁵ and joint operations in communications, information and cultural matters.³⁰⁶

Social provisions   The agreement on customs union and cooperation sets forth the principle of non-discrimination on grounds of nationality as regards working conditions and remuneration for Community and San Marinese workers in San Marino and the Community respectively.³⁰⁷ This principle does not include the right of free movement of workers. It furthermore provides for equal treatment in the field of social security for San Marinese workers and their families in the Community³⁰⁸ and for family allowances for these same workers.³⁰⁹ It should be noted that San Marino must accord to Community workers a 'treatment similar' to that accorded by the Community to San Marinese workers in the field of social security and family allowances.³¹⁰ There is therefore no absolute duty of reciprocity in these particular issues, but only a duty of similarity.³¹¹

---

[301] Information from the San Marinese department of foreign affairs, office for social and economic affairs. See also p. 230 above at n. 161 and accompanying text.
[302] Art. 14 of the agreement on customs union and cooperation.
[303] Art. 15 of the agreement on customs union and cooperation.
[304] Art. 16 of the agreement on customs union and cooperation.
[305] Art. 17 of the agreement on customs union and cooperation.
[306] Art. 18 of the agreement on customs union and cooperation.
[307] Art. 20 of the agreement on customs union and cooperation.
[308] Art. 21 (1) of the agreement on customs union and cooperation.
[309] Art. 21 (3) of the agreement on customs union and cooperation.
[310] Art. 21 (5) of the agreement on customs union and cooperation.
[311] The French text states 'Saint Marin accorde ... un régime analogue': Art. 21 (5) of the agreement on customs union and cooperation.

Cooperation Committee This Committee has the responsibility for administering the agreement and ensuring that it is properly implemented.[312] The Cooperation Committee is composed of representatives of the Commission, who are assisted by delegates of the Member States, except under the interim agreement, and representatives of San Marino.[313] Any dispute arising over the interpretation of the agreement shall be put before the Cooperation Committee.[314] If the Committee fails to settle the dispute at its next meeting, each Party may designate an arbitrator, while the Cooperation Committee appoints a third arbitrator.[315] The arbitrators' decision taken by majority vote is binding upon the Parties.[316] The existence of this arbitration procedure has strengthened San Marino's actual independent position vis-à-vis Italy considerably. Thus, if Italy does not pay at least the exact amount of the customs duties collected on behalf of and for San Marino, the European Community will be held responsible for the violation of the agreement on customs union and cooperation. In that event the arbitration procedure can be used by San Marino. This then implies that Italy has lost one of its practical means of pressure on San Marino, namely the withholding of the customs contribution, once used in the casino dispute.[317]

Final provisions and declarations The agreement on customs union and cooperation replaces provisions of agreements concluded between San Marino and EC Member States that conflict with it, or which are identical.[318] The agreement is concluded for an unlimited duration, with the possibility of amendment after five years, but can be denounced subject to six months' notice.[319] Several declarations have been attached to the agreement on customs union and cooperation.[320] One declaration by the Community deserves particular attention:

[312] Art. 23 (1) of the agreement on customs union and cooperation (Art. 13 (1) of the interim agreement).
[313] Art. 23 (4) of the agreement on customs union and cooperation (Art. 13 (4) of the interim agreement).
[314] Art. 24 (1) of the agreement on customs union and cooperation (Art. 14 (1) of the interim agreement).
[315] Art. 24 (2) of the agreement on customs union and cooperation (Art. 14 (2) of the interim agreement).
[316] Ibid.
[317] See p. 225 above.
[318] Art. 28 of the agreement on customs union and cooperation. Thus, Arts. 44–46 and 51 of the 1939 treaty of friendship with Italy are abolished.
[319] Arts. 26 and 27 of the agreement on customs union and cooperation (Arts. 16 and 17 of the interim agreement).
[320] Four declarations by the Community, one by the Member States concerning the transport of passengers and one joint declaration.

Where the scale of trade flows so warrants, the Community is prepared to negotiate on behalf of and for the Republic of San Marino with countries with which it has concluded preferential agreements for an appropriate form of recognition of equivalent treatment for products originating in San Marino and products originating in the Community.[321]

This had been one of the wishes expressed in the San Marinese memorandum of April 1990. Although San Marino constituted a part of the Community's customs territory, this did not guarantee that a third State would treat San Marino in its trade relations like a Community State, as San Marino was not a Member of the European Community. Certain customs conventions concluded by the Community with third States will now be adapted so that San Marinese products are assimilated with products from the Member States of the Community. This does not imply that the Community has a duty to seek this assimilation nor an exclusive right to do so. If therefore, for whatever reason, the Community does not negotiate on San Marino's behalf, San Marino may well conclude a customs convention with a third State in order to enjoy the same advantages as the Community Member States. This would not be contrary to the agreement on customs union and cooperation as long as the convention does not deviate from the Common Customs Tariff, the common commercial policy of the Community and certain Community legislation related to imports from third States.[322]

The agreement on customs union and cooperation concluded with the European Economic Community has changed San Marino's customs relations with Italy on several points. In the first place, San Marino has emphasized its legal distinctness from an ever more integrated European Community by concluding an agreement as a third State with the Community. In the second place, San Marino has gained a more advantageous trade position towards non-EC Member States and has secured an active negotiation position in relation to the Community on a permanent basis in the Cooperation Committee. It also has the option to settle customs disputes by arbitration, which was not automatically foreseen in the former customs relations with Italy. In the third place, the customs regime applied by San Marino does not differ markedly from the old regime. In the fourth and last

---

[321] Text in ECOJ no. C 302 (22.11.91) pp. 17–18 and ECOJ no. L 359 (9.12.91) pp. 20–21 for the interim agreement. Declaration attached both to the agreement on customs union and cooperation and to the interim agreement.
[322] Art. 7 (1) of the agreement on customs union and cooperation (Art. 6 (1) of the interim agreement).

place, San Marino has entered into a framework of cooperation with the EC Member States that did not exist before. It is remarkable that the Community has shown its preparedness to safeguard not only the separate legal existence of San Marino, but also the economic survival of the Republic in the long run.

United Nations

San Marino participated for the first time as an *ad hoc* observer in the 1951 session of the General Assembly, and in March 1987 it obtained a permanent observer status. The stronger financial position of San Marino and the acquired experience with the United Nations as a permanent observer led San Marino to submit an official application for membership in the United Nations on 19 February 1992.[323] The Security Council adopted a resolution without a vote recommending to the General Assembly that the Republic of San Marino be admitted to membership in the United Nations.[324] The adoption of this resolution did not give rise to any discussion in the Security Council.[325] The General Assembly accepted the recommendation of the Security Council by acclamation on 2 March 1992.[326] According to the San Marinese Secretary of State for foreign affairs the admission of San Marino to the United Nations represented 'a recognition of their [San Marino's] buffeted and ancient freedom'.[327]

The admission procedure of San Marino was subject to much less discussion than that of Liechtenstein.[328] San Marino emphasizes that it wants to keep its vote in the United Nations free from any influence by other States.[329] Yet again, as in the Council of Europe, particular efforts are needed in order to study all the United Nations documents and items on which a vote from San Marino will be required. In 1993 and 1994, San Marino gave particular attention to a reform of the

---

[323] UN Doc. S/23619 (1992).
[324] SC Res. 744 (1992) and UN Doc. S/23640 (1992). The Committee on the Admission of New Members recommended to the SC the admission of San Marino to the UN: UN Doc. S/23634 (1992). Its report was not preceded by any discussion or investigation into San Marino's statehood or capacity to sustain its financial contribution: UN Doc. S/C.2/SR.86 (1992).
[325] UN Doc. S/PV.3056 (1992).
[326] UN Doc. A/46/PV.82 (1992) p. 13 and GA Res. 46/231 of 2 Mar. 1992. San Marino had been admitted to the ECE in a consultative capacity in Apr. 1977: UN Doc. E/5944, E/ECE/928, ECOSOC OR (10 Apr. 1976–30 Apr. 1977) Suppl. no. 9, vol. I.
[327] UN Doc. A/46/PV.82 (1992) p. 51.
[328] Cf. pp. 196–197 above.
[329] Interview with Mrs M. A. Bonelli of 7 Oct. 1991.

Security Council, which according to the Republic should lead to an equitable distribution of its seats and a greater transparency of its work.[330]

Other international organizations

Besides the international governmental organizations already referred to in the preceding paragraphs, San Marino is also a Member State of the ITU, the UPU,[331] the ICAO, WIPO and UNCTAD. More recently, San Marino applied to become a member of the International Monetary Fund on 29 May 1992.[332] After a fact-finding mission of experts of the International Monetary Fund was sent to San Marino, the Fund's Assembly approved San Marino's admission by acclamation on 22 September 1992.[333] San Marino's entry into the International Monetary Fund was considered to be a recognition of San Marino's economic system and to have positive results for its productivity.[334]

Application of the criteria for statehood

The foundation of San Marino's international status is the treaty on friendship, extradition and commerce with the Kingdom of Italy, concluded on 22 March 1862. The main question which arose until 1971 concerned the clause on Italy's protective friendship and San Marino's obligation not to accept the protective friendship of any other Power.[335] In practice, this protective friendship did not imply a control by Italy over San Marino's internal and external affairs. San Marino was juridically free to regulate its internal order, conclude treaties with third States on, for example, extradition and free to enter into diplomatic or consular relations with States. The fact that San Marino did not become a member of numerous international organizations before the seventies and eighties was principally related to its restrictive budget. If Italy's protective friendship did not imply a certain permitted influence of Italy in San Marino in

---

[330] Information from the Permanent Mission of the Republic of San Marino to the UN.
[331] See p. 229 above.
[332] *Notizia* (1992) no. 6, p. 7.
[333] *Notizia* (1992) no. 7, pp. 2–3.
[334] Opinion of the San Marinese Secretary of State for finance and budget, ibid., p. 3.
[335] Art. XXIX of the 1862 treaty with Italy which was upheld in the 1939 treaty of friendship until its withdrawal in 1971.

whatever form, why then did Italy want to ensure that San Marino would not accept the protective friendship of any other Power? Could this mean that the protective friendship was considered a certain form of influence? How then was this influence felt in practice? It should not be forgotten that the protective friendship clause was aimed at the maintenance of San Marino's ancient freedom and independence.[336] This would imply in the first place that Italy would not try to annex San Marino, that it would help San Marino against any measures taken by third States which would compromise San Marino's freedom and independence, and that San Marino would not seek this same help from States other than Italy. In the second place, the protective friendship clause implied that it was not meant to restrict San Marino's independence but to maintain it, also in its relations with Italy. Therefore by definition the protective friendship stipulation could not establish a protectorate which was characterized by a lack of independence.[337] Italy's protection was no more than a diplomatic or perhaps even military effort to defend San Marino's freedom and independence in a world where a small State like San Marino could not appeal to an international court or exert any pressure on larger States with which it could enter into conflict. It is in this sense that Italy's permitted influence under the protective friendship clause should be understood. Other involvement by Italy in San Marino's internal or external affairs was explicitly regulated by the other treaty provisions we have discussed in preceding paragraphs.[338] Moreover, the deletion of the protective friendship clause in 1971 did not alter the independent position of San Marino.

The following can be inferred from the criteria for statehood applied to San Marino:[339]

Territory The relative smallness of San Marino's territory has never been used as an argument by the international community, whether by separate States or by Member States of international fora, to preclude San Marino's statehood. This has no bearing on the fact that, for example in 1952 FAO expressed some doubt about the utility and

---

[336] The stipulation ran: 'l'amicizia protettrice di S.M. il Re d'Italia per la conservazione della sua [San Marino's] antichissima libertà ed indipendenza', Art. XXIX of the 1862, and Art. 1, 2nd para. of the 1939 treaty of friendship before amendment in 1971.
[337] Compare with one form of protectorate between France and Tunisia in 1881, pp. 123–124 above at nn. 90–93 and accompanying text.
[338] See pp. 223–230 above.
[339] See for the general criteria for statehood pp. 116–127 above.

financial feasibility of Micro-States becoming members of that Organization.³⁴⁰

Population The existence of a fixed population in San Marino is unquestioned. The presence of 17.7 per cent foreign inhabitants has not led to any objections concerning San Marino's statehood either.

Government The San Marinese governmental organization is based on the institutions of centuries of autonomy. There is no doubt that the present administrative organs wield effective power within the territory.

Independence The degree of formal and real independence from Italy is the determinant factor of San Marino's statehood. The following foreign elements are present in the San Marinese governmental organization:

1. *Obligations towards Italy* These are at present reduced to two obligations,³⁴¹ namely the duty not to adopt any financial measures which could, directly or indirectly, in any form influence Italy's tax or monetary system and the obligation not to permit the establishment of gambling houses in San Marinese territory.
2. *Italian legislation which has to be made applicable in San Marino* This concerns primarily the postal legislation and the currency norms, although the latter legislation has only to be adopted substantially. A control by Italian financial institutions exists in the banking sector.
3. *EC customs legislation* What was previously the application of the customs regime in force in Italy has been substituted on 1 December 1992 by the EC customs legislation. One can therefore no longer speak of an Italian influence on San Marinese imports from third States. The EC customs legislation differs only in name from the Italian. However, as far as San Marino is concerned the Community involvement is not a control, but a rendering of services.³⁴²
4. *Consular representation by Italy only occurs in States where San Marino does not have its own consular or diplomatic representation* Due to the expansion of San Marino's diplomatic service, recourse to the Italian missions has reduced. It is clear that

---

³⁴⁰ See p. 237 above at n. 213 and accompanying text.
³⁴¹ Art. 47 of the 1939 treaty of friendship as amended in 1954 and taking into account the 1991 Convention on financial and currency relations and the 1987 Agreement of cooperation in the field of radio and television which overruled certain former obligations of Art. 47.
³⁴² See pp. 249–251 above.

the occasional representation by Italy constitutes no more than a temporary protection of the interests of a third State within the meaning of Article 46 of the Vienna Convention on Diplomatic Relations of 1961.[343]

5 *Most judges in San Marino are of Italian nationality* Their independence has been guaranteed by law and they are therefore inherently independent from Italy. Their foreign origin is seen as a necessity in order to secure their impartiality in a small community.[344]

6 *Radio and television stations in San Marino can only be established with joint San Marinese and Italian governmental capital* San Marino cannot seek any cooperation in this field with other States.[345]

In practice, San Marino's independence does not differ from the degree of independence flowing from the treaty relations with Italy. It has the possibility, in virtually all cases, to denounce the treaties within six months, which makes its commitments less burdensome.[346]

One should distinguish carefully between lack of actual independence due to a substantial control by a third State and lack of economic or functional independence which is used, in an illegal way, by a third State as a means of pressure to enforce its demands. Italy does not control San Marino's State functions in a substantial way. Yet Italy could, by illegally withholding its customs contribution between 1949 and 1951, force San Marino to make certain concessions.[347] If these measures are not justifiable under international law, they cannot prejudice a State's independence according to the maxim *ex injuria jus non oritur*. If it were otherwise, States acting in contravention of international law would have the discretionary power to nullify another State's statehood. As a consequence, the measures which Italy took against San Marino in the dispute over the casino had no effect on San Marino's actual independence and statehood.[348]

---

[343] San Marino ratified the 1961 Vienna Convention on Diplomatic Relations on 8 Sept. 1965. See pp. 227–228 above.
[344] See pp. 214–215 above.
[345] See p. 231 above.
[346] The 1987 Agreement of cooperation in the field of radio and television has been concluded for 15 years after which it can be denounced subject to six months' notice, Art. 9.
[347] See pp. 225–226 above.
[348] See also pp. 126–127 above.

Recognition The report on San Marino's statehood by the Council of Europe concluded that San Marino was sufficiently independent to be a State. As we have seen, the argument that San Marino's statehood needed to be completed by an international constitutive recognition cannot be upheld.[349] The need for a reparative constitutive recognition was not felt by other international organizations either, nor was such a necessity expressed by any State in its bilateral relations with San Marino.

It can be inferred that San Marino is a State within the meaning of international law and that its degree of formal and real independence falls within the criteria for statehood.

Self-determination of the San Marinese people

The San Marinese people has the right of self-determination because it constitutes a State and because the indigenous inhabitants of this State are a 'people' or a 'fraction of a people' within the meaning of international law.[350] The 21,296 San Marinese nationals who had their residence in the Republic in 1991[351] do not clearly distinguish themselves from their immediate neighbours on strictly objective criteria. There is no special San Marinese language, although cultural, traditional and historic characteristics of the group are noticeable. The subjective elements of the San Marinese population are particularly pronounced and derive from ages of togetherness. The attachment to the territory is unquestionable. The San Marinese nationals are to a great extent the descendants of families which have been established in San Marino for several centuries. The San Marinese feel like a separate people and intend to maintain this separateness in the future. Therefore, the San Marinese people has the right of self-determination without prejudice to whether it constitutes one people or a fraction of a people according to the emphasis laid on the objective characteristics.

---

[349] See p. 244 above.
[350] See the general conclusion p. 103 above.
[351] Centro Elaborazione Dati e Statistica, *Bollettino di Statistica* (Apr./May 1991) nos. 4–5, fig. 2.5, p. 9.

Conclusions

The following can be inferred for the purposes of the present study:

1. The delegation of certain State functions to the Italian authorities by San Marino is at present restricted to the postal and monetary union. The Italo-San Marinese relations are furthermore governed by cooperation and concessions made by San Marino. These special relations can partly be explained by the smallness of the San Marinese territory and its restrictive resources, but also by San Marino's geographical position as a small enclave within Italy. Italy's political desire not to have to suffer any political, economic or fiscal disadvantages from San Marinese actions and Italy's stronger negotiation position have prompted San Marino to make certain juridical concessions.
2. San Marino's statehood is well established and recognized.
3. The efforts which San Marino has made in order to fortify its international activities have helped to prove its statehood and independence from Italy. Its rapprochement with the European Community has strengthened its negotiation position towards Italy and made its independence juridically more defendable.
4. States, whether on a bilateral or on a multilateral basis, have accepted San Marino in the international community on the basis of sovereign equality, without expressed objections with regard to its statehood.
5. The presence of San Marino at the international level is not hampered by its legal relations with Italy. In this context the problems which have arisen were of a financial nature or related to staffing.

6 The Principality of Monaco

Territory, population and economy

The Principality of Monaco is situated on the coast of the Mediterranean Sea and surrounded by the French department of the Alpes-Maritimes. The Principality covers a total land area of 1.95 square kilometres[1] and 71.1 square kilometres of territorial sea.[2] In 1990, at the last census, Monaco had 29,972 inhabitants of whom 5,070 were of Monégasque nationality comprising 16.92 per cent of the population against 40.19 per cent French, 16.68 per cent Italian and 26.21 per cent other nationals.[3] The Monégasque economy is mainly based on a strongly developed service sector, including banking and tourism, an industrial sector and real estate, building and construction activities.[4] In 1994, Monaco had an import surplus of 99.4 million French francs.[5] The State budget for 1995 showed a

---

[1] Information from the 'Service des Statistiques et des Etudes Economiques' of the Principality of Monaco.
[2] Figure calculated on the basis of a 3.2 km coastline and 12 nautical miles of territorial sea determined by the Convention on maritime delimitation concluded between Monaco and France on 16 Febr. 1984, Sovereign Order no. 8403 of 30 Sept. 1985. Monaco has an Exclusive Economic Zone which extends about 48.5 nautical miles from the baseline from which the breadth of the territorial sea is measured, and which is equidistant from the French coast of Corsica: Art. 2 of the Convention on maritime delimitation.
[3] Information from the 'Service des Statistiques et des Etudes Economiques' of the Principality of Monaco.
[4] In 1991, 72.99 per cent of the private sector turnover was covered by tertiary activities, 12.03 per cent by industry, 11.22 per cent by real estate, building and construction, and 3.76 per cent by hotels. Department of Finance and Economy, *The Best of Monte-Carlo: Monaco's Economy and its Leading Companies* (1992) p. 56. The industry is, among other things, composed of metallurgical, plastic and chemical industry, as well as enterprises producing electronic and precision instruments.
[5] Information from the French customs office in Monaco.

deficit of 77.0 million francs.[6] The receipts from VAT and other indirect taxes on commercial transactions are the main source of income of the Monégasque State and covered 45.7 per cent of total receipts in 1995.[7] The Monégasque economy is relatively export-oriented as 37.1 per cent of the turnover in 1990 emanated from exports to other countries, including France.[8]

History

The history of Monaco is closely related to its location on a natural harbour, which became of strategic and commercial interest over the centuries. Monaco and its neighbouring communities were placed under Roman domination until the fall of the Roman Empire after which it was subject to several invaders. In 1191, the coast of Monaco was put under the feudal system and subordinated to the Republic of Genoa.[9] Within the Genoese Republic a struggle for power had arisen between two parties: the Guelphs and the Ghibellines. When in 1295 after combats the Ghibellines had won authority over Genoa, the Guelphs were expelled from the city, among whom were members of the Grimaldi family.[10] On 8 January 1297, François Grimaldi, disguised as a Franciscan monk, managed to penetrate the fortress of Monaco held by the Ghibellines. The fortress was seized and the Grimaldi family established its authority over Monaco.

In order to protect his territory from annexation in the Italian wars, the Lord of Monaco concluded a protection treaty with Charles V which turned him into a vassal of the King of Spain.[11] A Spanish garrison was installed in Monaco. At the beginning of the seventeenth century the Lord of Monaco had assumed the title of Prince, which was recognized by the Spanish Court in 1633.[12] As the Spanish protectorate became too dominant, the Prince of Monaco concluded the Treaty of Péronne on 14 September 1641 with King Louis XIII of France

---

[6] Figure calculated on the basis of the rectified budget for 1995, tables A to C, *Journal de Monaco* (1995) no. 7.209.
[7] Figure calculated on the basis of the rectified budget for 1995; 1,421,050,000.- francs of tax on commercial transactions in total receipts of 3,111,826,000.- francs: ibid.
[8] Figure calculated on the basis of information represented in *Rapport du Gouvernement de S.A.S. le Prince sur le Projet de Budget de l'Exercice 1992* (Oct. 1991) p. 13.
[9] L.-H. Labande, *Histoire de la Principauté de Monaco*, 2nd edn (1934) p. 19.
[10] Ibid., pp. 25–28.
[11] Ibid., pp. 104–105.
[12] Ibid., p. 143.

in order to establish a French garrison in Monaco which would replace the Spanish one and ensure the future protection of Monaco against foreign aggression. This form of protection, which left the Prince of Monaco full internal sovereignty over his communes,[13] was upheld until 1793 when, under the influence of the French revolution, Monaco, Menton and Roquebrune were attached to the French territory. It was after the deposition of Napoleon in 1814 that the Prince of Monaco regained his rights over the Principality under the same conditions as had been laid down in the Treaty of Péronne.[14] However, after the second deposition of Napoleon, the Congress of Vienna was convinced by the Kingdom of Sardinia that the Monégasque coast should not be left under French protection. Without consulting the Prince of Monaco, the Congress of Vienna therefore decided that Monaco, Menton and Roquebrune would be brought under the protection of the King of Sardinia under similar conditions to those embodied in the Treaty of Péronne.[15] In 1848, due to dissatisfaction with the burden of taxation, the communes of Roquebrune and Menton declared themselves free cities. A plebiscite was held in Menton and Roquebrune which resulted in an overwhelming acceptance of the incorporation into the French Empire.[16] Negotiations with France on this issue led to the conclusion of a treaty on 2 February 1861 by virtue of which the Prince of Monaco abandoned his rights over Menton and Roquebrune for the sum of four million francs.[17] The additional articles of this treaty furthermore provided that the King of Sardinia had renounced his protectorate over Monaco, that the Prince of Monaco would not ally his Principality with any Power other than France and would neither seek nor accept the protectorate of any Power other than France.[18] On 17 July 1918 a final treaty was signed on the basis of France's protective

---

[13] Art. VI of the Treaty of Péronne read: 'Sadite Majesté laissera ledit Prince en sa liberté & Souveraineté de Monaco, Manton & Roquebrune, sans que ladite Garnison Royale, ou autre l'y puissent troubler & s'ingerer jamais en ce qui est de ladite Souveraineté de terre & de mer, & moins encore au Gouvernement & Justice de ses peuples, ou administration de ses biens; mais seulement ladite Garnison s'employera à garder la Place, ainsi qu'il est dit ci-dessus.' Archives of the Palace of Monaco.
[14] Labande, *Histoire*, pp. 390–391.
[15] Ibid., p. 400.
[16] Ibid., p. 467.
[17] Arts. 1 and 2 of the Treaty of 1861. Text in *Codes et Lois de la Principauté de Monaco: Traités bilateraux avec la France*. Also in J.-P. Gallois, *Le Régime international de la Principauté de Monaco* (1964) p. 222.
[18] Additional Arts. 1 and 2 of the Treaty of 1861.

friendship and this is still the basis of the present Franco-Monégasque relationship.[19] As from 1867, Monaco had started to develop its economy and to strengthen its financial resources by opening a casino and encouraging luxury tourism. On 8 February 1869 all direct taxation was abolished.

During the First World War, Monaco declared its neutrality.[20] It also declared its neutrality when the Second World War broke out, but it was nevertheless bombed and occupied first by the Italians and then by the Germans. The period after the Second World War was characterized by rising prosperity, the inflow of foreign capital and foreign inhabitants, and the development of the construction and industrial sectors. In the seventies, 0.31 square kilometres of land were reclaimed from the sea, thus extending Monaco's land territory.

Constitutional and legal order

Form of government

The first Constitution of the Principality of Monaco was promulgated in 1911 and replaced by the Constitution of 17 December 1962.[21] Monaco is a hereditary and constitutional monarchy which respects the law and fundamental rights and freedoms.[22] The Government structure is based on the separation of the executive, legislative and judicial powers.[23]

The executive power is exercised by the Prince and the Government under the former's authority.[24] The succession to the throne is secured by the direct and legitimate descendants of the Prince Regnant with priority to male descendants. Prince Rainier III of Monaco has been the Prince Regnant since 1949. The Government is composed of the Minister of State ('Ministre d'Etat'), assisted by three Government Counsellors ('Conseillers de Gouvernement').[25] The Minister of State and the Government Counsellors are appointed by

---

[19] See pp. 274–282 below.
[20] Labande, *Histoire*, p. 525.
[21] Text in A. P. Blaustein and G. H. Flanz, eds., *Constitutions of the Countries of the World: Monaco*; also in Conseil National, *Constitution du 17 décembre 1962 et Textes Organiques* (1982) pp. 7 ff.
[22] Art. 2 of the Constitution.
[23] Art. 6 of the Constitution.
[24] Arts. 3, 43 and 44 of the Constitution.
[25] Art. 43 of the Constitution.

the Prince who also has the right to dismiss them. The Government is therefore not responsible to the Monégasque Parliament.[26] By virtue of a Franco-Monégasque Convention of 28 July 1930, the Minister of State and the Government Counsellor for the interior have to be of French nationality.[27] To this end, the French Government proposes several candidates from its own Administration from whom the Prince of Monaco makes his choice. For the Minister of State, usually a diplomat, three French candidates are presented.[28] The Minister of State and the Government Counsellor for the interior are each appointed for a period of five years which is renewable once.[29] Article 5 of the Convention of 1930 emphasizes that the French civil servants seconded to Monaco are immediately removed from the hierarchy of their own service.[30] The Minister of State represents the Prince and has a preponderant vote in the Government Council.[31] The two other Government Counsellors, the Counsellor for finance and economy and the Counsellor for public works and social affairs, are Monégasque nationals. A Sovereign Order has to be deliberated in the Government Council and countersigned by the Minister of State who presents the Order for approval to the Prince.[32] A Ministerial Decree is always deliberated in the Government Council and signed by the Minister of State. The Decree is, in general, promulgated in the absence of an objection by the Prince within ten days after it has been transmitted to him.[33]

---

[26] Art. 50 of the Constitution.
[27] Art. 5 of the 1930 Convention and exchange of letters of 7 May 1973, JORF (28 Febr. 1974) p. 2320. See also pp. 283–285 below.
[28] J. Pillon and J.-F. Vilotte, 'Les Institutions politiques de la Principauté de Monaco', 98 RDP (1982) p. 368.
[29] Art. 4 of the 1930 Convention as amended by exchange of letters of 9 Jan. 1985, JORF (10 Apr. 1985) p. 4158.
[30] Art. 5 of the 1930 Convention reads: 'Son Altesse Sérénissime continuera comme par le passé à ne faire appel qu'à des Français qui seront dorénavant détachés des cadres de l'Administration française pour remplir les emplois qui intéressent la sécurité, l'ordre public, les relations extérieures de la Principauté et l'exécution des accords conclus avec le Gouvernement Français.'
[31] Art. 44 of the Constitution.
[32] Art. 45 of the Constitution. Some Sovereign Orders are not subject to the approval of the Government Council and to the Ministerial countersignature, such as appointments to the diplomatic and consular corps, the appointment of the Minister of State and the Government Counsellors, the granting of the *exequatur* to consuls and the dissolution of the Monégasque Parliament: Art. 46.
[33] Art. 47 of the Constitution.

Legislative power is vested in the Prince and the Monégasque Parliament, the National Council ('Conseil National').[34] The National Council is composed of eighteen members elected by universal and direct suffrage for a period of five years.[35] The mandate of National Counsellor is incompatible with, *inter alia*, the functions of member of the Princely House and of Government Counsellor.[36] The Prince has the right to dissolve the National Council, after having consulted the Crown Council ('Conseil de la Couronne'), in which case new elections are called.[37] The National Council has the right to approve the budget and has to consent to any direct or indirect financial contributions except for those flowing from international conventions.[38] A law can only be promulgated with the approval of the National Council. The National Council does not, however, have the right of initiative, which belongs exclusively to the Prince.[39] A law has to be adopted both by the Prince and by the National Council.[40] The National Council may only make a proposition for a law or amendment of a law, which does not have the status of a draft law and which can be disregarded by the Prince and the Government.[41] Though the right of initiative belongs exclusively to the Prince, a draft law cannot be submitted to the National Council without the signature of the Minister of State. The Prince's right of initiative is therefore not absolute. The signature of the Minister of State should equally be obtained if a proposition for a draft law has emanated from the National Council or from the Government Council. Once a draft law has been approved by the Prince and by the Minister of State (after deliberation in the Government Council), the National Council has the right of amendment and the right to vote against or for the draft law. After being approved by the National Council, the Minister of State no longer intervenes as it is up to the Prince to decide the promulgation of the adopted law. Thus, although the Minister of State can bar the submis-

---

[34] Art. 4 of the Constitution.
[35] Art. 53 of the Constitution. All Monégasque nationals who have possessed this nationality for at least five years and are at least twenty-one years old have the right to vote. All Monégasque citizens of at least twenty-five years old are eligible for election: Art. 54.
[36] Art. 54 of the Constitution and Art. 14 of law no. 839 of 23 Febr. 1968 on national and municipal elections.
[37] Art. 74 of the Constitution.
[38] Art. 70 of the Constitution.
[39] Art. 66 of the Constitution.
[40] Ibid.
[41] Art. 67, 2nd para. of the Constitution.

sion of a draft law to the National Council, once a draft law has been referred to the National Council it can be amended at will without its having to be approved once again by the Minister of State. As the Government is not responsible to the National Council, the Monégasque legislation does not provide for an express right of interpellation and enquiry.

There are several commissions and councils which assist the Prince or the Government in the decision-making process. Thus, the Crown Council, an advisory committee, has to be consulted by the Prince on the conclusion of international treaties, the dissolution of the National Council, naturalizations and re-integrations as well as pardons and amnesty.[42] The opinion of the Crown Council is not binding. An international convention is signed and ratified by the Prince, who represents the Principality in its external relations, and is communicated to the National Council.[43] The Prince and the Minister of State can submit draft laws, decrees and orders for study to the State Council ('Conseil d'Etat').[44] There are moreover numerous consultative commissions like the Economic Council and specialized committees which can be consulted by the Government on specific issues.[45]

The Constitution can be amended by mutual agreement between the Prince and the National Council.[46] The National Council may, with the approval of two-thirds of its members, propose a partial or total revision of the Constitution.[47] As it does not have the right of initiative, such a proposal can be disregarded by the Prince and/or the Government. The amendment of the Constitution follows the same procedure as the adoption of an ordinary law, which does not imply that a subsequent ordinary law can invalidate provisions of the Constitution. Amendments of the Constitution should be explicitly voted on and promulgated as such.

---

[42] Art. 77, 2nd para. of the Constitution. The Crown Council is composed of seven Monégasque nationals, appointed by the Prince for three years, of whom three are proposed by the National Council: Art. 75 of the Constitution.

[43] Arts. 13 and 14 of the Constitution. Only treaties affecting the constitutional organization need to be ratified by law and are therefore subject to the approval of the National Council.

[44] Art. 52 of the Constitution and Art. 1 of Sovereign Order no. 3.191 of 29 May 1964 on the organization and functioning of the State Council. The twelve members of the State Council are appointed by the Prince, after consulting the Minister of State and the director of judicial services.

[45] G. Grinda, *Les Institutions de la Principauté de Monaco* (1975) pp. 31-32.

[46] Art. 94 of the Constitution.

[47] Art. 95 of the Constitution.

Judicial system

Judicial power is held by the Prince who has delegated it to the courts and tribunals which administer justice in his name.[48] By virtue of Article 6, first paragraph of the Franco-Monégasque Convention of 28 July 1930, the majority of the judges in the Monégasque courts and tribunals have to be French nationals seconded from the French judicial administration, except for the Criminal Tribunal ('Tribunal criminel').[49] The independence of the judges is guaranteed by the Constitution.[50] Monaco has an elaborate judicial system with several specialized commissions and tribunals.

Disputes concerning civil and commercial law can in certain cases, depending on the sum of money involved, be brought before the Justice of the Peace ('juge de paix') who, before giving judgment, attempts to reconcile the parties.[51] If neither the Justice of the Peace nor any other specialized commission or tribunal is competent, a civil dispute can be brought before the Tribunal of first instance and in second instance before the Court of Appeal.[52] Monaco's Civil Code dates from 21 December 1880 and is similar to, but not entirely identical with, the French Civil Code.

In criminal procedures, three different tribunals can be seized in first instance: the Justice of the Peace,[53] the Correctional Tribunal ('Tribunal correctionnel')[54] and the Criminal Tribunal which is composed of three French magistrates and three male Monégasques who are laymen.[55] An appeal can be lodged before the Court of Appeal against the sentences in first instance of the Correctional Tribunal,

---

[48] Arts. 5 and 88 of the Constitution.
[49] Art. 6 of the 1930 Convention and supplementary exchange of letters of 7 Jul. 1978, JORF (25 Oct. 1978) p. 3664. The French judges cannot have a permanent appointment in the Monégasque judiciary. The Procurator-General of the Court of Appeal ('Cour d'Appel') has to be a French national too: Exchange of letters of 7 May 1973, JORF (28 Febr. 1974) p. 2320.
[50] Art. 88, 2nd sentence of the Constitution.
[51] Art. 24 of the Code of Civil Procedure. There are in first instance three specialized jurisdictions which decide on specific legal matters. They are the Labour Tribunal ('Tribunal du Travail'), the Arbitration Commission on rents ('Commission arbitrale des loyers') and the Arbitration Commission on commercial rents ('Commission arbitrale des baux commerciaux'): Grinda, *Les Institutions*, pp. 78–80.
[52] Arts. 21 (1) and 22 of the Code of Civil Procedure.
[53] Art. 22 of the Code of Criminal Procedure.
[54] Art. 23 of the Code of Criminal Procedure. This trbunal also acts as court of appeal for sentences of the Justice of the Peace.
[55] Art. 25 of the Code of Criminal Procedure. See also Grinda, *Les Institutions*, p. 75.

but no further appeal lies against the verdict of the Criminal Tribunal.[56] The present Criminal Code dates from 28 September 1967 and, like the Civil Code, is not entirely identical to the French Penal Code. In civil as well as in penal cases, the Court of Judicial Revision ('Cour de Révision judiciaire') can reverse any judgment of last instance which violates the law.[57] Although Monaco has a prison, convicted persons of whatever nationality will serve their prison sentence in the French penitentiaries by virtue of the Franco-Monégasque Convention of vicinage of 18 May 1963.[58] The Monégasque prison is, in general, used to receive persons in preventive custody. The Prince has the right to grant a pardon or amnesty after consulting the Crown Council.[59]

In administrative proceedings, an action can be instituted before the Supreme Tribunal ('Tribunal Suprême')[60] against any decision or Sovereign Order emanating from any administrative authority taken with a view to implementing the laws.[61] No further appeal lies against the judgment of the Supreme Tribunal. If the action or failure to act of an administrative authority does not fall within the direct competence of the Supreme Tribunal, a legal action can be instituted before the Tribunal of first instance,[62] with the possibility of appeal to the Court of Appeal.[63] The Supreme Tribunal subsequently acts as a Court of Cassation.[64] It should furthermore be noted that any court or tribunal can ask the Supreme Tribunal for a preliminary ruling on the validity of an administrative decision or Sovereign Order.[65]

The Supreme Tribunal has more competences than the ones we have referred to above. Thus, it controls the constitutionality of the rules of procedure of the National Council and of the law.[66] However, a law can

[56] Art. 24 of the Code of Criminal Procedure.
[57] Art. 23 of the Code of Civil Procedure and Art. 30 of the Code of Criminal Procedure.
[58] Art. 14 of the 1963 Convention of vicinage.
[59] Art. 15 of the Constitution.
[60] The Supreme Tribunal is composed of five judges and two substitutes who are appointed by the Prince and proposed by the National Council, the State Council, the Crown Council, the Court of Appeal and the Tribunal of first instance: Art. 89 of the Constitution. The judges are appointed for four years and have to be confirmed in office if they are presented for a second time after this period: Art. 1, 1st para. of Sovereign Order no. 2.984 of 16 Apr. 1963.
[61] Art. 90 (B) (1) of the Constitution.
[62] Art. 21 (2) of the Code of Civil Procedure.
[63] Art. 22 of the Code of Civil Procedure.
[64] Art. 90 (B) (2) of the Constitution.
[65] Art. 90 (B) (3) of the Constitution.
[66] Art. 90 (A) of the Constitution.

only be annulled by the Supreme Tribunal if it violates the fundamental rights and freedoms embodied in the Constitution.[67] An appeal for annulment can therefore be brought before the Supreme Tribunal by any person whose fundamental rights and freedoms are violated by a law. Moreover, the Supreme Tribunal has to be seized by any other court or tribunal for a preliminary ruling if the infringement of a constitutional human right by a Monégasque law has been invoked by the parties.[68] Although the supremacy of the Constitution over the law has been established, the Supreme Tribunal does not consider the constitutionality of a law permitting the ratification or execution of an international convention.[69] Thus it recognizes the supremacy of international conventions within the national legal order.

Human rights situation

Monaco is a State Party to the International Convention for the Abolition of Slavery of 1926,[70] to the Convention on the Prevention and Punishment of the Crime of Genocide of 1948[71] and more recently to the Convention against Torture and other Cruel, Inhuman or Degrading Treatment or Punishment of 1984.[72] The Monégasque Constitution guarantees certain fundamental rights and freedoms of which certain rights are reserved to Monégasque nationals only. These include, *inter alia*, the equality of Monégasques before the law,[73] the priority of access of Monégasques to public and private jobs,[74] the right of peaceful assembly[75] and the right to freedom of association.[76]

In matters of public employment, vacancies are first offered to Monégasque nationals who have the required professional qualifications.[77] The Monégasque Government has moreover the right to ask

---

[67] Art. 90 (A) (2) of the Constitution.
[68] Grinda, *Les Institutions*, p. 84.
[69] Decisions of the Supreme Tribunal of 13 Apr. 1931, *Sieur Chiabaut* and of 6 May 1964, *Sieur Jama et autres*.
[70] Ratification in 1926 and amending Protocol of 1953 ratified on 12 Nov. 1954, *Journal de Monaco* (1954) no. 5.073.
[71] Ratification on 30 Mar. 1950, *Journal de Monaco* (1951) no. 4.873.
[72] Ratification on 6 Dec. 1991, with declaration accepting the competence of the Committee against Torture to receive communications from States and individuals under Arts. 21 (1) and 22 (1), reservation made concerning the possibility of arbitration, and therefore not bound by Art. 30 (1), *Journal de Monaco* (1992) no. 7.026.
[73] Art. 17 of the Constitution.
[74] Art. 25, 2nd para. of the Constitution.
[75] Art. 29 of the Constitution.
[76] Art. 30 of the Constitution.
[77] Art. 1 of the law on public offices of 18 Jul. 1934, *Journal de Monaco* (1934) no. 4.003.

for the recall of a French functionary if a Monégasque national is qualified to hold this office.[78] In the private sector a ratio has been fixed between the number of Monégasque and foreign employees according to the nature of the company or profession.[79] There is however one exception to the priority given to Monégasques in the public sector. As we have seen, certain important public offices are reserved for French nationals by virtue of the Franco-Monégasque Convention of 28 July 1930.[80] These positions include, *inter alia*, the Minister of State, the Government Counsellor for the interior, the director of the judicial services, the director of public security, the director of the registry office and police commissioners.[81] Monaco is not a State Party to the ICCPR. As we shall see later on, the exclusion of Monégasques does not directly serve the Principality's political interests, but is rather designed to secure certain French political interests.[82] If Monaco were to ratify the Covenant, it is doubtful whether the Human Rights Committee would accept the restrictions in question as 'reasonable' within the meaning of Article 25 (c) of the Covenant, as the right to have access to public service in one's country has been restricted, not in order to serve a defendable purpose of the country in whose jurisdiction the nationals are, but to meet the wishes of another State Party, namely France, which in turn has no duty to respect the human right in question in the other State.[83]

The ratification of the ICCPR by Monaco would however also imply that certain provisions of the Constitution would be extended to all persons under Monaco's jurisdiction. This then would mean that not only Monégasques but all persons would be equal before the law and

---

[78] Art. 4, 2nd para. of the 1930 Franco-Monégasque Convention on public offices.
[79] Art. 1 of the law on private employment of 18 Jul. 1934, *Journal de Monaco* (1934) no. 4.003 and Order no. 1911 of 13 Aug. 1936. In the private industrial sector, 80 per cent of the employees may be foreigners, compared to 70 per cent in the services sector. This law is not rigorously applied in practice.
[80] See p. 265 above and pp. 283-285 below.
[81] Exchange of letters of 7 May 1973 with respect to Art. 5 of the 1930 Convention on public offices, JORF (28 Febr. 1974) p. 2320.
[82] See pp. 274-285 below.
[83] The human rights laid down in the ICCPR are to be respected by a State Party with respect to 'all individuals within its territory and subject to its jurisdiction': Art. 2 (1). Monégasque nationals in Monaco do not fall under French jurisdiction as the restrictions on the access to public service are imposed under the authority of the Monégasque Government, although flowing from an international obligation. See also D. McGoldrick, *The Human Rights Committee: Its Role in the Development of the ICCPR* (1991) p. 282.

the courts.[84] The prohibition of discrimination included in Article 26 ICCPR would affect the Monégasque law on nationality which is not based on the equal treatment of men and women. The law on nationality was promulgated on 18 December 1992 and aimed to replace the former legislation which did not permit the transmission of the Monégasque nationality by a Monégasque mother to her children unless the father was unknown.[85] The new law of 1992 provides for the acquisition of Monégasque nationality for children born from a Monégasque father or a Monégasque mother who answers to certain conditions.[86] Unequal conditions also apply to the acquisition of nationality by marriage. A foreign woman may acquire the Monégasque nationality of her husband by declaration after five years of marriage,[87] whereas a foreign man married to a Monégasque woman can only obtain his wife's nationality by naturalization, that is after ten years of residence in Monaco or if the Prince so decides.[88] Article 14, first paragraph of the ICCPR would, in case of accession, oblige Monaco to delete the power to demand security for costs by a Monégasque defendant from a foreign plaintiff in court proceedings.[89] Lastly, the ratification of the ICCPR would lead to the extension of the right of peaceful assembly and of association to the Principality's foreign inhabitants.[90] At present the right of association has been used by the Monégasque citizens to establish a trade union, the 'Union des Syndicats de Monaco', which defends the right to strike and the freedom of work irrespective of the nationality of its members.[91]

As Monaco is not a State Party to the ECHR, a French national living in Monaco submitted an application against France to the European Commission of Human Rights.[92] The applicant claimed that he was

---

[84] Arts. 14 (1) and 26 of the ICCPR.
[85] Art. 8 (2) of the Civil Code, law no. 869 of 11 Jul. 1969.
[86] Art. 1 (2°) and (3°) of the law on nationality, *Journal de Monaco* (1992) no. 7.057, p. 1365. The mother must be a native Monégasque and possess that nationality the day her child is born or must be a Monégasque and have one direct ancestor who is a native Monégasque.
[87] Art. 3 of the law on nationality.
[88] Arts. 5 and 6, 1st para. of the law on nationality.
[89] Arts. 259–261 of the Code on Civil Procedure.
[90] Arts. 21 and 22 of the ICCPR.
[91] Arts. 1 and 2 of law no. 553 of 7 Febr. 1952. The right to strike does not apply to the civil servants of the public sector and, in general, the Minister of State has the right to prohibit a strike if it is likely to compromise public order or the interests of the national economy.
[92] Application no. 21392/93 (*J. M. v. France*), decision of the Commission of 28 Jun. 1993.

unjustly expelled from his Monégasque apartment by Monégasque judicial and administrative authorities. The applicant was of the opinion that France was responsible for the violations of the Convention of which he had been the victim. The Monégasque judicial and administrative authorities had all been French judges and civil servants who, so he argued, were seconded from the French Administration under Franco-Monégasque bilateral treaties and for whom France could be held responsible.[93] The Commission recalled the judgment of the European Court of Human Rights in the *Drozd and Janousek v. France and Spain* case[94] and estimated that 'les mêmes considérations sont applicables en l'espèce'.[95] Thus, just like the French and Spanish judges in Andorra, the Commission considered that the French judges in Monaco did not exercise judicial authority 'en qualité de juges français'. Therefore, 'les actes dont se plaint le requérant, faisant partie de l'exercice de fonctions judiciaires et administratives en Principauté de Monaco, ne sont pas imputables à la France'.[96] The Commission therefore implicitly recognized that the seconded French judges and civil servants in question did not fall under France's authority and declared the application inadmissible due to incompatibility *ratione personae* with the provisions of the Convention.

The compliance of a law with a human rights convention cannot be challenged before the Supreme Tribunal by a direct claim of nullity under Article 90, paragraph A, 2° of the Constitution, because this judicial process is restricted to the test of compatibility with human rights set forth in the Constitution. The convergence of a law, decision or order with a human rights convention to which Monaco is a party can in any case be tested through the normal civil, penal and administrative court procedures. The special character of Monaco's human rights situation is founded, on the one hand, on the fact that the Monégasque nationals constitute a minority of the population and therefore are granted a more advantageous legal position, and, on the other hand, on the obligations into which Monaco has entered towards France.

---

[93] Ibid., p. 3. The applicant claimed a violation of Arts. 3, 8 and 13 of the ECHR.
[94] European Court of Human Rights, Judgment of 26 Jun. 1992 (21/1991/273/344). See pp. 331–332 below.
[95] Application no. 21392/93, p. 4.
[96] Ibid.

Relations with States
Foreign policy
The foreign policy of the Principality of Monaco is closely related to the foreign policy of France. Monaco does not take a different attitude from the core of the French external relations policy.[97] The utilization of seconded French civil servants guarantees that there will not be a great divergence.[98] This implies that Monaco is not one of the traditionally neutral Micro-States, as its foreign policy is not only inspired by a political affinity with France, but also rooted in a treaty of 17 July 1918.[99] The basis of Monaco's foreign policy remains its desire to be recognized as an independent State. Article 1, first sentence of the Constitution provides:

> La Principauté de Monaco est un Etat souverain et indépendant dans le cadre des principes généraux du droit international et des conventions particulières avec la France.

Although it is not up to national legislation to determine whether a political entity possesses the characteristics of a State within the meaning of international law, this article nevertheless provides us with the basis of Monaco's adopted attitude towards France and the international community in general.

Relations with France
Friendly relations

The basic treaty on which the political relations between Monaco and France are founded is the treaty of 17 July 1918 and the complementary exchange of letters of the same date.[100] The negotiations on this treaty had started during the First World War and were prompted by France's desire to ensure that Monaco would not become subject to German or other foreign influence. It was feared that if the heir apparent Prince Louis, who fought in the French army during the war, and who was a bachelor, were to remain childless and die, the

---

[97] Interview with HE Mr Jacques Dupont, Minister of State of the Principality of Monaco, 3 Mar. 1992.
[98] Ibid.
[99] See pp. 275–282 below.
[100] *Codes et Lois de la Principauté de Monaco: Traités bilatéraux avec la France*; also in Gallois, *Le Régime international*, pp. 224–225. Text of the exchange of letters of 17 Jul. 1918 not published.

throne of Monaco would be ascended by the German branch of the Grimaldi family.[101]

The following principles govern the Franco-Monégasque relations:

France guarantees the defence of Monaco's independence and sovereignty and its territorial integrity as if the territory were a part of France[102] This duty of defence sets forth the basic principle that Monaco is considered by France a sovereign and independent territory.[103]

Political affiliation with France Article 1, second paragraph of the treaty states:

> De son côté, le Gouvernement de Son Altesse Sérénissime le Prince de Monaco s'engage à exercer ses droits de souveraineté en parfaite conformité avec les intérêts politiques, militaires, navals et économiques de la France.

This widely phrased clause raises two questions: what is covered by 'ses droits de souveraineté' and to what extent do these sovereign rights have to be in conformity with the French political, military, naval and economic interests, under which practically any French wish could be classified? An exchange of letters of 17 July 1918 is meant to interpret the treaty of the same date and emphasizes that its explanations 'ont la même valeur que le Traité et feront foi pour son interprétation'.[104] The exchange of letters sets forth with regard to Article 1, second paragraph of the treaty, that it has

> pour objet de définir d'une manière générale les obligations de réciprocité qui incombent au Prince en retour de l'appui amical de la France sans porter, par ailleurs, atteinte à la Souveraineté et à l'Indépendance de Son Altesse Sérénissime.[105]

This then implies that Monaco's obligations towards France are only invocable if in turn France lends its friendly support. Moreover, the exercise of Monaco's sovereign rights has to be in perfect conformity

---

[101] J. Laroche, 'Comment fut négocié le traité franco-monégasque du 17 juillet 1918', *Revue d'Histoire Diplomatique* (Oct.–Dec. 1955) p. 289; and Gallois, *Le Régime international*, pp. 103–104.

[102] Art. 1, 1st para. of the 1918 treaty reads: 'Le Gouvernement de la République française assure à la Principauté de Monaco la défense de son indépendance et de sa souveraineté et garantit l'intégrité de son territoire comme si ce territoire faisait partie de la France.'

[103] See further p. 290 below.

[104] Last para. of the 1918 exchange of letters, Archives of the Palace of Monaco.

[105] First para. of the 1918 exchange of letters.

with the French political, military, naval and economic interests only in so far as it does not prejudice the Principality's sovereignty and independence. It is in this light that the word 'intérêts' should be interpreted. There is however no clarification concerning the content of the sovereign rights: do they include the determination of Monaco's internal political as well as external political order? The ambiguity of the stipulation gives France the right to cover any of its demands under its political, military, naval or economic interests, while claiming the imperfect exercise of a sovereign right of whatever nature, and emphasizing that its demands do not detract from Monaco's independence. If Monaco argues that a French demand for conformity would be prejudicial to its independence, one may note the increased necessity to define clearly what degree of independence is still required in order to constitute a State in international law.

Proceeding from the basic principle of the treaty of 1918 that Monaco's independence should not be infringed upon, the customary rules of international law will determine the extent of France's right to demand conformity from Monaco, and not the other way round. This legal question is complicated by the fact that France has at its disposal certain legal means of pressure, such as the denunciation of treaties with Monaco and the adoption of unilateral laws and regulations, which can have a negative influence on the Monégasque economy and compel Monaco to give in to French demands. Nevertheless, if Monaco decides to meet illegal French requests and to conclude a treaty to this end, this later treaty cannot be invalidated. Both parties have given their consent to be bound, the later treaty takes precedence over the treaty of 1918 and the coercion of a State by non-use of force is not a legal ground to nullify a treaty.[106]

One case should be mentioned in which France has invoked a breach of Article 1, second paragraph of the treaty of 1918, because of Monaco's non-conformity with French economic interests. In 1962, France wanted to revise its relations with Monaco and initially

---

[106] Cf. Art. 52 of the Vienna Convention on the Law of Treaties. It should be noted that the UN Conference on the Law of Treaties, in its Final Act of 23 May 1969, adopted a Declaration on the Prohibition of Military, Political or Economic Coercion in the Conclusion of Treaties. It condemned 'the threat or use of pressure in any form ... by any State in order to coerce another State to perform any act relating to the conclusion of a treaty in violation of the principles of the sovereign equality of States and freedom of consent'. This declaration has, however, no binding force or legal effect on the validity of treaties outside the scope of Art. 52 of the Vienna Convention on the Law of Treaties.

requested an alignment of the Monégasque and French fiscal systems so that Monaco and France would constitute one territory from a fiscal point of view.[107] It moreover wished a more serious involvement of the Minister of State in the adoption procedure of Sovereign Orders.[108] This eventually led to the formulation of Articles 45 and 46 of the Constitution of 17 December 1962 which, in general, demands the countersignature of the Minister of State for Sovereign Orders.[109] The dispute over Monaco's fiscal system was prompted by the fact that Monaco had no direct taxes on revenues nor on company profits. As a consequence, certain enterprises and private persons had established their head office or residence in Monaco while in practice residing and functioning in France, so it was alleged.[110] France believed this was contrary to its economic interests. Monaco replied, *inter alia*, that France's demands were an infringement of Monaco's independence and sovereignty.[111] When the negotiations came to a deadlock, France took certain coercive measures.[112] As a result, frontier posts were established which controlled the circulation of goods and persons (although the customs union was maintained), Monaco was considered a third State for postal tariff purposes and the importation of pharmaceutical products in France was prohibited, which led to dismissals in Monaco's pharmaceutical laboratories.[113] The core of these measures was maintained between October 1962 and April/May 1963. At the end of this period six conventions were concluded redefining in particular Monaco's fiscal system. Monaco did not have to take over France's fiscal system entirely. A company tax on profits was to be established in Monaco[114] and French residents in Monaco

[107] Gallois, *Le Régime international*, p. 168.
[108] Ibid., pp. 163–164.
[109] See p. 265 above. Before 1963 a Sovereign Order was presented by the Prince to the Minister of State who transmitted it to the director of judicial services for promulgation by the Tribunal of Monaco.
[110] Gallois, *Le Régime international*, pp. 162 and 164–165.
[111] Ibid., pp. 166–167.
[112] Ibid., pp. 169–174. France denounced the Convention of 23 Dec. 1951, the Convention on pharmaceutical products of 28 Febr. 1952 and the Convention on transport by road of 20 Jan. 1955, respecting their respective terms of notice. It refused to register French citizens in Monaco, who after five registered years of residence could have been exempted from French taxes, no longer granted visas to foreigners wishing to take up residence in Monaco, withdrew its national decision not to consider Monégasques as foreigners in France and issued a decree prohibiting financial transactions between French legal and private persons and Monégasque banks.
[113] Ibid., pp. 175–178.
[114] Art. 5 of the fiscal Convention of 18 May 1963. See p. 287 below.

would be taxed under the French fiscal system by France.[115] Thus, Monaco was compelled to conclude conventions which led to the introduction of certain taxes in its territory without it in fact wanting this taxation.[116]

Did the French intervention into Monaco's sovereign right to decide on the constitutional relations between the Prince and the Minister of State with respect to the adoption of Sovereign Orders and its sovereign right to determine its own fiscal system constitute a violation of Monaco's independence? It should be noted in this context that France was careful to employ legal means of pressure, such as the denunciation of conventions and the adoption of French prohibitive laws, instead of using in principle illegal countermeasures justified by an alleged illegal Monégasque conduct. This is however no solid evidence that France believed its demands prejudiced Monaco's independence. As far as international customary law is concerned, it is unlikely that the French demands would be considered as non-prejudicial to Monaco's statehood. We recall that the ancient French protectorate over Tunisia imposed on the Bey the obligation to adopt, *inter alia*, any financial reform which the French Government considered useful.[117] In order to maintain Monaco's independence, France cannot have this same discretionary power as it had in Tunisia.

The legal implications of Article 1, second paragraph of the treaty of 1918 are also felt in Monaco's foreign policy. Article 5 of the treaty states:

Le Gouvernement français prêtera au Gouvernement princier ses bons offices pour lui faciliter l'accès à ses côtés des conférences et institutions internationales, notamment de celles ayant pour objet l'organisation de la Société des Nations.

The interpretative exchange of letters declares that Monaco maintains the right to have its own delegation in international conferences and institutions and explains that Article 5 in combination with Article 1:

a uniquement pour objet d'éviter, conformément à l'article Ier du Traité, qu'il y ait éventuellement opposition entre la représentation française et la représentation monégasque et laisse, sous cette réserve, à Son Altesse

---

[115] Art. 7 of the fiscal Convention. See p. 287 below.
[116] Declaration made in the National Council by the head of the Monégasque delegation to the negotiations, *Journal de Monaco* (1963) no. 5.498, annex, p. 7.
[117] See p. 124 above at n. 91.

Sérénissime toute liberté de manifester sa pensée sur les problèmes scientifiques, moraux ou sociaux.[118]

This rule should be read in connection with the general principle underlying Article 1, second paragraph, namely that Monaco's independence should be left untouched. The duty to prevent any discrepancy between the Monégasque and French positions in international conferences and organizations, except for scientific, moral or social problems, is therefore considered by France as non-prejudicial to Monaco's statehood and independence. Moreover, read in combination with Article 1, second paragraph of the treaty of 1918, the freedom left to the Prince in scientific, moral and social matters seems to be meant to cover all domains except the political, military, naval and economic ones. The sovereign rights referred to in Article 1, second paragraph of the treaty include therefore internal as well as international acts. The wording of Article 5 of the treaty of 1918 seems furthermore to suggest that Monaco may not enter into an international conference or organization if France does not participate in this same conference or organization. France will 'faciliter l'accès à ses côtés [emphasis added] des conférences et institutions internationales'.[119] The better interpretation is probably that the duty to facilitate access to international conferences and organizations can only be imposed on France if France takes part in these conferences or organizations itself. In any case, Monaco has the freedom to participate in international conferences and international organizations which treat of scientific, moral or social problems, whereas the prohibition on taking part in any other conferences or organizations in which France is not involved is not explicitly laid down. Although opposite positions of Monaco and France in international conferences and organizations are rare, this nevertheless occurred in the International Whaling Commission where Monaco in contradistinction to France favoured a total ban on whale hunting. If Monaco were to be clearly shocked by any French position, it would not endorse the French policy either.[120]

Prior agreement with France on international actions Article 2, first paragraph of the treaty of 1918 reads:

---
[118] Fifth para. of the 1918 exchange of letters.
[119] Art. 5 of the 1918 treaty.
[120] Interview with HE Mr Jacques Dupont, Minister of State of the Principality of Monaco, 3 Mar. 1992.

Les mesures concernant les relations internationales de la Principauté devront toujours faire l'objet d'une entente préalable entre le Gouvernement princier et le Gouvernement français.

The exchange of letters of 1918 enumerates three cases in which the prior agreement between the two Governments should be obtained:

Les ententes prévues au paragraphe Ier de l'article 2 auront pour objet:
1°) d'examiner l'établissement éventuel de Légations nouvelles de Son Altesse Sérénissime le Prince auprès de gouvernements étrangers;
2°) de déterminer le choix des chefs de mission, pour le recrutement desquels le Gouvernement de la République pourra mettre à la disposition du Prince, les agents diplomatiques des cadres actifs français;
3°) de constater que les Traités que le Prince se proposerait de conclure avec des Puissances étrangères n'ont rien de contraire aux stipulations du présent Traité.[121]

The exchange of letters explains the object of Article 2, first paragraph of the treaty of 1918 and therefore presents an exhaustive account of the international acts which are subject to a previous agreement. The third point includes any treaty which is contrary to French political, military, naval and economic interests within the meaning of Article 1, second paragraph of the treaty of 1918. It seems logical that France cannot refuse a prior agreement with Monaco for the ratification of a multilateral treaty to which France is also a party and which is therefore clearly not contrary to French interests. With regard to our findings on Monaco's participation in international conferences and organizations, the question arises whether the application to become a member of an international organization is also dependent on French approval. Adhering to an international organization implies the ratification of a multilateral treaty and therefore falls under the discussed point three of the exchange of letters. Supposing that Monaco wishes to become a member of an international organization of which France is not a member, a preceding agreement is required to ascertain its compatibility with the provisions of the treaty of 1918.[122]

---

[121] Second para. of the 1918 exchange of letters.
[122] This also applies to international organizations of a scientific, moral or social character. The freedom to determine its position in this field is held by Monaco once it has become a member of these organizations and has *a priori* no influence on the freedom to present its application for membership.

Prior agreement with France on the regency and succession to the throne With respect to the preceding agreement referred to in Article 2, first paragraph of the treaty of 1918, the second paragraph continues:

> Il en est de même des mesures concernant directement ou indirectement l'exercice d'une régence ou la succession à la couronne qui, soit par l'effet d'un mariage, d'une adoption ou autrement ne pourra être dévolue qu'à une personne ayant la nationalité française ou monégasque et agréée par le Gouvernement français.

The exchange of letters provides that the exclusion of persons who are not French or Monégasque nationals 'pourra être levée par la naturalisation française ou monégasque en suite d'un accord intervenu entre le Gouvernement de la République et Son Altesse Sérénissime le Prince'.[123] The regent or successor to the throne must be confirmed by France.[124]

Non-alienation of the Principality Article 3, first paragraph of the treaty of 1918 reiterates the obligation entered into by Monaco in the Additional Article 1 of the treaty of 1861 not to ally the Principality with any Power other than France.[125]

French protectorate in case of a vacancy on the throne Article 3, second paragraph of the treaty of 1918 states:

> En cas de vacance de la couronne, notamment faute d'héritier direct ou adoptif, le territoire monégasque formera, sous le protectorat de la France, un Etat autonome sous le nom d'Etat de Monaco.

This implies *a contrario* that, at present, the Principality of Monaco is not a French protectorate nor an autonomous State which is not the equivalent of an independent State. The exchange of letters explains moreover that in this case 'des dispositions tenant compte des droits politiques et des franchises d'impôt dont bénéficient actuellement les sujets monégasques seront arrêtées d'un commun accord entre les deux Gouvernements'.[126] It is probable that the vacancy of

---

[123] Third para. of the 1918 exchange of letters.
[124] To this end, for example, the Minister of State informed the French Government that by Sovereign Order of 2 Jun. 1944, Prince Rainier had become heir to the throne: *Journal de Monaco* (1944) no. 4.523.
[125] See p. 263 above at n. 18 and accompanying text.
[126] Fourth para. of the 1918 exchange of letters.

the crown may be caused not only by the absence of direct or adoptive heirs, but also by the absence of a French confirmation of a direct or adoptive heir, under Article 2, second paragraph of the treaty. The use of the word 'notamment' permits the existence of causes other than those enumerated. This would imply that, as France has the right to disapprove a regent or a successor to the Monégasque throne without having to justify its decision under the treaty, France can create a vacancy on the throne and thus turn Monaco into an autonomous State under a French protectorate. It may be wondered whether, under present international law, France could change Monaco's legal status without the approval of the Monégasque nationals.[127]

Article 7 foresees that the treaty would be 'porté, par les soins du Gouvernement français, à la connaissance des Puissances'. Accordingly, Article 436 of the Treaty of Versailles of 28 June 1919 states: 'Les Hautes Parties Contractantes reconnaissent avoir pris connaissance et donner acte du traité signé par le gouvernement de la République française le 17 juillet 1918 avec Son Altesse Sérénissime le Prince de Monaco, et définissant les rapports de la France et de la Principauté.'[128] This confirmation was meant to prevent any German claims for the Monégasque throne in favour of the German branch of the Grimaldi family and to prevent any new attempts of Italy to re-establish a protectorate over Monaco like the Sardinian one.[129] The Franco-Monégasque treaty of 1918 does not provide for a denunciation clause.

Diplomatic representation

In accordance with Article 2, first paragraph of the Franco-Monégasque treaty of 1918, the active right of legation is always exercised by Monaco subject to a prior agreement with France.[130] This includes the establishment of diplomatic or consular relations with third States as well as the choice of the head of the mission. France can place its diplomatic servants at Monaco's disposal, who become seconded from the French diplomatic corps.[131] The head of the mission can be either French or Monégasque.[132] It is not uncommon

---

[127] See on this question pp. 311–313 below.
[128] C. Parry, *The Consolidated Treaty Series*, vol. 225 (1919) pp. 189 ff.
[129] M. Moncharville, 'Le nouveau Statut franco-monégasque', RGDIP (1920) p. 229.
[130] See pp. 279–280 above.
[131] Art. 4 of the 1930 Convention and 2nd para. point 2° of the 1918 exchange of letters.
[132] Art. 4 of the 1930 Convention. Honorary consuls can have any nationality.

that a Minister of State at the end of his mandate becomes ambassador for Monaco. In 1995, Monaco had entered into diplomatic or consular relations with sixty-six States of which seven were at the ambassadorial level[133] and of which forty-nine had received an *exequatur* for a resident or non-resident consul or honorary consul to the Principality of Monaco.

Civil service

Certain public offices concerning the security, public order and external relations of Monaco are reserved to seconded French civil servants.[134] The nature of the relations between the Minister of State and the Government Counsellor for the interior on the one hand and France on the other hand is relevant to determining Monaco's independence of France, as both French civil servants are integrated into Monaco's constitutional organization. Pillon and Vilotte note that 'le Ministre d'Etat, bien qu'il s'en défende, assure à la France un contrôle politique discret qui préserve les apparences de l'indépendence monégasque'.[135] The Minister of State himself feels entirely like a Monégasque civil servant who maintains a good relationship with France.[136] The purpose of the secondment of any French civil servant working for the Monégasque authorities is to assure his independence of France from which he cannot receive instructions. Seconded French civil servants can be dismissed at any time by the Prince, who can also decide not to renew their five-year mandate.[137] The Convention of 1930 does not set forth an equivalent right for France vis-à-vis the French functionaries. France has no disciplinary power over the seconded civil servants in Monaco. After the termination of their mandates they can be re-integrated into the French civil

---

[133] Monaco has accredited ambassadors to Belgium (including the Netherlands and Luxembourg), France, Germany, the Holy See, Italy, Spain and Switzerland (and soon Liechtenstein): 'Service des Relations Extérieures' of the Principality of Monaco.

[134] Art. 5 of the 1930 Convention. These functions are enumerated in the exchange of letters of 7 May 1973, JORF (28 Febr. 1974) p. 2320. Besides the majority of the judges in Monaco, these positions include Minister of State, Director of judicial services, Government Counsellor for the interior, Director of public security, Procurator-General of the Court of Appeal, Director of the registry office, Inspector of the registry office, Chiefs of police, Director of the labour office, Head of the fiscal services and Director of the harbour.

[135] Pillon and Vilotte, 'Les Institutions politiques', p. 369.

[136] Interview with HE Mr Jacques Dupont, Minister of State of the Principality of Monaco, 3 Mar. 1992.

[137] Art. 4, 2nd para. of the 1930 Convention.

service.¹³⁸ The possibility remains that a seconded French civil servant will look more favourably upon French interests if he plans to continue his career in France after the accomplishment of his tasks in Monaco. The Ministers of State are usually, but not necessarily, at the end of their careers. This factor is however of a personal nature and is too changeable to draw any conclusions on the legal nature and independence of France's relationship with the seconded civil servants. Yet, France does have an interest in reserving certain public positions to French nationals to the exclusion of Monégasque nationals. The Minister of State and the Government Counsellor for the interior are seen as the guarantors of the correct application of the treaty of 1918.¹³⁹ This is, in terms of international law, an exceptional structure which assures the implementation of a treaty by another State. Nevertheless, if Monaco fails to meet its obligations under the treaty of 1918 its international responsibility will not be attenuated, as legally the Minister of State and the Government Counsellor for the interior are organs of the Monégasque State.

In this framework we should recall the decision of the European Commission of Human Rights of 28 June 1993 in the case of *J. M. v. France*.¹⁴⁰ The complaint concerned the acts of French functionaries who, just like the Minister of State and the Government Counsellor for the interior, were seconded from the French Administration. The functionaries in question were French judges, the French Procurator-General, a French bailiff and French policemen, all in the service of the Monégasque State. Though it is true that the independence of the French judges in Monaco has been guaranteed in the Constitution, no such explicit provision exists for the other seconded French civil servants. Yet, the European Commission of Human Rights considered that 'les actes dont se plaint le requérant, faisant partie de l'exercice de fonctions judiciaires et *administratives* [emphasis added] en Principauté de Monaco, ne sont pas imputables à la France'.¹⁴¹ This would only have been otherwise if the civil servants in question had not functioned autonomously, but had acted for France.¹⁴² The

---

¹³⁸ Interview with HE Mr Jean-Michel Dasque, Consul-General of France in Monaco, 22 Dec. 1992.
¹³⁹ Gallois, *Le Régime international*, p. 166.
¹⁴⁰ Application no. 21392/93. See pp. 272–273 above at nn. 92–96 and accompanying text.
¹⁴¹ Ibid., p. 4.
¹⁴² Compare with the decision of the European Commission of Human Rights and the European Court of Human Rights in the case of *Drozd and Janousek v. France and Spain*. The Commission had stated: 'The President of the French Republic does not act

Minister of State and the Government Counsellor for the interior are civil servants placed at Monaco's disposal by France, just like any other seconded French functionary covered by the Franco-Monégasque Convention of 28 July 1930. The European Commission of Human Rights obviously did not believe that the seconded French civil servants, whose acts were disputed, were acting, in law or in fact, on behalf of the French State.[143] The same consideration should apply to the Minister of State and the Government Counsellor for the interior, as they are *de jure* organs of the Monégasque State and as *de facto* there is absolutely no legally acceptable proof to the contrary. It should therefore be inferred that the seconded French civil servants in Monaco are legally independent of France.

The Convention of 1930 does not include a denunciation clause.

Postal union

The postal, telegraph and telephone relations with France are regulated by one of the six conventions of 18 May 1963.[144] The postal and telegraph services in Monaco fall under the authority of the French postal and telegraph administration,[145] whereas the telephone services are maintained by the Monégasque authorities.[146] The French postal and telegraph legislation is applicable in the Monégasque territory.[147] The employees of the Monégasque post offices are appointed by the French authorities and confirmed by the Monégasque Government which can ask for their replacement.[148] In case of a deficit the expenses are borne by Monaco, while a surplus is divided between Monaco and France at the ratio of 93 per cent to 7 per cent respectively.[149] The Convention can be denounced subject to six months' notice.[150]

---

for France any more than the Bishop of Urgel acts for Spain when they exercise the functions of co-prince.' Application no. 12747/87, Decision of the Commission of 11 Dec. 1990, p. 23, para. 110. The Court concluded that the Andorran courts 'exercise their functions in an autonomous manner; their judgments are not subject to supervision by the authorities of France and Spain'. Judgment of 26 Jun. 1992 (21/1991/273/344) p. 28, para. 96. See also pp. 331–332 below.

[143] Cf. Art. 8 of the 1980 Draft Articles on State Responsibility.
[144] Text in Gallois, *Le Régime international*, pp. 254–259.
[145] Art. 1 of the 1963 postal Convention.
[146] Art. 10 of the 1963 postal Convention.
[147] Art. 2 of the 1963 postal Convention.
[148] Art. 5 of the 1963 postal Convention. Both Monégasque and French nationals have access to these positions: Arts. III and IV of the Protocol to the 1963 postal Convention.
[149] Art. 7, 3rd para. of the 1963 postal Convention.
[150] Art. 14, 2nd para. of the 1963 postal Convention.

Customs union

The customs union between Monaco and France is regulated by the customs Convention of 18 May 1963.[151] The customs legislation and any other regulations which control imports or exports and which are in force in France are applicable in the Principality of Monaco.[152] The customs duties are levied by the French customs authorities.[153] One customs office has been established in Monaco of which all officers and other employees are French nationals appointed by the French Government and confirmed by the Monégasque Government which can ask for their replacement.[154] The total receipts of the customs duties are divided between Monaco and France in proportion to the number of inhabitants of each.[155]

The fact that the customs and customs-related legislation in force in France applies integrally in Monaco implies that the customs legislation of the European Community is applicable in Monaco. In contrast with San Marino,[156] Monaco is assimilated with a Community State by non-Community members which therefore apply the same customs tariffs to Monégasque exports as to the products of Member States of the European Community.[157] There is no apparent legal ground which explains the difference of treatment by non-Community States between Monaco and San Marino, even after the conclusion of the agreement on customs union and cooperation between San Marino and the European Economic Community.[158] Both San Marino and Monaco apply the Community customs legislation in their territory by virtue of their agreement with the Community and with France respectively. However, before falling under the exclusive competence of the European Community, both Italy and France concluded customs conventions with third States, with the difference that Italy did not refer to San Marino in the agreements and France did mention that Monaco was a part of its customs territory and

---

[151] Text in Gallois, *Le Régime international*, pp. 237–242. Modified by exchange of letters of 8 Nov. 1994, JORF (10 Mar. 1995) p. 3763.
[152] Art. 1, 2nd para. of the 1963 customs Convention and Art. I of the additional Protocol.
[153] Art. 6 of the 1963 customs Convention.
[154] Art. 8 of the 1963 customs Convention.
[155] Art. 7 of the 1963 customs Convention and Art. II of the additional Protocol. In addition, the total receipts of the customs duties in Monaco and France are raised by a fixed coefficient before the division, as Monaco has a higher import rate per inhabitant than France.
[156] See pp. 229–230 above.
[157] Information from the French customs office in Monaco.
[158] See pp. 252–253 above.

therefore enjoyed the results of, for example, the mutual most-favoured-nation clauses.[159] It seems possible that the third States with which France had concluded trade agreements maintained the assimilation of Monégasque products with Community products even when they concluded trade agreements, which did not refer to Monaco, with the Community later on. Nevertheless, this situation does not provide Monaco with a legal guarantee that non-Community States will, in all cases, continue to grant an equal treatment to Monégasque and Community products.

The customs Convention can be denounced subject to six months' notice.[160]

Taxes

The Franco-Monégasque fiscal Convention of 18 May 1963 has introduced two new direct taxes in Monaco: a company tax on profits and a tax on income for French residents in Monaco. The company tax on profits is levied by Monaco in accordance with its own fiscal legislation.[161] The fiscal Convention imposes the mandatory elements of the Monégasque fiscal legislation.[162] French inhabitants of Monaco are liable to direct taxes on revenues in France, unless they can prove five years of residence in Monaco before 13 October 1962.[163] The French legislation on taxes on incomes therefore has extraterritorial force and is applied by and for the benefit of France.[164]

The fiscal Convention also regulates the taxes on turnover which include VAT. Monaco applies and levies the taxes on turnover under the same conditions and at the same rates as in France.[165] VAT receipts

---

[159] Compare p. 230 above at n. 159. For instance, a trade and navigation treaty of 14 Dec. 1963 between France and Albania specifies that 'Les produits naturels ou fabriqués, originaires du territoire douanier français' include products from the Principality of Monaco, mentioned in the annex as a part of the French customs territory: Art. 2 (1) and Annex (1), JORF (21 Apr. 1965) p. 3101.

[160] Art. 13 of the 1963 customs Convention.

[161] Art. 1 of the 1963 fiscal Convention. Text in Gallois, *Le Régime international*, pp. 226–236.

[162] Thus, enterprises based in Monaco are to pay company tax on their profits if at least 25 per cent of their turnover arises from commercial transactions with persons situated outside Monaco: Art. 2 (a) of the 1963 fiscal Convention.

[163] Art. 7 of the 1963 fiscal Convention.

[164] Monaco is the only country in which the French inhabitants are liable to taxation in France. Andorra has no direct taxes either, but this regime also applies to French inhabitants as it is considered that the residence permits are granted more restrictively. See p. 341 below.

[165] Art. 15 of the 1963 fiscal Convention and Art. IV of the additional Protocol.

constitute the most essential part of the receipts from taxes on turnover,[166] which are divided between Monaco and France according to a fixed formula.[167] This formula apportions to Monaco a certain part of total receipts, of which one portion has already been levied and received by Monaco directly while the remaining part is paid by France, which accounts for the VAT collected by France on behalf of Monaco for its imported goods. In 1990, the Monégasque recoveries were almost equal to the French share.[168] The knowledge of this ratio is relevant in order to determine the financial dependence of Monaco on France. Since 1987, the French authorities have no longer strictly applied the division formula agreed to in 1963. This implies that the French Government pays several million francs a year less than it was due to contribute under the division formula.[169] France believed this unilateral measure was justified by the rapid increase of the Monégasque turnover compared with a slower increase of the French turnover. Although France violates at present the exchange of letters to the fiscal Convention of 1963, a new legal arrangement between the two countries has not yet been fixed.

The fiscal Convention has established a mixed consultative Commission which can meet at the request of either party and propose solutions to problems of interpretation arising from the Convention.[170] The fiscal Convention can be denounced subject to six months' notice.[171]

Aliens office

The Monégasque legislation on the sojourn and residence of foreigners has to be kept in harmony with the French legislation on

---

[166] *Rapport du Gouvernement de S.A.S. le Prince sur le Projet de Budget de l'Exercice 1992* (Oct. 1991) pp. 12 and 36.
[167] Art. 17 of the 1963 fiscal Convention and exchange of letters of 18 May 1963.
[168] *Rapport du Gouvernement de S.A.S. le Prince sur le Projet de Budget de l'Exercice 1992* (Oct. 1991) p. 12. As since 1 Jan. 1993 VAT for Community products is paid in the country in which the buying company is established, the Monégasque share of the total VAT receipts according to the division-formula will increase. France will only levy VAT on goods imported from outside the EU. The ratio of Monégasque recoveries and French contributions will therefore balance in favour of Monaco's financial independence.
[169] Calculation of the author based on Ministère de l'Economie, des Finances et du Budget, *Les Notes Bleues* (1992) 2ème suppl. trimestriel, pp. 17 and 19 and *Rapport du Gouvernement de S.A.S. le Prince sur le Projet de Budget de l'Exercice 1992* (Oct. 1991).
[170] Art. 25 of the 1963 fiscal Convention.
[171] Art. 26 of the 1963 fiscal Convention.

this matter.[172] In addition, a foreigner who wishes to stay more than three months in Monaco has to have a visa issued by France.[173] When issuing a visa to a non-French foreigner, the French authorities first assure themselves of the accord of the Monégasque authorities.[174] No non-Monégasque individual expelled from France can reside in the Principality.[175] The Monégasque Government has the right to expel a foreigner and request a prohibition of sojourn for a non-French national in the two French departments near the Principality.[176] In contrast with Liechtenstein, San Marino and Andorra,[177] there are no restrictions imposed on foreigners acquiring real estate in Monaco. The Convention of vicinage of 18 May 1963, which regulates the Franco-Monégasque relations on the sojourn of foreigners, can be denounced subject to six months' notice.[178]

Harmonized legislation

The monetary union between France and Monaco is regulated by a Convention of 14 April 1945 and supplementary exchanges of letters on exchange control.[179] The Convention stipulates that the legislation on exchange control, currency protection, the organization of the banking sector and the functioning of the financial market, which is in force in France, is fully applicable in Monaco.[180] The Bank of France has the same competence in Monaco as in France.[181] The French financial services can control the correct application of the French financial legislation in Monaco.[182] The establishment of a bank in Monaco is subject to the approval of the French banking authorities which

---

[172] Art. 1 of the 1963 Convention of vicinage. Text in Gallois, *Le Régime international*, pp. 243–248.
[173] Art. 2 of the 1963 Convention of vicinage and Art. 1, 1st para. of Sovereign Order no. 3.153 of 19 Mar. 1964 on the entry and sojourn of foreigners.
[174] Art. 3 of the 1963 Convention of vicinage.
[175] Art. 13, 1st para., 1st sentence of the 1963 Convention of vicinage.
[176] Art. 13, 1st para., 2nd sentence of the 1963 Convention of vicinage.
[177] See pp. 168 and 230–231 above and p. 341 below.
[178] Art. 24 of the 1963 Convention of vicinage.
[179] Exchanges of letters of 18 May 1963, JORF (3 Sept. 1963) pp. 8031–8032 and of 27 Nov. 1987, JORF (29 Jun. 1988) pp. 8535–8536. Convention on exchange control of 14 Apr. 1945, *Codes et Lois de la Principauté de Monaco: Traités bilatéraux avec la France*.
[180] Arts. 1, 2 and 4 of the 1945 Convention on exchange control and Art. 1 of the 1987 exchange of letters.
[181] Art. 3 of the 1945 Convention on exchange control.
[182] Art. 6 of the 1945 Convention on exchange control. In the event of an infraction, legal proceedings are instituted before the French tribunals: Art. 8 of the 1945 Convention on exchange control.

ascertain that the establishment of the bank is authorized by the Monégasque Government.[183] The Convention on exchange control of 1945 does not provide for a denunciation clause.[184]

The French laws and regulations on war material are automatically in force in Monaco.[185] Some other legal domains are regulated by Monégasque legislation which is to a certain extent, or completely, brought into line with the French rules. Thus we can mention the regulations on pharmacy which have to be fixed by Monaco as closely as possible to the French legislation.[186] The Monégasque legislation on arms and munitions which are not war material is to be harmonized as far as possible with the corresponding French legislation.[187] In matters of insurance the Monégasque and French regulations have to be coordinated.[188] The Monégasque Government should adopt the insurance legislation in force in France taking into account Monaco's special position and in mutual agreement.[189] French services of the Ministry of Finance have the right to check on the insurance companies operating in Monaco.[190]

Defence

Article 1, first paragraph of the Franco-Monégasque treaty of 1918 stipulates that the French Government assures the defence of Monaco's independence and sovereignty, and guarantees the integrity of its territory as if it were a part of France. France has the right in times of peace to traverse the Monégasque territory with its army, subject to a prior agreement with the Monégasque Government.[191] Monaco has no army nor a general conscription.

---

[183] Art. 3, para. 4 of the 1987 exchange of letters. One representative of the Monégasque Government participates with the right to vote in these banking committees in case of an application of a future Monégasque bank.
[184] Art. 10 of the 1945 Convention on exchange control.
[185] Art. 16, 1st para. of the 1963 Convention of vicinage.
[186] Art. 1 of the 1963 Convention on pharmacy. French inspectors are appointed by the Monégasque Government to control the pharmaceutical products produced in Monaco: Art. 4.
[187] Art. 16, 2nd para. of the 1963 Convention of vicinage.
[188] Art. 1 of the 1963 Convention on insurances. Text in Gallois, *Le Régime international*, pp. 251-253.
[189] Para. 1 to Art. 1 of the exchange of letters to the 1963 Convention on insurances. An insurance company can function in the Monégasque territory if so authorized by the Minister of State and the French Minister of Finance: Para. 1 to Art. 2 of the exchange of letters to the 1963 Convention on insurances.
[190] Interpretation of Art. 4 of the exchange of letters to the 1963 Convention on insurances.
[191] Art. 22 of the 1963 Convention of vicinage.

Relations with international organizations
League of Nations
In Article 5 of the Franco-Monégasque treaty of 1918, the French Government had promised to offer its good offices in order to facilitate Monaco's access to international conferences and organizations together with France, and more particularly to conferences which prepared the organization of the League of Nations.[192] Monaco therefore informed France of its wish to be invited to the preparatory conferences of the League of Nations in 1919. Although the French Ministry of Foreign Affairs transmitted the request to President Woodrow Wilson,[193] the latter omitted to send an invitation to Monaco for the conference with the neutral countries regarding the League of Nations, in which Monaco would have liked to participate.[194] When Monaco asked to be represented at the first meeting of the League of Nations, President Wilson replied that it was beyond his competence to determine what States would be asked to send representatives.[195] Thereupon, Monaco informed the French Government of its wish to be included in the Annex of the Covenant of the League of Nations so that it could become an original member under Article 1 of the Covenant, but this effort too was unavailing.[196] Finally, Monaco submitted an application for membership of the League of Nations on 6 April 1920 through the intermediary of the French Government.[197] The Permanent Advisory Commission of the League on Military, Naval and Air questions had requested information on Monaco's naval force, to which Monaco replied that it did not need a naval force because it was neutral.[198] However, without waiting for the League's decision on the application of Liechtenstein, Monaco withdrew its application on 22 October 1920.[199] Objections had mainly been raised by the United Kingdom which did not want to

---
[192] See pp. 278–279 above.
[193] Letter from the French Ministry of Foreign Affairs to HSH Prince Albert I of Monaco of 9 Apr. 1919. Archives of the Palace of Monaco.
[194] Letter of apology from President Wilson to the Monégasque plenipotentiary minister in Paris of 18 Apr. 1919. Archives of the Palace of Monaco.
[195] Letter from President Wilson to HSH Prince Albert I of Monaco of 21 Apr. 1919. Archives of the Palace of Monaco.
[196] Letter from the Monégasque plenipotentiary minister in Paris to the French Minister of Foreign Affairs of 15 Apr. 1919. Archives of the Palace of Monaco.
[197] League of Nations Off. J. (1920) pp. 265–266.
[198] Letter from the League of Nations to the Consul-General of Monaco of 18 Aug. 1920 and Monégasque answer of 25 Sept. 1920. Archives of the Palace of Monaco.
[199] See for Liechtenstein pp. 170–174 above and for San Marino, pp. 233–234 above.

accord another supplementary vote to France and which had doubts about Monaco's full independence.[200]

As in 1924 Monaco believed it detected a more forthcoming position of the League of Nations towards Micro-States and the universal participation of States in its Organization, it decided to submit a new application for membership. The Monégasque Government had informed France of its intentions and, according to the French Consul-General in Monaco, it had stated: 'La France devait, d'après le Gouvernement Monégasque, trouver son intérêt à cette admission, puisqu'elle disposerait ainsi d'une voix de plus, le Gouvernement princier s'étant engagé à conformer sa politique extérieure à celle du Gouvernement de la République.'[201] France had no objections to Monaco's candidacy provided that the application would be submitted by France and not by Monaco, and that the head of the Monégasque delegation in the League would be appointed with the consent of France.[202] As it was believed that the Monégasque application would be more successful if it was presented by Monaco itself, France eventually did not object to a direct Monégasque submission of its application for membership.[203] Accordingly, Monaco applied for membership of the League of Nations on 8 September 1924 and bolstered its candidacy with an additional document in which it pleaded its own sovereignty and financial capacity.[204] Apart from objections, especially British ones, concerning Monaco's independence of France, problems of a technical nature seemed to have arisen. Monaco was the only applicant for membership in 1924 and it was considered unfortunate and humiliating for the League Assembly that a small State like Monaco would be considered by the League of Nations while States like Germany and Turkey had not yet applied.[205]

---

[200] 'Ière Note sur la candidature de la Principauté à la Société des Nations' of 29 Aug. 1924. Archives of the Palace of Monaco.
[201] Letter from the Consul-General of France in Monaco to the Monégasque Government of 20 Jul. 1924. Archives of the Palace of Monaco.
[202] Ibid.
[203] Letter from the Vice-Consul of France in Monaco to the Monégasque Secretary of State (at present Minister of State) of 1 Sept. 1924. Archives of the Palace of Monaco.
[204] 'Note à l'appui de la demande d'admission de la Principauté à la Société des Nations' of 1924. Archives of the Palace of Monaco. Apart from the objections raised concerning its independence, which Monaco defended by pleading its participation in international conferences and the existence of diplomatic and consular relations, Monaco also defended itself against presumptions that it had immoral financial resources from the casino. It received only 12 per cent of the game profits in 1924, so it was argued.
[205] Note from the Monégasque representative in Geneva of 18 Sept. 1924. Archives of the Palace of Monaco.

The Monégasque representative who pleaded Monaco's cause in the League of Nations had hoped that the Turkish Government would apply for membership soon, so that the League of Nations and the press 'n'apporteraient qu'une attention distraite à la candidature de la Principauté qui aurait alors quelques chances de succès'.[206] On 1 May 1925 Monaco withdrew its application for membership, for the second time.[207]

Not all Member States of the League of Nations had been against Monaco's possible membership.[208] Like Liechtenstein and San Marino, Monaco suffered from the League's general opposition to the entry of Micro-States into the Organization.[209] Yet, in addition, Monaco's application was complicated by the fact that it seemed to have intended to conform its vote and its head of delegation to French wishes. Under these conditions States like the United Kingdom were reluctant to give France a supplementary vote.

International courts

Permanent Court of International Justice

Like Liechtenstein and San Marino, Monaco was among the non-Member States of the League of Nations which received an invitation from the registrar of the Permanent Court of International Justice to become a State Party to the Court's Statute.[210] On 22 April 1937, Monaco used this possibility by ratifying the Statute of the Permanent Court of International Justice and accepted its compulsory jurisdiction, under Article 36, paragraph 2 of the Statute, for a period of five years.[211] Monaco never brought a dispute before the Permanent Court of International Justice, nor were any proceedings instituted against it.

International Court of Justice

After it became known that Liechtenstein had submitted a request to be admitted as a party to the Statute of the International Court of

---

[206] Ibid.
[207] Letter from the Monégasque Secretary of State (at present, Minister of State) to the Secretary-General of the League of Nations of 1 May 1925. Archives of the Palace of Monaco.
[208] A note of the Monégasque representative in Geneva of 19 Sept. 1924 refers to the support of Uruguay and a hesitant consideration of Romania.
[209] See pp. 133–134, 170–174 and 233–234 above.
[210] See pp. 174 and 234 above. *Rapport Annuel de la Cour Permanente de Justice Internationale* (1 Jan. 1992–15 Jun. 1925) series E, No. 1, pp. 139–140.
[211] *Seizième Rapport de la Cour Permanente de Justice Internationale* (1 Jan. 1939–31 Dec. 1945) series E, No. 16, p. 348.

Justice on 24 March 1949, Monaco considered the opportunity to adhere to the Statute as well, invoking Liechtenstein as a precedent.[212] *A priori*, Monaco had no reason to believe that its application would be rejected given the fact that it had already been a State Party to the Statute of the Permanent Court of International Justice, which did not demand more independence and statehood than the Statute of the International Court of Justice. A separate application by Monaco was in the end not submitted.

WHO

Together with San Marino's first application, Monaco applied for the membership of WHO in 1948.[213] Both applications were submitted to the Legal Committee of the World Health Assembly which referred them for preliminary examination to a working group.[214] The report of the Legal Committee does not show an investigation by the Committee or the working group into the degree of independence and the statehood of Monaco. The Legal Committee confined itself to the considerations that Monaco's application complied with the required conditions and that a decision for admission was only valid for this particular case and should not serve as a precedent for the future.[215] On 2 July 1948, the Assembly of WHO approved the conclusions of the Legal Committee and unanimously decided to admit Monaco as a full member of the Organization.[216] Monaco has always sent its own delegations to the meetings of the World Health Assembly and regional meetings.[217]

UNESCO

On 19 July 1947, the Principality of Monaco applied for admission to membership of UNESCO. As by virtue of Article II of the Agreement

---

[212] The Monégasque Government considered 'que le Liechtenstein ne possède pas toujours les compétences étatiques qu'exerce la Principauté, il n'a pas, notamment, de représentation diplomatique à l'étranger. La demande monégasque devrait donc être aisément retenue si le précédent de Liechtenstein pouvait être invoqué': Report of the Minister of State to HSH Prince Rainier III of Monaco of 21 Nov. 1949. Archives of the Palace of Monaco.

[213] See on San Marino, pp. 239–240 above.

[214] WHO OR (1948) 1st Assembly, p. 332.

[215] Ibid.

[216] Ibid., p. 76.

[217] A Monégasque physician forms part of the delegation. Interview with HE Mr Jacques Dupont, Minister of State of the Principality of Monaco, 3 Mar. 1992.

between the United Nations and UNESCO the admission of States which were not members of the United Nations still needed to be approved by the Economic and Social Council, Monaco's application was first transmitted to this Council.[218] Canada proposed a draft resolution which was adopted by the Economic and Social Council on 5 February 1948, informing UNESCO 'that it has no objection to the admission of Monaco to the Organization' and that UNESCO should 'take into account what contribution Monaco can make in furthering the programme of the Organization' and should also consider 'the general problem of the admission of similar diminutive States'.[219] The Canadian representative in the Economic and Social Council had no doubts about Monaco's statehood, but nevertheless believed that 'the Principality did not in fact exercise all the prerogatives of sovereignty because of the treaty binding it to France'.[220] The Executive Board of UNESCO considered Monaco's application on 24 September 1948 and examined three aspects:[221]

Legal status of Monaco The Executive Board examined the effects of the treaty of 17 July 1918 between Monaco and France, without referring to its interpretative exchange of letters, and concluded that this treaty

can hardly be regarded as infringing the independence and sovereignty of Monaco. Internationally, the Principality enjoys the right to conclude treaties with other Powers, the right to a flag, and the right to both active and passive diplomatic and consular representation. In practice, it exercises these rights to the full.[222]

The Executive Board added that the obligations undertaken in virtue of the treaty of 1918

do not imply for the Principality a status such as would prevent, from a legal point of view, its admission to an international organization

and finally inferred:

The Principality of Monaco is therefore essentially a small independent State which has bound itself to a more powerful neighbour as regards the exercise

---

[218] Art. II of the Agreement between UNESCO and the UN has not been in effect since 1962.
[219] ECOSOC Res. 137 (VI) of 5 Febr. 1948, ECOSOC OR (1948), UN Doc. E/568/Add. 1 (1948). Also in UNESCO Doc. 8 EX/6 (24 Jun. 1948).
[220] ECOSOC OR (1948) 6th Session, pp. 53–55.
[221] UNESCO Doc. 8 EX/6 (24 Jun. 1948), Executive Board, 8th Session.
[222] Ibid., p. 2.

of certain rights, but whose position as a sovereign State has not been prejudiced by the limitation of its freedom of action to which, in certain respects, it has agreed.[223]

The Executive Board also emphasized that Monaco had signed a number of international social and cultural conventions, had been the scene of several international conferences and was a member of the ITU, the International Union for the Protection of Literary and Artistic Works and the International Hydrographic Union.[224] The considerations of the Executive Board of UNESCO are the most elaborate ones provided by an international organization with respect to Monaco's legal status. Its conclusions show that the international recognition of Monaco was not determinant for its statehood and that the treaty of 1918 was not considered an infringement of Monaco's independence. Nevertheless, the latter conclusion was based on the erroneous argument that in practice Monaco exercised the right to conclude treaties and the right to both active and passive diplomatic or consular representation 'to the full'. We have already seen that the right to conclude treaties and in any case the active right of legation cannot be exercised by Monaco without the previous agreement of France, according to the interpretative exchange of letters of 1918.[225] This principle is in practice officially applied.

What contribution could Monaco make in furthering the programme of UNESCO? This second question considered by the Executive Board, like the first one, fell into the category of questions generally raised when considering a State's application for membership. Monaco had submitted a document on the achievements of the Principality in the fields of culture, science, art and radio, which was considered satisfactory by the Executive Board.[226]

Possible effect of Monaco's admission on the future admission of other diminutive States This point was discussed in the light of possible applications of Andorra, Liechtenstein and San Marino in the future. The Executive Board adopted a United States draft resolution placing the general problem of the admission of diminutive States and the status of associate membership on the agenda of the General Conference, thus deferring Monaco's application pending a decision

---

[223] Ibid.
[224] Ibid., p. 3.
[225] See p. 280 above.
[226] UNESCO Doc. 8 EX/6 (24 Jun. 1948) p. 3 and Annex III.

on this problem by the General Conference.²²⁷ However, as this was considered, by France and others, an inexcusable delay of the decision on Monaco's application, the Executive Board eventually submitted a resolution to the General Conference recommending Monaco's admission subject to the condition that 'this decision shall in no way be invoked as a precedent in the event of an application for admission to membership by any other diminutive State'.²²⁸ The General Conference of UNESCO unanimously endorsed the recommendation of the Executive Board on 9 December 1948.²²⁹ It should be remembered that many fields of the work of UNESCO fall within Monaco's freedom to express its opinion on scientific, moral or social problems without the need to concord with the French position.²³⁰

IAEA

The Principality of Monaco was an initial member of the IAEA on 19 September 1957.²³¹ The question of its statehood and independence was thus never raised in the IAEA.

In 1961, the IAEA established an international laboratory of marine radioactivity in Monaco and concluded to this end a special agreement with the Principality defining the laboratory's privileges and immunities.²³² The agreement also provides for exemption from customs duties with respect to material needed for the functioning of the laboratory.²³³ This exemption is to be applied by France if a product destined for the laboratory arrives at one of its customs offices. In principle, the exemption from customs duties would be contrary to Article 1, second paragraph of the Franco-Monégasque customs union Convention as it does not constitute a French customs

---

²²⁷ UNESCO Doc. 8 EX/SR.8 (rev.) (27 Sept. 1948) pp. 6–8.
²²⁸ UNESCO Doc. 3C/96 (1948).
²²⁹ *Records of the General Conference of UNESCO: Proceedings*, 3rd Session (1948) vol. III, pp. 156–157. Res. 3C/Rev. IV. National Commission of UNESCO in 1950 established by Sovereign Orders no. 292 of 16 Oct. 1950 and no. 450 of 11 Sept. 1951.
²³⁰ Exchange of letters of 17 Jul. 1918, see p. 279 above.
²³¹ It took advantage of the possibility offered in Article IV (A) of the Statute of the IAEA by virtue of which States, which were a member of any of the UN specialized agencies, could become a member of the IAEA if they deposited their instrument of ratification with the Government of the United States and signed the Statute before 24 Jan. 1957.
²³² Agreement between Monaco and the IAEA on the international laboratory of marine radioactivity and the privileges and immunities of the Agency on the territory of the Principality of 16 May 1986. Replaces a previous agreement between the IAEA, the Oceanographic Institute and the Principality of Monaco of 7 Apr. 1961.
²³³ Art. 8 (1) (b) of the Agreement between Monaco and the IAEA.

regulation in force in France. Given the fact that France must have given its consent to the conclusion of the Agreement between Monaco and the IAEA, under Article 2, first paragraph of the treaty of 1918, France has approved this exceptional customs regulation and is therefore compelled not to obstruct the implementation of this exemption.

OSCE

The Principality of Monaco did not participate in the preparatory talks of the CSCE. On 28 May 1973, the French delegate to the CSCE preliminaries requested that Monaco be invited to the Conference.[234] This request met with certain objections, especially from the Soviet Union which had some reservations about Monaco's independence, but was eventually agreed to.[235] Thus, Monaco participated with one official in the Conference of Helsinki and since then has regularly attended the CSCE meetings and summits. Monaco does not, like Liechtenstein and San Marino, participate in the group of neutral and non-aligned States.[236] As the OSCE is an international political conference, Monaco always adopts the same position as France within the OSCE.[237] The interests which Monaco can find in taking part in the OSCE are in the first place the recognition of its statehood and the acceptance by the European States of its participation, on a par with the other European States, in a political organism. In the second place, the Helsinki Declaration (Final Act of the CSCE) and the Charter of Paris for a New Europe are legally non-binding instruments which nevertheless have permitted Monaco to enter into relations with other European States on the basis of the enumerated principles of international law and security.

Apart from the appreciation of the work of the OSCE for security reasons, the institutionalization of the CSCE has entailed other legal and political advantages for Monaco. Like Liechtenstein and San Marino, it has two seats in the OSCE Parliamentary Assembly[238] and covers 0.20 per cent of the costs for the OSCE institutions.[239] In

---

[234] L. V. Ferraris, ed., *Report on a Negotiation – Collection de Relations internationales* (1979) p. 38.
[235] Information from a French diplomatic source.
[236] See for Liechtenstein pp. 177–179 above and for San Marino pp. 235–236 above.
[237] Interview with HE Mr Jacques Dupont, Minister of State of the Principality of Monaco, 3 Mar. 1992.
[238] Art. 1 (I) of the final resolution of the Madrid Conference concerning the establishment of the CSCE Parliamentary Assembly, 3 Apr. 1991, 30 ILM (1991) p. 1346.
[239] Part III (2) of the Supplementary Document to give effect to certain provisions in the Charter of Paris for a New Europe, 30 ILM (1991) p. 220.

addition, the Dispute Settlement Mechanism adopted at Valletta in 1991 and the Arbitral Tribunal are frameworks in which Monaco can seek the settlement of a dispute with one of the other OSCE Member States, such as France.[240] Unfortunately, neither France nor Monaco has so far accepted the compulsory jurisdiction of the OSCE Arbitral Tribunal.[241]

Council of Europe

Monaco is neither a member nor a permanent observer of the Council of Europe. When the Statute of the Council of Europe had been adopted and before the first meeting of the Consultative Assembly in August 1949, Monaco had made serious efforts to become a member of the Council of Europe. A draft ratification of the Statute of the Council of Europe had been prepared, as well as a memorandum of 25 July 1949 in which: 'La Principauté Souveraine de Monaco a l'honneur de demander son admission au "Conseil de l'Europe", et plus particulièrement à "l'Assemblée Consultative"'.[242] The memorandum explained that the Principality was a sovereign State because it fulfilled the three essential conditions set by public international law:

une Population sédentaire et autonome, un Territoire délimité, une Organisation Gouvernementale, Administrative et judiciaire. La Principauté jouit de la 'Souveraineté Intérieure' par l'équilibre de ses trois Pouvoirs: Exécutif, Législatif, Judiciaire; elle jouit de la 'Souveraineté Extérieure' classique, puis-qu'elle conclut des Traités et accrédite des Représentants diplomatiques parmi les Puissances Souveraines; elle en reçoit par réciprocité les Représentants.[243]

The Monégasque memorandum also indicated the interests for the Council of Europe in admitting Monaco as a member and emphasized that Monaco's exclusion from the Council of Europe would isolate the Principality and would 'pénaliser sans raison sa "Souveraineté" en

---

[240] Report of the CSCE Meeting of Experts on Peaceful Settlement of Disputes, Valletta 8 Febr. 1991, 30 ILM (1991) pp. 382 ff. and Convention on Conciliation and Arbitration within the CSCE signed by Monaco on 15 Dec. 1992, 32 ILM (1993) p. 551.
[241] Art. 26 (2) of the Convention on Conciliation and Arbitration within the CSCE. As the acceptance of the compulsory jurisdiction of a Tribunal is not an act similar to the conclusion of a treaty, it will not be subject to prior consent of France under Art. 2, 1st para. of the Franco-Monégasque treaty of 1918.
[242] 'Mémoire aux fins d'admission de la Principauté Souveraine de Monaco au Conseil de l'Europe', 25 Jul. 1949. Archives of the Palace of Monaco.
[243] Ibid., Section I.

l'écartant du rôle d'entr'aide que remplissent les autres Etats Souverains de l'Europe et qu'en fait elle remplit'.²⁴⁴ The memorandum suggests that Monaco did not necessarily envisage a full membership of the Council of Europe, but also considered an associate membership under Article 5 (a) of the Statute of the Council of Europe and therefore mentioned its admission to the Consultative Assembly. When it became clear that the associate membership was rather designed for entities which were not entirely independent, the associate membership was considered to be to the detriment of Monaco's statehood. An application for full membership of the Council of Europe was never carried through.²⁴⁵

The attitude of the Council of Europe towards Liechtenstein and San Marino reveals certain obstacles to the admission of Monaco. During the debate on Liechtenstein's admission in the Parliamentary Assembly, the British representative declared that Liechtenstein would not create a precedent and added that no other Micro-State would fulfil the required conditions. Speaking about Monaco he added:

> Let us take, for example, Monaco. Monaco is not sovereign. It cannot make a treaty with any other country without the permission of France, and France proposes the name of the Prime Minister of Monaco to the Prince of Monaco who then nominates that person, who is normally a French civil servant. Therefore, Monaco is in no sense a sovereign state parallel to Liechtenstein.²⁴⁶

The Council of Europe could raise certain objections concerning the interest of admitting Monaco as a full member if Monaco always conforms its position to the French one. Except for the economic cooperation, Monaco is completely free to act in the other domains of common action of the Council of Europe, namely, social, cultural, scientific, legal and administrative matters as well as the realization of human rights and fundamental freedoms.²⁴⁷ Liechtenstein had assured the Council of Europe that it would combat tax offences and evasion²⁴⁸ and San Marino had agreed not to become a tax haven.²⁴⁹

---

²⁴⁴ Ibid., Section IV.
²⁴⁵ The French Minister of Foreign Affairs, Robert Schuman, declared in 1949 that '[t]oute demande d'admission exige une préparation prudente' and assured Monaco that he would do his best: Letter from the French Minister of Foreign Affairs to the Minister of State of 4 Aug. 1949. Archives of the Palace of Monaco.
²⁴⁶ Council of Europe, *Parliamentary Assembly, Official Report* (27 Sept.–5 Oct. 1978) vol. II, 30th Session (2nd part), 11th mtg (28 Sept. 1978) p. 386.
²⁴⁷ Cf. Art. 1 (b) of the Statute of the Council of Europe and fifth para. of the 1918 Franco-Monégasque exchange of letters.
²⁴⁸ See p. 183 above.
²⁴⁹ See p. 243 above.

The same would be expected from Monaco. Furthermore, although Monaco is a State which accepts the rule of law, its democracy is not as complete as in certain other European States. Nevertheless, during the discussion on the admission of Andorra to the Council of Europe, the chairman of the Committee on Relations with European Non-Member Countries stated that he looked 'forward to another country, Monaco – which is in a similar situation – making progress towards accession to the Council of Europe'.[250]

Monaco is a State Party to two European conventions concluded in the framework of the Council of Europe.[251]

European Community

As with San Marino, the Council of the European Communities established in 1968 that the Principality of Monaco was a part of the Community's customs territory as defined by its customs union Convention with France.[252] In 1986, in its reply to a question raised by an Irish member of the European Parliament, the Commission had explained that, like San Marino, Monaco did not have to apply the Community legislation concerning the free movement of workers, the freedom of establishment and the free movement of services.[253]

Apart from the Vatican City, Monaco is the only European Micro-State which until now has not concluded a customs union agreement with the European Community and has not entered into negotiations to that end. Nevertheless, the Principality of Monaco, of all the European Micro-States, is the one which maintains the closest legal relations with the European Community and which therefore would raise the least complications if an agreement with the Community were to be concluded. Much depends on whether France looks favourably on such a customs union agreement. Considering that France has the right to bar the conclusion of a treaty between Monaco and other States only in so far as the treaty would be contrary to the Franco-Monégasque treaty of 1918,[254] juridically speaking it cannot be

---

[250] Council of Europe, *Parliamentary Assembly, Official Report* (3 Oct. 1994), Doc. AS (1994) CR 24, 4th part, p. 29.
[251] In 1994, it adhered to the Berne Convention on the Conservation of European Wildlife and Natural Habitat (1979) no. 104 and the European Cultural Convention (1954) no. 18.
[252] Art. 2 and annex point 2 of the Council Regulation no. 1496/68, ECOJ no. L 238 (28.9.68) p. 1. See also pp. 286–287 above.
[253] Answer given by Mr Delors in name of the Commission to written question no. 900/86 of 14 Jul. 1986, ECOJ no. C 54 (2.3.87) p. 31.
[254] Art. 2 (1) of the 1918 treaty and 2nd para. at point 3° of the interpretative exchange of letters of 1918. See further p. 280 above.

accepted that France does not agree with an agreement concluded between Monaco and the Community which in essence does not alter the existing customs regime under the Franco-Monégasque customs union Convention of 1963. Taking into account the negotiations and agreements between the European Economic Community and two other European Micro-States, Andorra and San Marino,[255] a customs union agreement between the Community and Monaco would have the advantage that the payment of the collected customs duties would be assured under the legal responsibility of the Community and subject to negotiations in a Joint Committee and the possibility of arbitration.[256] The Community could undertake the realization of the assimilation of Monégasque and Community products in its relations with third States, which, although existing in practice, has no fixed legal basis.[257] It should furthermore be noted that the European Parliament, when approving the agreement on customs union and cooperation with San Marino, had emphasized that San Marino was not a tax haven.[258] One may wonder what value this argument could have for the conclusion of a customs union agreement. If an agreement between the Community and a tax haven could not be accepted by the European Parliament, this would be a political and not a legal reason as direct taxation does not fall within the competences of the European Community. Moreover, the absence of direct taxation on revenues and company benefits has not prevented the conclusion of a customs union agreement between the European Economic Community and Andorra.[259]

The growing European integration will lead to a loss of France's commercial and monetary competence and will therefore inevitably require an agreement between the Community and Monaco.[260] The existence of a customs union agreement between the European Community and Monaco would enable Monaco to negotiate directly with the Community in a Joint Committee and could be a framework for any future Community legislation which affects Monaco and on which it wants to be heard. The protection of its economic interests is

---

[255] Cf. San Marino, pp. 246–254 above and Andorra, pp. 359–364 below.
[256] Cf. Art. 24 of the San Marino–EEC agreement on customs union and cooperation and Art. 18 of the Andorra–EEC customs union agreement.
[257] See pp. 286–287 above.
[258] See p. 249 above, n. 288 and accompanying text.
[259] See pp. 359–364 below.
[260] See Declaration on monetary relations with the Republic of San Marino, the Vatican City and the Principality of Monaco (7 Febr. 1992), 31 ILM (1992) p. 365.

usually undertaken by France within the European Commission or Council. However, this arrangement lacks any legal foundation. Article 1, second paragraph read in connection with Article 2, first paragraph of the Franco-Monégasque treaty of 1918 obliges Monaco to respect France's economic interests and not the other way round.

United Nations

Since 1956, the Principality of Monaco has maintained a permanent observer mission to the United Nations in New York.[261] It has participated in certain United Nations programmes such as the International Control of Narcotic Drugs. Following in the footsteps of Liechtenstein and San Marino, Monaco was the third European Micro-State to apply for membership of the United Nations. The application of Monaco for admission to membership in the United Nations was received by the Secretary-General on 18 May 1993.[262] The President of the Security Council referred the application to the Committee on the Admission of New Members which recommended the admission of Monaco without much discussion.[263] Thereupon, the Security Council approved, without voting, Monaco's admission to membership on 26 May 1993.[264] On 28 May 1993, the General Assembly welcomed Monaco's membership of the United Nations by acclamation.[265] The representatives of the regional groups emphasized the principle of universality of the United Nations and believed that the admission of Monaco would add to the realization of the principles of the Organization. Thus the Italian delegate, speaking in the name of the Group of Western European States, stated that 'all member states – be they large or small, ancient or new – bear a responsibility to strengthen the role of the United Nations'.[266]

The importance of Monaco's admission to the United Nations lies in the fact that the other Member States did not consider that its relations with France precluded membership of this political organization. In addition, Monaco's statehood has been firmly recognized, which strengthens its position in the long term, while at the same time it can benefit from the legal and political facilities which the United Nations offers.

[261] United Nations, *Permanent Missions to the United Nations* (1988) no. 263, p. 272.
[262] UN Doc. S/25796 (1993).
[263] UN Doc. S/25842 (1993).
[264] SC Res. 829 (1993) and UN Doc. S/PV.3219 (1993).
[265] GA Res. 47/231.
[266] UN Doc. A/47/PV.104 (1993) pp. 19–20.

Monaco has participated in the Working Group on the question of equitable representation in the Security Council, proposing the increase of the number of non-permanent Members from ten to twenty, divided into two categories.[267] This proposition would have made it possible, theoretically, for Monaco to be elected on to the Security Council. The Principality also proposed the drafting of a convention by which the States Parties would undertake in advance to authorize in case of a conflict the establishment of protection and security zones reserved for defenceless children, women and the elderly, guarded by unarmed volunteers wearing white helmets.[268] So far the General Assembly has not acted upon the proposal.

Other international organizations

Monaco is a Member State of several other governmental international organizations. We may mention Monaco's membership of the ITU, the UPU, the ICAO, WIPO, INTELSAT and EUTELSAT.

By virtue of its membership of the United Nations specialized organizations, Monaco was invited and has participated in United Nations conferences of which we can mention the Vienna Conference on the Law of Treaties, the United Nations Conferences on the Law of the Sea and the United Nations Conference on Environment and Development.

Application of the criteria for statehood: first analysis

The Principality of Monaco has generally been classified as a protectorate of Spain between 1524 and 1641, a protectorate of France between 1641 and 1817 and a protectorate of Sardinia between 1817 and 1861. Guggenheim continued to call Monaco a protectorate of France after the treaty of 1918 because Monaco cannot conclude treaties without France's permission and because France takes over the governmental organization of Monaco in case of a vacancy of the throne.[269] The international status of the Principality of Monaco after

---

[267] Declaration of the permanent representative of Monaco to the UN: ten semi-permanent Members, per regional group, elected by two-thirds of the GA for five years and ten Members, two per regional group, elected by simple majority for one year: UN Doc A/48/264 (1993) and Add. and supplementary information from the Permanent Mission of the Principality of Monaco to the UN.
[268] UN Doc. A/49/SR.13 (1994) p. 6.
[269] P. Guggenheim, *Lehrbuch des Völkerrechts*, vol. I (1948) p. 254.

the treaty of 1861, by which it ceded the communes of Menton and Roquebrune to France, should be determined on the basis of the criteria for statehood:[270]

Territory The Principality of Monaco has a relatively small land territory, which, except for the Vatican City, is the smallest in the world. It has defined its maritime boundaries and airspace in agreements with France.[271] Smallness has never been an argument for the international community to deny Monaco its statehood.

Population The Monégasque nationals constituted 16.92 per cent of the inhabitants in 1990 and are therefore a minority of the population. The existence of a majority of foreign inhabitants has not been considered a reason for denying the existence of a permanent population in Monaco.

Government Monaco's governmental organization is firmly established by the Constitution and wields effective power within the territory.

Independence The crucial element of Monaco's international status is its degree of formal and actual independence. Three factors are determinant for the acceptance or denial of Monaco's independence under international law: the number and legal value of foreign elements in the exercise of the sovereign rights of the putative State, the position of France towards Monaco's international position and the attitude of the international community as a whole towards Monaco. We have established the following foreign elements in Monaco's functioning as a State:

1. *A majority of French judges in the Monégasque courts and tribunals* As in the cases of Liechtenstein and San Marino, the presence of foreign judges in a State's judicial system cannot be considered an infringement of a State's independence, as judges, whether foreigners or nationals, are by definition independent.[272] Their independence is guaranteed by law and they do not act under the instructions of any Government.
2. *French civil servants in certain important public positions and a majority vote of French nationals in the Monégasque Government*

---

[270] See for the general criteria for statehood, pp. 116–127 above.
[271] Convention on maritime delimitation of 16 Febr. 1984 and Convention on air traffic between Monaco and France of 24 Jan. 1991.
[272] Cf. Liechtenstein, p. 201 above and San Marino, p. 258 above.

These French civil servants are seconded from the French Administration and can be dismissed by the Prince from whom they receive instructions. We have already seen that the seconded French civil servants are legally independent of the French Government.[273]

3. *Extraterritorial application of French legislation* The issues which fall into this domain are the legislation on war material, on banking, on customs matters and on postal tariffs. The French tax on revenues is applicable in Monaco only in so far as it concerns certain French inhabitants.[274]

4. *Monégasque laws harmonized with French legislation* Monaco has adopted in full or to a substantial degree the French laws on the residence and sojourn of aliens, on VAT, on arms and munitions, on insurances and on pharmacy.[275] The legislation referred to under points 3 and 4, is in certain cases subject to disciplinary control by French administrative services, but can be withdrawn by Monaco within six months. Monaco can freely denounce, subject to this six months' notice, the conventions which oblige it to adopt and apply the laws in question. The only exception to this principle is the French banking legislation. As we have seen in the cases of Liechtenstein and San Marino, certain treaty obligations which imply the application or adoption of foreign legislation do not prejudice a State's independence if the treaty can be freely denounced by either party.[276] However, French banking legislation applicable in Monaco does not in itself restrict Monaco's formal independence in a substantial way. It concerns a part of Monaco's economic life without prejudice to other economic domains in which Monaco is free to legislate as it wishes, possibly subject to the denunciation of conventions with France (customs matters, insurance companies and pharmacies).

5. *Residence permit* A foreigner, who is not French, cannot reside in Monaco without having obtained a French visa. This condition can be withdrawn by denouncing the Franco-Monégasque Convention of vicinage of 1963.[277] Monaco's independence would thus seem not to be compromised.

6. *Defence* France's duty of defence is not linked to the presence of military forces in Monaco, which cannot traverse the Monégasque territory in times of peace without the previous agreement of the

---

[273] See pp. 283–285 above.
[274] See further pp. 285–287 and 289–290 above.
[275] See further pp. 285–290 above.
[276] Cf. Liechtenstein, pp. 201–202 above and San Marino, p. 258 above at n. 346 and accompanying text.
[277] See p. 289 above.

Monégasque Government. The duty of defence concerns a defence of Monaco's independence and is therefore not considered prejudicial to Monaco's independence.[278]

7 *Duty of non-alienation* The obligation not to ally the Monégasque territory with any Power other than France does not alter Monaco's present international status, but aims to preserve it in the long term. Strictly speaking the duty of non-alienation cannot be considered a restriction of Monaco's independence as it leaves the present choice of the Monégasque people to constitute a State intact.

8 *Obligations under the 1918 treaty* The core of the problem lies in the Franco-Monégasque treaty of 1918 which sets forth three provisions which compromise Monaco's independence. On the one hand, Monaco has to keep the exercise of its sovereign rights (internal as well as international acts) in perfect conformity with French political, military, naval and economic interests, it has to seek France's previous consent if it wants to establish a consular or diplomatic mission abroad, appoint a head of the mission or conclude a treaty (the consent is presumed if France is itself a party to that treaty) and France has the right to disapprove a regent or successor to the Monégasque throne, which can lead to a vacancy on the throne and thus to the imposition of a French protectorate. On the other hand, the same treaty of 1918 stipulates that France shall assure the defence of Monaco's independence and sovereignty,[279] whereas the interpretative exchange of letters of 1918, which has the same legal value as the treaty of 1918 and which determines its interpretation, states that the duty to comply with certain French interests should not prejudice Monaco's independence and sovereignty.[280] If it were not for those latter provisions, one would be forced to conclude that Monaco lacks sufficient formal independence and only enjoys a considerable measure of autonomy. France would seem to have the right to demand that Monaco conforms all Monégasque acts, whether internal or international, to its political, military, naval or economic interests, while at the same time certain Monégasque acts would need special French approval. Moreover, though France cannot dethrone a ruling Prince, it can nevertheless bar the access to the throne to any pretender to the throne, thus provoking a vacancy, leading to a Monégasque autonomous State under French protectorate. This would lead to a large discretionary power of

---

[278] See p. 290 above.
[279] Art. 1, 1st para. of the treaty of 1918. See p. 275 above at n. 102 and p. 290 above.
[280] First para. of the 1918 exchange of letters. See p. 275 above at n. 105 and accompanying text.

France to intervene in Monégasque internal and international affairs which under present international law would not leave Monaco a sufficient margin of formal independence.

This international legal consequence contrasts sharply with the intention of the parties. Does the duty to defend Monaco's independence and the wish not to prejudice Monaco's independence, through its compliance with certain French interests, contradict the actual duties imposed on Monaco under the treaty of 1918? In other words, does the intention of the parties conflict with the wording of the treaty of 1918? According to customary international law, a treaty shall be interpreted 'in good faith in accordance with the ordinary meaning to be given to the terms of the treaty in their context and in the light of its object and purpose'.[281] One may presume that the contracting parties did not intend to include contradictory obligations in the 1918 treaty and in the exchange of letters. By analogy with the *Nuclear Tests* case,[282] treaties limiting a State's freedom of action should be interpreted in a restrictive manner. The key provision of the treaty of 1918 is Article 1, second paragraph according to which Monaco has to comply with French political, military, naval and economic interests.[283] This article does not disclose whether the duty of compliance is a permanent one nor how vital the French interests must be in order to be respected. Moreover, French approval of certain international acts by Monaco can only be refused if French political, military, naval or economic interests are at stake. Article 2, first paragraph of the treaty of 1918 does not grant an arbitrary right of refusal to France, but should be read in the light of the general obligation of Monaco under Article 1, second paragraph, namely to observe certain French interests. Article 2, first paragraph ensures that this is done in the international field through the duty to seek France's consent. It therefore lays down a supplementary technical guarantee for France. It cannot however be forgotten that the purpose of the treaty of 1918 is also to preserve Monaco's indepen-

---

[281] Art. 31 (1) of the Vienna Convention on the Law of Treaties codifying a rule of customary international law. Neither France nor Monaco are parties to this Convention.

[282] ICJ Reports (1974) para. 44. See also M. Ris, 'Treaty Interpretation and ICJ Recourse to *Travaux préparatoires*: Towards a Proposed Amendment to Articles 31 and 32 of the Vienna Convention on the Law of Treaties', *Boston College International and Comparative Law Review* (1991) pp. 111–136; and in general E. S. Yambruzic, *Treaty Interpretation* (1987).

[283] See for precise text pp. 275–279 above.

dence. This flows from the fact that France has promised to defend Monaco's independence by force if the need arises. One presumes that France would therefore also be prepared to defend and respect Monaco's independence by less aggressive means. In addition, France has explicitly stated in the interpretative exchange of letters to the treaty of 1918 that the duty to comply with certain French interests should not prejudice Monaco's independence. The parties to the treaty were not obliged to emphasize this point. However, as they have done so, the obligations imposed on Monaco should be interpreted in the light of this intended maintenance of independence. As a consequence, the following interpretation of the provisions of the treaty of 1918 was intended by the parties:

1. Monaco has to comply, in its internal and international order, with French political, military, naval and economic interests as long as it does not consider that its independence has disappeared. This implies, from an international legal point of view, that the duty of compliance should not be absolute nor permanent and that only primary French interests of the most essential importance are to be respected by Monaco, and only as long as fundamental interests of the Monégasque State do not prevail. This would be the meaning of the term 'intérêts' in Article 1, second paragraph of the treaty of 1918. Accordingly, Monaco has no legal duty to conform its vote in international conferences or organizations in a permanent manner to the French vote or position.
2. French consent for certain international actions to be taken by Monaco may not be refused if essential French political, military, naval or economic interests are not at stake within the meaning of point 1.
3. France can only disapprove a regent or successor to the Monégasque throne by reason of extremely compelling French national interests.

This does not solve the question of what 'essential or primary French interests' are. It may well be that, in practice, France demands an absolute compliance with all interests whatever their value. Though having the colour of right such demands would legally violate the treaty of 1918 as they would prejudice Monaco's formal independence. France has promised to defend and not to prejudice Monaco's independence. If *de facto* it does not keep its promise, there is no reason to 'reward' this illegal action by France by concluding that Monaco has therefore no formal independence. By virtue of the maxim *ex injuria jus non oritur*, Monaco's formal independence is maintained if France intervenes illegally in its internal or international affairs.

Before drawing final conclusions on Monaco's statehood it should first be considered whether the Monégasque people has the right of self-determination with force of *jus cogens*. This question is answered in the next paragraph and enables us to solve the question of Monaco's formal and actual independence.

Self-determination of the Monégasque people

At this point of the analysis we have not yet determined whether or not Monaco is a State under international law. We have concluded in Chapter 1 (p. 103) that a people will have the right of self-determination with force of *jus cogens* if the full exercise of this right does not disrupt, partially or totally, the territorial integrity of an existing State. The territory of the Principality of Monaco has been defined by the Franco-Monégasque treaty of 2 February 1861 (by which Menton and Roquebrune were ceded to France) and by the Franco-Monégasque Convention on maritime delimitation of 16 February 1984.[284] It has therefore been established that Monaco is not an integral part of France nor a part of the territory of any other existing State.[285] Monaco has been a separate territory at least since the sixteenth century, though receiving military protection from other States. Moreover, since its admission to the United Nations, there can be no doubt that Monaco is a State entitled to the legal protection flowing from the principle of self-determination.[286] If therefore Monaco were to have a people within the meaning of the right of self-determination, it would have a *jus cogens* right of self-determination. The 5,070 Monégasque nationals distinguish themselves from their neighbouring people on historical, traditional, cultural and to a certain extent on linguistic grounds. There exists a distinct Monégasque language which is not the official language of the State and is no longer spoken by all Monégasque nationals. The objective characteristics of the Monégasque nation have been formed by ages of togetherness, relative autonomy and an attachment to the

---

[284] See p. 261 above.
[285] Cf. the right of self-determination of the Andorran people, pp. 372–373 below.
[286] Art. 1 (2) of the UN Charter. See pp. 12–17 above.

traditional organization and reign of the Grimaldi family. The subjective element is present in the we-consciousness of the Monégasque nationals who want to be considered a people desirous to live in a separate State. The core of the Monégasque people is composed of the descendants of families who have lived in the Monégasque territory for centuries, some since the Grimaldi family took possession of Monaco. The objective characteristics, though not striking, are noticeable and strengthened by a traditional attachment to the territory and the monarchy. Therefore, the Monégasque people has a *jus cogens* right of self-determination without prejudice to whether it constitutes one people or a fraction of a people.

Application of the criteria for statehood: final analysis

In the event of a vacancy on the throne, whether provoked by a French refusal of all pretenders to the throne or by reason of an absence of direct or adoptive heirs, Monaco will be turned into an autonomous State under French protectorate.[287] The question arises whether this preformed legal solution has been accepted by the Monégasque people, which holds the right of self-determination with force of *jus cogens*.[288] At the time of the drafting of the Franco-Monégasque treaty of 1918 the right of self-determination was not yet accepted as a legally binding right.[289] The treaty of 1918 was concluded by the Prince of Monaco who did not need the approval of the National Council for its ratification.[290] What would be the legal consequence if a vacancy on the throne were ever to occur and if the Monégasque people, by virtue of its right of self-determination, were to refuse a French protectorate and prefer to maintain its statehood? The decision of the Monégasque people could contradict the automatic imposition of the French protectorate under Article 3, second paragraph of the treaty of 1918. This in turn could conflict with a peremptory norm of general international law and be declared void within the meaning of Article 64 of the Vienna Convention on the

---

[287] Art. 3, 2nd para. of the treaty of 1918. See pp. 281–282 above.
[288] See p. 310 above.
[289] See pp. 9–10 above.
[290] In 1919, one member of the National Council had sent a letter to the *Journal de Genève* in which he openly protested against the treaty of 1918 and claimed that the Monégasque nationals had not been given 'la faculté des peuples à disposer d'eux-mêmes'. Protest of L. Auréglia, 'Monaco et le Traité de Paix', *Journal de Genève* (4 Oct. 1919).

Law of Treaties of 1969, if the Monégasque people, by virtue of its right of self-determination with force of *jus cogens*, were to decide to maintain its statehood.

Neither France nor Monaco is a State Party to the Vienna Convention on the Law of Treaties. Moreover, both France and Monaco voted against draft Article 50, according to which a treaty was void if it was in conflict with a peremptory norm of general international law.[291] France explained at the time that the notion *jus cogens* was too vague and might impose upon States international obligations of which they had no clear knowledge and to which they had not subscribed by treaty.[292] Although some States like France and Monaco had doubts about the content and existence of *jus cogens*, there was a general consensus among the participating States in the Vienna Conference that *if* a norm of *jus cogens* were to be established, a treaty which would conflict with this norm would become void.[293] The rule that a treaty is void when it conflicts with a peremptory norm of general international law, whether at its conclusion or because a new rule of *jus cogens* has emerged (as is the case of the treaty of 1918), can be accepted as a customary rule of international law, even if the debate on the content of *jus cogens* has not been closed. We have already demonstrated that the people of a State has the right of self-determination with force of *jus cogens*.[294] As the Monégasque people holds this right too, Article 3, second paragraph of the treaty of 1918 can be declared void, if the Monégasque people so wishes, by virtue of a customary rule in international law and despite the fact that neither France nor Monaco has ratified the Vienna Convention on the Law of Treaties.[295]

---

[291] *United Nations Conference on the Law of Treaties, Official Records*, Second Session (1969) p. 107.
[292] Ibid., pp. 94–95. See also O. Deleau, 'Les Positions françaises à la Conférence de Vienne sur le Droit des Traités', AFDI (1969) pp. 16–30.
[293] L. Hannikainen, *Peremptory Norms (Jus Cogens) in International Law* (1988) p. 178.
[294] See p. 103 above.
[295] By virtue of Art. 44 (3) of the Vienna Convention on the Law of Treaties only Art. 3, 2nd para. of the 1918 treaty is void and not the treaty as a whole, as the clause is separable from the other provisions, does not seem to be an essential basis of the consent of the parties to be bound by the whole treaty and because the continued performance of the remainder of the treaty would not be unjust. As neither France nor Monaco are State Parties to the Vienna Convention on the Law of Treaties a possible dispute on the nullity of Art. 3, 2nd para. of the 1918 treaty cannot be brought before the ICJ under Art. 66 (a) of the Vienna Convention.

Under these circumstances the possibility of France turning Monaco into a French protectorate cannot be considered prejudicial to Monaco's present formal independence as under modern international law the French protectorate cannot be imposed without the express approval of the Monégasque people. It can be inferred that Monaco's obligations towards France under the Franco-Monégasque treaty of 1918 do not derogate from its formal independence. France has no discretionary authority to rule upon and intervene in the internal and external affairs of Monaco.[296]

Does Monaco also have actual independence? France's duty to respect Monaco's independence also extends to the protection of its actual independence, without which Monaco's independence and statehood will not be complete. If France meets its commitments, Monaco's actual independence will not be impinged upon. What are the legal consequences for Monaco's statehood if France nevertheless uses or threatens to use coercive measures to compel Monaco to adopt certain legislation or to take certain actions which are prejudicial to its independence? We have stated that, in the case of San Marino, one should distinguish between lack of actual independence and lack of economic and functional independence which can be used by a third State, in an illegal way, as a means of pressure to enforce its demands.[297] The latter situation should not impinge upon a putative State's actual independence.[298] An official protest by the people in question against the concessions it has been compelled to make is a *conditio sine qua non* in order to preserve its independence and statehood, otherwise its consent to be bound by the imposed obligations can be seen as an expression of its right of self-determination. It may be difficult to determine whether Monaco has made just one concession too many, for due to French threats of pressure certain concessions may become 'voluntary' concessions. In practice France may be the judge of its own interests, especially as the 1918 treaty does not include a denunciation clause, nor an arbitral procedure in case of a dispute on the interpretation of the provisions. The mechanisms provided for the peaceful settlement of disputes in the OSCE and the UN are therefore a clear advancement of the defence of Monaco's independence, although none of them can be effective

---

[296] *Contra*, J. Crawford, *The Creation of States in International Law* (1979) p. 56. See also p. 123 above at nn. 86–87 and accompanying text.
[297] See p. 258 above.
[298] See pp. 126–127 above.

without France's cooperation. In the absence of this and of Monaco's protests against attacks on its independence, international recognition will have the value of affirming its statehood in the long term – a constitutive effect of recognition, which will only turn fully declaratory once Monaco has all legal and practical means to defend its independence in all circumstances.[299] Due to lacking means of international judicial control, Monaco's actual independence will not be fully guaranteed in practice, even if it has formal independence. It cannot impose a restrictive and correct interpretation of the treaty of 1918.

Monaco maintains diplomatic or consular relations with sixty-six States which have recognized its statehood. This fact does not indicate whether these States recognized Monaco as a State because they considered that Monaco was sufficiently independent or despite its lack of independence and therefore by constitutive recognition. The only international organization which examined Monaco's statehood was UNESCO. It concluded that Monaco was sufficiently independent to be a State, regardless of its recognition.[300] Its conclusions were unfortunately based on erroneous arguments and a summary investigation into the Franco-Monégasque relations. Nevertheless we can infer that Monaco has in any case been firmly recognized as a State by the Member States of the United Nations. As a consequence, the Principality of Monaco is a State under international law reinforced by international recognition.

Conclusions

In the light of the purposes of this study we can draw the following conclusions with regard to the legal situation of the Principality of Monaco:

---

[299] It should furthermore be remembered that if France nevertheless does not respect Monaco's independence by imposing obligations which are too burdensome, it violates the Franco-Monégasque treaty of 1918. Given the fact that respect for Monaco's independence is essential to the accomplishment of the object and purpose of this treaty, Monaco could invoke this material breach as a ground for terminating the treaty of 1918 or for suspending its operation in whole or in part: Art. 60 (1) and (3) of the Vienna Convention on the Law of Treaties, codifying customary law according to the ICJ in its advisory opinion on *Legal Consequences for States of the Continued Presence of South Africa in Namibia (South West Africa) notwithstanding Security Council Resolution 276 (1970)*, ICJ Reports (1971) p. 47, para. 94.

[300] See pp. 295–296 above.

1   Certain historical, political and practical reasons have prompted Monaco to establish close contractual relations with France. Franco-Monégasque relations are in principle based on respect for and defence of Monaco's independence and statehood. The treaty obligations imposed on Monaco have to be fulfilled and interpreted in this light. France has therefore, legally, no discretionary right to intervene in Monaco's internal and external relations. Monaco is a State under international law and is recognized as such by a large number of States with constitutive effect, that is, its actual independence needs to be secured in practice. This constitutive effect will turn fully declaratory once Monaco has the judicial means to enforce a correct interpretation of the Franco-Monégasque treaty of 1918.
2   The extent of Monaco's obligations towards France is to be determined according to the general rules of international law with respect to the minimum degree of independence required in order to be a State. Accordingly, Monaco's duty to respect France's political, military, naval and economic interests is of an exceptional nature and only concerns primary French national interests of essential value, as long as Monégasque national interests do not prevail.
3   By virtue of the right of self-determination of the Monégasque people, the statehood of the Principality is guaranteed even in the case of a vacancy on the throne.

7 The Principality of Andorra

Territory, population and economy

The Principality of Andorra is a political entity with a land area of 467.76 square kilometres enclosed by France and Spain.[1] At the last census of 1989, Andorra comprised 46,166 inhabitants, of whom 11,218 were Andorran nationals, that is, 24.3 per cent, against 54.7 per cent Spanish and 6.5 per cent French citizens.[2] In 1989, the official statistics showed an import surplus of 102.5 thousand million pesetas.[3] There is, nevertheless, no doubt that the Andorran economy is strongly export-oriented due to the development of its tourist sector and the inflow of capital which this entails.[4] Most of Andorra's

---

[1] M. I. Consell General, ed., *Estadistiques de les Valls d'Andorra* (1977) p. 23. It has been stated that the frontiers of the Principality of Andorra are not fixed as there is no delimitation laid down by treaty. The borderline is thus formed, on the French side, by the frontiers of the French department and the Andorran parishes as based on the Treaty of Corbeil of 1258, and, on the Spanish side, by the delimitation line set forth in a treaty between Andorra and Spain of 1863 initially not recognized by France. See B. Bélinguier, *La Condition juridique des Vallées d'Andorre* (1970) p. 210; K. Zemanek, *Le Statut international de l'Andorre: Situation actuelle et Perspectives de Réforme* (1980) p. 4; and P. Raton, *Le Statut international de la Principauté d'Andorre*, 2nd edn (1990) p. 46.

[2] The remaining inhabitants are composed of 8.5 per cent Portuguese, 1.6 per cent English and 4.4 per cent other nationals. The official Catalan language in Andorra is spoken by 44.5 per cent of the inhabitants: G. Martínez Díez, ed., *Recull Estadístic General de la Població d'Andorra 1989, 1ers Resultats* (1989) no page numbering. Another source, which seems less precise, notes that on 31 Dec. 1988 Andorra had 50,528 inhabitants of whom there were 53 per cent Spanish, 17 per cent Andorran, 8 per cent French and 5 per cent Portuguese nationals: *Pla de Salut per Andorra (1990–1991)* (Oct. 1989) p. 25.

[3] Andorra Govern, *Estadístiques de Comerç Exterior, Importacions–Exportacions Any 1989* (1990) p. 8.

[4] A. Pes, 'El Sistema Financiero de Andorra', in A. Sabater Tomas, ed., *La Notaria: Estudios Monograficos Dedicados al Derecho Civil del Principado de Andorra (1982–1983)* (1986) p. 502. Of the residents in Andorra 75.9 per cent are active in the service sector

exports are directed towards France (61.5 per cent) and Spain (25.6 per cent).[5] The State budget of the Principality of Andorra of 1995 foresaw a deficit of 4.0 thousand million pesetas.[6] The indirect taxes are the main source of income of the State, covering 86.5 per cent of the total receipts in 1995.[7] There are no direct taxes on revenues or company earnings in Andorra.[8]

History

According to legend, Andorra was conquered by Charlemagne from the Moors, but the true origins of the Principality are contested.[9] In 819, Louis I, Charlemagne's son, granted the Valleys of Andorra to the Count of Urgell[10] whose descendant exchanged his possessions in Andorra with the Bishop of Urgell for other parishes in 988.[11] In the eleventh century, the Bishop of Urgell granted Andorra in fief to the Caboet family of France in order to strengthen the military protection of his possessions in the Valleys. Subsequently, their feudal rights were passed by marriage to the Count of Foix in 1208.[12] As the Count of Foix strongly contested the supreme authority of the Bishop of Urgell over Andorra in the subsequent period, it was decided that the ongoing disputes should be settled by agreement and through the intervention of the Bishop of Valencia. Thus on 6 September 1278, the Bishop of Urgell and the Count of Foix signed an agreement, the

---

(including trade, hotels, government administration and professions), while 22.9 per cent work in the industrial sector and 1.2 per cent in the agricultural sector. Martínez Díez, *Recull Estadístic General*, no page numbering.

[5] Andorra Govern, *Estadístiques Any 1989*, p. 39. Of the exports 10.2 per cent is directed towards other EC States, thus making a total of 97.3 per cent exportation to the EC as a whole, against 2.7 per cent to other countries. Ibid. In 1989, clothing comprised 39 per cent of exports, against 12.3 per cent for alcoholic beverages and 10.3 per cent for electrical appliances and machines.

[6] BOPA (1995) no. 15, pp. 297–304.

[7] Ibid. See further on new indirect taxes since 1 Jul. 1991, p. 362 below.

[8] Enterprises in Andorra pay a fixed annual sum dependent on the number of employees and the nature of their commercial activities. Landlords have to pay up to 10 per cent of their revenues from rents to the parishes (the 'Inquilinat'). Interview with Mr Josep Miquel Vila Barstida, inspector of taxes Andorran Government ('interventor') of 19 Dec. 1990.

[9] J. A. Brutails, *La Coutume d'Andorre*, 2nd edn (1965) p. 23.

[10] A. Blaustein and G. Flanz, eds., *Constitutions of the Countries of the World* (1976): Andorra, p. 1.

[11] Raton, *Le Statut international*, p. 11.

[12] Ibid., p. 12 and O. Casanovas i La Rosa, *Andorra devant el Dret Internacional* (1972) p. 3.

Pariatge, by virtue of which they defined their corresponding rights.[13] The basis of the *Pariatge* of 1278 remained that the Count of Foix held the feud of Andorra from the Bishop of Urgell in perpetuity.[14] The Count had the right to send a permanent representative to Andorra, the *veguer*. In addition, the Count and the Bishop were to receive a biennial contribution, the *qüèstia*, from the Andorran population. Up to present times, the Andorrans have insisted on paying the *qüèstia* to the co-Princes personally and not to their neighbouring States.[15] The stipulations of the *Pariatge* were not scrupulously implemented, which led to new disputes and uncertainties.[16] A second *Pariatge* was therefore concluded on 6 December 1288.[17] The *Pariatges* are the founding documents of the present institutions of Andorra, although they did not expressly set forth the equal rights of the Count of Foix and the Bishop of Urgell in every legal domain. The development of the shared sovereignty over Andorra has been primarily of a customary nature.

A significant event for the institutional development of Andorra was the coming to the French throne of the Count of Foix who became King Henry IV of France in 1590. In 1607, by the 'Edit de Réunion' he incorporated all his lands in the French Crown.[18] It is since this date that the Head of the French State has been at the same time a co-Prince of Andorra. When the monarchy was abolished in France, the French President took over the rights of the King, including his co-sovereignty over Andorra. It was only during a brief period between 1793 and 1806 that the French co-Prince, due to the abolition of the feudal rights in France, refused to receive his biennial

---

[13] Original Latin text and Catalan translation in J. Riera i Simó, *El Pariatge d'Andorra* (1978) pp. 3 ff.

[14] Art. IV of the 1278 *Pariatge* reads (in modern Catalan): '[el] comte de Foix i tots els seus successors tinguin en feu, perpètuament, del bisbe d'Urgell i dels seus successors, tot el que té i rep, i tot el que ha de tenir i rebre en la Vall o les Valls i homes d'Andorra'.

[15] Art. I of the 1278 *Pariatge*. The Bishop could receive 4,000 monetary units ('sous') every even year and the Count of Foix could fix his contribution at his discretion for every odd year. The Bishop receives at present 450 pesetas and the French President 960 francs. The Andorrans refused to pay the *qüèstia* to the French State and since 1963 present the symbolic sum of money at a ceremony in the Elysée Palace. Raton, *Le Statut international*, p. 53 at n. 14.

[16] The Pope had come too late with his confirmation provided for in Art. IX of the 1278 *Pariatge*. N. Marquès i Oste, *La Reforma de les Institucions d'Andorra (1975-1981): Aspectes Interns i Internacionals* (1989) p. 201.

[17] Arts. I, IV and VI of the 1288 *Pariatge*. Catalan text in J. Bartumeu i Cassany et al., *L'Estat Andorrà: Recull de Textos Legislatius i Constitucionals d'Andorra* (1977) pp. 30 ff.

[18] Raton, *Le Statut international*, p. 18.

contribution, the *qüèstia*, from the Andorrans.[19] Due to the lack of a clear written document the rights of both co-Princes in Andorra remained an unsolved and disputed question, which only found an answer in the factual situation.

Between 1931 and 1933 there was a climate of political unrest in Andorra due to certain political events in the neighbouring countries and internal movements. When in 1931 the Spanish monarchy was overthrown and replaced by a Republican Government, Spain asked the Bishop of Urgell to cede his rights over Andorra to it.[20] The Bishop refused and was supported by the French co-Prince. The tension was also of an internal order. In 1931, the General Council (Andorra's Parliament) had at its own initiative authorized the establishment of a gambling house in Andorra. This unlawful authorization was immediately cancelled by the co-Princes which generated violent protests from the General Council.[21] In addition, the General Council had granted a concession to Spain to install Andorra's telephone network, which again was cancelled by the co-Princes.[22] The controversy between the General Council and the co-Princes was accentuated in 1933 because of the General Council's wish to introduce universal male suffrage. The General Council therefore adopted a new electoral law which was considered void by the co-Princes. The General Council was dissolved and a provisional one installed.[23] In the same year, new elections were called and the co-Princes approved by Decree the establishment of universal male suffrage.[24]

---

[19] J. M. Vidal i Guitart, *Història d'Andorra* (1984) pp. 99–102. The Andorrans did not favour the non-use of the French co-Prince's rights in Andorra, as they feared that if in practice they would only be subject to the authority of the Bishop, they would be treated as foreigners in France and would not be assured of the customs exemptions on imported goods from France. They addressed therefore an official petition to Napoleon I demanding, *inter alia*, the re-establishment of the relations between Andorra and the French co-Prince as they had been before 1793. By Imperial Decree of 27 Mar. 1806 Napoleon restored the ancient administrative, police and trade relations with France, appointed a *veguer* and accepted the *qüèstia*.

[20] M. J. Pelaez and J. Guillamet i Anton, 'La Situación Politica de los Valles de Andorra en Abril de 1936: El Informe de Joaquim Saltor i Madorell', *Cuadernos Informativos de Derecho Historico Publico, Procesal y de la Navegación* (Jun. 1990) nos. 12–13, p. 2848.

[21] L. Armengol Vila, *Approche à l'Histoire de l'Andorre* (1983) p. 28.

[22] Pelaez and Guillamet i Anton, 'La Situación Politica', pp. 2849–2850. In the end the co-Princes decided that the construction would be realized by France.

[23] A. Morell, 'Una Revolució Andorrana: 1933', 2 *Quaderns d'Estudis Andorrans* (1977) pp. 67–70.

[24] Ibid., pp. 78–79 with full text of the Decree modifying the electoral system.

During the First World War, the Second World War and the Spanish Civil War Andorra remained neutral territory. From 1936 to 1940 the co-Princes agreed to send French troops to the Spanish–Andorran border in order to protect the territory against possible Spanish intrusion.[25] In 1944, French troops entered Andorran territory again and at the request of the Bishop the Spanish civil guard did the same. The Spanish guards were eventually withdrawn, leaving the French troops under the common authority of the co-Princes.[26] After the Second World War, the situation in Andorra was characterized by strong economic growth, occasional differences of opinion between the co-Princes on the delimitation of their rights in the international field, a codification of Andorran customary law and, in general, by the development of a codified legal system with defined institutions the areas of competence of which were laid down and restricted by law.

Constitutional and legal order
Form of government

Institutional reforms of the Andorran legal order were initiated in 1975, when the permanent commission of the General Council, the General Syndicate, addressed a letter to the co-Princes requesting a reconsideration and adaptation of the Andorran institutions.[27] This petition, which received a favourable reply from the co-Princes, aimed to solve the problems emanating from the gaps in the Andorran legal order, the absence of codified laws and the uncertainties in the delimitation of the area of competence of each institution. Although all parties agreed that a restructuring of the Andorran legal order was necessary, the process of reform took eighteen years to complete. During the first stage, up till 1990, the institutional improvements were only of an internal order, while after 1990 the reform also endeavoured to strengthen Andorra's international status so as to permit a greater international representation and activity. This latter purpose had, before 1990, always been thwarted by the French co-Prince.[28]

---

[25] Armengol Vila, *Approche à L'Histoire*, p. 31. Andorra's neutrality during the Spanish Civil War was confirmed in an agreement with Spain of 1940: J. Aznar Sánchez, 'Los Interesos de España en la cuestión de Andorra', *Revista de Política Internacional* (Nov.–Dec. 1974) no. 136, p. 75.

[26] D. Mas, *Les Valls d'Andorra i el Maquis Antifranquista* (1985) pp. 124–139.

[27] Text in Marquès i Oste, *La Reforma*, pp. 309–310.

[28] Ibid., pp. 110–113.

The first effective changes were made in 1978 through the creation of a seventh parish and in 1981 through the establishment of an Executive Council, predecessor of the Andorran Government, which was a step towards the separation of powers.[29] The next stage was announced by the Head of the Executive Council in his declaration of 1990 to the General Council. It was believed to be incumbent upon the Andorran Government to draft and adopt a Constitution based upon the separation of powers and approved by referendum.[30] This act was supposed to assure Andorra's independence.[31] Accordingly, a tripartite commission was created composed of representatives of the General Council and of the two co-Princes which started the process of drafting the Constitution in December 1990. The text of the Constitution was unanimously approved by the General Council on 2 February 1993 and submitted to the Andorran electorate by referendum on 14 March 1993.[32] The draft Constitution was approved by 74.2 per cent of the votes.[33] The Constitution was promulgated and entered into force on 4 May 1993.[34] The main innovations which the Constitution introduced concern the international status of Andorra, a clear acceptance of human rights[35] and the transfer of powers from the co-Princes to the General Council and the Government. Andorra's form of Government has become a compilation of the remnants of the feudal system and the values of modern democracy.

Article 1, paragraph 1 of the Constitution sets forth that the Principality of Andorra is an independent democratic and social State, based on the rule of law.[36] The sovereignty resides in the Andorran people.[37] Andorra's political regime is a parliamentary co-Principality.[38] The co-Princes are, as had been the tradition, jointly and

---

[29] Ibid., pp. 28 and 53 and M. Duverger, *La Reforma de les Institucions d'Andorra* (1981) p. 27. See also *Actes Consell General*, Consell Extraordinari (22 Jan. 1981).
[30] *Declaració sobre l'Orientació Política General del Govern* (1 Jun. 1990) p. 5.
[31] Ibid., p. 6.
[32] Law on the referendum concerning the Constitution of the Principality of Andorra of 5 Febr. 1993, BOPA (1993) no. 7.
[33] Information from the 'Viguerie Française en Andorre', whose functions have been taken over in 1993 by the 'Représentation du co-Prince français en Andorre'.
[34] Original Catalan text in BOPA (1993) no. 24, French translation by the 'Viguerie Française en Andorre'.
[35] See pp. 329–334 below.
[36] Art. 1 (1) of the Constitution states: 'Andorre est un Etat indépendant, de Droit, Démocratique et Social. Son appelation officielle est la Principauté d'Andorre.'
[37] Art. 1 (3) of the Constitution.
[38] Art. 1 (4) of the Constitution.

indivisibly the Head of the State and assume its highest representation.[39] The Bishop of Urgell and the President of the French Republic are, personally and exclusively, the co-Princes who exercise their equal powers in accordance with the Constitution.[40] They commit the Andorran State in the international arena.[41] This provision clearly excludes the hegemony and monopoly of the French co-Prince with regard to the international representation of Andorra, thus burying a controversy which had lasted more than a century. The powers of the co-Princes are limited by the introduction of the countersignature for acts which do not belong to the free prerogatives of the co-Princes. The organ which has countersigned the acts of the co-Princes bears responsibility for them.[42] Another change in the traditional position of the co-Princes introduced by the Constitution is of a financial nature. Before the promulgation of the Constitution, the Bishop of Urgell received a financial contribution from Spain and the French President from the French Republic for the indemnification of their official expenses.[43] At present, the services of the co-Princes are paid from the Andorran State budget which fixes an equal amount for both of them.[44] The Constitution has abolished the institutions of the *veguers* and the permanent delegates of the co-Princes, to replace them by one personal representative of each co-Prince in Andorra.[45] In case of a vacancy of one of the co-Princes, the Andorran Constitution recog-

---

[39] Art. 43 (1) of the Constitution.

[40] Art. 43 (2) of the Constitution. There are three exceptions to the principle that every decision emanating from the co-Princes must be adopted by both of them: the appointment of their representatives, laws and treaties which have been declared in conformity with the Constitution by the Constitutional Tribunal and acts which have not been sanctioned within the prescribed time limits by one of the co-Princes due to circumstances notified by his representative: Art. 45 (2, 2nd para.) and (3).

[41] Art. 44 (1) of the Constitution.

[42] Art. 44 (3) of the Constitution. The Head of the Government, the responsible Minister or the Syndic countersigns, *inter alia*, decisions regarding the dissolution of the General Council, the accreditation and reception of diplomatic representatives, the appointment of the Head of the Government and other State organs, the promulgation of laws and the ratification of international treaties: Art. 45 (1) (c–h). Exempt from the countersignature are, *inter alia*, requests on the constitutionality of laws and treaties before their promulgation or ratification, and the approval of a treaty, in whose drafting the co-Princes have participated, before its parliamentary adoption: Art. 46 (1) (e, f and h).

[43] The Spanish contribution was considered justified in order to compensate the financial facilities of the French co-Prince. Interview with Mr Josep Miquel Vila Barstida, inspector of taxes Andorran Government, 19 Dec. 1990.

[44] Art. 47 of the Constitution.

[45] Art. 48 of the Constitution. The Prefect of the 'Pyrénées-Orientales' used to be the permanent delegate of the French co-Prince, whereas the vicar-general of the diocese of

nizes the substitution mechanisms of their respective organizations, that is, the French Constitution or canon law.[46] There are, in general, no meetings and discussions between the two co-Princes.[47]

The Andorran Parliament, the General Council ('Consell General de les Valls'), is composed of twenty-eight Counsellors of whom one half consists of an equal number of delegates for each of the seven parishes and the other half is elected by national constituency.[48] The General Council is elected for a period of four years by and from the Andorran nationals possessing political rights.[49] The General Council represents the Andorran people, exercises legislative power, approves the State budget and controls the political actions of the Government.[50] In contrast with the pre-existing customary rule, the legislative power no longer belongs to the co-Princes, but to the General Council and the Government.[51] The 1993 Rules of the General Council distinguish two procedures of legislative initiative: on the one hand, draft laws which are submitted to the General Council by the Government[52] and, on the other hand, propositions for draft laws which can be submitted by a parliamentary group, three General Counsellors, three parish councils or a tenth of the national electorate.[53] The essence of their proposition for a draft law will not be voted upon until the General Council has deemed it necessary to take it into consideration.[54] Once a law, including a budgetary law, has been adopted by the General Council, it has to be sanctioned and promulgated by the co-Princes and countersigned by, in general, the

---

Urgell used to be the permanent delegate of the Bishop of Urgell. The representatives acquire Andorran nationality as long as they hold their official positions: Art. 14 of the 1995 Code on Andorran nationality, BOPA (1996) no. 8, p. 158.

[46] Art. 49 of the Constitution.
[47] Interview with HE Mgr Joan Martí I Alanis, Bishop of Urgell, 11 Dec. 1990.
[48] Art. 52 of the Constitution and present state.
[49] Art. 51 (1) and (3) of the Constitution. Andorrans of at least eighteen years old may vote and are eligible for election at the age of twenty-five or thirty for the Syndic and Head of the Government respectively. Women were granted the right to vote in 1970 and have been eligible since 1973. Art. 9 of the Code on Andorran nationality of 7 Sept. 1985 eliminated any discrimination between men and women, and between regular and first generation Andorrans with respect to their political rights: R. Viñas i Farré, *Nacionalitat i Drets Polítics al Principat d'Andorra* (1989), pp. 92–93.
[50] Art. 50 of the Constitution.
[51] Art. 58 (1) of the Constitution. The Government has the exclusive right of initiative for the State budget: Art. 61 (1).
[52] Arts. 92–101 of the Rules of the General Council, BOPA (1993) no. 51, p. 922.
[53] Arts. 102–104 of the Rules of the General Council.
[54] If the General Council refuses to consider a proposition for a draft law, this law would normally stand little chance of being adopted by the General Council in another way.

Head of the Government.[55] The co-Princes or their delegates have the right to request an opinion from the Constitutional Tribunal on the constitutionality of the draft law.[56] International treaties will, in general, need the approval of the General Council in order to be ratified by the co-Princes.[57] The co-Princes ratify the treaties subject to the countersignature of the Head of the Government, but in certain instances they must also participate in the negotiations of the treaty and approve it before its submission to the General Council.[58]

The Government of Andorra is composed of the Head of the Government, appointed by the co-Princes after having been elected by the General Council,[59] and six Ministers. The Government conducts the national and international policy of Andorra, provides the State administration and exercises regulative power.[60] The Government is responsible to the General Council which, under certain conditions, can dismiss the Head of the Government.[61] The Head of the Government may ask the co-Princes to dissolve the General Council subject to his countersignature.[62] The members of the Government cannot at the same time be General Counsellors.[63]

> The only exception can be that the decision whether or not to take a proposition for a draft law into consideration must be taken by simple majority of the members present in the General Council, whereas the final debate of a draft law should be concluded in a plenary session and adopted by simple majority (which is therefore necessarily an absolute majority): Art. 104 (1) *juncto* Arts. 70 (1) and 101 (1) of the Rules of the General Council.
>
> [55] Arts. 45 (1) (g) and 63 of the Constitution. The laws and decrees have been published in an official statute book since 1989. Before that time, the Andorran laws and decrees were often published by private publicists such as A. Sabater Tomas, ed., *La Notaria: Estudios Recopilados de Legislación y Jurisprudencia Correspondiente al Derecho Civil del Principado de Andorra (1982–1983)* (1986).
> [56] Arts. 46 (1) (e) of the Constitution.
> [57] If they treat territorial matters, human rights, diplomatic representations, concern relations with international organizations or create financial obligations. If legislative, executive or judicial powers are devolved to international organizations an approval by a two-thirds majority of the members of the General Council is required: Arts. 64 (1) (a, c–e and g) and 65 of the Constitution.
> [58] Arts. 64 (b, c and g) and 66 (1) of the Constitution. It concerns exclusively treaties with neighbouring States relating to internal security, defence, the territory of Andorra, consular and diplomatic relations and judicial or penitentiary cooperation.
> [59] Arts. 68 and 73 of the Constitution.
> [60] Art. 72 (2) of the Constitution.
> [61] Art. 69 of the Constitution. Through a vote of no-confidence or by rejecting a vote of confidence demanded by the Head of the Government: Art. 70.
> [62] Art. 71 (1) of the Constitution.
> [63] Art. 78 (2) of the Constitution and Art. 63 of the 1993 law on the electoral regime and on referenda, BOPA (1993) no. 51, pp. 876 ff.

The Andorran people has acquired more political rights under the Constitution than it had before. Thus, besides the right of legislative initiative, the co-Princes, at the request of the Government and subject to approval by the General Council, can hold a referendum on any political question.[64] A referendum is mandatory for an amendment of the Constitution which has been approved by at least two-thirds of the members of the General Council.[65]

A Constitutional Tribunal composed of four judges has special competences to ensure the correct implementation of the Constitution.[66] The Constitutional Tribunal can be consulted, *inter alia*, in the following proceedings:

1. Proceedings on unconstitutionality of laws or legislative decrees.[67]
2. Preliminary requests for a judgment concerning the constitutionality of international treaties, before their ratification.[68]
3. Preliminary rulings if a tribunal has, in the course of a proceeding, doubts about the constitutionality of a law or legislative decree.[69]
4. Protection of the Constitutional Tribunal against the acts of public authorities which infringe upon the fundamental human rights.[70]

The protection and the supremacy of the Constitution have certain limits. The Constitutional Tribunal cannot examine the constitutionality of norms which are not laws or legislative decrees, such as customary rules and edicts, except for its general competence to hear claims concerning the violation of fundamental human rights by acts

---

[64] Art. 76 of the Constitution.

[65] Art. 106 of the Constitution. If the constitutional reform has been approved by referendum, the co-Princes are obliged to sanction and promulgate the new text: Art. 107. The reform of the Constitution can only be initiated by the co-Princes jointly or by a third of the members of the General Council: Art. 105 of the Constitution and Art. 115 (1) of the Rules of the General Council.

[66] Each co-Prince appoints one judge, without countersignature, and the two other judges are appointed by the General Council: Art. 96 (1) of the Constitution and Art. 10 (1) of the law on the Constitutional Tribunal, BOPA (1993) no. 51, pp. 852 ff.

[67] Arts. 45 (2), 46 (1) (e), 98 (b) and 99 (1) of the Constitution. At the request of a fifth of the members of the General Council, of the Head of the Government or of three *Comúns* (within thirty days of their publication) or at the request of the co-Princes jointly or separately (before the publication of a law).

[68] Art. 101 (1) of the Constitution. At the request of the co-Princes jointly or separately, of the Head of the Government or of a fifth of the members of the General Council.

[69] Art. 100 (1) of the Constitution.

[70] Art. 102 of the Constitution. See p. 328 below. This proceeding can be instituted by individuals, also before the coming into force of acts of the General Council, and by the Public Prosecutor in case of a violation of fundamental rights in the judicial process.

of public authorities.[71] Treaties which before their ratification were not tested on their constitutionality cannot be examined by the Constitutional Tribunal if their unconstitutionality becomes apparent only after ratification. Under Andorra's constitutional order, the main elements of the legislative and executive powers have been transferred from the co-Princes to the General Council and the Government, without, however, abandoning the co-Princes' right of veto for the promulgation of laws, the ratification of treaties and the appointment of the Head of the Government.

Judicial system

The Andorran Constitution of 1993 has introduced a considerable reform of the judicial organization. In the first place, justice is no longer administered in the name of the co-Princes, but in the name of the Andorran people.[72] In the second place, all special jurisdictions are prohibited.[73] In the third place, one Supreme Tribunal of Justice has been established in Andorra to replace the dual jurisdiction of, on the one hand, the Supreme Tribunal of Perpignan and, on the other hand, the Supreme Tribunal of the Mitre in Urgell, which both used to be competent to judge civil matters in third instance.[74] In the fourth place, the judges of the tribunals are no longer appointed by the co-Princes, but by a newly established Supreme Council of Justice.[75] The Supreme Council of Justice controls the independence

---

[71] Arts. 41 (2), 98 (c) and 102 of the Constitution.
[72] Art. 85 (1) of the Constitution.
[73] Art. 85 (2) of the Constitution. This meant the abolition of several recently established tribunals, such as the Administrative and Fiscal Tribunal (established by law of 7 Sept. 1991, BOPA (1991) no. 38, p. 703) and the 'Tribunal Superior de Corts', a court of appeal in penal cases (created by Decrees of 12 Jul. 1990 and 16 Apr. 1991, BOPA (1991) no. 17, p. 319).
[74] The Supreme Tribunal of Perpignan was composed of the President of the Perpignan Regional Court, the French *veguer* and two other members appointed by the French co-Prince, namely a member of the Perpignan Bar and a person chosen for his knowledge of the language and customs of Andorra. The Supreme Tribunal of the Mitre comprised six judges appointed by the Bishop of Urgell. Sabater Tomas, *La Notaria: Estudios Recopilados*, pp. XVI–XVII.
[75] Art. 89 (3) of the Constitution. Only the four judges of the Constitutional Tribunal are not appointed by the Supreme Council of Justice. All judges are appointed each time for a period of six years: Art. 90 (1). The Supreme Council of Justice is composed of five members, one appointed by each co-Prince, one by the Syndic, one by the Head of the Government and one by the judges and Bailiffs ('Battles') for a period of six years: Art. 89 (2) of the Constitution. The members of the Supreme Council of Justice have to be Andorran nationals: Art. 89 (1), except for the representatives of the co-Princes during the first six years after the establishment of the Supreme Council: para. 5 of the second transitional provision.

and proper functioning of the judiciary.[76] It can take disciplinary action against judges within the limits of the law.[77] The independence of the judiciary is guaranteed by the Constitution.[78]

Since October 1993, the Andorran judiciary has been composed of three courts which judge penal, civil and administrative cases. These courts are: the Bailiffs (sitting as a Tribunal of three Bailiffs or as a Sole Bailiff) who are at least eight in number,[79] the 'Tribunal de Corts' composed of three judges and the Supreme Tribunal of Justice ('Tribunal Superior de Justicia') comprising nine judges.[80]

In penal cases, a Sole Bailiff judges small infringements of the law, whereas the Tribunal of Bailiffs and the 'Tribunal de Corts' consider minor and serious offences, respectively, in first instance.[81] Appeal against the sentences of the Sole Bailiff or the Tribunal of Bailiffs lies before the 'Tribunal de Corts'.[82] The judgment of the 'Tribunal de Corts' acting in first instance can be challenged before the Supreme Tribunal of Justice.[83] There is no third instance, though a request for a revision of its own judgment can be submitted before the Supreme Tribunal of Justice, whether in penal, civil or administrative cases.[84]

Andorra has had a codified Code of Criminal Procedure since 1984 and a Penal Code since 1990.[85] A person sentenced to an imprisonment of less than three months will serve his sentence in the prison of Andorra.[86] In other cases, the convicted person may choose between a French or a Spanish prison.[87] The right of pardon is a prerogative held by the co-Princes jointly.[88]

---

[76] Art. 89 (1) of the Constitution.
[77] Art. 89 (3) and (4) of the Constitution and Arts. 79–87 of the 1993 law on the judicial system, BOPA (1993) no. 51, pp. 864 ff.
[78] Art. 85 (1) of the Constitution.
[79] They have to be Andorran, whereas judges should be preferably, but not necessarily, of Andorran nationality: Art. 31 of the 1993 law on the judicial system and para. 1 of the second transitional provision of the Constitution. Foreign judges should be either French or Spanish nationals.
[80] Arts. 47, 53 and 57 of the 1993 law on the judicial system, BOPA (1993) no. 51, p. 864.
[81] Arts. 49 (2) and 52 (1) of the 1993 law on the judicial system.
[82] Art. 52 (4) of the 1993 law on the judicial system.
[83] Art. 56, 2nd para. of the 1993 law on the judicial system.
[84] Art. 56, 3rd para. of the 1993 law on the judicial system.
[85] Code of Criminal Procedure amended on 16 Febr. 1989 and on 16 Jul. 1990, and Penal Code of 11 Jul. 1990, BOPA (1990) no. 21, pp. 377 ff. Before their codification the criminal procedure and penal legislation were based on customary law, decrees of the *veguers* and jurisprudence.
[86] Art. 234 of the Code of Criminal Procedure.
[87] Customary rule applied since the twelfth century.
[88] Art. 46 (1) (a) of the Constitution.

Civil jurisdiction is exercised in first instance by a Sole Bailiff or the Tribunal of Bailiffs depending on the amount of money which is claimed or involved in the dispute.[89] The Supreme Tribunal of Justice will act as a court of appeal against all civil judgments pronounced by the Bailiffs (alone or in the Tribunal).[90] There is no Civil Code nor a Code of Civil Procedure in Andorra.[91]

Any person whose rights have been prejudiced by a decision, or a failure to act, of a public authority can ask for a revision from the authority which has taken or failed to take the action, with the possibility of appeal before the Andorran Government.[92] If the complainant is still dissatisfied, the dispute can be brought before the Bailiffs.[93] Their judgments are open to appeal before the Supreme Tribunal of Justice.[94] In last resort, whether in civil, penal or administrative cases, the Constitutional Tribunal can be seized by the parties if they claim that a fundamental human right guaranteed by the Constitution has been violated.[95] If it concerns the acts of public authorities only the violation of 'le contenu essentiel' of the civil and political rights will be considered.[96] It is only in the case of resolutions or acts of the General Council which do not have the character of a law and which are claimed to violate fundamental human rights that an individual can institute direct proceedings before the Constitutional Tribunal, without having to go through other court instances.[97]

Andorra's judicial system provides more legal security than before due to the constitutional guarantees for the independence of the judges and for the observance of the principles of fair trial,[98] and due

---

[89] Art. 49 (3) of the 1993 law on the judicial system.
[90] Art. 56, 2nd para. of the 1993 law on the judicial system.
[91] Civil disputes are settled on the basis of customary law supplemented by jurisprudence or, alternatively, according to Catalan law, canon law, Roman law or Castilian law: Brutails, *La Coutume*, pp. 48 ff. Customary Andorran civil law has been codified by certain scholars of which the *Manual Digest* of 1748 and the *Politar* of 1763 are the best-known documents: A. Sabater i Tomas, *Legislació Civil: Legislació i Jurisprudència del Principat d'Andorra* (1981) pp. 93 ff.
[92] Art. 124 of the Code of Administration, BOPA (1989) no. 6, pp. 133 ff.
[93] Art. 49 (4) of the 1993 law on the judicial system.
[94] Art. 56, 2nd para. of the 1993 law on the judicial system.
[95] Arts. 85 and 86 of the law on the Constitutional Tribunal. Only the rights of Chapters III and IV, except Art. 22, of the Constitution are thus protected. See pp. 333–334 below.
[96] Art. 41 (2) of the Constitution. In this case a preferential and emergency procedure is foreseen: Art. 6 of the 1993 law on the judicial system.
[97] Art. 95 (1) of the law on the Constitutional Tribunal and Art. 102 (b) of the Constitution.
[98] See on the human rights situation pp. 329–334 below.

to the legal proceedings which can be instituted in order to strengthen these guarantees in practice.

Human rights situation

The protection of certain human rights in Andorra was, before the promulgation of the Constitution, recognized by customary law only. The General Council in a memorandum for an institutional reform of 1978 had requested the incorporation of the Universal Declaration of Human Rights of 1948 in the Andorran legal order.[99] The main obstacle to the recognition of the fundamental human rights in Andorra concerned the freedom of association. In general, only Andorran nationals can carry on commerce or industry in the Principality and at least two-thirds of the capital of Andorran enterprises must be controlled by Andorran nationals.[100] The ownership of the Andorran enterprises and shops is thus concentrated in the hands of the Andorran families and combined with a relatively liberal labour system. There is no unemployment act in Andorra and associations 'wishing to pursue class revindications or political or social struggle' as well as those supplanting or intimidating the General Council were prohibited.[101] This prevented the formation of trade unions, collective bargaining and certain political parties. This legal situation was however not only inspired by economic reasons but also by social reasons due to the fact that Andorran nationals constitute a minority of the population, needing special protection against foreign immigrants.[102]

The human rights situation in Andorra became the object of discussion in the Parliamentary Assembly of the Council of Europe in 1987 due to complaints made by Andorran inhabitants.[103] After a fact-finding mission to Andorra, the Parliamentary Assembly adopted a recommendation inviting the co-Princes and the General Council, *inter alia*, to accept the freedom of association and to bring the labour law and the social security system into line with European

---

[99] M. I. Consell General, *Memoria de Reforma Institucional* (Mar. 1978) p. 23.
[100] Art. 3 (1) of the Regulation on commercial enterprises of 19 May 1983. Foreigners who have lived in Andorra for a solid period of twenty years are assimilated with Andorran nationals: Art. 2 (2) of the Regulation on commercial enterprises of 19 May 1983. See also Viñas i Farré, *Nacionalitat*, pp. 79 and 87.
[101] Ordinance I of 1 Jun. 1950 and Ordinance III of 28 Jun. 1968.
[102] Considerations of the Commission on Political Questions of the Parliamentary Assembly of the Council of Europe, Doc. 6146 (16 Nov. 1989) p. 24, paras. 102–103.
[103] Council of Europe, Doc. 5742 (7 May 1987).

norms.¹⁰⁴ Despite initial opposition by the French co-Prince and by Andorran shop and factory owners,¹⁰⁵ a law on the rights of the person was promulgated by the permanent delegates of the co-Princes on 29 March 1989.¹⁰⁶

Article 5 of the Constitution states that the Universal Declaration of Human Rights is in force in Andorra. Nonetheless, Article 5 of the Constitution is not one of the articles setting forth human rights which are protected by the ordinary Tribunals or the Constitutional Tribunal, if the plaintiff is an individual.¹⁰⁷ The rights of the Universal Declaration of Human Rights remain non-enforceable under the Constitution for individuals.¹⁰⁸

Which therefore are the human rights which can be invoked by individuals under the Constitution? There are two main categories of rights: on the one hand civil rights which can be freely exercised by all, including foreigners, and political rights for Andorrans, which are directly applicable, and, on the other hand, economic, social and cultural rights which are only invocable within the terms fixed by the law.¹⁰⁹ Our attention will be focused on two legal domains which in the past have led to certain difficulties, namely the guarantee of a fair

---

¹⁰⁴ Parliamentary Assembly Recommendation 1127 (11 May 1990). See further pp. 357–359 below.

¹⁰⁵ Interview with HE Mgr Joan Martí I Alanis, Bishop of Urgell, 11 Dec. 1990.

¹⁰⁶ BOPA (1989) no. 6, p. 133. An attempt to include these fundamental rights in the Code of Administration failed. These rights were therefore included in a separate law promulgated on the same date as the Code of Administration. This law declares that the fundamental rights as defined by the Universal Declaration of Human Rights of 1948 are incorporated in the legal order of the Principality. The legal effects of this stipulation are immediately invalidated by another provision which states that the laws will define the conditions under which these human rights will be exercised, taking into account the particular character of Andorra: Arts. 1 and 2. As no such law was adopted until the promulgation of the Constitution, the Universal Declaration of Human Rights acquired no binding force in Andorra.

¹⁰⁷ Art. 41 of the Constitution assures the legal protection of the fundamental rights set forth in Chapters III and IV of the Constitution, i.e., civil rights and political rights of the Andorrans. The Universal Declaration of Human Rights is enclosed in Chapter I.

¹⁰⁸ This is without prejudice to any other legal action concerning unconstitutionality instituted by a State organ before the Constitutional Tribunal. Every State organ is obliged to respect the Constitutional provisions, including therefore the Universal Declaration of Human Rights, under penalty of unconstitutionality of its acts. A law, a legislative decree or a treaty can be declared unconstitutional by the Constitutional Tribunal if they are attacked in the procedures provided for in Art. 98 (a) and (b) of the Constitution, because of their non-compliance with the Universal Declaration of Human Rights. These procedures are not open to individuals, although they may benefit from their results. See also pp. 325–326 above.

¹⁰⁹ Art. 39 of the Constitution.

trial and the right of association. Before Andorra became a party to the ECHR, complaints against the conduct of the Andorran judiciary in penal cases were received by the European Commission of Human Rights in 1986.[110] The applicants, Jordi Drozd, a Spanish national, and Pavel Janousek, a Czechoslovakian national, had been sentenced by the Andorran 'Tribunal de Corts' to fourteen years' imprisonment for armed robbery. The applicants alleged violations of Article 6 of the ECHR by France and Spain since they considered that 'France and perhaps Spain exercise sovereign powers and in particular supervisory powers over justice in the "non-autonomous" territory such that at the very least France must – internationally – be held responsible for the violations perpetrated under the authority of its *viguier* and, more generally, in the Valleys of Andorra.'[111] In addition, the applicants, who had chosen to serve their prison sentences in France, claimed that France had violated Article 5, paragraph 1 (a) of the ECHR because their detention had not been 'lawful' within the meaning of Article 5, paragraph 1 (a) as no French legislation authorized the enforcement in France of a sentence pronounced in Andorra.[112] With respect to the absence of a fair trial, the applicants had alleged that the 'Tribunal de Corts' had lacked independence because the episcopal Bailiff ('Battle') in charge of the investigation had been present at the Tribunal's deliberations, the French member of the Tribunal had an inadequate knowledge of Catalan, the language of the proceedings, the witnesses and the victim had not been isolated before giving evidence, two judges were representatives of the co-Princes and superior officers of the police and because one applicant had not received full assistance of an interpreter or a lawyer during the investigation, nor a complete translation during the trial.[113] These facts were contested by the Spanish and French Governments. The European Commission of Human Rights as well as the European Court of Human Rights which pronounced a judgment on this case in 1992 held that neither France nor Spain was

---

[110] Application no. 12747/87, *Jordi Drozd and Pavel Janousek against France and Spain*, Report of the Commission adopted on 11 Dec. 1990. Andorra will soon ratify the ECHR and Protocol no. 6. It underlined in a general Declaration that the fact of constituting a State of limited territorial dimensions demanded special concern with respect to residence, work and social measures for foreigners, even if these questions were not covered by the ECHR: BOPA (1995) no. 82, p. 1752.
[111] Ibid., p. 2, para. 4.
[112] Ibid., p. 24, para. 123.
[113] Ibid., pp. 14–15, paras. 64–71.

internationally responsible for the acts of the Andorran judicial authorities and that the detention in France was lawful within the meaning of Article 5, paragraph 1 (a) of the ECHR, because the Andorran criminal proceedings did not violate 'essential guarantees of the rights of defence', according to the Commission,[114] and did not constitute 'a flagrant denial of justice', according to the Court.[115]

The value of the opinion of the European Commission of Human Rights and of the judgment of the European Court of Human Rights for the subsequent development of the human rights situation in Andorra does not lie in the conclusions themselves, but in the dissenting opinions. Four of the sixteen members of the Commission had held both France and Spain responsible for the violation of Article 6 of the ECHR. They based their opinion on the fact that 'France, through organs of the French state, exercises the right of legislating on questions concerning the organisation and procedure of the Tribunal des Corts, and appoints French judges to serve as judges of that Court. Spain allows a person under Spanish jurisdiction to legislate in Andorra and appoints a judge to sit on the Tribunal des Corts.'[116] They underpinned their opinion by arguing that Spain and France placed at the disposal of the Bishop of Urgell and the French President units of the 'guardia civil' and the French 'gendarmerie' respectively under the command of the *veguers* who also acted as judges in the 'Tribunal de Corts'.[117] The dissenting opinions of eight members of the Commission and of eleven judges of the Court relating to the violation of Article 5, paragraph 1 (a) of the ECHR by France were all based on the general conclusion that the 'Tribunal de Corts' had lacked independence and impartiality because two members of the Tribunal, the *veguers*, simultaneously exercised legislative, administrative and judicial authority.[118] Partly due to these dissenting opinions, the Constitution of Andorra introduced the necessary reforms to guarantee a greater independence of the judiciary, which we have discussed in the preceding paragraph.[119]

---

[114] Ibid., p. 29, para. 149.

[115] European Court of Human Rights, *Case of Drozd and Janousek v. France and Spain* (21/1991/273/344), Judgment of 26 Jun. 1992, p. 32, para. 110.

[116] Dissenting opinion of Mr J. A. Frowein, joined by MM. J. C. Soyer, H. Vandenberghe and L. Rozakis. Application no. 12747/87, p. 32.

[117] Ibid.

[118] See the dissenting opinions, ibid., pp. 33, 35, 37–40 and Judgment (21/1991/273/344) pp. 35 and 38–43.

[119] The *veguers* no longer sit in the Andorran courts, the judges are no longer appointed by the co-Princes and the Supreme Council of Justice controls the independence and impartiality of the judges. See pp. 326–327 above.

These reforms have definitely eliminated the arguments which could lead to the conclusion that France and/or Spain are responsible for the conduct of the Andorran judiciary. The Constitution provides also for the transfer of the authority over the police from the *veguers* to the Andorran Government.[120] In addition to these measures which concern the technical functioning of the judicial system, the Constitution sets forth certain fundamental rights to ensure a fair trial.[121]

The Constitution reserves four articles to facilitate the functioning and creation of trade unions: the right of peaceful assembly and demonstration for lawful purposes,[122] the freedom of association equally for lawful purposes,[123] such as the creation and functioning of professional or trade unions in enterprises,[124] and the right of workers and employers to defend their economic and social interests, which allows collective bargaining.[125] The preferential rights of Andorrans in matters of commerce, construction and ownership of houses have been maintained.

The Andorran Constitution has improved the legal protection of human rights considerably. Nevertheless, there are two drawbacks. In the first place, civil and political rights will only be protected by the Constitutional Tribunal if an act of a public authority violates 'le contenu essentiel' of these rights.[126] Moreover, the expulsion of a resident which leads to the violation of any civil right cannot be considered by the Constitutional Tribunal.[127] In the second place, two fundamental rights do not fall under the protection of the Tribunals

---

[120] Para. 2 of the third transitional provision.
[121] These rights include the right to a trial by an impartial Tribunal with the possibility of appeal, legal assistance, the right of defence, of a trial within a reasonable time, of the presumption of innocence, of being informed of the charge and the right not to make declarations against oneself, the right to liberty and security of person, including a preventive custody of no more than forty-eight hours, with the possibility of appeal to a judicial organ against any detention, the rule of *nulla poena sine lege*, the prohibition of torture or other cruel, inhumane or degrading treatment or punishment and the prohibition of the death penalty: Arts. 8–10 of the Constitution. Although no longer used in practice the death penalty was officially and *de jure* abolished in 1990 through the promulgation of the Penal Code. See also L. Armengol, 'La Pena de Mort a Andorra, segons el "Manual Digest"', *Quaderns d'Estudis Andorrans* (1977) no. 2. The maximum term of imprisonment is thirty years: Art. 39 of the Penal Code.
[122] Art. 16 of the Constitution.
[123] Art. 17 of the Constitution.
[124] Art. 18 of the Constitution.
[125] Art. 19, 1st sentence of the Constitution.
[126] Art. 41 (1) of the Constitution.
[127] Ibid.

in case of an individual petition, namely equality before the law and the prohibition of discrimination on grounds of birth, race, sex, origin, religion, opinion or any other personal or social condition.[128] With regard to this latter principle it should be noted that Andorra has eliminated any discrimination on the ground of sex from its code of nationality since 1985.[129] It is legally possible to restrict the principle of equality before the law and the prohibition of discrimination, as the exercise of all the fundamental rights and freedoms enumerated in the Constitution can be regulated by the law.[130] The Constitution does not state for which purposes the rights should be regulated. Civil and political rights can only be 'regulated', but not limited by a law.[131] In principle, the Andorran Constitution respects the international rules on fundamental human rights and accepts but few restrictions.

Relations with States
Foreign policy

The Principality of Andorra has for a long time been unable to develop an elaborate foreign policy, because the French co-Prince claimed sole responsibility for Andorra's international relations while at the same time maintaining that Andorra was not a State and

---

[128] Art. 6 (1) of the Constitution is embodied in Chapter I of the Constitution which therefore falls outside the scope of the judicial protection of the rights of Chapters III and IV: Art. 41 of the Constitution. The rights of Chapter I remain subject to any other non-individual proceeding of unconstitutionality instituted by a State organ.

[129] Code on Andorran nationality modified by law of 7 Sept. 1985. Text in Viñas i Farré, *Nacionalitat*, pp. 142–147. Not only the discrimination between men and women has been eliminated, but also that between those Andorran women who are not and those who are heiresses ('pubilla'). Under the 1985 Code foreigners could not easily acquire Andorran nationality. This was changed in Sept. 1993 by a new Code on Andorran nationality which permits the integration of persons born in Andorra of foreigners born in Andorra as well or living in Andorra for at least twenty years, and allows naturalization of foreigners living in Andorra at least since 31 Dec. 1959: Arts. 2, 5, 8 and 9 of the 1993 Code on Andorran nationality, BOPA (1993) no. 51, pp. 887 ff. Art. 2 (1) and (2) was declared contrary to the Constitution by the Constitutional Tribunal, Judgment of 15 Mar. 1994, BOPA (1994) no. 21. According to the new law on nationality of 5 Oct. 1995, BOPA (1996) no. 8, children born of foreign parents who had had their principal and permanint residence in Andorra for eighteen years at the time the child was born, foreigners who marry an Andorran and who live and are integrated in Andorra for at least three years and foreigners who live in Andorra for twenty-five years can aquire Andorran nationality: Arts. 6, 10 and 11.

[130] Art. 40, 1st sentence of the Constitution.

[131] Art. 39 (1), 2nd sentence and Art. 40, 2nd sentence of the Constitution.

could not therefore enter into normal international relations.¹³² The Constitution of Andorra has however marked a considerable change of position and has shifted the authority in international political matters from the co-Princes to the Head of the Government.¹³³ The following principles are present in Andorra's recent foreign policy:

Neutrality The neutrality of Andorra in times of war has been a centuries-old tradition. The *Manual Digest* of 1748 laid down the maxim that Andorra should always remain neutral in case of a war between its neighbouring countries France and Spain.¹³⁴ The neutrality of Andorra extends also to armed conflicts in which neither France nor Spain is involved.

Confirmation of its statehood Even before the coming into force of the Constitution some learned publicists argued that Andorra was a State in international law, while the General Council did not hide its wish to be fully recognized as such and to participate in international conferences and organizations.¹³⁵ The Constitution contains several provisions which enable Andorra to set up its own diplomatic representation and to adhere to international conventions and organizations.¹³⁶

Relations with France

Friendly relations

The institutional reforms of the Principality of Andorra were completed by a treaty of vicinage, friendship and cooperation of 3 June 1993 concluded between Andorra, France and Spain.¹³⁷ It defines the framework of Andorra's relations with its two neighbouring States. France and Spain recognize the Principality of Andorra as a sovereign State.¹³⁸ Moreover, both France and Spain 'facilitent la participation de la Principauté aux conférences et organisations

---

[132] See pp. 354–357 below.
[133] Art. 72 (2) of the Constitution states: 'Sous l'autorité de son Chef, il [le Gouvernement] dirige la politique nationale et internationale de l'Andorre.'
[134] Maxim no. 37 in Sabater i Tomas, *Legislació Civil*, p. 108.
[135] See further pp. 354–357 and 366–371 below.
[136] Arts. 44 (1), 45 (1) (e and h), 46 (1) (f and h), 64–67 and 72 (2) of the Constitution. See also pp. 322 and 324 above.
[137] Catalan text in BOPA (1993) no. 37, pp. 683 ff, French text in 98 RGDIP (1994) pp. 525–527. Treaty provisionally applied as of date of signature, entered into force on 1 Dec. 1994.
[138] Art. 1 of the treaty of vicinage.

internationales ainsi que son accession aux conventions internationales'.[139] This implies that France and Spain may not obstruct Andorra's participation in and accession to international organizations, conferences and conventions.

Andorra's absolute freedom in its international relations is restricted in two ways. In the first place, Andorra on the one hand and France and Spain on the other hand:

> s'engagent à veiller au respect mutuel de leurs intérêts fondamentaux respectifs et à coopérer pour le règlement des difficultés qui pourraient survenir dans ces matières, y compris au regard des engagements pris par la République française et le Royaume d'Espagne dans le cadre de la Communauté Européenne.[140]

When the need arises, this cooperation takes the form of bilateral or trilateral accords where Andorra adheres to international conventions to which France or Spain is also a party.[141] The essential domains in which a cooperation agreement between Andorra and the neighbouring States seems necessary will be determined by exchanges of notes.[142] In the second place, Andorra:

> s'engage à ne rien entreprendre depuis son territoire ou sur celui-ci, qui soit de nature à porter atteinte à la sécurité intérieure et extérieure de la République française ou du Royaume d'Espagne, ou à leurs engagements internationaux en ce domaine.[143]

Andorra's obligations under Article 4, first paragraph of the treaty of vicinage may raise certain difficulties of interpretation due to the vagueness of the text. Thus, Andorra has to respect the fundamental interests of both France and Spain and has to cooperate in the settlement of any difficulty which may arise in this matter. It may be asked what the fundamental interests of the neighbouring States are and how far the duty of cooperation stretches. This question becomes all the more relevant as the treaty of vicinage does not provide for arbitration or other dispute settlement mechanisms. How fundamental should the interests of France and Spain be? Does this stipulation imply that Andorra cannot adopt any measure or take any action in

---

[139] Art. 2, 2nd para. of the treaty of vicinage.
[140] Art. 4, 1st para. of the treaty of vicinage.
[141] Art. 4, 2nd para. of the treaty of vicinage.
[142] Art. 4, 3rd para. of the treaty of vicinage. The exchanges of notes will be signed after the entry into force of the treaty of vicinage.
[143] Art. 5 of the treaty of vicinage.

its internal and external affairs which would be deemed contrary to the fundamental interests of France or Spain? The situation may, in addition, be rendered more complicated if the fundamental interests of Andorra, France and Spain do not coincide. In theory it could be possible that a measure adopted by Andorra would respect a fundamental interest of, for example, France, but be contrary to a Spanish fundamental interest, whereas, conversely, the same measure, if it were not adopted, would respect Spanish interests but impinge upon French interests. In any case, Article 4, first paragraph of the treaty of vicinage mentions the obligations of France and Spain within the framework of the European Community as a fundamental interest. Article 5 of the treaty of vicinage sets forth, separately, Andorra's duty not to prejudice France's and Spain's internal and external security. The fact that these security interests are mentioned in a separate article and not included in the 'fundamental interests' of Article 4, first paragraph could imply that Andorra's duty of cooperation and respect under Article 4 is not as stringent as its duty not to encroach on its neighbours' security interests under Article 5. Unlike Article 4, Article 5 does not provide for a duty of cooperation.

It should furthermore be noted that France and Spain have undertaken to respect the independence of Andorra.[144] Therefore, the duty to respect the fundamental interests of both France and Spain should be read in this light. Article 4, first paragraph of the treaty of vicinage should not be invoked to justify a continuous obligation to bring Andorran internal and external matters into line with French and Spanish wishes, as this would be to the detriment of Andorra's independence.[145] Where the fundamental interests of a neighbouring State are at stake, Andorra has a duty to cooperate in the settlement of the problem. It is, in general, difficult to conceive the content of a duty of cooperation without a clear obligation to achieve a final result. Thus, a duty to negotiate will have no real value under international law without the determination of the duties of the negotiating parties. The duty to respect the fundamental interests of the States Parties is the main element of Article 4, first paragraph of the treaty of vicinage, whereas the duty of cooperation is of secondary importance, defining the formal framework to settle difficulties.

---

[144] Art. 3, 1st para. of the treaty of vicinage stating: 'La République française et le Royaume d'Espagne respectent la souveraineté et l'indépendance de la Principauté d'Andorre, ainsi que l'intégrité de son territoire.' See further pp. 342-345 and 348-350 below.
[145] Cf. the Franco-Monégasque relations pp. 308-309 above.

However, with the exception of internal and external security matters, the treaty of vicinage does not provide for a definite solution in case of clashing fundamental interests between Andorra on the one hand and France or Spain on the other.

Bilateral treaties which Andorra plans to conclude with either France or Spain are to be communicated to the other neighbouring State which does not participate in their negotiation.[146] In a case of common interests a trilateral treaty can be concluded.[147] The treaty of vicinage does not provide for a denunciation clause.

Diplomatic representation

The trilateral treaty of vicinage between Andorra, France and Spain regulates the position and tasks of the French diplomatic service with respect to Andorra's international representation.[148] In the past, France has always readily extended its diplomatic and consular services to Andorran nationals in third States. In theory, France maintained that Andorran nationals living outside Andorra or France should be registered by the French consulates or embassies and should receive diplomatic protection exclusively from France.[149] In practice, help and diplomatic protection in third States could be obtained both from the French and from the Spanish diplomatic service.[150] This practice was not officially based on a delegation of the co-Princes and it is not clear how it was justified towards the receiving States.[151] At present, France, like Spain, has undertaken to establish diplomatic relations with the Principality of Andorra.[152] In third States, or in international conferences or organizations, where Andorra has not set up its own diplomatic representation, the Principality may charge either France or Spain with its representation

---

[146] Art. 8 of the treaty of vicinage. A regular and complete information has to be provided from the beginning of the negotiations to the conclusion.
[147] Art. 9 of the treaty of vicinage.
[148] See for Spain p. 347 below.
[149] J. M. Vidal i Guitart, *Institucions Polítiques i Sociales d'Andorra* (1984) p. 294 and Zemanek, *Le Statut international*, pp. 81-82.
[150] Ibid. See p. 347 below.
[151] R. Viñas Farré, 'El "Treaty Making Power" y la Representación Internacional del Principado de Andorra', *Revista Jurídica de Cataluña* (Apr.-Jun. 1976) no. 2, pp. 337-339 and Zemanek, *Le Statut international*, pp. 82-83.
[152] Art. 2, 1st para. of the treaty of vicinage. At the end of 1993, both France and Spain had sent their resident ambassador to Andorra. At the beginning of 1995, an Andorran ambassador was appointed to France; an ambassador to Spain had been designated in 1994.

in accordance with the Vienna Convention on Diplomatic Relations.¹⁵³ The representative tasks of France and Spain must be evenly divided and will be supplemented by special agreements regulating the exact framework of the representation.¹⁵⁴ It remains clear that neither France nor Spain may conduct Andorra's foreign relations at will. At any time Andorra can assume its proper diplomatic representation. In States where Andorra does not have any consular representation, Andorran nationals may turn to either French or Spanish consulates, if the receiving State in question so allows.¹⁵⁵ By 1995, Andorra had established diplomatic relations with forty-eight States.¹⁵⁶ In order to be accredited to the Principality of Andorra, an *exequatur* must be signed by both co-Princes.¹⁵⁷

Postal union

In 1878, the Conference of the UPU approached Spain on the organization of a postal service in Andorra. After that time both France and Spain developed a small courier service, but it was only in 1906 that the UPU entrusted the organization of a proper postal service in Andorra to Spain.¹⁵⁸ Due to protests from the General Council against the unilateral Spanish actions, the French delegation to the Conference of the UPU in 1929 claimed that Spain had no rights over Andorra. The Conference of the UPU recognized France's rights and invited it to enter into negotiations with Spain to settle the matter.¹⁵⁹ As a result of these negotiations an agreement was signed on 30 June 1930 according to which the postal service in Andorra would be maintained simultaneously by the French and by the Spanish postal

---

[153] Art. 6, 1st para. of the treaty of vicinage.
[154] Art. 6, 2nd para. of the treaty of vicinage.
[155] Art. 7 of the treaty of vicinage.
[156] The British honorary consul, the French ambassador and the Spanish ambassador and consul are resident in Andorra. Information from the Andorran Ministry of Foreign Affairs.
[157] Vidal i Guitart, *Institucions Polítiques*, p. 301 and Marquès i Oste, *La Reforma*, pp. 251-252. Before 1977, consuls accredited in France needed, apart from their French *exequatur* signed by the French President and countersigned by the French Minister of Foreign Affairs, an *exequatur* from the French co-Prince only. It has happened that Spain has granted the *exequatur* for Andorra to consuls accredited to it: Vidal i Guitart, *Institucions Polítiques*, p. 299. After objections from the Bishop of Urgell, who would not extend his services to consuls unilaterally received by the French co-Prince, an *exequatur* signed by both co-Princes has to be obtained.
[158] Anon., *Vallée d'Andorre: Catalogue national spécialisé* (1978) p. 16.
[159] Ibid.

administrations.¹⁶⁰ The post offices in Andorra depend exclusively on the Spanish or French postal authorities and employ, in principle, Andorran nationals.¹⁶¹ The Spanish post offices and the French post offices in Andorra apply the postal legislation in force in Spain and France respectively.¹⁶² Due to this division of tasks, Andorra could not become a member of the UPU.

Customs regime

Since 1 July 1991, the date of entry into force of the customs union agreement signed by Andorra and the European Economic Community on 28 June 1990, the customs regime as applied by France by virtue of the exchange of letters of 1967 has been abolished.¹⁶³ Traditionally, Andorran products could be freely exported to France, which did not guarantee that other EC States would grant the same franchise, whereas products originating from the European Communitiy could be imported into Andorra without French customs duties.¹⁶⁴ France levied the common customs tariff of the European Community on any product imported by Andorra from outside the Community.¹⁶⁵ This practice was believed to be contrary to the rule of freedom of transit set forth in article V, paragraph 2 of the General Agreement on Tariffs and Trade (GATT).¹⁶⁶ The customs duties levied by France were not granted to the Andorran Government. Nevertheless, Andorra had adopted a law in 1985 which imposed an indirect tax on all imported products. This Andorran customs duty,

---

[160] Art. I of the postal agreement between France and Spain. Text in ibid., p. 17. The Bishop of Urgell delegated the postal organization to Spain and the French co-Prince to France.
[161] Art. III of the postal agreement.
[162] Art. V of the postal agreement. In contrast to Spain, France does not keep the profits of its post offices in Andorra to itself. Since 1965, 50 per cent of the benefits are granted to the Andorran Government: Raton, *Le Statut international*, p. 38 at n. 6.
[163] Art. 25 of the customs union agreement between Andorra and the EEC. See pp. 359-364 below. Exchange of letters of 1967, reiterating an exchange of letters of 1867, between the Secretariat-General of the French President, his permanent delegate and the French Minister of Economy and Finance: see Zemanek, *Le Statut international*, p. 63, n. 14.
[164] Ibid., p. 63 at n. 20.
[165] Ibid., p. 63 at n. 21. The EC common customs tariff was also applied to Andorran products exported to France which had previously been imported by Andorra from a non-EC State.
[166] France as the State of transit could not impose charges on products in transit originating from a contracting party to GATT. See also V. Pou, *Negociacions Andorra-Mercat Comú Europeu: Anàlisi i Documentació sobre les Relacions entre Andorra i la CEE* (1986) p. 95.

called 'Taxes de Consum', is still applied to products which are not covered by the customs union agreement with the European Economic Community.[167]

The French franc is legal tender in Andorra although this monetary union is not based on any treaty. In practice, the Spanish peseta is used more often, as, for example, in the State budget. Andorra has recently adopted a bank act.[168]

Aliens office

The Andorran legislation concerning the sojourn and residence of aliens aims to limit a large inflow of foreigners and to protect the social and economic interests of Andorran nationals. The General Council fixes every year an immigration quota for the residence and work permits, while the residence permits without authorization to work and the permits for cross-border workers are not subject to any quantitative restrictions.[169] The Andorran Government can thus balance Andorra's need for foreign labour with its desire to preserve the living conditions of the Andorrans and to control the housing market. Foreigners who have lived in Andorra for twenty consecutive years acquire the same privileges concerning ownership rights of enterprises, houses and constructions as Andorrans.[170] A long-term residence in Andorra does not necessarily permit naturalization.[171]

---

[167] See pp. 362–363 below.
[168] Law of 27 Sept. 1993, BOPA (1993) no. 70, p. 1210. Bank secrecy is guaranteed. In 1989 a National Andorran Institute of Finance was established which under the authority of the Government controls the financial health of the Andorran banks, BOPA (1989) no. 13, p. 293 and BOPA (1993) no. 51, p. 892.
[169] The entry, work and sojourn of aliens has been regulated by Decrees of 26 Jun. 1980, 25 Apr. 1984 and 25 Jul. 1991: BOPA (1991) no. 31, p. 595. Residence and work permits which concern a position in the Andorran administration or official services can only be granted to nationals of the EC countries: edict of 26 Jun. 1991, BOPA (1991) no. 28, p. 539.
[170] Viñas i Farré, *Nacionalitat*, pp. 78–79.
[171] A foreign adult can only become Andorran if he is married to an Andorran for at least three years, is born in Andorra of a parent who has lived eighteen years in Andorra or if he has lived in the Principality for twenty-five years: Arts. 6, 10 and 11 of the 1995 Code on Andorran nationality. The new Code makes the acquisition of Andorran nationality more dependent on residence in the Principality than the 1985 Code, see n. 129, p. 334 above.

Co-Prince

The President of the French Republic is personally and exclusively a co-Prince of Andorra according to the Andorran Constitution.[172] By virtue of the Andorran legal order, the French President when acting as a co-Prince is considered an Andorran public authority who is bound only by the Andorran Constitution. From this formal point of view, the presence of the French State and the French co-Prince's position therein seems irrelevant to the Andorran legal status. Nevertheless, the French co-Prince's legal title in Andorra will only be a personal and exclusive one if French public legislation allows it. However, neither the French Constitution nor any other French legislative text provides for a legal framework in which the personal and exclusive rights of the French President over Andorra can be exercised. The French Constitution of 1958 sets forth a limited number of cases in which presidential decrees and ordinances are exempted from the obligation of countersignature by the Prime Minister or other Ministers.[173] There is no reference to the acts of the President as co-Prince of Andorra. The relations between the French co-Prince and the French State are entirely based on practice. Accordingly, the French State has accepted that the French President when taking decisions as a co-Prince of Andorra is not subject to the countersignature of a French Minister, with the only exception that 'le contreseing est exigé dans la seule mesure où les décisions du coprince français ont des répercussions financières sur le budget de l'Etat français'.[174]

The question arises whether the French President when determining his position towards Andorra has the legal obligation to bring it into line with the policy of the French State towards Andorra. Under the French Constitution it is the Government which determines the foreign policy of the French State,[175] although the ratification of treaties is left to the President.[176] The French Government cannot

---

[172] Art. 43 (2) of the Constitution.

[173] These presidential acts concern personal powers of the President: Arts. 8 (1), 11, 12, 16, 18, 54, 56 and 61 of the 1958 French Constitution. Exhaustive enumeration in Art. 19 of the Constitution.

[174] Bélinguier, *La Condition juridique*, p. 247 and affirmed by Marquès i Oste, *La Reforma*, p. 213. It is to be expected that this latter category of decisions will be less frequent, as the services of the co-Prince will no longer be paid by the French State, but, by virtue of the Andorran Constitution, they will be covered by the Andorran State budget: Art. 47 of the Andorran Constitution.

[175] Art. 20 of the 1958 French Constitution. See A. Cocatre-Zilgien, 'Constitution de 1958, Droit international, Relations extérieures et Politique étrangère', 4 AFDI (1958) p. 658.

[176] Art. 52 of the 1958 French Constitution.

constitutionally impose a foreign policy upon the President, except for the fact that the President is the guarantor of national independence, of territorial integrity and of respect for the treaties concluded by France.[177] Within these limits, the French President is free to take any decision concerning Andorra. In practice, it has not yet been demonstrated that the French co-Prince has adopted a position contrary to that of the French Government towards Andorra. This is partly due to the fact that the French President may, in practice, determine the broad lines of the foreign policy of the State.[178]

The French co-Prince has in the past often used the services of the French governmental authorities. We can cite in this context the case of Radio Andorra. This radio station, which functioned from 1939 on the basis of a revocable concession granted by the two co-Princes, used frequencies which had been reserved to other countries. When in 1947 these countries raised objections against France, the French co-Prince withdrew the concession without the approval of the Bishop of Urgell.[179] As Radio Andorra continued to broadcast, it was decided in the French Council of Ministers under the presidency of the French co-Prince to jam the radio's transmissions.[180] In this case there was no divergence of opinion between the President and the Government, but it should, in general, be noted that the Council of Ministers could very well have taken the decision to jam Radio Andorra without the approval of the French President.[181] In the cases of *Société 'Le Nickel'* and *Radio Andorre*, the French 'Conseil d'Etat' maintained that the forfeiture of a concession pronounced by the French President acting as co-Prince of Andorra did not constitute a decision of a French administrative authority.[182] This position was followed by the French courts in other cases, so that the French co-Prince cannot be regarded as a French administrative authority.[183] Paradoxically, certain French courts justified the granting of special privileges to Andorran

---

[177] Art. 5 of the 1958 French Constitution.
[178] F. Luchaire and G. Conac, eds., *La Constitution de la République française: Analyses et Commentaires*, 2nd edn (1987) pp. 577–580.
[179] Bélinguier, *La Condition juridique*, pp. 179–180.
[180] Decision of 22 Apr. 1948. Ibid., p. 180.
[181] Although the President chairs the meetings of the Council of Ministers (Art. 9 of the French Constitution), the deliberation of the Council is secret and its decisions can only have legal effect if translated into a ministerial act or decree.
[182] *Société 'Le Nickel'*, *Recueil Lebon* (1933) p. 1132 and *Radio Andorre*, Judgment of 2 Febr. 1950, *Recueil Lebon* (1950) p. 652.
[183] See, e.g., *Porché v. Société de Gérance et de Publicité*, Cour d'Appel de Paris, 24 May 1949, *Gazette du Palais* (29 Jul. 1949).

nationals in France by arguing that 'nous y exerçons un droit de souveraineté'[184] and 'le territoire des Vallées d'Andorre ne constituait pas, au regard de la France, un pays étranger'.[185] These arguments were refuted by Bélinguier who contended that Andorra was not French territory and was not directed by France.[186] This has traditionally also been the official position of the French Government.[187]

The personal representative of the French co-Prince in Andorra is a French diplomat appointed for an indefinite period.[188] He does not receive orders from the French Ministry of Foreign Affairs.

It can be concluded that the relations between the French co-Prince and the French State are primarily defined by practice, but lack any legal guarantees. The absence of any legislative text defining the rights and privileges of the French co-Prince in French public law creates a legal insecurity with regard to the personal and exclusive character of the French co-Prince's position in Andorra. It has already been demonstrated that in the past the sovereign rights of the French co-Prince were transferred from the Caboets family to the President of the French Republic according to rules of succession which were not Andorran.[189] Any further transfers of rights or any amendment of the French Constitution affecting the position of the French President could have repercussions on the status of the French co-Prince in Andorra. The obligation of countersignature by the French Prime Minister can at any time be extended to every decision taken by the French President in his capacity of co-Prince of Andorra. There is no principle of French public law which could prevent such reform. It is therefore essential to note that according to the treaty of vicinage France has undertaken to respect 'la souveraineté et l'indépendance de la Principauté d'Andorre' and, if this independence were to be

---

[184] *Duedra*, Judgment of 22 Nov. 1905, Tribunal Correctionnel de Toulouse, *Revue de Droit international privé et de Droit penal international* (1906) p. 538.

[185] *Massip v. Cruze*, Cour d'Appel de Montpellier, Judgment of 23 Jul. 1952, cited by Bélinguier, *La Condition juridique*, p. 212.

[186] Ibid., pp. 214–216. Bélinguier argued that Andorra could not be French territory as the French laws were not applicable in Andorra, while the sovereignty over Andorra was exercised by the two co-Princes jointly and personally. He continues however by stating: 'En ce qui concerne la responsabilité internationale de l'Andorre, il ne fait pas de doute que la France en est investie.' Ibid., p. 191.

[187] Recently invoked by the French Government before the European Commission of Human Rights in Application no. 12747/87, *Jordi Drozd and Pavel Janousek against France and Spain*, Report of 11 Dec. 1990, p. 20, para. 96.

[188] Information from the 'Viguerie Française en Andorre'.

[189] See p. 318 above.

violated or threatened to be violated, to consult with the Andorran Government 'en vue d'examiner les mesures qui pourraient se révéler nécessaires afin d'en assurer le respect'.[190] It can be inferred that by virtue of Article 3 of the treaty of vicinage, France may not place the French co-Prince in a position which could be to the detriment of Andorra's independence. In this sense French public law is restricted by an international obligation which implies, for example, that the French President may never be forced, either in practice or by virtue of an institutional obligation, to follow the French Government's policy towards Andorra. The status of the French co-Prince is thus defined by the provisions of the Andorran Constitution and by the freedom which is left to the French President under the French Constitution, in practice and by virtue of the treaty of vicinage.

Defence

The Principality of Andorra, though a traditionally neutral country, has concluded an implicit defence agreement with its neighbouring States. Thus, by virtue of Article 3, second paragraph of the treaty of vicinage, France and Spain:

s'engagent en cas de violation, de menace de violation de la souveraineté, de l'indépendance ou de l'intégrité territoriale de la Principauté, à procéder entre eux et avec le Gouvernement andorran, à des consultations en vue d'examiner les mesures qui pourraient se révéler nécessaires afin d'en assurer le respect.

The defence agreement is implicit, because France and Spain will not lend military support to Andorra automatically in case of an attack on its territory, but only after consultations. The Andorran Constitution does not provide for a right of the co-Princes to request foreign military aid. The Andorran Government, however, with the consent of the General Council, can proclaim a state of emergency in case of an interruption of the normal functioning of democracy in Andorra.[191]

Other relations

In 1971, the French 'Cour de Cassation' determined that the decisions of the Andorran courts were not subject to the formal requirement of an enforcement order in France, because they 'ne peuvent être

---

[190] Art. 3 of the treaty of vicinage.
[191] Art. 42 (1) of the Constitution.

considérées comme ayant été prononcées au nom d'une souveraineté étrangère'.[192] Nevertheless, since 1971 other lower French courts have maintained that, as Andorran judicial decisions could not be assimilated with the French jurisdiction, an enforcement order remained necessary in order for them to be applied in France.[193] As under the Andorran Constitution justice is no longer administered in the name of the co-Princes, and as France has recognized that Andorra is a State under international law, there will be no room left for doubt that the judicial decisions of the Andorran courts constitute foreign judgments subject to an enforcement order in France.[194]

By virtue of the Regulations on social security in Andorra, the Andorran social security authority has been empowered by the co-Princes to conclude agreements with the competent social security organs of other States.[195] In 1970, such an agreement was signed with France in the form of an administrative accord without the status of a treaty.[196]

France has established a number of schools in Andorra. Their status, which is assimilated with that of public schools in France, is defined by a decree of 1917 of the French Minister of Public Education and approved by the Minister of Foreign Affairs.[197] By virtue of a 1993 law on education, Andorran schools can be established in the Principality alongside the French and Spanish ones.[198]

Relations with Spain

Friendly relations

The relations of vicinage, friendship and cooperation between Andorra and Spain are based on the same stipulations of the trilateral treaty of vicinage of 3 June 1993 as those between Andorra and

---

[192] Cour de Cassation, Judgment of 6 Jan. 1971, *Recueil Dalloz-Sirey* (1971) p. 338.
[193] Cour d'Appel de Montpellier, Judgment of 29 May 1972, *Elsen et autres v. Boudet*, AFDI (1973) p. 1014 and Tribunal de Grande Instance de Béziers, Judgment of 28 Nov. 1977, *Mandement v. Consorts Gianesini*, I *Gazette du Palais* (1978) p. 216.
[194] Art. 546 of the French Code of Civil Procedure.
[195] Art. 9 of the 1967 General Regulations relating to the Andorran social security. Zemanek, *Le Statut international*, p. 56 at n. 34.
[196] Viñas Farré, 'El "Treaty Making Power"', pp. 336–337.
[197] Decree of 18 Jun. 1917 concerning schools in the territory of the Principality of Andorra.
[198] Art. 1 of the 1993 law on education recognizes the right to basic education of all persons. The Government has the right of inspection in Andorran schools, but also in foreign schools according to the agreements which recognize their presence in Andorra, BOPA (1993) no. 51, pp. 883 ff.

France. We therefore refer to our discussion in a preceding paragraph.[199]

Diplomatic representation

The possible use of Spanish diplomats and consulates for the international representation of the Principality of Andorra has been regulated by the trilateral treaty concluded between Spain, France and Andorra which we have already discussed.[200] Since the end of 1993, Spain has had an embassy in Andorra. In the past the Bishop of Urgell has used the diplomatic service of Spain in order to be represented in certain international conferences, especially in the period during which France claimed to hold the monopoly of the international representation of Andorra.[201] Andorrans residing in a third State can traditionally receive diplomatic or consular protection from the Spanish diplomatic or consular missions.[202]

Postal union

Since the agreement concluded between France and Spain in 1930, the postal organization in Andorra has been divided between the French and the Spanish postal administrations.[203] Unlike France, Spain does not grant all or a part of the profits made by its post offices in Andorra to the Andorran State.

Customs regime

Traditionally, Spain has allowed the importation and exportation of products to and from Andorra free from customs duties. For certain products a quota was fixed annually by an interministerial commission. The importation of Spanish products or goods from third States into Andorra was also exempted from customs duties, but subject to quantitative restrictions in the form of annual quotas.[204] This

---

[199] See pp. 335–338 above.
[200] See pp. 338–339 above.
[201] In 1984, the ITU organized a Regional Conference on Radio Broadcasting in which Andorra participated, but in which the French delegation claimed to be the sole representative of the Principality, while Spain, delegated by the Bishop of Urgell, filed an official protest against this position: Marquès i Oste, *La Reforma*, pp. 280–282. See p. 356 below.
[202] Interview with HE Mgr Joan Martí I Alanis, Bishop of Urgell, 11 Dec. 1990. This practice is at present codified in Arts. 6 and 7 of the treaty of vicinage.
[203] See further pp. 339–340 above.
[204] Art. 2 of the Spanish Decree of 18 Oct. 1922 and Art. 119 (h) of the Spanish customs ordinance. See Zemanek, *Le Statut international*, pp. 76–77 at nn. 20–21 and Bélinguier, *La Condition juridique*, pp. 175–177.

customs regime is no longer applied since the entry into force of the customs union agreement between Andorra and the European Economic Community on 1 July 1991.[205]

Aliens office

The Andorran legislation on residence and sojourn of aliens does not, as we have seen, discriminate between Spanish and other nationals.[206] Before the enactment of the Spanish law on aliens in 1985, Andorrans living in Spain were assimilated with Spanish residents. After 1985, they had to obtain a residence permit and a work permit unless they were in possession of diplomas issued by educational establishments based on the Spanish system.[207]

Co-Prince

The status of the episcopal co-Prince differs from that of the French co-Prince as the Bishop of Urgell does not hold a public governmental position in Spain. His relations with the Spanish State are therefore of a different nature. The rights and duties of the Bishop of Urgell in Spain are defined by canon law, the concordat concluded by the Holy See and Spain, and by an agreement of 23 July 1993 concluded by Spain and Andorra defining the status of the episcopal co-Prince.[208] The present Bishop of Urgell was appointed in 1971 according to the procedure prescribed by a concordat of 1953. The apostolic nuncio, having received the accord of the Spanish Government, presented six candidates to the Pope who made a choice of three persons from which the Head of the Spanish State designated one Bishop to be appointed by the Pope.[209] The involvement of the Spanish civil authorities in the appointment of Bishops has disappeared by an agreement on juridical questions of 3 January 1979 with the Holy See, which will

---

[205] Art. 25 of the customs union agreement between Andorra and the EEC. See pp. 359–364 below.

[206] See p. 341 above.

[207] Second additional provision of the 1985 Spanish law on aliens ('lei de estranjería'), cited in Viñas i Farré, *Nacionalitat*, p. 18. Andorran nationals have access to the Spanish public service situated in Andorran territory, such as the Spanish schools and post offices. They can acquire Spanish nationality after two consecutive years of residence in Spain, as against ten years for other foreigners: Art. 22 of the Spanish Civil Code.

[208] Entered into force on 1 Dec. 1994, BOPA (1994) no. 72, p. 1588.

[209] Art. VII of the 1953 Concordat between Spain and the Holy See maintained the appointment procedure of the preceding Concordat of 1941. Text of the Concordats in AAS (1953) pp. 625 ff. and AAS (1941) pp. 480 ff. respectively.

therefore determine the designation of any episcopal co-Prince in the future.²¹⁰ The Bishops of Urgell are, in general, Catalans.²¹¹

The Bishop of Urgell when exercising his authority over Andorra does not act as an ecclesiastic power, but possesses a temporal sovereignty. In his capacity as co-Prince of Andorra it is not only the relations between the Church and the Spanish State which are involved, but also those between the State and its national. As a Spanish national, the Bishop of Urgell is not obliged to follow the Spanish foreign policy towards Andorra. Spain has officially recognized the Bishop of Urgell, in his capacity of co-Prince of Andorra, as having the status of internationally protected person.²¹² His person is inviolable and he enjoys penal, civil and administrative immunity on Spanish territory.²¹³ His home, office documents and correspondence are equally protected.²¹⁴

It cannot be denied that in certain periods of history Spain tried to exert some influence in Andorra if only to counterbalance a feared French interference. In 1934, despite the opposition of the Bishop of Urgell, the Spanish Government established a delegation in the Seu d'Urgell which aimed to increase its influence in Andorra. The Spanish delegate at the time wrote to the Spanish Minister of State that for historic reasons Spain had exerted its influence in Andorra through the Bishop of Urgell, which at times had been to the detriment of Spanish national interests.²¹⁵ He therefore admitted that the interposal of the Bishop of Urgell provided insufficient guarantees for Spanish interests. In 1941, a circular letter of the Spanish Minister of Foreign Affairs concerning the treatment of Andorrans in Spain referred to Andorra as a non-foreign country, which ultimately depended upon the superior sovereignty of the

---

²¹⁰ See pp. 350–352 below.
²¹¹ The last three Bishops of Urgell were Catalans. Interview with HE Mgr Joan Martí I Alanis, Bishop of Urgell, 11 Dec. 1990.
²¹² Art. 1 of the 1993 agreement on the status of the episcopal co-Prince.
²¹³ Art. 2 of the 1993 agreement on the status of the episcopal co-Prince.
²¹⁴ Arts. 3 and 4 of the 1993 agreement on the status of the episcopal co-Prince.
²¹⁵ Letter from the Spanish delegate in the Seu d'Urgell to the Spanish Minister of State, in which he states: ' Nuestro problema se plantea concretamente en el siguiente dilema: ¿ Debe España ejercer su influencia en Andorra directamente o a través de la Mitra d'Urgel? Por circunstancias históricas, que no he de detallar, siempre ha ejercitado España su influencia mediante los obispos de Urgel. Y también es cierto que esta circunstancia, consecuencia de los sentimientos e ideas dominantes en cada época, ha sido abiertamente desfavorable al interés nacional'. Marquès i Oste, *La Reforma*, p. 195 at n. 535.

Spanish nation.²¹⁶ After the end of the Franco regime the position of Spain towards Andorra changed, and it supported the Bishop of Urgell in his arguments that France did not have the exclusive right to represent Andorra in the international field.²¹⁷

Defence

Like France, Spain agreed to an implicit defence arrangement with Andorra, and has traditionally respected the neutrality of the Andorran territory.²¹⁸

Other relations

Certain relations between Spain and Andorra used to be directly maintained with the Andorran authorities without the interference of the French co-Prince. Thus in 1863, Spain and Andorra concluded a treaty delimiting their frontiers which was not recognized by France which claimed that it was the only competent organ to conclude treaties in the name of Andorra.²¹⁹ The Andorran social security authority has concluded several administrative agreements concerning social security with Spain.²²⁰ Like France, Spain also maintains schools in Andorra which are integrated into its education system.

Relations with the Holy See

The founding documents of Andorra's traditional feudal status, the *Pariatges* of 1278 and 1288, were both confirmed by the Pope.²²¹ By doing so the Pope gave his consent to the exercise of temporal powers

---

²¹⁶ The circular letter read: 'Se hace indispensable tener presente que los Valles de Andorra no constituyen Nación o Estado soberano é independiente, sino que geográfica, económica, etnográfica é históricamente forman parte integrante de la comarca de Urgel de la Provincia de Lérida ... Por consiguiente, no tratándose de un país extranjero, sino de un territorio fronterizo sometido a un régimen de derecho feudal – señoría jurisdiccional – dependiente en último término de la superior soberanía de la nación Española'. Ibid., pp. 195–196 at n. 535.

²¹⁷ When on 6 Jan. 1971 the French 'Cour de Cassation' had observed with respect to Andorra 'l'Etat français y exerçant les droits qui lui sont dévolus', the Spanish Government officially objected to the French Minister of Foreign Affairs who reaffirmed that the co-Princes were the personal and exclusive sovereigns and that therefore 'ni l'Etat français ni aucun autre état ne sont en droit d'exercer leur souveraineté dans les Vallées'. Ibid., p. 194 at n. 534.

²¹⁸ Art. 3, 2nd para. of the treaty of vicinage. See pp. 320 and 345 above.

²¹⁹ Bélinguier, *La Condition juridique*, p. 203.

²²⁰ Administrative agreements of 1968, 1971 and 1978. Zemanek, *Le Statut international*, p. 56 and Viñas Farré, 'El "Treaty Making Power"', p. 336.

²²¹ See p. 318 above at n. 16.

by the Bishop of Urgell and his successors in the territory of Andorra. The main element of the relations between the traditionally catholic Principality and the Holy See lies in the position of the episcopal co-Prince. The Holy See intervenes in the status of the Bishop of Urgell with respect to three aspects: the appointment of the Bishop, his rights and duties and his hierarchical position.

It is possible that the Pope, when designating the Bishop of Urgell, takes into consideration the fact that he will at the same time become co-Prince of Andorra. The present Bishop of Urgell has stated that if this were to be the case, the Pope's considerations would end after the appointment, as the Pope does not give the episcopal co-Prince instructions.[222] Moreover, the influence of the Holy See is also present in the case of a vacancy of the episcopal see of Urgell. The Andorran Constitution has recognized the legal validity of the substitution mechanism provided for by canon law in case of a vacancy.[223]

The second domain in which the Holy See exerts a certain influence on the position of the episcopal co-Prince in Andorra concerns the ecclesiastic rights and duties of the Bishop. The Andorran territory is included in the diocese of Urgell. The Bishop of Urgell is therefore also the Bishop of Andorra. The Code of Canon Law provides that Bishops in their diocese have all the powers which are required for the accomplishment of their pastoral tasks, except for the powers legally reserved to the Sovereign Pontiff or other ecclesiastic authorities.[224] Bishops 'direct their dioceses freely under the authority of the Pope as their proper ordinaries and immediate pastors', but the papal representative in the State concerned can intervene at any moment in the name of the higher authority in the debates and discussions of the Bishops, although his power is not 'despotic'.[225] The Bishop of Urgell, when acting as the co-Prince of Andorra, exercises worldly authority which in principle is not covered by the duties imposed upon him by virtue of canon law. The only exception remains, however, that the Bishop of Urgell in all his actions, including those in the capacity of co-Prince of Andorra, has to respect the principles of divine law and should not commit any crimes under canon law.[226]

---

[222] Interview with HE Mgr Joan Martí I Alanis, Bishop of Urgell, 11 Dec. 1990.
[223] Art. 49 of the Constitution and Cans. 416–430 of the 1983 Code of Canon Law, AAS (1983) vol. 75.
[224] Can. 381 (1) of the 1983 Code of Canon Law.
[225] H. E. Cardinale, *The Holy See and the International Order* (1976) p. 50.
[226] In practice, this has implied that the Bishop of Urgell has always been a strong proponent of respect for fundamental human rights in Andorra. Moreover, the Catholic

Finally, the Holy See has the right to deprive the episcopal co-Prince of his rank of Bishop or can transfer him to another diocese and appoint a new Bishop of Urgell.[227] This measure, as a disciplinary sanction, is only used in extreme cases. It is evident that the acts of the Bishop of Urgell, in his capacity of co-Prince of Andorra, would have to constitute a severe violation of divine or canon law before the Holy See decided to take disciplinary measures. This situation can fairly be compared with the case of high treason in French law leading to the deposition of the President.[228] As a consequence of the hierarchical power which the Pope exercises over the Bishop of Urgell, it has been argued that the consent of the Holy See has to be sought in order to permit the Bishop of Urgell to become a co-Head of the Andorran State.[229] Within the above limits the Pope does not intervene in Andorran affairs.[230]

Relations with international organizations
League of Nations
In 1925, the Secretary-General of the League of Nations sent an invitation to the Syndic of the General Council to adhere to the International Opium Convention of 19 February 1925.[231] The same year,

---

Church in Andorra has been guaranteed a special position in the Constitution. It can freely and publicly exercise its activities and maintain its traditional and particular cooperation with the Andorran State, whereas the legal capacity of Church entities under canon law is recognized in the Andorran legal order: Art. 11 (3) of the Constitution.

[227] This action leads to a temporary vacancy of the episcopal see: Can. 416 of the 1983 Code of Canon Law.

[228] In case of a conviction for high treason under Art. 68 of the French Constitution, the French Government can request the Constitutional Council to declare that the President is not able to fulfil his functions: Art. 7 of the French Constitution.

[229] Zemanek, *Le Statut international*, p. 182. It is not likely that the Holy See will conclude a concordat with Andorra, because, even if Andorra is recognized as a State, for ecclesiastic purposes its territory falls under the Spanish church organization and therefore under the concordat with Spain.

[230] The only exception known concerned a petition from the Andorrans directly addressed to the Pope in 1894, in which they requested his intervention in the actions of the Bishop of Urgell. The Andorrans objected to the fact that the Bishop, possibly masking Spanish aspirations, had taken up the title of sovereign prince and tended to consider himself sole ruler over Andorra, thus destabilizing the balance between the two co-Princes and jeopardizing Andorran privileges and institutional rights. The petition was heard and the Bishop moderated his position: W. Pieshold, *Principat d'Andorra: Das Land des ewigen Friedens* (1964) pp. 152–153.

[231] An earlier contact had been made by a Spanish national, Miret Y Sans, who approached the Peace Conference of 1919 with a plan to annex Andorra to Catalonia in exchange

the Syndic notified the Secretary-General of Andorra's accession to the International Opium Convention, but France asked the Secretary-General to annul Andorra's ratification because the Syndic had not been competent to undertake international obligations for Andorra, a right reserved to France.[232] This in turn provoked the reaction of Spain which protested against the French hegemony in the international relations of Andorra. Nevertheless, Andorra did not manage to become a party to the International Opium Convention.

As a result of the internal political unrest in Andorra in 1933, fifty French policemen had been sent to the Valleys to secure public order.[233] A telegram was sent to the League of Nations in the name of the General Council and the Andorran people with their 'énergique protestation pour violation territoire andorran par la gendarmerie française'.[234] The General Council, which had adopted a protest document against the occupation of Andorra by French troops, claimed that France had violated the Briand–Kellogg Pact and had sent an official representative to discuss the question with the Secretary-General of the League of Nations.[235] The legal counsel of the League of Nations concluded that 'the external relations of the Republic [sic] can probably be conducted only by one or both of the Co-Princes ... it appears that no one save the Co-Princes or their authorised representatives can validly appeal to the League' and that therefore 'no official action can be taken on this telegram'.[236] As a result, the Andorran question was not considered by the League of Nations.[237]

Unlike Liechtenstein, San Marino and Monaco, Andorra was not one of the non-Member States of the League of Nations to receive a letter from the registrar of the Permanent Court of International Justice informing it of the possibility of adherence to the Statute of this Court.[238] Nevertheless, the acceptance of the Statute of the Permanent Court of International Justice by Andorra was registered

---

for the Spanish Valley of Aran which was to be granted to France. This initiative was however not supported by the Andorran authorities and received no attention from the Peace Conference. Bélinguier, *La Condition juridique*, p. 164.

[232] Ibid., p. 169.
[233] See p. 319 above.
[234] Telegram of P. Font received by the League of Nations on 21 Aug. 1933, cited in Zemanek, *Le Statut international*, p. 115 at n. 5.
[235] Ibid., pp. 116–117.
[236] Ibid., pp. 115–116.
[237] See also R. Toureng, *Statut juridique des Vallées d'Andorre* (1939) pp. 185–186.
[238] Cf. pp. 174, 234 and 293 above.

by the registry although, at the request of France, Andorra was erased from the list of parties to the Statute in 1926.[239] No attempts were made by the co-Princes to apply for membership of the League of Nations. This was to a great extent due to the French position that Andorra was not a State in international law.[240]

International conferences

The international conferences, often organized by international organizations, in which the co-Princes of Andorra were represented by the French and/or Spanish delegation, led in virtually all cases to a controversy between the French and Spanish representatives concerning their competence to represent Andorra in the international field. As a consequence, the international conventions, which were adopted by the international conferences, were either signed by France and Spain in the name of the French and the episcopal co-Prince respectively or signed by France alone and extended to the territory of Andorra.

The former situation arose in 1952 with respect to the Universal Copyright Convention, in 1954 regarding the Hague Convention for the Protection of Cultural Property in the Event of Armed Conflict and in 1984 during the ITU Regional Conference on Radio Broadcasting. During the Universal Copyright Conference in 1952, Spain had signed the Convention in the name of the Bishop of Urgell, who had *a posteriori* approved its actions and authorized it to ratify the Convention in his name as well.[241] France had signed the Universal Copyright Convention in the name of the French co-Prince and had declared to the Director-General of UNESCO that it considered the signature and ratification in the name of the Bishop of Urgell as 'nulle et non avenue', because only the French co-Prince was competent to sign and ratify treaties applicable in Andorra.[242] Despite this controversy

---

[239] Letter from the registrar of the Permanent Court of International Justice to the Secretary-General of the League of Nations of 20 Febr. 1926. Zemanek, *Le Statut international*, p. 108 at n. 5.

[240] Information from the French Government to the Secretary-General of the League of Nations concerning the unlawful ratification of the International Opium Convention by Andorra. Ibid., p. 108. Toureng, *Statut juridique*, p. 186 argues that Andorra could not have become a member of the League of Nations because of its traditional neutrality. It should be noted that apart from the problems raised concerning Andorra's statehood, the League of Nations was not forthcoming towards Micro-States in general. See, e.g., pp. 133–134, 170–174, 233–234 and 291–293 above.

[241] Zemanek, *Le Statut international*, pp. 109–110.

[242] Ibid., p. 110.

relating to the international competence to represent Andorra, UNESCO has registered Andorra as a contracting State of the Universal Copyright Convention of 1952.[243] When, in 1971, both the French and the Spanish delegations were charged to represent the French and episcopal co-Prince respectively in the Conference for a revision of the Universal Copyright Convention, the French delegation initially contested the Spanish delegation's right to represent the Bishop of Urgell, invoking its own monopoly. However, eventually France admitted that 'pour siéger valablement au nom de la République d'Andorre, les représentants devraient avoir l'aval des deux Co-Princes'.[244] The Committee on Credentials of the Conference therefore decided to await a previous agreement between the co-Princes settling the question of representation. This accord was never reached.

The Conference on the Protection of Cultural Property in the Event of Armed Conflict of 1954 gave rise to a similar dispute between France and Spain concerning the international representation of Andorra. However, this time France did not claim to represent the French co-Prince, but to sign the Convention on the Protection of Cultural Property in the Event of Armed Conflict with effect in Andorra. France directly invoked Article 35 of the Convention, a so-called colonial clause, in order to make the Convention applicable in Andorra and therefore adopted the position that France bore international responsibility for Andorra.[245] Spain had signed the Convention in the name of the Bishop of Urgell, but it was never ratified by him. The episcopal co-Prince had raised objections to the Director-General of UNESCO concerning the application of the colonial clause by France and claimed that the Convention had to be ratified by both co-Princes in order to come into force in Andorra.[246] The Director-General of UNESCO, in his capacity of depositary of the Convention, refused to accept France's notification on the application of the colonial clause to Andorra, which was therefore not communicated to the other States Parties.[247] As a consequence, Andorra was registered as a signatory of the Convention, but not as a party due to the lack of a proper ratification.[248]

---

[243] France ratified Protocols nos. 1, 2 and 3 to the Universal Copyright Convention of 1952 while Spain ratified only Protocols nos. 2 and 3 in the name of the Bishop of Urgell. Vidal i Guitart, *Institucions Polítiques*, p. 287.
[244] Ibid., p. 249 at n. 740.
[245] JORF (25 Oct. 1960) p. 9646.
[246] Viñas Farré, 'El "Treaty Making Power"', p. 333 at n. 44.
[247] Zemanek, *Le Statut international*, p. 112.
[248] D. Schindler and J. Toman, eds., *The Laws of Armed Conflict* (1988) p. 769.

Although it was generally believed that after 1973 the two co-Princes, through their *veguers*, had agreed to appoint their representatives to international conferences jointly,[249] France did not abandon its position that the French co-Prince was the only competent body to represent Andorra in the international field. Thus in 1984, France again emphasized this point, contested by Spain, during the ITU Regional Conference on Radio Broadcasting.[250] Andorra could therefore not fully participate in the work of this Conference.

Two conventions were signed by France subject to the declaration that 'la signature de la Convention par la France vaudra également pour l'Andorre dont elle assume la représentation'.[251] These two conventions were the Convention on Road Traffic of 1949 and the International Convention for the Protection of Performers of 1961. Andorra has not officially been registered as a State Party to these Conventions.

The participation of Andorra in certain international conferences and the signature of international conventions in its name prompted the French Minister of Foreign Affairs to declare to the Director-General of UNESCO in 1970:

> Si l'Andorre a pu participer à certaines conférences internationales, y signer et y ratifier des conventions et être, ainsi ... considérée comme une entité distincte, cela n'implique pas que ce soit sur un pied d'égalité avec les Etats. De même, si l'Andorre a été mentionnée dans divers documents de l'Unesco aux côtés d'Etats contractants ou parmi des Etats signataires, il s'agit d'une erreur ou d'une inadvertance qui ne peuvent conférer à ce territoire le statut d'Etat souverain.[252]

France, when participating in international conferences for Andorra, has interchangeably either claimed to represent the French co-Prince or claimed the right to sign a convention because it (without reference to the French co-Prince) is internationally responsible for Andorra. France was of the opinion that as Andorra had no right of active or passive diplomatic representation and was not recognized as a State, it could not constitute a State and therefore could not participate in international conferences on the same footing as States.[253]

---

[249] Zemanek, *Le Statut international*, p. 54.
[250] Marquès i Oste, *La Reforma*, pp. 280–282. See n. 201, p. 347 above.
[251] Zemanek, *Le Statut international*, p. 113.
[252] Communication of the French Minister of Foreign Affairs to the Director-General of UNESCO of 8 Dec. 1970, ibid., pp. 146–147.
[253] Bélinguier, *La Condition juridique*, p. 223.

This argument implies a complete assimilation of the French co-Prince and the French State. Even if it had been admitted that the French co-Prince held the exclusive right of international representation of Andorra, this fact would not *a priori* have prevented Andorra's statehood, if the French co-Prince acted in his personal and exclusive capacity. The French position was however that Andorra did not have its own international competence, which implies that the French co-Prince lacked independence.

Council of Europe

The first contacts between Andorra and the Council of Europe were made in 1987 and led to a draft resolution presented by a member of the Parliamentary Assembly inviting the co-Princes and the authorities of Andorra to reform the political institutions in order to turn Andorra into a modern State respecting human rights.[254] A working group was formed in 1988 composed of four members of the Parliamentary Assembly who produced a report and made certain draft resolutions concerning the Principality of Andorra. The Council of Europe was interested in the legal situation in Andorra not only because its attention had been unofficially drawn to it by the Andorran side, but also because geographically, historically and traditionally Andorra was an integral part of Western Europe.[255] On 11 May 1990, the Parliamentary Assembly adopted a resolution on the Principality of Andorra in which it recommended certain reforms with regard to the protection of human rights, the integration of foreigners, the electoral law and a constitutional democratization.[256]

The recommendations of the Parliamentary Assembly supported those who favoured a democratization in Andorra. All of the Parliamentary Assembly's suggestions have been followed in the Andorran Constitution. Thus, fundamental human rights are guaranteed

---

[254] Council of Europe Doc. 5742 (7 May 1987).
[255] Council of Europe Doc. 6146 (16 Nov. 1989) 'Report on the situation in Andorra', p. 3.
[256] Parliamentary Assembly Res. 946 (1990). It had also recommended to the Committee of Ministers that they determine to which conventions of the Council of Europe Andorra could adhere without being a member of the Organization and define the intergovernmental activities of the Council of Europe in which Andorra could participate: Res. 947 and 1127 (1990). Although in Oct. 1990, the Committee of Ministers had asked the Secretary-General to contact the two co-Princes to define the areas suitable for cooperation between the Council of Europe and the Principality of Andorra, no regular contacts were established at the time and Andorra did not accede to any of the conventions of the Council of Europe.

constitutional protection, the freedom of association has been expressly recognized, more powers have been transferred from the co-Princes to the General Council in order to create a democratic Parliament and Government and the electoral system has been changed so as to permit a national representation and not just a representation for every parish in the General Council.[257] Andorra even relaxed its Code on Andorran nationality so as to facilitate the naturalization of foreigners and their integration in the Andorran society, although this was subsequently annulled by the Constitutional Court.[258]

Shortly after becoming a member of the United Nations, Andorra expressed the wish to be invited to become a member of the Council of Europe.[259] The Parliamentary Assembly referred the matter to a rapporteur of the Political Affairs Committee[260] and entrusted a judge of the European Court of Human Rights and a member of the European Commission of Human Rights with preparing a report on the human rights legislation in Andorra.[261] Both reports concluded that there were no obstacles to Andorra's admission, though it was urged to adopt a new text of the law on nationality making the conditions required for acquisition of the nationality much more flexible.[262] It is remarkable that, contrary to the studies of the admission of Liechtenstein and San Marino, the rapporteur did not examine the international legal status of the applicant State. Andorra's statehood was not questioned, probably due to the fact that it was already a member of the United Nations – Liechtenstein and San Marino were not at the time of their applications – and because Andorra had followed the legal reforms which the Parliamentary Assembly had recommended in 1990, which were believed sufficient to make Andorra fulfil the membership conditions of the Council of Europe. At the plenary meeting of the Assembly, it was however made clear by

---

[257] Ibid. See also pp. 320–326 and 329–334 above.
[258] See n. 129, p. 334 above.
[259] Letter of 22 Nov. 1993, Committee of Ministers Res. (94) 1, Council of Europe Doc. 6988. Previously, it had invited representatives of the Parliamentary Assembly to visit the Principality during the Dec. 1993 general elections. The *ad hoc* Committee concluded that the elections were completely democratic, free and fair, which could not pose problems for Andorra's membership: Council of Europe Doc. 6996, Add. I.
[260] Mr Reddemann, same rapporteur as for the applications of Liechtenstein and San Marino, Council of Europe Doc. 7152.
[261] Information report on the legislation of the Principality of Andorra, Council of Europe Doc. 7080, Add. III.
[262] Council of Europe Doc. 7080, Add. III, p. 11 and Doc. 7152, paras. 33–34 and 42.

many speakers that Andorra should adopt a new version of the articles of the law on nationality, annulled by the Constitutional Court, facilitating access to Andorran nationality, in order to overcome the difficulties of integrating the non-Andorran residents.[263] This point was emphasized in the Assembly's opinion inviting Andorra to become a member of the Council of Europe.[264] Thus Andorra became a member of the Council of Europe on 10 November 1994, with two representatives in the Assembly.[265]

European Community

Andorra has always been considered a third country with respect to the European Community. In 1965, the ambassador of the Federal Republic of Germany officially asked the French Minister of Foreign Affairs whether by virtue of Article 227, paragraph 4 of the EC Treaty, Andorra was a part of the European Economic Community. France replied that Andorra did not fall within the Community because of its special customs regime and international status.[266] This position implies that, contrary to its policy in other cases concerning Andorra, France did not consider that it assumed the external relations of Andorra so as to make the EC Treaty applicable in Andorran territory within the meaning of Article 227, paragraph 4 of the EC Treaty. In 1978, in response to a written question from a member of the European Parliament, the Commission declared that the exchange of letters between France and Andorra defining Andorra's customs regime was one of the rights and obligations which was not affected by the EC Treaty by virtue of Article 234 of the EC Treaty.[267] Again, in 1986, the Commission emphasized that the provisions of the EC Treaty concerning the free movement of workers, the right of establishment and the freedom of services did not apply to Andorra.[268]

---

[263] Council of Europe, *Parliamentary Assembly, Official Report* (3 Oct. 1994), Doc. AS (1994) CR 24, pp. 23–35. France and Spain were convinced that the rights of foreign residents would be better protected if Andorra became a member, Council of Europe Doc. 7152, para. 42. New law on nationality adopted on 5 Oct. 1995, BOPA (1996) no. 8.
[264] Parliamentary Assembly Opinion no. 182 (1994), para. 7. When ratifying the ECHR it was considered essential that Andorra also ratify Prot. no. 11: para. 4.
[265] Committee of Ministers Res. (94) 26, instrument of ratification deposited on 10 Nov. 1994.
[266] Viñas Farré, 'El "Treaty Making Power"', p. 326 at n. 16.
[267] Answer of the Commission to written question no. 191/78, ECOJ no. C 238 (15.9.78) pp. 14–15.
[268] Answer of the Commission to written question no. 900/86, ECOJ no. C 54 (2.3.87) p. 31.

The first contacts between the European Economic Community and Andorra were made in 1984. The Head of the Andorran Government had turned to the two co-Princes proposing negotiations with the European Economic Community in order to fix future trade relations with the participation of representatives of the Andorran people. The Bishop of Urgell notified his willingness to accept the proposal of the Head of the Government to the French co-Prince who gave no response.[269] Thereupon, the French ambassador to the European Communities informed the Commission that 'les relations extérieures de celles-ci [the Valleys of Andorra] sont assurées par le Président de la République Française en sa qualité de co-prince'.[270] The Bishop of Urgell for his part notified the Commission that an international agreement would require the approval of both co-Princes and that nothing should be arranged with the Community without the participation of the Andorran people.[271] France had wished to find a settlement for the Andorran customs regime through the Act of Accession of Spain to the European Communities. The Community had therefore prepared three projects based on the principle that Andorra was a third country in its relations with the Community and that no EC Member State bore responsibility for its international relations.[272] The General Council and the Government, supported by the Bishop of Urgell and Spain, opposed the inclusion of Andorra in Spain's Act of Accession to the European Economic Community in a similar way to the Channel Islands and the Isle of Man.[273] The Government and the General Council wanted to participate in direct negotiations with the Community and seek recognition of Andorra's statehood.[274] It was therefore decided, in a joint declaration annexed to the Act of Accession of Spain to the European

---

[269] Marquès i Oste, *La Reforma*, p. 283.
[270] Letter from the French ambassador to the EC, to the Commission, 2 May 1984. Ibid., p. 284.
[271] Memorandum of the episcopal co-Prince to the Commission of 18 Jul. 1984. Ibid., p. 285.
[272] All three projects held on to the position that the French co-Prince was the sole representative in the international field. The first project classified Andorra as a State under the personal, exclusive, joint and indivisible sovereignty of its co-Princes, the second project considered Andorra as an exclusive, joint and indivisible suzerainty of the co-Princes, whereas the third project stated that Andorra was not a State, but a suzerainty. Marquès i Oste, *La Reforma*, p. 287.
[273] Ibid., p. 286.
[274] Document of information from the Executive Council and the General Council of 16 Apr. 1986. Ibid., pp. 288–289.

Economic Community, that within two years of Spain's accession a regime would be established regulating commercial relations between the Community and Andorra destined to replace the present national regimes in force, which would remain applicable until the new regime came into effect.[275]

In 1988, the contacts between Andorra and the European Economic Community were renewed. The French co-Prince had approved the participation of Andorran representatives in the delegation of negotiators which would also include representatives of both co-Princes.[276] On 14 December 1988, the Commission issued a press release stating that 'Andorra is an independent State placed under the joint sovereignty of the President of the French Republic and the Bishop of Urgel.'[277] After having received a memorandum from the Andorran delegation and a recommendation from the Commission, the Council adopted a decision on 20 March 1989 authorizing the Commission to open negotiations with Andorra.[278] In the mean time the European Parliament's Committee on Institutional Affairs had adopted its 'resolution on the rights of the citizens of small States and territories in Europe'. It had concluded that the resources of Andorra would be prejudiced due to the unification of the European market and the reduction of VAT percentages in France and Spain.[279]

The trade agreement between the European Economic Community and Andorra was signed by the Council, the co-Princes and the Andorran Government on 28 June 1990.[280] The European Parliament approved the customs agreement with Andorra on 23 November 1990.[281] The agreement came into force on 1 July 1991.[282]

The customs agreement between Andorra and the European Economic Community reconciles on the one hand the Community's wish to abolish discriminatory taxes and to apply the Community customs tariffs, and on the other hand Andorra's desire to remain a

---

[275] Joint declaration of the EEC and Spain, annexed to the Act of Accession of 1985, no. A-8. ECOJ no. L 302 (1985).
[276] Marquès i Oste, *La Reforma*, p. 290.
[277] EP Doc. A3-0256/90, European Parliament, *Session Documents* (18 Oct. 1990) p. 5, para. 2.
[278] Bull. EC (3-1989) point 2.2.11, p. 53.
[279] EP Doc. A2-86/89, European Parliament, *Session Documents* (20 Apr. 1989) p. 7.
[280] The legal basis for the customs agreement with Andorra was found in Arts. 99, 113 and 228 of the EC Treaty.
[281] EP Legislative Resolution A3-256/90, ECOJ no. C 324 (24.12.90) p. 329.
[282] Text of the EEC-Andorra customs union agreement in ECOJ no. L 374 (31.12.90) pp. 16 ff. Council Decision 90/680/EEC of 26 Nov. 1990. Text also in BOPA (1992) extra no. 3.

country with competitive prices in order to attract tourism and foreign buyers. The following customs regime has therefore been instituted:

Industrial products A customs union is established between the European Community and Andorra for industrial products only.[283] For these products, the Principality has also adopted the provisions on import formalities applied by the Community to third countries.[284] The customs offices listed in Annex I to the customs union agreement are authorized to levy on behalf of and for Andorra the import duties payable on goods imported from non-EC countries.[285] The Community assigns the amounts thus collected to the Andorran exchequer after deduction of administrative costs.[286] Andorra had to abolish all customs duties and charges having equivalent effect on imports from the Community.[287] This implied that the tax on imported goods ('Taxes de Consum') had to be abolished at least on industrial products imported from the Community. In order to compensate for this loss of revenues, Andorra introduced an Indirect Tax on Merchandise ('Impost de Mercaderies Indirecte') applicable to every imported good and to domestic products.[288]

Agricultural products Agricultural products which are not covered by the customs union and which originate in Andorra are nevertheless exempt from import duties when imported into the Community.[289] The appendix to the customs union agreement defines restrictively the concept of originating products.[290] Andorra is not

---

[283] Those are the products covered by Chapters 25 to 97 of the Harmonized System: Art. 2 of the customs union agreement.
[284] Art. 7 (1) of the customs union agreement and Decision no. 2/91 of the EEC–Andorra Joint Committee of 12 Jul. 1991, ECOJ no. L 250 (7.9.91) p. 24.
[285] Art. 8 (1) of the customs union agreement.
[286] Art. 8 (3) (b) of the customs union agreement and Decision no. 5/91 of the EEC-Andorra Joint Committee of 12 Jul. 1991, ECOJ no. L 250 (7.9.91) p. 32. The percentage of administrative costs to be deduced was fixed at 10 per cent: Art. 1 (g) of Decision no. 5/91.
[287] Art. 6 (2) of the customs union agreement.
[288] Law on Indirect Tax on Merchandise of 26 Jun. 1991, BOPA (1991) extra no. 7, pp. 498 ff. The tariffs vary from 1 to 12 per cent.
[289] Those are the products covered by Chapters 1 to 24 of the Harmonized System: Art. 11 (1) of the customs union agreement.
[290] Art. 1 of the Appendix to the customs union agreement. This definition has however been extended by the EEC–Andorran Joint Committee so as to include certain products originating in Andorra which would otherwise not have enjoyed the tax exemption, such as biscuits, chocolates and pastry which can be imported from Andorra into the EC duty-free up to a quantitative limit: Decisions nos. 7/91 and 8/91 of the EEC–Andorra

allowed to apply a more favourable arrangement to agricultural products from third countries than to those from the Community.[291] Agricultural products imported from the Community into Andorra remain subject to the Andorran tax on imported goods.[292] As Andorra constitutes a third country for the European Community, agricultural products imported from non-EC countries into Andorra will not be subject to the Community tariffs.[293]

Joint Committee A Joint Committee has been set up to ensure the proper implementation of the agreement and to settle questions of interpretation.[294] The Joint Committee is composed of representatives of the Community and Andorra, the latter being appointed by the Andorran Government.[295] If the Joint Committee does not succeed in settling a dispute, an arbitration procedure can be instituted.[296] The customs union agreement has been concluded for an unlimited duration, but can be denounced by either party subject to six months' notice.[297]

Andorra has gained several advantages from its agreement with the European Community. In the first place, it now receives the import duties on industrial products from third countries collected on its behalf by the Community, whereas agricultural products imported from third countries into Andorra are exempt from Community customs duties.[298] In the second place, the European Community has

---

Joint Committee of 31 Dec. 1991, ECOJ no. L 43 (19.2.92) p. 33 and Decision no. 1/92 of 19 Oct. 1992, ECOJ L 321 (6.11.92) p. 27.

[291] Art. 12 (1) of the customs union agreement.
[292] The tax on imported goods varies from 2 to 60 per cent. By virtue of Art. 12 (2) of the customs union agreement, Community raw tobacco is eligible, when imported into Andorra, for a preferential rate, 60 per cent lower than the rate applied to third countries: Law of 26 Jun. 1991 modifying the tax on imported goods, BOPA (1991) extra no. 7, pp. 509–510.
[293] Special tax exemptions have been laid down for imports by travellers: Art. 13 of the customs union agreement.
[294] Art. 17 (1) of the customs union agreement.
[295] Art. 17 (4) of the customs union agreement.
[296] Art. 18 (2) of the customs union agreement.
[297] Arts. 20 and 21 of the customs union agreement. Within five years of the entry into force of the customs union agreement, the parties shall begin consultations to examine the results of its application and, if necessary, to open negotiations on its amendment: Art. 20.
[298] This constitutes a financial improvement compared to the former French customs regime applied to Andorra which did not provide for assigning the collected customs duties to Andorra, and did not exempt agricultural products, imported from third States, from the Community charges. See p. 340 above.

treated Andorra like a State.[299] The relations between the Community and Andorra are maintained directly with the Andorran institutions (Government and co-Princes), without the need for the legal intervention of either France or Spain.

United Nations

On 3 June 1993, the date of the signature of the trilateral treaty of vicinage, the Head of the Andorran Government announced the Government's intention of applying for membership of the United Nations. By letter of 9 June 1993, the application for membership in the United Nations was submitted to the Secretary-General.[300] The Security Council, having consulted its Committee on the Admission of New Members, recommended, on 8 July 1993, that Andorra be admitted as a Member State.[301] The General Assembly approved Andorra's admission on 28 July 1993 by acclamation.[302] Though no organ of the United Nations had examined Andorra's statehood, the representative of the Group of Western European States declared in the General Assembly that Andorra's admission 'témoigne également de la reconnaissance, par la communauté internationale, de la souveraineté de la Principauté d'Andorre'.[303] The United Nations thus became the very first political international governmental organization to accept Andorra as a Member State.

In June 1994, the Andorran representative acted as chairman of the Western European and Other States Group in the General Assembly. In October 1994, Andorra co-sponsored a draft resolution calling for the abolition of the death penalty by all Member States.[304] Despite its small delegation, Andorra makes every effort to enhance the goals of the United Nations and is of the opinion that much can be learned from Micro-States, because of their respect for diversity and coexistence.[305]

---

[299] There is no difference between EC–San Marinese relations and EC–Andorran relations with respect to the procedure of the negotiations, the legal form of the agreement and the wish to protect each side's basic economic interests. Cf. pp. 246–254 above.
[300] UN Doc. S/26039 (1993).
[301] SC Res. 848 (1993).
[302] GA Res. 47/232.
[303] Luxembourg delegate: UN Doc. A/47/PV.108 (1993) p. 13.
[304] UN Doc. A/49/234 (1994), draft resolution not adopted, UN Docs. A/C.3/49/SR.35 and 39 (1994).
[305] UN Doc. A/49/PV.6 (1994).

Other international organizations

In 1932, the General Council, at its own initiative, instructed a representative to request the admission of the 'Republic of Andorra' as a full member of the UPU. The Swiss Government as depositary of the Universal Postal Convention refused to comply with this request, arguing that

> le statut de la République des Vallées d'Andorre [sic] est, en droit des gens, celui d'un Etat soumis simultanément à la suzeraineté de la France et à la souveraineté ecclésiastique de l'Evêque d'Urgel en Espagne. ... un Etat soumis à la suzeraineté d'autres Puissances n'est pas capable d'accomplir sans autre – c'est-à-dire sans le concours du suzerain – des actes de droit des gens d'une grande portée, comme par exemple l'adhésion à une convention internationale.[306]

The accord of the co-Princes was not obtained.

Much later, in 1978, the General Council informed the permanent delegates of the co-Princes of its desire to become a full member of the World Tourism Organization. The representatives of the French co-Prince emphasized that the General Council had no competence in international questions and stated that the status of associate member would correspond better to Andorra's international position, as Andorra could not be recognized as a State.[307] The episcopal representatives opposed associate membership of the World Tourism Organization for Andorra, because they considered that Andorra possessed full responsibility for its international relations. No further action was therefore taken until 1995 when Andorra joined the Organization as a full member.[308]

Andorra almost became a Member State of the ITU in 1983. After the approval of the General Council, the two co-Princes had agreed by exchange of notes that they would jointly apply for membership of the ITU. In order to become a member of the ITU at least two-thirds of the State Members should have approved Andorra's application.[309] This number was not achieved before the deadline which had been

---

[306] Cited in Zemanek, *Le Statut international*, pp. 118–119. It should be remembered that the General Council's initiative was placed in the context of internal political disputes between the General Council and the co-Princes. See p. 319 above.
[307] Marquès i Oste, *La Reforma*, p. 125. Art. 6 (1) of the Statute of the World Tourism Organization reserves the status of associate member to territories or groups of territories which are not responsible for the conduct of their international relations.
[308] Accession on 17 Oct. 1995. Information from the Andorran Ministry of Foreign Affairs.
[309] Art. 6 of the International Telecommunication Convention of 1973.

set, although afterwards many more favourable votes were received which would have secured the required two-thirds majority, if they had been on time.[310] Andorra's application was however not renewed due to a lack of willingness of the French co-Prince.[311] Later, Andorra had no difficulties in joining the ITU on 12 November 1993.[312]

After assuring its statehood, Andorra was admitted to UNESCO on 20 October 1993, without much discussion.[313] The Director-General declared that 'thanks to its rich potential of human resources' Andorra would no doubt play a significant role in the Organization.[314]

More recently, Andorra has adhered to EUTELSAT and WIPO.[315]

Application of the criteria for statehood

The Andorran Constitution of 1993 states that Andorra is an independent State.[316] It should at present be examined whether, according to the criteria for statehood in international law, the same conclusion can be drawn.[317] The following elements should be examined:

Territory The territory of the Principality of Andorra is larger than that of the other four Micro-States considered. Bearing in mind that the international community has not doubted the statehood of these other Micro-States by reason of the smallness of their territory, it can be concluded that Andorra satisfies the territorial condition of statehood in international law.[318] It has moreover been maintained by both Spain and France that the Andorran territory does not constitute a part of the Spanish or French territory respectively.[319] Both France and

---

[310] On the deadline of 8 Jun. 1983, 83 out of 147 favourable votes were received, while 20 more votes were received up to 17 Jun. 1983. Marquès i Oste, *La Reforma*, p. 278 at nn. 855–856.
[311] The episcopal co-Prince informed the Head of the Andorran Government that he was prepared to reiterate Andorra's application for membership of the ITU: ibid., p. 278.
[312] Information from the Department of external relations of the Andorran Government, BOPA (1994) nos. 50 and 65.
[313] UNESCO Doc. 27 C/VR.2 (25 Oct. 1993) p. 9 and 27 C/Resolution 0.60.
[314] UNESCO Doc. DG/16.1.6/499 (25 Oct. 1993).
[315] On 28 Oct. 1994; information from the Department of external relations of the Andorran Government, BOPA (1994) nos. 50 and 65.
[316] Art. 1 (1) of the Constitution.
[317] See for the general criteria for statehood pp. 116–127 above.
[318] See pp. 200, 256 and 305 above and p. 411 below.
[319] See n. 187, p. 344 above, and n. 219, p. 350 above, and accompanying text regarding the treaty of 1863 between Spain and Andorra delimiting the frontier between the two countries.

Spain have undertaken to respect the territorial integrity of Andorra, which implies recognition of an Andorran territory.[320]

Population The Andorran nationals who comprise 24.3 per cent of the inhabitants of the Principality are a minority group which has been long-established in the territory. They constitute a permanent population within the meaning of the criteria for statehood.[321]

Government Since the promulgation of the Andorran Constitution in 1993, Andorra possesses a codified governmental legal system. The powers of each constitutional organ have been clearly defined so as to guarantee a more democratic Government based on the rule of law. The Constitution has eliminated the uncertainties concerning the delimitation of powers and has thus increased the effective control of the governmental institutions. It is beyond doubt that the Government of Andorra, in the widest sense, wields effective power in the territory.[322]

Independence There are four domains in which foreign States could claim to have certain rights of interference in Andorran affairs, thus limiting the Principality's formal independence:[323]

1. *Postal union* The postal agreement which met with the approval of the co-Princes cannot be denounced by Andorra.[324] However, the delegation of the postal administration to another State is not considered by the international community as a factor which *a priori* precludes independence.[325]
2. *Diplomatic representation* The Andorran Constitution provides for a proper Andorran diplomatic or consular service.[326] The use of any other diplomatic service is a subsidiary means of representation, only acceptable to the Principality if dependent upon its instructions. The freedom of Andorra is complete as France and Spain, when putting their diplomatic service at Andorra's disposal, have provided a legal guarantee that their agents will act according to the Principality's wishes in accordance with the Vienna Convention on Diplomatic Relations.[327]

---

[320] Art. 3 of the treaty of vicinage.
[321] See p. 316 above.
[322] See pp. 320–329 above.
[323] See p. 123 above.
[324] See pp. 339–340 and 347 above.
[325] Cf. Liechtenstein, San Marino, Monaco and the Vatican City, pp. 163–164, 228–229 and 285 above and pp. 390–391 below.
[326] Art. 45 (1) (e) of the Constitution.
[327] Art. 6 of the treaty of vicinage. See pp. 338–339 and 347 above. Such guarantees have not always been provided in the past, as Spain has at times acted independently

3   *Co-Princes*   The two co-Princes of the Andorran State hold their rights in their personal and exclusive capacity according to the Andorran Constitution.[328] We have observed that their rights are nevertheless restricted by virtue of their special relations with, on the one hand, Spain and the Holy See and, on the other, France.[329] The relations between Spain and the Bishop of Urgell are very liberal. Spain has no legal rights to impose its policies upon the episcopal co-Prince. Spain has granted the privileges and immunities of foreign Heads of State under international law to the Bishop of Urgell.[330] A certain influence of the Holy See on the Bishop of Urgell cannot be denied. This interference is restricted to the appointment of the episcopal co-Prince, his rights and duties under canon and divine law and the transfer or removal of the Bishop for serious ecclesiastic reasons. The Holy See does not instruct the Bishop of Urgell in Andorran affairs.[331] The relations between the French co-Prince and the French State are more ambiguous. Under the French Constitution, the French President cannot legally be obliged to follow the French State's policy towards Andorra. In this sense the French co-Prince is free to determine his actions in Andorra. However, the French Constitution does not oppose the use of the countersignature by the French Prime Minister for any act of the French President in his capacity of co-Prince of Andorra. The legal uncertainty concerning the formal independence of the French co-Prince of the French State would have remained if no legal instrument, binding Andorra and France, had guaranteed the personal and exclusive exercise of the French co-Prince's rights within French public law. Such a legal guarantee, rather than simply a custom open to change, is all the more necessary because of the French position in certain periods of Andorran history and because Andorra's lack of independence of France has been one of the major objections raised in doctrine to Andorra's statehood.[332] Moreover, for those learned writers who have contended that Andorra was not a

of the Bishop of Urgell or sought his approval *a posteriori*, whereas France has occasionally claimed to represent Andorra without reference to the French co-Prince, see p. 356 above.

[328] Art. 43 (2) of the Constitution.
[329] See pp. 342–345 and 348–352 above.
[330] 1993 Agreement on the status of the episcopal co-Prince. See p. 349 above.
[331] See p. 351 above.
[332] See in this light Anon., 'La Principauté d'Andorre et son Statut international', 10 *Chronique de Politique Etrangére* (May 1957) pp. 385–391; Bélinguier, *La Condition juridique*, pp. 224–225; J. Crawford, 'The International Legal Status of the Valleys of Andorra', 55 RDI (1977) p. 267; J. Roca, *De la Condition internationale des Vallées d'Andorre* (1908); G. Riera, 'L'Andorre', 72 RGDIP (1968) pp. 361–380; C. Rousseau, 'Les Vallées d'Andorre: Une Survivance féodale dans le Monde contemporain', *Symbolae Verzijl* (1958) p. 343; Toureng, *Statut juridique*, p. 177; and P. Vellas, 'Les Etats exigus en Droit international public', 58 RGDIP (1954) p. 569.

State because its international relations were assumed by France through the French co-Prince, the Andorran Constitution has brought only a partial change: the French co-Prince still has a substantial control over the promulgation of laws, the ratification of treaties and the maintenance of diplomatic relations. If therefore the French co-Prince lacks independence of France, no law can be adopted, no treaty ratified and no diplomatic relations maintained without the consent of France. France has at times adopted contradictory positions. In 1971, the French co-Prince wrote to the Bishop of Urgell:

> L'Andorre n'étant pas un Etat reconnu internationalement, les deux Co-Princes n'ont, en tant que tels, aucun pouvoir sur le plan international; ils ne peuvent de ce fait ni parler au nom des Vallées ni confier à d'autres le soin de le faire puisqu'on ne peut déléguer un pouvoir qu'on ne possède pas.[333]

France has, however, often claimed that the French co-Prince possessed the exclusive power to represent Andorra in the international field,[334] whereas it has also occurred that France has declared that it, without reference to the French co-Prince, assumed international responsibility for Andorra.[335] Under these circumstances the formal independence of Andorra will only be firmly established in international law if France guarantees that the French co-Prince will be able to exercise his rights in Andorra independently of the French State. France's obligation to respect Andorra's independence under Article 3 of the treaty of vicinage is therefore a determinant element of Andorra's formal, and actual, independence which can be translated into an obligation to guarantee the French co-Prince's independent position of France in French public law. France has no right to intervene in the French co-Prince's decisions and may not alter his position in French public law so as to create a situation of dependence on the French Government, like, for example, the introduction of a countersignature.

4 *Fundamental interests* Andorra has to respect the internal and external security interests of France and Spain. In addition, it should respect the fundamental interests of France and Spain, which in turn will respect Andorran fundamental interests.[336] The former obligation comprises, in fact, a duty of absolute neutrality. The latter duty is relativized by its reciprocal application and by

---

[333] Memorandum of the French co-Prince to the episcopal co-Prince of 8 Jun. 1971, cited in Marquès i Oste, *La Reforma*, p. 263.
[334] See, for example, French declaration to the Commission of the EC in 1984, n. 270, p. 360 above, and accompanying text.
[335] See, for example, the use of the 'colonial clause' of the Hague Convention on the Protection of Cultural Property in the Event of Armed Conflict of 1954, p. 355 above.
[336] See pp. 336–338 above.

the obligation of France and Spain to respect Andorra's independence. As a consequence, the mutual respect for each other's fundamental interests implies that France and Spain may not in law demand more from Andorra than Andorra demands from them. The result of this obligation should therefore not lead to loss of formal independence of Andorra, or indeed of France and Spain.[337] It is in this sense that the fundamental character of the parties' interests should be interpreted and determined. By virtue of the trilateral treaty of vicinage there are sufficient legal guarantees for us to accept Andorra's formal independence.

It is more complicated to ascertain whether Andorra enjoys actual independence of any other country. It is clear that the duty to respect Andorra's independence also extends to Andorra's actual independence. In any case the political affiliation of the co-Princes or indeed any other Andorran public organ with the policy of another State is of a personal nature and not imposed by that other State. In the past, the actual independence of Andorra has been of a variable nature, depending on the periods of its history or the questions treated.[338] As Andorra's formal independence has been assured, its actual independence will be stabilized in the future.

Recognition France and Spain were the first States to recognize Andorra as a State in international law. Due to the conflict between the Bishop of Urgell and the French co-Prince regarding the competence to represent Andorra in the international field, the occasions on which Andorra could seek to affirm its international status before 1993 were rare. The early bilateral agreements concluded by Andorra and Spain or France were usually kept in the form of an administrative agreement so as not to constitute an implicit recognition of Andorra's statehood.[339] At least up to the conclusion of the trilateral treaty of vicinage, the international recognition of Andorra as a State has not been unequivocal. Of all the modes of recognition accepted in international law, those used in the case of Andorra were not the most unambiguous ones.[340] Thus in 1990, the French representative

---

[337] Art. 3 of the treaty of vicinage.
[338] See, for example, the French involvement in the question of Radio Andorra, p. 343 above and attempts of direct or indirect interference by Spain, pp. 319, 349–350 and 352, n. 230 above.
[339] See pp. 340, 346, and 350 above.
[340] It is, in general, difficult to infer recognition in case of non-political treaties dealing with technical matters, such as the Universal Copyright Convention of 1952 or the International Telecommunications Convention. Opinions differ as to whether the

in the Council of the European Communities approved the conclusion of the customs union agreement with Andorra, but in the same year, before the European Commission of Human Rights, the French Government had contended that there could be no neighbourhood agreement between France and Andorra 'since Andorra is not a sovereign power'.[341] At the time when Andorra lacked formal independence, its international recognition as a State was still too weak to compensate the non-fulfilment of all criteria for statehood. The implied acts of recognition had only the effect of recognizing the Principality as a separate entity in international law which at least did not constitute an integral part of the French or Spanish State.

The Commission of the European Community has been the first international organ to declare expressly in a press release that Andorra was 'an independent State'.[342] However, the opinions of the Commission are not necessarily those of the Member States of the European Community, as it has its own power of decision.[343] The agreement concluded between the European Economic Community and Andorra in the form of an exchange of letters could nevertheless imply recognition of Andorra's statehood, as the agreement has been approved by the Council which does represent the opinions of the Governments of the EC Member States. The European Community has not treated Andorra differently from San Marino as far as the respect for its legal status is concerned. Neither the United Nations, UNESCO, nor the Council of Europe considered it necessary to examine whether Andorra was a State.[344] Legally, Andorra became a State in international law when it signed the trilateral treaty of vicinage by which France and Spain engaged to respect the Principality's independence.

---

receipt of a consular *exequatur* implies recognition by the sending State. Even if recognition were to be accepted, it would be weakened by the fact that the receiving State did not in turn send consular missions to other States, as in the case of Andorra, thus not taking the opportunity to seek a second direct recognition. There is however a stronger assumption of recognition where the accession to a multilateral treaty needs the approval of other States Parties, as in the ITU. It should nevertheless not be forgotten that Andorra eventually did not become a member of the ITU in 1983. See also P. K. Menon, 'Some Aspects of the Law of Recognition. Part V: Modes of Recognition', RDI (1991) no. 1, pp. 17–49.

[341] Application no. 12747/87, *Jordi Drozd and Pavel Janousek against France and Spain*, Report of the Commission adopted on 11 Dec. 1990, p. 25, para. 127.
[342] See n. 277, p. 361 above, and accompanying text.
[343] Art. 155, 4th para. of the EC Treaty.
[344] See pp. 358, 364 and 366 above.

Self-determination of the Andorran people

Despite the fact that the Principality of Andorra had not yet been clearly established as a State in international law prior to the conclusion of the trilateral treaty of vicinage, its people already had the right of self-determination with force of *jus cogens*. It has been concluded that under international law the right of self-determination is a *jus cogens*, as long as the territorial integrity of an existing State is not partially or totally disrupted by the exercise of this right.[345] As has been clearly established by both Spain and France, the territory of Andorra does not constitute an integral part of either the Spanish or the French territory.[346] As a consequence, if the Andorran people were to hold the right of self-determination, this right would have the force of *jus cogens*. The Andorran people has the right of self-determination within the Principality if it constitutes a 'people' or a 'fraction of a people' according to the conditions laid down in international law. Both the General Council and Zemanek have argued that the institutional reforms leading to the confirmation of Andorra's statehood were the expression of the right of self-determination of the Andorran people.[347] Does the Andorran people distinguish itself on objective and subjective grounds? The objective characteristics which distinguish Andorran nationals from the Catalan people are tradition, culture and history. Catalan being the official language, there is no specific Andorran language. The subjective feeling of togetherness has traditionally been well pronounced. Over the ages the Andorran people has emphasized its separateness and its attachment to long-standing customs and to its institutional organization. The Andorran nationals are descendants of long-established Andorran families who have a particular attachment to the territory. Comparing the Andorran people with the Liechtenstein, San Marinese and Monégasque peoples, who, admittedly, do not possess striking objective characteristics but who nevertheless are peoples or fractions of peoples, it should be inferred that the Andorran people are also a people or a fraction of a people within the meaning of the right of self-determination.[348] The Andorrans meet the objective and subjective criteria in order to be a people or a fraction of a people,

---

[345] See pp. 103 and 310 above.
[346] See in general pp. 366–367 above.
[347] M. I. Consell General, *Memoria de Reforma Institucional* (Mar. 1978) pp. 8–10 and Zemanek, *Le Statut international*, p. 161.
[348] See pp. 204–205, 259 and 310–311 above.

coupled with a strong attachment to the territory. Therefore, the Andorran people has the right of self-determination with force of *jus cogens*.

Conclusions

The following conclusions can be drawn with respect to the legal implications of Andorra's international legal status:

1. Due to institutional reforms and the promulgation of a written Constitution, Andorra has introduced within its territory a modern legal system based on human rights and democracy, which has been brought into line with Western European standards and which has relativized its feudal heritage.
2. The internal reforms have increased Andorra's independence of its neighbouring States by clarifying and restricting the powers of the co-Princes, and giving them more financial independence.
3. The independence and statehood of Andorra are only clearly established under international law if the powers of the co-Princes are guaranteed to be exercised independently of the States with which the co-Princes maintain special relations. It is due to the legal guarantees provided in the trilateral treaty of vicinage that Andorra has become a State in international law.
4. The restrictions of Andorra's absolute independence are not prompted by the smallness of its territory, but by the special relations which the co-Princes maintain with Spain and the Holy See or France respectively and by its direct relations with its neighbouring States, which are not particularly burdensome.
5. Although the presence of Andorra in the international field has been limited in the past, the Constitution and the trilateral treaty of vicinage have created a legal framework which permits a more active participation in the future.

8 The State of the Vatican City

Territory, population and economy

The existence of the Vatican City is closely and indissolubly connected with the existence of the Holy See and the Roman Catholic Church. In this chapter our attention will be primarily focused on the temporal activities of the Vatican City and the Holy See. The State of the Vatican City ('lo Stato della Città del Vaticano') has a territory of 0.44 square kilometres and is therefore the smallest territorial entity to claim statehood. There are 508 residents in the Vatican City of whom 165 have Vatican citizenship.[1] There are two main budgets under which the State activities are financed: the budget of the Vatican City and the budget of the Holy See which includes the financing of the international activities of the Holy See. The provisional budget of the Holy See forecast a deficit of 105,732 million lire in 1992.[2] Although the budget of the Vatican City is not readily available, it generally shows a deficit too.[3] There are no direct or indirect taxes in the Vatican City. The budget of the Vatican City is covered by the receipts from the State monopoly on salt and tobacco, the patrimonial revenues which include the sale of goods and the rents of immovable property, levies on the rendering of services regarding vehicles and intellectual and industrial properties, and the postal, telephone and telegraph receipts.[4] The financial structure of the Vatican City cannot be

[1] There are in total 431 Vatican citizens (of whom 266 live outside the Vatican City), 184 are of Italian and 108 of Swiss origin. Status as at 2 Dec. 1991. Information from the Apostolic Nunciature in France.
[2] *Osservatore Romano* (8 Nov. 1991).
[3] Interview with Mgr Alain Lebeaupin, auditor of nunciature first class ('uditore di nunziatura di prima classe'), 16 Oct. 1991.
[4] F. Cammeo, *Ordinamento Giuridico dello Stato della Città del Vaticano* (1932) pp. 455–459.

compared with the economy of other States, because of the lack of industrial activities. Commercial dealings in the Vatican territory leading to the importation of capital are in general restricted to the sale of souvenirs and stamps, and to the revenues from the Vatican museums.

History

The Apostolic See became a territorial entity gradually, mostly by bequests of land, and increased its wealth after AD 395 when the Roman Emperor Constantine recognized the Christian Church as a corporate body.[5] The Papal lands gained protection against the Lombards from Charlemagne, after the Pope had crowned him Holy Roman Emperor, thus legitimizing the Carolingian usurpation of the Merovingian throne. After 962 and until the eleventh century the Ottonian emperors had taken practical control over the Papal States though recognizing the theoretical supremacy of the Pope.[6] Although after this period the Papal States, comprising the present Italian regions of the Romagna, Marche, Umbria and the Patrimony of Saint Peter including Rome, suffered several attacks especially from the French kings, it was only in 1807 that Napoleon I invaded the Papal States. Rome was occupied in 1808 and the whole of the Papal States annexed by a Decree of 17 May 1809.[7] The Pope was kept prisoner in Savona until the Congress of Vienna restored the Papal States. Due to revolutionary influences and the beginning of the 'Risorgimento' which was to lead to the unification of Italy, the Pope fled to the Kingdom of Naples in 1848. Mazzini proclaimed the Roman Republic. With the help of Napoleon III, the Pope returned to Rome in 1850 and kept his remaining territories under the protection of French garrisons. The French troops were however withdrawn in 1870 in order to be deployed in the Franco-Prussian war. Immediately, the remaining Papal States were annexed by Italy.[8] The Italian law of guarantees of 13 May 1871 provided that the Pope could freely use the Vatican, the Lateran palaces and the Villa of Castel Gandolfo, leaving

---

[5] A. P. Blaustein and P. M. Blaustein, eds., *Constitutions of Dependencies and Special Sovereignties* (Dec. 1988): Vatican City State, p. 1.
[6] Ibid., p. 2.
[7] Bibliothèque Apostolique Vaticane, *Le Saint-Siège et la France: Douze Siècles d'Histoire* (1987) p. 57.
[8] Blaustein and Blaustein, *Constitutions of Dependencies*, p. 3.

him in addition the freedom of communication and the right to receive diplomatic missions accredited to the Holy See.[9] The Pope, who felt like a prisoner in the Vatican, rejected the Italian law of guarantees as a solution for what was to become known as the Roman question. The temporal power of the Holy See had been abrogated, although the Pope continued to exercise his spiritual sovereignty as the Head of the Catholic Church.

During the First World War solutions were sought for the Roman question.[10] Eventually, the Kingdom of Italy and the Holy See signed the Lateran Agreements on 11 February 1929 under which the Holy See acquired its present land territory.[11] The State of the Vatican City was established with a view to securing a temporal power to the Holy See which would assure it a real independence from any State and thus would facilitate the religious tasks of the Holy See in the world.[12] The fate of the State of the Vatican City thus became dependent on the existence of the Holy See. During the Second World War the Holy See declared the Vatican City neutral territory. The diplomatic efforts of the Holy See in world politics are disproportionate to the size of its territory, due to the special nature of its religious tasks. Nevertheless, the Vatican City remains a Micro-State which, like any other Micro-State, has managed to establish a legal order and treaty relations with a larger neighbouring State in order to wield temporal power in its territory.

Constitutional and legal order
Form of government

On 7 June 1929, when the Lateran Agreements were ratified and entered into force, the Pope promulgated seven constitutional laws which regulate the temporal sovereignty of the Pope in the Vatican City.[13] According to the first law, the fundamental law of the Vatican

---

[9] H. E. Cardinale, *The Holy See and the International Order* (1976) p. 100.
[10] M. Angelo-Comnemo, *Ragioni, Significato e Origini dei Patti Lateranensi e il Problema del Divorzio in Italia* (1970) p. 7.
[11] See p. 389 below.
[12] Preamble of the 1929 Lateran Treaty. See also Catholic Truth Society, *How the "Roman Question" was settled: Explained by the Pope Himself* (1929).
[13] The Constitutional laws are numbered 1 to 7. Law no. 7 was a temporary law on the entry into the Vatican City and was abrogated on 30 Jun. 1929. AAS Suppl. (1929) no. 5. Italian text of the Constitutional laws in AAS Suppl. (1929) no. 1, English text in Cardinale, *The Holy See*, pp. 341 ff.

City (hereafter, fundamental law), the Sovereign Pontiff, ruler of the Vatican City State, has full legislative, executive and judicial powers.[14] The Pope is appointed by the Sacred College of Cardinals sitting in conclave, according to the Sacred Constitutions.[15] Since 22 October 1978, Pope John Paul II has been the Head of the Vatican City State. During a vacancy of the Papal See the legislative, executive and judicial powers are delegated to the Sacred College of Cardinals.[16] This legislative authority can only be used in cases of emergency for the period of the vacancy, and the laws thus promulgated lapse after the vacancy has been filled unless the Pope confirms them. Legislative power during the vacancy is usually delegated to a small commission of Cardinals.[17]

The Vatican State structure is not based on separation of the legislative, executive and judicial powers. The Pope has the right to delegate his legislative power, except for certain reserved domains, to another institution. Until 1952, certain questions were delegated to the State Governor who was appointed by the Pope.[18] Since 1952, the position of State Governor has been vacant and in his absence his legislative and executive tasks have been taken over by the Pontifical Commission.[19] The Pontifical Commission was established in 1939 and is at present composed of seven Cardinals appointed by the Pope for a five-year term.[20] Since 1969, the Pope has directly delegated his legislative and executive powers, except for the reserved domains, to the Pontifical Commission.[21] The Pontifical Commission can seek the advice of the 'Consulta' which is composed of twenty-four experts, including laymen, appointed by the Pope on any legislative matter.[22] In addition, general consultative authority of the Vatican City is vested in the State General Counsellor who is appointed by and responsible to the Pope. Both the Pope and the Pontifical Commission can ask him for

---

[14] Art. 1, 1st para. of the fundamental law (Constitutional law no. 1).
[15] Art. 1, 2nd para. of the fundamental law. Apostolic Constitution of Pius XII, *Vacantis Apostolicae Sedis* (8 Dec. 1945), AAS (1946) vol. 38, pp. 65 ff.
[16] Art. 1, 2nd para. of the fundamental law.
[17] On 18 Aug. 1978 three Cardinals were entrusted with the legislative power in monetary and postage stamps matters, AAS Suppl. (1978) nos. 8 and 9.
[18] Art. 5 of the fundamental law. The State Governor had a case to case legislative authority and a general executive power, except for the reserved domains of the Pope.
[19] Law no. LXXII of 9 Jun. 1952, AAS Suppl. (1952) no. 3.
[20] AAS (1939) vol. 31, p. 176 and AAS Suppl. (1943) no. 2.
[21] Law no. LI of 24 Jun. 1969, AAS Suppl. (1969) no. 5.
[22] *Motu Proprio* of the Pope, 28 Mar. 1968, AAS Suppl. (1968) no. 2.

advice, also in those cases prescribed by law.[23] The legislative domains which fall under the exclusive competence of the Pope are the full powers he exercises with regard to the various organs and tribunals of the Apostolic See according to the Code of Canon Law, all that concerns his Court, the administration of the property of the Holy See, the Vatican Library and Archives, the printing press, book shops, the conclusion of treaties and diplomatic relations by means of the State Secretariat and the approval of the budgets.[24] The Secretariat of the Governor, the 'Governatorato', adopts certain administrative measures for the execution of the laws promulgated by the Pope or the Pontificial Commission.[25] The 'Governatorato' is thus the administrative organ which assists the Pontifical Commission in its executive powers.

The legislative and executive powers of the Pontifical Commission are, except for the reserved domains of the Pope, also restricted by the legislative and executive tasks of the Secretary of State, in the fields of residence permits[26] and judicial organization.[27] The Secretary of State is a Cardinal appointed by the Pope who has both external and internal functions. The Pope's right of representation of the State of the Vatican with foreign Powers is exercised through the Secretary of State.[28] He usually signs treaties with third States in the name of the Vatican City or the Holy See, which are subsequently ratified by the Pope. It should be borne in mind that the delegated legislative, executive and judicial powers can at any time be withdrawn by the Pope, by a subsequent law, and all power is taken back into his own hands. The delegation of powers does not alter the fact that all power is vested in the Sovereign Pontiff. The fundamental law is not hierarchically superior to any other temporal law.

---

[23] Art. 8 of the fundamental law.
[24] Arts. 2-4 of the fundamental law.
[25] The Pontifical Commission decreed in 1981 that administrative actions which have external effects should be signed by the responsible delegate or secretary-general and validated by the Secretary of State: Decree no. XXVI of 7 Jan. 1981, AAS Suppl. (1981) no. 14. Disciplinary and administrative measures are adopted by the Cardinal President of the Pontifical Commission, by the secretary-general or the special delegate, in the name of the Pontifical Commission: Order of the Pontifical Commission no. CXCV codifying the existing practice, AAS Suppl. (1992) no. 14.
[26] Art. 3 of the law on the right of citizenship and sojourn (Constitutional law no. 3).
[27] On 6 Apr. 1984, the Pope delegated certain legislative power to the Secretary of State which enabled him to adopt the law on the judicial organization of the State of the Vatican City: Law no. CXIX of 21 Nov. 1987, AAS Suppl. (1987) no. 12.
[28] Art. 3 of the fundamental law.

Judicial system

The fundamental law of the State of the Vatican City provided for a civil, penal and administrative jurisdiction which was in part exercised by ecclesiastic courts such as the Sacred Roman Rota and the Supreme Tribunal of the Segnatura.[29] The law on the judicial organization of the Vatican City of 1987 has introduced a strict separation of ecclesiastic and temporal courts. The ecclesiastic courts are therefore no longer charged with dispensing justice in temporal civil, penal or administrative cases, although some temporal courts remain composed of Cardinals.

The judges of the temporal courts are appointed by the Pope.[30] They are only submitted to the law, but are hierarchically dependent on the Sovereign Pontiff or other organs to which he has delegated legislative power.[31] Although the judges only base their decisions on the law, there is no legal guarantee that they are independent of the Head of the State and therefore of the legislative and executive power. Every judge has to swear an oath that he shall be true and obedient to the Sovereign Pontiff.[32] This obedience seems however only to be due if the Pope transmits his wishes in the form of a law. Except for the Court of Cassation, there are no general norms which guide the appointment of a judge. With the exception of the Sole Judge, the judges do not have to be Vatican citizens, are either clergymen or laymen, and are usually male catholics with technical and moral capacities.[33] The general judicial power is vested in four courts: the Sole Judge, the Tribunal, the Court of Appeal and the Court of Cassation, which administer justice in the name of the Sovereign Pontiff.[34]

---

[29] Arts. 10-14 of the fundamental law.
[30] Art. 7, 1st para. and Art. 12 of the law on judicial organization, AAS Suppl. (1987) no. 12.
[31] Art. 2 of the law on judicial organization.
[32] Art. 9 of the law on judicial organization.
[33] Cammeo, *Ordinamento Giuridico*, p. 146.
[34] Art. 1 of the law on judicial organization. The Sole Judge has to be a Vatican citizen. The Tribunal judges a case in a college of three judges. The Court of Appeal hears its cases by a bench of three judges. The judges of the Court of Appeal are appointed by the Pope for a period of five years. The Court of Cassation comprises the Prefect of the Supreme Tribunal of the Apostolic Segnatura and two other Cardinals of the same Supreme Tribunal, appointed by the Prefect at the beginning of each judicial year: Arts. 3, 4, 12 and 18.

Civil actions and penal cases are, in first instance, within the competence of either the Sole Judge[35] or the Tribunal,[36] depending on the amount of the damages claimed or the seriousness of the offence. Appeal lies normally before the Court of Appeal.[37] In third instance, the Court of Cassation decides on any claims of procedural faults and errors of form of a judgment pronounced in second instance.[38] In the event of temporal penal offences committed by a Cardinal or a Bishop only the Court of Cassation is competent, subject to the consent of the Sovereign Pontiff.[39] In case of a mixed crime which is punishable both under the temporal penal legislation and under the Code of Canon Law, the punishments can be accumulated or only a temporal punishment can be imposed if this is thought sufficient.[40] The Sovereign Pontiff always reserves the right to grant pardons, amnesties, dispensations and remissions.[41] The Vatican City has a prison in its territory which is rarely used.

The civil legislation applicable in the Vatican City has three sources of law: the Code of Canon Law, the laws promulgated by the Sovereign Pontiff or another authority to which he has delegated his legislative power and Italian law.[42] Accordingly, the Civil Code of the Kingdom of Italy which was in force on 7 June 1929 – the date of the entry into force of the constitutional laws – is applicable in the Vatican City providing that it is not contrary to divine law, the general principles of canon law, the Lateran Treaty or Concordat and that it is applicable to the existing situation in the Vatican City.[43] If no source of law

---

[35] Art. 15, 1st para. of the law on the sources of the legal code (Constitutional law no. 2) and Cammeo, *Ordinamento Giuridico*, pp. 148–149.

[36] Ibid., p. 148.

[37] Art. 10 of the fundamental law. The Court of Appeal has replaced the Sacred Roman Rota in civil proceedings. In civil cases, judgments of the Sole Judge are subject to appeal before the Tribunal: Art. 15, 3rd para. of the law on the sources of the legal code. The Tribunal has replaced the Court of first instance in temporal jurisdiction.

[38] The Court of Cassation has replaced the Supreme Tribunal of the Segnatura in civil proceedings. See also I. Cardinale, *Le Saint-Siège et la Diplomatie* (1962) p. 61.

[39] Art. 23 of the law on judicial organization.

[40] Cammeo, *Ordinamento Giuridico*, p. 162.

[41] Art. 18 of the fundamental law.

[42] Arts. 1 and 3 of the law on the sources of the legal code.

[43] Art. 3 of the law on the sources of the legal code. There are certain specific civil law domains which remain regulated by canon law, such as the ability to perform juridical acts, to acquire or dispose of property, marriages, adoptions, registers of citizenship and civil status and the recording of mortgages: Art. 11 (a to j). The Italian Commercial Code in force on 7 Jun. 1929 is in general also applicable in the Vatican City although the Pontifical Commission when granting its permission for a commercial enterprise can decide otherwise: Art. 12.

contains a precise juridical ruling or if that source is not applicable, the judge may, in civil lawsuits, base his decision on the precepts of divine and natural law, as well as on general principles of canon law, as if he were the legislator.[44] The Italian Code of Civil Procedure valid on 7 June 1929 is also applied in the Vatican City under the general condition that it is not contrary to divine law, canon law or the Lateran Agreements.[45] If the Pope adopts a law which is meant to interpret or amend the applicable Italian Civil Code or Code of Civil Procedure, this law takes precedence over the latter Codes.[46]

The Italian Code of Penal Procedure as in force on 7 June 1929 is in general applied in the Vatican City, and supplemented by special Vatican laws on penal procedure.[47] The Italian Penal Code of 1889 which was valid on 7 June 1929 is the source of the Vatican City's penal legislation, as long as it does not contradict divine law, general principles of canon law, the Lateran Treaty or Concordat and is applicable to the existing situation in the Vatican City.[48] There are special Vatican penal regulations which derogate from the Italian Penal Code.[49] There are also offences which are considered as crimes under Vatican law only.[50] Moreover, even if an act is not punishable under any applicable penal law, an imprisonment of up to six months can still be imposed, if the act violates the principles of religion, the public order or the safety of people or property.[51] The principle *nullum crimen, nulla poena sine lege* is not strictly applied in the Vatican City.[52]

---

[44] Art. 22 of the law on the sources of the legal code.
[45] Arts. 13–15 and 17 of the law on the sources of the legal code.
[46] See, for example, on civil procedure: 'Motu Proprio de ordine udiciali et de ratione procedendi in causis civilibus in statu civitatis Vaticanae servandis' of 1 Nov. 1946, AAS (1946) p. 170.
[47] Art. 7 of the law on the sources of the legal code, and additional laws no. L of 21 Jun. 1969, AAS Suppl. (1969) no. 4 and no. LII of 10 Jan. 1983, AAS Suppl. (1983) no. 11.
[48] Arts. 3 and 4, 1st para. of the law on the sources of the legal code.
[49] Thus, an attack in Vatican territory against the life, safety or liberty of a Head of State or a Head of the Government of any State receives the same punishment as the one which would have been imposed if the attack had been committed in the State of the victim. Attacks against the life, safety or liberty of the Sovereign Pontiff are punished by analogy with an attack against the King of Italy: Art. 4, 2nd para. of the law on the sources of the legal code.
[50] This concerns, for example, the exportation of goods without permission and the importation of goods without compliance with the formalities. See pp. 391–392 below.
[51] Art. 23 of the law on the sources of the legal code.
[52] Cammeo mentions as a justification of the violation of the *nullum crimen, nulla poena sine lege* principle that in a small State like the Vatican City many people and treasures

If a temporal administrative decision, whatever the organ which has taken it, violates, threatens to violate or denies the right of a person, two different legal actions can be instituted. The first possibility is to bring an action before the normal civil courts. The judicial authorities can however neither annul nor modify the administrative act or refusal to act.[53] The courts can neither suspend the effects of the administrative act nor demand that the administrative institution in question undo the negative effects of its action. They can only declare that an administrative act is illegal and fix a compensation for any loss incurred.[54] The second recourse can be addressed within thirty days of the publication or notification of the measure, to the Sovereign Pontiff through the mediation of the State General Counsellor.[55] The State General Counsellor transmits his opinion on a case to the Pope for a final decision. This legal action has the advantage that a case can also be judged on its merits, that the effects of the disputed measure can be suspended and that the Sovereign Pontiff can replace the measure with his own. In addition, the Sovereign Pontiff has the right at any moment to annul, revoke or reform any order emanating from an administrative authority if it is contrary to the general or social laws or regulations.[56] The use of one of the two legal remedies against administrative decisions precludes recourse to the other.

The supremacy of the Sovereign Pontiff in judicial matters is reflected in the rule that in all civil or penal cases, and Cammeo argues also in administrative cases,[57] the Pope may, during all the phases of a trial, refer the examination and the judgment to a special commission empowered to give a verdict in conformity with justice and to exclude any further recourse to an appeal.[58] Given this general prerogative of the Sovereign Pontiff and given the fact that in first instance the legislative and executive powers are vested in him, it can

are accumulated which could constitute a threat to the public order. It is also meant to prevent scandals. He gives one example of a morally punishable offence, viz., the adultery of a husband in the marital home. Cammeo, *Ordinamento Giuridico*, p. 229.

[53] Art. 15 of the fundamental law.
[54] Cammeo notes that the courts can issue a writ of attachment to secure the indemnification, but a great number of the properties of the Vatican City or the Holy See cannot legally be seized. Cammeo, *Ordinamento Giuridico*, pp. 372–373.
[55] Art. 16 of the fundamental law and Art. 3 of the law on the administration organization (Constitutional law no. 4).
[56] Art. 2 of the law on the administration organization.
[57] Cammeo, *Ordinamento Giuridico*, pp. 373–374.
[58] Art. 17 of the fundamental law.

be concluded that the judiciary of the Vatican City is not strictly independent of the legislative and executive authority.

Human rights situation

The Holy See is a Contracting Party to the Convention relating to the Status of Refugees of 1951[59] and to the Convention on the Rights of the Child of 1989.[60] The Holy See made reservations to both Conventions which aimed to apply the Conventions only in so far as certain stipulations are in practice compatible with the particular nature of the State of the Vatican City and do not prejudice its legislation on citizenship, entry and sojourn.[61] Thus, citizenship and a permit of entry or residence can be withdrawn by the Sovereign Pontiff, or by an organ with delegated powers, at any moment and at his discretion.[62] No State has made objections to the reservations made by the Holy See.

No other human rights convention is applicable in the territory of the Vatican City. The special nature of the Vatican City as an accommodation of the Holy See has led to the juridical situation that generally accepted human rights are not explicitly laid down in the law but are usually subject to a previous authorization by the executive power.[63] The close correlation between the Vatican City and the Holy See has implied the principle that the residents and citizens of the Vatican City are subjected to the authority of the Holy See and that it is not the State which is established for the better functioning of its nationals and inhabitants. However justifiable this principle may be from the point of view of the doctrine of the Holy See and of canon law, the Vatican City also acts as an international person in the community of States and is therefore subjected to international law, including general human rights.

We shall first examine whether the human rights situation in the Vatican City is contrary to human rights which could possibly

---

[59] Signed on 21 May 1952, ratified on 8 Mar. 1957.
[60] Signed and ratified on 20 Apr. 1990.
[61] *Multilateral Treaties deposited with the Secretary-General*, Status as at 31 Dec. 1993 (1994) pp. 197 and 212. The reservation to the Convention relating to the Status of Refugees only concerns Art. 42 (1) whereas the reservation to the Convention on the Rights of the Child applies to the Convention as a whole.
[62] Arts. 9 and 19 of the law on the right of citizenship and sojourn. Due notice is given of the revocation unless immediate measures have to be taken for reasons of public order, service, morality or discipline.
[63] See also H. Leising, *La Città del Vaticano und ihre Bürger*, Inaugural Dissertation (1933) pp. 57–58.

constitute *jus cogens* under international law. One human right from which no derogation under certain human rights conventions is permitted deserves our attention in the present context: the rule that 'no one shall be held guilty of any criminal offence on account of any act or omission which did not constitute a criminal offence, under national or international law, at the time when it was committed'.[64] This human right, which aims to prevent retroactive criminal laws, can be said to be violated by Article 23 of the Vatican law on the sources of the legal code, because national law provides for certain criminal offences which violate the principle of religion, public order or safety of people or property.[65] This prohibition is of a general nature and does not specify the exact act which is prohibited. The general prohibition does not provide the citizens with an absolute legal security and impinges on the strict interpretation of the wording of Article 7, first paragraph of the ECHR and Article 15, first paragraph of the ICCPR, because persons could be convicted for acts of which they could not foresee the illegality and for which no one has been convicted before.[66]

The employees of the State of the Vatican City, who are not clergymen, have to profess the catholic faith and its principles, also in their private life.[67] They should not adhere to any association or institution the goals of which are contrary to the doctrine and discipline

---

[64] Art. 15 (1) of the ICCPR, no derogation under Art. 4 (2) and Art. 7 (1) of the ECHR, no derogation under Art. 15 (2).

[65] See p. 381 above at n. 52.

[66] Cf. the decision of admissibility of the European Commission of Human Rights in a case concerning the unforeseeable meaning of 'contempt of court', *Herman v. UK*, decision of 11 May 1984, D & R, Oct. 1984, no. 38, pp. 53–63. The case was settled amicably. Hannikainen argues that the prohibition of retroactive criminal laws does not fulfil the criteria of *jus cogens*, because a derogation of this prohibition is permitted if the act constituted a crime according to 'general principles of law recognized by the community of nations' or by 'civilised nations' within the meaning of Art. 15 (2) of the ICCPR and Art. 7 (2) of the ECHR: L. Hannikainen, *Peremptory Norms (Jus Cogens) in International Law* (1988) p. 442. The second paragraphs of the two articles mentioned do not constitute a derogation or an exception to the first paragraphs, as even in the case of a crime according to general principles of law recognized by the community of nations, the act must be committed at the time when it was prohibited by the general principles of law, which is no more than international law itself and therefore a repetition of the first paragraphs. Considering furthermore the wide acceptance of the ICCPR, its Art. 15 seems to lay down a rule of *jus cogens*.

[67] Arts. 9 (1) (1) and 16 (4) of Decree no. CCXXXI of the Pontifical Commission on the general regulations for the employees of the State of the Vatican City, AAS Suppl. (1995) no. 3.

of the Catholic Church.⁶⁸ The fact that non-catholics will not be employed in the Vatican City does however not constitute a 'severe' discrimination on the ground of someone's religion nor a violation of a *jus cogens*.⁶⁹

The ratification of human rights conventions like the ICCPR and the ECHR by the Vatican City could not be without effect for the human rights situation in the Vatican City. It should thus be borne in mind that the freedom of religion cannot be exercised in full unless it is supplemented by a freedom of expression and a freedom of assembly. Yet, these two latter freedoms are dependent upon the authorization of the Pontifical Commission. No printed matter can be distributed in the Vatican City without authorization of the Pontifical Commission, which is a limitation of the freedom of expression.⁷⁰ All public meetings are forbidden without authorization by the Pontifical Commission and private meetings are prohibited under the same condition if they are 'disguised' public meetings.⁷¹ Moreover, no association may be formed without the Pontifical Commission's authorization.⁷² It follows from canon law that printings, assemblies and associations which are contrary to canon law and the doctrine of the Catholic Church in general will always be prohibited.⁷³ Foreigners and Vatican citizens are not in all cases equal before the law. Foreigners may be arrested for any offence,⁷⁴ whereas Vatican citizens may only be detained if the alleged crime can be punished with imprisonment.⁷⁵ There is no absolute freedom of movement in the Vatican City as permission of entrance is granted for specific parts of the territory⁷⁶ and a person residing in the Vatican City needs a letter of lodgings which can be revoked or changed at any time.⁷⁷ A certain

---

[68] Art. 19 (9) of Decree no. CCXXXI.
[69] Hannikainen suggests that only 'severe' discrimination is under a peremptory prohibition and that public positions reserved to persons of the official State religion are not severe discriminations under customary international law. Hannikainen, *Peremptory Norms*, pp. 478 and 481.
[70] Art. 8 of the law on public safety (Constitutional law no. 6). The Pontifical Commission replaces the Governor.
[71] This depends on the number of people invited to the private meeting and the object of the meeting: Art. 4 of the law on public safety.
[72] Art. 3 of the law on public safety.
[73] Cammeo, *Ordinamento Giuridico*, pp. 402–403 and J.-H. Fragonard, *La Condition des Personnes dans la Cité du Vatican* (1930) pp. 34–36.
[74] Art. 8 of the law on the sources of the legal code.
[75] Fragonard, *La Condition*, p. 112.
[76] Art. 12 of the law on the right of citizenship and sojourn.
[77] Art. 20 of the law on the right of citizenship and sojourn.

interference in the family life of Vatican citizens is also possible by law. The members of a family residing in the Vatican City can be refused residence at any time because of the smallness of the territory.[78] Sons must usually leave the Vatican City at the age of twenty-five and daughters on marriage.[79] The above-cited human rights can, according to international law, be restricted by law if it is necessary to protect public safety, order, health, or morals, or the fundamental rights and freedoms of others.[80] In the Vatican City the exercise of most fundamental rights and freedoms is subordinated to a previous authorization by the Pontifical Commission for reasons of public safety, order and morals. The Pontifical Commission has also the general right to take any measure for the maintenance of public order, safety and morality.[81] If the Vatican City or the Holy See were to ratify the ICCPR or the ECHR, the question would arise whether reasons of public safety, order or morals permitting the restriction of a human right can be accepted as more imperative in the Vatican City than in any other State.

Relations with States
Relations with the Holy See

The Holy See is not a State in international law, but has an international legal personality of its own which permits it to take international actions such as the conclusion of treaties and the maintenance of diplomatic relations. Due to the principle that the Vatican City is subordinated to the existence of the Holy See, it is generally the Holy See which takes care of its international representation even if its acts can have effects for the territory of the Vatican City. Article 3 of the Lateran Treaty signed by Italy and the Holy See on 11 February 1929 states that Italy recognizes full possession, exclusive and absolute power and sovereign jurisdiction of the Holy See over the Vatican,

---

[78] Art. 7 of the law on the right of citizenship and sojourn.
[79] Art. 4 (b, c) of the law on the right of citizenship and sojourn. Their citizenship lapses, with the possibility to be granted a residence permit without citizenship, but this remains at the discretion of the Pontifical Commission: Art. 17 (a).
[80] See, e.g., for the right to liberty of movement Art. 12 (3), for the freedom to manifest one's religion Art. 18 (3), for the freedom of expression Art. 19 (3), for the right of peaceful assembly Art. 21 and for the right to freedom of association Art. 22 (2) of the ICCPR.
[81] Art. 1 of the law on public safety. Most restrictions of fundamental rights and freedoms are set forth in this law.

creating the Vatican City for such purpose with its special aims in connection with the Treaty.[82] Although the Holy See has full sovereignty over the Vatican City, it is not the Government of the State of the Vatican City. According to the Code of Canon Law, the Holy See comprises the Sovereign Pontiff, the Roman Curia and that which appears from natural law or the context.[83] The Roman Curia includes the Secretary of State, the Council for public ecclesiastic affairs, the Sacred Congregations (commissions of Cardinals with specific tasks), the ecclesiastic Tribunals and other institutions as defined by special law.[84] The Sovereign Pontiff and the Secretary of State are positions which the Holy See and the worldly governmental institutions of the Vatican City have in common. Neither the Pontifical Commission, the 'Consulta', the State General Counsellor nor the secular judicial organs, which have been separated from the ecclesiastic tribunals since 1987, can be considered a part of the Holy See, as they are not incorporated in the Roman Curia by special law and do not belong to the Holy See through natural law or the context due to their exclusively secular tasks.[85] As a consequence, if the State of the Vatican City were to disappear, the governmental institutions of the Vatican City would cease to function too, except for the Sovereign Pontiff and the Secretary of State who are organs of the Holy See. The Vatican City and the Holy See are therefore two legal persons of which the former has been established for the better functioning of the latter. The Holy See can take international actions in the name of the Vatican City which will be applicable in the territory of the Vatican City, because the external relations of both the Holy See and the Vatican City are maintained by the Sovereign Pontiff in cooperation with the Secretary of State. It is the Pope, as the Head of the Roman Catholic Church and the Head of the Vatican Government, who decides on the hierarchical relation between the Holy See and the Vatican Government. Given the fact that the Vatican City is at the service of the Holy See, the supremacy of the authority of the Holy See over the Vatican Government cannot be affected.

---

[82] Art. 3, 1st sentence of the Lateran Treaty, AAS (1929) no. 6, pp. 209 ff. English text of the Lateran Agreements in Cardinale, *The Holy See*, pp. 319 ff.
[83] Can. 361 of the 1983 Code of Canon Law states: 'Nomine Sedis Apostolicae vel Sanctae Sedis in hoc Codice veniunt non solum Romanus Pontifex, sed etiam, nisi ex rei natura vel sermonis contextu aliud appareat, Secretaria Status, Consilium pro publicis Ecclesiae negotiis, aliaque Romanae Curiae Instituta.' AAS (1983) vol. 75.
[84] Can. 360 of the 1983 Code of Canon Law.
[85] See pp. 376–383 above.

The distinct legal personality of the Holy See was a point of debate, especially during the Italian occupation between 1870 and 1929. Some international lawyers argued that the Holy See had continued to exist as a subject of international law, because it had not ceased to conclude concordats, receive and send diplomatic representations and settle certain disputes by arbitration.[86] Others contended that the international legal status of the Holy See had only been established and recognized by the conclusion of the Lateran Agreements.[87] However, according to the Lateran Treaty, Italy has recognized the sovereignty of the Holy See in the international field as an inherent attribute of its nature.[88] The most widely accepted view therefore is that the Holy See is an international legal person independently of any exercise of temporal sovereignty over a certain territory.

Foreign policy

The foreign policy of the Holy See and therefore inherently of the Vatican City is based on two main principles:

Christian diplomacy The international position of the Holy See is founded on the defence of Roman Catholic values which include the doctrine of divine law. The divine law established by God comprises natural divine law, which flows from what is just according to natural values, and positive divine law, which emanates from the institutions of the Holy See.[89] As a result, the Holy See is opposed to the use of force and in favour of the peaceful settlement of disputes, solidarity between nations, human rights and the prosperity of mankind.[90] The Holy See's diplomatic efforts are focused both on worldly affairs and on problems relating to the relationship between a State and the Catholic Church.

---

[86] Y. de la Brière, 'La Souveraineté du Saint-Siège et le Droit des Gens', 20 RDI (1937) pp. 29–48; Cardinale, *Le Saint-Siège*, pp. 38–39; L. le Fur, *Le Saint-Siège et le Droit des Gens* (1930); H. F. Köck, *Die völkerrechtliche Stellung des Heiligen Stuhls* (1975); J. L. Kunz, 'The Status of the Holy See in International Law', 46 AJIL (1952) pp. 308–314; and E. Ruffini, *La Personalità Giuridica Internazionale della Chiesa* (1936). See also on the relation between the Holy See and the Vatican City J. Crawford, *The Creation of States in International Law* (1979) pp. 157–160 and pp. 413–414 below.

[87] See, e.g., G. Arangio-Ruiz, 'La Città del Vaticano', 11 *Revista di Diritto Pubblico e Giustizia Amministrativa* (1929) p. 4.

[88] Art. 2 of the Lateran Treaty.

[89] Cammeo, *Ordinamento Giuridico*, p. 207.

[90] Interview with Mgr Alain Lebeaupin, auditor of nunciature first class, 16 Oct. 1991. See also Cardinale, *Le Saint-Siège*, p. 14 and E. Midgley, *The Natural Law Tradition and the Theory of International Relations* (1975) pp. 388–392.

Neutrality In Article 24 of the Lateran Treaty, the Holy See has declared that it will remain extraneous to all temporal disputes between States and to international congresses held for such objects, unless the contending parties make concordant appeal to its mission of peace. The Vatican City will always and in every case be considered neutral.[91] The principle of neutrality implies in practice a non-alignment with certain blocs or groups of States, but does not mean an inactivity.[92] The international actions of the Holy See are not in the first place inspired by the wish to remain neutral, but by the moral values prescribed by divine law. In appealing to certain governments, the Holy See does not make any distinction on grounds other than the problems concerned.[93]

Relations with Italy

Territorial sovereignty

The basis of the independent position of the Vatican City and the Holy See in relation to Italy is laid down in the Lateran Agreements of 11 February 1929, which comprise the Lateran Treaty with four annexes and a concordat.[94] The Lateran Treaty aims to guarantee to the Holy See absolute independence in the fulfilment of its high mission in the world.[95] Italy has recognized full and exclusive sovereignty of the Holy See over the Vatican City, which implies that there cannot be any interference on the part of the Italian Government and that within the Vatican City there is no authority other than the Holy See.[96] The Holy See possesses a number of buildings outside the Vatican City which are in Italian territory but exempt from Italian expropriation and fiscal legislation. Some of them enjoy the same immunity as that recognized by international law to seats of diplomatic agents of foreign States.[97] Italy assures the Vatican's supply of water and railway communication.[98]

[91] Art. 24, 2nd para. of the Lateran Treaty.
[92] Interview with Mgr Alain Lebeaupin, auditor of nunciature first class, 16 Oct. 1991.
[93] Cardinale, *The Holy See*, p. 127.
[94] Italian text in AAS (1929) no. 6, pp. 209–295. English text in Cardinale, *The Holy See*, pp. 319 ff.
[95] Preamble to the Lateran Treaty.
[96] Arts. 3 and 4 of the Lateran Treaty. A special regime applies to St Peter's Square. During opening hours, the Italian police can enter St Peter's Square up to the foot of the steps leading into the St Peter basilica. When the Square is not open to the public it remains subject to the authority of the Vatican police corps.
[97] Arts. 14–16 and annexes 2–3 of the Lateran Treaty.
[98] Art. 6 of the Lateran Treaty.

Diplomatic representation

The first pontifical nunciature was established in Venice in 1500.[99] Papal diplomacy flourished especially in the seventeenth century and after the Congress of Vienna. By virtue of the Lateran Treaty, Italy has recognized to the Holy See the active and passive right to maintain diplomatic relations even with States with which Italy has no diplomatic contacts. The diplomatic missions of foreign Governments enjoy all diplomatic immunities according to international law in Italian territory.[100] Diplomatic relations are always maintained in the name and on behalf of the Holy See, not of the Vatican City. The diplomatic corps of the Holy See is regulated by canon law and is composed of three ranks.[101] Italian nationals who are Papal diplomatic representatives are considered to have permanent residence in the Vatican City.[102] The diplomatic agents of the Holy See have two main tasks: the worldly diplomatic mission in the receiving State and the ecclesiastic mission to the local Catholic Church.[103] An apostolic delegate has no diplomatic mission, but controls the conditions of the local Catholic Churches in general and keeps the Pope informed.[104] Diplomatic missions received by the Holy See are always at the ambassadorial level, but they do not reside in the Vatican City. The double mandate of the Holy See's diplomatic missions – the worldly and ecclesiastic tasks – explains the fact that diplomatic relations are never entered into by the State of the Vatican City.

Postal union

A convention for the maintenance of postal services in the Vatican City was concluded on 29 July 1929 between Italy and the State of the

---

[99] Cardinale, *Le Saint-Siège*, p. 32.
[100] Art. 12, 1st para. of the Lateran Treaty.
[101] Cans. 362–367 of the 1983 Code of Canon Law. The apostolic nuncio is the general head of a mission with a grade of ambassador, the inter nuncio acts as a nuncio in the absence of the latter, and the apostolic delegate is the personal representative of the Sovereign Pontiff without diplomatic character. The diplomatic agents of the Holy See maintain their Vatican citizenship abroad as they have their legal residence in the Vatican City: see p. 394 below.
[102] Exchange of letters of 23 Jul./17 Aug. 1940 between the Holy See and Italy. *Patti Lateranensi, Convenzioni e Accordi Successivi fra il Vaticano e l'Italia fino al 31 Dicembre 1945* (1946) vol. I, p. 291.
[103] See p. 388 above and Cardinale, *The Holy See*, p. 50.
[104] *Annuario Pontificio per l'Anno 1991*, p. 1736. An apostolic delegate has been sent to Angola, the Antilles, Palestine, Libya, Mexico and the Region of the Red Sea.

Vatican City.¹⁰⁵ The Vatican State has established its own post offices and issues its own stamps.¹⁰⁶ The Italian internal postal tariffs are adopted by the Vatican City.¹⁰⁷ The international postal tariffs used by the Vatican City are those imposed by international conventions and agreements.¹⁰⁸ The postal receipts are divided between the parties by mutual agreement.¹⁰⁹ The postal convention can be denounced subject to six months' notice.¹¹⁰

On 18 November 1929, a convention relating to telegraph and telephone services was concluded between Italy and the State of the Vatican City.¹¹¹ The Italian tariffs are applicable in the territory of the Vatican City and are levied by and in favour of the Vatican Government.¹¹² The Vatican City has to adhere to the international telegraph and telephone conventions which are in force in Italy.¹¹³ The convention on telegraph and telephone services can equally be denounced subject to six months' notice.¹¹⁴

Customs regime

Merchandise coming to the Vatican City from outside is fully exempted from Italian customs duties and indirect taxation according to the Lateran Treaty.¹¹⁵ This rule has been supplemented by a customs convention concluded by Italy and the State of the Vatican City on 30 June 1930 and implemented by national Vatican legislation. Both products imported from a third State and Italian goods can be introduced in the Vatican City free from customs duties, VAT and other indirect taxes.¹¹⁶ The importation without charges and

---

¹⁰⁵ Text in *Patti Lateranensi, Convenzioni e Accordi Successivi fra il Vaticano e l'Italia fino al 31 Dicembre 1945* (1946) vol. I, pp. 89 ff.
¹⁰⁶ Art. 1 of the postal convention.
¹⁰⁷ Exchange of letters of 23 Jan. 1952. *Convenzioni ed Accordi fra il Vaticano e l'Italia dal 1° Gennaio 1946 al 31 Dicembre 1954* (1955) vol. II, pp. 115–117. The postal tariffs are automatically adapted by the Pontifical Commission.
¹⁰⁸ Art. 9, 1st para. of the postal convention. Art. 20 (c) (5) of the law on the sources of the legal code states that the postal treaties concluded by Italy and in force on 7 Jun. 1929 apply to the Vatican City if it consents to these.
¹⁰⁹ Art. 14, 2nd para. of the postal convention.
¹¹⁰ Art. 18 of the postal convention.
¹¹¹ Text in *Patti Lateranensi, Convenzioni e Accordi Successivi fra il Vaticano e l'Italia fino al 31 Dicembre 1945* (1946) vol. I, pp. 103 ff.
¹¹² Art. 13 of the telegraph and telephone convention.
¹¹³ Art. 5 of the telegraph and telephone convention.
¹¹⁴ Art. 18 of the telegraph and telephone convention.
¹¹⁵ Art. 20 of the Lateran Treaty.
¹¹⁶ Art. 1 of the customs convention. Text in *Patti Lateranensi, Convenzioni e Accordi Successivi fra il Vaticano e l'Italia fino al 31 Dicembre 1945* (1946) vol. I, pp. 121 ff.

indirect taxes has to meet certain administrative regulations. A resident of the Vatican City or an inhabitant of its extraterritorial buildings has to ask the competent Vatican merchandise office, which falls under the authority of the Pontifical Commission, for permission to introduce a product free from charges in the Vatican City.[117] The merchandise office notifies the customs office of Rome, takes care of the transportation of the product to the Vatican City and confirms its arrival to the Italian customs office.[118] Products for which customs duties and Italian indirect taxes have been paid can be freely introduced into the Vatican City if they are for personal use and proof is offered of the payment of the said charges.[119] In order to avoid tax evasion through the re-introduction of Vatican imported products into Italy or an illegal exportation to a third State, the exportation of goods from the Vatican City is, in general, prohibited.[120] In any case, the exportation is subject to the authorization of the Vatican merchandise office,[121] which seeks the previous accord of the customs office of Rome.[122] The customs convention does not provide for a denunciation clause.

The postal and customs regime of the Vatican City is supplemented by a monetary union with Italy and San Marino. Monetary conventions between the State of the Vatican City and Italy have laid down the acceptance of the Italian lira and the Vatican coins in both territories.[123]

---

[117] Art. 3 of Governor's Decree no. XVII, AAS Suppl. (1930) no. 5.
[118] Art. 4 of the customs convention and Art. 6 of Governor's Decree no. XVII.
[119] Art. 5 of the law on the economic, commercial and professional organization (Constitutional law no. 5).
[120] Art. 6 of the law on the economic, commercial and professional organization. There are however exceptions such as products used by the Pope as gifts, products for which the Italian taxes have been paid and temporarily exported goods which are meant to be re-imported after processing in Italy: Art. 17 (a, b, c) of Governor's Decree no. XVII.
[121] Art. 18 of Governor's Decree no. XVII. Products sold in the Vatican City to non-residents are in practice not conditional upon a case by case export permission of the merchandise office if they are for personal use. Also Art. 6, 2nd para. of the law on the economic, commercial and professional organization, relating to objects for personal use necessary for a journey.
[122] Art. 8, 2nd para. of the customs convention.
[123] Monetary convention of 2 Aug. 1930. Text in *Patti Lateranensi, Convenzioni e Accordi Successivi fra il Vaticano e l'Italia fino al 31 Dicembre 1945* (1946) vol. I and monetary convention of 21 Apr. 1951. Text in *Convenzioni ed Accordi fra il Vatican e l'Italia dal I° Gennaio 1946 al 31 Dicembre 1954* (1955) vol. II, pp. 83 ff.

Italian legislation

The principal sources of the legal code in the State of the Vatican City are the Code of Canon Law and the laws promulgated by the Sovereign Pontiff or by the authorities to which he has delegated his legislative powers.[124] Any legal domain which has not been regulated by the aforesaid legal sources shall be governed by Italian legislation, as long as no specific canon law or Vatican law has been adopted on this matter.[125] Italian legislation in force in the Vatican City may in no way be contradictory to the precepts of divine law, the general principles of canon law or the rules of the Lateran Treaty and Concordat and must be applicable to the existing situation in the Vatican City.[126] The applicable Italian legislation can be divided into Italian rules specifically mentioned in the constitutional laws of the Vatican City[127] and undetermined Italian laws which fill legal gaps. The former category usually consists of the Italian legislation in force at the time of the promulgation of the constitutional laws, whereas the latter category is not expressly specified and consists simply of the 'laws promulgated by the Kingdom of Italy'.[128]

In certain cases the Vatican penal legislation will be applied by Italian courts as it does not necessarily coincide with the Italian Penal Code. Such a situation will arise if the Holy See requests Italy to punish suspects who have committed a crime in Vatican territory. This mandate is provided for in the Lateran Treaty.[129] In addition, a perpetrator of a crime committed in the Vatican City who flees into Italian territory, which for this purpose includes St Peter's Square when it is open to the public, is prosecuted in Italian courts according to Vatican penal laws but Italian rules of

---

[124] Art. 1 of the law on the sources of the legal code.
[125] Art. 3 of the law on the sources of the legal code.
[126] Art. 3 of the law on the sources of the legal code. Not applicable to the existing situation in the Vatican City would be the Italian commercial and administrative rules on internal navigation. However, the Vatican City has a regulation on maritime navigation under the Vatican flag: AAS Suppl. (1951) no. 10.
[127] *Inter alia*, the Civil Code, the Commercial Code, the Code of Civil Procedure, the Penal Code, the Code of Penal Procedure and Italian legislation relating to expropriation, antiquities and fine arts, intellectual property, railways, aviation, motor cars, contagious diseases, hygiene and the security and safety of persons and property: Art. 20 of the law on the sources of the legal code.
[128] Art. 3, 1st sentence of the law on the sources of the legal code. Cammeo, *Ordinamento Giuridico*, pp. 174–175, concludes that even in the latter case only Italian legislation in force on 7 Jun. 1929 is meant to apply.
[129] Art. 22 of the Lateran Treaty.

procedure.¹³⁰ In any case, the Italian rules concerning the public organization, the treatment of officials and employees, the armed forces and the fiscal system are excluded from the Vatican legal order.¹³¹ It should be borne in mind that the Italian legislation is made applicable in the Vatican City only by virtue of a Vatican wish and can at any time unilaterally be replaced by a proper Vatican rule.

Aliens office

The residence permit for the State of the Vatican City is always directly or indirectly related to the official position which the person in question holds. Citizenship of the State of the Vatican City, that is, Vatican nationality, is in general a *ius officii*. Vatican citizenship implies the right to reside in the Vatican City. Cardinals resident in the Vatican City or in Rome are Vatican citizens, as well as those who reside permanently in the City by virtue of their office or employment and whose residence is authorized or prescribed by law, all who are so authorized by the Sovereign Pontiff and under certain conditions the married partner, children, parents, brothers and sisters of the Vatican citizen.¹³² Members of the family of a Vatican citizen who do not fulfil the conditions for citizenship, domestic staff and servants of the Vatican citizens or residents and extraordinary cases for reasons of absolute necessity may reside in the Vatican City without Vatican citizenship.¹³³ The Sovereign Pontiff can decide to accord a residence permit for an indefinite time.¹³⁴ Vatican citizenship lapses if a citizen gives up his residence, resigns or if the authorization to reside in the Vatican City is revoked.¹³⁵ The residence permit can be withdrawn at any time.¹³⁶

Possible statelessness is solved by Article 9, second paragraph of the Lateran Treaty. Anyone who is no longer a resident of the Vatican City, which includes persons whose Vatican citizenship has lapsed, is

---

[130] Ibid. Arangio-Ruiz, 'La Città del Vaticano', p. 11, argues that criminals who have fled from the Vatican City are punished according to the Italian Penal Code, unless the Vatican penal laws are different.

[131] Art. 20 (d, 1st para.) of the law on the sources of the legal code.

[132] Arts. 1 and 2 of the law on the right of citizenship and sojourn.

[133] The residence permits are conferred by the competent service of the 'Governatorato' in the name of the Pontifical Commission or by the Secretary of State if it concerns a member of the Papal Court: Arts. 3 and 17 of the law on the right of citizenship and sojourn.

[134] Art. 16 of the law on the right of citizenship and sojourn.

[135] Art. 6 of the law on the right of citizenship and sojourn.

[136] Art. 19 of the law on the right of citizenship and sojourn.

considered an outright Italian citizen in Italy, when not in possession of other citizenship.[137]

Concordat

Besides the Lateran Treaty, Italy and the Holy See also concluded the Lateran Concordat on 11 February 1929,[138] which has been replaced by another concordat signed on 18 February 1984.[139] Although the relations between the Catholic Church and Italy fall outside the scope of this study, the arguments which have led to the amendment of the Lateran Concordat are nevertheless relevant to the relations between the two States. In 1967 a motion was adopted in the Italian Parliament inviting the Government to revise the Lateran Agreements.[140] After several years of negotiations[141] the new Concordat was signed, reiterating, *inter alia*, the fact that the State and the Catholic Church are, each within its own order, independent and sovereign.[142] This principle was meant in the first place to exclude the interference of the Catholic Church in Italy's political life and in the second place to abolish Article 1 of the Lateran Treaty under which the Roman Catholic Church was the State Church.[143] Thus, the State and the Catholic Church in Italy were separated. The independence of the Catholic Church and, in consequence, of the Holy See was expressly reaffirmed, while the existence of the State of the Vatican City was left unaffected.

---

[137] Art. 9, 3rd para. of the Lateran Treaty has been cited by Cardinale, *The Holy See*, p. 110 in order to demonstrate the possibility of survival of the nationality of non-Italian nationals who are at the same time Vatican citizens. This article provides for the use of Italian legislation with respect to persons subject to the sovereignty of the Holy See (which means all persons having fixed residence in the Vatican City) when they are in Italian territory or the use of the legislation of another State, if they are citizens of that State. This argument is however not convincing, as 'persons subject to the sovereignty of the Holy See' also includes persons who do not possess Vatican citizenship and therefore do not have dual nationality.

[138] English text in Cardinale, *The Holy See*, pp. 328 ff., original Italian text in AAS (1929) no. 6, pp. 209 ff.

[139] Entered into force on 3 Jun. 1985. English text in Blaustein and Blaustein, *Constitutions of Dependencies*, pp. 9 ff. Original Italian text in G. Dalla Torre, *Revisione del Concordato: Trattati, Concordati, Accordi ecc.* (1985) pp. 25 ff.

[140] P. Ciprotti and A. Talamanca, *La Revisione del Concordato nelle Discussioni Parlamentari I* (1975) p. 1.

[141] Dalla Torre, *Revisione del Concordato*, p. 18. See also R. Coppola, ed., *Atti del Convegno Nazionale di Studio su il Nuovo Accordo tra Italia e Santa Sede* (1987).

[142] Art. 1 of the 1984 Concordat.

[143] Point 1 of the Additional Protocol to the 1984 Concordat.

Defence

The territory of the Vatican City has not been the object of a defence agreement with Italy, as this would be contrary to the neutrality of the Vatican City. Moreover, Italy has a duty of non-interference in the Vatican City, within the meaning of Article 4 of the Lateran Treaty, although this does not necessarily prevent Italian defensive actions, were the Vatican City to be attacked by a third Power, if the Pope so requests.

The Vatican police force consists of the Swiss Guard, which guards the Apostolic Palace and the border crossings of the Vatican City, and the Central Surveillance Office ('Ufficio Centrale di Vigilanza') which has general police tasks.[144] In case of an armed conflict it should be remembered that the Vatican City has ratified the Hague Convention for the Protection of Cultural Property in the Event of Armed Conflict of 1954, and has registered every building in its territory in the International Register of Cultural Property under Special Protection, thus making its territory in principle immune from armed attack.[145]

Relations with other States

The relations between the Holy See and other States, besides Italy, are based on the principle that the Holy See is in general willing to establish contacts with other States 'regardless of their religious or philosophical beliefs, provided they are ready to grant the Church a reasonable measure of freedom in the exercise of her mission and to respect the fundamental human rights'.[146] The position of another State towards the Holy See depends in general on the policy of that State towards the Catholic Church and therefore on non-temporal reasons, except for certain periods of history such as the First and Second World Wars during which contacts with the Holy See were kept up for diplomatic purposes. The interest in establishing diplomatic relations with the Holy See does not flow from the worldly aspects of the existence of the Vatican City, although the number of diplomatic missions to the Holy See has increased since the

---

[144] The Central Surveillance Office falls under the authority of the Pontifical Commission, law no. CLXVIII, AAS Suppl. (1991) no. 3. Its general security and police tasks are defined in Art. 2 of Decree no. XXXVIII, AAS Suppl. (1981) no. 12. The Swiss Guard has been in existence since the fifteenth century and depends directly on the Sovereign Pontiff: Art. 2 of the fundamental law.

[145] Art. 8 of the Hague Convention for the Protection of Cultural Property in the Event of Armed Conflict of 1954. Registration received by UNESCO.

[146] Cardinale, *The Holy See*, p. 188.

conclusion of the Lateran Treaty.[147] The treaty relations between the Holy See and third States usually take the form of concordats and not of temporal conventions.

The diplomatic efforts of the Holy See are sometimes solicited by States with a view to its acting as mediator in, usually, territorial disputes. Thus the mediation of the Holy See led to an agreement between Germany and Spain relating to the Caroline Islands in 1885 and to the settlement of the territorial dispute concerning the Beagle Channel between Argentina and Chile, mediation of which started in 1979.[148]

Relations with international organizations
Hague International Peace Conferences

At the time when the International Peace Conferences were held in the Hague in 1899 and 1907, the Vatican City State had not yet been established. Initially, the Holy See had been invited to participate in the international conference on, *inter alia*, good offices, mediation and arbitration which was to be held in the Hague in 1899, but due to strong Italian protests it did not receive a definite invitation.[149] Italy feared that the Holy See would take the opportunity of the Conference to invoke the Roman question and argued that the Holy See had no interest in participating in the Conference as it no longer had any temporal power.[150] It was for the same reasons that the Holy See was also excluded from the International Peace Conference in 1907. Nevertheless, at the last plenary meeting of the Hague Conference in 1899, at the request of the Government of the Netherlands, the President of the Conference read a letter from the Queen of the Netherlands addressed to the Pope in which she asked the 'précieux appui moral' of the Sovereign Pontiff for the work of the Conference and to which the Pope replied that he would not only 'prêter un appui moral, mais d'y coopérer effectivement' and briefly evoked

---

[147] In 1929 the Holy See maintained diplomatic relations with 37 States, against 134 in 1991. See *Annuario Pontificio per l'Anno 1991*, pp. 1266–1285 and Köck, *Die völkerrechtliche Stellung*, p. 266.
[148] See S. Benadava, 'La Mediación de la Santa Sede en el Diferendo Chileno–Argentino sobre la Zona Austral', in Y. Dinstein, ed., *International Law at a Time of Perplexity: Essays in Honour of Shabtai Rosenne* (1989) pp. 33 ff.
[149] J. Puente Egido, *Personalidad Internacional de la Ciudad del Vaticano* (1965) p. 86.
[150] Ibid., p. 86 at n. 40 and Köck, *Die völkerrechtliche Stellung*, pp. 616–620.

'l'anormale condition où nous sommes réduits pour l'heure'.[151] Except for Italy, and to a certain extent Germany and Austro-Hungary, the participating States of the Hague Conference were not *a priori* opposed to the participation of the Holy See, even though it had no territorial sovereignty.[152]

League of Nations

The Sovereign Pontiff in a peace message of 1 August 1917 had pleaded for the creation of an international organization with compulsory dispute settlement mechanisms and international sanction possibilities.[153] There was therefore in first instance no reason for the Holy See to oppose the establishment of the League of Nations. Certain events and the opposition felt against it eventually led the Holy See to adopt a more averse position towards the League of Nations. In the first place, the Holy See had been explicitly excluded from the Paris Peace Conference of 1919 at the request of Italy, which was supported by France, the United Kingdom and the Soviet Union.[154] In the second place, the Holy See believed that the League of Nations would be used by anti-catholic movements such as freemasonry and socialism.[155] In the third place, all attempts of the Holy See to participate in the preparatory conferences of the League of Nations and in the League of Nations itself met with strong opposition. Not all States, however, favoured the exclusion of the Holy See.[156]

---

[151] *Conférence internationale de la Paix* (La Haye 18 mai–29 juillet 1899) Ière Partie, Séances plénières, pp. 210–211.

[152] At the initiative of a French delegate, the 1899 Hague Convention for the peaceful settlement of international conflicts and all other Hague Conventions were left open for accession by the Holy See as the initially used word 'Etats' was replaced by the term 'puissances' (Art. 60 of the 1899 Hague Convention for the peaceful settlement of international conflicts). The same applied to the 1907 Hague Conventions, but due to continued Italian opposition, the Holy See did not attempt to become a party to any of them. See also Puente Egido, *Personalidad Internacional*, p. 86 at n. 40 and Köck, *Die völkerrechtliche Stellung*, p. 620.

[153] Köck, *Die völkerrechtliche Stellung*, p. 622.

[154] This exclusion was agreed to in Art. 15 of the secret London Treaty of 26 Apr. 1915: ibid., p. 623.

[155] Ibid., p. 627.

[156] Germany did support the Holy See's participation in the League of Nations during the Paris Peace Conference and it has been alleged that Germany intended to propose in its counter-project for a peace treaty that the Sovereign Pontiff be permitted to take part in the League of Nations. This proposal was however not realized in practice: newspaper article of 30 May 1919, no name of the newspaper mentioned. Vatican Secret Archives ('Archivio Segreto Vaticano'), Archive no. St. Eccl. 216 XV.

At the International Conference on the League of Nations of March 1919, held in Berne, the cooperation of the Holy See with the League of Nations was the object of a motion which was accepted by a Commission and adopted by the plenary meeting.[157] It was feared that this motion would be interpreted as the recognition of the Holy See's temporal power, but the majority of the Commission in which the motion had been presented believed that this issue remained outside the scope of the motion which aimed to permit a general cooperation between the League of Nations and the Holy See.[158] In general, voices in favour of the Holy See's admission to the League of Nations were heard especially in Belgium[159] and catholic circles in Switzerland, while the United Kingdom and Italy were among the opponents.[160] There was no doubt that the Holy See had planned and wished to be admitted to the League of Nations and regretted its exclusion.[161] When it concluded that the League of Nations would not live up to expectations, the Holy See took a more cautious position, although it did not advise, for example, catholics in Switzerland to vote against their membership of the League of Nations.[162] The Holy See took a different attitude towards the League of Nations in 1923 when, following a request of a British functionary of the League of

---

[157] The United States, Bohemia, Bulgaria, Egypt and one member of the British delegation voted against. Letter of the Swiss nuncio of 12 Mar. 1919, no. 2054. Vatican Secret Archives.

[158] A proposed amendment of the motion with a view to restricting the cooperation between the Holy See and the League of Nations to cultural and social domains was not upheld. Ibid.

[159] Discussions in the Belgium Senate show a division among opponents and supporters of the Holy See's membership of the League of Nations, *Sénat-Annales Parlementaires*, Séance du 7 mai 1919, pp. 321 ff.

[160] It was alleged that English freemasonry wished to specify that the delegations to the Assembly of the League of Nations would be appointed by the national parliaments of each State, thus excluding *de facto* a representation of the Holy See. Letter of the Belgian nuncio to the Secretary of State of 8 Dec. 1919, no. 382. Vatican Secret Archives.

[161] Letter of the Papal delegate to the Swiss representative to the Conference on the League of Nations of 9 Apr. 1920, Doc. 5869. Vatican Secret Archives. Köck, *Die völkerrechtliche Stellung*, p. 628 concluded that the Holy See did not seem interested in taking part in the League of Nations; also Kunz, 'The Status of the Holy See', p. 312.

[162] Letter of the nuncio in Paris to the Secretary of State of 21 Aug. 1921, Doc. 25143 and letter of the Papal delegate to the Swiss representative to the Conference on the League of Nations of 9 Apr. 1920, Doc. 5869. The Holy See did not establish a permanent representative in Geneva to follow the League's work and never pronounced itself definitely in favour of the League of Nations despite British requests to make such a pronouncement. Letter of a British ambassador to a Cardinal of 14 Jul. 1920, Doc. 8413. Vatican Secret Archives.

Nations for the establishment of formal relations between the Holy See and the League of Nations, it replied that it was only competent in matters of 'elucidation of questions of principle in morality and public international law; [and in] assistance to the League's relief work'.[163] On 6 September 1924, a British delegate in the League of Nations had proposed to invite the Holy See to become a member of the League, but this proposition received no official reaction from the other Member States.[164]

In general, the arguments raised against the admission of the Holy See to the League of Nations fell into three main categories: the Holy See was not a State, it had adopted a position towards Germany during the First World War which was considered too favourable and it was feared that the Holy See would have too much influence on the votes of the catholic Member States of the League of Nations. It is remarkable that objections such as the fact that the Holy See cannot by definition be subjected to the decisions of another forum and the impossibility of it implementing collective sanctions by virtue of its principle of neutrality did not initially prevent the Holy See from seeking participation in the League of Nations.

United Nations organizations

Membership

The State of the Vatican City or the Holy See is a member of a number of United Nations specialized organizations. In general, it is always the Holy See which concludes treaties and which becomes a member of an international organization unless it has been expressly indicated that it is not the Holy See, but the State of the Vatican City which is bound.[165] If the State of the Vatican City is mentioned as the member of an international organization or a party to a multilateral treaty, it is the Holy See which signs the treaty 'on behalf of the State of the Vatican City' and which represents the Vatican City. Such has been the practice in the ITU, the UPU and, outside the context of the United Nations, the International Wheat Council, EUTELSAT and INTELSAT.

The relations between the Vatican City and the ITU date back to the establishment of the World Telegraph Union in 1865 of which the Papal States became a member in 1866.[166] Due to the loss of its

---
[163] J. Eppstein, *The Catholic Tradition of the Law of Nations* (1935) p. 320.
[164] Köck, *Die völkerrechtliche Stellung*, pp. 645–646.
[165] Interview with Mgr Alain Lebeaupin, auditor of nunciature first class, 16 Oct. 1991.
[166] S. Ferlito, *L'Attività Internazionale della Santa Sede* (1988) p. 145 at n. 92.

temporal power in 1870, the Papal States were no longer present at the successive conferences of the World Telegraph Union. After the conclusion of the Lateran Agreements, the State of the Vatican City was admitted to the World Telegraph Union on 1 June 1929 by simple deposition of the instrument of ratification of the Telegraph Convention of 1875.[167] The Holy See also ratified in the name of the Vatican City the Radiotelegraph Convention of 1927, which enabled it to join the Radiotelegraph Service in 1931.[168] When in 1932 the World Telegraph Union and the Radiotelegraph Service merged into the ITU, the Vatican City remained a member and adhered to the International Telecommunication Convention of Montreux in 1968, accepting its optional protocol concerning mandatory procedures for the settlement of disputes.[169] The Vatican City was obliged to adhere to certain telecommunications conventions by virtue of Article 5 of its telegraph and telephone convention with Italy.[170]

As the Holy See was restrained by the Italian occupation when the UPU was founded in 1874, it was only on 1 June 1929 that the State of the Vatican City joined the UPU by becoming a State Party of the Stockholm Postal Convention of 1924.[171] The Vatican's accession to the UPU facilitated the implementation of the postal convention with Italy.[172]

In 1953 the International Wheat Council approved the admission of the State of the Vatican City as a Member State. The Holy See ratified on behalf of the State of the Vatican City the Wheat Trade Convention and in the annex of this Convention it is referred to as a 100 per cent wheat importing country.[173] The reason for becoming a member of the International Wheat Council was not only to secure nutritive interests of the Vatican City, but also the general concern which the Holy See shows for famine in the world.

The fact that the State of the Vatican City and not the Holy See became a member of the ITU, the UPU and the International Wheat Council can be explained in the first place by the exclusively temporal character of these organizations and the territorial implications of

---

[167] Köck, *Die völkerrechtliche Stellung*, pp. 491–492.
[168] Ibid., p. 493.
[169] Ibid., p. 494.
[170] See p. 391 above.
[171] Ferlito, *L'Attività Internazionale*, p. 145 at n. 92 and Köck, *Die völkerrechtliche Stellung*, p. 496.
[172] See p. 391 above.
[173] Köck, *Die völkerrechtliche Stellung*, pp. 512–513.

their underlying conventions. This is however an indicative argument as the interests to be represented in the International Wheat Council were partly of a humanitarian and ecclesiastic nature. In the second place, the Vatican membership of the ITU and the UPU was prompted by the telegraph and telephone convention and the postal convention concluded between Italy and the State of the Vatican City. There is no strict delimitation between purely worldly conventions signed by the Vatican City and conventions which can evoke religious interests signed by the Holy See. Thus, the Holy See ratified the Convention of WIPO on 20 January 1975 in order to become a full member, after having taken the opportunity given by the WIPO Convention to participate in WIPO without membership but with the same rights.[174] This possibility had been created for Member States of the Paris Union for the protection of intellectual property and of the Berne Union for the protection of literary and artistic property whose functions were to be taken over by WIPO. The Vatican City had been listed as a member of the Paris Union, while the Holy See was mentioned as a member of the Berne Union.[175] This dualistic situation had led to confusion concerning the Holy See's membership of WIPO, especially as in a conference organized by WIPO in 1973 the Holy See had presented its credentials 'acting in name and on behalf of the Vatican City State'.[176] The subsequent practice has however been unified so as to consider only the Holy See a member of WIPO.[177]

The Holy See participated in the founding Conference of the IAEA in 1956, although the secretariat of the Conference listed its representatives as the delegates of the Vatican City.[178] The Holy See became an original member of the IAEA in 1957. The United States Department of State, depositary of the ratifications, made the mistake however of informing the Secretary-General of the IAEA of the receipt of the ratification of 'the Vatican City'.[179] After an intervention of the Secretary of State of the Holy See, the Director-General of the IAEA in a circular note of 7 January 1960 informed the Member States of the IAEA that not the Vatican City but the Holy See was a member of the Agency.[180] No objections were raised by the other

[174] Art. 21 (2) (a) of the WIPO Convention.
[175] Köck, *Die völkerrechtliche Stellung*, p. 506.
[176] Ibid., p. 507 at n. 35.
[177] Ibid., p. 506 at n. 34.
[178] Ibid., p. 735 and Ferlito, *L'Attività Internazionale*, p. 149.
[179] Information from the IAEA archives.
[180] Text in E. Gallina, *Le Organizzazioni Internazionali e la Chiesa Cattolica* (1967) p. 77.

Member States of the IAEA, even if the Holy See could not juridically speaking have become an initial member because it was a member neither of the United Nations nor of a United Nations specialized organization according to Article IV, paragraph A of the Statute of the IAEA. The Holy See's membership of the IAEA guaranteed that the Holy See would be invited to all United Nations conferences in its own right and not as the Vatican City which would not have sufficiently reflected its universal religious mission. Another reason for joining the IAEA was that the Holy See wanted to lend its moral support to the work of the Organization in order to reduce the risks of nuclear wars and to promote the peaceful use of atomic energy.[181] Consequently, the Holy See became a party to the Treaty on the Non-Proliferation of Nuclear Weapons on 25 February 1971 and as a non-nuclear power concluded, this time on behalf of the Vatican City, a Safeguard-Agreement with the IAEA on 26 June 1972 which gives the IAEA certain rights of control on the absence of nuclear weapons in the Vatican City.[182]

It is noticeable that the Holy See became a member of the IAEA and WIPO without being subjected to a vote by a general conference and that no other Member State has raised the legal objection that the Holy See is not a 'State' and cannot therefore be admitted as a 'State Member' under either the WIPO Convention or the Statute of the IAEA. For at least the purposes of these international organizations the Holy See has been assimilated to a State with the same rights and duties. Mindful of the difficulties raised during the foundation of the League of Nations,[183] it is likely that if the Holy See, due to a lack of direct ratification possibilities, had been obliged to submit an application for membership, it could have met considerable opposition from most communist and anti-catholic minded States, especially in the fifties and sixties. As for the Vatican City, its participation in certain international organizations has not led to particular discussions or objections.

Permanent Observer

The Holy See, and this time there has been no confusion with the Vatican City State, has acquired the status of permanent observer to a number of United Nations specialized organizations as well as to the

---

[181] Interview with Mgr Alain Lebeaupin, auditor of nunciature first class, 16 Oct. 1991.
[182] Köck, *Die völkerrechtliche Stellung*, pp. 737–739.
[183] See pp. 398–400 above.

United Nations itself. The Holy See attaches value to its permanent observer status for several reasons. In the first place, it ensures its spiritual freedom without being subordinated to majority votes.[184] In the second place, observer status is less costly than membership status while at the same time the Holy See can issue declarations, receive all the documents of the organization and be present at the decision-making process. In the third place, an observer status can be indicated whenever the Holy See encounters technical obstacles such as a likely refusal of membership or problems of incompatibility with the nature of the Holy See as, for example, the inclusion of representatives of employers' and workers' organizations in the ILO delegation.

FAO was the first United Nations specialized agency to grant the Holy See the status of permanent observer, in 1948. It was expressly underlined in the Conference of FAO that the Holy See had obtained this status because of its special religious nature and without reference to its territorial sovereignty over the Vatican City.[185] As from 1951, the Holy See attended as an *ad hoc* observer certain meetings of the General Assembly of the United Nations, the Assembly of WHO and the General Conference of UNESCO. In 1964, the Holy See informed the Secretary-General of the United Nations that it would have a permanent observer in New York.[186] In 1967, a permanent observer of the Holy See was accredited to the United Nations Office in Geneva and at the same time he obtained the status of permanent observer to ILO and WHO. The Director-General of ILO was requested to invite the Holy See to the annual sessions of the International Labour Conference as an observer.[187] After a period of *ad hoc* observation, the Holy See was also confirmed as a permanent observer of UNESCO.[188] Moreover, in 1976 the Holy See, at the same time as Liechtenstein, was admitted to participate in the work of the United Nations Economic Commission for Europe in a consultative capacity.[189]

---

[184] Interview with Mgr Alain Lebeaupin, auditor of nunciature first class, 16 Oct. 1991.

[185] Invoked by the Conference of FAO during San Marino's request for an analogous observer status. FAO Doc. 51/11/4137, *Conference of FAO, Sixth Session* (29 Nov. 1951) C51/PV7, pp. 18–19. Also p. 237 above.

[186] Exchange of notes of 21 Mar./6 Apr. 1964. Full text in Gallina, *Le Organizzazioni Internazionali*, p. 75.

[187] Authorization by the ILO Governing Body, ILO Doc. GB 170/21/22, 170th Session of the Governing Body (17 Nov. 1967) pp. 1–2.

[188] *Annuario Pontificio per l'Anno 1991*, pp. 1286–1287.

[189] ECOSOC OR (25 Apr. 1975–9 Apr. 1976) Suppl. no. 8, UN Doc. E/5781, E/ECE/909, p. 93. The Economic Commission for Europe agreed to the request without discussion: ECE Res. N (XXXI) of 5 Apr. 1976.

The Holy See gave special attention to conferences and organizations with economic aims as it considered that such economic interests served its mission of peace.[190] Therefore, when in 1964 UNCTAD was installed, the Holy See participated fully. The Holy See joined UNCTAD as a full member in 1964 and it also became a member of UNIDO, set up in 1966.[191] In 1975, the Holy See unilaterally renounced its membership of UNIDO and transformed it into the status of permanent observer. This action, though heavily criticized by developing countries, did not raise any legal objection. Although the exact reasons for the abandonment of UNIDO membership were not clarified by the Holy See, Ferlito suggests that they were probably of a financial nature and related to the burden of the annual contribution.[192]

Outside the context of the United Nations organizations, the Holy See is a permanent observer to the OAS and to the World Tourism Organization.[193] In every situation mentioned above the Holy See opted in favour of a permanent observer status and acted primarily on religious grounds. It is for this reason that no confusion was created between the participation of the Holy See and the Vatican City, a distinction which was also observed by the Member States of the organizations.

United Nations

In the practice of the United Nations, the Holy See was at times listed as the Vatican City.[194] By exchange of letters between the Secretary of State of the Holy See and the Secretary-General of the United Nations in 1957, it was definitively determined that the relations of the United Nations were maintained with the Holy See.[195]

---

[190] Köck, *Die völkerrechtliche Stellung*, p. 520 at n. 17.
[191] The Holy See fulfilled the condition of membership of the UN or of a UN specialized organization, as it was a member of the IAEA. Though not legally a UN specialized organization, IAEA membership was in practice considered sufficient to be able to join UNIDO. Also pp. 402–403 above.
[192] Ferlito, *L'Attività Internazionale*, p. 140.
[193] *Annuario Pontificio per l'Anno 1991*, pp. 1286–1287.
[194] E.g. UN Yearbook (1958) pp. 103 and 254. Apart from being a permanent observer to the UN and participating in a consultative capacity to the ECE, the Holy See also lends its support to UNICEF and has been seated in advisory committees of the UNHCR. Particular attention has always been given to the status of Jerusalem, the protection of the Holy Places and the humane treatment of the Palestinian people and refugees. Köck, *Die völkerrechtliche Stellung*, pp. 722–728.
[195] Exchange of letters of 16/29 Oct. 1957 cited by H. F. Köck, 'Aktuelle Probleme der Völkerrechtlichen Präsenz des Heiligen Stuhls', *Profide et Iustitia* (1984) p. 307 at n. 39.

The aim of the United Nations, namely the universal promotion of peace, is a principle shared by the Holy See and therefore a common ground for cooperation. Contrary to what has generally been believed, the Holy See was not, at least initially, uninterested in becoming a full member of the United Nations. In October 1944, just after the Conference of Dumbarton Oaks, the Sovereign Pontiff asked the personal representative of the United States President to the Holy See what would be the conditions of membership of the future United Nations.[196] The United States Secretary of State replied that 'it would seem undesirable that the question of membership of the Vatican be raised now'.[197] He referred to several difficulties such as the neutrality of the Vatican City according to Article 24 of the Lateran Treaty, the incapacity of fulfilling all responsibilities of membership for a diminutive State like the Vatican City and the fact that 'original members not maintaining diplomatic relations with the Vatican State would in some instances probably oppose its admission', like the Soviet Union, while at the same time 'the question would be likely to raise a political controversy in the United States'.[198] The United States Secretary of State considered the question of membership of the State of the Vatican City, although it was more likely that the Sovereign Pontiff envisaged a possible United Nations membership of the Holy See, which would have a greater moral weight than the membership of the Vatican City.

Setting aside the problem of opposition by certain Member States of the United Nations, there are other obstacles which are intrinsic to the nature of the Holy See. The Holy See has a religious value for a part of the world population living in different States. For this reason it would be out of the question for the Holy See to adopt a position against this or that State.[199] Yet in the United Nations the members are often compelled to define their position. The Holy See would by its very nature often be forced to abstain from voting.[200] In addition, as under Article 24 of the Lateran Treaty the Holy See has to remain extraneous to all temporal disputes between States, it could not endorse sanctions imposed by the Security Council under Chapter VII

---

[196] *Papers relating to the Foreign Relations of the United States* (1944) vol. I, pp. 963–964, also mentioned by Ferlito, *L'Attività Internazionale*, pp. 133–134.
[197] *Papers relating to the Foreign Relations of the United States* (1944) vol. I, p. 962.
[198] Ibid.
[199] Interview with Mgr Alain Lebeaupin, auditor of nunciature first class, 16 Oct. 1991.
[200] Ibid.

of the United Nations Charter. Lastly, although in principle the Holy See does not accept a higher jurisdiction than itself, an accession to the Statute of the International Court of Justice would not be entirely excluded. The Holy See does not have to accept the compulsory jurisdiction of the Court under Article 36, paragraph 2 of the Statute of the International Court of Justice or can make a reservation to the Court's jurisdiction for matters which fall under divine law. Until now, the Holy See seems to have obtained satisfactory results which serve its mission through its permanent observer position in the United Nations.

OSCE

In 1969, the consultative political Committee of the Warsaw Pact invited the Holy See to participate in a pan-European conference, the CSCE. The reasons for inviting the Holy See were believed to be related to the presence of the Vatican City in Europe and therefore to a territorial argument, but, in the end, the participating States valued foremost the spiritual, non-political contribution of the Holy See.[201] As the Holy See does not pursue political aims and is bound by the principle of political neutrality in disputes between States according to Article 24 of the Lateran Treaty, the Holy See's delegate to the Helsinki consultations made an interpretative declaration on 28 November 1972, concerning the rule of consensus of the Helsinki rules of procedure, in which he stated that the Holy See would abstain from taking a position when resolutions related to 'concrete problems of political character' were adopted.[202] This abstention would imply neither an agreement nor a disagreement and would not prevent an adoption by consensus. This principle of the relations between the Holy See and the CSCE has been underlined and followed ever since.

At the Helsinki conferences which led to the adoption of the Final Act of the CSCE in 1975, the Holy See particularly advocated respect for human rights, including the freedom of religion. It is due to the actions and proposals of the Holy See that the freedom of thought, conscience, religion or belief is the one human right which has been elaborated in more precise terms than the other human rights set

---

[201] Address of Mgr Agostino Casaroli, special delegate of Pope Paul VI, to the CSCE in Helsinki on 1 Aug. 1975. Text in A. Carrascosa Coso, *La Santa Sede y la Conferencia sobre la Seguridad y la Cooperación en Europa*, 2nd edn (1991) p. 365.

[202] CSCE Doc./HS/5 (29 Nov. 1972). Reiterated by an address of Mgr Zabkar on 4 Dec. 1972, ibid., p. 352.

forth in the Final Act of the CSCE. Although the Holy See had preferred to confer on the CSCE principles juridical value instead of only a moral importance, the Final Act of the CSCE gave the Holy See the opportunity to be on a level with two other world Powers – the United States and the Soviet Union – and to ameliorate its relations with the communist States.[203]

In the drafting process of the Charter of Paris for a New Europe, the Holy See was only present in the working groups which treated matters of moral and ethical interest.[204] The Holy See remained outside the group which prepared the new institutions of the CSCE, as it was considered incompatible with the Holy See's non-political nature. The final resolution of the 1991 Madrid Conference concerning the establishment of the CSCE Parliamentary Assembly provides that '[the] Holy See may send two representatives to the Assembly's meetings as guests of honour'.[205] They do not have the right to vote. Hence, in the OSCE Parliamentary Assembly the Holy See is a permanent observer, or 'guest of honour', due to the absence of a Holy See parliament. The Holy See, like Liechtenstein, San Marino and Monaco, covers 0.20 per cent of the OSCE institutional costs.[206] The institutionalization of the CSCE prompted the Holy See to send a memorandum to all the participating States in the CSCE on 2 June 1992 explaining its position and suggesting a future framework for its relations with the CSCE. The Holy See notes: 'The Holy See's contribution to decision-making and implementation will stop at the point Member States approve initiatives of political–military character, for example in matters of crisis solving and peacekeeping.'[207] The Holy See therefore wishes to come to a solution agreed with the other Member States in order to 'achieve a formal "modus vivendi" according to which the Conference would take note of the specific contribution of the Holy See and state that this would not constitute a precedent for other participants, since the "modus vivendi" will be based on the specific nature of the Holy See'.[208] The *modus vivendi*

---

[203] Ibid., pp. 308–311.
[204] Address of Mgr Alain Lebeaupin of 29 Oct. 1990. Information from the CSCE.
[205] Last para. of Art. 1 of the final resolution of the Madrid Conference concerning the establishment of the CSCE Parliamentary Assembly, 3 Apr. 1991, 30 ILM (1991) p. 1346.
[206] Part III (2) of the Supplementary Document to give effect to certain provisions in the Charter of Paris for a New Europe, 30 ILM (1991) p. 220.
[207] Holy See memorandum entitled: 'Considerations on the participation of the Holy See to the CSCE' (2 Jun. 1992), not published.
[208] Ibid.

would consist of 'reservations or interpretative statements' which would not reduce the Holy See to an observer in every domain. The result of the membership conditions of the Holy See in the OSCE could become an example or precedent for the Holy See's participation in other political international fora, such as the United Nations.

Council of Europe

Since the inception of the Council of Europe, the Holy See has given its moral support to this European movement. When in May 1948 a preparatory conference was held in the Hague which in the end would lead to the establishment of the Council of Europe, the Pope sent a personal representative 'afin de montrer la sollicitude et de porter l'encouragement du Saint-Siège pour l'union des peuples'.[209] The Holy See has frequently shown its favourable position towards the Council of Europe, especially with regard to the Council of Europe's efforts in the protection of human rights.[210] It is not publicly known whether the Holy See or the Vatican City has ever envisaged becoming a full member of the Council of Europe. Such participation would undoubtedly encounter technical objections. As one British parliamentarian in the Parliamentary Assembly observed, during the debate on the admission of Liechtenstein to the Council of Europe: 'Except for the election of His Holiness the Pope, the Vatican is not a democracy.'[211] Moreover, as far as the membership of the State of the Vatican City is concerned, it is doubtful whether the fundamental human rights are sufficiently protected in the Vatican City.[212]

The Holy See has become a party to several European conventions[213] and has appointed a permanent observer to the Council of Europe since November 1970.[214]

---

[209] Consistorial allocution of Pope Pius XII, of 2 Jun. 1948, *Osservatore Romano* (3 Jun. 1948), also cited in Köck, *Die völkerrechtliche Stellung*, pp. 741–742.
[210] Ibid., p. 742.
[211] Council of Europe, *Parliamentary Assembly, Official Report* (27 Sept.–5 Oct. 1978) vol. II, p. 386.
[212] See pp. 383–386 above.
[213] The European Cultural Convention (1954) no. 18, the European Convention on the Academic Recognition of University Qualifications (1959) no. 32, the European Convention on the Protection of the Archeological Heritage (1969) no. 66 and the European Convention on Transfrontier Television (1989) no. 132 (signed, not ratified).
[214] Köck, *Die völkerrechtliche Stellung*, p. 743.

European Community

The State of the Vatican City finds itself in a different position vis-à-vis the European Community from the other European Micro-States.[215] The basic difference lies in the fact that the Vatican City does not constitute a part of the European Community's customs territory by virtue of its customs convention with Italy.[216] As with the other three European Micro-States, the European Commission clarified in 1986 that the free movement of workers, the right of establishment and the free movement of services under the EC Treaty did not apply to the Vatican City.[217] The fact that the Vatican City does not form a customs union with Italy and the particular nature of the Vatican City have led the European Parliament to believe that it was not likely that the Vatican City would conclude a customs union agreement with the European Community.[218] The special customs regime and exceptional customs enclave in the European Community has not led to any objections from the Member States of the Community. The only common ground for an agreement between the Vatican City and the European Community could be the introduction of the ECU as a single currency. A declaration on monetary relations with, *inter alia*, the Vatican City has been joined to that end to the Maastricht Treaty on European Union. Since November 1970, the Holy See has accredited an apostolic nuncio to the European Union, who is particularly interested in the moral, social and cultural aspects of the Community.

Application of the criteria for statehood

In the light of the above considerations, the statehood of the Vatican City will be examined.[219] We shall only take into account the legal status of the Vatican City as from its creation in 1929 by virtue of the Lateran Treaty, because it is from this date on that the Vatican City

---

[215] Cf. San Marino, pp. 246–254 above, Monaco, pp. 301–302 above, and Andorra, pp. 359–364 above.

[216] See pp. 391–392 above.

[217] Answer of Mr Delors in name of the Commission to written question no. 900/86, ECOJ no. C 54 (2.3.87) p. 31.

[218] The European Parliament's Commission for Institutional Affairs stated in its 'resolution on the rights of the citizens of small States and territories in Europe' that as the activities of the Vatican City are in the spiritual sphere and as its economic role is small, the Vatican City would be left outside the Commission's considerations.: EP Doc. A2-86/89, European Parliament, *Session Documents* (20 Apr. 1989) p. 7.

[219] See for the general criteria for statehood, pp. 116–127 above.

has functioned in the international community. The following aspects are therefore taken into account:

Territory With its 0.44 square kilometres of land territory, the Vatican City is the smallest political entity in the world. It may be wondered whether this small territorial size is sufficient to meet the criterion for statehood. In this context it should be observed that the Holy See and Italy were of the opinion that the Holy See needed a territory in order to be politically sovereign,[220] because 'the world today recognizes no form of sovereignty other than the territorial form'.[221] They clearly agreed that even a minimal territory like the Vatican City would provide an international legal basis for statehood. Some scholars have argued that the exiguity of the Vatican territory cannot constitute a cause for denying the Vatican City's statehood.[222] Unfortunately, they did not advance clear legal arguments based on the attitude of the international community to support their position. The difficulty lies in the fact that even if the Vatican City is a member of the ITU and the UPU, and a party to certain international conventions, this may well be considered a recognition of the Vatican City's statehood, but does not determine once and for all that the recognition was declaratory. Certain hard facts should however be retained: Italy and the Holy See were convinced that the Vatican territory was a necessary and sufficient element in order to fulfil the territorial criterion for statehood in international law, while no third State has ever made a reservation concerning the territorial element of the State of the Vatican City. There is therefore no proof acceptable under international law that the smallness of the territory of the Vatican City precludes its statehood, without reparative recognition.

Population We have found in Chapter 2 that the inhabitants of a State must constitute a permanent population.[223] There are 508 persons effectively residing in the Vatican City of whom 165 are Vatican citizens.[224] There are several elements which distinguish the inhabitants of the Vatican City from those of other States. It cannot be maintained that the inhabitants of the Vatican City are not a

---

[220] C. A. Biggini, *Storia Inedita della Conciliazione* (1942) pp. 87–88.
[221] D. A. Binchy, *Church and State in Fascist Italy* (1941) p. 229, citing Pope Pius XI.
[222] P. Vellas, 'Les Etats exigus en Droit international public', 58 RGDIP (1954) pp. 561–563 and M. H. Mendelson, 'Diminutive States in the United Nations', 21 ICLQ (1972) p. 612.
[223] See pp. 117–118 above.
[224] State as at 2 Dec. 1991. Information from the Apostolic Nunciature in France.

population within the meaning of the criteria for statehood, because they are practically all in the service of the Holy See or because the population is not 'capable of maintaining and reproducing itself'.[225] These elements do not *a priori* exclude the permanent establishment of the Vatican citizens, although in the long run one cannot speak of a permanent succession of generations established in the Vatican City. One noteworthy principle of the Vatican legal order is that every inhabitant of the Vatican City, whether or not possessing Vatican citizenship, can be expelled from the Vatican territory at any time.[226] This factor prejudices the development of a permanent population and demonstrates that the Vatican Government does not consider the inhabitants of the Vatican City a fixed population to whose presence it attaches distinctive value for the governmental structure. Although Article 9 of the Lateran Treaty foresees the existence of persons subject to the sovereignty of the Holy See, it also provides for a legal status for persons who cease to be subject to the sovereignty of the Holy See. It was therefore implicitly recognized that the Vatican inhabitants would not have a permanent attachment to the Vatican territory. Moreover, according to the Lateran Treaty, the Vatican City State was created for special purposes, namely to assure absolute visible independence to the Holy See in order to guarantee it indisputable sovereignty also in the international field.[227] The presence of a fixed population was of secondary interest. Even if the Vatican City did not comprise any inhabitant, except for the Sovereign Pontiff representing the governmental power of the Vatican City and the Head of the Roman Catholic Church, the State of the Vatican City would still be considered a State for special purposes according to the Lateran Treaty. It is not the object of the Holy See to wield effective power over a population in the Vatican territory. The Vatican City lacks a human society stably united in its territory.[228] It can therefore be inferred that the Vatican City does not have a population within the meaning of the criteria for statehood.

Government Despite the fact that there is no permanent population in the Vatican City, the Government of the Vatican City wields effective temporal power over its inhabitants and employees. As we have

---

[225] Mendelson, 'Diminutive States', p. 612.
[226] See p. 394 above.
[227] Preamble and Art. 3 of the Lateran Treaty.
[228] Arangio-Ruiz, 'La Città del Vaticano', p. 4.

concluded in preceding paragraphs, the Vatican City possesses a governmental organization which is proper to itself and which juridically speaking cannot be identified with the Holy See.[229] There is no doubt that the governmental institutions of the Vatican City exercise effective authority, within their own legal framework, in the Vatican territory.

Independence A number of lawyers have argued that the Vatican City did not fulfil the conditions for statehood, because it had been established in the service of the Holy See.[230] This argument corresponds to a denial of the Vatican City's independence of the Holy See. The criterion of independence aims to distinguish one State from another so that one territorial entity is not just the continuation of another territorial entity. The Holy See however is neither a State nor a territorial entity. Moreover, it is an authority which partly coincides with certain Vatican temporal governmental institutions and which operates from inside the Vatican City. Thus the presence of the Holy See cannot preclude the Vatican City's statehood, because the Vatican City is not subject to any *external* influence.

However, the argument needs to be taken further as in the international field the Holy See and the Vatican City are often confused and interchanged. It is only in its relations with Italy that the Holy See clearly distinguishes between its own actions, actions in the name of the Vatican City or actions taken directly by the Vatican City through, for example, the Governor.[231] The question arises whether an international commitment entered into by the Holy See in its own capacity has legally binding effects for the Vatican Government and should therefore be implemented in the Vatican City by the latter. The Holy

---

[229] See pp. 376–383 and 386–388 above.

[230] Puente Egido, *Personalidad Internacional*, p. 99 states that the State of the Vatican City is 'un sujeto soberano de carácter territorial no estatal, creado al servicio de la Santa Sede y como tal reconocido por los Estados'. Kunz, 'The Status of the Holy See', p. 313 concludes with regard to the Vatican City: 'Its constitution is not autonomous, but derived from the Holy See. It is a vassal state of the Holy See.' N. Nuccitelli, *Le Fondement juridique des Rapports diplomatiques entre le Saint-Siège et les Nations Unies* (1956) p. 52 believes that, due to the presence of the Holy See in the Vatican City and the exercise of the latter's sovereignty by the Holy See, the Vatican City State must be 'un Etat sui generis'.

[231] The postal, telegraph and telephone conventions of 1929 between the Vatican City and Italy have, for example, been concluded by the Governor of the Vatican City, i.e., without interposition of an organ of the Holy See. See pp. 390–391 above. Such direct representation has never been used with other States, except in the relations with Italy.

See has absolute power and sovereign jurisdiction over the Vatican City.[232] It should nevertheless not be forgotten that the Holy See cannot be identified with the Vatican City. They are two distinct international legal persons. The Holy See is the hierarchically highest organ of the Roman Catholic Church with its own religious jurisdiction, while the Vatican temporal Government only has jurisdiction over the Vatican territory. The Vatican Government, ultimately the Pope, is only subordinated to the decisions of the Holy See, which in the end is again the Pope as the supreme authority of the Roman Catholic Church,[233] if the Holy See so determines. This flows from the Holy See's absolute power over the Vatican City. The existence of two international legal persons implies however that international legal actions taken by the Holy See will have no binding effect for the Vatican temporal authorities, unless the Holy See so decides. Therefore, strictly juridically speaking, the international conventions ratified by the Holy See in its own name do not bind the Vatican City's temporal Government, unless they have been concluded in the name of the Vatican City. This would only be different if the Holy See had promised to apply the convention in the Vatican City, a promise which can also be implicit, such as a reservation made to the convention aiming to restrict a full application of the treaty provisions in the Vatican City.[234]

Is the Vatican City formally and actually independent of Italy? According to Article 4 of the Lateran Treaty, Italy recognizes that it cannot interfere in any way in the Vatican City and that there is no authority within the Vatican City other than the Holy See. The very purpose of the creation of the Vatican City was to guarantee the greatest independence to the Holy See. Nevertheless, certain 'foreign elements' are present in the territory of the Vatican City, due to arrangements which had to be made to solve problems linked to the smallness of the territory. Compared with the other European Micro-States, these 'foreign elements' have been kept to a minimum:[235]

---

[232] Art. 3 of the Lateran Treaty.
[233] Can. 331 of the 1983 Code of Canon Law. See also p. 387 above.
[234] E.g. reservations with respect to the Vatican legislation on entry and sojourn, to the Convention relating to the Status of Refugees of 1951 and to the Convention on the Rights of the Child of 1989 (point c of the reservation). *Multilateral Treaties deposited with the Secretary-General*, Status as at 31 Dec. 1993 (1994) pp. 197–198 and 212.
[235] Cf. pp. 200–204, 255–259, 304–314 and 366–371 above.

1 *Special regime for St Peter's Square* The Italian police is charged with the security surveillance in St Peter's Square when it is open to the public.[236] This restricted interference has been chosen by the Holy See for practical purposes relating to the number of persons to be controlled each day and the relatively easy access to St Peter's Square. Although this regulation cannot be denounced unless by common accord of both parties to the Lateran Treaty, Italy's rights do not restrict the authority of the Holy See considerably. The closed part of the Vatican City remains at all times under the Holy See's jurisdiction.

2 *Italian legislation* Certain legal domains in the Vatican City are regulated by Italian legislation which has thus an extraterritorial application.[237] In these cases, newly introduced Italian laws will not automatically be adopted in the Vatican City. Moreover, the applicable Italian legislation can at any time be abolished by means of the promulgation of Vatican legislation on the same subject. By virtue of the 1929 postal, telegraph and telephone conventions, the Vatican City applied relevant Italian legislation and is in principle obliged to adhere to the international telegraph and telephone conventions. This obligation does not exist for postal matters[238] and seems restricted to the treaties to which Italy was a party in 1929 for telegraph and telephone questions.[239] In any case, the fundamental law provides that the treaties ratified by Italy which concern postal, telegraph and telephone matters can only be implemented in the Vatican City if the Vatican City consents.[240] Considering that the postal, telegraph and telephone conventions with Italy can be denounced within six months, the Vatican City's independence is not compromised by these conventions. The Vatican City's formal independence is not restricted either by the extraterritorial effects of certain Italian legislation.

The formal independence of the Vatican City is supplemented by an actual independence. Italy does not in practice exercise any substantial control over the Vatican City. Such interference is prohibited by Article 4 of the Lateran Treaty. Rousseau has been the only scholar to deny the Vatican City's statehood on the ground that the 'Vatican ne

---

[236] Art. 3 of the Lateran Treaty. See p. 389 above.
[237] See pp. 393–394 above.
[238] Art. 9 of the postal convention only states that the tariffs of the 'Accordi Internazionali' shall apply to certain correspondence from the Vatican City. This implies that the international postal conventions concluded by Italy are also applied in the Vatican City. The Vatican City has not been prevented from adhering to these postal conventions itself in the framework of the UPU.
[239] Art. 5, 2nd para. of the telegraph and telephone convention.
[240] Art. 20 (c) of the fundamental law.

possède pas l'autonomie de ses services publics'.[241] He argued that the Vatican City was not sufficiently independent, as Italy provided it with water and energy, had installed the railway station and the telephone network, while the Vatican police force employed only Italians, and children of the Vatican City had to attend schools in Italy.[242] Rousseau's argumentation is however based on too wide a notion of a State's independence. Admittedly, Italy has practical means of exerting pressure on the Vatican City, such as withholding water and energy supplies or obstructing the postal, telegraph and telephone correspondence, but it has never used these methods. It cannot be maintained that Italy exercises any control over the functioning of the Vatican City. The Vatican City's Government has therefore formal and actual independence of Italy.

Recognition In the light of the above considerations, it should be concluded that the Vatican City is not a State in international law, because it does not meet the criterion of a permanent population. Any international recognition of the Vatican City's statehood would have a constitutive and reparative effect. The State of the Vatican City was first of all recognized by Italy under the clear condition however that it would serve the independence of the Holy See.[243] It seems evident that without the presence of the Holy See as the highest organ of the Roman Catholic Church, Italy would not have recognized the Vatican City's statehood, especially if the inhabitants of the Vatican City had remained a non-permanent population. The international community of States seems to have adopted the same position, as during its participation in international conferences and organizations, such as the IAEA and WIPO, the State of the Vatican City was smoothly replaced by the Holy See without international objections. The international community appeared to admit that the State of the Vatican City was created at the service of the Holy See with which it could be identified, despite its separate international legal status. The Vatican City was recognized as a State through its participation in the UPU, the ITU, the International Wheat Council, EUTELSAT, INTELSAT, and in the United Nations Conferences before the Holy See's accession to the IAEA. The statehood of the Vatican City has not been recognized by means of the maintenance of diplomatic relations, as these have

---

[241] C. Rousseau, 'Etat de la Cité du Vatican', 37 RGDIP (1930) p. 150.
[242] Ibid., pp. 150–152.
[243] Art. 3 of the Lateran Treaty recognizes the Holy See's sovereignty over the Vatican City which is created for such purpose with the special aims of the Lateran Treaty.

always been entered into by the Holy See. Nevertheless, as the Holy See was often regarded as the Government of the Vatican City, the diplomatic relations of the Holy See were at times interpreted as an implicit recognition of the Vatican City, even by States which did not maintain diplomatic relations with the Holy See.[244] This reasoning is juridically incorrect as the recognition of the Holy See's international status does not imply the recognition of another international entity – the Vatican City – however close the functional relations between these two entities may be.

As a consequence, it should be concluded that the Vatican City was recognized as a State by the international community for special purposes relating to the presence of the Holy See in the Vatican territory.[245] It cannot therefore be argued that the Vatican City was recognized as a State because it fulfilled all criteria for statehood, nor that international law does not require a permanent population in order to be a State. One State cannot be superimposed on another State in the same territory; thus the international recognition of the Holy See does not imply that the Holy See is regarded as a State, but that it has been granted certain rights which are normally inherent in statehood.

Self-determination of the Vatican population

In the discussion relating to the right of self-determination of independent peoples, that is, of States, no attention was given to the question of whether or not the States accommodating such peoples had to be recognized.[246] It seems therefore that the general criteria for statehood in international law must be followed, so that the people of a State can have the right of self-determination if the State fulfils these

---

[244] Accordingly the United States Department of State observed in 1939: 'The Vatican City State is a state in the international sense and the Holy See, as the sovereign authority of that state, maintains diplomatic relations with a number of countries ... While ... this [the United States] Government has not established diplomatic relations with the Government of the Vatican City State, it nevertheless is a sovereign state': Petition of the United States Department of State to the District of Columbia Board of Commissioners for tax exemption for property owned by the Holy See. Text in M. M. Whiteman, *Digest of International Law*, vol. VII (1963) p. 316.

[245] ILC Rapporteur Fitzmaurice of the draft Convention on the Law of Treaties had foreseen the case of the Vatican City in his draft Art. 3 of 1956 on used terms, which defined a State also as '(iii) entities recognized as being States ... on special grounds'. ILC Yearbook (1956) vol. II, p. 107, para. 4 and p. 118.

[246] See in general, Chapter 1 above.

general criteria. As a State can also be established by means of a constitutive recognition with reparative effect, there is *a priori* no reason to withhold the right of self-determination from the Vatican citizens.[247] In order to exercise this right, the Vatican citizens must constitute a people within the meaning of the right of self-determination.[248] Do the Vatican citizens have common objective characteristics? Two factors preclude the development of common objective characteristics among the Vatican citizens: every Vatican citizen is originally a foreigner, that is a non-Vatican citizen, and there is, in principle, no succession of generations of Vatican citizens. Admittedly, the Vatican citizens share common elements, because they are all Roman Catholics and in the service of the Roman Catholic Church, but these elements are not reinforced by a common tradition, culture or history linked to the Vatican City and passed on from generation to generation. The absence of ancestors and descendants implies that, apart from their religious beliefs, Vatican citizens, each with their different cultures, traditions and historical backgrounds of origin, do not develop a common Vatican history, culture, tradition or even language, proper to the Vatican City. As a consequence, Vatican citizens do not feel like a Vatican people and have no objective characteristics to preserve. Whatever the importance of the Vatican City for its citizens from a religious point of view, Vatican citizens have no personal attachment to the Vatican territory. This argument is reinforced by the fact that any Vatican citizen can at any time be expelled from the Vatican City.[249] Considering the lack of objective and subjective characteristics, and the absence of a personal link with the Vatican territory, it should be inferred that Vatican citizens are not a people or a fraction of a people within the meaning of the right of self-determination.

Conclusions

The State of the Vatican City is a Micro-State which has been created, not for the convenience of its population, but in order to guarantee independence to another international legal person, the Holy See. It is nevertheless an entity which has been recognized by the international community as a State for special purposes and is in this

---

[247] See for our conclusions on the Vatican City's statehood, pp. 410–417 above.
[248] See pp. 77–84 above.
[249] See 394 above.

capacity submitted to international law. The following conclusions can be drawn:

1. The Holy See is not the Government of the Vatican City, although the Government of the Vatican City is ultimately subordinated to the decisions of the Holy See.
2. The Vatican City is a State in international law, because it has been recognized as such due to the presence of the Holy See in its territory. This international recognition has a constitutive effect, as the Vatican City possesses no permanent population and therefore no people with the right of self-determination.
3. The Vatican City's 0.44 square kilometres of land territory is up to now the smallest territory still to be accepted as fulfilling the territorial criterion for statehood.
4. The functional relations between the Vatican City and Italy which aim to meet practical difficulties related to the smallness of the Vatican territory, such as postal, telegraph and telephone communications, customs regulations and energy supply, have not prejudiced the Vatican City's formal and actual independence. This proves that the exiguity of a State's territory does not necessarily lead to a reduction or minimization of independence.
5. The State of the Vatican City and the Holy See are two separate international legal persons which are strictly juridically speaking not interchangeable. As a consequence, international obligations entered into by either the Vatican City or the Holy See do not bind the other legal entity, unless the Holy See so decides.

PART III

General conclusions

9 General conclusions

After having examined the present international legal content of the right of self-determination and the criteria for statehood as well as the international legal status of five European Micro-States, our findings can be combined in order to enlighten certain legal questions in three domains, namely the question of autonomy as distinct from statehood, the international attitude to be adopted towards secession and the expected consequences of fragmentation.

Autonomy

Peoples and fractions of peoples have a *jus cogens* right to autonomy as long as this autonomous status does not partially or totally disrupt the territorial integrity of an existing State.[1] When soliciting autonomy, a people does not at the present stage have to prove a special reason to justify its demand, for the right of self-determination entitles a people to freely determine its internal political status. Autonomy can thus become an alternative to seceding or a preparatory step to a gradual secession. Once a State is faced with a claim for full autonomy by a people on its territory it becomes essential to distinguish between the limits of autonomy and those of statehood and independence. In other words, what is the maximum degree of autonomy, short of independence, which does not lead to the disruption of a State's territorial integrity?

The status of Micro-States is pertinent in this context, as, apart from being the smallest State units, they also represent border cases of independence. On this basis it can be concluded that there are two

---

[1] See pp. 77–84 and 105 above.

legal domains which will determine the level of independence or autonomy of a political entity, namely internal and external affairs. National defence and security matters may be listed as a third factor, but this is not a mandatory State activity. A State may decide not to have an army and delegate the defence of its territory to another State by a bilateral or collective defence agreement.[2] The Micro-States which have opted for this formula did not see their statehood denied for this reason. Full autonomy will therefore comprise:

Internal affairs A recent and clear enumeration of matters which may be governed by a local authority is given by Articles 31 to 35 of the 1994 Draft United Nations Declaration on the Rights of Indigenous Peoples.[3] Indigenous peoples are peoples who have been officially recognized as entities entitled to a high degree of autonomy. Their autonomy covers matters relating to culture, religion, education, information, media, health, housing, employment, social welfare, economic activities, land and resources management, environment,[4] citizenship[5] and institutional structures.[6] Autonomous entities may have their own government and parliamentary assembly which may cover substantial political, legal and financial domains independently of the central State authorities.

External affairs The freedom of an autonomous entity in external affairs is the main element which will decide when autonomy glides into independence. It is not uncommon that autonomous regions, like the Swiss cantons, have the right to establish contacts, also in contractual form, with neighbouring foreign regions or States.[7] The

---

[2] Micronesia, the Marshall Islands, Palau and Monaco have concluded an explicit defence agreement with the USA and France respectively, pp. 139-140 and 290 above, San Marino and Andorra an implicit one with Italy and France and Spain respectively, pp. 233 and 345 above, while Liechtenstein and the Vatican City have no army nor a defence agreement with another State, pp. 169 and 396 above.

[3] UN Doc. E/CN.4/1995/2 and E/CN.4/Sub.2/1994/56, 34 ILM (1995) pp. 546 ff. See also pp. 46-48 above.

[4] Art. 31 of the Draft Declaration on the Rights of Indigenous Peoples.

[5] Art. 32 of the Draft Declaration on the Rights of Indigenous Peoples.

[6] Art. 33 of the Draft Declaration on the Rights of Indigenous Peoples.

[7] Thus W. Burckhardt, *Kommentar der schweizerischen Bundesverfassung vom 29. Mai 1874* (1931) p. 81 notes that the Swiss federal authority has the right to conclude international treaties on whatever subject even if this has been reserved to the cantons. On less important subjects, cantons may conclude international agreements, providing that, according to the Federal Council, Swiss international interests or the rights of other cantons are not prejudiced. Thus, Swiss cantons could conclude intercantonal agreements with Liechtenstein on the trade of cattle (not published), on medicines,

subjects treated by such agreements should remain of a minimal national interest. The rights of autonomous regions should not enable the establishment of consular or diplomatic contacts with foreign States, the conclusion of international agreements on matters of high State interest, nor admission to international governmental organizations. When according a certain freedom in external relations to autonomous regions, the central State authorities should also take into account that legal constructions which fall short of independence may nevertheless foster international constitutive recognition and admission to the United Nations, which in turn will disrupt the territorial integrity of the State which has granted the autonomy. Thus, Micronesia, the Marshall Islands and Palau, self-governing entities which have to 'consult' the United States in the conduct of their foreign affairs, without an explicit guarantee of independence, have been admitted as members of the United Nations.[8] Monaco, though recognized as independent by France, lacks actual independence because it has problems enforcing these guarantees of independence in practice, but has been admitted to the United Nations.[9] Particularly in these cases where the restrictions on the external relations of a putative State are not clearly and unambiguously phrased, international recognition is no longer withheld and admission to the United Nations is not *a priori* excluded, even if according to the criteria for statehood the entity lacks independence.

In addition, some States are more prone to concede judicial means of settling disputes than others.[10] If there are no means of judicial redress and if bilateral treaties restrict the independence of a small State, that State may be better off with a very high degree of autonomy while remaining a part of another State, than with

---

LGBl (1973) no. 20, and on financial contributions to the Swiss 'Hochschule', LGBl (1982) no. 47.

[8] See pp. 139–140 above, at nn. 35–37.
[9] See pp. 304–314 above.
[10] Nauru could settle its dispute with Australia before the ICJ and Liechtenstein can submit customs, monetary and VAT problems with Switzerland to an arbitration commission. This latter option is of rather recent origin. See pp. 140–141 and 164–167 above. France (and Spain) have not permitted arbitration or denunciation clauses in their political treaties with Monaco and Andorra respectively, although Spain has accepted the ICJ's compulsory jurisdiction. See pp. 274–282 and 335–338 above. Micronesia, the Marshall Islands and Palau can bring their disputes, except for defence and security matters, under their Compacts of Free Association before an Arbitration Board: Title 4, Art. II, Section 424 of the Compacts of Free Association. See also pp. 139–140 above at nn. 35–37.

statehood. The reason for this argument is that within a State the autonomous community may have more constitutionally framed judicial means to have its legal position guaranteed than it would have outside the national framework. In this sense international judicial control is not yet as well developed and obvious as domestic legal remedies.

The unresolved problem remains the determination of the communities that will have a *jus cogens* right to autonomy. So far States have been very reluctant to take any steps in the direction of defining such groups, fearing that a discussion on autonomy could potentially lead to a dismemberment of existing States.[11] The only exception to this attitude is the drafting of the Declaration on the Rights of Indigenous Peoples. The United Nations envisages the creation of a high-level body with special competences, with the direct participation of indigenous peoples, to promote respect for and full application of the provisions of the Declaration.[12] The experience of this body could serve as an example for any other international organ to be established charged with hearing the legitimacy of claims for autonomy.

Secession

Given the fact that so far the attitude of the international community towards secessions has not permitted the filling of the legal vacuum created, on the one hand, by the right of self-determination and, on the other, by the duty to respect the territorial integrity of existing States, two aspects should be borne in mind in the future development of the right to secession:[13]

Use of force As we have concluded in Chapter 1, the present international legal situation encourages the use of force in order to make demands for secession successful.[14] The international response towards wars of secession, especially in the former Yugoslavia, has confirmed two points: first, military interference by third States to help secessionists is prohibited[15] and, secondly, States are in principle

---

[11] See pp. 107–108 and 198 above.
[12] Art. 41 of the Draft Declaration on the Rights of Indigenous Peoples.
[13] See in general pp. 104–109 above.
[14] Ibid.
[15] In an EPC Statement on Bosnia and Hercegovina of 16 Apr. 1992, the EC condemned 'any attempts from outside to destabilize Bosnia and Hercegovina', EPC Press Release 51/92. By SC Res. 752 (1992), the Security Council demanded that interference from

entitled to use police enforcement measures to impose the continuation of their territorial integrity and to prevent secessions.¹⁶ This latter point is counterbalanced by the duty to respect fundamental human rights and international humanitarian law. Yet, as soon as a seceding part is recognized as being a State, the so-called police actions become acts of international aggression. As an example of what could be called a police enforcement measure, one may cite the Croatian Government offensive to restore its authority in the Serb-held Krajina region on 4 August 1995. Neither the United Nations nor the European Union officially condemned the offensive as such.¹⁷ In other parts of the world, the prevention of secession by military means has not always led to international condemnation either.¹⁸

If the purpose of the international community is to prevent the use of force by secessionists, the question is complicated by the fact that so far the international community has not clearly and consistently condemned the use of violence by such groups so as to create an *opinio juris*. It cannot be denied that in the case of Abkhazia, Bosnia-Herzegovina and Nagorno Karabakh the international community has condemned the use of force or demanded the end of

> outside Bosnia-Herzegovina, including by units of the Yugoslav National Army and elements of the Croatian army, cease immediately and that its neighbours respect the territorial integrity of Bosnia-Herzegovina. This is nothing more than the reiteration of the principle of non-intervention in a State's internal affairs. According to Art. II (f) of GA Res. 36/103 (Declaration on the Inadmissibility of Intervention and Interference in the Internal Affairs of States) States have the duty 'to refrain from the promotion, encouragement or support ... of rebellious or secessionist activities within other States'. The EC countries did not support this Declaration as a whole.

[16] See also M. Weller, 'The International Response to the Dissolution of the Socialist Federal Republic of Yugoslavia', 86 AJIL (1992) p. 572.

[17] The Security Council condemned 'in the strongest terms' the 'unacceptable' Croatian acts against UN personnel, but only in the considerations, not in the operative part of SC Res. 1009 (1995). It demanded an end to the military actions at a moment when those actions had already ceased – SC Res. 1009 is dated 10 Aug. 1995 – without asking for the withdrawal of the Croatian troops. The EU 'expressed its profound concern about the offensive', condemning only the military actions which had led to death and injuries of innocent civilians, and asked for an immediate end to military operations: EU Declaration regarding the Resumption of Hostilities in Croatia (4 Aug. 1995). In May 1995, during the Croatian offensive in Western Slavonia, the Security Council demanded by Presidential Statement that the Croatian Government immediately end its offensive: UN Doc. S/PRST/1995/23. SC Res. 994 (1995) asked all parties to refrain from any further military measures or actions that could lead to the escalation of the situation in Western Slavonia.

[18] The Russian offensive in Chechnya has so far not been treated in the UN, though the OSCE has offered its mediation.

hostilities,[19] but this has not been the reaction in other secession cases, nor was it made clear what would be the source of this obligation to refrain from the use of force. Are intra-State (civil) wars now illegal under international law or should no conflict involving international legal principles (such as the right of self-determination and the respect for the territorial integrity of States) lead to the use of force by non-State actors? If the international community of States does not solve this question unequivocally, wars of secession will be more difficult to outlaw. The matter becomes even more precarious if one considers that it is not impossible to defend the legal use of force by peoples entitled to a *jus cogens* right of self-determination, for the purpose of attaining autonomy, if they can prove that they have been forcibly deprived of that right. Given the *jus cogens* character of their right to autonomy, police enforcement actions by the State aimed at depriving them of this right may justify armed resistance by peoples seeking autonomy.[20] In view of the sliding scale between full autonomy and independence, where then would be the line between a legitimate armed struggle for a high degree of autonomy and an illegal armed struggle for independence?

Gradual secession Rapid secessions may lead to an insufficiently crystallized popular and genuine will for separation, facilitate the success of demagogic political supporters of secession, create economic and minority problems, as well as border conflicts. The

---

[19] By SC Res. 876 (1993) the Security Council demanded that all parties in the Abkhaz conflict 'refrain from the use of force'. The CSCE appealed for an immediate end of hostilities in Bosnia-Herzegovina: Statement adopted at the Helsinki Follow-up Meeting (15 Apr. 1992), CSCE Press Office, Helsinki. In a Presidential Statement, the Security Council condemned the use of force in Bosnia-Herzegovina: UN Press Release SC/5398 (1992). SC Res. 752 (1992) demanded that all parties stop fighting immediately. By EPC Statement the EC condemned 'the use of force, intimidation and provocations perpetrated by national extremists' in Bosnia-Herzegovina: EPC Statement on Bosnia and Hercegovina (16 Apr. 1992), EPC Press Release 51/92. SC Res. 822 (1993) demanded the 'immediate cessation of all hostilities' in Nagorno Karabakh and SC Res. 853 (1993) condemned 'all hostile actions in the [Nagorno Karabakh] region'.

[20] Art. 7 of the Definition of Aggression, GA Res. 3314 (XXIX), states: 'Nothing in this Definition ... could in any way prejudice the right to self-determination ... of peoples forcibly deprived of that right ... nor the right of these peoples to struggle to that end and to seek and receive support, in accordance with the principles of the Charter and in conformity with the above-mentioned Declaration.' Peoples under colonial and racist regimes or other forms of alien domination are mentioned as 'particularly' appertaining to this category of peoples. The right to struggle for self-determination thus belongs especially to peoples who are entitled to a *jus cogens* right of self-determination.

right to gradual secession, as proposed before,[21] can prevent these disadvantages. The dissolution of the Soviet Union and Yugoslavia led to rather rapid international recognitions of the newly established States. Given the fact that the international community has held on to the *uti possidetis juris* principle in these cases,[22] the risk has been created that internal administrative borders, which have not necessarily been stable during a long period of time and which in theory could have been changed only days before the secession, can become internationally protected borders, without this being foreseeable well in advance.[23] The use of the *uti possidetis juris* principle in the colonial context was in a way more moderate, as the decolonization process took a much longer time than the dissolution processes in Eastern Europe and parties knew well beforehand that the old colonial borders would preferably be maintained. In the case of a rapid secession, there is a high risk that former administrative borders will be contested and result in the use of force, especially if, during negotiations, the new State has the right to refuse any border changes now that they are internationally protected.

Fragmentation

It is not likely that the international community will look favourably upon the creation of very small enclaved States which have not constitute separate political entities over the centuries. This can be concluded by analogy with the attitude of States towards small colonial enclaves.[24] However, as no similar case has been put to the test so far, it remains possible that small entities secede. The United Nations considers that if there is no limit to fragmentation, peace, security and economic well-being for all will be more difficult to achieve.[25] There are several factors which put this conclusion in perspective. In the first place fragmentation, by means of secessions or dissolutions, will only engender violence if the weighing process between self-determination and respect for the territorial integrity of a State has not been properly regulated by international law. Such is the present situation. In the second place, whether a fragmented world community

---

[21] See pp. 106–109 above.
[22] See pp. 68–70 and 84 above.
[23] See also p. 108 above.
[24] See pp. 84–88 above.
[25] An Agenda for Peace, UN Doc. A/47/277 (1992) para. 17 and p. 1 above.

will be more prone to the occurrence of wars may depend on a number of factors, including the development of international judicial control, the existence of multilateral security arrangements and economic unions. In the last place, the feared disadvantages of fragmentation depend on a factor of relativity, that is, are all the world's States disintegrated or only some of them and how many? Bearing these factors in mind and the general tendency of stronger States to dominate weaker ones, one may discern the following aspects from the existence of Micro-States.

Very small States have little means to put pressure on other (neighbouring) States in order to have their demands complied with or to protect themselves from external interference in their internal affairs. It is therefore essential for a Micro-State to conclude treaties with its neighbouring State which include arbitration and denunciation clauses, especially if the agreements cover political and economic subjects. This has particularly been demanded by Liechtenstein and has been used in the relations between the European Micro-States and the European Community. In the absence of such clauses, Micro-States will be at the mercy of the stronger State which in practice will be able to impose its policies. Compulsory judicial protection prevents arbitrary interpretations of bilateral treaties and preserves actual independence.[26] International recognition of a Micro-State can remedy any non-fulfilment of criteria for statehood, but cannot change the practical dependence of Micro-States on their neighbouring States.

One cannot maintain in a general way that everyday life in a Micro-State is more prosperous than in a larger State. There is a great variety among Micro-States: some are developing island States needing financial assistance, others are wealthy but have not always known such wealth in the past, like the European Micro-States. The economic survival of a Micro-State may well depend on exceptional circumstances, such as a relatively mild tax system. Contrasts can then offer the financial advantages required. But there is certainly no assurance that Micro-States will be able to survive, economically and politically, in a community comprising only small States if there is no political or economic international organization to secure their long-term existence.

---

[26] See especially pp. 313–314 above.

The human rights situation in Micro-States is in general not unfavourable.[27] The smallness of the territory demands sometimes special privileges for the nationals, which have however lessened in recent years.[28] Whatever the form of government of the Micro-State, the smallness of the population and the territory means that relations between the leaders and the governed are closer than in other countries, though there is in practice the risk that the political system turns into an oligarchy of families.

The main international role which Micro-States can play is that of contributor to ideas for a peaceful international society ruled by international law. In the absence of political and economic means of pressure, this is their only method, which should be used in a neutral way so as to acquire serious attention from other States. The international community and, as a consequence, international organizations have accepted full participation of Micro-States in every domain of international activities to the effect that Micro-States are no longer 'tolerated' subjects of international law. This rather recent development gives Micro-States a unique opportunity to secure a full existence in the community of States and to prove that the principle of universality is not hollow.

Micro-States are accepted as full members of the international community and are eligible for membership of international organizations on the same footing as larger States. In contrast with the League of Nations and the United Nations in the seventies, which were reluctant to admit Micro-States to their organization,[29] at present – that is since the seventies – international organizations, including political international organizations, no longer object to the admission of Micro-States as full members. The ultimate proof of the full acceptance of the principle of universality has been furnished by the United Nations through the admission of four European Micro-States (Liechtenstein, San Marino, Monaco and Andorra) in the nineties.[30] The fact that Micro-States are given the same right to vote

---

[27] But see the exceptional situation of the Vatican City pp. 383–386 above. In Nauru the death penalty can be prescribed by law. The deprivation of a person's life is also permitted 'for the purpose of suppressing a riot, an insurrection or mutiny': Art. 4 (2) (d) of the Nauruan Constitution in A. P. Blaustein and G. H. Flanz, eds., *Constitutions of the Countries of the World* (1986): Nauru.

[28] More access to Andorran nationality, p. 334 above at n. 129, and free movement of workers and services in Liechtenstein as a consequence of the EEA, pp. 188–190 above.

[29] See pp. 133–138 above.

[30] See for Liechtenstein pp. 195–198 above, for San Marino pp. 254–255 above, for Monaco 303–304 above and for Andorra p. 364 above.

as larger States in the United Nations General Assembly and are allowed to participate in international conferences such as the CSCE which bases its decisions on consensus, is to a large extent due to the international behaviour of the Micro-States themselves. In the first place, after the Second World War the European Micro-States acquired greater financial means to develop their international relations and to meet the obligations imposed by the membership of an international organization.[31] In the second place, some Micro-States desirous of confirming their international status made membership of international organizations one of the priorities of their foreign policy. The first Micro-State to be admitted to a given international organization not only created a precedent facilitating the entry of other Micro-States, but also demonstrated that the votes of the Micro-States were not amenable to bribery, that their participation did not obstruct the decision-making process of the organization and that the cooperation of a Micro-State could add to the overall work of the organization.

The potential strength of a Micro-State as a member of an international organization lies in the use of its vote in favour of the development of international law, respect for human rights, the general development of the international community and the correct implementation of internal procedural rules. They can exploit these possibilities more than larger States which might have to consider national interests in more domains. Nevertheless, certain restrictions can be imposed on this 'ideal' use of vote: the restrictions imposed by the neighbouring State (Franco-Monégasque relations)[32] and practical limitations due to limited national expertise and the fact that the small delegations are often compelled to make choices between the different aspects of the work of the organization.

The European Community has shown its willingness to respect the economic divergence of the European Micro-States.[33] The existence of the European Community has strengthened the international legal position of the European Micro-States, because the Community replaces the neighbouring State in customs matters with the possibility of arbitration in case of conflicts and because the European Micro-States have not been absorbed by the European integration.

---

[31] See, for example, the fruitless attempts of San Marino to become a member of FAO, UNESCO, WHO and ILO in the late forties, due to lack of financial means, pp. 236–242 above.

[32] See pp. 275–280 and 307 at point 8 above but not in the UN, pp. 139–140 above.

[33] See for San Marino pp. 246–254 above and for Andorra pp. 359–364 above.

The international legal relations between a Micro-State and its neighbouring State have, in general, grown from the political and economic interest which each party has in the existence of the other. This results in practical, economic and political cooperation. The existence of a Micro-State depends on its economic viability and on its international legal survival. With respect to the first aspect the position of a neighbouring State cannot be ignored. It may be concluded that the level of independence of a Micro-State depends on the will of the larger neighbouring State. Thus, Italy leaves considerable freedom to the Vatican City, Switzerland and Italy – both used to some degree of decentralization in their own country – are rather indulgent towards Liechtenstein and San Marino respectively, Andorra gains a political and legal advantage from the mutual power surveillance and balance of France and Spain, whereas Monaco is faced with France and its traditional centralism.

Micro-States are one of the first entities to benefit from the advancement of international law and particularly from the international control on its implementation. Given the relative weakness of their negotiating position, the existence of dispute settlement mechanisms ameliorates the relations of Micro-States with their neighbouring States. The development of international law contributes strongly to the legal maintenance of Micro-States. The more the protection of international law advances, the less Micro-States will need tacit or explicit 'protector' States and the less fragmentation will lead to breaches of the peace.

Bibliography

The bibliography does not include documents or general documentary books

INTRODUCTION
D. Ehrhardt, *Der Begriff des Mikrostaats im Völkerrecht und in der internationalen Ordnung*, Aalen (1970)

CHAPTER 1. RIGHT OF SELF-DETERMINATION
R. Afonso and F. Gonçalves Pereira, 'The Political Status and Government Institutions of Macao', 16 *Hong Kong Law Journal* (1986) pp. 28-57
J. Allan, 'Hong Kong's Future and the Uncertainty Principle', 21 *Anglo-American Law Review* (1992) pp. 372-385
E. M. Amberg, 'Self-Determination in Hong Kong: A New Challenge to an Old Doctrine', 22 *San Diego Law Review* (1985) pp. 839-858
S. J. Anaya, 'The Capacity of International Law to advance Ethnic or Nationality Rights Claims', 75 *Iowa Law Review* (1990) no. 4, pp. 837-844
B. Bagwell, 'Yugoslavian Constitutional Questions: Self-Determination and Secession of Member Republics', 21 *Georgia Journal of International and Comparative Law* (1991) pp. 489-523
R. L. Barsh, 'The Challenge of Indigenous Self-Determination', 26 UMJLR (1993) pp. 277-312
L. Berat, *Walvis Bay: Decolonization and International Law*, New Haven (1990)
K. N. Blay, 'Self-Determination versus Territorial Integrity in Decolonization Revisited', 25 *Indian Journal of International Law* (1985) pp. 386-410
A. B. Bologna, *Los Derechos de la Republica Argentina sobre las Islas Malvinas, Georgia de Sur (San Pedro) y Sandwich del Sur*, Buenos Aires (1989)
C. Brandt et al., *A Documentary History of Chinese Communism*, Cambridge, Mass. (1952)

J. Broested et al., *Native Power: The Quest for Autonomy and Nationhood of Indigenous Peoples*, Bergen (1985)
I. Brownlie, *Principles of Public International Law*, Oxford, 4th edn (1990)
  'The Rights of Peoples in Modern International Law', in J. Crawford, ed., *The Rights of Peoples*, Oxford (1988) pp. 1–16
  Treaties and Indigenous Peoples, Oxford (1992)
L. C. Buchheit, *Secession: The Legitimacy of Self-Determination*, New Haven (1978)
J. Burger and P. Hunt, 'Indigenous Peoples' Rights', 12 NQHR (1994) pp. 405–423
W. E. Butler, *Basic Documents on the Soviet Legal System*, New York, 2nd edn (1991)
M. Cahen, 'Mozambique 1990: Dernière Année de Guerre civile?', in D. Hermant and D. Bigo, eds., *Approches polémologiques: Conflits et Violence politique dans le Monde au tournant des Années quatre-vingt-dix*, Paris (1991) pp. 122–131.
A. J. Caroll and B. Rajagopal, 'The Case for the Independent Statehood of Somaliland', 8 *American University Journal of International Law and Policy* (1992–93) pp. 653–681
A. Cassese, 'Political Self-Determination – Old Concepts and New Developments', in A. Cassese, ed., *UN Law/Fundamental Rights: Two Topics in International Law*, Alphen aan den Rijn (1979) pp. 137–165
  Self-Determination of Peoples: A Legal Reappraisal, Cambridge (1995)
P. Chapleau, 'Entre le Renouveau et le Chaos: Une Analyse des Situations conflictuelles en Afrique du Sud en 1990', in D. Hermant and D. Bigo, eds., *Approches polémologiques: Conflits et Violence politique dans le Monde au tournant des Années quatre-vingt-dix*, Paris (1991) pp. 109–121
C. Chinkin, 'East Timor moves into the World Court', 4 EJIL (1993) pp. 206–222
  'The Merits of Portugal's Claim against Australia', 15 *University of New South Wales Law Journal* (1992) p. 423
S. R. Chowdhury, 'The Status and Norms of Self-Determination in Contemporary International Law', 24 NILR (1977) pp. 72–84
R. Y. Chuang, 'The Joint Declarations on Hong Kong and Macao and the Draft Basic Law for Hong Kong', 68 RDI (1990) pp. 139–155
R. S. Clark, 'Some International Law Aspects of the East Timor Affair', 5 LJIL (1992) pp. 265–271
  'Timor Gap: The Legality of the "Treaty on the Zone of Cooperation in an Area between the Indonesian Province of East Timor and Northern Australia"', *Pace Yearbook of International Law* (1992) pp. 69–95
A. M. Connelly, 'The Right of Self-Determination and International Boundaries', in D. S. Constantopoulos, ed., *Thesaurus Acroasium*, Thessaloniki, vol. XIV (1985) pp. 545–573
B. Covic, *Croatia between War and Independence*, Zagreb (1991)

J. Crawford, *The Creation of States in International Law*, Oxford (1979)
Democracy in International Law, Cambridge (1994)
'Islands as Sovereign Nations', 38 ICLQ (1989) pp. 277-298
'Outside the Colonial Context', in W. A. J. Macartney, ed., *Self-Determination in the Commonwealth*, Aberdeen (1988), pp. 1-22
P. A. Dagati, 'Hong Kong's Lost Right to Self-Determination: A Denial of Due Process in the United Nations', 13 *New York Law School Journal of International and Comparative Law* (1992) pp. 153-179
J. Diez-Hochleitner, 'Les Relations hispano-britanniques au Sujet de Gibraltar', 35 AFDI (1989) pp. 167-187
Y. Dinstein, 'Collective Human Rights of Peoples and Minorities', 25 ICLQ (1976) pp. 102-120
J. Dugard, 'Secession: Is the Case of Yugoslavia a Precedent for Africa?', 5 *African Journal of International and Comparative Law* (1993) pp. 163-175
'Walvis Bay and International Law: Reflections on a Recent Study', 108 *South African Law Journal* (1991) pp. 82-92
L. S. Eastwood, 'Secession: State Practice and International Law after the Dissolution of the Soviet Union and Yugoslavia', 3 *Duke Journal of Comparative and International Law* (1992-93) pp. 299-349
D. Ehrhardt, *Der Begriff des Mikrostaats im Völkerrecht und in der internationalen Ordnung*, Aalen (1970)
A. Eide, 'In Search of Constructive Alternatives to Secession', in C. Tomuschat, ed., *Modern Law of Self-Determination*, Dordrecht (1993) pp. 139-176
R. Emerson, *From Empire to Nation: The Rise to Self-Assertion of Asian and African Peoples*, Massachusetts (1960)
T. Eriksson, *Åland an Autonomous Province*, Mariehamn (1978)
R. Falk, 'The Rights of Peoples (in particular Indigenous Peoples)', in J. Crawford, ed., *The Rights of Peoples*, Oxford (1988) pp. 17-37
A. Fenet, ed., *Droits de l'Homme, Droits des Peuples*, Paris (1982)
L. Foscaneanu, 'La Déclaration conjointe du Gouvernement de la République populaire de Chine et du Gouvernement de la République du Portugal sur la Question de Macao', 91 RGDIP (1987) pp. 1279-1303
R. W. Gomulkiewicz, 'International Law Governing Aid to Opposition Groups in Civil War: Resurrecting the Standard of Belligerency', 63 *Washington Law Review* (1988) pp. 43-68
R. Goy, 'La Réunification du Yémen', 36 AFDI (1990) pp. 249-265
D. W. Greig, 'Sovereignty and the Falkland Island Crisis', AYIL (1986) pp. 20-70
H. Grotius, *De Jure Bellis Ac Pacis Libri Tres*, Amsterdam, vol. II (1651)
J. F. Guilhaudis, *Le Droit des Peuples à disposer d'eux-mêmes*, Grenoble (1976)
'Le Droit positif à l'Autodétermination', in Institut Européen des Hautes Etudes Internationales, *Le Droit à l'Autodétermination: Actes du*

Colloque international de Saint-Vincent, Nice (1980) pp. 11–39
A. Guillaume-Gentil, 'Le Liberia: Un Pays déchiré par une Année de Guerre civile', in D. Hermant and D. Bigo, eds., *Approches polémologiques: Conflits et Violence politique dans le Monde au tournant des Années quatre-vingt-dix*, Paris (1991) pp. 132-144
L. S. Gustafson, *The Sovereignty Dispute over the Falkland (Malvinas) Islands*, Oxford (1988)
M. van Haegendoren, 'Ethnicity, Language and State', 13 *Plural Societies* (1982) nos. 1-4, pp. 47-56
L. Hannikainen, *Peremptory Norms (Jus Cogens) in International Law*, Helsinki (1988)
H. Hannum, *Autonomy, Sovereignty and Self-Determination: The Accommodation of Conflicting Rights*, Philadelphia (1990)
G. Héraud, 'Les Communautés linguistiques en quête d'un Statut', 13 *Plural Societies* (1982) nos. 1-4, pp. 91-120
 'Modèle pour une Application générale du Droit d'Autodétermination', in Institut Européen des Hautes Etudes Internationales, *Le Droit à l'Autodétermination: Actes du Colloque international de Saint-Vincent*, Nice (1980) pp. 41-63
B. R. Howard, 'Human Rights and Indigenous People: On the Relevance of International Law for Indigenous Liberation', 35 GYIL (1992) pp. 105-156
C. J. Iorns, 'Indigenous Peoples and Self-Determination: Challenging State Sovereignty', 24 *Case Western Reserve Journal of International Law* (1992) pp. 199-348
R. Jennings and A. Watts, eds., *Oppenheim's International Law*, London, 9th edn (1992)
H. Kelsen, *The Law of the United Nations: A Critical Analysis of its Fundamental Problems*, London (1950)
O. Kimminich, 'A "Federal" Right of Self-Determination?', in C. Tomuschat, ed., *Modern Law of Self-Determination*, Dordrecht (1993) pp. 83-100
J. Klabbers and R. Lefeber, 'Africa: Lost between Self-Determination and *Uti Possidetis*', in C. Brölmann et al., eds., *Peoples and Minorities in International Law*, Dordrecht (1993) pp. 37-76
K. Klüpfel, *Selbstbestimmung durch Assoziation*, Frankfurt am Main (1987)
P. H. Kooijmans, 'In the Shadowland between Civil War and Civil Strife', in A. Delissen and G. Tanja, eds., *Humanitarian Law of Armed Conflict: Challenges Ahead*, Dordrecht (1991) pp. 225-247
F. E. Kranz, *International Enclaves and Rights of Passage*, Geneva (1961)
H. S. Levie, *The Status of Gibraltar*, Boulder, Colo. (1983)
M. C. Maffei, 'The Case of East Timor before the International Court of Justice', 4 EJIL (1993) pp. 223-238
G. Marchildon and E. Maxwell, 'Quebec's Right of Secession under Canadian and International Law', 32 *Virginia Journal of International Law* (1992) pp. 583-623
M. Maung, *Burma's Constitution*, The Hague (1961)

R. McCorquodale, 'Self-Determination: A Human Rights Approach', 43 ICLQ (1994) pp. 857–885

R. W. McGee and D. King-Kong Lam, 'Hong Kong's Option to Secede', 33 Harv. Int'l LJ (1992) pp. 427–440

D. McGoldrick, 'Canadian Indians, Cultural Rights and the Human Rights Committee', 40 ICLQ (1991) pp. 658–669

The Human Rights Committee: Its Role in the Development of the ICCPR, Oxford (1991)

L. A. McKibben, 'The Political Relationship between the United States and the Pacific Islands Entities: The Path to Self-Government in the Northern Mariana Islands, Palau and Guam', 31 Harv. Int'l LJ. (1990) pp. 257–293

D. Miller, *The Drafting of the Covenant*, New York, vol. II (1928)

D. S. Morris and R. H. Haigh, *Britain, Spain and Gibraltar 1945–90: The Eternal Triangle*, London (1992)

G. T. Morris, 'In Support of the Right of Self-Determination for Indigenous Peoples under International Law', 29 GYIL (1986) pp. 277–316

D. Murswiek, 'The Issue of a Right of Secession – Reconsidered', in C. Tomuschat, ed., *Modern Law of Self-Determination*, Dordrecht (1993) pp. 21–40

V. P. Nanda, 'Self-Determination under International Law: Validity of Claims to Secede', 13 *Case Western Reserve Journal of International Law* (1981) no. 1, pp. 257–280

G. Nettheim, 'Peoples and Populations: Indigenous Peoples and the Rights of Peoples', in J. Crawford, ed., *The Rights of Peoples*, Oxford (1988) pp. 107–126

A. N'Kolombua, 'L'Ambivalence des Relations entre le Droit des Peuples à disposer d'eux-mêmes et de l'Intégrité territoriale des Etats en Droit international contemporain', in M. Lachs et al., *Mélanges offerts à Charles Chaumont: Le Droit des Peuples à disposer d'eux-mêmes*, Paris (1984) pp. 433–463

M. Nowak, 'The Right of Self-Determination and Protection of Minorities in Central and Eastern Europe in the Light of the Case Law of the Human Rights Committee', 1 Int'l JGR (1993) pp. 6–16

J. A. de Obieta Chalbaud, *El Derecho Humano de la Autodeterminación de los Pueblos*, Madrid (1985)

A. Oraison, 'Quelques Réflections critiques sur la Conception française du Droit des Peuples à disposer d'eux-mêmes à la Lumière du Différend franco-comorien sur l'Ile de Mayotte', 17 RBDI (1983) pp. 655–698

J. T. Paxman, 'Minority Indigenous Populations and their Claims for Self-Determination', 21 *Case Western Reserve Journal of International Law* (1989) pp. 185–202

S. Pierré-Caps, *Nation et Peuples dans les Constitutions modernes*, Nancy, vol. II (1987)

M. Pomerance, *Self-Determination in Law and Practice: The New Doctrine in*

the United Nations, The Hague (1982)
G. Prunier, 'Les Conflits de la Corne de l'Afrique 1989-1990', in D. Hermant and D. Bigot, eds., *Approches polémologiques: Conflits et Violence politique dans le Monde au tournant des Années quatre-vingt-dix*, Paris (1991) pp. 99-108
P. Raton, 'Les Enclaves', 4 AFDI (1958) pp. 186-195
E. Renan, *Qu'est-ce qu'une Nation?*, Amsterdam (1882)
L. Rohr, 'El Principio de la Auto-Determinación de los Pueblos en el Derecho Internacional', 1 *Annuario de Derecho Internacional Publico* (1981) pp. 60-71
V. Rudrakumaran, 'The Legitimacy of Lithuania's Claim for Secession', 10 *Boston University International Law Journal* (1992) pp. 33-60
M. Sarin, *The Case of Goa (1961) and the Controversy regarding Gandhian Non-Violent Resistance (Satyagraha) and International Law Involved in it*, Inaugural Dissertation, Marburg/Lahn (1973)
H. O. Schoenberg, 'Limits of Self-Determination', 6 *Israel Yearbook on Human Rights* (1976) pp. 91-103
A. M. Scholz, *Die Behandlung der Goa-Frage durch die Vereinten Nationen*, Inaugural Dissertation, Würzburg (1970)
Secretariat of the International Commission of Jurists, *The Events in East Pakistan*, Geneva (1972)
M. N. Shaw, 'The Definition of Minorities in International Law', 20 Israel Yrb. HR (1990) pp. 13-43
Title to Territory in Africa: International Legal Issues, Oxford (1986)
R. Sisson and L. E. Rose, *War and Secession: Pakistan, India and the Creation of Bangladesh*, Berkeley (1990)
C. Spencer, *The Former Yugoslavia: Background to Crisis*, Toronto (1993)
A. Sprudzs, ed., *The Baltic Path to Independence: An International Reader of Selected Articles*, New York (1994)
H. J. Steiner, 'Political Participation as a Human Right', 1 HRY (1988) pp. 77-134
E. Suzuki, 'Self-Determination and World Public Order: Community Response to Territorial Separation', 16 *Virginia Journal of International Law* (1976) no. 4, pp. 779-862
B. Szajkowski, *Encyclopaedia of Conflicts, Disputes and Flashpoints in Eastern Europe*, London (1993)
D. Thürer, *Das Selbstbestimmungsrecht der Völker*, Berne (1976)
C. Tomuschat, 'Self-Determination in a Post-Colonial World', in C. Tomuschat, ed., *Modern Law of Self-Determination*, Dordrecht (1993) pp. 1-20
M. E. Turpel, 'Indigenous Peoples' Rights of Political Participation and Self-Determination: Recent International Legal Developments and the Continuing Struggle for Recognition', 25 *Cornell International Law Journal* (1992) pp. 579-602
J. Verhoeven, 'Peuples et Droit international', in F. Rigaux, ed., *Le Concept de*

Peuple, Brussels (1988) pp. 39–64
J. H. W. Verzijl, *International Law in Historical Perspective*, Leiden, vol. I (1968)
M. Weller, 'The International Response to the Dissolution of the Socialist Federal Republic of Yugoslavia', 86 AJIL (1992) pp. 569–607
P. Wesley-Smith, *Unequal Treaty, 1898–1997: China, Great Britain and Hong Kong's New Territories*, Oxford (1983)
R. C. White, 'Self-Determination: Time for a Re-assessment?', 28 NILR (1981) pp. 147–170
H. Wright, 'The Goa Incident', 56 AJIL (1962) pp. 616–621

CHAPTER 2. CRITERIA FOR STATEHOOD

M. Akehurst, *A Modern Introduction to International Law*, London, 6th edn (1987)
G. Arangio-Ruiz, *L'Etat dans le Sens du Droit des Gens et la Notion du Droit international*, Bologna (1975)
T. Baty, 'Can an Anarchy be a State?', 28 AJIL (1934) pp. 444–455
I. Brownlie, *Principles of Public International Law*, Oxford, 4th edn (1990)
L. Cavaré, *Le Droit international public positif*, Paris, vol. I (1967)
J. Crawford, *The Creation of States in International Law*, Oxford (1979)
   'The Criteria for Statehood in International Law', 48 BYIL (1976–1977) pp. 93–182
   'Islands as Sovereign Nations', 38 ICLQ (1989) pp. 277–298
T. Darsow, *Zum Wandel des Staatsbegriffs: Unter besonderer Burücksichtigung der Lehre und Praxis internationaler Organisationen, der Mikrostaaten und der PLO*, Frankfurt am Main (1984)
D. J. Devine, 'Recognition, Newly Independent States and General International Law', 10 *South African Yearbook of International Law* (1984) pp. 18–34
   'The Requirements of Statehood Re-examined', 34 *Modern Law Review* (1971) pp. 410–417
J. Dugard, *Recognition and the United Nations*, Cambridge (1987)
J. E. S. Fawcett, *The Law of Nations*, London, 2nd edn (1971)
P. Guggenheim, *Lehrbuch des Völkerrechts*, Basle, vol. I (1948)
L. Hannikainen, *Peremptory Norms (Jus Cogens) in International Law*, Helsinki (1988)
F. H. Hinsley, *Sovereignty*, Cambridge, 2nd edn (1986)
A. James, *Sovereign Statehood: The Basis of International Society*, London (1986)
G. Jellinek, *Allgemeine Staatslehre*, Berlin (1914)
A. Kamanda, *A Study of the Legal Status of Protectorates in Public International Law*, Dissertation, Ambilly-Annmasse (1961)
H. Lauterpacht, *Recognition in International Law*, Cambridge (1947)
M. H. Mendelson, 'Diminutive States in the United Nations', 21 ICLQ (1972) pp. 609–630

P. K. Menon, 'Some Aspects of the Law of Recognition; Part I: Theories of
 Recognition', RDI (1989) pp. 161-182
 'Some Aspects of the Law of Recognition; Part II: Recognition of States',
 RDI (1990) pp. 9-16
C. N. Okeke, *Controversial Subjects of Contemporary International Law*,
 Rotterdam (1974)
L. Oppenheim, *International Law: A Treatise*, London, 8th edn
 (H. Lauterpacht, ed.) vol. I (1955)
S. von Pufendorf, *De Iure Naturae et Gentium Libri Octo* (1672), English
 translation C. H. and W. A. Oldfather, Oxford (1934)
E. Rouard de Card, *Les Traités de Protectorat conclus par la France en
 Afrique 1870-1895*, Paris (1897)
C. Rousseau, *Droit International Public*, Paris, vol. III (1977)
 'L'Indépendance de l'Etat dans l'Ordre international', 2 Hague Recueil
 (1948) pp. 171-253
J. D. van der Vyver, 'Statehood in International Law', 5 *Emory International
 Law Review* (1991) pp. 9-102
M. Weller, 'The International Response to the Dissolution of the Socialist
 Federal Republic of Yugoslavia', 86 AJIL (1992) pp. 569-607
M. J. Whiteman, *Digest of International Law*, Washington, vol. I (1963)

CHAPTER 3. THE GENERAL QUESTION OF MICRO-STATES IN
INTERNATIONAL ORGANIZATIONS

R. Adam, 'Micro-States and the United Nations', 2 *Italian Yearbook of
 International Law* (1976) pp. 80-101
R. P. Anand, 'Sovereign Equality of States in International Law', 2 Hague
 Recueil (1986) pp. 9-228
P. W. Blair, *The Ministate Dilemma*, Washington (1967)
B. Conforti, 'L'Arrêt de la Cour Internationale de Justice dans l'Affaire de
 certaines Terres de Phosphates à Nauru (Exceptions préliminaires)', 38
 AFDI (1992) pp. 460-467
J. Crawford, 'Islands as Sovereign Nations', 38 ICLQ (1989) pp. 277-298
D. Ehrhardt, 'Mikrostaaten als UN-Mitglieder? Zum Strukturproblem der
 Weltorganisation', *Vereinte Nationen* (1970) no. 4, pp. 111-116
R. Fisher et al., 'The Participation of Microstates in International Affairs',
 PASIL (1968) pp. 164-188
E. M. Fitzgerald, 'Nauru v. Australia: A Sacred Trust Betrayed?', 6 *Connecticut
 Journal of International Law* (1990) pp. 209-249
R. Goy, 'Le dernier Territoire sous Tutelle: Les Iles du Pacifique', 34 AFDI
 (1988) pp. 454-474
M. M. Gunter, 'The Problem of Ministate Membership in the United Nations
 System: Recent Attempts towards a Solution', 12 *Columbia Journal of
 Transnational Law* (1973) pp. 464-486
 'What happened to the United Nations Ministate Problem?', 71 AJIL (1977)
 pp. 110-124

W. L. Harris, 'Microstates in the United Nations: A Broader Purpose', 9 *Columbia Journal of Transnational Law* (1970) pp. 23-53

J. Hinck, 'The Republic of Palau and the United States: Self-Determination becomes the Price of Free Association', 78 *California Law Review* (1990) pp. 915-971

B. Macdonald, *In Pursuit of the Sacred Trust: Trusteeship and Independence in Nauru*, Wellington (1988)

P. W. Manhard, *The US and Micronesia in Free Association: A Chance to do Better?*, Washington (1979)

L. A. McKibben, 'The Political Relationship between the United States and the Pacific Islands Entities: The Path to Self-Government in the Northern Mariana Islands, Palau and Guam', 31 Harv. Int'l LJ (1990) pp. 257-293

M. H. Mendelson, 'Diminutive States in the United Nations', 21 ICLQ (1972) pp. 609-630

J. G. Rapoport et al., 'The Participation of Ministates in International Affairs', PASIL (1968) pp. 155-188

Small States and Territories: Status and Problems, UNITAR study, New York (1971)

Y.-L. Sage, 'Le Système juridique de l'île de Nauru', 46 *Revue Juridique et Politique Indépendance et Coopération* (1992) pp. 458-466

B. Saint-Girons, 'L'Organisation des Nations Unies et les Micro-Etats', 76 RGDIP (1972) pp. 446-474

S. M. Schwebel, 'Mini-States and a more Effective United Nations', 67 AJIL (1973) pp. 108-116

I. Scobbie, 'Case concerning Certain Phosphate Lands in Nauru (Nauru v. Australia), Preliminary Objections Judgment', 42 ICLQ (1993) pp. 710-719

R. I. Starr et al., 'The Future Relationship between Small States and the United Nations', 3 Int'l L (1969) pp. 58-74

Y. van de Steen, 'De Verenigde Naties en de Microstaten: Problemen omtrent de Toetreding van Microstaten tot de Verenigde Naties', 7 RBDI (1971) pp. 578-618

D. W. Wainhouse, *Remnants of Empire: The United Nations and the End of Colonialism*, New York (1964)

C. Weeramantry, *Nauru: Environmental Damage under International Trusteeship*, Oxford (1992)

U. Whitaker, 'Proliferation in the UN: Mini-Membership for Mini-States', 7 *War/Peace Report* (1967) pp. 3-5

INTRODUCTION TO PART II

C. Amelunxen, *Die kleinstaaten Europas*, Hamburg (1964)

A. Astraudo, *Les petits Etats d'Europe*, Nice, 3rd edn (1938)

P. W. Blair, *The Ministate Dilemma*, Washington (1967)

J. de Clerq, *Les petites Souverainetés d'Europe*, Louvain (1936)

G. Gschnitzer, 'Lebensrecht und Rechtsleben des Kleinstaates', in A. P. Goop, *Gedächtnisschrift Ludwig Marker*, Zurich (1963) pp. 19-52

R. O. Keohane, 'Lilliputians' Dilemmas: Small States in International Politics', 23 *International Organization* (1969) pp. 291-310

H. C. Luke, 'Freaks of Freedom', 131 *Fortnightly Review* (1932) pp. 600-621

E. Plischke, *Microstates in World Affairs: Policy Problems and Options*, Washington (1977)

G. L. Reid, *The Impact of Very Small Size on the International Behavior of Microstates*, Beverly Hills (1974)

CHAPTER 4. THE PRINCIPALITY OF LIECHTENSTEIN

T. Allgäuer, *Die parlamentarische Kontrolle über die Regierung im Fürstentum Liechtenstein*, Dissertation no. 1097, Vaduz (1989)

C. Amelunxen, 'Schwierige Vaterländer – Aspekte der liechtensteinisch-deutschen Beziehungen in Vergangenheit und Gegenwart', 2 *Liechtenstein Politische Schriften* (1973) pp. 57-74

Anon.,'Can Liechtenstein's Lawyers survive the EEA?', 11 Int'l Fin. Law Review (1992) pp. 21-24

'Der internationale Erfolg der Liechtensteinischen Wirtschaft ist kein Zufall', *VN Magazin Extra* (1986)

'Die Organisation der Strafgerichte und der Strafvollzug im Fürstentum Liechtenstein', 4 *Der Strafvollzug in der Schweiz* (1980) no. 112, pp. 204-206

Die Aussenpolitik des Fürstentums Liechtenstein: Standort und Zielsetzungen, Schriftenreihe der Regierung, Vaduz (1988) no. 1

A. Batliner and R. J. Proksch, 'Changes on the Way for Liechtenstein Banks?', 10 Int'l Fin. Law Review (1991) pp. 28-29

M. Beck et al., *Die Vereinten Nationen – Ein Thema für Liechtenstein*, St Gallen (1988)

T. Bruha, 'Liechtenstein and an All-European System of Human Rights Protection', 1 All-Eur. HR Yearb. (1991) pp. 55-61

C. Chinkin, *Third Parties in International Law*, Oxford (1993)

Council of Europe, *The Protection of Human Rights in Europe*, Strasbourg (1981)

H. Frennered, 'The Protocols adjusting the EEA Agreement and the EFTA Agreements', *EFTA Bulletin* (1993) no. 2, pp. 9-11

P. Guggenheim, 'Völkerrecht', 7 ASDI (1950) pp. 176-184

M. M. Gunter, 'Liechtenstein and the League of Nations: A Precedent for the United Nations' Ministate Problem?', 28 AJIL (1974) pp. 496-501

W. B. Gyger, *Das Fürstentum Liechtenstein und die Europäische Gemeinschaft*, Vaduz (1975)

N. Jansen, 'Liechtenstein und die Vereinte Nationen', 18 *Liechtenstein Wirtschaftsfragen* (1991)

P. Kaiser, *Geschichte des Fürstentums Liechtenstein*, 1847 edn, Ruggell (1983)

F. Kneschaurek, 'Entwicklungsperspektiven der liechtensteinischen Volkswirtschaft in den neunziger Jahren', 17 *Liechtenstein Wirtschaftsfragen* (1990)

K. Kohlegger, 'Als österreichischer Richter in Liechtenstein', in *Herbert Battliner Festgabe zum 60. Geburtstag*, Vaduz (1988) pp. 281-290

W. Kranz, ed., *The Principality of Liechtenstein: A Documentary Handbook*, Vaduz, 5th edn (1981)

V. Lanfranconi, *Die Staatsverträge und Verwaltungsabkommen zwischen der Schweiz und dem Fürstentum Liechtenstein unter besonderer Berücksichtigung der daraus entstandenen völkerrechtlichen Konsequenzen*, Dissertation, Basle (1969)

M. von Ledebur, 'Licht und Schatten über der KSZE', 10 *Liechtenstein Politische Schriften* (1984) pp. 133-193

E. von und zu Liechtenstein, *Liechtensteins Weg von Oesterrreich zur Schweiz: eine Rückschau auf meine Arbeit in der Nachkriegszeit 1918-1921*, Vaduz (1945)

N. von Liechtenstein, 'Liechtensteins Mitgliedschaft im Europarat', 10 *Liechtenstein Politische Schriften* (1984) pp. 195-225

Liechtensteinische Fremdenpolizei und Passamt, *Wohnen und Arbeiten im Fürstentum Liechtenstein / Living and Working in the Principality of Liechtenstein*, Vaduz (1984)

B. M. Malunat, 'Die Verträge zwischen dem Fürstentum Liechtenstein und der Schweizerischen Eidgenossenschaft, politische Implikationen und völkerrechtliche Beurteilung', 36 *Oesterreichische Zeitschrift für Oeffentliches Recht und Völkerrecht* (1986) pp. 329-363

P. Marxer et al., *Companies and Taxes in Liechtenstein*, Vaduz, 4th edn (1988)

D. J. Niedermann, *Liechtenstein und die Schweiz; Eine völkerrechtliche Untersuchung*, Vaduz (1976)

A. Oehry, 'Fürst und Volk bei der Bestellung der liechtensteinischen ordentlichen Gerichte', 7 *Liechtensteinische Juristen Zeitung* (1986) pp. 145-146

P. Raton, *Liechtenstein: History and Institutions of the Principality*, Vaduz (1970)

Staat und Geschichte, Vaduz (1969)

P. Reuter, *Introduction to the Law of Treaties*, London (1989)

A. Rougier, 'La première Assemblée de la Société des Nations (Genève, novembre-décembre 1920)', 28 RGDIP (1921) pp. 230-231

G. Scelle, 'L'Admission des nouveaux Membres de la Société des Nations par l'Assemblée de Genève', 28 RGDIP (1921) pp. 136-137

H. G. Schermers and D. Waelbroek, *Judicial Protection in the European Communities*, Deventer (1987)

O. Seger, *Überblick über die Liechtensteinische Geschichte*, Vaduz (1974)

H. Thévenaz, 'La Suisse, Etat mandataire', 6 ASDI (1949) pp. 15-16

CHAPTER 5. THE REPUBLIC OF SAN MARINO

R. Ago, 'La Neutralità di S. Marino', *Libera Orizzonte* (31 Jul. 1963) no. 7, pp. 3-12

T. Ballarino, 'L'Evoluzione della Personalità Internazionale di San Marino', *Studi Sammarinese* (1987) pp. 7-63

F. Bindi, 'Gli Anni del Fascismo', *Storia e Ordinamento della Repubblica di San Marino* (Febr.-Apr. 1982) pp. 149-152

M. A. Bonelli, *I Rapporti Convenzionali Italo-Sammarinesi: Con Notizie sulle Relazione Internazionali della Reppublica di San Marino (1862-1942)*, San Marino (1985)
    'La Politica Estera e i Rapporti con gli altri Stati Europei', in E. R. Iwanejko, ed., *La Tradizione Politica di San Marino: Dalle Origini dell'Indipendenza al Pensiero Politico di Pietro Franciosi*, San Marino (1988) pp. 327-341

R. Bonelli, *Gli Organi dei Poteri Pubblici nell'Ordinamento della Repubblica di San Marino*, San Marino (1984)

C. Buscarini, 'Dal Comune allo Stato: Note sulla Formazione della Soggettività Internazionale di San Marino', *Storia e Ordinamento della Repubblica di San Marino* (Febr.-Apr. 1982) pp. 63-77
    'Gli Organi della Giurisdizione nell'Ordinamento di San Marino', 3 *IGS Miscellanea* (Jul. 1992) pp. 79-107

Commissione per lo Studio dei Problemi Istituzionali dell'Ordinamento Sammarinese, *Relazione*, Rome (1972)

P. Giorgeri, *Conflittualità nelle Relazioni Italo - Sammarinesi*, Tesi di Laurea, Urbino (1987-88)

P. Guggenheim, *Lehrbuch des Völkerrechts*, Basle, vol. I (1948)

R. Higgins, *The Development of International Law through the Political Organs of the United Nations*, Oxford (1963)

J. M. Le Besnerais, *Le Statut international de la République de Saint-Marin*, Thèse de Doctorat, Paris (no date mentioned, about 1968)

T. Masi, 'L'Analisi e il Commento del Testo', *Forum* (1991) no. 1, pp. 19-39

H. Maza, *Neuf Meneurs internationaux: De l'Initiative individuelle dans l'Institution des Organisations internationales*, Paris (1965)

G. Ramoino and M. Bonelli, *Supplemento alla Raccolta delle Leggi e Decreti della Repubblica di San Marino*, Castello, 1st edn (1915)

G. Rossi, 'I Rapporti della Repubblica di San Marino con lo Stato Italiano', in E. R. Iwanejko, ed., *La Tradizione Politica di San Marino: Dalle Origini dell'Indipendenza al Pensiero Politico di Pietro Franciosi*, San Marino (1988) pp. 313-325

A. Sottile, 'L'Ordinamento Politico e Giuridico della Repubblica di San Marino e la sua Situazione Internazionale', 51 RDI (1973) pp. 319-346

E. Spagna Musso and R. Lipparini, 'L'Ordinamento Costituzionale di San Marino', *Archivio Giuridico 'Filippo Serafini'*, vol. CCVI (1986) pp. 5-78

G. Vedovato, *Le Relazioni Italia-San Marino*, Florence, 2nd ser. X (1960)

CHAPTER 6. THE PRINCIPALITY OF MONACO

L. Auréglia, 'Monaco et le Traité de Paix', *Journal de Genève* (4 Oct. 1919)
J. Crawford, *The Creation of States in International Law*, Oxford (1979)
O. Deleau, 'Les Positions françaises à la Conférence de Vienne sur le Droit des Traités', AFDI (1969) pp. 16-30
Department of Finance and Economy, *The Best of Monte-Carlo: Monaco's Economy and its Leading Companies*, Monaco (1992)
P. Erlanger, *Fascinant Monte Carlo*, Monaco, 3rd edn (1986)
L. V. Ferraris, ed., *Report on a Negotiation – Collection de Relations internationales*, Dordrecht (1979)
J.-P. Gallois, *Le Régime international de la Principauté de Monaco*, Paris (1964)
G. Grinda, *Les Institutions de la Principauté de Monaco*, Monaco (1975)
P. Guggenheim, *Lehrbuch des Völkerrechts*, Basle, vol. I (1948)
L. Hannikainen, *Peremptory Norms (Jus Cogens) in International Law*, Helsinki (1988)
L.-H. Labande, *Histoire de la Principauté de Monaco*, Monaco, 2nd edn (1934)
J. Laroche, 'Comment fut négocié le traité franco-monégasque du 17 juillet 1918', *Revue d'Histoire Diplomatique* (Oct.-Dec. 1955) pp. 289-292
D. McGoldrick, *The Human Rights Committee: Its Role in the Development of the ICCPR*, Oxford (1991)
M. Moncharville, 'Le nouveau Statut franco-monégasque', RGDIP (1920) pp. 229-235
J. Pillon and J.-F. Vilotte, 'Les Institutions politiques de la Principauté de Monaco', 98 RDP (1982) pp. 355-375
M. Ris, 'Treaty Interpretation and ICJ Recourse to Travaux préparatoires: Towards a Proposed Amendment to Articles 31 and 32 of the Vienna Convention on the Law of Treaties', *Boston College International and Comparative Law Review* (1991) pp. 111-136
E. S. Yambruzic, *Treaty Interpretation*, Lanham (1987)

CHAPTER 7. THE PRINCIPALITY OF ANDORRA

Anon.,'La Principauté d'Andorre et son Statut international', 10 *Chronique de Politique Etrangère* (May 1957) pp. 385-391
  Vallée d'Andorre: Catalogue national spécialisé, Paris (1978)
E. Aranzadi, *Repertorio Cronológico de Legislación*, Madrid (1978)
A. Aristot i Gomà, ed., *Andorra el meu País*, Andorra (1963)
L. Armengol, 'La Pena de Mort a Andorra, segons el "Manual Digest"', *Quaderns d'Estudis Andorrans* (1977) no. 2, pp. 49-63
L. Armengol Vila, *Approche à l'Histoire de l'Andorre*, Andorra (1983)
  Aprocimació a la Història d'Andorra, Andorra (1989)
J. Aznar Sánchez, 'Los Intereses de España en la cuestión de Andorra', *Revista de Política Internacional* (Nov.-Dec. 1974) no. 136, pp. 59-80
C. Barate and G. Riera, 'Le Dépassement des Contradictions en Andorre: Un Scénario de l'Impossible?', 96 RDP (1980) pp. 367-407

J. Bartumeu i Cassany et al., *L'Estat Andorrà: Recull de Textos Legislatius i Constitucionals d'Andorra*, Andorra (1977)
B. Bélinguier, *La Condition juridique des Vallées d'Andorre*, Paris (1970)
J. A. Brutails, *La Coutume d'Andorre*, Andorra, 2nd edn (1965)
H. E. Cardinale, *The Holy See and the International Order*, Gerrards Cross (1976)
O. Casanovas i La Rosa, *Andorra devant el Dret Internacional*, Andorra (1972)
A. Cocatre-Zilgien, 'Constitution de 1958, Droit international, Relations extérieures et Politique étrangère', 4 AFDI (1958) pp. 645–659
J. Crawford, 'The International Legal Status of the Valleys of Andorra', 55 RDI (1977) pp. 258–272
M. Duverger, *La Reforma de les Institucions d'Andorra*, Andorra la Vella (1981)
General Council, *Notes on the Juridical Situation of the Principality of Andorra*, Andorra (1989)
F. Luchaire and G. Conac, eds., *La Constitution de la République française: Analyses et Commentaires*, Paris, 2nd edn (1987)
N. Marquès i Oste, *La Reforma de les Institucions d'Andorra (1975–1981): Aspectes Interns i Internacionals*, Lleida (1989)
G. Martínez Díez, ed., *Recull Estadístic General de la Població d'Andorra 1989, 1ers Resultats*, Andorra (1989)
D. Mas, *Les Valls d'Andorra i el Maquis Antifranquista*, Andorra (1985)
P. K. Menon, 'Some Aspects of the Law of Recognition. Part V: Modes of Recognition', RDI (1991) no. 1, pp. 17–49
A. Morell, 'Una Revolució Andorrana: 1933', 2 *Quaderns d'Estudis Andorrans* (1977) pp. 65–76
M. J. Pelaez and J. Guillamet i Anton, 'La Situación Politica de los Valles de Andorra en Abril de 1936: El Informe de Joaquim Saltor i Madorell', *Cuadernos Informativos de Derecho Historico Publico, Procesal y de la Navegación* (Jun. 1990) nos. 12–13, pp. 2848–2883
A. Pes, 'El Sistema Financiero de Andorra', in A. Sabater Tomas, ed., *La Notaria: Estudios Monograficos Decicados al Derecho Civil del Principado de Andorra (1982–1983)*, Barcelona (1986) pp. 497–509
W. Pieshold, *Principat d'Andorra: Das Land des ewigen Friedens*, Andorra (1964)
V. Pou, *Negociacions Andorra – Mercat Comú Europeu: Anàlisi i Documentació sobre les Relacions entre Andorra i la CEE*, Andorra (1986)
P. Raton, *Le Statut international de la Principauté d'Andorre*, Andorra, 2nd edn (1990)
G. Riera, 'L'Andorre', 72 RGDIP (1968)
J. Riera i Simó, *El Pariatge d'Andorra*, Andorra (1978)
J. Roca, *De la Condition internationale des Vallées d'Andorre*, Thèse de Doctorat, Antibes (1908)
C. Rousseau, 'Les Vallées d'Andorre: Une Survivance féodale dans le Monde

contemporain', *Symbolae Verzijl* (1958) pp. 337-346
A. Sabater Tomas, ed., *La Notaria: Estudios Monograficos Dedicados al Derecho Civil del Principado de Andorra (1982-1983)*, Barcelona (1986)
La Notaria: Estudios Recopilados de Legislación y Jurisprudencia Correspondiente al Derecho Civil del Principado de Andorra (1982-1983), Barcelona (1986)
A. Sabater i Tomas, *Legislació Civil: Legislació i Jurisprudència del Principat d'Andorra*, Andorra la Vella (1981)
F. Taillefer, *L'Ariège et l'Andorre*, Toulouse (1985)
R. Toureng, *Statut juridique des Vallées d'Andorre*, Thèse de Doctorat, Toulouse (1939)
P. Vellas, 'Les Etats exigus en Droit international public', 58 RGDIP (1954) pp. 559-581
J. M. Vidal i Guitart, *Història d'Andorra*, Barcelona (1984)
Institucions Polítiques i Sociales d'Andorra, Andorra (1984) no. 4
R. Viñas Farré, 'El "Treaty Making Power" y la Representación Internacional del Principado de Andorra', *Revista Jurídica de Cataluña* (Apr.-Jun. 1976) no. 2, pp. 319-342
R. Viñas i Farré, *Nacionalitat i Drets Polítics al Principat d'Andorra*, Avui (1989)
K. Zemanek, *Le Statut international de l'Andorre: Situation actuelle et Perspectives de Réforme*, Vienna (1980)

CHAPTER 8. THE STATE OF THE VATICAN CITY

M. Angelo-Comnemo, *Ragioni, Significato e Origini dei Patti Lateranensi e il Problema del Divorzio in Italia*, Rome (1970)
G. Arangio-Ruiz, 'La Città del Vaticano', 11 *Revista di Diritto Pubblico e Giustizia Amministrativa* (1929) pp. 1-19
S. Benadava, 'La Mediación de la Santa Sede en el Diferendo Chileno-Argentino sobre la Zona Austral', in Y. Dinstein, ed., *International Law at a Time of Perplexity: Essays in Honour of Shabtai Rosenne*, Dordrecht (1989) pp. 33-50
Bibliothèque Apostolique Vaticane, *Le Saint-Siège et la France: Douze Siècles d'Histoire*, Vatican City (1987)
C. A. Biggini, *Storia Inedita della Conciliazione*, Milan (1942)
D. A. Binchy, *Church and State in Fascist Italy*, London (1941)
Y. de la Brière, 'La Souveraineté du Saint-Siège et le Droit des Gens', 20 RDI (1937) pp. 29-48
F. Cammeo, *Ordinamento Giuridico dello Stato della Città del Vaticano*, Florence (1932)
H. E. Cardinale, *The Holy See and the International Order*, Gerrards Cross (1976)
I. Cardinale, *Le Saint-Siège et la Diplomatie*, Paris (1962)
A. Carrascosa Coso, *La Santa Sede y la Conferencia sobre la Seguridad y la Cooperación en Europa*, Vatican City, 2nd edn (1991)

A. Casaroli, *Der Heilige Stuhl und die Völkergemeinschaft: Reden und Aufsätze*, Berlin (1981)
Catholic Truth Society, *How the "Roman Question" was settled: Explained by the Pope Himself*, London (1929)
P. Ciprotti and A. Talamanca, *La Revisione del Concordato nelle Discussioni Parlamentari I*, Milan (1975)
R. Coppola, ed., *Atti del Convegno Nazionale di Studio su il Nuovo Accordo tra Italia e Santa Sede*, Milan (1987)
J. Crawford, *The Creation of States in International Law*, Oxford (1979)
G. Dalla Torre, *Revisione del Concordato: Trattati, Concordati, Accordi ecc.*, Vatican City (1985)
J. Eppstein, *The Catholic Tradition of the Law of Nations*, London (1935)
S. Ferlito, *L'Attività Internazionale della Santa Sede*, Milan (1988)
J.-H. Fragonard, *La Condition des Personnes dans la Cité du Vatican*, Paris (1930)
L. le Fur, *Le Saint-Siège et le Droit des Gens*, Paris (1930)
E. Gallina, *Le Organizzazioni Internazionali e la Chiesa Cattolica*, Rome (1967)
L. Hannikainen, *Peremptory Norms (Jus Cogens) in International Law*, Helsinki (1988)
H. F. Köck, 'Aktuelle Probleme der Völkerrechtlichen Präsenz des Heiligen Stuhls', *Profide et Iustitia* (1984) pp. 301–318
Die völkerrechtliche Stellung des Heiligen Stuhls, Berlin (1975)
J. L. Kunz, 'The Status of the Holy See in International Law', 46 AJIL (1952) pp. 308–314
H. Leising, *La Città del Vaticano und ihre Bürger*, Inaugural Dissertation, Erlangen (1933)
J. Lucien-Brun, 'Les nouveaux Etats africains et le Saint-Siège', AFDI (1961) pp. 808–813
'Le Saint-Siège et les Etats communistes', AFDI (1966) pp. 106–109
M. H. Mendelson, 'Diminutive States in the United Nations', 21 ICLQ (1972) pp. 609–630
E. Midgley, *The Natural Law Tradition and the Theory of International Relations*, London (1975)
N. Nuccitelli, *Le Fondement juridique des Rapports diplomatiques entre le Saint-Siège et les Nations Unies*, Paris (1956)
J. Puente Egido, *Personalidad Internacional de la Ciudad del Vaticano*, Madrid (1965)
C. Rousseau, 'Etat de la Cité du Vatican', 37 RGDIP (1930) pp. 145–153
E. Ruffini, *La Personalità Giuridica Internazionale della Chiesa*, Isola del Liri (1936)
P. Vellas, 'Les Etats exigus en Droit international public', 58 RGDIP (1954) pp. 559–581

CHAPTER 9. GENERAL CONCLUSIONS
W. Burckhardt, *Kommentar der schweizerischen Bundesverfassung vom 29. Mai 1874*, Berne, 3rd edn (1931)
M. Weller, 'The International Response to the Dissolution of the Socialist Federal Republic of Yugoslavia', 86 AJIL (1992) pp. 569-607

Index

Aaland Islands 56–57, 107
Abkhazia 89, 98, 100, 427–428
Agenda for Peace 1, 429
Aggression
 definition of 35, 112, 129, 428
 entities resulting of 97, 129–130
 prohibition of 129–130
 See also Use of force
Alberoni, Cardinal 209, 211
Aliens Act
 Andorra 341, 348, 357
 Liechtenstein 167–168, 188–189, 202
 Monaco 288–289, 306
 San Marino 217, 230–231
 Vatican City, residence 383, 386, 395–396
Alsace-Lorraine 74
American Samoa 48
Andorra 112, 126, 127, 138–141, 162, 205, 222, 247, 273, 287, 289, 296, 301, 302, 316–373, 424, 425, 431–433
Anguilla 48
Apartheid 120, 131–132
Apostolic See 375, 378
 See also Holy See *and* Pope
Arbitration Commission on Yugoslavia 67–72, 79, 91, 97, 115, 119, 130
Arengo 213
Argentina
 and Falkland Islands 51–52, 87
Armenia 93–94, 96
Arms embargo 90
Assam 94
Atlantic Charter (1941) 10–11, 15
Austria
 and Liechtenstein 149, 154, 159, 161–164, 169–170, 172–173, 183, 201
Austro-Hungarian Empire 9–10, 160
Autonomous regions 93–94, 98, 106, 424–425

Autonomy 104–109, 423–426
 claims for 94, 428
 forcible denial of 93, 428
 high degree of 105. 423–426, 428
 and independence 93, 423–426, 428
 Liechtenstein initiative 107–108, 198
 limits to 423–426, 428
 and micro-peoples 107, 424–425
 minority rights 43–44, 105
 self-determination 44, 47, 105–106, 108
 use of force 428
Azerbaijan 93–94, 96

Baltic States 99
 See also Estonia, Latvia *and* Lithuania
Bangladesh 83, 95, 130
Banks
 Andorra 341
 Liechtenstein 147, 166, 189–190
 Monaco 261, 289–290, 306
 San Marino 232, 257
Bantustans 130–131
Barstida, J. M. 317, 322
Beagle Channel 397
Belize 84
Belligerent occupation
 and independence 124, 126
Bengali people 83
Bermuda 48
Biafra 89, 93, 95, 101
Bishop of Urgell
 and Andorra 317–319, 322–323, 326, 330, 332, 339–340, 343, 347–352, 354–355, 360, 368, 370
 and Holy See 348–352
 and Spain 319, 322, 348–350
 rights of 320–326
 See also Co-Princes *and* Holy See
Bonelli, M. A. 222–223, 236, 246, 254

Bosnia-Herzegovina 68–70, 72, 96, 130–131, 426–428
British Virgin Islands 48
Budget
 Andorra 317, 323, 341–342
 Holy See 374, 378
 Liechtenstein 148, 161
 Monaco 261–262, 266
 San Marino 207–208, 211, 241, 255
 Vatican City 374, 378
Burma 90

Canon law 215, 323, 348, 351–352, 378, 380–381, 383, 385, 387, 390, 393
Cantons, Swiss
 and autonomy 424–425
 and Liechtenstein 155, 424–425
Captains Regent
 rights of, San Marino 211–213
Caroline Islands 397
Casino dispute
 San Marino 126, 225–226, 252, 258
Castel Gandolfo 375
Catholic Church 351–352, 374, 376, 385, 387–388, 390, 395–396, 414, 416, 418
Cautio judicatum solvi
 San Marino 220
Cayman Islands 48
Charlemagne 148, 317, 375
Charter of Economic Rights and Duties of States (1974) 35
Charter of Paris for a New Europe (1990) 179, 236, 298
 and Holy See 408
 and self-determination 36, 97
Charter of the United Nations
 Arts. 1 (2), 55 12–16, 33, 36, 85
 Arts. 73 (b), 76 (b) 16–17
Checheno-Ingush 98
Chechnya 98, 101, 427
China
 secession in Constitution 90
China, Republic of 112
Christmas Islands 50
Civil servants
 French, in Monaco 265, 271, 283–285, 305–306
Civil war 95, 101, 118, 428
 See also Spanish Civil War *and* Use of force
Co-Princes
 delimitation of powers 320, 342–345, 348–352, 354–357, 360–361, 368–370, 373
 rights of 319, 320–326, 339
 See also Bishop of Urgell *and* French President

Cocos (Keeling) Islands 50–51
Colonialism 17, 22, 49
Commonwealth of Independent States 96
Communism 95
Community
 and autonomy 108, 198, 426
 definition of 59, 70–72, 79, 198, 426
Concordat
 Andorra 352
 Italy 395
 Spain 348
Conference on Security and Cooperation in Europe
 and Bosnia-Herzegovina 428
 and Chechnya 427
 and Nagorno Karabakh 89, 94
 See also Organization for Security and Cooperation in Europe
Congo 92, 118
Congress of Vienna (1815) 149, 178, 209–210, 263, 375, 390
Consent, prior
 of France in Monaco 279–282, 296, 299, 307–309
Constitutional reform
 Andorra 320–321, 325, 332–333, 357–358, 373
Cooperation of Micro-States/neighbour States
 economic 125–126
 political 126
 practical 125
Council of Europe
 Andorra 112, 329, 357–359, 371
 declaration on voting 182, 245
 Holy See 409
 Liechtenstein 160–162, 170, 179–184, 196–197, 201, 203, 205
 Monaco 299–301
 San Marino 242–246, 254, 259
Council of Twelve
 rights of, San Marino 212–213, 215–217, 230
Criteria for statehood. *See* Statehood
Croatia 68–70, 72, 96, 105, 427
Customs regime
 Vatican City 391–392
Customs union
 Andorra 340–341, 347–348
 Liechtenstein 164–167, 201–202
 Monaco 286–287, 306
 San Marino 229–230, 246–250, 253, 257
Czech Republic 91
 and Liechtenstein 161, 179
Czechoslovakia 91, 161, 179

Daman 85

INDEX 453

Dasque, J.-M. 284
Declaration on the Granting of
    Independence (GA Res. 1514 (XV))
    17–19, 34, 47, 52–54, 62, 78, 80, 86
Declaration on Principles of International
    Law (GA Res. 2625 (XXV)) 19–26, 68, 76,
    78, 80, 82–83, 89, 95
Declaration of the Rights of Man and the
    Citizen (1789) 8–9
Declaration on the Rights of Minorities (GA
    Res. 47/135) 44
Decolonization 18, 61–62, 68, 75, 84, 86,
    135
Defence
    Andorra 345, 350
    Liechtenstein 169
    Monaco 290, 306–307
    San Marino 233
    Vatican City 396
Diet
    rights of, Liechtenstein 150–154
Diplomatic relations
    Andorra 335, 338–339, 347, 356, 367
    Holy See 376, 378, 388, 390, 396–397, 417
    Liechtenstein 161–163, 184, 196, 201
    Monaco 282–283, 307, 314
    San Marino 222, 227–228, 239, 255,
        257–258
Dissolution 67–68, 89, 91, 96–97, 101, 104,
    119, 128, 169, 429
    See also Secession, Soviet Union *and*
    Yugoslavia
Diu 85
Divine law 380–381, 388–389, 393, 407
Domestic jurisdiction 22, 56, 89–90, 93–94
    See also Secession
Dominion, indirect 208–209
Dupont, J. 274, 279, 283, 294, 298

East Pakistan 83
East Timor 48, 62, 84
Eastern Carelia 58
Economic Commission for Europe
    Holy See 404–405
    Liechtenstein 197
    San Marino 254
Economy
    Andorra 316–317, 320, 329
    Liechtenstein 147–148, 150, 188
    Monaco 261–262, 264
    San Marino 207–208, 210
    Vatican City 375
Edit de Réunion (1607) 318
Effective government 98, 118–120, 132, 200,
    257, 305, 367, 412–413
Elections
    Andorra 319, 323, 357–358

Liechtenstein 150, 152, 157, 182, 183
Monaco 266
San Marino 211, 217–218, 221, 224–225
Electors, Council of 149
Enclaves, small colonial 84–88, 107, 429
Equality before the law
    Andorra 334
    Liechtenstein 159
    Monaco 270–271
    San Marino 220–221
    Vatican City 385
Equality of men and women
    Andorra 323, 334
    Liechtenstein 157, 181–183
    Monaco 272
    San Marino 218, 220–221, 244–245
Eritrea 101
Estonia
    independence of 99
Estrada doctrine 120
European Bank for Reconstruction and
    Development
    Liechtenstein 200
European Commission of Human Rights,
    applications
    Andorra 331–332, 344, 371
    Liechtenstein 158–159, 168, 194
    Monaco 272–273, 284–285
    San Marino 221
European Community
    Andorra 359–364
    Liechtenstein 185
    Monaco 301–303
    San Marino 229–230, 246–254, 257, 260
    Vatican City 410
European Court of Human Rights, cases
    Andorra 273, 284–285, 331–332
European Currency Unit 232, 410
European Economic Area
    Liechtenstein 153–154, 157, 159–160,
        163–165, 167–168, 185–190, 195,
        201–202, 205
    protective measures 189–191
European Free Trade Association
    Liechtenstein 162, 164, 184–188, 190–191,
        201, 205
European Union
    Liechtenstein 162, 190–191
EUTELSAT
    Andorra 366
    Monaco 304
    Vatican City 400, 416
Export
    Andorra 316–317
    Liechtenstein 147
    Monaco 261
    San Marino 207

Vatican City 381, 392
External control
  and independence 124–127, 202

Fair trial
  guarantees, Andorra 330–333
Falkland Islands
  invasion of 51, 87
  and self-determination 48, 51–53, 86, 88
Fiscal dispute
  Monaco 126, 276–278
Food and Agriculture Organization
  Holy See 237, 404
  San Marino 236–239, 256
Foreign policy
  Andorra 334–335
  Holy See 388–389
  Liechtenstein 153–154, 160–161, 196–197, 203, 205
  Monaco 274, 278
  San Marino 222–223
  Vatican City 388–389
Fragmentation
  consequences of 40, 429–433
  See also Secession
France
  and Andorra 126–127, 140, 322, 331–333, 335–346, 347, 350, 353–357, 359–361, 364, 366–373, 433
  and Monaco 123–124, 126–127, 140, 263, 265, 268, 274–292, 295, 297–299, 301–315, 433
French President
  and Andorra 320–322, 330, 332, 334, 339–340, 342–345, 352, 354–357, 360–361, 365–366, 368–370, 373
  and France 342–345
  rights of 320–326, 342–345
  See also Co-Princes
French revolution 263
Friendly relations
  Andorra 335–338, 346–347
  Monaco 274–282
  San Marino 223–227

General Agreement on Tariffs and Trade
  Andorra 340
  Liechtenstein 199, 200
General Council
  rights of, Andorra 323–326
German Federation 149, 169
German occupation 210, 264
Germany
  unification of 81, 82
Gibraltar
  and self-determination 48, 51–55, 79, 86, 88

Goa 85–86
Golan Heights 129
Government, form of
  Andorra 320–326, 367
  Liechtenstein 150–154, 200
  Monaco 264–267, 305
  San Marino 211–214, 257
  Vatican City 376–378, 387
  See also Effective government and Statehood
Great and General Council
  rights of, San Marino 211–216
Guam 48
Guatemala 84
Guidelines on the Recognition of New
  States in Eastern Europe 97, 130

Hans-Adam II, Prince of Liechtenstein 151, 163, 178, 182, 183, 184, 195
Helsinki Declaration (1975) 178, 181, 298
  and Holy See 407–408
  and self-determination 35–36, 68, 97
History
  Andorra 317–320
  Liechtenstein 148–150
  Monaco 262–264
  San Marino 208–210
  Vatican City 375–376
Holy See 117, 177, 208, 210
  and Bishop of Urgell 348, 350–352, 368, 373
  international legal status of 386–388
  international relations of 162, 376, 386, 388, 396–400, 402–409
  and Vatican City 374, 376, 378, 383, 386–388, 389, 390, 411–414, 416–419
Hong Kong 87–88
Human rights
  Andorra 321, 325, 328, 329–334, 357–358, 373
  Liechtenstein 156–160
  Monaco 270–273
  San Marino 217–221, 244–245
  Vatican City 383–386
  See also Secession
Human Rights Committee 31, 41, 63–66, 104, 107, 271
  San Marino 218–220
  See also Self-determination
Human rights violations 47, 75–76, 83, 92–95, 104, 236
  See also Secession

Ibo people 92–93, 95
Ifni 86
Illegal entities 120, 124, 127–132
  See also Statehood

INDEX   455

Independence
　actual 122–126, 202, 257–259, 305, 310, 313–315, 369–370, 414, 416, 419, 430
　Andorra 126–127, 321, 337, 344–345, 367–371, 373
　and belligerent occupation 124, 126
　and external control 124–127
　formal 122–126, 202, 257, 259, 305–310, 313, 367–370, 414–415, 419
　Holy See 376, 389, 412, 416, 418
　and illegal origin 124, 127–132
　Liechtenstein 126, 169, 180, 184, 196, 201–202, 204, 205
　limits to 125–127
　Marshall Islands 139–140
　Micronesia 139–140
　and Micro-States (general) 49, 120–127, 433
　Monaco 123–124, 126–127, 276–279, 283, 290, 292, 294, 296–298, 305–310, 313–315
　Nauru 125
　Palau 139–140
　San Marino 126, 244, 256–259
　Vatican City 125, 413–416, 419
　See also Autonomy, Statehood and Trusteeship system
India
　and Bangladesh 83, 130
　and small colonial enclaves 85–86
Indigenous peoples 43, 46–48, 55, 79, 424, 426
　See also Peoples and Self-determination
Inhabitants of
　Andorra 316, 367
　Liechtenstein 147, 200
　Monaco 261, 305
　San Marino 207, 257
　Vatican City 374, 411–412
INTELSAT
　Monaco 304
　Vatican City 400, 416
International Agriculture Institute 236
International Atomic Energy Agency
　Holy See 402–403, 405, 416
　Liechtenstein 199
　Monaco 297–298
　Vatican City 402–403, 416
International Civil Aviation Organization
　Monaco 304
　San Marino 255
International conferences
　Andorra 354–357
International Court of Justice
　and definition of State 115–116, 177
　Holy See 407
　Liechtenstein 175–177, 178, 181, 197, 203, 205
　Monaco 140–141
　Nauru 293–294
　San Marino 227, 235
　and self-determination 59–63, 103
International Hydrographic Union 296
International laboratory of marine radioactivity 297
International Labour Organisation
　Holy See 404
　San Marino 221, 239, 241–242
International Law Commission
　and definition of State 112–114
　and self-determination 102
International Monetary Fund
　San Marino 233, 255
International Peace Conferences, the Hague
　Holy See 397–398
International responsibility
　of Liechtenstein 192–195
International Telecommunication Union
　Andorra 347, 354, 356, 365–366, 371
　Liechtenstein 199
　Monaco 296, 304
　San Marino 255
　Vatican City 400–402, 411, 416
International Union for the Protection of Literary and Artistic Works 296
International Wheat Council
　Vatican City 400–402, 416
Intervention, foreign military 129–130, 426–427
　See also Secession
Isaq people 94
Italy
　Kingdom of 209, 210, 255, 376
　and Holy See 375–376, 386, 388, 397–399
　and San Marino 209, 210, 222–233, 250, 252, 253, 255–258, 260, 286, 433
　and Vatican City 386, 388, 389–396, 411, 413–416, 419, 433

Jerusalem 129, 405
John Paul II, Pope 377
Judges
　Andorra 327, 332
　Liechtenstein 154–156, 201
　Monaco 268, 283–284, 305
　San Marino 214–215, 220, 225, 258
　Vatican City 379
Judicial system
　Andorra 326–329, 345–346
　Liechtenstein 154–156
　Monaco 268–270
　San Marino 214–217
　Vatican City 379–383
Jus cogens

and Monaco 310–312
and self-determination 102–103, 126, 130, 204, 423, 426, 428
and Vatican City 384–385

Kashmir 94
Katanga 92, 118
Kowloon Peninsula. *See* Hong Kong
Krajina 101, 427
Kurds 94
Kuwait
 invasion of 120, 129

Labour market
 Andorra 329, 333
 Liechtenstein 147–150
 Monaco 270–271
 San Marino 207, 218, 224
 Vatican City 384–385
Land, ownership of
 Andorra 329, 333, 341
 Liechtenstein 168, 189, 190
 Monaco 289
 San Marino 217, 220, 231
 See also Territorial sovereignty
Lateran palaces 375
Latvia
 independence of 99
League of Nations
 Andorra 352–354
 'associated' status 134
 Holy See 398–400, 403
 Liechtenstein 123, 133, 170–174, 197, 202–203
 'limited participation' 134
 Monaco 133, 291–293
 position of small State 133–134, 431
 'represented' status 134
 San Marino 133, 233–234, 242
 See also Aaland Islands
Lebeaupin, A. 374, 388, 389, 400, 403, 404, 406, 408
Legislation
 harmonized, Monaco 289–290, 306
 Italian, Vatican City 380, 381, 393–394, 415
Lenin, V. I. 9
Liberia
 Gios, Manos and Krahns 95
Liechtenstein 123, 107–108, 133, 138, 141, 147–206, 234, 235, 243, 244, 245, 246, 254, 289, 291, 293, 294, 296, 298, 300, 303, 305, 306, 353, 358, 367, 404, 408, 409, 410, 424, 425, 430, 431, 433
Lithuania
 independence of 99

Macao 87–88
Macedonia 68, 69, 96
Malaysian Federation 91
Maldive Islands 136, 141
Mali Federation 91
Manchukuo 124
Manchuria 92
Marshall Islan 138–140, 424, 425
 See also Trusteeship system
Martí I Alanis, J. 323, 330, 347, 349, 351
Mayotte, Island of 84
Micro-States
 definition of 2–3, 136, 138
 general conclusions on 429–433
 international attitude towards (general) 133–142, 145–146, 431–433
 See also Self-determination
Micronesia 138–140, 424, 425
 See also Trusteeship system
Minister of State
 rights of, Monaco 264–267
Minorities
 definition of 38, 40–46, 58–59, 70–72, 79
 and secession 31–32, 89, 97
 and Serbs 69–72, 131
 Sub-Commission on 25, 37–48
Minority rights 40–45, 57, 66, 70–71, 97, 101, 104, 107, 109
 See also Autonomy *and* Secession
Monaco 117, 123, 124, 126, 127, 133, 138–140, 141, 162, 205, 247, 261–315, 353, 367, 408, 410, 424, 425, 431–433
Monetary union
 Andorra 341
 Liechtenstein 166–167, 201–202
 Monaco 289
 San Marino 231–233, 257, 260
 Vatican City 392
Montenegro 69
Montevideo formula 112–113, 116, 118
Montserrat 48
Morocco
 and Ifni 86
Mozambique 95

Nagorno Karabakh 89, 93–94, 100, 101, 427, 428
Namibia
 and Walvis Bay 87
Napoleon I 149, 209, 263, 319, 375
National Council
 rights of, Monaco 266–267
Nationalities 71
Nationality
 Andorra 323–324, 341, 350, 358–359, 431
 Liechtenstein 157, 177
 Monaco 272

INDEX 457

San Marino 213-214, 217, 221, 224, 244-245, 251
  Vatican City 395
Nations 13-14, 32, 39, 40, 71, 74, 75
Nauru 112, 117, 125, 140-141, 425, 431
  See also Trusteeship system
Neutrality
  Andorra 320, 345, 354, 370
  Liechtenstein 149-150, 160-161, 169, 171, 179
  Monaco 264, 274, 291
  San Marino 210, 222, 224, 233
  Vatican City 376, 389, 396, 406, 407
New Caledonia 48
New Territories. *See* Hong Kong
Nigeria 89, 92, 93
Non-alienation
  Monaco 263, 281, 307
  San Marino 223-224, 255-256
Non-recognition of statehood 356, 365
  See also Secession
Non-Self-Governing Territories
  definition of 50, 83
  list of 48
  self-determination 16-19, 21, 33, 48-55, 78-79, 82-83, 103, 130
  separate status 22, 25, 82
  small 18-19, 40, 45, 48-55, 84-88, 135, 138
  See also Self-government
Norway
  union with Sweden 91
Nullum crimen, nulla poena sine lege
  Liechtenstein 159
  Vatican City 381, 384

Observer status
  Holy See 403-405, 409
  Liechtenstein 180
  San Marino 237-242, 244, 246, 254
Ogadeni refugees 94
Organization of American States
  Holy See 405
Organization for Security and Cooperation in Europe
  Holy See 177, 407-409
  Liechtenstein 161, 162, 177-179, 196, 197, 203, 205
  Monaco 298-299, 314
  San Marino 235-236
  See also Conference on Security and Cooperation in Europe
Ottonian emperors 9, 375

Palau 138-140, 424, 425
  See also Trusteeship system
Papal States
  and San Marino 208-209
  and Vatican City 375
Pariatges 318, 350
Parliaments
  exercise of self-determination 82, 91
  See also Elections
Peoples
  colonial 18, 21-23, 26, 37-38, 52, 54-55, 82
  definition of 14, 21, 31-33, 38-39, 44-46, 55, 66, 71-77, 79
  independent 22-24, 37-38, 81
  See also Indigenous peoples
Permanent Court of International Justice
  Andorra 353-354
  Liechtenstein 174
  Monaco 293
  San Marino 234
Pitcairn 48, 50, 118
Police enforcement measures 427-428
  See also Secession *and* Use of force
Political affiliation
  Monaco with France 274
Pontifical Commission
  rights of, Vatican City 377-378, 385-386
Pope
  powers of 376-383
Population
  composition of 200, 257, 305, 367, 411-412
  and Micro-States 55, 117-118
  See also Statehood
Portugal
  and Daman, Diu and Goa 85-86
  and East Timor 62, 84
Postal union
  Andorra 339-340, 347, 367
  Liechtenstein 163-164, 167, 201, 202
  Monaco 285, 306
  San Marino 228-229, 257, 260
  Vatican City 390-391
Prince of
  Liechtenstein, family council 150-154, 198, 204
  Monaco 264-267, 281-282, 311
  See also Co-Princes
Protective friendship
  San Marino 210, 223-224, 242, 255-256
Protectorate
  of France 123-124, 256, 278, 281-282, 304, 307-308, 311-313
  of Italy 223-224, 243
Public office
  Monaco 265, 268, 270-271, 283-285
  San Marino 224-225
Punjab 94

Quebec 106
Qüèstia 318, 319

Racial discrimination 22, 92, 131–132
Radio and television
　Andorra 343
　Liechtenstein 163, 199
　San Marino 226, 231, 245, 258
Radiotelegraph service 401
Rainier III, Prince of Monaco 264, 281, 294
Recognition
　of Andorra 335, 360, 367, 370–371
　constitutive 110–115, 127, 181, 259, 314, 315, 416, 418, 419, 425
　declaratory 111–115, 202, 244
　of Holy See 417
　of Liechtenstein 160, 171, 181, 184, 202–203
　of Monaco 274, 296, 298, 303, 314–315
　non-recognition 92–95, 98–101, 115, 119–120, 127
　of San Marino 222, 243, 244, 259
　by United Nations 111–112, 139, 142
　of Vatican City 411, 416–419
　See also Secession and Statehood
Referendum
　Andorra 321, 325
　Liechtenstein 151–154, 155, 187, 188, 195
　San Marino 213–214
　and self-determination 68, 72, 77, 93, 99, 108, 131, 139
Rhine Confederation 149
Risorgimento 223, 375
Roman Curia 387
Roman question 376, 397
Roman Republic 209, 375

Sacred College of Cardinals 377
Salt water theory 76, 83
San Marino 126, 133, 138, 141, 205, 207–260, 286, 289, 291, 293, 294, 296, 298, 300, 301, 302, 303, 305, 306, 313, 353, 358, 367, 371, 392, 404, 408, 410, 424, 431, 432, 433
Sardinia
　and Monaco 263, 282, 304
Schools
　Andorra 346, 350
Secession
　in Africa and Asia 100
　domestic jurisdiction 22, 56, 89–90, 93–94
　foreign military intervention 129–130, 426–427
　human rights violations 75–76, 83, 92–95
　justification of 24–25, 39, 75–77, 83,
　　89–106
　minority rights 40–41, 43–44
　non-recognition 92–95, 98, 100–101
　police enforcement measures 427–428
　procedural rules 77, 90–91, 96–97, 100, 104, 106
　representative government 24–25, 76, 83, 89, 94–96, 105
　right of 14, 22–23, 31–32, 39, 41, 57–58, 89–109
　right of gradual 106–107, 423, 428–429
　See also Use of force and Territorial integrity
Secretary of State
　rights of, Vatican City 378
Security Council
　Working Group on equitable representation 255, 304
Self-determination
　of Andorra 372–373
　autonomy 44, 47, 93–94, 104–109
　collective/individual right 30, 39, 64–66
　first settlers 50–51, 53–55, 79
　historical background 7–11
　holders of the right 26, 31–33, 37–40, 44, 49–51, 53–55, 77–84
　Human Rights Committee 31, 41, 63–66, 107
　indigenous peoples 47, 55, 79, 424, 426
　internal (form of government) 15, 11, 17, 25, 33–34, 36, 47, 80–81, 95, 105–106
　jus cogens 102–103, 126, 130, 204, 423, 426, 428
　of Liechtenstein 204–205
　Micro-States 40, 49, 88, 107, 126–127
　of Monaco 310–312
　Non-Self-Governing Territories 16–19, 21, 48–55, 78–79, 82–83, 103, 130
　of San Marino 259
　secession 14–15, 31–32, 47, 57, 67–68, 75–77, 89–109, 426–429
　small colonial enclaves 84–88, 107, 429
　territorial integrity 18, 34, 55, 60–62, 79, 80–81, 89–104, 106, 423, 425, 426
　Trust Territories 16–17, 21, 28, 33, 78–79, 82, 103
　use of force 92, 98, 100–102, 104–106, 108–109, 426–429
　of Vatican City 417–418
Self-government 16–18, 47, 140
Senegal 91
Serbia 69, 72
Serbian Republic of Bosnia-Herzegovina 68, 72, 100, 101, 131
Services, movement of
　Liechtenstein 190, 431
　Monaco 301

INDEX 459

San Marino 246
Vatican City 410
See also Banks
Shaumyan district 93
Singapore 91
Slovak Republic 91
Slovenia 68, 69, 96
Social security
  Andorra 329, 346, 350
  Liechtenstein 157, 159
  San Marino 221, 241, 251
Solomon Islands 141
Somali National Movement 94
Somalia 95
Somaliland Republic 94
South Ossetia 98
South West Africa. *See* Namibia
Southern Rhodesia 92, 128, 130–131
Southern Sudan 94
Sovereign equality 138, 140–142, 178, 236, 260
Sovereignty 110, 120–121
Soviet Union
  dissolution of 95, 96, 100, 101, 108, 429
  secession in legislation 90, 94, 98
Spain
  and Andorra 126, 140, 319, 322, 331–333, 335, 336–339, 340, 345–350, 353–356, 360, 361, 364, 366–373, 433
  and Gibraltar 52–55
  and Monaco 262, 304
Spanish Civil War 320
Special Committee of Twenty-Four 48–55, 79, 82, 86, 87
Sri Lanka 94
St Helena 48, 50
St Peter's Square 389, 393, 415
State succession 67, 89, 97, 128
Statehood
  Andorra 335, 357–358, 364, 366–371, 373
  continuation of 118–119
  criteria for 110–132
  government 118–120
  illegal origin 124, 127–132
  independence 98, 120–127
  Liechtenstein 160, 171–172, 175–178, 181, 184, 196, 200–204, 205
  Monaco 294–297, 300, 303, 304–314
  population 117–118
  recognition 91–95, 97–101, 110–115, 119, 127, 160, 181, 184
  San Marino 239–240, 242–244, 254, 255–260
  territory 116–117
  Vatican City 117, 410–417
Stonecutters Island. *See* Hong Kong
Sub-Commission on Minorities 25, 37–48

See also Minorities
Sustainable development
  small island States 40, 142
Suzerainty 360, 365
Sweden
  union with Norway 91
Switzerland
  and Liechtenstein 149, 150, 159, 161–169, 170, 171–173, 181, 183, 184–188, 191–195, 199, 201–202, 205, 433
Syria 91

Taiwan. *See* China, Republic of
Tamils 94
Tax haven
  Liechtenstein 183
  Monaco 300–302
  San Marino 243, 249, 300, 302
Taxes
  Andorra 317, 340–341, 362–363
  Liechtenstein 148, 150, 182, 191
  Monaco 262, 277–278, 287–288, 306
  San Marino 207–208, 250
  Vatican City 374
  See also Value-Added Tax
Telecommunication
  Andorra 319, 343, 347
  Liechtenstein 163, 199
  Monaco 285
  Vatican City 391, 401
  See also International Telecommunication Union
Territorial integrity
  GA Res. 1514 (XV) 18, 34, 55, 62, 80
  ICCPR 34, 100
  partial or total disruption 34, 44, 80, 83, 89, 91–92, 94, 96–97, 423, 425–426
  use of force 92, 100–102, 104, 426–428
  Western Sahara 60–62, 84
Territorial sovereignty
  Vatican City 389
Territory
  Andorra 316, 366
  Liechtenstein 147, 200
  and Micro-States 117
  Monaco 261, 305
  San Marino 207, 256–257
  Vatican City 274, 411
Territory, size of
  Andorra 316
  Liechtenstein 147
  Monaco 261
  San Marino 207
  Vatican City 374
Throne
  vacancy on, Monaco 281–282, 304, 307–308, 311–312, 315

Tibet 94
Tokelau 48, 50
Trusteeship system
  independence 16
  Marshall Islands 138–140
  Micronesia 138–140
  Nauru 140–141
  Palau 138–140
  self-determination 16–17, 21, 28, 33, 78–79, 82, 103
Tunisia
  Bey of Tunis 123–124, 278
  See also Protectorate of France
Turkish Republic of Northern Cyprus 130
Turks and Caicos Islands 48, 50

Unification 81–82, 91
  See also Germany and Yemen
United Arab Republic 91
United Kingdom
  and Falkland Islands 51–52
  and Gibraltar 52–55
United Nations
  Andorra 138–141, 358, 364, 371
  associated member 135, 137–138
  freedom of voting 139–140, 432
  GA Res. 1514 (XV) 17–19
  GA Res. 2625 (XXV) 19–26
  Holy See 405–407, 404, 409
  Liechtenstein 138, 141, 160–162, 170, 195–198, 201, 203, 205
  Marshall Islands 138–140
  Micronesia 138–140
  Monaco 138–141, 303–304, 310, 314
  Nauru 140
  Non-Self-Governing Territories 16–19, 21–22, 25, 33, 40, 135, 138
  Palau 138–140
  principle of self-determination 12–17
  question of Micro-States 134–139, 431
  San Marino 138, 141, 238, 254–255
  Vatican City 405–406
  See also Charter of the United Nations
United Nations Conference on Trade and Development
  Holy See 405
  Liechtenstein 199
  San Marino 255
United Nations Educational, Scientific and Cultural Organization
  Andorra 366, 371
  Holy See 404
  Monaco 294–297, 314
  San Marino 238–239
United Nations Industrial Development Organization
  Holy See 405

United States Declaration of Independence (1776) 8
United States Virgin Islands 48
Universal Declaration of Human Rights (1948) 29, 329–330
Universal Declaration on the Rights of Indigenous Peoples 46–48, 424, 426
Universal Postal Union
  Andorra 339–340, 365
  Liechtenstein 199
  Monaco 304
  San Marino 229, 255
  Vatican City 400–402, 411, 415–416
Upper Silesia 58, 71
Use of force
  and autonomy 428
  and secessionists 98, 100–102, 104, 106, 108, 109, 426–429
  and territorial integrity 92, 100–102, 104, 106, 108, 109, 426–429
Uti possidetis juris 68–70, 84, 97, 100, 101, 108–109, 429

Value-Added Tax
  Liechtenstein 165–166, 191
  Monaco 262, 287–288, 306
  San Marino 230, 250
  Vatican City 391
Vanuatu 141
Vatican City 117, 125, 301, 305, 367, 374–419, 424, 431, 433
Veguers 318, 319, 322, 326, 327, 332, 333, 356
Vienna Declaration and Programme of Action (1993) 27

Walvis Bay 87
War. See Aggression, Civil war and Use of force
West Bank 129
West Irian 84
West Pakistan 83, 95
Western Sahara 48, 60–62, 84
Western Samoa 141
Western Slavonia 427
Wilson, W. 9–10, 234, 291
World Health Organization
  Holy See 404
  Monaco 294
  San Marino 239–240
World Intellectual Property Organization
  Andorra 366
  Holy See 402–403, 416
  Liechtenstein 199
  Monaco 304
  San Marino 255
  Vatican City 402–403, 416

INDEX   461

World Telegraph Union 400–401
World Tourism Organization
  Andorra 365
  Holy See 405
World Trade Organization
  Liechtenstein 200
World War I 9, 149, 160, 161, 166, 169, 171, 210, 222, 264, 274, 320, 376, 396, 400
World War II 11, 150, 160, 162, 210, 222, 227, 264, 320, 376, 396, 432

Yemen
  secession 91
  unification of 82, 91
Yugoslavia
  dissolution of 67, 89, 95–97, 100–101, 119, 429
  Socialist Federal Republic of 67, 69, 71, 105, 108
  See also Arbitration Commission on

CAMBRIDGE STUDIES IN INTERNATIONAL AND COMPARATIVE LAW

Books in the series

1 **Principles of the institutional law of international organisations**
   C.F. Amerasinghe
2 **Fragmentation and the international relations of Micro-states**
   Jorri Duursma
3 **The polar regions and the development of international law**
   Donald Rothwell

For EU product safety concerns, contact us at Calle de José Abascal, 56–1°,
28003 Madrid, Spain or eugpsr@cambridge.org.